Empirical Corporate Finance
Volume I

The International Library of Critical Writings in Financial Economics

Series Editor: Richard Roll

Allstate Professor of Economics
The Anderson School at UCLA, USA

This major series presents by field outstanding selections of the most important articles across the entire spectrum of financial economics – one of the fastest growing areas in business schools and economics departments. Each collection has been prepared by a leading specialist who has written an authoritative introduction to the literature.

Future titles will include:

Wherever possible, the articles in these volumes have been reproduced as originally published using facsimile reproduction, inclusive of footnotes and pagination to facilitate ease of reference.

For a list of all Edward Elgar published titles visit our site on the World Wide Web at
http://www.e-elgar.co.uk

Empirical Corporate Finance
Volume I

Edited by

Michael J. Brennan

Goldyne and Irwin Hearsh Professor of Banking and Finance,
University of California, Los Angeles, USA and Professor of Finance,
London Business School, UK

THE INTERNATIONAL LIBRARY OF CRITICAL WRITINGS IN FINANCIAL ECONOMICS

An Elgar Reference Collection
Cheltenham, UK • Northampton, MA, USA

© Michael J. Brennan 2001. For copyright of individual articles, please refer to the Acknowledgements.

Published by
Edward Elgar Publishing Limited
Glensanda House
Montpellier Parade
Cheltenham
Glos GL50 1UA
UK

Edward Elgar Publishing, Inc.
136 West Street
Suite 202
Northampton
Massachusetts 01060
USA

A catalogue record for this book is available from the British Library.

Library of Congress Cataloguing in Publication Data

Empirical corporate finance / edited by Michael J. Brennan.
     p. cm. — (The international library of critical writings in financial economics; 7)
  Includes bibliographical references and index.
  1. Corporations—Finance. I. Brennan, Michael J. II. Series.

HG4026 .E475 2001
658.15—dc21

00–066245

ISBN   1 85898 484 X (4 volume set)

Printed and bound in Great Britain by MPG Books Ltd, Bodmin, Cornwall

Contents

Acknowledgements

The editor and publishers wish to thank the authors and the following publishers who have kindly given permission for the use of copyright material.

Blackwell Publishers for articles: Eugene F. Fama, Lawrence Fisher, Michael C. Jensen and Richard Roll (1969), 'The Adjustment of Stock Prices to New Information', *International Economic Review*, **10** (1), February, 1–21; Michael J. Brennan and Patricia J. Hughes (1991), 'Stock Prices and the Supply of Information', *Journal of Finance*, **XLVI** (5), December, 1665–91; Laurie Simon Bagwell (1992), 'Dutch Auction Repurchases: An Analysis of Shareholder Heterogeneity', *Journal of Finance*, **XLVII** (1), March, 71–105; Roni Michaely, Richard H. Thaler and Kent L. Womack (1995), 'Price Reactions to Dividend Initiations and Omissions: Overreaction or Drift?', *Journal of Finance*, **L** (2), June, 573–608; Raghuram Rajan and Henri Servaes (1997), 'Analyst Following of Initial Public Offerings', *Journal of Finance*, **LII** (2), June, 507–29; Alon Brav and Paul A. Gompers (1997), 'Myth or Reality? The Long-Run Underperformance of Initial Public Offerings: Evidence from Venture and Nonventure Capital-Backed Companies', *Journal of Finance*, **LII** (5), December, 1791–1821; John D. Lyon, Brad M. Barber and Chih-Ling Tsai (1999), 'Improved Methods for Tests of Long-Run Abnormal Stock Returns', *Journal of Finance*, **LIV** (1), February, 165–201.

Elsevier Science Ltd for articles: Stephen J. Brown and Jerold B. Warner (1980), 'Measuring Security Price Performance', *Journal of Financial Economics*, **8** (3), September, 205–58; Francis Koh and Terry Walter (1989), 'A Direct Test of Rock's Model of the Pricing of Unseasoned Issues', *Journal of Financial Economics*, **23** (2), August, 251–72; William A. Sahlman (1990), 'The Structure and Governance of Venture-Capital Organizations', *Journal of Financial Economics*, **27**, 473–521; Joshua Lerner (1994), 'Venture Capitalists and the Decision to go Public', *Journal of Financial Economics*, **35**, 293–316; Kathleen Weiss Hanley and William J. Wilhelm, Jr. (1995), 'Evidence on the Strategic Allocation of Initial Public Offerings', *Journal of Financial Economics*, **37** (2), 239–57; David Ikenberry, Josef Lakonishok and Theo Vermaelen (1995), 'Market Underreaction to Open Market Share Repurchases', *Journal of Financial Economics*, **39** (2 & 3), October–November, 181–208; Bernard S. Black and Ronald J. Gilson (1998), 'Venture Capital and the Structure of Capital Markets: Banks versus Stock Markets', *Journal of Financial Economics*, **47** (3), March, 243–77.

Journal of Financial and Quantitative Analysis for article: Theo Vermaelen (1984), 'Repurchase Tender Offers, Signaling, and Managerial Incentives', *Journal of Financial and Quantitative Analysis*, **19** (2), June, 163–81.

Oxford University Press for articles: Roni Michaely and Wayne H. Shaw (1994), 'The Pricing of Initial Public Offerings: Tests of Adverse-Selection and Signaling Theories', *Review of Financial Studies*, **7** (2), Summer, 279–319; Pyung Sig Yoon and Laura T. Starks (1995),

'Signaling, Investment Opportunities, and Dividend Announcements', *Review of Financial Studies*, **8** (4), Winter, 995–1018; N.R. Prabhala (1997), 'Conditional Methods in Event Studies and an Equilibrium Justification for Standard Event-Study Procedures', *Review of Financial Studies*, **10** (1), Spring, 1–38.

Every effort has been made to trace all the copyright holders but if any have been inadvertently overlooked the publishers will be pleased to make the necessary arrangement at the first opportunity.

In addition the publishers wish to thank the Marshall Library of Economics, Cambridge University and the Library of Indiana University at Bloomington, USA, for their assistance in obtaining these articles.

Foreword

In his introduction to these volumes, Professor Brennan suggests there has been a paradigm shift in scholarly research about corporate finance, a shift away from regarding the corporation as '... an autonomous set of cash flows...' to '... a social organization, directed by intelligent, self-interested individuals.' This is an interesting contention. The classical literature certainly held that market forces constrained the freedom of individual actions. Offsetting market transactions could effectively 'undo' individually motivated corporate decisions. Newer literature seems to regard the market as a less potent antidote to manager self-indulgence.

By the editor's design, almost all the articles in these volumes are recent. Only seven of 72 were published before 1990 and many appeared within the past several years. Consequently, he has taken a potentially rewarding but risky stance by selecting articles well before the time usually required by science to deem an article truly important. In this regard, Professor Brennan has given more than a usual amount of service to the profession.

Volume I is devoted mainly to raising new capital, through venture capital and initial public offerings, and to equity management (dividends, share repurchases, secondary offerings, and splits). In both areas, the new paradigm is strongly in evidence. Many of these papers speak of 'signaling' and some offer empirical evidence which seems to violate basic principles of market efficiency – thereby suggesting that it is quite easy to make large profits by trading on public information.

Corporate investment policy is the focus of the first section of Volume II. Most of these papers seem to support a more market-oriented view of corporate finance. The exceptions are papers by Lamont and by Blanchard, *et al.*, which contain empirical analyses suggesting the existence of intra-firm constraints on decisions. The second section of Volume II covers organizational structure, which has not traditionally been a finance topic, falling instead within the purview of a strategy or organizational behavior group in the business school. The fact that a number of recent papers on this topic have appeared in leading finance journals is indeed very good evidence in support of the editor's contention about a paradigm shift. Volume II follows with a section on agency problems, particularly compensation arrangements.

Volume III focuses directly on corporate financial policy and financing. The first section covers such traditional topics as taxation and leverage. The papers are all recent, only two of 21 before 1995, so they are probably not very well known to many readers. Some of these papers offer evidence of behavioral phenomena, for instance, that managerial entrenchment can resist market-based extermination efforts. Other papers purport to find evidence of signaling – for example, firms with better private information issue shorter-term debt.

Volume IV begins with a section on the modern technique of corporate risk management and is followed by a section on acquisitions and divestitures. Professor Brennan summarizes these latter selections as follows:

> These [papers] suggest that diversifying acquisitions tend to be unprofitable, that they are often driven by managerial rather than shareholder objectives, and the value destroying acquisitions tend to be punished by subsequent acquisitions of the acquiring firm.

In other words, corporate decision-makers can ignore shareholders only at their peril. The puzzle here is why they apparently fail to learn about this. Surely business schools should be teaching a new generation of managers about the retribution exacted by the market for self-interested actions.

The collection terminates with a selection of articles on bankruptcy and related issues. Not surprisingly, managers involved in such distressed situations do not fare well personally.

Professor Brennan concludes his introduction, 'It is [the] emphasis on incentives and constraints that marks the divide between the classical Modigliani-Miller theories of corporate finance and their modern counterparts.' I would put it slightly differently: the older literature assumed, perhaps with inadequate empirical support, that shareholder incentives were sufficient to impose binding constraints on recalcitrant managers.

Most collections in this series on Critical Writings in Financial Economics are of greater interest to scholars, students, and business specialists than to general managers. This collection is an exception. It should help managers assess how much they can get away with before being in jeopardy of reassignment to oblivion.

Richard Roll

Introduction

M.J. Brennan[1]

This book of readings covers the main issues in the field of empirical corporate finance that are the subject of contemporary interest and research. Inevitably, it has not been possible to cover all issues; for example, I have not included anything related to the international dimension of corporate finance, nor, more narrowly, to the role of preferred shares or convertible bonds, nor to the interesting issues raised by the mode of payment in corporate takeovers. And within each of the general topics within which I have arranged the subject, it has been necessary to be highly selective in choosing readings, even though there are more than 70 papers in this collection.

In deciding which papers to be included I have generally leant towards more recent ones for two reasons. Firstly, the more recent papers allow the reader to trace back the development of an area of study through the bibliographies – moving in the reverse direction is decidedly more difficult. Secondly, in a progressive discipline like corporate finance, more recent papers tend to represent advances that are not reflected in earlier papers; this is not to say, of course, that later papers, even the ones chosen for this selection, necessarily subsume their predecessors. Scientific development is not a linear process, and innovations are, by their nature, haphazard, so that recent papers on a particular issue may neither reflect the points of view of, nor deal with the issues raised in, earlier papers. There is no remedy for this. The reader who wishes to become an expert in a particular area must read beyond the papers we have been able to include.

In compiling an edited work of this kind one becomes aware of Kuhn's (1970) observation that a paradigm shift often involves a change in world view which raises new issues and renders old issues irrelevant.[2] Such a paradigm shift is evident in empirical corporate finance over the past 30 years. A natural starting point for the modern era in empirical corporate finance is the classic paper of Fama, Fisher, Jensen and Roll (1969) which was made possible by the, slightly earlier, compilation of the CRSP tapes at the University of Chicago. At the time of the FFJR paper, and for a long time thereafter, the efficient markets hypothesis reigned supreme, and much of empirical corporate finance was concerned, either with assessing market reactions to specific corporate events,[3] or with tests of the Modigliani-Miller propositions concerning dividend and financial structure policies, and assessing the implications of personal and corporate tax codes for these propositions. The event study technique that they pioneered has continued to play a significant role in empirical investigations. However, its influence has diminished for at least three reasons. Firstly, the increasing evidence of slow adjustment of stock prices to corporate events casts doubt on the market efficiency assumption which underlies the standard interpretations of event studies. Secondly, there has been an enormous resurgence of cross sectional studies of the relation between stock prices and firm characteristics[4] which had been largely eclipsed by the development of the event study. Thirdly, as the papers in this collection attest, the scope of corporate financial theories has expanded far beyond models that predict simply the relation between certain variables and stock prices, so that there has been a natural reduction in the relative proportion of papers devoted to analyzing stock prices or stock price changes.[5]

Even more dramatic perhaps than the relative decline of the event study, has been the shift away from empirical concerns with the implications of capital structure and dividend policies for firm valuation. One reason for this, perhaps, has been the realization that the information content of these policies introduces an insuperable errors in variables problem into empirical analysis of, for example, the tax-associated valuation consequences of these policies.[6] But the most important reason is the paradigm shift that took place in the late 1970s; whereas the classical model treated the firm as an autonomous set of cash flows to be distributed by a choice of securities, the new model treats the firm as a social organization, directed by intelligent, self-interested individuals; these individuals, the managers of the firm, can convey signals about their private information, are influenced by the web of contracts which engages them, including those related to the firm's financial structure, and can even use this financial structure as a tool to precommit their own future actions.[7]

The subject matter ordering that I have chosen largely reflects the life-cycle of the firm, starting with venture capital and initial public offerings, moving on to topics such as dividend policy and capital structure that are relevant for the mature firm, and ending with acquisition, bankruptcy and liquidation. As a prelude to this journey through the life of the typical firm, Part I of Volume I contains four papers that are concerned with the techniques used in event studies, which are still the predominant investigative tool of empirical corporate finance. The classic paper of FFJR which is included as (I.1) analyzed monthly stock price changes using the 'market model' of security returns which had originally been used by William Sharpe (1963) to simplify portfolio construction algorithms for computational ease. In (I.2) Brown and Warner analyze the statistical properties of abnormal event period returns estimated from monthly stock returns using a variety of techniques, including the market model.[8] Prabhala (I.3) analyzes the biases that are introduced into event study measures of the value consequences of corporate actions by the fact that the actions are chosen by the firm and are at least partly forecastable from the firm's observable situation. Lyon *et al.* (I.4) is concerned with the statistical properties of various estimators of the *long-run* abnormal returns of firms following particular events; this issue has become important because of increasing, though still disputed,[9] evidence that stock prices do not adjust instantaneously to new information.

The role of venture capital in facilitating the rapid exploitation of new ideas and technologies by providing finance and advice to new firms is now widely recognized. Black and Gilson (I.5) argue that the existence of a market for initial public offerings (IPOs) is important for venture capital financing because it allows the venture capitalist to exit, while leaving the entrepreneur with control over the firm; they support their thesis by comparing developments in Germany and Japan with those in the USA. Sahlman (I.6) shows how the contractual structure of venture capital organizations has evolved to overcome the informational and agency problems that are particularly acute for new ventures. Lerner (I.7) shows that venture capitalists in the biotechnology industry were able to take their firms public at market peaks, and tended to rely on private equity financings when market valuations were lower; the more experienced were the venture capital firms the better was their market timing. One puzzle in the IPO market is the underpricing that leads to very high returns for investors who purchase at the offer price: rival explanations include the winners' curse model of Rock (1986) and the signaling model of Grinblatt and Hwang (1989) and others. Michaely and Shaw (I.8) provide evidence in favor of the winners' curse model by showing that certain IPOs in which informed institutional investors are less likely to participate experience significantly less underpricing; they find no support for the signalling hypothesis which predicts that firms that are likely to seek subsequent public financing will underprice by more. Koh and Walter (I.9) provide additional evidence that is consistent with Rock's model by showing that uniformed investors who subscribe to IPOs in Singapore earn only normal returns because of the winners' curse that causes the allotments they receive to be highest in the least successful offerings. Hanley and Wilhelm (I.10) study the allotment of shares in US IPOs where, in contrast to the rule-based system in Singapore, individual allotments are at the discretion of the underwriter. They show that a US underwriter who employs the book-building system allocates a large proportion of IPOs to institutional investors but that, in contrast to the winners' curse hypothesis, the fraction of shares purchased by the institutions is not significantly related to the amount of underpricing. They suggest that the underwriter requires institutions to participate in all offerings in order to receive shares in underpriced offerings, and that this ameliorates the winners' curse problem and accounts for the increasing predominance of the book-building approach over the fixed price offer that has been common in other jurisdictions. Rajan and Servaes (I.11) find that the number of investment analysts who follow a firm in the first year after its IPO is strongly increasing in the degree of underpricing; that the analysts are systematically over-optimistic about the firms' future earnings;[10] that the number of IPOs in an industry is related to the optimism of analysts about that industry; and that the firms about which analysts are most optimistic in the short run have the worst long-run stock price performance. Brav and Gompers (I.12) take on the issue of the apparent long-run underperformance of IPOs.[11] They show that the underperformance comes primarily from the returns of small low book to market firms that have not received venture capital backing. They find that the returns of IPO firms are highly correlated in calendar time even if the firms go public in different years, and suggest that the returns on small firms may be influenced by investor sentiment.

Part III of Volume I is concerned with the role of dividends, share repurchases, and stock splits. Michaely *et al.* (I.13) show that stock prices drop by an average 7 per cent when a dividend omission is announced, and rise by 3 per cent when dividends are initiated. This is consistent with Miller and Modigliani's (1961) information content of dividends hypothesis, which was later formalized in the signaling models of Miller and Rock (1985) among others; however, the authors report that the stock price continues to drift up for initiations and down for omissions for two to three years after the announcement, with the effect being particularly significant for omissions. Yoon and Starks (I.14) examine evidence for the signaling hypothesis and for a free cash flow hypothesis which is based on the notion that cash flows retained by the firm tend to be 'wasted' on unprofitable investment projects. They find evidence which is consistent with the signaling hypothesis and which is inconsistent with the free cash flow hypothesis.

Vermaelen (I.15) examines the stock price response to announcements of tender offer repurchases and finds evidence consistent with the fact that the tender offers also convey inside information; more importantly, he is able to interpret the magnitude of the stock price change as a rational response to the information contained in the terms of the offer. Ikenberry *et al.* (I.16) examine stock price responses to announcements of open market repurchases. Consistent with the signaling hypothesis, they find an initial stock price response of around 3 per cent, but their most striking finding is that the information in the repurchase announcement is largely ignored, for the announcing firms have abnormal returns of around 45 per cent over the next four years. This is consistent with the finding of Michaely *et al.* (*op. cit.*) and others that, contrary to the predictions of the efficient markets hypothesis, stock prices exhibit slow adjustment to new firm specific information.[12] Bagwell's paper (I.17) reports that firms face upward-sloping supply curves when they repurchase shares in a Dutch auction, and that the supply elasticity is larger for firms with large trading volume, firms included in the S&P500 Index, and takeover targets. This contradicts the conventional wisdom that developed from Scholes (1972) that the elasticity of demand for corporate stock was infinite.[13] Brennan and Hughes (I.18) find that stock splits are associated with an increase in the number of investment analysts who follow a firm; they argue that this is a rational response since the brokerage houses who employ the analysts typically make higher returns from trading low-priced stocks.[14]

Part I of Volume II contains studies that are related to corporate investment decisions. McConnell and Muscarella (II.1) is a classic event study that shows that announcements of changes in corporate capital budgets are generally accompanied by stock price changes of the same sign. This is consistent with firms adopting positive net present value projects and having private information about their opportunities. The major exception is public utilities for which the stock price response is insignificant; this is consistent with regulation enforcing only normal profits for these firms. Kaplan and Ruback (II.2) use data on highly leveraged transactions to assess the ability of the discounted cash flow approach, which is widely used in corporate capital budgeting,[15] to yield values which approximate those found in the marketplace: they find that discounted cash flow valuation methods provide reliable estimates of market value.

Fama and French (II.3) use a three factor model to derive estimates of the costs of equity capital for different industries; in doing so, they emphasize the imprecision to which such studies are subject. The classical discounted cash flow approach to capital budgeting is increasingly supplanted by the 'real options' approach which, building on the intuitions of the Black-Scholes (1973) model, takes account of the decision-contingent nature of project cash flows.[16] Berger *et al.* (II.4) show that, in valuing firms, investors do take account of the options that the firms possess – in this case the option of the firm to abandon its current line of business and liquidate. Lamont (II.5) explores the relation between corporate investment and corporate profitability and cash flow; he finds that, when oil firms experienced a negative price shock, they cut back investment in their non-oil divisions; this suggests that corporate investment is influenced not only by conditions in the external capital market, but also by conditions in the *intra*-firm capital market.

This conclusion is reinforced by Blanchard *et al.* (II.6) who examine what unprofitable firms do with the cash windfalls that arise from successful lawsuits. They find that the windfall is typically kept inside the firm rather than distributed to investors; if anything, the firms borrow more as a result of the windfall, and use the proceeds to finance acquisitions or make other investments that do not create value. They conclude that the evidence is consistent with an agency model of the firm in which the managers use the windfalls to strengthen their own positions as managers of an independent firm.

Part II of Volume II is concerned with the control mechanisms that restrain managements' tendency to run firms in their own interest. Morck *et al.* (II.7) assess the effectiveness of boards of directors in monitoring corporate managements; they find that boards are likely to replace the managements of firms that underperform relative to other firms in the same industry, but that boards have not been the main force in replacing unresponsive managements in poorly performing industries; in these industries hostile takeovers have been the main agent of change.

Zingales (II.8) studies the determinants of the value of the voting rights associated with common shares, and finds that the major determinant is the expected additional payment the shareholders will receive for their votes in a control contest, which depends in turn on the probability that a vote is pivotal in a control contest and the magnitude of the private benefits obtainable by controlling the company. Mikkelson and Partch (II.9) find evidence that both takeover activity and managerial turnover declined from 1984–88 to 1989–93, and that the decline in managerial turnover was most marked among poorly performing firms. While not conclusive, the evidence suggests that the intensity of managerial discipline in the form of board decisions to replace top management, depends on the level of activity in the external market for corporate control.[17]

Bethel *et al.* (II.10) provide evidence that partial corporate control by large blockholders can also exert an important disciplinary influence on management; they find that block purchases by activists are followed by increases in asset divestitures, reductions in merger and acquisition activity, and share price increases. Esty (II.11) shows that the allocation of rights to cash flows, and to control in an organization can have an important effect on firm performance. He finds that stock thrifts and mutual thrifts behaved quite differently in the turbulent period of the 1980s, with the former taking on significantly more risk; this is consistent with control rights in the latter being vested in shareholders, the value of whose cash flow rights increases with risk because of the convex payoff function associated with equity claims. Brickley and Dark (II.12) study the choice of the organizational form that allocates control and cash flow rights. They find that the choice between franchising and direct ownership is determined by a trade-off between different types of agency cost and inefficiencies in risk bearing that are associated with the franchise form.

Part III of Volume II is concerned with the role of incentives and ownership in controlling managerial agency problems. Jensen and Murphy (1990) had argued that the pay performance sensitivity of US executives had declined significantly since the 1930s because of political constraints. Hadlock and Lumer (II.13) show that, once proper account is taken of size effects,[18] the sensitivity has remained constant for large firms and has actually risen for small firms. Moreover, the rate of managerial turnover in the 1930s was only about half the modern rate and was quite insensitive to stock returns. Like Mikkelson and Partch (II.9), they attribute the lower level of turnover to the lack of an active external market for corporate control in the 1930s. Hall and Liebman (II.14) show that pay-performance sensitivity has increased dramatically since 1969–83, the Jensen-Murphy sample period, primarily on account of a dramatic growth in stock option grants. Aggarwal and Samwick (II.15) test a key prediction of the agency model of executive compensation, that pay-performance sensitivity will be less in riskier firms because of risk-sharing considerations; they find strong support for this. Himmelberg *et al.* (II.16) take issue with the literature that has found a non-monotone relation between Tobin's q and the fraction of equity owned by the management and interpret it in terms of incentive-alignment and entrenchment effects.[19] The authors argue and provide evidence, that managerial ownership and Tobin's q are both endogenous variables that are determined by observable and unobservable firm characteristics; this endogeneity makes parameter estimates from simple regressions of Tobin's q on managerial ownership inconsistent. Taking account of the endogeneity with instrumental variables, the authors find only weak evidence of a causal relation from managerial equity ownership to Tobin's q. Denis *et al.* (II.17) provide evidence that value destroying diversification strategies are the result of agency problems;[20] they find that the level of firm diversification is negatively related to managerial and outside block equity ownership, and that decreases in diversification follow external control threats and managerial turnover.[21]

Part I of Volume III is concerned with corporate financing policies, its determinants and its effects. While the old Modigliani-Miller (1963) framework allowed only for tax and bankruptcy cost effects, the modern theory is much richer and the empirical literature reflects this, taxation and bankruptcy or liquidation costs receiving relatively little attention. La Porta *et al.* (III.1) are concerned with financial structure at the macro level. They demonstrate that the amounts of both external equity and debt financing in an economy depend on the legal environment. Countries with legal systems that provide strong protections for minority shareholders and creditors have the most developed debt and equity capital markets.

Graham (III.2) tests the implications of the traditional tax based theories of capital structure[22] that firms with higher effective marginal tax rates will issue more debt. He estimates the effective marginal tax rates of individual firms taking account of loss carryforwards, tax credits, alternative minimum tax, profit uncertainty etc., and finds, after controlling for other factors, that there is a strong relation between a firm's marginal tax rate and its propensity to issue additional debt. Graham *et al.* (III.3) uses a similar procedure to estimate the firm's effective tax rate before (debt and lease) financing, and shows that there is a positive relation between the firm's amount of debt financing and its marginal tax rate, and a negative relation between the firm's use of operating leases (which effectively allow firms to transfer depreciation allowances to other firms) and its marginal tax rate. There is no relation between a firm's use of capital leases (which are tax neutral) and a firm's tax status. These two studies provide strong evidence of the importance of tax considerations for a firm's financial policy.

Alderson and Betker (III.4) examine the capital structures that are chosen by firms emerging from Chapter 11 Bankruptcy and find that the debt ratio is strongly positively related to the ratio of the firm's estimated liquidation value to its going concern value. The difference between going concern value and liquidation value corresponds to the traditional concept of 'bankruptcy costs',[23] so their results support the traditional view that higher bankruptcy costs will be associated with lower leverage ratios. Hoven Stohs and Mauer (III.5) examine the characteristics of firms that are associated with longer term debt issues. In addition to asset maturity matching, they find strong evidence for Diamond's (1991) liquidity risk theory which predicts that firms with very high or low bond ratings will issue lower maturity debt; they find less support for the Myers (1977) hypothesis that agency cost considerations will lead firms with more investment opportunities to issue short-term debt. Their results also support Flannery's (1986) signaling hypothesis that firms with good private information will tend to issue shorter maturity debt.

Jensen (1986) argued that debt exerts a disciplinary role on management by forcing the firm to pay out its free cash flow which would otherwise be at the management's discretion; this suggests that managers will prefer lower debt levels, other things equal. Berger *et al.* (III.6) provide evidence that confirms this. They find that firms tend to have lower leverage when the CEO appears to be entrenched, does not face strong monitoring because the board is either large or contains few outsiders, and has low pay-performance sensitivity. Consistent with this, managerial turnover and acquisition threats lead to subsequent increases in debt. Safieddine and Titman (III.7) confirm that firms that have successfully resisted takeover attempts tend to increase their leverage. They find that the firms with the largest leverage increases then reduce capital expenditures, sell assets, reduce employment and improve performance; they are also less likely to be taken over subsequently. The authors interpret their findings as consistent with the theory that debt precommits the firm's management to take value increasing actions.[24]

While the classical Modigliani-Miller theories of capital structure took the assets of the firm as exogenous and unaffected by the way they were financed,[25] the subsequent papers of Jensen and Meckling (1976), Myers (1977), Jensen (1986) and others recognized that the value of an asset could be affected by the way in which it is financed and in which control is allocated. McConnell and Servaes (III.8) show that, consistent with the these theories, Tobin's q is positively associated with leverage for firms with low growth opportunities (Jensen), and is negatively associated with q for firms with strong growth opportunities (Myers). They also find evidence that inside and institutional ownership is a significant determinant of q.[26] Chevalier (III.9) provides evidence that suggests that firms compete less aggressively after taking on additional debt;[27] she finds that the leveraged buyout of a supermarket chain tended to be associated with stock price increases for the chain's competitors, and for more entry and expansion by competitors in the chain's markets.[28]

Kovenock and Phillips (III.10) show, in similar vein, that increases in leverage by firms in concentrated industries are followed by increased plant closings, while rival firms are less likely to close plants. However, they stress that the leverage changes are endogenous responses to long run changes in industry supply and demand conditions, so that causality from leverage to product market behavior cannot be inferred. Since the leverage effects are apparent only in concentrated industries, they conjecture that agency problems are more important in these industries where competition is less intense, so that debt is required to discipline managers in these industries.[29] Zingales (III.11) attempts to address the problem caused by the endogeneity of leverage by studying the effects of pre-deregulation leverage of trucking firms on their post-deregulation survival and profitability.[30] He finds that higher leverage is associated with lower levels of investment, which is consistent with the Myers (1977) underinvestment theory, and lower probability of survival, and that high leverage led to more aggressive price competition in the price-war that followed deregulation.[31]

Part II of Volume III deals with issues related to the choice of timing and type of security issue. Jung *et al.* (III.12) investigate the choice between debt and equity issuance. They find that equity issues are more likely the higher the firm's market to book ratio and its past returns, the lower its tax payments,[32] and the higher its existing long-term debt, but there is no significant evidence that the security choice is associated with subsequent security returns as might be expected if firms were able to time their equity issues. They interpret their results as consistent with a theory in which the agency costs of debt are higher for firms with good growth opportunities (high market to book ratio) because of the Myers (1977) underinvestment problem, so that such firms tend to issue debt. However, a significant proportion of firms in their sample issues equity even though they have debt capacity and their growth prospects (as measured by the market to book ratio) are not good; these firms experience a strong negative price reaction to the issue and, despite their poor growth prospects, their subsequent asset growth is high. The authors interpret these results as consistent with the role of managerial agency in which firms that wish to expand despite a lack of profitable investments issue equity to avoid the disciplinary role of debt.

Loughran and Ritter (III.13) provide detailed evidence that the average firm making initial or secondary public offerings of common stock is significantly overpriced. This is strong evidence that equity issuers are able to time the market.[33] In (III.14) the same authors demonstrate that the operating performance of firms making secondary equity issues deteriorates following the issue relative to the operating performance of non-issuers and argue that investors do not properly allow for this so that firms are able to take advantage of windows of opportunity to time their issues. Houston and Ryngaert (III.15) present evidence that is consistent with adverse selection or market timing in seasoned equity issues. They examine the market response to stock-financed bank merger announcements, and find that the price reaction is more favorable the greater the extent to which the bidder guarantees the target against adverse movements in the bidder's stock price.

Lang *et al.* (III.16) study another source of finance for firms, the sale of existing assets. They find that firms selling assets typically have high leverage, low earnings and low stock prices; moreover the stock price response to the sale announcement is strongly related to the use of the sale proceeds: they find that the price response is positive if the firm is planning to use the proceeds to pay down debt but negative if the proceeds are to be used to finance investment in these poorly performing firms. They conclude that asset sales are driven by a firm's financing needs and the high cost of alternative sources to firms with poor performance.

Part III of Volume III is concerned with the role of financial intermediaries in corporate finance. Hoshi *et al.* (III.17) compare the sensitivity of investment to liquidity for two sets of Japanese firms, one which has close ties to a bank which serves as its main source of finance, and one which has only weak bank ties. They find that investment is much less sensitive to liquidity for the first set, and conclude that banks may be able to mitigate informational and other imperfections in the capital market. Petersen and Rajan (III.18) document the importance of banking relationships for small US firms. They find that while the cost of bank credit is unrelated to the strength of the banking relationship (except that firms with multiple banks pay higher rates), the availability of credit increases in the length and extent of the firm's relationship with the bank, as would be predicted by information based theories of financial intermediation.

Carey *et al.* (III.19) compare the lending of banks and finance companies; they find that, while there are no significant differences in terms of information complexity[34] between bank borrowers and finance company borrowers, finance companies tend to lend to more highly levered companies than banks. Their results suggest that not only is the private-public debt distinction important, but that the type of private debt is also important. While the authors offer regulatory and reputational stories for the specialization in private lending, this appears to be an area in which empirical findings have at present outrun theory. Petersen and Rajan (III.20) analyze trade credit which is also an important source of corporate finance.[35] Theories of trade credit have been based on the informational advantages of suppliers, on the superior collateral value of goods to their sellers, and on its role as an instrument for price discrimination,[36] and the authors find support for all three theories. Sharpe and Nguyen (III.21) explore the determinants of lease finance. They find that the share of leasing in the total financing of a firm is higher for firms that face substantial financial contracting costs because of their weak financial position, and for firms that have low tax rates or significant loss carryforwards.[37]

Part I of Volume IV contains three papers that are concerned with management of the firm's risk exposure. Proposed benefits of risk management include benefits to shareholders through avoidance of the costs of financial distress including lost investment opportunities, and reductions in expected taxes due to the convexity of the corporate tax schedule, as well as purely managerial benefits associated with managerial risk aversion.[38] Tufano (IV.1) examines risk management practices in the gold mining industry in light of these theories.[39] He finds that the major determinants of risk management practices are the risk exposures through stock and options of the management; there is little evidence in favor of hypotheses based on shareholder benefits of hedging. An interesting finding is that managerial stock ownership leads to more hedging while managerial option ownership leads to less hedging. This finding is confirmed by Schrand and Unal (IV.2) who examine changes in the risk management of thrifts as they convert from mutual to stock form. In addition to the influence of the managerial ownership structure, they find evidence consistent with hedging policies being designed also to benefit all shareholders. Firstly, there is an increase in the total risk of the firm following conversion; secondly, they find that this is due to an increase in credit risk and a reduction in interest rate risk. They argue that the firms are co-ordinating their management of the different types of risk, reducing interest rate risk which they have no special advantage in bearing, and increasing credit risk which allows them to make profitable commercial loans. Petersen (IV.3) argues that a firm's risk is affected by whether it chooses a defined benefit or a defined contribution pension plan since there is more flexibility in the firm's contributions to the latter. Consistent with this, he finds that firms with high operating risk and for which the costs of financial distress are likely to be higher are significantly more likely to choose defined contribution pension plans.

Part II of Volume IV is concerned with the acquisitions and divestitures. Morck *et al.* (IV.4) show that if acquiring firm announcement returns are lower, the lower is the growth rate of the acquirer and the higher is the growth rate of the target; announcement returns are also lower for diversifying acquisitions in the 1980s. The authors argue that these unprofitable acquisitions are precisely the ones that are most likely to be driven by managerial career considerations and not by shareholder objectives. While Morck *et al.* show that takeovers may be one manifestation of a managerial agency problem, Mitchell and Lehn (IV.5) demonstrate that takeovers are also a solution to managerial agency problems. They show first that the announcement price response to acquisitions which are subsequently divested is significantly below that associated with acquisitions which are not subsequently divested. Thus the market appears to be able to distinguish good acquisitions from bad acquisitions. Moreover, the firms that make bad acquisitions are significantly more likely to be acquired later by other firms, so that the takeover market acts as a disciplinary mechanism.

Kaplan and Weisbach (IV.6) report that 44 per cent of large acquisitions are subsequently divested; however, using accounting data, they estimate that only about 34 per cent of the divestitures represent unsuccessful acquisitions so that divestiture itself is not a sign of an unsuccessful acquisition. The market is apparently able to recognize unsuccessful acquisitions, for the announcement returns are significantly lower for these than for successful divestitures and for acquisitions that are not subsequently divested. Finally, divestitures are about four times as likely for diversifying acquisitions as for related acquisitions.

Consistent with the evidence of Morck *et al.* (IV.4) that diversifying acquisitions are less profitable than related ones, Lang and Stulz (IV.7) find that diversified firms have lower values of Tobin's q than a similarly weighted portfolio of firms in the same industries: there appears to be a 'diversification discount'; there is some evidence that diversifying firms are relatively poor performers before they diversify which suggests that diversification may be driven by lack of growth opportunities in the current line of business.

Overall, these papers suggest that diversifying acquisitions tend to be unprofitable, that they are often driven by managerial rather than shareholder objectives, and that value destroying acquisitions tend to be punished by subsequent acquisition of the acquiring firm.

Bradley *et al.* (IV.8) report that the total value gain for bidder and target firms around tender offer announcements remained quite constant over the period 1963–84. However, the lion's share of the gains was captured by target stockholders, and their share increased significantly following the passage of the Williams Act in 1968 and the development of state anti-takeover statutes which strengthened the bargaining position of targets. This, and increasing competition between bidders, appears to have driven the returns to bidders negative in the period 1981–84. Warga and Welch (IV.9) provide empirical evidence of the bondholder expropriation effect associated with leveraged buyouts that reduce bond coverage ratios; the average affected bond drops in price by around 6 per cent. However, bond losses are poor predictors of stockholder gains, and on average represent only about 7 per cent of the gains to stockholders in LBOs. Ippolito and James (IV.10) examine pension fund terminations, another source of potential gains to shareholders in LBOs. They find no evidence that LBOs are driven by the potential gains from defined pension plan terminations; rather, consistent with other studies, the main precipitating factors are takeover threats and potential tax benefits. However, the termination of a defined benefit plan and its replacement by a defined contribution plan, which is consistent with the breach of an implicit pension contract, is about 2.5 times more likely for a firm that has undergone an LBO than for a similarly situated non-LBO firm.

Spinoffs are divestitures that are effected by distributing shares in a division to the firm's shareholders. Krishnaswami and Subramaniam (IV.11) test an information-based theory of spinoffs that argues that a spinoff enhances value because it mitigates information asymmetry in the market about the value of different divisions of a firm. They measure information asymmetry by variables such as the accuracy and dispersion of analysts' earnings forecast and find, consistent with the hypothesis, that firms that complete spinoffs have higher measures of information asymmetry than a control sample and that, following the spinoff, the measures of information asymmetry decline. Moreover, the spinoff announcement return is strongly related to the pre-spinoff measures of information asymmetry. These spinoff results are consistent with the diversification discount discussed by Lang and Stulz (IV.7) above.

Part III of Volume IV deals with issues of bankruptcy and liquidation. Pulvino (IV.12) provides evidence on one element of the bankruptcy costs that supported the classical theory of capital structure. He shows that airlines that are financially constrained receive lower prices for their aircraft than better financed firms.[40] Moreover, consistent with the industry debt equilibrium model of Shleifer and Vishny (1992), distressed airlines are more likely to sell their aircraft during recessions to leasing companies and other industry outsiders; these outsiders pay around 30 per cent less than other airlines. There is also evidence that well capitalized airlines were able to profit by purchasing aircraft from their distressed rivals during recessions. Franks and Torous (IV.13) compare voluntary debt restructurings with those which take place under Chapter 11 of the US Bankruptcy Code. They find that many firms resort to Chapter 11 only after attempting voluntary restructurings, and that creditors' recovery rates are much lower in Chapter 11 than in voluntary restructurings (51 per cent versus 80 per cent) because firms reorganizing under Chapter 11 are less solvent and less liquid than those that effect voluntary restructurings. The payoffs that equity investors receive in excess of their entitlement under the absolute priority rule are larger in voluntary exchanges than in Chapter 11 reorganizations;

the differences in payoffs suggesting that the incremental costs of Chapter 11 are of the order of 4.5 per cent of firm value.

Asquith *et al.* (IV.14) examine how distressed firms attempt to avoid bankruptcy through asset sales and debt restructurings; they find that firms with a combination of secured private debt and several public issues are least likely to avoid bankruptcy and, consistent with Pulvino (IV.12), that firms in distressed and highly levered industries are less able to avoid bankruptcy through asset sales, presumably because there are few potential purchasers for their assets. Gilson (IV.15) studies changes in corporate ownership and control following bankruptcy or voluntary re-organizations. He finds that over half of the board of directors and CEOs are removed following these events, and that directors who are retired serve less often as directors of other companies, so that financial distress imposes significant non-pecuniary costs on management.[41] In addition to changes in control, these events lead to significant changes in ownership structure, with significant increases in the proportion of the equity owned by blockholders and creditors. In the final paper of these volumes, Mehran *et al.* (IV.16) study corporate liquidations. Liquidations have been found by previous researchers to be associated with increases in shareholder wealth.[42] The authors confirm this finding and show that liquidation decisions are significantly influenced by the CEO incentive plan, the proportion of outside board members, as well as threats to the current management control.

The Mehran *et al.* paper is an appropriate paper on which to end this collection. Not only does it mark the end of the corporate life as well as the end of the collection, but it also reflects the major theme of the collection, that in understanding corporate finance it is necessary to understand the incentives of entrepreneurs, venture capitalists, investment bankers, investment analysts, boards of directors and managers, and investors, as well as the legal and contractual frameworks within which these actors perform. It is this emphasis on incentives and constraints that marks the divide between the classical Modigliani-Miller theories of corporate finance and their modern counterparts. The role of the seminal article of Jensen and Meckling (1976) in effecting this paradigm shift cannot be over-estimated.

Notes

1. I am grateful to Paul Gompers, Stuart Gilson, John McConnell, Henri Servaes, Ivo Welch, and Sheridan Titman for their suggestions in compiling this work. However, the selections are largely the product of my own views about what is important in the field.
2. 'It is rather as if the professional community had been suddenly transported to another planet where familiar objects are seen in a different light and are joined by unfamiliar ones as well.' (Kuhn, 1970, p. 111).
3. So popular has the event study approach that they developed become, that the *Journal of Economic Literature* now has a separate classification for event studies.
4. This approach was initially largely displaced by the event study approach and was subject to significant criticism on technical grounds (Keenan (1970); this criticism has been muted in recent years.
5. At a generous count, no more than a score of the 72 papers in these volumes can be thought of as explaining stock prices or stock price changes.
6. The paper at the cusp of the transition of the analysis of capital structure from a tax-based to an informational perspective is Masulis (1980).
7. See Safieddine and Titman (III.7).

8. For a subsequent analysis of estimators using daily stock returns see Brown and Warner (1985).
9. See Fama (1998).
10. One reason for this is that analysts are generally reluctant to make sell recommendations (Womack (1996)).
11. See Loughran and Ritter (III.13).
12. For example Loughran and Ritter (III.13). Fama (1998) treats such evidence with scepticism. However, it is interesting to note that Vermaelen is currently running a mutual fund whose stock selections are based on repurchase announcements.
13. Other papers that report evidence of downward-sloping demand curves for corporate stock include Shleifer (1986) and Loderer *et al.* (1991).
14. Brennan and Subrahmanyam (1995) show that increased analyst coverage enhances liquidity. For a discussion of liquidity and stock prices see Brennan and Tamarowski (2000).
15. See Gitman *et al.* (1977).
16. For an excellent survey of the real options model see Dixit and Pindyck (1994).
17. A similar conclusion is reached by Denis and Denis (1995).
18. Jensen and Murphy (1990) emphasized the relation between the dollar change in CEO wealth and the dollar change in the value of the firm; the more recent analyses focus on the relation between the dollar change in CEO wealth and the *proportional* change in the value of the firm.
19. See Morck *et al.* (1988) and McConnell and Servaes (1990).
20. See Lang and Stulz (IV.7) for evidence that diversification is value destroying.
21. See also Bethel *et al.* (II.10).
22. See for example DeAngelo and Masulis (1980).
23. Modern theories recognize the distinction between bankruptcy and liquidation which was frequently neglected in early theories of capital structure.
24. See Grossman and Hart (1982) and Jensen (1986).
25. With the modest exception of bankruptcy costs which were a peripheral element of the classical theory.
26. However, see the comments on Himmelberg *et al.* (II.16) above.
27. See also Chevalier (1995).
28. This is consistent with the predictions of Bolton and Scharfstein (1990), but contrary to those of Brander and Lewis (1986) and Maksimovic (1988) who predicted that leverage increases would make for tougher product market competition.
29. Their evidence is also consistent with that of Safieddine and Titman (III.7) who argue that debt is used as a precommitment device.
30. He argues that since the pre-deregulation leverage was unlikely to have been optimal for the post-deregulation environment it can legitimately be treated as exogenous.
31. This effect, which is concentrated in the less competitive segments of the industry is consistent with Brander and Lewis (1986) and Maksimovic (1988); see note 27.
32. See Graham (III.2).
33. While Jung *et al.* (III.12) were unable to find statistically significant differences between post issue returns of debt and equity issuers, this is most likely due to lack of power. See also Lerner (I.7) for evidence that venture capitalists can time the market. However, Brav and Gompers (1997) demonstrate that the underpricing of initial public offerings is almost exclusively confined to the smallest firms (below $50 million in market capitalization), and that the returns on these firms match those of non-issuers with the same combination of small size and high market to book ratio.
34. As measured by firm size, R&D intensity, market-to book ratio etc.
35. Around 15 per cent of total financing according to Rajan and Zingales (1995).
36. See Smith (1987), Brennan *et al.* (1988), Mian and Smith (1992).
37. See Graham *et al.* (III.3).
38. See for example, Smith and Stulz (1985), Froot *et al.* (1993).
39. In Tufano (1998) he shows that the firms' hedging policies have a significant effect on equity risk.
40. In Pulvino (1999) he shows that the prices received are even lower for firms in bankruptcy.
41. These non-pecuniary costs are fundamental to the debt signaling model of Ross (1977).
42. Hite *et al.* (1987) and Kim and Schatzberg (1987).

References

Black, F. and M. Scholes, 1973, 'The Pricing of Options and Corporate Liabilities', *Journal of Political Economy*, **81**, 637–59.

Bolton, P. and D.S. Scharfstein, 1990, 'A Theory of Predation Based on Problems in Financial Contracting', *American Economic Review*, **80**, 93–106.

Brander, J.A. and T.R. Lewis, 1986, 'Oligopoly and Financial Structure', *American Economic Review*, **76**, 956–70.

Brav, A. and P.A. Gompers, 1997, 'Myth or Reality? The Long-Run Underperformance of Initial Public Offerings: Evidence from Venture and Nonventure Capital-Backed Companies', *Journal of Finance*, **52**, 1791–821.

Brennan, M.J., V. Maksimovic and J. Zechner, 1988, 'Vendor Financing', *Journal of Finance*, **43**, 1127–141.

Brennan, M.J. and A. Subrahmanyam, 1995, 'Investment Analysis and Price Formation in Securities Markets', *Journal of Financial Economics*, **38**, 361–81.

Brennan, M.J. and C. Tamarowski, 2000, 'Investor Relations, Liquidity and Stock Prices', *Journal of Applied Corporate Finance*, **12**, 26–37.

Brown, S.J. and J.B. Warner, 1985, 'Using Daily Stock Returns: the Case of Event Studies', *Journal of Financial Economics*, **14**, 3–31.

Chevalier, J.A., 1995, 'Do LBO Supermarkets Charge More? An Empirical Analysis of the Effects of LBOs on Supermarket Pricing', *Journal of Finance*, **50**, 1095–112.

Denis, D.J. and D.K. Denis, 1995, 'Performance Changes following Top Management Dismissals', *Journal of Finance*, **50**, 1029–57.

Diamond, D.W., 1991, 'Debt Maturity Structure and Liquidity Risk', *Journal of Political Economy*, **106**, 709–37.

Dixit, A. and R.S. Pindyck, 1994, *Investment under Uncertainty*, Princeton University Press, Princeton, NJ.

Fama, E.F., 1998, 'Market Efficiency, Long-term Returns, and Behavioral Finance', *Journal of Financial Economics*, **49**, 283–306.

Fama, E.F., L. Fisher, M.C. Jensen and R. Roll, 1969, 'The Adjustment of Stock Prices to New Information', *International Economic Review*, **10**, 1–21.

Flannery, M.J., 1986, 'Asymmetric Information and Risky Debt Maturity Choice', *Journal of Finance*, **41**, 19–37.

Froot, K.A., D.S. Scharfstein and J.C. Stein, 1993, 'Risk Management: Co-Ordinating Corporate Investment and Financing Policies', *Journal of Finance*, **48**, 1629–58.

Gitman, L.J. and J.R. Forrester, 1977, 'A Survey of Capital Budgeting Techniques Used by Major U.S. Firms', *Financial Management*, **6**, 66–71.

Grinblatt, M. and C. Hwang, 1989, 'Signaling and the Pricing of New Issues', *Journal of Finance*, **44**, 393–420.

Grossman, S. and O. Hart, 1982, 'Corporate Financial Structure and Managerial Incentives', in J. McCall (ed.), *The Economics of Information and Uncertainty*, University of Chicago Press, Chicago.

Hite, G., J. Owers and R. Rogers, 1987, 'The Market for Interfirm Asset Sales', *Journal of Financial Economics*, **18**, 229–52.

Jensen, M.C. and W.H. Meckling, 1976, 'Theory of the Firm: Managerial Behavior, Agency Costs and Ownership Structure', *Journal of Financial Economics*, **3**, 305–60.

Jensen, M.C. and K.J. Murphy, 1990, 'Performance Pay and Top Management Incentives', *Journal of Political Economy*, **98**, 225–64.

Keenan, M., 1970, 'Models of Equity Valuation: the Great SERM Bubble', *Journal of Finance*, 243–73.

Kim, E. and J. Schatzberg, 1987, 'Voluntary Corporate Liquidation', *Journal of Financial Economics*, **19**, 311–28.

Kuhn, T.S., 1970, *The Structure of Scientific Revolutions (2nd edn)*, University of Chicago Press, Chicago, IL.

Loderer, C., J. Cooney and L. Van Drunen, 1991, 'The Price Elasticity of Demand for Common Stock', *Journal of Finance*, **46**, 621–51.

Maksimovic, V., 1988, 'Capital Structure in Repeated Oligopolies', *Rand Journal of Economics*, **19**, 389–407.

Masulis, R., 1980, 'The Effects of Capital Structure Changes on Security Prices: A Study of Exchange Offers', *Journal of Financial Economics*, **8**, 139–78.

McConnell, J.J. and H. Servaes, 1990, 'Additional Evidence on Equity Ownership and Corporate Value', *Journal of Financial Economics*, **27**, 595–612.

Mian, S. and C.W. Smith, 1992, 'Accounts Receivable Management Policy: Theory and Evidence', *Journal of Finance*, **47**, 169–200.

Miller, M.H. and F. Modigliani, 1961, 'Dividend Policy, Growth and the Valuation of Shares', *Journal of Business*, **34**, 235–64.

Modigliani, F. and M.H. Miller, 1963, 'Corporate Income Taxes and the Cost of Capital: A Correction', *American Economic Review*, **53**, 433–43.

Morck, R., Shleifer, A. and R. Vishny, 1988, 'Management Ownership and Market Valuation', *Journal of Financial Economics*, **20**, 293–315.

Myers, S.C., 1977, 'Determinants of Corporate Borrowing', *Journal of Financial Economics*, **5**, 147–75.

Pulvino, T., 1999, 'Effects of Bankruptcy Court Protection on Asset Sales', *Journal of Finance*, **52**, 151–86.

Rajan, R. and L. Zingales, 1995, 'What Do We Know about Capital Structure? Evidence from International Data', *Journal of Finance*, **50**, 1421–60.

Rock, K., 1986, 'Why New Issues are Underpriced', *Journal of Financial Economics*, **20**, 187–212.

Ross, S.A., 1977, 'The Determinants of Financial Structure: the Incentive Signalling Approach', *Bell Journal of Economics and Management Science*, **8**, 23–40.

Scholes, M., 1972, 'The Market for Securities: Substitution versus Price Pressure Effects', *Journal of Business*, 179–211.

Sharpe, W.F., 1963, 'A Simplified Model for Portfolio Analysis', *Management Science*, **9**, 277–93.

Shleifer, A., 1986, 'Do Demand Curves for Stock Slope Down?', *Journal of Finance*, **41**, 579–90.

Smith, C.W. and R. Stulz, 1985, 'The Determinants of Firms's Hedging Policies', *Journal of Financial and Quantitative Analysis*, **20**, 391–405.

Smith, J., 1987, 'Trade Credit and Information Asymmetry', *Journal of Finance*, **42**, 863–69.

Tufano, P., 1996, 'The Determinants of Stock Price Exposure: Financial Engineering and the Gold Mining Industry', *Journal of Finance*, **53**, 1015–52.

Womack, K.L., 1996, 'Do Brokerage Analysts' Recommendations have Investment Value?', *Journal of Finance*, **51**, 137–68.

Part I
Methodology

[1]

INTERNATIONAL
ECONOMIC
REVIEW

February, 1969
Vol. 10, No. 1

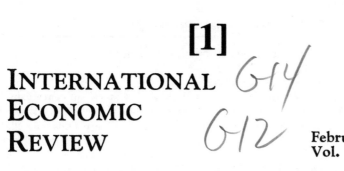

THE ADJUSTMENT OF STOCK PRICES
TO NEW INFORMATION*

By Eugene F. Fama, Lawrence Fisher,
Michael C. Jensen and Richard Roll[1]

1. INTRODUCTION

THERE IS an impressive body of empirical evi
successive price changes in individual common st
pendent.[2] Recent papers by Mandelbrot [11] and
ously that independence of successive price chan
"efficient" market, i.e., a market that adjusts rap

It is important to note, however, that in the en
usual procedure has been to *infer* market efficien
pendence of successive price changes. There h
testing of the speed of adjustment of prices to *sp*
mation. The prime concern of this paper is to ex_____ ___ p_____ __ w____
common stock prices adjust to the information (if any) that is implicit in a
stock split.

2. SPLITS, DIVIDENDS, AND NEW INFORMATION: A HYPOTHESIS

More specifically, this study will attempt to examine evidence on two related
questions: (1) Is there normally some "unusual" behavior in the rates of
return on a split security in the months surrounding the split?[3] and (2) if
splits are associated with "unusual" behavior of security returns, to what
extent can this be accounted for by relationships between splits and changes

* Manuscript received May 31, 1966, revised October 3, 1966.

[1] This study way suggested to us by Professor James H. Lorie. We are grateful
to Professors Lorie, Merton H. Miller, and Harry V. Roberts for many helpful comments and criticisms.

The research reported here was supported by the Center for Research in Security
Prices, Graduate School of Business, University of Chicago, and by funds made
available to the Center by the National Science Foundation.

[2] Cf.Cootner [2] and the studies reprinted therein, Fama [3], Godfrey, Granger, and
Morgenstern [8] and other empirical studies of the theory of random walks in speculative prices.

[3] A precise definition of "unusual" behavior of security returns will be provided
below.

in other more fundamental variables?[4]

In answer to the first question we shall show that stock splits are usually preceded by a period during which the rates of return (including dividends and capital appreciation) on the securities to be split are unusually high. The period of high returns begins, however, long before any information (or even rumor) concerning a possible split is likely to reach the market. Thus we suggest that the high returns far in advance of the split arise from the fact that during the pre-split period these companies have experienced dramatic increases in expected earnings and dividends.

In the empirical work reported below, however, we shall see that the highest average monthly rates of return on split shares occur in the few months immediately preceding the split. This might appear to suggest that the split itself provides some impetus for increased returns. We shall present evidence, however, which suggests that such is not the case. The evidence supports the following reasoning: Although there has probably been a dramatic increase in earnings in the recent past, in the months immediately prior to the split (or its announcement) there may still be considerable uncertainty in the market concerning whether the earnings can be maintained at their new higher level. Investors will attempt to use any information available to reduce this uncertainty, and a proposed split may be one source of such information.

In the past a large fraction of stock splits have been followed closely by dividend increases—and increases greater than those experienced at the same time by other securities in the market. In fact it is not unusual for the dividend change to be announced at the same time as the split. Other studies (cf. Lintner [10] and Michaelsen [14]) have demonstrated that, once dividends have been increased, large firms show great reluctance to reduce them, except under the most extreme conditions. Directors have appeared to hedge against such dividend cuts by increasing dividends only when they are quite sure of their ability to maintain them in the future, i.e., only when they feel strongly that future earnings will be sufficient to maintain the dividends at their new higher rate. Thus dividend changes may be assumed to convey important information to the market concerning management's

---

[4] There is another question concerning stock splits which this study does not consider. That is, given that splitting is not costless, and since the only apparent result is to multiply the number of shares per shareholder without increasing the shareholder's claims to assets, why do firms split their shares? This question has been the subject of considerable discussion in the professional financial literature. (Cf. Bellemore and Blucher [1].) Suffice it to say that the arguments offered in favor of splitting usually turn out to be two-sided under closer examination — e.g., a split, by reducing the price of a round lot, will reduce transactions costs for some relatively small traders but increase costs for both large and very small traders (i.e., for traders who will trade, exclusively, either round lots or odd lots both before and after the split). Thus the conclusions are never clear-cut. In this study we shall be concerned with identifying the factors which the *market* regards as important in a stock split and with determining how market prices adjust to these factors rather than with explaining why firms split their shares.

ADJUSTMENT OF STOCK PRICES 3

assessment of the firm's long-run earning and dividend paying potential.

We suggest, then, that unusually high returns on splitting shares in the months immediately preceding a split reflect the market's anticipation of substantial increases in dividends which, in fact, usually occur. Indeed evidence presented below leads us to conclude that when the information effects of dividend changes are taken into account, the apparent price effects of the split will vanish.[5]

3. SAMPLE AND METHODOLOGY

a. *The data.* We define a "stock split" as an exchange of shares in which at least five shares are distributed for every four formerly outstanding. Thus this definition of splits includes all stock dividends of 25 per cent or greater. We also decided, arbitrarily, that in order to get reliable estimates of the parameters that will be used in the analysis, it is necessary to have at least twenty-four successive months of price-dividend data around the split date. Since the data cover only common stocks listed on the New York Stock Exchange, our rules require that to qualify for inclusion in the tests a split security must be listed on the Exchange for at least twelve months before and twelve months after the split. From January, 1927, through December, 1959, 940 splits meeting these criteria occurred on the New York Stock Exchange.[6]

b. *Adjusting security returns for general market conditions.* Of course, during this 33 year period, economic and hence general stock market conditions were far from static. Since we are interested in isolating whatever *extraordinary* effects a split and its associated dividend history may have on returns, it is necessary to abstract from general market conditions in examining the returns on securities during months surrounding split dates. We do this in the following way: Define

P_{jt} = price of the j-th stock at end of month t.

$P'_{jt} = P_{jt}$ adjusted for capital changes in month $t + 1$. For the method of adjustment see Fisher [5].

D_{jt} = cash dividends on the j-th security during month t (where the dividend is taken as of the ex-dividend data rather than the payment date).

$R_{jt} = (P_{jt} + D_{jt})/P'_{j,t-1}$ = price relative of the j-th security for month t.

L_t = the link relative of Fisher's "Combination Investment Performance Index" [6, (table A1)]. It will suffice here to note that L_t is a com-

---

[5] It is important to note that our hypothesis concerns the information content of dividend changes. There is nothing in our evidence which suggests that dividend *policy* per se affects the value of a firm. Indeed, the information hypothesis was first suggested by Miller and Modigliani in [15, (430)], where they show that, aside from information effects, in a perfect capital market dividend policy will not affect the total market value of a firm.

[6] The basic data were contained in the master file of monthly prices, dividends, and capital changes, collected and maintained by the Center for Research in Security Prices (Graduate School of Business, University of Chicago). At the time this study was conducted, the file covered the period January, 1926 to December, 1960. For a description of the data see Fisher and Lorie [7].

4   FAMA, FISHER, JENSEN AND ROLL

plicated average of the R_{jt} for all securities that were on the N.Y.S.E. at the end of months t and $t-1$. L_t is the measure of "general market conditions" used in this study.[7]

One form or another of the following simple model has often been suggested as a way of expressing the relationship between the monthly rates of return provided by an individual security and general market conditions:[8]

$$(1) \qquad \log_e R_{jt} = \alpha_j + \beta_j \log_e L_t + u_{jt} ,$$

where α_j and β_j are parameters that can vary from security to security and u_{jt} is a random disturbance term. It is assumed that u_{jt} satisfies the usual assumptions of the linear regression model. That is, (a) u_{jt} has zero expectation and variance independent of t; (b) the u_{jt} are serially independent; and (c) the distribution of u_j is independent of $\log_e L$.

The natural logarithm of the security price relative is the rate of return (with continuous compounding) for the month in question; similarly, the log of the market index relative is approximately the rate of return on a portfolio which includes equal dollar amounts of all securities in the market. Thus (1) represents the monthly rate of return on an individual security as a linear function of the corresponding return for the market.

c. *Tests of model specification.* Using the available time series on R_{jt} and L_t, least squares has been used to estimate α_j and β_j in (1) for each of the 622 securities in the sample of 940 splits. We shall see later that there is strong evidence that the expected values of the residuals from (1) are non-zero in months close to the split. For these months the assumptions of the regression model concerning the disturbance term in (1) are not valid. Thus if these months were included in the sample, estimates of α and β would be subject to specification error, which could be very serious. We have attempted to avoid this source of specification error by excluding from the estimating samples those months for which the expected values of the

[7] To check that our results do not arise from any special properties of the index L_t, we have also performed all tests using Standard and Poor's Composite Price Index as the measure of market conditions; in all major respects the results agree completely with those reported below.

[8] Cf. Markowitz [13, (96–101)], Sharpe [17, 18] and Fama [4]. The logarithmic form of the model is appealing for two reasons. First, over the period covered by our data the distribution of the monthly values of $\log_e L_t$ and $\log_e R_{jt}$ are fairly symmetric, whereas the distributions of the relatives themselves are skewed right. Symmetry is desirable since models involving symmetrically distributed variables present fewer estimation problems than models involving variables with skewed distributions. Second, we shall see below that when least squares is used to estimate α and β in (1), the sample residuals conform well to the assumptions of the simple linear regression model.

Thus, the logarithmic form of the model appears to be well specified from a statistical point of view and has a natural economic interpretation (i.e., in terms of monthly rates of return with continuous compounding). Nevertheless, to check that our results do not depend critically on using logs, all tests have also been carried out using the simple regression of R_{jt} on L_t. These results are in complete agreement with those presented in the text.

ADJUSTMENT OF STOCK PRICES   5

residuals are apparently non-zero. The exclusion procedure was as follows: First, the parameters of (1) were estimated for each security using all available data. Then for each split the sample regression residuals were computed for a number of months preceding and following the split. When the number of positive residuals in any month differed substantially from the number of negative residuals, that month was excluded from subsequent calculations. This criterion caused exclusion of fifteen months before the split for all securities and fifteen months after the split for splits followed by dividend decreases[9].

Aside from these exclusions, however, the least squares estimates $\hat{\alpha}_j$ and $\hat{\beta}_j$ for security j are based on all months during the 1926–60 period for which price relatives are available for the security. For the 940 splits the smallest effective sample size is 14 monthly observations. In only 46 cases is the sample size less than 100 months, and for about 60 per cent of the splits more than 300 months of data are available. Thus in the vast majority of cases the samples used in estimating α and β in (1) are quite large.

Table 1 provides summary descriptions of the frequency distributions of the estimated values of α_j, β_j, and r_j, where r_j is the correlation between monthly rates of return on security j (i.e., $\log_e R_{jt}$) and the approximate monthly rates of return on the market portfolio (i.e., $\log_e L_t$). The table indicates that there are indeed fairly strong relationships between the market and monthly returns on individual securities; the mean value of the $\hat{r}_j$ is 0.632 with an average absolute deviation of 0.106 about the mean.[10]

TABLE 1

SUMMARY OF FREQUENCY DISTRIBUTIONS OF ESTIMATED COEFFICIENTS
FOR THE DIFFERENT SPLIT SECURITIES

Statistic	Mean	Median	Mean absolute deviation	Standard deviation	Extreme values	Skewness
$\hat{\alpha}$	0.000	0.001	0.004	0.007	−0.06, 0.04	Slightly left
$\hat{\beta}$	0.894	0.880	0.242	0.305	−0.10*, 1.95	Slightly right
$\hat{r}$	0.632	0.655	0.106	0.132	−0.04*, 0.91	Slightly left

* Only negative value in distribution.

Moreover, the estimates of equation (1) for the different securities conform fairly well to the assumptions of the linear regression model. For example,

[9] Admittedly the exclusion criterion is arbitrary. As a check, however, the analysis of regression residuals discussed later in the paper has been carried out using the regression estimates in which no data are excluded. The results were much the same as those reported in the text and certainly support the same conclusions.

[10] The sample average or mean absolute deviation of the random variable x is defined as

$$\frac{\sum\limits_{t=1}^{N} |x_t - \bar{x}|}{N}$$

where $\bar{x}$ is the sample mean of the x's and N is the sample size.

6   FAMA, FISHER, JENSEN AND ROLL

the first order auto-correlation coefficient of the estimated residuals from (1) has been computed for every twentieth split in the sample (ordered alphabetically by security). The mean (and median) value of the forty-seven coefficients is -0.10, which suggests that serial dependence in the residuals is not a serious problem. For these same forty-seven splits scatter diagrams of (a) monthly security return versus market return, and (b) estimated residual return in month $t+1$ versus estimated residual return in month t have been prepared, along with (c) normal probability graphs of estimated residual returns. The scatter diagrams for the individual securities support very well the regression assumptions of linearity, homoscedasticity, and serial independence.

It is important to note, however, that the data do not conform well to the normal, or Gaussian linear regression model. In particular, the distributions of the estimated residuals have much longer tails than the Gaussian. The typical normal probability graph of residuals looks much like the one shown for Timken Detroit Axle in Figure 1. The departures from normality in the distributions of regression residuals are of the same sort as those noted by Fama [3] for the distributions of returns themselves. Fama (following

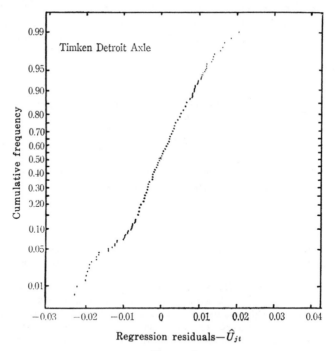

FIGURE 1

NORMAL PROBABILITY PLOT OF RESIDUALS*

* The lower left and upper right corners of the graph represent the most extreme sample points. For clarity, only every tenth point is plotted in the central portion of the figure.

Mandelbrot [12]) argues that distributions of returns are well approximated by the non-Gaussian (i.e., infinite variance) members of the stable Paretian family. If the stable non-Gaussian distributions also provide a good description of the residuals in (1), then, at first glance, the least squares regression model would seem inappropriate.

Wise [19] has shown, however, that although least square estimates are not "efficient," for most members of the stable Paretian family they provide estimates which are unbiased and consistent. Thus, given our large samples, least squares regression is not completely inappropriate. In deference to the stable Paretian model, however, in measuring variability we rely primarily on the mean absolute deviation rather than the variance or the standard deviation. The mean absolute deviation is used since, for long-tailed distributions, its sampling behavior is less erratic than that of the variance or the standard deviation[11].

In sum we find that regressions of security returns on market returns over time are a satisfactory method for abstracting from the effects of general market conditions on the monthly rates of return on individual securities. We must point out, however, that although (1) stands up fairly well to the assumptions of the linear regression model, it is certainly a grossly over-simplified model of price formation; general market conditions alone do not determine the returns on an individual security. In (1) the effects of these "omitted variables" are impounded into the disturbance term u. In particular, if a stock split is associated with abnormal behavior in returns during months surrounding the split date, this behavior should be reflected in the estimated regression residuals of the security for these months. The remainder of our analysis will concentrate on examining the behavior of the estimated residuals of split securities in the months surrounding the splits.

3. "EFFECTS" OF SPLITS ON RETURNS: EMPIRICAL RESULTS

In this study we do not attempt to determine the effects of splits for individual companies. Rather we are concerned with whether the process of splitting is in general associated with specific types of return behavior. To abstract from the eccentricities of specific cases we can rely on the simple process of averaging; we shall therefore concentrate attention on the behavior of cross-sectional averages of estimated regression residuals in the months surrounding split dates.

a. *Some additional definitions.* The procedure is as follows: For a given split, define month 0 as the month in which the effective date of a split occurs. (Thus month 0 is not the same chronological date for all securities, and indeed some securities have been split more than once and hence have more than one month 0).[12] Month 1 is then defined as the month immediately

[11] Essentially, this is due to the fact that in computing the variance of a sample, large deviations are weighted more heavily than in computing the mean absolute deviation. For empirical evidence concerning the reliability of the mean absolute deviation relative to the variance or standard deviation see Fama [3, (94-8)].

[12] About a third of the securities in the master file split. About a third of these split more than once.

8   FAMA, FISHER, JENSEN AND ROLL

following the split month, while month -1 is the month preceding, etc. Now define the average residual for month m (where m is always measured relative to the split month) as

$$u_m = \frac{\sum_{j=1}^{N_m} \hat{u}_{jm}}{N_m}$$

where $\hat{u}_{jm}$ is the sample regression residual for security j in month m and n_m is the number of splits for which data are available in month m.[13] Our principal tests will involve examining the behavior of u_m for m in the interval $-29 \leq m \leq 30$, i.e., for the sixty months surrounding the split month.

We shall also be interested in examining the cumulative effects of abnormal return behavior in months surrounding the split month. Thus we define the cumulative average residual U_m as

$$U_m = \sum_{k=-29}^{m} u_k .$$

The average residual u_m can be interpreted as the average deviation (in month m relative to the split month) of the returns of split stocks from their normal relationships with the market. Similarly, the cumulative average residual U_m can be interpreted as the cumulative deviation (from month -29 to month m); it shows the cumulative effects of the wanderings of the returns of split stocks from their normal relationships to market movements.

Since the hypothesis about the effects of splits on returns expounded in Section 2 centers on the dividend behavior of split shares, in some of the tests to follow we examine separately splits that are associated with increased dividends and splits that are associated with decreased dividends. In addition, in order to abstract from general changes in dividends across the market, "increased" and "decreased" dividends will be measured relative to the average dividends paid by all securities on the New York Stock Exchange during the relevant time periods. The dividends are classified as follows: Define the dividend change ratio as total dividends (per equivalent unsplit share) paid in the twelve months after the split, divided by total dividends paid during the twelve months before the split.[14] Dividend "increases" are then defined as cases where the dividend change ratio of the split stock is greater than the ratio for the Exchange as a whole, while dividend "decreases" include cases of relative dividend decline.[15] We then define u_m^+, u_m^- and U_m^+,

[13] Since we do not consider splits of companies that were not on the New York Stock Exchange for at least a year before and a year after a split, n_m will be 940 for $-11 \leq m \leq 12$. For other months, however, $n_m < 940$.

[14] A dividend is considered "paid" on the first day the security trades ex-dividend on the Exchange.

[15] When dividend "increase" and "decrease" are defined relative to the market, it turns out that dividends were never "unchanged." That is, the dividend change ratios of split securities are never identical to the corresponding ratios for the Exchange as a whole.

(*Continued on next page*)

ADJUSTMENT OF STOCK PRICES   9

U_m^- as the average and cumulative average residuals for splits followed by "increased" (+) and "decreased" (−) dividends.

These definitions of "increased" and "decreased" dividends provide a simple and convenient way of abstracting from general market dividend changes in classifying year-to-year dividend changes for individual securities. The definitions have the following drawback, however. For a company paying quarterly dividends an increase in its dividend rate at any time during the nine months before or twelve months after the split can place its stock in the dividend "increased" class. Thus the actual increase need not have occurred in the year after the split. The same fuzziness, of course, also arises in classifying dividend "decreases." We shall see later, however, that this fuzziness fortunately does not obscure the differences between the aggregate behavior patterns of the two groups.

b. *Empirical Results.* The most important empirical results of this study are summarized in Tables 2 and 3 and Figures 2 and 3. Table 2 presents the average residuals, cumulative average residuals, and the sample size for each of the two dividend classifications ("increased," and "decreased") and for the total of all splits for each of the sixty months surrounding the split. Figure 2 presents graphs of the average and cumulative average residuals for the total sample of splits and Figure 3 presents these graphs for each of the two dividend classifications. Table 3 shows the number of splits each year along with the end of June level of the stock price index.

Several of our earlier statements can now be substantiated. First, Figures 2a, 3a and 3b show that the average residuals (u_m) in the twenty-nine months prior to the split are uniformly positive for all splits and for both classes of dividend behavior. This can hardly be attributed entirely to the splitting process. In a random sample of fifty-two splits from our data the median time between the announcement date and the effective date of the split was 44.5 days. Similarly, in a random sample of one hundred splits that occurred between 1/1/1946 and 1/1/1957 Jaffe [9] found that the median time between announcement date and effective date was sixty-nine days. For both samples in only about 10 per cent of the cases is the time between announcement date and effective date greater than four months. Thus it seems safe to say that the split cannot account for the behavior of the regression residuals as far as two and one-half years in advance of the split date. Rather we suggest the obvious—a sharp improvement, relative to the market, in the earnings prospects of the company sometime during the years immediately preceding a split.

Thus we conclude that companies tend to split their shares during "abnormally" good times—that is during periods of time when the prices of their shares have increased much more than would be implied by the normal

---

In the remainder of the paper we shall always use "increase" and "decrease" as defined in the text. That is, signs of dividend changes for individual securities are measured relative to changes in the dividends for all N.Y.S.E. common stocks.

TABLE 2
ANALYSIS OF RESIDUALS IN MONTHS SURROUNDING THE SPLIT

(1) Month m	Splits followed by dividend "increases"			Splits followed by dividend "decreases"			All splits		
	(2) Average u_m^+	(3) Cumulative U_m^+	(4) Sample size N_m^+	(5) Average u_m^-	(6) Cumulative U_m^-	(7) Sample size N_m^-	(8) Average u_m	(9) Cumulative U_m	(10) Sample size N_m
−29	0.0062	0.0062	614	0.0033	0.0033	252	0.0054	0.0054	866
−28	0.0013	0.0075	617	0.0030	0.0063	253	0.0018	0.0072	870
−27	0.0068	0.0143	618	0.0007	0.0070	253	0.0050	0.0122	871
−26	0.0054	0.0198	619	0.0085	0.0155	253	0.0063	0.0185	872
−25	0.0042	0.0240	621	0.0089	0.0244	254	0.0056	0.0241	875
−24	0.0020	0.0259	623	0.0026	0.0270	256	0.0021	0.0263	879
−23	0.0055	0.0315	624	0.0028	0.0298	256	0.0047	0.0310	880
−22	0.0073	0.0388	628	0.0028	0.0326	256	0.0060	0.0370	884
−21	0.0049	0.0438	633	0.0131	0.0457	257	0.0073	0.0443	890
−20	0.0044	0.0482	634	0.0005	0.0463	257	0.0033	0.0476	891
−19	0.0110	0.0592	636	0.0102	0.0565	258	0.0108	0.0584	894
−18	0.0076	0.0668	644	0.0089	0.0654	260	0.0080	0.0664	904
−17	0.0072	0.0739	650	0.0111	0.0765	260	0.0083	0.0746	910
−16	0.0035	0.0775	655	0.0009	0.0774	260	0.0028	0.0774	915
−15	0.0135	0.0909	659	0.0101	0.0875	260	0.0125	0.0900	919
−14	0.0135	0.1045	662	0.0100	0.0975	263	0.0125	0.1025	925
−13	0.0148	0.1193	665	0.0099	0.1074	264	0.0134	0.1159	929
−12	0.0138	0.1330	669	0.0107	0.1181	266	0.0129	0.1288	935
−11	0.0098	0.1428	672	0.0103	0.1285	268	0.0099	0.1387	940
−10	0.0103	0.1532	672	0.0082	0.1367	268	0.0097	0.1485	940
− 9	0.0167	0.1698	672	0.0152	0.1520	268	0.0163	0.1647	940
− 8	0.0163	0.1862	672	0.0140	0.1660	268	0.0157	0.1804	940
− 7	0.0159	0.2021	672	0.0083	0.1743	268	0.0138	0.1942	940
− 6	0.0194	0.2215	672	0.0106	0.1849	268	0.0169	0.2111	940
− 5	0.0194	0.2409	672	0.0100	0.1949	268	0.0167	0.2278	940
− 4	0.0260	0.2669	672	0.0104	0.2054	268	0.0216	0.2494	940
− 3	0.0325	0.2993	672	0.0204	0.2258	268	0.0289	0.2783	940
− 2	0.0390	0.3383	672	0.0296	0.2554	268	0.0363	0.3147	940
− 1	0.0199	0.3582	672	0.0176	0.2730	268	0.0192	0.3339	940
0	0.0131	0.3713	672	−0.0090	0.2640	268	0.0068	0.3407	940
1	0.0016	0.3729	672	−0.0088	0.2552	268	−0.0014	0.3393	940
2	0.0052	0.3781	672	−0.0024	0.2528	268	0.0031	0.3424	940
3	0.0024	0.3805	672	−0.0089	0.2439	268	−0.0008	0.3416	940
4	0.0045	0.3851	672	−0.0114	0.2325	268	0.0000	0.3416	940
5	0.0048	0.3898	672	−0.0003	0.2322	268	0.0033	0.3449	940
6	0.0012	0.3911	672	−0.0038	0.2285	268	−0.0002	0.3447	940

(Continued on next page)

ADJUSTMENT OF STOCK PRICES   **11**

TABLE 2
(continued)

(1) Month m	Splits followed by dividend "increases"			Splits followed by dividend "decreases"			All splits		
	(2) Average u_m^+	(3) Cumulative U_m^+	(4) Sample size N_m^+	(5) Average u_m^-	(6) Cumulative U_m^-	(7) Sample size N_m^-	(8) Average u_m	(9) Cumulative U_m	(10) Sample size N_m
7	0.0008	0.3919	672	−0.0106	0.2179	268	−0.0024	0.3423	940
8	−0.0007	0.3912	672	−0.0024	0.2155	268	−0.0012	0.3411	940
9	0.0039	0.3951	672	−0.0065	0.2089	268	0.0009	0.3420	940
10	−0.0001	0.3950	672	−0.0027	0.2062	268	−0.0008	0.3412	940
11	0.0027	0.3977	672	−0.0056	0.2006	268	0.0003	0.3415	940
12	0.0018	0.3996	672	−0.0043	0.1963	268	0.0001	0.3416	940
13	−0.0003	0.3993	666	0.0014	0.1977	264	0.0002	0.3418	930
14	0.0006	0.3999	653	0.0044	0.2021	258	0.0017	0.3435	911
15	−0.0037	0.3962	645	0.0026	0.2047	258	−0.0019	0.3416	903
16	0.0001	0.3963	635	−0.0040	0.2007	257	−0.0011	0.3405	892
17	0.0034	0.3997	633	−0.0011	0.1996	256	0.0021	0.3426	889
18	−0.0015	0.3982	628	0.0025	0.2021	255	−0.0003	0.3423	883
19	−0.0006	0.3976	620	−0.0057	0.1964	251	−0.0021	0.3402	871
20	−0.0002	0.3974	604	0.0027	0.1991	246	0.0006	0.3409	850
21	−0.0037	0.3937	595	−0.0073	0.1918	245	−0.0047	0.3361	840
22	0.0047	0.3984	593	−0.0018	0.1899	244	0.0028	0.3389	837
23	−0.0026	0.3958	593	0.0043	0.1943	242	−0.0006	0.3383	835
24	−0.0022	0.3936	587	0.0031	0.1974	238	−0.0007	0.3376	825
25	0.0012	0.3948	583	−0.0037	0.1936	237	−0.0002	0.3374	820
26	−0.0058	0.3890	582	0.0015	0.1952	236	−0.0037	0.3337	818
27	−0.0003	0.3887	582	0.0082	0.2033	235	0.0021	0.3359	817
28	0.0004	0.3891	580	−0.0023	0.2010	236	−0.0004	0.3355	816
29	0.0012	0.3903	580	−0.0039	0.1971	235	−0.0003	0.3352	815
30	−0.0033	0.3870	579	−0.0025	0.1946	235	−0.0031	0.3321	814

relationships between their share prices and general market price behavior. This result is doubly interesting since, from Table 3, it is clear that for the exchange as a whole the number of splits increases dramatically following a general rise in stock prices. Thus splits tend to occur during general "boom" periods, and the particular stocks that are split will tend to be those that performed "unusually" well during the period of general price increase.

It is important to note (from Figure 2a and Table 2) that when all splits are examined together, the largest positive average residuals occur in the three or four months immediately preceding the split, but that after the split the average residuals are randomly distributed about 0. Or equivalently, in Figure 2b the *cumulative* average residuals rise dramatically up to the split month, but there is almost no further systematic movement thereafter. Indeed during the first year after the split, the cumulative average residual

12   FAMA, FISHER, JENSEN AND ROLL

TABLE 3

NUMBER OF SPLITS PER YEAR AND LEVEL OF THE STOCK MARKET INDEX

Year	Number of splits	Market Index* (End of June)
1927	28	103.5
28	22	133.6
29	40	161.8
1930	15	98.9
31	2	65.5
32	0	20.4
33	1	82.9
34	7	78.5
35	4	73.3
36	11	124.7
37	19	147.4
38	6	100.3
39	3	90.3
1940	2	91.9
41	3	101.2
42	0	95.9
43	3	195.4
44	11	235.0
45	39	320.1
46	75	469.2
47	46	339.9
48	26	408.7
49	21	331.3
1950	49	441.6
51	55	576.1
52	37	672.2
53	25	691.9
54	43	818.6
55	89	1190.6
56	97	1314.1
57	44	1384.3
58	14	1407.3
59	103	1990.6

* Fisher's "Combination Investment Performance Index" shifted to a base January, 1926=100. See [6] for a description of its calculation.

changes by less than one-tenth of one percentage point, and the total change in the cumulative average residual during the two and one-half years following the split is less than one percentage point. This is especially striking since 71.5 per cent (672 out of 940) of all splits experienced greater percentage dividend increases in the year after the split than the average for all securities on the N.Y.S.E.

We suggest the following explanation for this behavior of the average residuals. When a split is announced or anticipated, the market interprets this (and correctly so) as greatly improving the probability that dividends

ADJUSTMENT OF STOCK PRICES 13

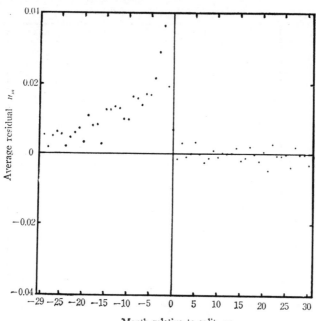

FIGURE 2a
AVERAGE RESIDUALS—ALL SPLITS

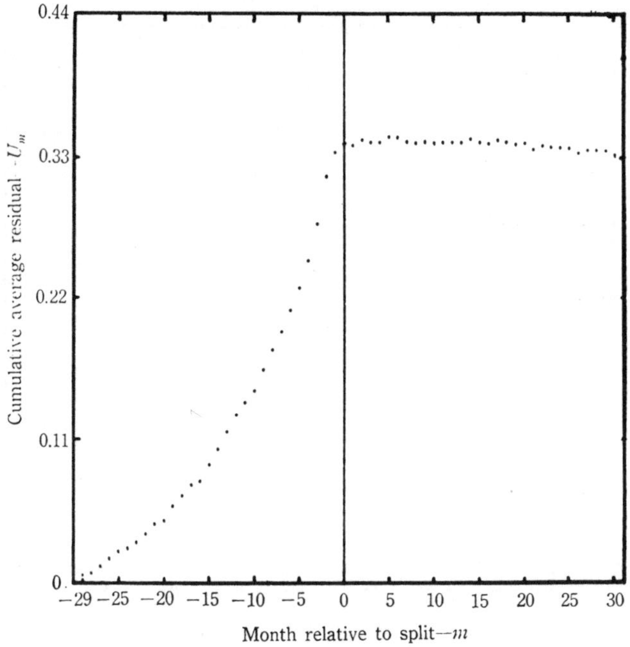

FIGURE 2b
CUMULATIVE AVERAGE RESIDUALS—ALL SPLITS

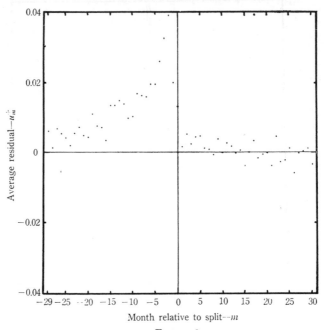

FIGURE 3a

AVERAGE RESIDUALS FOR DIVIDEND "INCREASES"

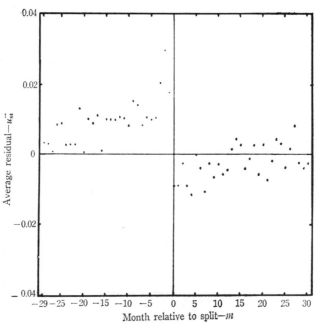

FIGURE 3b

AVERAGE RESIDUALS FOR DIVIDEND "DECREASES"

ADJUSTMENT OF STOCK PRICES   15

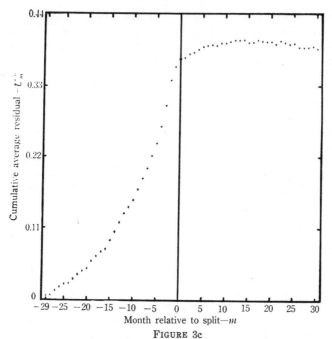

FIGURE 3c

CUMULATIVE AVERAGE RESIDUALS FOR DIVIDEND "INCREASES"

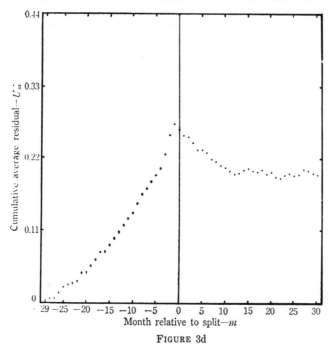

FIGURE 3d

CUMULATIVE AVERAGE RESIDUALS FOR DIVIDEND "DECREASES"

will soon be substantially increased. (In fact, as noted earlier, in many cases the split and dividend increase will be announced at the same time.) If, as Lintner [10] suggests, firms are reluctant to reduce dividends, then a split, which implies an increased expected dividend, is a signal to the market that the company's directors are confident that future earnings will be sufficient to maintain dividend payments at a higher level. If the market agrees with the judgments of the directors, then it is possible that the large price increases in the months immediately preceding a split are due to altering expectations concerning the future earning potential of the firm (and thus of its shares) rather than to any intrinsic effects of the split itself.[16]

If the information effects of actual or anticipated dividend increases do indeed explain the behavior of common stock returns in the months immediately surrounding a split, then there should be substantial differences in return behavior subsequent to the split in cases where the dividend increase materializes and cases where it does not. In fact it is apparent from Figure 3 that the differences are substantial—and we shall argue that they are in the direction predicted by the hypothesis.

The fact that the cumulative average residuals for both dividend classes rise sharply in the few months before the split is *consistent* with the hypothesis that the market recognizes that splits are usually associated with higher dividend payments. In some cases, however, the dividend increase, if it occurs, will be declared sometime during the year after the split. Thus it is not surprising that the average residuals (Figure 3a) for stocks in the dividend "increased" class are in general slightly positive, in the year after the split, so that the cumulative average residuals (Figure 3c) drift upward. The fact that this upward drift is only very slight can be explained in two (complementary) ways. First, in many cases the dividend increase associated with a split will be declared (and the corresponding price adjustments will take place) before the end of the split month. Second, according to our hypothesis when the split is declared (even if no dividend announcement is made), there is some price adjustment in anticipation of future dividend increases. Thus only a slight *additional* adjustment is necessary when the dividend increase actually takes place. By one year after the split the returns on stocks which have experienced dividend "increases" have resumed their normal relationships to market returns since from this point onward the average residuals are small and randomly scattered about zero.

The behavior of the residuals for stock splits associated with "decreased" dividends, however, provides the strongest evidence in favor of our split

[16] If this stock split hypothesis is correct, the fact that the average residuals (where the averages are computed using all splits (Figure 2) are randomly distributed about 0 in months subsequent to the split indicates that, on the average, the market has *correctly* evaluated the implications of a split for future dividend behavior and that these evaluations are fully incorporated in the price of the stock by the time the split occurs. That is, the market not only makes good forecasts of the dividend implications of a split, but these forecasts are fully impounded into the price of the security by the end of the split month. We shall return to this point at the end of this section.

hypothesis. For stocks in the dividend "decreased" class the average and cumulative average residuals (Figures 3b and 3d) rise in the few months before the split but then plummet in the few months following the split, when the anticipated dividend increase is not forthcoming. These split stocks with poor dividend performance on the average perform poorly in each of the twelve months following the split, but their period of poorest perform- ance is in the few months immediately after the split—when the improved dividend, if it were coming at all, would most likely be declared.[17] The hy- pothesis is further reinforced by the observation that when a year has passed after the split, the cumulative average residual has fallen to about where it was five months prior to the split which, we venture to say, is probably about the earliest time reliable information concerning a possible split is likely to reach the market.[18] Thus by the time it has become clear that the anticipated dividend increase is not forthcoming, the apparent effects of the split seem to have been completely wiped away, and the stock's returns have reverted to their normal relationship with market returns. In sum, our data suggest that once the information effects of associated dividend changes are properly considered, a split *per se* has no net effect on common stock returns.[19]

Finally, the data present important evidence on the speed of adjustment of market prices to new information. (a) Although the behavior of post-split returns will be very different depending on whether or not dividend "increases" occur, and (b) in spite of the fact that a substantial majority of split securities *do* experience dividend "increases," when all splits are examined together (Figure 2), the average residuals are randomly distributed about 0 during the year after the split. Thus there is no net movement either up or down in the cumu- lative average residuals. According to our hypothesis, this implies that on the average the market makes unbiased dividend forecasts for split securities and these forecasts are fully reflected in the price of the security by the end of the split month.

5. SPLITS AND TRADING PROFITS

Although stock prices adjust "rapidly" to the dividend information implicit in a split, an important question remains: Is the adjustment so rapid that splits can in no way be used to increase trading profits? Unfortunately our

---

[17] Though we do not wish to push the point too hard, it is interesting to note in Table 2 that after the split month, the largest negative average residuals for splits in the dividend "decreased" class occur in months 1, 4, and 7. This "pattern" in the residuals suggests, perhaps, that the market reacts most strongly during months when dividends are declared but not increased.

[18] In a random sample of 52 splits from our data in only 2 cases is the time be- tween the announcement date and effective date of the split greater than 162 days. Similarly, in the data of Jaffe [9] in only 4 out of 100 randomly selected splits is the time between announcement and effective date greater than 130 days.

[19] It is well to emphasize that our hypothesis centers around the information value of dividend changes. There is nothing in the empirical evidence which indicates that dividend policy *per se* affects the market value of the firm. For further dis- cussion of this point see Miller and Modigliani [15, (430)].

data do not allow full examination of this question. Nevertheless we shall proceed as best we can and leave the reader to judge the arguments for himself.

First of all, it is clear from Figure 2 that expected returns cannot be increased by purchasing split securities after the splits have become effective. After the split, on the average the returns on split securities immediately resume their normal relationships to market returns. In general, prices of split shares do not tend to rise more rapidly after a split takes place. Of course, if one is better at predicting which of the split securities are likely to experience "increased" dividends, one will have higher expected returns. But the higher returns arise from superior information or analytical talents and not from splits themselves.

Let us now consider the policy of buying splitting securities as soon as information concerning the possibility of a split becomes available. It is impossible to test this policy fully since information concerning a split often leaks into the market before the split is announced or even proposed to the shareholders. There are, however, several fragmentary but complementary pieces of evidence which suggest that the policy of buying splitting securities as soon as a split is *formally announced* does not lead to increased expected returns.

First, for a sample of 100 randomly selected splits during the period 1946–1956, Bellemore and Blucher [1] found that in general, price movements associated with a split are over by the day after the split is announced. They found that from eight weeks before to the day after the announcement, 86 out of 100 stocks registered percentage price increases greater than those of the Standard and Poor's stock price index for the relevant industry group. From the day after to eight weeks after the announcement date, however, only 43 stocks registered precentage price increases greater than the relevant industry index, and on the average during this period split shares only increased 2 per cent more in price than nonsplit shares in the same industry. This suggests that even if one purchases as soon as the announcement is made, split shares will not in general provide higher returns than nonsplit shares.[20]

Second, announcement dates have been collected for a random sample of 52 splits from our data. For these 52 splits the analysis of average and cumulative average residuals discussed in Section 4 has been carried out first using the split month as month 0 and then using the announcement month as month 0. In this sample the behavior of the residuals after the announcement date is almost identical to the behavior of the residuals after the split date. Since the evidence presented earlier indicated that one could

---

[20] We should note that though the results are Bellemore and Blucher's, the interpretation is ours.

Since in the vast majority of cases prices rise substantially in the eight weeks prior to the announcement date, Bellemore and Blucher conclude that if one has advance knowledge concerning a contemplated split, it can probably be used to increase expected returns. The same is likely to be true of all inside information, however.

ADJUSTMENT OF STOCK PRICES   **19**

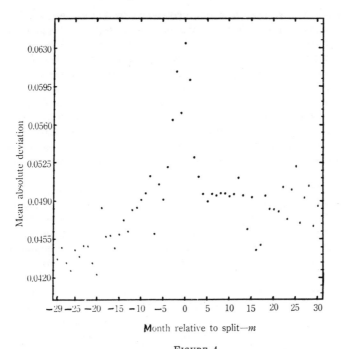

FIGURE 4

CROSS SECTIONAL MEAN ABSOLUTE DEVIATION OF RESIDUALS—ALL SPLITS

not systematically profit from buying split securities after the effective date of the split, this suggests that one also cannot profit by buying after the announcement date.

Although expected returns cannot in general be increased by buying split shares, this does not mean that a split should have no effect on an investor's decisions. Figure 4 shows the cross-sectional mean absolute deviations of the residuals for each of the sixty months surrounding the split. From the graph it is clear that the variability in returns on split shares increases substantially in the months closest to the split. The increased riskiness of the shares during this period is certainly a factor which the investor should consider in his decisions.

In light of some of the evidence presented earlier, the conclusion that splits cannot be used to increase expected trading profits may seem a bit anomalous. For example, in Table 2, column (8), the cross-sectional average residuals from the estimates of (1) are positive for at least thirty months prior to the split. It would seem that such a strong degree of "persistence" could surely be used to increase expected profits. Unfortunately, however, the behavior of the *average* residuals is not representative of the behavior of the residuals for *individual securities*; over time the residuals for individual securities are much more randomly distributed about 0. We can see this more clearly by comparing the average residuals for all splits (Figure 2a) with the month by month behavior of the cross-sectional mean absolute deviations of residuals for all splits (Figure 4). For each month before the split the mean absolute deviation of residuals is well over twice as large as the corresponding average residual, which indicates that for each month the residuals for many *individual* securities are negative. In fact, in examining residuals for individual securities the following pattern was typical: Prior to the split, successive sample residuals from (1) are almost completely independent. In most cases, however, there are a few months for which the residuals are abnormally large and positive. These months of large residuals differ from security to security, however, and these differences in timing explain why the signs of the *average* residuals are uniformly positive for many months preceding the split.

Similarly, there is evidence which suggests that the extremely large positive average residuals in the three or four months prior to the split merely reflect the fact that, from split to split, there is a variable lag between the time split information reaches the market and the time when the split becomes effective. Jaffe [9] has provided announcement and effective dates for the 100 randomly chosen splits used by herself and Bellemore [1]. The announcement dates occur as follows: 7 in the first month before the split, 67 in the second and third months, 14 in the fourth month, and 12 announcements more than four months before the split. Looking back at Table 2, column (8), and Figure 2a we see that the largest average residuals follow a similar pattern: The largest average residuals occur in the second and third months before the split; though smaller, the average residuals for one and four months before the split are larger than those of any other months.

This suggests that the pattern of the average residuals immediately prior to the split arises from the averaging process and thus cannot be assumed to hold for any particular security.

6. CONCLUSIONS

In sum, in the past stock splits have very often been associated with substantial dividend increases. The evidence indicates that the market realizes this and uses the announcement of a split to re-evaluate the stream of expected income from the shares. Moreover, the evidence indicates that on the average the market's judgments concerning the information implications of a split are fully reflected in the price of a share at least by the end of the split month but most probably almost immediately after the announcement date. Thus the results of the study lend considerable support to the conclusion that the stock market is "efficient" in the sense that stock prices adjust very rapidly to new information.

The evidence suggests that in reacting to a split the market reacts only to its dividend implications. That is, the split causes price adjustments only to the extent that it is associated with changes in the anticipated level of future dividends.

Finally, there seems to be no way to use a split to increase one's expected

ADJUSTMENT OF STOCK PRICES   21

returns, unless, of course, inside information concerning the split or subsequent dividend behavior is available.

University of Chicago, University of Rochester, and
Carnegie-Mellon University, U.S.A.

REFERENCES

[1] BELLEMORE, DOUGLAS H. and Mrs. LILLIAN BLUCHER (JAFFE), "A Study of Stock Splits
in the Postwar Years," *Financial Analysts Journal,* XV (November, 1956), 19-26.

[2] COOTNER, PAUL H., ed., *The Random Character of Stock Market Prices* (Cambridge,
Mass.: M.I.T. Press, 1964).

[3] FAMA, EUGENE F., "The Behavior of Stock-Market Prices," *Journal of Business,*
XXXVIII (January, 1965), 34-105.

[4] ———, "Portfolio Analysis in a Stable Paretian Market," *Management Science,*
XI (January, 1965), 404-19.

[5] FISHER, LAWRENCE, "Outcomes for 'Random' Investments in Common Stocks
Listed on the New York Stock Exchange," *Journal of Business,* XXXVIII (April,
1965), 149-61.

[6] ———, "Some New Stock Market Indexes," *Journal of Business,* XXXIX (Supplement, January, 1966), 191-225.

[7] ——— and JAMES H. LORIE, "Rates of Return on Investments in Common
Stocks," *Journal of Business,* XXXVII (January, 1964), 1-21.

[[8] GODFREY, MICHAEL D., CLIVE W. J. GRANGER and OSKAR MORGENSTERN, "The
Random Walk Hypothesis of Stock Market Behavior," *Kyklos,* XVII (1964), 1-30.

[9] JAFFE (BLUCHER), LILLIAN H., "A Study of Stock Splits, 1946-1956," Unpublished
Master's Thesis, Graduate School of Business Administration, New York University (1957).

[10] LINTNER, JOHN, "Distribution of Incomes of Corporations Among Dividends,
Retained Earnings and Taxes," *American Economic Review,* XLVI (May, 1956),
97-113.

[11] MANDELBROT, BBNOIT, "Forecasts of Future Prices, Unbiased Markets, and
'Martingale' Models," *Journal of Business,* XXXIX (Supplement, January, 1966),
242-255.

[12] ———, "The Variation of Certain Speculative Prices," *Journal of Business,*
XXXVI (October, 1963), 394-419.

[13] MARKOWITZ, HARRY, *Portfolio Selection: Efficient Diversification of Investments*
(New York: Wiley, 1959).

[14] MICHAELSEN, JACOB B., "The Determinants of Dividend Policies: A Theoretical
and Empirical Study," Unpublished Doctoral Dissertation, Graduate School of
Business, University of Chicago (1961).

[15] MILLER, MERTON H. and FRANCO MODIGLIANI, "Dividend Policy, Growth and the
Valuation of Shares," *Journal of Business,* XXXIV (October, 1961), 411-33.

[16] SAMUELSON, PAUL A., "Proof That Properly Anticipated Prices Fluctuate Randomly," *Industrial Management Review* (Spring, 1965), 41-49.

[17] SHARPE, WILLIAM F., "Capital Asset Pricing: A Theory of Market Equilibrium
under Conditions of Risk," *Journal of Finance,* XIX (September, 1964), 425-42.

[18] ———, "A Simplified Model for Portfolio Analysis," *Management Science,* IX
(January, 1963), 277-93.

[19] WISE, JOHN, "Linear Estimators for Linear Regression Systems Having Infinite
Variances," paper presented at the Berkeley-Stanford Mathematical Economics
Seminar (October, 1963).

Journal of Financial Economics 8 (1980) 205–258. © North-Holland Publishing Company

MEASURING SECURITY PRICE PERFORMANCE*

Stephen J. BROWN

Bell Laboratories, Murray Hill, NJ 07974, USA

Jerold B. WARNER

University of Rochester, Rochester, NY 14627, USA

Received January 1980, revised version received April 1980

Event studies focus on the impact of particular types of firm-specific events on the prices of the affected firms' securities. In this paper, observed stock return data are employed to examine various methodologies which are used in event studies to measure security price performance. Abnormal performance is introduced into this data. We find that a simple methodology based on the market model performs well under a wide variety of conditions. In some situations, even simpler methods which do not explicitly adjust for marketwide factors or for risk perform no worse than the market model. We also show how misuse of any of the methodologies can result in false inferences about the presence of abnormal performance.

1. Introduction and summary

The impact of particular types of firm-specific events (e.g., stock splits, earnings reports) on the prices of the affected firms' securities has been the subject of a number of studies. A major concern in those 'event' studies has been to assess the extent to which security price performance around the time of the event has been abnormal — that is, the extent to which security returns were different from those which would have been appropriate, given the model determining equilibrium expected returns.

Event studies provide a direct test of market efficiency. Systematically nonzero abnormal security returns which persist after a particular type of event are inconsistent with the hypothesis that security prices adjust quickly to fully reflect new information. In addition, to the extent that the event is unanticipated, the magnitude of abnormal performance at the time the event actually occurs is a measure of the impact of that type of event on the wealth of the firms' claimholders. Any such abnormal performance is consistent with market efficiency, however, since the abnormal returns would only have been

*Financial support for this research was provided to J.B. Warner by the Managerial Economics Research Center, University of Rochester, and the Institute for Quantitative Research in Finance, Columbia University. We are indebted to numerous colleagues for their help on this paper. We are especially grateful to Michael Gibbons and Michael Jensen for their assistance.

attainable by an investor if the occurrence of the event could have been predicted with certainty.

In this paper, observed stock return data are employed to examine various methodologies which are used in event studies to measure security price performance. Abnormal performance is introduced into this data. We assess the likelihood that various methodologies will lead to Type I errors — rejecting the null hypothesis of no abnormal performance when it is true, and Type II errors — failing to reject the null hypothesis of no abnormal performance when it is false. Our concern is with the power of the various methodologies. Power is the probability, for a given level of Type I error and a given level of abnormal performance, that the hypothesis of no abnormal performance will be rejected. Since a test's power indicates its ability to discern the presence of abnormal performance, then all other things equal, a more powerful test is preferred to a less powerful test.

The use of various methodologies is simulated by repeated application of each methodology to samples which have been constructed by random selection of securities and random assignment of an 'event-date' to each. Randomly selected securities should not, on average, exhibit any abnormal performance. Thus, for a large number of applications of a given methodology, we examine the frequency of Type I errors. Abnormal performance is then artificially introduced by transforming each sample security's return around the time it experiences a hypothetical event. Each methodology is then applied to a number of samples where the return data have thus been transformed. For each methodology, and for various levels of abnormal performance, this technique provides direct measures of the frequency of Type II errors. Since, for any given level of abnormal performance, the power of a test is equal to one minus the probability of a Type II error, this technique thus allows us to examine the power of the methodologies and the ability to detect abnormal performance when it is present.

Overview of the paper

General considerations which are relevant to measuring abnormal security price performance are discussed in section 2. Performance measures in event studies are classified into several categories: Mean Adjusted Returns, Market Adjusted Returns, and Market and Risk Adjusted Returns. In section 3, we specify methodologies which are based on each of these performance measures and which are representative of current practice. We then devise a simulation procedure for studying and comparing these methods, and their numerous variations.

Initial results are presented in section 4. For each methodology, the probability of Type I and Type II errors is assessed for both parametric and non-parametric significance tests. In addition, the distributional properties of the test statistics generated by each methodology are examined. We also focus on different ways in which actual event studies take into account the systematic risk of the sample securities. The risk adjustment methods we compare are based on market model residuals, Fama–MacBeth residuals, and what we call Control Portfolios.

In section 5, we discuss the effect of imprecise prior information about the timing of the event on the power of the tests. The use of the Cumulative Average Residual procedure suggested by Fama, Fisher, Jensen and Roll (1969) is also investigated.

In section 6, two forms of sample security 'clustering' are examined. We first look at the calendar time clustering of events, and examine the characteristics of the tests when all sample securities experience an event during the same calendar time period. We then examine how the tests are affected when all sample securities have higher than average (or lower than average) systematic risk.

Section 7 examines the effect of the choice of market index on the various tests. Section 8 reports additional simulation results. The sensitivity of earlier simulation results to the number of sample securities is investigated. Evidence is also presented on the likelihood that the various test methods will, for a given sample, lead to the same inference.

Our conclusions, along with a summary of the paper's major results, are presented in section 9; an appendix contains a more detailed discussion of the specific performance assessment methods used in the study.

2. Measuring abnormal performance: General considerations

2.1. Defining abnormal performance for a security

A security's price performance can only be considered 'abnormal' relative to a particular benchmark. Thus, it is necessary to specify a model generating 'normal' returns before abnormal returns can be measured. In this paper, we will concentrate on three general models of the process generating *ex ante* expected returns. These models are general representations of the models which have been assumed in event studies. For each model, the abnormal return for a given security in any time period t is defined as the difference between its actual *ex post* return and that which is predicted under the assumed return-generating process, The three models are as follows.

(1) Mean Adjusted Returns

The Mean Adjusted Returns model assumes that the *ex ante* expected return for a given security i is equal to a constant K_i which can differ across securities: $E(\tilde{R}_i) = K_i$. The predicted *ex post* return on security i in time period t is equal to K_i. The abnormal return ε_{it} is equal to the difference between the observed return, R_{it}, and the predicted return K_i: $\varepsilon_{it} = R_{it} - K_i$.

The Mean Adjusted Returns model is consistent with the Capital Asset Pricing Model; under the assumption that a security has constant systematic risk and that the efficient frontier is stationary, the Asset Pricing Model also predicts that a security's expected return is constant.

(2) Market Adjusted Returns

This model assumes that *ex ante* expected returns are equal across securities, but not necessarily constant for a given security. Since the market portfolio of risky assets M is a linear combination of all securities, it follows that $E(\tilde{R}_{it}) = E(\tilde{R}_{mt}) = K_t$ for any security i. The *ex post* abnormal return on any security i is given by the difference between its return and that on the market portfolio: $\varepsilon_{it} = R_{it} - R_{mt}$. The Market Adjusted Returns model is also consistent with the Asset Pricing model if all securities have systematic risk of unity.

(3) Market and Risk Adjusted Returns

This model presumes that some version of the Capital Asset Pricing Model generates expected returns. For example, in the Black (1972) two-parameter Asset Pricing Model, $E(\tilde{R}_{it}) = E(\tilde{R}_{zt}) + \beta_i[E(\tilde{R}_{mt}) - E(\tilde{R}_{zt})] = K_{it}$ for any security i, where R_{zt} is the return on a minimum variance portfolio of risky assets which is uncorrelated with the market portfolio. In the Black model, the abnormal return ε_{it} is equal to $R_{it} - [R_{zt}(1 - \beta_i) + \beta_i R_{mt}]$.

For each of these three models, the return which will be realized on security i in period t, $\tilde{R}_{it}$, is given by

$$\tilde{R}_{it} = K_{it} + \tilde{\varepsilon}_{it},$$

where K_{it} is the expected return given by the particular model, and $\tilde{\varepsilon}_{it}$, which is unknown at the beginning of period t, is the component which is abnormal or unexpected.

2.2. Evaluating alternative performance measures

Under each model of the return generating process, there will be times when the realized return on a given security is different from that which was predicted. However, returns in an efficient market cannot systematically differ from those which are predicted. That is, the expected value of the unexpected component, $\tilde{\varepsilon}_{it}$, of a security's return cannot systematically differ from zero.

Let I be an integer which is equal to 0 when no 'event' takes place, and equal to 1 when a particular event does take place. In an efficient market, the abnormal return measure ε_{it}, if correctly specified, must be such that

$$E(\tilde{\varepsilon}_{it}) = [E(\tilde{\varepsilon}_{it} \mid I=0)]p(I=0) + [E(\tilde{\varepsilon}_{it} \mid I=1)]p(I=1) = 0;$$

abnormal returns conditional on the event can systematically be non-zero, as can abnormal returns conditional on no event. The only restriction is that a security's abnormal return, weighted by its magnitude and probability of occurrence, have an expected value of zero. Under each model just discussed, the abnormal performance measure for every security has an unconditional mean of 0 if the model is correct. In that sense, the abnormal performance measures are unbiased for each model.

Of course, another major purpose of specifying the 'correct' model for expected returns is to reduce the variance of the abnormal return component ε_{it}. For example, in the Market and Risk Adjusted Returns model, a contemporaneous relationship between realized security returns and realized market returns is predicted by the *ex ante* model. In an event study, where the market return which was observed at the time of each firm's event is known, the variance of the abnormal component of returns will be lower if a model takes into account the *ex post* relationship between a security's return and that of the market. When the *ex post* return generating process is correctly specified, abnormal performance, which is just the difference between returns conditional on the event and returns unconditional on the event, should be easier to detect.[1] Thus, if the Capital Asset Pricing model is correct, then the Market and Risk Adjusted Returns method, by bringing to bear additional information about the determinants of realized returns, such as the security's systematic risk and the market's return, could increase the power of the tests over the Mean Adjusted Returns method.[2]

---

[1]Our definition of abnormal performance as the difference between conditional (expected) and unconditional (expected) returns is consistent with the abnormal performance metric used in studies where the event is associated with either good news ($I=1$) or bad news ($I=0$) [e.g., Ball and Brown (1968)]. In such studies, abnormal performance is often measured as the average of the deviation from unconditional returns when there is good news and the deviation from unconditional returns when there is bad news, where the deviation from unconditional returns when there is bad news is first multiplied by -1. It can be shown that this abnormal performance measure is equal to our definition of abnormal performance conditional on good news, multiplied by twice the probability of good news. If good news has probability 0.5, the two abnormal performance measures will be identical; in general, the two measures differ only by a factor of proportionality. See Patell (1979, p. 536) for a related discussion.

[2]This line of argument has been pushed still further. The Asset Pricing model allows a security's return to be contemporaneously related to additional 'factors' as well. For example, a security's realized return could be related to the return on the securities of a particular industry. Even though there is no 'industry factor' in the *ex ante* Asset Pricing model, under certain conditions taking into account such an *ex post* relationship leads to more powerful tests. For a further discussion, see Warner (1977, p. 259) and Langetieg (1978). Fama and MacBeth (1973, pp. 634–635) and Roll and Ross (1979) also discuss related issues in the context of multiple factor models.

2.3. On the role of simulation

Unfortunately, specifying a more precise model of the processs generating realized returns is not sufficient for that model to generate a more powerful test for abnormal performance. Even if the Capital Asset Pricing model is the correct specification of the return generating process, it does not follow that a performance measure based upon that model will dominate performance measures based on the Mean Adjusted Returns method.

First, there is measurement error in each of the variables upon which abnormal returns depend in the Asset Pricing model. Not only is a security's risk measured with error, but, as Roll (1977) has argued, the market portfolio cannot be observed directly. Such measurement error need not introduce any systematic bias in event studies.[3] However, with small samples, the measurement error in these variables may be so large that it renders inconsequential any potential efficiency gains from more precise specification of the return-generating process.[4]

Second, the efficiency of using a particular model of the return-generating process will depend critically on the appropriateness of the additional peripheral assumptions about the $\tilde{\varepsilon}_{it}$ which must be made in order to test the hypothesis of 'no abnormal performance' conditional on a particular event. For example, with each method, a test statistic such as a t-statistic must be computed and compared to the distribution of test statistics which is assumed to obtain under the null hypothesis. To the extent that the assumed sampling distribution under the null hypothesis differs from the true distribution, false inferences can result. If the assumed properties of the test statistic under the Mean Adjusted Returns Method are more appropriate than those under the Market and Risk Adjusted Returns Method, the Mean Adjusted Returns Method can be preferred even if the second method is 'correct'.

Finally, there are a variety of ways of measuring abnormal returns under different variants of the Asset Pricing model. These include market model residuals, Fama–MacBeth residuals, and control portfolios. The differences in the predictive ability of such alternative methods could be substantial; the usefulness of the Asset Pricing model is not independent of the specific method of implementing the Market and Risk Adjusted Returns model.

Even if it were possible to analytically derive and compare the properties of alternative methods for measuring abnormal performance in event studies, conclusions from the comparison would not necessarily be valid if the actual data used in event studies were generated by a process which differed from that which the comparison assumed. For this reason, the performance of the

---

[3]See Mayers and Rice (1979) for a more detailed discussion of how the unobservability of the true market portfolio affects the measures of abnormal performance. Bawa, Brown, and Klein (1979) present an extensive discussion of how measurement error can be taken into account by using the predictive distribution of returns [see also Patell (1976, p. 256)].

[4]Brenner (1979) makes a similar point.

alternative methods is an empirical question. To address the question, we will employ simulation techniques which use actual security return data (presumably generated by the 'true' process) to examine the characteristics of various methodologies for measuring abnormal performance.

3. The experimental design

3.1. Sample construction

Our study concentrates on abnormal performance measurement using monthly data.[5] To simulate methodologies based on the three general models just discussed, we first construct 250 samples, each containing 50 securities. The securities are selected at random and with replacement from a population consisting of all securities for which monthly return data are available on the files of the Center for Research in Security Prices (CRSP) at the University of Chicago.[6] For each security, we generate a hypothetical 'event' month. Events are assumed to occur with equal probability in each month from June 1944 through February 1971.[7] Events can occur in different

[5]For our simulation study, monthly data offers several advantages over daily data. The use of monthly data enables us to consider those studies which have employed Fama–MacBeth (1973) residuals; the data necessary for readily computing daily Fama–MacBeth residuals are not to our knowledge available, and such daily residuals have not been used in any event study.

Furthermore, the use of daily data involves complications whose treatment is largely beyond the scope of this paper. Daily stock returns depart more from normality than do monthly returns [Fama (1976, ch. 1)]. In addition, the estimation of parameters (such as systematic risk) from daily data is a non-trivial matter due to the non-synchronous trading problem [see Scholes and Williams (1977)]. Any conclusions from simulations using daily data could be sensitive to specific procedures we employed to handle the complications associated with non-normality and non-synchronous trading.

We have no strong reason to believe that our conclusions about the relative performance of various methods for measuring abnormal performance would be altered by the use of daily data. However, in the absence of problems such as non-normality and non-synchronous trading, all of the methods for measuring abnormal performance are potentially more powerful with daily data. First, daily returns have smaller standard deviations than do monthly returns. The mean standard deviation of monthly returns for randomly selected securities is about 7.8% [Fama (1976, p. 123)], whereas the corresponding mean standard deviation of daily returns will be approximately 1.8% if daily returns are serially independent. In addition, as we later indicate, the power of all the methodologies increases with knowledge about precisely when an event occurs; use of daily data is potentially useful in that it permits the researcher to take advantage of prior information about the specific day of the month on which an event took place. Performance measurement with daily data is the subject of a separate study we are currently undertaking.

[6]We used a combination congruential and Tausworthe (shift register) algorithm to generate uniformly distributed random numbers on the [0, 1) interval. See Marsaglia, Ananthanarayanan and Paul (1973) for a description of the algorithm.

[7]Given the other data requirements we will discuss, including the requirement that Fama–MacBeth residuals be computed, these are the calendar months whose selection maximizes the length of the calendar time period over which our simulations can be performed. With the exception of mutual funds, all CRSP listed securities are eligible for selection. Each CRSP security initially has the same probability of being selected, subject to data availability. A security can be selected more than once for inclusion in a given sample or in a different sample. In both cases, whenever a security already selected is again selected, it is treated as a 'different' security in the sense that a new event-date is generated.

calendar months for different securities. This set of sample securities and hypothetical event dates will be used in most of the present study.

Define month '0' as the month in which the firm has been assigned an event. For a given sample, we use 100 return observations on each security for the period around the time of the event. We use 100 months of data, from month -89 through month $+10$.[8]

Introducing abnormal performance

Return data for the 250 samples which have been chosen is based on randomly selected securities and event dates, and, as indicated in section 2, should not systematically exhibit any abnormal performance. However, an important question we want to investigate is how different methodologies perform when some abnormal performance is present. It is thus necessary to specify a procedure for introducing a known level of abnormal performance into the sample securities.

A particular level of abnormal performance is artificially introduced into a given sample by transforming its actual return data. To introduce, say, 5% abnormal performance for each security of a sample, 0.05 is added to the actual return on each sample security in the particular calendar month in which its event is assumed to occur. Abnormal performance is thus introduced by adding a constant to a security's observed return.[9]

---

[8]If a security does not have this 100 months of return data surrounding its event-date, it is not included in the sample. To handle such cases, we continue to select securities and event-dates until, for a given sample, we have found 50 securities with a sufficient amount of data. With this selection procedure, the probability of being included in our sample will depend upon the amount of data which is available for a security. For example, a security with continuous return data from 1935 through 1971 will be included with a higher frequency than one with a smaller amount of available data. Thus, our data requirements introduce a bias towards including only surviving companies; none of our simulation results suggest that the bias is of importance.

[9]Three points about the procedure for introducing abnormal performance are worth mentioning. First, note that the level of abnormal performance associated with an actual event could itself be stochastic; an event could thus affect not only the conditional mean of a security's return, but higher-order moments as well. Introducing a constant represents a simple case which enables us to focus on the detection of mean shifts when an event takes place, holding constant the conditional variance. The detection of mean shifts is the relevant phenomenon to study when investigating how well different methodologies pick up the impact of an event on the value of the firm.

Second, although it is not critical for our purposes, it should also be noted that if for a given security there is positive abnormal performance conditional on an event, there should also be negative abnormal performance conditional on no event. Otherwise, the unconditional expected return on the security will be abnormal, which is inconsistent with an efficient market. However, for simulations introducing positive abnormal performance in month '0', the appropriate downward adjustment to security returns in those months when the event does not occur is not obvious. The adjustment which leaves expected returns unaltered will depend upon the *ex ante* probability of the event, which in an actual event study is unobservable.

For all results reported in this paper, in order to leave mean returns unaltered across all levels of abnormal performance, for each sample security the observed return for each month in the

3.2. Abnormal performance measures for a given sample

For every sample, we have a set of security returns which is transformed to reflect various levels of abnormal performance. For each sample, we calculate performance measures based on the three models of the return-generating process discussed in section 2. The performance measures are briefly summarized here; further details are contained in the appendix.

(a) *Mean Adjusted Returns* — To implement this model, we focus on the returns to each sample security around the time of its event. We examine whether or not the returns on the sample securities in month '0' are statistically significantly different from the returns on the securities in the time period surrounding the event. As discussed below, several different significance tests are used. The Mean Adjusted Returns method is used by Masulis (1978).

(b) *Market Adjusted Returns* — Unlike the Mean Adjusted Returns methodology, this method takes into account marketwide movements which occurred at the same time that the sample firms experienced events. The variable of interest is the *difference* between the return on a sample security and the corresponding return on the market index. We initially use the Fisher Equally Weighted Index to represent the market portfolio, and we will later examine the results when the CRSP Value Weighted Index is employed. The performance measures are the differences between the sample security returns and the market index in month '0'. Again, the statistical significance of the measures is assessed in several different ways. The Market Adjusted Returns method is used by Cowles (1933) and Latane and Jones (1979).

(c) *Market and Risk Adjusted Returns* — This method takes into account both market-wide factors and the systematic risk of each sample security. Although we will examine a number of different variations of this

---

(-89, $+10$) period is reduced by the level of abnormal performance divided by 100. Roughly speaking, this transformation presumes that for each sample security the *ex ante* probability of the event in any one month is 0.01. Simulations have also been carried out with no such adjustment, and the results do not appear to be sensitive to whether or not such an adjustment procedure is used.

Finally, it should be noted that our simulations are directly applicable to the case where there is 'good news' or 'bad news'. We are implicitly examining abnormal performance for those securities which had good news; if month '0' had unconditional abnormal performance equal to zero, then there need be no adjustment to returns in the (-89, $+10$) period. Furthermore, we have also simulated a situation where, for a given sample security, good news (positive abnormal performance) or bad news (negative abnormal performance) occur with equal probability at month '0', and where the abnormal performance measure conditional on a bad news realization is multiplied by -1 before the null hypothesis of no abnormal sample security returns is tested. The results from such alternative simulations are quite similar to those reported in the paper, although there is a slight reduction in the degree of misspecification in the non-parametric tests.

method, we initially use the 'market model'.[10] For each sample security, we use ordinary least squares to regress its return over the period around the event against the returns on the Equally Weighted Index for the corresponding calendar months. The 'market model' regression which is performed yields a residual in each event related month for each sample security. The significance of the month '0' market model residuals is then examined.

Detecting Type I and Type II errors for a given sample

For a given sample, when no abnormal performance has been introduced we test whether or not, under each performance measure, the hypothesis of no abnormal performance is rejected. This null hypothesis should indeed be true if randomly selected securities do not, on average, exhibit any abnormal performance given a particular benchmark. We classify rejection of the null hypothesis here as a Type I error — rejecting it when it is true.

We then investigate how the methodologies perform when the null hypothesis is not true for the sample, that is, when the returns of the sample securities have been transformed to reflect abnormal performance. For a given level of abnormal performance introduced into every sample security, each methodology is applied and the hypothesis of no abnormal performance then tested. If the null hypothesis fails to be rejected, this is classified as a Type II error — failure to reject the null hypothesis of no abnormal performance when it is false.

4. Simulating the methodologies across samples: Procedure and initial results

Whether a particular performance measure happens to result in a Type I or Type II error for a given sample and a given level of abnormal performance yields little insight into the likelihood that a particular type of error will *systematically* be made with a given methodology. To get direct measures of the *ex ante* probability of Type I and Type II errors, the procedure of introducing abnormal performance and then testing for it must be applied to each of the 250 samples. For a specific level of abnormal performance introduced into each security of every sample, we examine the overall performance of a methodology when it is applied to each sample — that is, when the methodology is replicated 250 times. We concentrate on the frequency of Type I and Type II errors in these 250 trials.

For each methodology, table 1 shows the frequency with which the hypothesis of no abnormal performance in month '0' is rejected using several different significance tests. The results are reported for 0, 1, 5, 15 and 50% levels of abnormal performance introduced into each security of every sample

---

[10]See Fama (1976, chs. 3 and 4) for a discussion of the market model.

in month '0'.[11] The frequency of rejections is reported when the null hypothesis is tested at both the 0.05 and 0.01 significance levels using a one-tailed test.[12]

4.1. Rejection frequencies using t-tests

One set of significance tests for which results are reported in table 1 are *t*-tests.[13] When there is no abnormal performance, for all of the performance measurement methods the *t*-tests reject the null hypothesis at approximately the significance level of the test. For example, for the tests at the 0.05 level, the rejection rates range from 3.2% for the Market Adjusted Returns method

Table 1

A comparison of alternative performance measures. Percentage of 250 replications where the null hypothesis is rejected. One-tailed test. H_0: mean abnormal performance in month '0' = 0.0. Sample size = 50 securities.

Method	Test level: $\alpha = 0.05$			Test level: $\alpha = 0.01$		
	Actual level of abnormal performance in month '0'					
	0%	1%	5%	0%	1%	5%
Mean Adjusted Returns						
t-test	4.0	26.0	100.0	1.6	8.8	99.2
Sign test	0.8	6.4	96.0	0.0	1.6	90.8
Wilcoxon signed rank test	1.6	12.8	99.6	0.4	4.4	97.6
Market[a] Adjusted Returns						
t-test	3.2	19.6	100.0	1.6	5.2	96.4
Sign test	0.0	9.2	99.2	0.0	2.0	97.6
Wilcoxon signed rank test	1.6	17.2	99.6	0.4	4.4	98.8
Market[a] and Risk Adjusted Returns						
t-test	4.4	22.8	100.0	1.2	6.8	98.4
Sign test	0.4	7.2	99.6	0.0	2.4	98.0
Wilcoxon signed rank test	2.8	16.4	100.0	0.0	4.4	99.2

[a]Fisher Equally Weighted Index. Note that for 15 and 50% levels of abnormal performance, the percentage of rejections is 100% for all methods.

[11]The range of these levels of abnormal performance corresponds roughly to the range of estimated abnormal performance reported in Fama, Fisher, Jensen and Roll (1969, table 2). For example, for their sample of stock splits followed by divided increases, estimated abnormal performance ranged from about 1% in month '0' to 38% when the performance measure is cumulated over a 30-month period before and including month '0'.

[12]Throughout most of the paper, results will be reported for one-tailed tests. In a one-tailed test at any significance level α, the critical value of the test statistic at or above which the null hypothesis is rejected is given by the $(1 - \alpha)$ fractile of the frequency distribution of the test statistic which is assumed to obtain under the null. In section 5, results for two-tailed tests will be discussed.

[13]The assumptions underlying the *t*-tests are discussed in the appendix. For an example of *t*-tests in event studies, see Jaffe (1974). Although different variations of the *t*-tests are examined in section 6, results for the initial simulations are not sensitive to the specific variation employed.

to 4.4% for the Market and Risk Adjusted Returns method; for tests at the 0.01 level of significance, the rejection rates for the three methods range from 1.2 to 1.6%.[14]

With 1% abnormal performance, using t-tests the Mean Adjusted Returns method rejects the null hypothesis in 26.0% of the 250 replications when testing at the 0.05 level of significance. This compares to a 22.8% rejection rate with the Market and Risk Adjusted Returns method, and a 19.6% rejection rate with the Market Adjusted Returns method. This result is striking: it suggests that the simplest method, the Mean Adjusted Returns method, is no less likely than either of the other two to detect abnormal performance when it is present.[15]

Furthermore, the results which obtain with 1% abnormal performance are robust with respect to seemingly minor variations in the simulation procedure. For example, the relative rankings of the tests do not seem to be very sensitive to the significance level at which the null hypothesis is tested: at the 0.01 level of significance, the Mean Adjusted Returns method rejects 8.8% of the time, compared to a rejection rate of 6.8% for the Market and Risk Adjusted Returns method and a 5.2% rate for the Market Adjusted Returns method. It should also be emphasized that our conclusions about the relative

[14]Even if the empirical sampling distribution of a particular test statistic corresponds exactly to the assumed theoretical distribution, the proportion of rejections when the null hypothesis is true will not be exactly equal to the test level: The proportion of rejections is itself a random variable with a sampling distribution. Suppose that, under the null hypothesis, the outcomes of the hypothesis tests for each of the 250 replications are independent. Then at the 0.05 test level, the proportion of rejections for such a Bernoulli process has a mean of 0.05 and a standard deviation of 0.014. If the proportion of rejections is normally distributed, then the percentage of rejections reported in table 1 for 0% abnormal performance should, if the test statistics are properly specified, be between 2 and 8% approximately 95% of the time when testing at the 0.05 level. At the 0.01 level, the proportion of rejections should be between 0 and 2.2% approximately 95% of the time.

In calculating the proportion of rejections to be observed under the null hypothesis, it should be kept in mind that our 250 samples or 'trials' cannot be regarded as literally independent. A given security can be included in more than 1 of the 250 replications. To investigate the degree of dependence, for each of the 250 samples we computed an equally weighted average return for the sample securities for event months −89 through +10. We then computed the 31125 pairwise correlation coefficients for the 250 samples. The correlation coefficient between sample 1 and sample 2, for example, is computed from the 100 equally weighted returns on each sample in event time.

The largest of the 31125 pairwise correlation coefficients is 0.42, and the smallest is −0.34. Using a two-tailed test, only 485, or about 1.5% of the correlation coefficients are significant at the 0.01 level, compared to an expected proportion of 1%. While the hypothesis that the samples are pairwise independent is rejected, the degree of linear dependence appears to be small.

[15]In comparing rejection frequencies across methodologies, it is necessary to gauge the magnitude of the differences in rejection proportions, either pairwise or jointly. If, for each replication, the results for two different test methods are independent of each other, then the difference in the proportion of rejections in 250 replications could be as large as about 4% merely due to chance; hence the difference between the 26.0% rejection rate for Mean Adjusted Returns need not be regarded as significantly different from the 22.8% rejection rate for the Market and Risk Adjusted Returns method.

performance of the Market Adjusted Returns and Market and Risk Adjusted Returns methods have not been induced by the use of the Equally Weighted Index. For example, with 1% abnormal performance, the rejection rate we obtain for the Market and Risk Adjusted Returns with the Equally Weighted Index is 22.8%; with the Value-Weighted Index, the rejection rate is even lower, 15.2%. Differences between the use of the Equally Weighted and Value Weighted Indices are examined in detail in section 7.[16]

When the level of abnormal performance is increased from 1 to 5% in each sample security, all three methods detect the abnormal performance almost all of the time: at the 0.05 significance level, all three methods reject the null hypothesis 100% of the time, and at the 0.01 level, the minimum rejection rate is 96.4% for the Market Adjusted Returns method. Similarly, when the level of abnormal performance is again increased first to 15% and then to 50%, all three methods reject virtually 100% of the time. While this high frequency of rejections suggests that the tests for abnormal performance are quite powerful when there is 5% or more abnormal performance, it should be kept in mind, as we will later discuss, that these results are critically dependent on the assumption that the precise time at which the abnormal performance occurs is known with certainty. Furthermore, as we will also discuss, the relatively favorable performance of the Mean Adjusted Returns method will not obtain under all experimental conditions.

4.2. Parametric vs. non-parametric significance tests

Implicit in the *t*-tests which are used to assess abnormal performance are a number of strong assumptions: for example, in order for the test statistics to be distributed Student-*t* in the Mean Adjusted Returns method, security returns must be normally distributed. If such an assumption is not met, then the sampling distribution of test statistics assumed for the hypothesis tests could differ from the actual distribution, and false inferences could result. If the distribution of the test statistic is misspecified, then the null hypothesis, when true, could be rejected with some frequency other than that given by the significance level of the test.

To examine the usefulness of significance tests which make less restrictive assumptions than the *t*-tests, we also employ two non-parametric tests of the

---

[16]In an Asset Pricing model context, there is no clear *a priori* justification for use of an equally weighted index. However, even if their use is viewed as an *ad hoc* procedure, the fact that such indices are employed in actual event studies [e.g., Fama, Fisher, Jensen and Roll (1969), Watts (1978)] suggests that the consequences of their use are of interest. In addition, there are strong reasons for reporting initial simulation results with the Equally Weighted Index. As we later discuss, some of the performance measures under study can actually be biased when used with the Value-Weighted Index. If we reported our initial simulation results using the Value-Weighted Index, biases associated with the use of that index would make it difficult to standardize the level of Type I errors across test methods; valid comparisons of the power of different methodologies would thus not be possible with our simulation procedure.

performance measures which have been used in actual event studies: (1) a sign test, and (2) a Wilcoxon signed rank test.[17] In the sign test for a given sample, the null hypothesis is that the proportion of sample securities having positive measures of abnormal performance (e.g., positive residuals) is equal to 0.5; the alternative hypothesis (for any particular level of abnormal performance) is that the proportion of sample securities having positive performance measures is greater than 0.5. In the Wilcoxon test, both the sign *and* the magnitude of the abnormal performance are taken into account in computing the test statistic.[18]

Table 1 indicates the frequency with which the two non-parametric tests reject the hypothesis of no abnormal performance in month '0' for each methodology and for 0, 1, 5, 15 and 50% abnormal performance. From the results with 0% abnormal performance, it appears that there is a serious problem with the use of these non-parametric tests: under the null hypothesis, the tests do not reject at the 'correct' level. For example, for tests at the 0.05 level, the rejection rates range from a low of 0% for the sign test in the Market Adjusted Returns method to a high of 2.8% for the Wilcoxon test used in conjunction with the Market and Risk Adjusted Returns method. For tests at the 0.01 level, four of the six rejection rates are equal to 0%, and the other two are equal to 0.4%. Compared to the significance level of the test, the sign and Wilcoxon tests do not appear to reject the null hypothesis often enough. Although they are used to avoid the problem of possible misspecification of the *t*-tests, it appears that the non-parametric tests themselves suffer from such a problem of misspecification.

Distributional properties of the test statistics

To further examine the properties of the *t*, sign, and Wilcoxon tests, in table 2 we report summary measures for the actual frequency distribution of each test statistic, based on the 250 replications. Even when there is no abnormal performance, in many cases there appear to be significant differences between the empirical sampling distribution of the test statistic and the distribution which is assumed for the hypothesis tests. That such differences are substantial implies that tests for abnormal security price performance can be misleading and must be interpreted with great caution.

For the *t*-tests, the differences between the actual and assumed distribution of the test statistics seem small. For example, when there is no abnormal performance, the average *t*-statistics are approximately 0, ranging from a low of -0.13 in the Mean Adjusted Returns method to a high of -0.04 in the Market Adjusted Returns method. There is also evidence that the *t*-statistics

[17]See, for example, Kaplan and Roll (1972), Ball, Brown and Finn (1977), and Collins and Dent (1979).
[18]Details of the calculation of these test statistics are contained in the appendix.

are leptokurtic and slightly skewed to the right. However, at the 0.05 significance level it is only for the Mean Adjusted Returns method that the Kolmogorov–Smirnov test rejects the hypothesis that the distribution of t-values is indeed t. For both the Mean Adjusted Returns and Market and Risk Adjusted Returns methods, it also appears that the t-tests result in slightly 'too many' extreme negative t-values.[19]

For the sign and Wilcoxon tests, in large samples the test statistics should be distributed unit normal. However, table 2 indicates that the mean of the test statistics is generally significantly less than 0 under the null hypothesis; the mean test statistics ranges from a low of -0.52 for the sign test in the Market and Risk Adjusted Returns method to a high of -0.42 for the Wilcoxon test in Market and Risk Adjusted Returns method; the χ^2 and Kolmogorov–Smirnov tests reject the hypothesis of normality with mean 0 for all the tests.

Our finding for the non-parametric tests that the average test statistic is significantly negative is not difficult to explain: the sign and Wilcoxon tests assume that the distribution of a security specific performance measure (such as a market model residual) is symmetric, with half of the observations above the mean and half below the mean. However, there is evidence of right skewness in security specific performance measures such as market model residuals [Fama, Fisher, Jensen and Roll (1969, p. 6)]. With fewer positive than negative performance measures, the median performance measure will

---

[19]There are two related points about the frequency distributions of the t-statistics, summarized in table 2, which should be mentioned. First, note that the t-statistics in the Mean Adjusted Returns method have an estimated variance of 1.32, higher than the variance of the t-statistics of either of the other methods. The higher variance is indicative of the troubling behavior of the Mean Adjusted Returns t-tests in the left-hand tail region. There, 21 of the 250 t-statistics fall in the 5% left-hand tail of a t distribution, compared to an expected number of 12.5, and 41 of the test statistics fall in the 10% lower tail of a t distribution, compared to an expected number of 25. This large fraction of test statistics in the lower tail region implies that a test of the hypothesis that there is no abnormal performance (compared to an alternative hypothesis that abnormal performance is negative) will result in rejection of that hypothesis at a rate almost twice that of the significance level of the test when the null hypothesis is true. Similar left-hand tail behavior is obtained in later simulations where the Value-Weighted Index is employed for computing market model residuals. Use of the Jaffe–Mandelker dependence adjustment procedure, which we will later discuss, also yields such left-hand tail behavior in the t-statistics even when market model residuals are computed from the Equally Weighted Index.

Second, note that when there is 1% abnormal performance, the distributions of the t-statistics for all methods are quite different from the t distribution, which is the distribution which should obtain under the null hypothesis; that there are such differences merely indicates that the t-tests do in fact pick up abnormal performance when it is present. When there is abnormal performance, one could also compare the distributions of test statistics to the non-central t, which is the distribution which would be expected under the alternative hypothesis if the test statistics were correctly specified. However, since even the null distributions are at least slightly misspecified, it also seems reasonable to anticipate some misspecification in the distribution which should obtain under the alternative hypothesis. Given such misspecification, analytically deriving power functions under the assumptions of the various tests is not a reliable way of understanding the actual power functions for the tests. A simulation technique such as ours is necessary.

Table 2

Summary measures for the actual frequency distribution of each test statistic, based on the 250 replications. Upper and lower lines indicate 0 and 1% abnormal performance, respectively.

Method	Mean	Variance	t-statistic for mean	$\beta_1 = \mu_3^2/\mu_2^3$	Kurtosis	Pearson skewness	χ^2 statistic (20 equally spaced intervals)	χ^2 statistic (9 tail region intervals)[a]	Kolmogorov–Smirnov D-statistic
Mean Adjusted Returns									
t-test values 0% abnormal performance	−0.13	1.32	−1.80	0.02	3.20	0.06	29.0	24.1	0.09
1% abnormal performance	0.92	1.30	12.8	0.03	3.18	0.07	284.0	280.0	0.33
Sign test values	−0.51	0.83	−8.89	0.00	3.01	0.03	325.0	90.2	0.29
	0.25	0.79	4.45	0.00	3.01	0.02	282.0	13.0	0.20
Wilcoxon test values	−0.42	0.96	−6.87	0.01	2.78	0.05	88.2	64.5	0.18
	0.66	0.96	9.14	0.00	2.75	0.01	107.0	60.7	0.25
Market Adjusted Returns									
t-values	−0.04	1.04	−0.59	0.01	4.18	0.04	13.6	5.65	0.06
	0.92	1.06	14.1	0.04	4.17	0.06	246.8	212.2	0.35
Sign test values	−0.52	0.87	−8.83	0.11	2.71	0.24	304.5	86.6	0.26
	0.39	0.79	6.84	0.05	2.98	0.12	283.1	27.5	0.24
Wilcoxon test values	−0.43	1.01	−6.66	0.02	2.79	0.07	75.1	81.5	0.17
	0.69	1.01	1.08	0.05	2.93	0.12	149.1	103.9	0.30

Market and Risk Adjusted Returns

t-values								
−0.05	1.01	−0.77	0.07	3.72	0.09	20.1	9.06	0.06
0.91	1.03	14.1	0.08	3.61	0.10	259.4	227.0	0.34
Sign test values								
−0.48	0.82	−8.51	0.10	2.93	0.18	347.7	84.3	0.29
0.48	0.73	8.91	0.00	3.01	0.03	287.1	18.8	0.30
Wilcoxon test values								
−0.42	1.02	−6.66	0.00	2.77	0.00	79.9	61.5	0.18
0.72	0.97	11.6	0.02	2.78	0.07	166.6	115.1	0.30

[a] For tests concentrating on the tail regions, the 9 intervals are: 0–0.01, 0.01–0.02, 0.02–0.05, 0.05–0.1, 0.1–0.9, 0.9–0.95, 0.95–0.98, 0.98–0.99, 0.99–1.0.

Upper percentage points

	0.95	0.99
$\chi^2(8)$	15.5	20.1
$\chi^2(19)$	30.1	36.2
D ($N = 250$)	0.086	0.103
β_1 (assuming normality, $N = 250$)	0.063	0.129
Kurtosis (normality, $N = 250$)	3.52	3.87

be negative even when the average performance measure is equal to 0. The non-parametric tests will tend to reject the null 'too often' (compared to the significance level of the test) when testing for negative abnormal performance and 'not often enough' when testing for positive abnormal performance.[20]

The non-parametric tests could, in principle, take asymmetry in the distribution of the performance measure into account and test the null hypothesis that the proportion of positive performance measures is equal to some number other than 0.5. However, such a test would first require a procedure for determining the proportion of positive security-specific performance measures which obtains in the absence of abnormal performance. We know of no event study which has employed such a test.[21]

4.3. Different risk adjustment methods

In the initial simulations reported in table 1, we concluded that tests which used risk-adjusted returns were no more powerful than tests which used returns which had not been adjusted for systematic risk. However, that conclusion was predicated on the assumption that the 'market model residual' method we chose represented the appropriate method of risk adjustment. To investigate the robustness of those earlier results, it is useful to simulate other risk adjustment methods which have also been used in actual event studies. We will examine two alternative methods; specific details of each method are discussed in the appendix.

Fama–MacBeth Residuals — Instead of computing a market model residual for each sample security, a 'Fama–MacBeth' (1973) residual is computed instead. Average residuals are then computed and abnormal performance is assessed in the same way as with the Market Model Residual method.[22]

Market model residuals are an appropriate performance measure if security returns are multivariate normal. For Fama–MacBeth residuals to be

---

[20]Even a small degree of asymmetry will lead to such a result. For example, if a sample of 50 securities has 27 negative and 23 positive market model residuals in month '0', the test statistic in the sign test will be approximately -0.5. This is about equal to the average value of -0.48 reported in table 2. Note that the use of continuously compounded (rather than arithmetic) returns is likely to reduce the extent of the asymmetry in market model residuals.

[21]Residual based techniques focusing on median (rather than mean) residuals could presumably use estimation procedures other than ordinary least squares to perform the market model regressions [see Bassett and Koenker (1978), and Cornell and Dietrich (1978)]. However, even if the non-parametric tests were properly calibrated by focusing on differences from medians, it is not obvious that the tests would be more powerful (against specific alternatives) than the t-tests, particularly since the t-tests, with their additional restrictions, seem reasonably well specified. But it should be kept in mind that there do exist distributions of the security-specific performance measures for which tests such as the sign test will be more efficient, particularly distributions with sufficiently heavy tails. See Lehman (1975, pp. 171–175) for a further discussion of the power of the t, sign, and Wilcoxon tests.

[22]Fama–MacBeth residuals have been used by, for example, Jaffe (1974) and Mandelker (1974).

an appropriate performance measure, it is also necessary for equilibrium expected returns to be generated according to the Black (1972) version of the Asset Pricing model. A comparison of the performance of the market model and Fama–MacBeth residual techniques will indicate the benefits, if any, which are associated with the restrictive assumptions (and additional data requirements) implicit in using the Fama–MacBeth residuals.

Control Portfolios — This method forms the sample securities into a portfolio with an estimated β of 1. Regardless of the risk level of each sample security, the portfolio thus formed should have the same risk as the market portfolio. Those securities comprising the market portfolio become a 'control portfolio' in the sense that the market portfolio has the same risk level as the sample securities, but is not experiencing the 'event' under study. The performance measure for month '0' is the difference between the return on a portfolio of sample securities (formed so that $\hat{\beta}=1$) and the average return on the market portfolio in the calendar months in which the sample securities experience events.

Variations of the Control Portfolio technique have been used by, for example, Black and Scholes (1973), Gonedes, Dopuch and Penman (1976), Warner (1977) and Watts (1978).[23] By concentrating on the difference in mean returns, this method makes no particular assumption about which version of the Asset Pricing model is correct.

Simulation results for alternative risk adjustment methods

To compare the different methods for risk adjustment, table 3 indicates the simulation results for 250 replications of each risk adjustment method with 0, 1 and 5% levels of abnormal performance. Two important results emerge from the simulation.

Compared to using Market Model residuals, the use of Fama–MacBeth residuals does not increase the power of the tests. Earlier, for example, using the Equally Weighted Index and with 1% abnormal performance, the Market Model Residual method rejected 22.8% of the time; the rejection rate using Fama–MacBeth residuals is 21.6%. Even if the Black model is corrent, there appears to be sufficient measurement error in the parameter estimates on which Fama–MacBeth residuals are based so that the tests based on those residuals are no more useful than those based on the multivariate normality assumption of the Market Model. Furthermore, use of the Control Portfolio method also results in no increase in the proportion of rejections which take place under the alternative hypotheses: With 1% abnormal performance, the Control Portfolio method rejects the null hy-

---

[23]The Control Portfolio technique has also been used to control for factors other than systematic risk. See Gonedes, Dopuch and Penman (1976, p. 113) for a discussion.

pothesis in 18.0% of the 250 replications. These results for alternative risk adjustment procedures are consistent with our earlier conclusion that the Mean Adjusted Returns method performs no worse than those methods which explicitly adjust for systematic risk.[24]

Table 3

Different methods for risk adjustment. Percentage of 250 replications where the null hypothesis is rejected ($\alpha = 0.05$). One-tailed t-test results. H_0: mean abnormal performance in month '0' $= 0.0$. Sample size $= 50$ securities.

Method	Actual level of abnormal performance in month '0'			Mean t-statistic with 1% abnormal performance
	0%	1%	5%	
Methods making no explicit risk adjustment				
Mean Adjusted Returns	4.0	26.0	100.0	0.92
Market Adjusted Returns	3.2	19.6	100.0	0.92
Methods with market and risk-adjusted returns				
Market Model Residuals	4.4	22.8	100.0	0.91
Fama–MacBeth Residuals	4.0	21.6	100.0	0.89
Control Portfolio	4.4	18.0	100.0	0.86

5. The use of prior information

The simulations which have been performed thus far make the strong assumption that the time at which abnormal security price performance occurs is known with complete certainty. However, if it is only known when, for example, the *Wall Street Journal* announced that the 'event' had taken place, then the calendar date of the event cannot be pinpointed exactly and the date itself becomes a random variable; in that case, abnormal returns for a number of periods before the 'announcement date' will typically be scrutinized for evidence of 'abnormal' performance. Similarly, even when it can be established with certainty when the event occurred, one is often concerned with whether or not there exists a profitable trading rule which could be implemented conditional on an event. In such a situation, it is necessary to study abnormal price performance for the period following time '0'.

[24]We have also examined the properties of the test statistics generated with Fama–MacBeth residuals and the Control Portfolio method. For both methods, the distribution of t-statistics is reasonably close to Student-t, and the properties of the test statistics are very similar to those reported in table 2 for the market model residual methodology.

5.1. Assessing abnormal performance when its precise date is unknown

We now examine how uncertainty about the precise date of the abnormal performance affects the power of the tests. For every security in each of the 250 samples, abnormal performance is generated in one specific month in the interval from month -10 through $+10$. The event month of abnormal performance can differ across securities; for a given security, the event month of abnormal performance is a drawing from a uniform distribution.[25] In this experiment, 0, 1, 5, 15% and 50% abnormal performance is introduced for each security for one month in the $(-10, +10)$ interval. This experimental situation corresponds to one where abnormal performance occurs (a) at some time in the 21-month interval up to and including month '0', or (b) at some time in the 21-month interval including and following the event. The null hypothesis to be tested is that the mean level of abnormal performance over the entire 21-month interval is equal to 0.

Table 4 shows the frequency with which each test method results in a rejection of the null hypothesis of no abnormal performance. The results are dramatic: even at high levels of abnormal performance, the hypothesis of no abnormal performance often fails to be rejected. For example, with 5% abnormal performance, the rejection rates range from 16.0% with the Control Portfolio method to a high of 28.4% with the Mean Adjusted Returns method. With 15% abnormal performance, the rejection rates increase and are on the order of 70 to 80% for the various test methods; however, these rejection rates are still much lower than those obtained in the earlier simulations, where the precise date of abnormal performance was known with certainty. There, using t-tests even 5% abnormal performance was detected 100% of the time by all of the test methods.[26]

To further illustrate how prior information can be used to increase the power of the tests, in table 4 we also show the results of a simulation where all abnormal performance occurs in the $(-5, +5)$ interval and is uniformly distributed. When prior information can be used to narrow the time interval in which the abnormal performance could have occurred, in this case from $(-10, +10)$ to $(-5, +5)$, the rejection rates increase substantially in the presence of a given level of abnormal performance. With 5% abnormal performance, the rejection rates increase from 28.4 to 35.2% for the Mean Adjusted Returns method, and from 24.4 to 39.6% using Market Model residuals.

---

[25]When other distributions (e.g., normal, exponential) were used, the qualitative conclusions of this section remained unchanged.

[26]Furthermore, the rejection rates in table 4 cannot be markedly increased if the researcher is merely willing to tolerate a slightly higher probability of Type I error — that is, if one is willing to conduct the hypothesis test at a higher significance level. For example, in the Mean Adjusted Returns method, the rejection rate with 5% abnormal performance is 28.4%. To obtain a rejection rate of 50%, the significance level would have to be increased to about 0.20; to obtain a 75% rejection rate, the significance level would have to be increased to about 0.35.

Table 4

Alternative performance measures when the precise date of the abnormal performance is unknown.[a] Percentage of 250 replications where the null hypothesis is rejected ($\alpha = 0.05$). One-tailed *t*-test results using Equally Weighted Index. H_0: mean abnormal performance in the interval $(-10, +10) = 0.0$

Method	Actual level of abnormal performance in interval $(-10, +10)$				
	0%	1%	5%	15%	50%
Mean Adjusted Returns	7.6	9.2	28.4	82.0	100.0
	(9.2)	(13.6)	(35.2)	(94.4)	(100.0)
Market Adjusted Returns	3.6	5.6	18.4	73.2	100.0
	(5.2)	(6.8)	(35.2)	(96.4)	(100.0)
Market Model Residuals	7.2	10.8	24.4	86.4	100.0
	(7.6)	(10.4)	(39.6)	(96.8)	(100.0)
Fama–MacBeth Residuals	3.6	5.2	16.4	74.8	100.0
	(8.8)	(15.6)	(45.6)	(97.6)	(100.0)
Control Portfolio	4.8	6.4	16.0	70.0	100.0
	(5.6)	(6.8)	(32.0)	(91.2)	(100.0)

[a]For each security, abnormal performance is introduced for one month in the interval $(-10, +10)$ with each month having an equal probability of being selected. The rejection rates shown in brackets are for the case where (1) for each security, abnormal performance is introduced for one month in the $(-5, +5)$ interval, with each month having an equal probability of being selected, and (2) the null hypothesis is that the mean abnormal performance in the $(-5, +5)$ interval is equal to 0.

Table 5

The behavior of two-tailed tests. Percentage of replications, for the 0.025 significance level, where a one-tailed *t*-test rejects the null hypothesis of no abnormal performance. This rejection rate is identical to the percentage of replications where a two-tailed test at the 0.05 level rejects the null and detects positive abnormal performance. Rejection rates from table 4, for a one-tailed test with $\alpha = 0.05$, are shown in brackets. H_0: mean abnormal performance in the interval $(-10, +10) = 0.0$.[a]

Method	Actual level of abnormal performance in interval $(-10, +10)$			
	0%	1%	5%	15%
Mean Adjusted Returns	4.8	5.6	17.6	74.4
	(7.6)	(9.2)	(28.4)	(82.0)
Market Adjusted Returns	1.0	2.4	9.2	58.0
	(3.6)	(5.6)	(18.4)	(73.2)
Market Model Residuals	3.2	5.2	18.4	78.8
	(7.2)	(10.8)	(24.4)	(86.4)
Fama-MacBeth Residuals	2.0	2.0	9.2	60.4
	(3.6)	(5.2)	(16.4)	(74.8)
Control Portfolio	2.0	2.4	8.0	48.4
	(4.8)	(6.4)	(16.0)	(70.0)

[a]For each security, abnormal performance is introduced for one month in the $(-10, +10)$ interval, with each month having an equal probability of being selected.

Rejection rates for two-tailed significance tests

There is yet another assumption about prior information which all of our simulations make and whose consequences can also be studied: the hypothesis tests we perform throughout this paper are one-tailed tests. An implicit assumption in such tests is that the sign of the abnormal performance is also known. However, if one cannot use prior information to impose this restriction, the appropriate test is two-tailed. For a given significance level, the power of the tests is thus reduced.[27]

In table 5, we report rejection rates for one-tailed tests conducted at both the 0.05 and 0.025 significance levels. The rejection rate for a one-tailed test at the 0.025 level also represents the percentage of replications in which a two-tailed test at the 0.05 level will pick up positive abnormal performance. Thus, comparing the rejection rates for one-tailed tests at the 0.05 and 0.025 levels is equivalent to comparing the frequency with which one-tailed and two-tailed tests, each conducted at the 0.05 level, will lead the researcher to conclude that positive abnormal performance is present.

When the sign of the abnormal performance is not known *a priori*, the ability to discern abnormal performance is reduced markedly. For example, with 5% abnormal performance in the $(-10, +10)$ interval, a two-tailed test at the 0.05 significance level picks up positive abnormal performance 17.6% of the time for the Mean Adjusted Returns method, compared to a rate of 28.4% for the corresponding one-tailed test. With 15% abnormal performance in the $(-10, +10)$ interval, a two-tailed test with that method detects positive abnormal performance in 74.4% of the replications, compared to a rate of 82.0% for a one-tailed test. While such results are hardly surprising, they serve to underscore the importance of using all available prior information in testing for abnormal performance.

5.2. Using cumulative average residuals

One method frequently used to investigate abnormal performance when there is incomplete prior information about when it occurs is the 'cumulative average residual' (CAR) technique employed by Fama, Fisher, Jensen and Roll (1969).[28] The technique focuses on the average market model residuals of the sample securities for a number of periods around the event. The

[27]Similarly, to obtain a particular rejection frequency when there is abnormal performance of a given sign and magnitude, the level of Type I error must be increased in moving from a one-tailed to a two-tailed test. For example, two-tailed tests would have to be conducted at the 0.1 level to pick up positive abnormal performance with the same frequency as that which has been reported throughout this paper for one-tailed testes at the 0.05 significance level.

[28]A similar technique involves construction of an Abnormal Performance Index [e.g., Ball and Brown (1968)]. In simulations not reported here, the abnormal performance measures of Ball–Brown, Pettit, and Beaver–Dukes [see Ohlson (1978, p. 184) for a description of these measures] were also examined. The properties of the confidence bands traced out by such alternative metrics were similar to those discussed for the CARs.

cumulative average residual for a given event-related month t is defined as the value of the cumulative average residual in the previous event-month plus the current value of the average residual, AR_t,

$$CAR_t = CAR_{t-1} + AR_t. \qquad (1)$$

Examining the CAR of a set of sample securities as of any given event-related month t is a way of looking at whether or not the values of the average residuals, starting from the month of cumulation and up to that point, are systematically different from 0.[29]

To simulate the CAR technique for various levels of abnormal performance, we use the values of the average market model residuals which were obtained for the simulations reported in table 4, where abnormal performance is uniformly distributed in the $(-10, +10)$ interval. For a given sample and a given level of abnormal performance, we take the average market model residuals and begin cumulating them in month -10; cumulation then continues for every month through month $+10$. For each sample, the procedure yields a set of 21 cumulative average residuals, one for each event-related month from -10 through $+10$. For a given event-related month, repeated application of the procedure to each of the 250 samples yields 250 cumulative average residuals.

Cumulative average residuals when there is no abnormal performance

To understand the properties of CARs under the null hypothesis, in fig. 1 we trace selected fractiles of the 250 CARs in each event-related month for the case where no abnormal performance is introduced. As the figure indicates, the 0.05 and 0.95 fractiles of the 250 CARs depart more and more from 0 as the cumulation process continues. By the end of month $+10$, the 0.95 fractile takes on a value of over 9%, and the 0.05 fractile takes on a value of about -9%. This suggests that the CAR for a given sample could appear to wander a great deal from 0, even in the absence of abnormal performance.[30]

The behavior of the CAR is consistent with a simple explanation. As eq. (1) indicates, the CAR for a given sample is by construction a random walk.[31] Like any process which follows a random walk, the CAR can easily

[29]Examining the CAR as of any event month is equivalent to examining the significance of the mean average residual over the cumulation period. However, looking at the entire set of event-time CARs on a month by month basis is not very meaningful unless the significance test explicitly takes into account the fact that CARs are, by construction, highly serially dependent.

[30]In table 2, we presented evidence that average residuals were skewed to the right. The slight apparent downward drift in the 0.5 fractile of the CAR would thus be expected.

[31]CARs will be a random walk if the average residuals in event time are independent and identically distributed. A confidence band such as that traced out by the 0.05 and 0.95 fractiles in fig. 1 should increase with the square root of the number of months over which cumulation takes place.

give the *appearance* of 'significant' positive or negative drift, when none is present. However, even if no abnormal performance were present, neither the seemingly significant upward drift indicated by the 0.95 fractile or the downward drift of the 0.05 fractile could be considered outside of the realm of chance. Indeed, in 5% of the 250 samples, the value of the CAR exceeds the values taken on by the 0.95 fractile reported in fig. 1; in another 5% of the samples, the value of the CAR is less than that taken on by the 0.05 fractile. The pattern of CAR fractiles in fig. 1 serves to underscore the necessity for statistical tests on the performance measures, since merely looking at a picture of CARs can easily result in Type I errors.

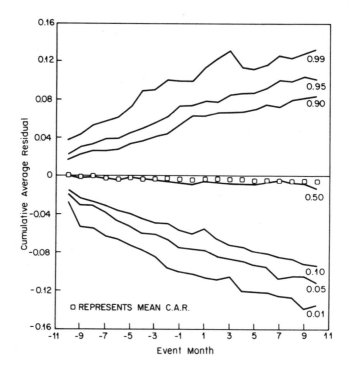

Fig. 1. Fractiles of cumulative average residual under null hypothesis of no abnormal performance.

Cumulative average residuals when abnormal performance is present

In fig. 2, we show selected fractiles of the CARs for the case where 5% abnormal performance occurs for each sample security, and the month of abnormal performance is uniformly distributed in the $(-10, +10)$ interval.

230   *S.J. Brown and J.B. Warner, Measuring security price performance*

The value of each fractile as of month $+10$ is higher by approximately 0.05 than the corresponding value in fig. 1, when no abnormal performance was present; however, the 0.5 fractile, that is, the median CAR as of month $+10$ still falls well within the bounds which were shown in fig. 1, and which obtain under the null hypothesis. Moreover, since for a given sample the

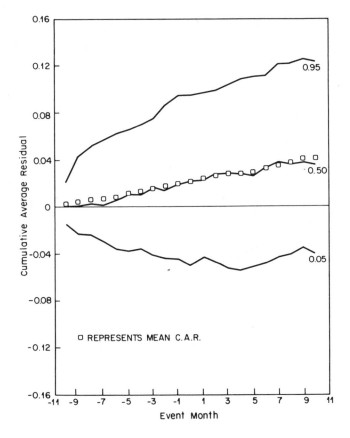

Fig. 2. Fractiles of cumulative average residual with 5% excess return distributed uniformly on months -10 to $+10$.

month of abnormal performance is uniformly distributed across securities and not on average large in any one month, CAR plots for the individual samples would tend to show a pattern not strikingly different from what would be expected under the null hypothesis. In such a case, there is little information which the CAR for the sample provides in helping to decide whether abnormal performance is present.

However, in fig. 3 we show fractiles of CARs when 5% abnormal performance occurs in month '0' for all sample securities. Although the fractiles at the end of the cumulation period take on values similar to those shown in fig. 2, there is an apparent 'spike' at month '0'; such a spike shows up not only in the selected fractiles, but in the CAR plot for any given

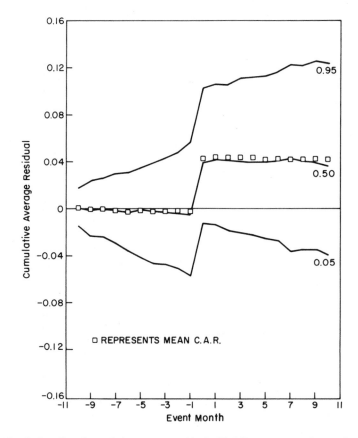

Fig. 3. Fractiles of cumulative average residual with 5% excess return in month zero.

sample. Given some prior information that month '0' is of particular interest to focus on, the existence of such a spike in the CAR pattern could reasonably suggest to the researcher that a hypothesis test for abnormal performance in month '0' rather than the entire $(-10, +10)$ period would be appropriate. The test on month '0' picks up abnormal performance 100% of the time, as indicated in table 1, whereas the test in the $(-10, +10)$ interval only yields the rejection rate of 24.4% shown in table 4. Thus, when the timing of the abnormal performance is not uniform over the period under study, the precise pattern of estimated abnormal returns is conveniently summarized by a CAR plot; the pattern can provide useful information beyond that given by the value of the CAR at the end of an arbitrary 'cumulation period'.[32]

6. The effect of clustering

6.1. Event month clustering

The securities of a sample will frequently each experience an event during the same calendar time period. For example, as Schwert (1978) and Foster (1980) discuss, government regulation or mandated accounting procedures will often have a simultaneous impact on a number of different securities whose price performance around the time of an event is being examined. We refer to the close or simultaneous spacing of events as event month clustering.

Clustering has implications for the characteristics of the test methods being examined in this paper. The general impact of clustering is to lower the number of securities whose month '0' behavior is independent. The month '0' dependence is important for two reasons. First, if performance measures such as the deviation from historical mean returns or market model residuals are positively correlated across securities in calendar time, then such clustering will increase the variance of the performance measures (e.g., the average residual) and hence lower the power of the tests. Secondly, the month '0' dependence in security-specific performance measures must explicitly be taken into account in testing the null hypothesis of no abnormal performance. Otherwise, even in the absence of abnormal performance, the null

---

[32]Our discussion of CAR plots touches on a deeper set of issues which arises in connection with all tests for abnormal performance: *a priori*, the researcher often does not know when the abnormal performance would have occurred, nor perhaps even the frequency distribution of the time of the abnormal performance. Lacking that information, the choice of time period over which to conduct the hypothesis test is arbitrary, and one's inferences can be sensitive to the choice.

For example, if for all securities the abnormal performance occurs in month '0' or a few months surrounding it, a hypothesis test conducted over the entire $(-10, +10)$ period is less likely to pick up abnormal performance than one concentrating on month '0'. Conversely, if the event month of abnormal performance is uniformly distributed over the $(-10, +10)$ period, but the hypothesis test is performed for month '0', the abnormal performance is also less likely to be detected. In general, the hypothesis test should give weights to event months which are the same as those implicit in the actual frequency distribution of the time of abnormal performance. However, in the absence of a plausible *a priori* reason for doing so, it is dangerous to infer the frequency distribution of the time of abnormal performance by merely looking at CAR plots and the estimated level of abnormal performance in each event-related month: if one puts enough weight on 'outliers', the null can always be rejected even when it is true.

hypothesis will be rejected too frequently if security specific performance measures are positively correlated.[33]

Inducing clustering in event-dates of the sample securities

To examine the effect of clustering, we must specify a new procedure for generating event-dates. For each of the securities in a given sample, month '0' is restricted to fall in a particular calendar time month which is common to all securities in the sample. The month is randomly selected. For each sample, a new calendar month is selected.[34] The effect of clustering is simulated with the same levels of abnormal performance which were used previously: 0, 1, 5 and 15%. All abnormal performance is generated in month '0'.

Testing for abnormal performance when there is clustering

For each performance measurement method, t-tests for month '0' abnormal performance are conducted using three different methods, each of which is discussed in the appendix. The t-tests are first conducted under the assumption that the performance measures (e.g., residuals) are independent across securities. The t-tests are also performed using two different methods for taking into account cross-sectional dependence.

One procedure, which we call 'Crude Dependence Adjustment', focuses on the series of event-time average performance measures (e.g., average residuals). A second, more complicated method we simulate has been employed by Jaffe (1974) and Mandelker (1974); that method forms various portfolios of sample securities in calendar time; as discussed in the appendix, the portfolios are formed so as to make their performance measures independent and homoscedastic, and the hypothesis test is actually performed on the independent performance measures of the portfolios. In table 6, we present simulation results for the different tests. From the numbers presented in the table, several results are apparent.

First, event-month clustering has a substantial impact on rejection frequencies for the Mean Adjusted Returns method. For example, when the t-tests ignore cross-sectional dependence in security specific performance measures,

---

[33]This consequence of the independence assumption has recently been discussed by, for example, Beaver (1979) and Collins and Dent (1978). Note that for the simulations presented thus far, cross-sectional dependence is unimportant because the degree of clustering is small: Since event dates are independent draws from a uniform distribution comprised of over 300 different calendar months, the likelihood that many securities in a given sample will have a common event date is small. Previous simulations have been performed both with and without dependence adjustment of the types to be discussed in this section; the differences in Type I error frequencies under the null hypothesis are generally small.

[34]The month is between June 1944 and March 1968. For a given sample, any month in that period has an equal probability of being selected; for the purpose of maintaining sample to sample independence, the selection of calendar months is carried out without replacement.

the Mean Adjusted Returns method rejects the null hypothesis 32.4% of the time when there is no abnormal performance;[35] this compares to rejection rates of about 3% using either Crude Dependence Adjustment or the Jaffe–Mandelker procedure. Clustering also reduces the power of the Mean Adjusted Returns method against specific alternative hypotheses: with highly correlated security specific performance measures, the variance of the mean

Table 6

The effect of event-month clustering.[a] Percentage of 250 replications where the null hypothesis is rejected ($\alpha = 0.05$). One-tailed t-test results. H_0: mean abnormal performance in month '0' $= 0.0$.

Method	Actual level of abnormal performance in month '0'		
	0%	1%	5%
Mean Adjusted Returns			
No Dependence Adjustment	32.4	44.4	74.0
Crude Adjustment	3.2	4.8	31.6
Jaffe–Mandelker	3.6	5.6	34.4
Market Adjusted Returns			
No Dependence Adjustment	3.6	22.8	99.6
Crude Adjustment	4.0	23.6	99.6
Jaffe–Mandelker	5.2	24.4	99.6
Market Model Residuals			
No Dependence Adjustment	4.0	23.2	99.2
Crude Adjustment	5.6	24.8	99.6
Jaffe–Mandelker	6.0	26.8	99.6
Fama–MacBeth Residuals			
No Dependence Adjustment	4.0	25.2	100.0
Crude Adjustment	4.8	24.4	98.8
Jaffe–Mandelker	4.8	26.4	99.2
Control Portfolio			
Crude Adjustment	4.4	23.2	99.2

[a]For a given replication, month '0' falls on the same calendar date for each security. The calendar date differs from replication to replication. Equally Weighted Index.

[b]Methodology not readily adapted to other dependence adjustment procedures.

[35]Event month clustering is not the only stochastic process generating events which would lead to 'too many' rejections for the Mean Adjusted Returns method. When there is no clustering, but the event tends to occur only in those months when the market return is abnormally high, then rejection rates using Mean Adjusted Returns will also be too high with a one-tailed test for positive abnormal performance. Furthermore, in an actual event study involving only one security, an analogous situation arises. For that case, the Mean Adjusted Returns method will not yield the probability of Type I error assumed in the hypothesis tests if the market return at the time of the event happened to have been abnormally high (or abnormally low).

performance measure, computed across sample securities, is higher, and the power of the tests is expected to be lower. With 5% abnormal performance, the Mean Adjusted Returns method rejects the null hypothesis 31.6% of the time using Crude Dependence Adjustment, and 34.4% of the time using the Jaffe–Mandelker procedure. These numbers are much lower than the rejection rate of 100% we obtained in the analogous earlier simulation without clustering.

Secondly, in marked contrast to the results for the Mean Adjusted Returns method, clustering appears to have little impact on rejection frequencies for any of the other performance measurement methods, and thus our earlier conclusions about the relatively favorable performance of Mean Adjusted Returns do not apply if there is clustering. When the null hypothesis is true, for our simulations it makes little difference whether or not cross-sectional dependence is taken into account. For example, in the Market Adjusted Returns method, the rejections rate with no dependence adjustment is 3.6%, compared to rejection rates of 4.0% using Crude Dependence Adjustment and 5.2% with the Jaffe–Mandelker procedure.

Furthermore, when abnormal performance is present, the rejection rates when there is clustering are not markedly different from those when there is no clustering: With 1% abnormal performance, the rejection rates with clustering are on the order of 20 to 25%, slightly higher than was the case in earlier simulations without clustering. It thus appears that for all methods taking into account market-wide factors, with the Equally Weighted Index the degree of cross-sectional dependence in the performance measures is negligible for randomly selected securities.[36] However, in an actual event study, a sample of securities whose events are clustered in calendar time may be nonrandom; the sample securities might be drawn from a common industry group having positively correlated performance measures. In such a case, the power of the tests is reduced even if a particular methodology abstracts from the market, and taking into account cross-sectional dependence in order to assure the 'correct' proportion of rejections is appropriate in such a case.

Third, it appears that the differences in simulation results between the Crude Adjustment procedure and the Jaffe–Mandelker procedure are small. In the presence of abnormal performance, there is a slight increase in rejection frequencies with the Jaffe–Mandelker procedure, and the increase

---

[36]Note that our finding of negligible cross-sectional dependence is specific to the Equally Weighted Index. With that index, randomly selected securities would not be expected to exhibit systematic positive cross-sectional dependence in performance measures. For example, if all securities in the market had positively correlated market model residuals, then the market model has really not abstracted from marketwide influences. With the Value Weighted Index, the unweighted average of pairwise covariances between residuals can be positive; in fact, simulations of clustering with the Value Weighted Index result in rejection rates under the null of about 15% (for $\alpha = 0.05$) when cross-sectional dependence is ignored.

takes place for every test method. The increase is consistent with our discussion in the appendix, where we suggest that the Jaffe–Mandelker procedure will be more precise than Crude Dependence Adjustment.

6.2. Security risk clustering

Another form of clustering which is pertinent to our study is clustering by systematic risk: a particular sample may consist of securities which tend to have higher than average (or lower than average) systematic risk. Since for individual securities there is a positive empirical relationship between the variance of returns and systematic risk (as well as between market model residual variance and systematic risk),[37] it seems reasonable to expect that tests for abnormal performance will be more powerful for low risk securities than for high risk securities; the intuition is simply that a given level of abnormal performance should be easier to detect when 'normal' fluctuations in sample security returns (and the standard errors of parameter estimates such as $\hat{\beta}$) are small rather than large.

Security risk clustering: Sample selection procedure

To see the effect of security risk clustering, we construct two sets of 250 samples, where all 500 samples have 50 securities each. We call the first 250 samples low-risk samples, and the second 250 samples high-risk samples.

The samples are constructed as follows. Securities are picked and event dates generated as discussed in section 3. In addition to data availability requirements imposed earlier, it is also required that a security have data from event-months -149 through -90. Based on an estimate of β in that 60-month period, a security is assigned to a sample in either the high-risk or low-risk set, depending on whether its estimated β is greater than 1 or less than 1.[38] The procedure of picking securities and event dates, and then of assigning securities to samples based on $\hat{\beta}$, is continued until both the low-risk set of samples and the high-risk set of samples each has 250 samples of 50 securities.

Simulation results for risk-clustered samples

For each set of 250 samples, various methodologies are simulated as in previous experiments not involving either security-risk or event-month clus-

---

[37]See Fama (1976, pp. 121–124). Note that empirically there is also a negative relationship between $\hat{\beta}$ (and hence variance of returns) and firm size. We have not examined the separate, independent effect of firm size on the power of the tests. However, to the extent that β merely proxies for firm size, tests for abnormal performance would be expected to be more powerful for large firms than for small firms.

[38]By selecting on the basis of previous $\hat{\beta}$, the expected value of the measurement error in $\hat{\beta}$ over the $(-89, -11)$ period should be zero for both the high-$\hat{\beta}$ and low-$\hat{\beta}$ samples. See Black, Jensen and Scholes (1972) for a discussion.

Table 7

The effect of clustering by risk.[a] Percentage of 250 replications where the null hypothesis is rejected ($\alpha = 0.05$). One-tailed t-test results. H_0: mean abnormal performance in month '0' = 0.0.

Method	Rejection rates				Mean t-statistics			
	Abnormal performance				Abnormal performance			
	0%		1%		0%		1%	
	$\hat{\beta}<1$	$\hat{\beta}>1$	$\hat{\beta}<1$	$\hat{\beta}>1$	$\hat{\beta}<1$	$\hat{\beta}>1$	$\hat{\beta}<1$	$\hat{\beta}>1$
Mean Adjusted Returns	6.8	6.0	26.8	24.4	−0.03	−0.02	1.18	0.89
Market Adjusted Returns	7.6	7.2	31.6	24.8	−0.02	0.07	1.14	0.99
Market Model Residuals	8.0	5.6	29.6	21.6	−0.02	0.01	1.18	0.91
Fama–MacBeth Residuals	8.4	5.6	30.0	20.0	0.02	−0.02	1.19	0.88
Control Portfolio	8.4	5.2	17.6	14.0	0.11	0.03	0.74	0.54

	Mean $\hat{\beta}$ ($N = 12500$)
250 samples with $\hat{\beta}<1$	0.81
250 samples with $\hat{\beta}>1$	1.24

[a]CRSP Equally Weighted Index. There are 500 samples, each having 50 securities. $\hat{\beta}<1$ refers to the 250 samples formed from securities with estimated βs less than 1. $\hat{\beta}>1$ refers to the 250 samples formed from securities with estimated βs greater than 1.

tering. In table 7, for both the low-$\hat{\beta}$ set of samples and the high-$\hat{\beta}$ set of samples, we show rejection rates and mean t-statistics when various methodologies are applied to each set of 250 samples, and when all abnormal performance is introduced in month '0'.

When there is no abnormal performance, neither the rejection rates nor the mean t-statistics seem particularly out of line for any of the test methods. It is a bit surprising that the Market Adjusted Returns method does not reject 'too often' for the $\hat{\beta}>1$ samples and 'not often enough' when $\hat{\beta}<1$; however, it should be kept in mind that the rejection proportions shown in the table are merely estimates of the true proportions; in addition, there is some overlap in the sets of samples in the sense that individual securities in the high-$\hat{\beta}$ set can have true βs less than 1, and securities in the low-$\hat{\beta}$ set can have βs greater than 1.

With 1% abnormal performance, for all test methods both the rejection rates and the mean t-statistics are higher for the $\hat{\beta}<1$ set of samples than for the $\hat{\beta}>1$ set of samples. But the rejection rates for the high-$\hat{\beta}$ and low-$\hat{\beta}$ samples are generally not markedly different from each other, averaging 27.1% (across test methods) for the $\hat{\beta}<1$ samples and 21.0% for the $\hat{\beta}>1$ samples. Nor are these rejection rates much different from the 21.6% average rejection rate (across test methods) we obtained earlier for samples where the average $\hat{\beta}$ was approximately 1. Furthermore, the Mean Adjusted Returns method continues to perform well, rejecting the null 26.8% of the time for the $\hat{\beta}<1$ samples, and 24.4% of the time for the $\hat{\beta}>1$ samples.

Our risk clustering simulations also provide some new insight into the relative efficacy of various test methods. A careful look at table 7 reveals that while the rejection rates and mean t-statistics for the Control Portfolio method are indeed higher for $\hat{\beta}<1$ sample than for $\hat{\beta}>1$ samples when there is abnormal performance, both sets of numbers are lower than for previous samples with $\hat{\beta}$s averaging 1. For example, using the Control Portfolio method, the mean t-statistic in our earlier results was 0.86 with 1% abnormal performance; the figures are 0.74 and 0.54, respectively, for the $\hat{\beta}<1$ and $\hat{\beta}>1$ sets of samples. While the relative rankings of most of the test methods are not very sensitive to sample security β, the version of the Control Portfolio method we have simulated performs noticeably worse, relative to both itself and to the other methods, when β departs from 1.

The unfavorable performance of the Control Portfolio method when average $\hat{\beta}$ is different from 1 is related to the manner in which the methodology forms portfolios.[39] The Control Portfolio method we simulate is likely to involve short selling of some sample securities when average $\hat{\beta}$ is much different from 1. With short selling, the weights applied to the two subportfolios of sample securities will be vastly different from each other, and the variance of returns on the portfolio thus formed will be quite large;

[39]Gonedes, Dopuch and Penman (1976) and Gonedes (1978) discuss a related issue.

compared to a situation where each subportfolio has the same positive weight, the performance measure, which is the difference between portfolio returns and market returns, will also have a higher variance.

In addition, portfolio residual variance tends to be lowest when β is 1 [Black, Jensen and Scholes (1972, table 2)]. Portfolios of sample securities which have βs much different from 1 will have greater estimation error in subportfolio β and hence greater estimation error in calculating appropriate weights for subportfolios. This will also increase the variance of the performance measure and lower the power of the tests.

7. The choice of market index

Simulation results reported thus far have been based on use of the Equally Weighted Index. However, while the Equally Weighted Index is often employed in actual event studies, the Asset Pricing Model provides no justification for its use: the Asset Pricing model specifies an *ex ante* relationship between security expected returns and systematic risk measured with respect to the Value-Weighted Index. To examine the sensitivity of our earlier results to the choice of market index, we replicate the experiment reported in table 4 using the Value-Weighted (rather than the Equally Weighted) Index. As in the table 4 simulations, the event-month of abnormal performance is a drawing from a uniform distribution in the interval from month -10 through $+10$. For each methodology, results using the Value Weighted Index, along with the corresponding earlier results for the Equal Weighted Index, are reported in table 8.

7.1. Estimates of systematic risk using different market indices

One way in which the simulation results using the Value-Weighted Index differ from those using the Equally Weighted Index is related to the estimates of sample security systematic risk. To focus on the differences, which will play an important role in our discussion, for each of the 250 replications the average and standard deviation of the market model βs using each index are computed; summary statistics are shown at the bottom of table 8.

For the Equally Weighted Index, the mean of the 250 average βs is equal to 0.993, which is insignificantly different from 1. That the average $\hat{\beta}$ is approximately equal to 1 is hardly surprising, since our simulation procedure involves random selection of securities.

However, with the Value-Weighted Index, estimates of sample security βs are systematically different from 1. With that Index, the mean of the 250 average βs is 1.13, with a standard deviation of 0.031. At the 0.01 level of significance, the hypothesis that the mean average β is equal to 1 must be rejected.

Table 8

The effect of the choice of market index. Percentage of 250 replications where the null hypothesis is rejected ($\alpha = 0.05$). One-tailed t-test results. H_0: mean abnormal performance in interval $(-10, +10) = 0.0$. VW = CRSP Value Weighted Index. EW = Equally Weighted Index.

Method	Actual level of abnormal performance in the interval $(-10, +10)$[a]							
	0%		1%		5%		15%	
	VW	EW	VW	EW	VW	EW	VW	EW
Mean Adjusted Returns	7.6	7.6	9.2	9.2	28.4	28.4	82.0	82.0
Market Adjusted Returns	20.4	3.6	24.0	5.6	44.8	18.4	94.8	73.2
Market Model Residuals	4.0	7.2	6.0	10.8	18.8	24.4	76.4	86.4
Fama–MacBeth Residuals	1.2	3.6	2.0	5.2	7.2	16.4	54.8	74.8
Control Portfolio	14.0	4.8	15.6	6.4	29.6	16.0	78.0	70.0

[a] For each security, abnormal performance is introduced for one month in the interval $(-10, +10)$, with each month having an equal probability of being selected.

Summary Statistics, Systematic Risk Estimates

	VW	EW
Mean estimate of β	1.13	0.993
Average cross-sectional standard deviation of β	0.49	0.43
Standard deviation of average βs for the 250 samples	0.031	0.027

There is no necessity for $\hat{\beta}$s computed from a value-weighted (rather than an equally weighted) index to have an unweighted average of 1; the only requirement is that the value-weighted average of all security $\hat{\beta}$s (computed with respect to the value-weighted index) be equal to 1. For randomly selected securities, an unweighted average $\hat{\beta}$ greater than 1 would be expected if securities with low value weights have relatively high $\hat{\beta}$s, and vice versa. Hence an average $\hat{\beta}$ of 1.13 results from a particular cross-sectional distribution of β, and does not imply that our selection procedure is somehow biased toward including high risk securities.

7.2. Type I errors with the value-weighted index

Our finding that the unweighted average of $\hat{\beta}$s computed from the Value-Weighted Index is not equal to 1, along with the fact that not all securities have the same value weights in the market portfolio, turns out to have significant implications for the behavior of one performance measurement method under study: the Market Adjusted Returns method implicitly assumes that security βs average to one, and looks at the average differences between security returns and those on the Value-Weighted Market Index. However, since average β is greater than 1, an equally weighted portfolio of randomly selected stocks is expected to have returns which are greater than those of the Value-Weighted Index. The unweighted average difference between security returns and returns on the Value-Weighted Market Index will tend to be positive for any sample of randomly selected securities. Using the Value-Weighted Index, the Market Adjusted Returns method will reject the null hypothesis 'too often'.

This potential problem with the Market Adjusted Returns method does not result from the use of the Value-Weighted Index itself. Rather, a potential bias is induced by the failure to appropriately value weight security returns and security specific performance measures.[40] To our knowledge no

---

[40]For the Market Model Residuals method, under the null hypothesis there is no bias inherent in not value-weighting the residuals: Since for every security the expected value of the residuals is zero, the average residual is expected to be zero for any set of weights applied to the individual residuals. On the other hand, for the Market Adjusted Returns method, some securities have performance measures which on average will be positive, (e.g., $\beta > 1$) and others have performance measures which will be negative (e.g., $\beta < 1$). Equal weighting of the security specific performance measures will not guarantee an average performance measure of zero because the number of securities with positive performance measures is greater than the number with negative performance measures.

For Fama–MacBeth residuals, there could well be biases in our simulations with the Value-Weighted Index. Note that Fama–MacBeth residuals are computed on the basis of estimates of γ_0 and γ_1 derived from the Equally-Weighted Index. If a security's $\hat{\beta}$ is computed from the Value-Weighted Index, and Fama–MacBeth residuals then calculated from $\hat{\gamma}_0$ and $\hat{\gamma}_1$ based on the Equally Weighted Index, there is no reason for a security's Fama–MacBeth residual to have an expected value of 0 under the null hypothesis of no abnormal performance. Furthermore, deriving estimates of γ_0 and γ_1 for the Value-Weighted Index would require more than a mere replication of the Fama–MacBeth procedure; the use of value-weighting procedures (e.g., for portfolio formation) would also be indicated.

event study employing the Market Adjusted Returns method has used such value-weighting. Furthermore, as a practical matter the bias can be substantial. As table 8 indicates, when there is no abnormal performance, the Market Adjusted Returns method rejects the null hypothesis a whopping 20.4% of the time using the Value-Weighted Index, and the mean t-statistic for 250 replications is 0.77; if the hypothesis test is performed at the 0.1 rather than the 0.05 level, the rejection rate increases to 27.2%.[41]

From table 8, it also appears that the Control Portfolio method exhibits a positive bias in the performance measure. For that methodology, the rejection rate under the null hypothesis is 14.0% (for $\alpha = 0.05$), and the mean t-statistic is 0.36. However, the problem of 'too many' rejections when using the Value-Weighted Index cannot be attributed to the failure to value-weight the security-specific performance measures; this is because the Control Portfolio method, unlike the Market Adjusted Returns method, applies weights to securities such that the portfolio thus formed has a β of 1 and an expected return equal to that of the Value-Weighted Market Index.[42]

7.3. Type II errors with the value-weighted index

Because some of the performance measurement methods do not, under the null hypothesis, reject at the significance level of the test when used with the Value-Weighted Index, legitimate comparisons of the power of the tests for the Equally Weighted versus Value-Weighted Index are not possible for those methods, since the probability of Type I errors differs according to the index being used. However, the one method which does not suffer from 'too high' a frequency of Type I errors using the Value-Weighted Index is the Market Model Residuals method. Some clue as to the relationship between

[41]The rejection frequencies reported in table 8 for the Market Adjusted Returns method will not always be applicable because the magnitude of the bias in the method is critically dependent on several parameters of the experimental situation. For example, for randomly selected securities, the propensity for rejecting 'too often' under the null will be positively related to sample size and the length of time over which abnormal performance is being measured: if a given performance measure, averaged over sample securities, is positive, whether one can reject the null hypothesis that the average performance measure is zero depends on the number of independent observations over which the average is computed. For example, when the null hypothesis being tested is that month '0' (rather than months -10, $+10$) abnormal performance is 0, the rejection rates using the Value-Weighted Index are not much different from those which obtained in simulations using the Equally Weighted Index.

Note also that the bias in the Market Adjusted Returns method is not always positive. The sign of the bias is related to the systematic risk of the sample securities. If the value-weighted average $\hat{\beta}$ is greater than 1, the bias will be positive; if it is less than 1, it will be negative.

[42]The computation of the test statistic in the Control Portfolio method is discussed in the appendix. The distributional properties of the test statistic in repeated sampling will depend upon the sampling properties of the weights which are estimated and applied to the returns on individual securities; the properties could differ according to the index employed, particularly since the degree of measurement error in $\hat{\beta}$ (and hence in the weights) can be a function of the index. Conditions on the weights sufficient for the test statistic to be distributed Student-t have not to our knowledge been discussed in the event study literature.

the power of the tests and the specific market index is provided by the results for that method.

As shown in table 8, for each of several different levels of abnormal performance, the rejection rates using Market Model Residuals are higher with the Equally Weighted Index than with the Value-Weighted Index. With 1% abnormal performance, the rejection rates are 10.8 and 6.0%, respectively; with 5% abnormal performance, the rejection rates are 24.4 and 18.8%, respectively.

It thus appears that use of the Equally Weighted Index is no less likely, and in fact slightly more likely, to pick up abnormal performance than use of the Value-Weighted Index. Such a finding is consistent with the argument that the returns on randomly selected securities are on average more highly correlated with the Equally Weighted Index than the Value-Weighted Index. If for a majority of sample securities the precision with which β and hence residuals are measured is higher with the Equally Weighted Index, abnormal performance would be easier to detect using that benchmark.

8. Additional simulation results

8.1. Simulation results for different sample sizes

All results reported thus far in this paper are for sample sizes of 50 securities. However, it is of interest to examine the sensitivity of our results to sample size. For the case where all sample securities experience abnormal performance in month '0', table 9 reports simulation results for sample sizes of 12, 25, and again for 50 securities.[43]

As would be expected, the power of the tests increases with sample size. However, the rejection frequencies are not especially sensitive to the number of sample securities. For example, with the Mean Adjusted Returns method, doubling the sample size from 12 to 25 securities increases the rejection frequency with 1% abnormal performance from 14.0 to 15.2%. Doubling sample size again to 50 securities increases the rejection frequency to 26.0%. Furthermore, the relatively favorable performance of the Mean Adjusted Returns method seems to be independent of sample size, and the rejection frequencies still do not appear to be dramatically different than those for methods which adjust returns for market performance and risk.

8.2. The relationship among the tests

In many of the simulations we have performed, the rejection frequencies are not dramatically different for different methodologies. However, even if

---

[43]When we attempt to examine larger samples as well, the computing costs were found to be prohibitively high. For sample sizes of 100, the cost of performing just a third of the 250 replications was in excess of $1,000.

two methods have the same rejection frequency for any level of abnormal performance, this does not imply that the two methods will always lead a researcher to the same conclusion. For example, if each of two methods rejects the null hypothesis in 50 of the 250 samples, the samples on which the first method rejects the null hypothesis need not be the same as the samples on which the second method rejects the null hypothesis.[44] To assess the likelihood that the various methods will lead to results which are consistent

Table 9

The effect of sample size on rejection frequencies. Percentage of 250 replications where the null hypothesis is rejected ($\alpha = 0.05$). One-tailed *t*-test results. H_0: mean abnormal performance in month '0' $= 0.0$. Equally Weighted Index.

Method	Actual level of abnormal performance in month '0'		
	0%	1%	5%
Mean Adjusted Returns			
$N = 12$	5.2	14.0	79.2
$N = 25$	6.0	15.2	94.8
$N = 50$	4.0	26.0	100.0
Market Adjusted Returns			
$N = 12$	2.8	8.4	72.4
$N = 25$	3.6	13.2	91.6
$N = 50$	3.2	19.6	100.0
Market Model Residuals			
$N = 12$	3.2	9.6	72.4
$N = 25$	4.4	13.6	91.6
$N = 50$	4.4	22.8	100.0
Fama–MacBeth Residuals			
$N = 12$	2.8	8.4	56.8
$N = 25$	4.8	15.2	93.2
$N = 50$	4.0	21.6	100.0
Control Portfolio			
$N = 12$	2.8	8.4	56.8
$N = 25$	2.4	12.8	84.8
$N = 50$	4.4	18.0	100.0

for a given sample, it is necessary to examine the results of our earlier hypothesis tests in more detail. In table 10, for the case where all abnormal performance occurs in month '0', we indicate the frequency with which the results of the hypothesis tests for a given sample are the same for different methodologies.

[44]Charest (1978), Langetieg (1978), and Brenner (1979) have all conducted event studies where the results of the hypothesis tests appear to be somewhat sensitive to the particular test method which is used.

When the null hypothesis is true, it appears that the test methods typically lead to results which are somewhat, but not perfectly consistent. For example, in the simulations we presented in table 1, under the null hypothesis the Mean Adjusted Returns method rejected in 4.0% of the samples, and the Market Adjusted Returns method rejected the null hypothesis in 3.2% of the 250 samples. However, as indicated in table 10, the frequency with which *both* methods reject the null hypothesis when it is true

Table 10

The relationship among the tests. For 1% abnormal performance in month '0', the table shows the frequency (in 250 replications) with which a given combination of methods resulted in (a) at least one rejection ($R \geq 1$), and (b) an inconsistency (one rejection, one failure to reject; $R = 1$). The third entry is the frequency with which both methods reject the null hypothesis when it is true ($R = 0$). The number in parentheses is the product of the individual rejection frequencies which obtained for each method under the null hypothesis. H_0: mean abnormal performance in month '0' $= 0.0$ ($\alpha = 0.05$). One-tailed t-test results. Equally Weighted Index.

	Market Adjusted Returns	Market Model Residuals	Fama–MacBeth Residuals	Control Portfolios
Mean Adjusted Returns				
$R \geq 1$	45.6%	48.8	47.6	44.0
$R = 1$	33.2	33.2	33.6	33.2
$R = 0$	1.6(0.13)	2.0(0.18)	1.6(0.16)	1.2(0.18)
Market Adjusted Returns				
$R \geq 1$		42.4	41.2	37.6
$R = 1$		25.2	25.6	22.4
$R = 0$		2.4(0.15)	2.8(0.13)	2.8(0.14)
Market Model Residuals				
$R \geq 1$			44.4	40.8
$R = 1$			25.2	26.4
$R = 0$			3.2(0.18)	2.4(0.19)
Fama–MacBeth Residuals				
$R \geq 1$				39.6
$R = 1$				25.6
$R = 0$				2.8(0.18)

is 1.6%, which is approximately 10 times the frequency which would be expected if the two methods were independent. Furthermore, for all of the pairwise combinations of methods shown in table 10, it appears that the results of the hypothesis tests are also highly correlated; the frequency with which two given methods reject the null hypothesis when it is true ranges from 1.2 to 3.2%. This high correlation suggests that rejecting the null hypothesis using two different methods is much more likely than would be expected by assuming independence of the test methods.

When the null hypothesis is not true, the test methods are still not perfectly consistent. With 1% abnormal performance, the likelihood that one method will reject the null hypothesis but the other will fail to reject ranges from 22.4 to 33.6%; inconsistencies between two methods seem least likely for the combination of Control Portfolios and Market Adjusted Returns.

Our finding that the test methods are not always consistent when there is abnormal performance opens up the possibility that there are sets of methodologies which, when used jointly, are more likely to detect abnormal performance than any one method alone. For example, as table 10 indicates, with 1% abnormal performance, the frequency with which *at least* one of two methods rejects the null hypothesis of no abnormal performance ranges from 37.6 to 48.8%, which is higher than the rejection rates which typically obtain for the individual tests. However, we hasten to add that the higher rejection rates are not themselves evidence of a more powerful test. It should be kept in mind that the significance level of the test (that is, the probability of *falsely* rejecting at least one of two null hypotheses) also increases when methodologies are used in combination with each other. The probability of at least one Type I error increases with the number of tests, and cannot be assessed unless the dependence of the tests is taken into account.

9. Summary and conclusions

In this paper, observed monthly stock return data were employed to examine various methodologies with which event studies measure security price performance. Abnormal performance was artificially introduced into this data. Our conclusions about the performance of the different methodologies can be summarized as follows.

9.1. Simulation results for the 'no clustering' case

Initially, we simulated a situation where securities and event dates were randomly selected, and event dates for different securities were not clustered in calendar time. When abnormal performance was present, the differences between methodologies based on Mean Adjusted Returns, Market Adjusted Returns, and Market and Risk Adjusted Returns were quite small; the simplest methodology, Mean Adjusted Returns, picked up abnormal performance no less frequently than did the other methodologies, and the power of the tests did not appear to be enhanced using risk adjustment procedures suggested by the Asset Pricing model. For example, when 1% abnormal performance was introduced in month '0' for every security in a sample of 50, each of the methodologies rejected the null hypothesis of no abnormal month '0' performance about 20% of the time when performing a one-tailed *t*-test at the 0.05 level of significance. Such a result also indicates that if the researcher is working with a sample size of 50 and the event under study is not expected *a priori* to have changed the value of the affected securities by 1% or more, the use of monthly data is unlikely to detect the event's impact.

The use of prior information

With 5% or more abnormal performance in month '0', rejection rates for a sample size of 50 were 100% for all of the methodologies. However, that simulation result does not imply that an event study using monthly data will always pick up 5% or more abnormal performance using a sample size of 50: if the researcher is unable to identify the specific time at which the abnormal performance would have occurred, the power of the tests for abnormal performance falls off dramatically. For example, we simulated a situation where each of 50 sample securities had 5% abnormal performance in a particular month surrounding month '0', but the precise month was uncertain and different across securities. When the time of the abnormal performance could only be narrowed to an 11 month 'window', the null hypothesis of no abnormal performance over the window was rejected only 30 to 40% of the time with the different methodologies. Thus, unless the time of the abnormal performance can be narrowed using prior information, the null hypothesis often fails to be rejected even when the sample securities experience high levels of abnormal performance.

9.2. Performance measurement when event dates or systematic risk estimates are clustered

Calendar time clustering of events

Our conclusions about the relatively favorable performance of the Mean Adjusted Returns method were found to be highly sensitive to the specification of the stochastic process generating events. For example, when we simulated a situation in which event dates were randomly selected, but clustered in calendar time, the Mean Adjusted Returns method performed very poorly compared to those methods which explicitly adjusted for market performance and for systematic risk. In the extreme example of clustering we examined, all securities of a given sample were assigned a common event date, and the *t*-tests were adjusted to take into account cross-sectional dependence in the security-specific performance measures. The Mean Adjusted Returns method detected 5% abnormal performance in month '0' only about 35% of the time, compared to rejection rates of 98.8 to 100.0% for all the other test methods. On the basis of such results, it is difficult to argue that the use of the Mean Adjusted Returns method will always be appropriate. When there is event month clustering, methodologies which incorporate information about the market's realized return perform substantially better than Mean Adjusted Returns.

Sample security risk clustering

Within the class of methodologies which adjust for marketwide factors, we examined several alternatives. These included a one-factor market model, a two-factor model utilizing Fama–MacBeth residuals, and a Control Portfolio technique in which the return on a portfolio of sample securities was compared to that of another portfolio with the same estimated systematic risk. For randomly selected securities, which were of 'average' risk, the differences between these methodologies were small, regardless of whether or not there was calendar time clustering of events. However, when securities were not randomly selected, and sample security systematic risk estimates were systematically 'clustered' and different from 1, an important difference between the methodologies emerged: with systematic risk clustering, the Control Portfolio method was much less likely to pick up a given level of abnormal performance than either a one-factor or a two-factor model. In fact, when there was risk clustering but not event month clustering, even the simple Mean Adjusted Returns method outperformed the seemingly complicated Control Portfolio method. Thus, under plausible conditions the researcher can actually be made worse off using explicit risk adjustment procedures.

9.3. Additional simulation results

The choice of market index

Although use of the Equally Weighted Index is an *ad hoc* procedure, that index led to no notable difficulties in our simulations; however, improper use of the Value-Weighted Index was shown to cause considerable problems which have not been recognized in extant event studies. For example, when some methodologies (including the widely used 'Control Portfolio' methodology) were used with the Value-Weighted Index, the null hypothesis was rejected too often, in some cases over 20% of the time (when testing at the 0.05 significance level) even when there was no abnormal performance. Furthermore, we find no evidence that the use of the Value-Weighted Index increases the power of the tests.

The appropriate statistical test

For methodologies using the Equally Weighted Index, and for many of those using the Value-Weighted Index, we found that *t*-tests focusing on the average month '0' performance measure (e.g., the average residual) are reasonably well-specified. Although stated significance levels should not be taken literally, when the null hypothesis is true the *t*-tests typically reject at approximately the significance level of the test; the differences between the empirical frequency distribution of the test statistics and the *t*-distribution are generally not large.

On the other hand, certain non-parametric tests used in event studies are not correctly specified. We indicated how the sign and Wilcoxon tests will not give the 'correct' number of rejections unless asymmetry in the distribution of security specific performance measures is taken into account; as far as we can determine, no event study using non-parametric tests has recognized how sensitive the tests can be to departures from the symmetry assumption.

9.4. The bottom line: What's the best methodology?

Our goal in this paper has not been to formulate the 'best' event study methodology, but rather, to compare different methodologies which have actually been used in event studies and which constitute current practice. Even among the methods we have studied, it is difficult to simulate every conceivable variation of each methodology, and every plausible experimental situation; while we cannot, therefore, indicate the 'best' methodology (given some set of criteria), our simulations do provide a useful basis for discriminating between alternative procedures.

A 'bottom line' that emerges from our study is this: beyond a simple, one-factor market model, there is no evidence that more complicated methodologies convey any benefit. In fact, we have presented evidence that more complicated methodologies can actually make the researcher worse off, both compared to the market model and to even simpler methods, like Mean Adjusted Returns, which make no explicit risk adjustment. This is not to say that existing techniques cannot be improved; indeed, our results have led us to suggest a number of ways in which such improvements can be made. But even if the researcher doing an event study has a strong comparative advantage at improving existing methods, a good use of his time is still in reading old issues of the *Wall Street Journal* to more accurately determine event dates.

Appendix: Methodologies for measuring security price performance

In this appendix, we discuss in more detail the different methods for measuring security price performance which are used in the study. For all of the methodologies, securities are selected as discussed in section 3. For a given security i, its monthly arithmetic return, R_{it}, is available over a period beginning in the 89th month prior to the event ($t = -89$) and terminating at the end of the tenth month following the event ($t = +10$). There are two observation periods over which return behavior is examined: a single month (month 0) and a series of event-related months (typically, months -10 through $+10$). For a particular level of abnormal performance, a given method computes the performance measures for individual securities in each of the 250 samples and, for each sample, assesses the statistical significance of those measures.[45]

A.1. Mean adjusted returns

For each security i, the mean K_i, and standard deviation $\sigma(R_i)$ of its return in months -89 through -11 are estimated:

$$\hat{K}_i = \frac{1}{79} \sum_{t=-89}^{-11} R_{it}, \tag{A.1}$$

$$\hat{\sigma}(R_i) = \left[\frac{1}{78} \sum_{t=-89}^{-11} (R_{it} - \hat{K}_i)^2 \right]^{\frac{1}{2}}. \tag{A.2}$$

The measure of abnormal performance for a given security in a given event-related month, A_{it}, is the difference between its realized return and the estimate of its mean return in the $(-89, -11)$ period, where this difference is standardized by the estimated standard deviation of the security's return in the $(-89, -11)$ period,[46]

$$A_{it} = (R_{it} - \hat{K}_i)/\hat{\sigma}(R_i). \tag{A.3}$$

---

[45]For all statistical tests reported in the paper, the $(-10, +10)$ period is ignored in estimating parameters such as the variance of the various performance measures. The simulations presented in tables 1 through 3 have also been replicated using the additional returns from the $(-10, +10)$ period. The additional 21 months of data provided by this period do not appear to have a marked impact on the rejection frequencies or on the distributional properties of the test statistics under the null hypothesis.

However, in an actual event study, the results can be sensitive to the inclusion (or exclusion) of the period surrounding the event. If high levels of abnormal performance are present, then including observations from around the time of the event gives more weight to apparent 'outliers', tending to increase the variance of the security-specific performance measures, and, as borne out by simulations not reported here, lowering the power of the tests. In addition, if there are abnormal returns in the event period, it is difficult to infer 'normal' returns, particularly if the period of the abnormal performance is long and includes an amount of data which is substantial relative to the total available. For a further discussion of reasons to exclude the 'event' period, see Brown, Durbin and Evans (1975). Note that if the event period is excluded in computing parameter estimates which are then used to predict returns into that period, the variance of the performance measure can be adjusted to reflect the predictive nature of the excess returns [see Patell (1976)]. However, event studies typically make no such adjustment; to be consistent with those studies, our simulations, as discussed in this appendix, also make no such adjustment.

[46]The standardization is similar to that which is performed in the Jaffe–Mandelker procedure. Earlier, we noted that the t-statistics for the Mean Adjusted Returns method had too much mass in the left-hand tail. That behavior becomes more pronounced without the standardization, making comparisons of power difficult because the level of Type I error is not constant across methodologies.

For month '0', and every month, this procedure yields one performance measure for each of the N securities in the sample.

The t-tests

The t-test for month '0' examines whether or not the average value of the performance measure in month '0' (i.e., the average month '0' standardized difference) is equal to 0. Except when otherwise specified, the t-test in the Mean Adjusted Returns method takes into account cross-sectional dependence in the security specific performance measures via a procedure we call Crude Dependence Adjustment.

For all methods using Crude Dependence Adjustment, the standard deviation of the month '0' average performance measure is estimated from the values of the average performance measures in months -49 through -11. Any cross-sectional dependence in the performance measures is thus taken into account. If the average performance measures for each event-related month are normal, independent,[47] and identically distributed, then under the null hypothesis the ratio of the month '0' average performance measure to the estimated standard deviation is distributed Student-t with 38 degrees of freedom.

With Crude Dependence Adjustment, the test statistic is given by

$$\frac{\frac{1}{N}\sum_{i=1}^{N} A_{i0}}{\left[\frac{1}{38}\left(\sum_{t=-49}^{-11}\left[\left(\frac{1}{N}\sum_{i=1}^{N} A_{it}\right) - A^*\right]^2\right)\right]^{\frac{1}{2}}}, \tag{A.4}$$

where

$$A^* = \left[\sum_{t=-49}^{-11}\sum_{i=1}^{N} A_{it}\right] \cdot \frac{1}{39N}. \tag{A.5}$$

In the t-test for abnormal performance in the $(-10, +10)$ interval, the numerator in (4) becomes

$$\frac{1}{21N}\sum_{t=-10}^{+10}\sum_{i=1}^{N} A_{it}, \tag{A.6}$$

---

[47]Note that, in general, the average performance measures will not literally be independent, which is one reason we refer to our procedure as a crude one. For example, suppose security A had an event in January and security B had an event in March of the same year. Then the average standardized difference in event months spread two months apart (-2 and 0, -1 and $+1$, etc.) will be calculated on the basis of observations from the same calendar month, and which are likely to be positively correlated. That the Mean Adjusted Returns method does not appear to reject the null hypothesis 'too often' suggests that the degree of dependence is small with this procedure.

and the denominator is the same as that shown in (4), divided by $\sqrt{21}$. This test statistic is also assumed to be distributed Student-t with 38 degrees of freedom.

Non-parametric tests

The test statistic in the sign test for month '0' abnormal performance is given by

$$Z = \frac{|P - 0.5| - 1/2N}{\sqrt{(0.5(0.5)/N)}},$$

(A.7)

where P is the proportion of A_i's in month '0' having positive signs.[48] The test statistic is assumed unit normal under the null hypothesis. The Wilcoxon test is carried out as in Lehmann (1975, pp. 128–129).

A.2. Market adjusted returns

For month '0', the performance measure for a given sample security is the difference between its return and the corresponding return on the market index,

$$A_{it} = R_{it} - R_{mt}.$$

(A.8)

An assumption sufficient for using such a performance measure is that the systematic risk for each sample security is equal to 1. In that case, the expected value of the difference between the return on a security and the return on the market index should, in an asset pricing model framework, be equal to zero.[49] The significance of the month '0' and months $(-10, +10)$ abnormal performance is assessed exactly as in the Mean Adjusted Returns method. For the month '0' t-test, the performance measure for a sample is the average difference.

A.3. Market model residuals

For each security in the sample, we regress its return in months -89 through -11 against the returns on the market portfolio during the corresponding calendar months. This 'market model' regression yields a 'residual' in each event-related month for each security. For a given security, the market model residual is its measure of abnormal performance. For the

---

[48] The sign of Z is equal to the sign of the difference between P and 0.5.

[49] For the average difference to be zero, it is not necessary for *all* sample securities to have $\beta = 1$. It is required only that the average β be equal to 1.

t-test on month '0', the performance measure is the average market model residual. Thus, we examine the significance of

$$\frac{1}{N} \sum_{i=1}^{N} A_{i0},$$ (A.9)

where

$$A_{it} = R_{it} - \hat{\alpha}_i - \hat{\beta}_i R_{mt}.$$ (A.10)

Because residual cross-correlation in calendar time is likely to be small (and would generally be even smaller in event time), simulations with Market Model Residuals make no dependence adjustment, unless otherwise stated. For procedures making no dependence adjustment, the significance test on the average residual (or average security specific performance measure) is carried out under the assumption that residuals (or other performance measures) are uncorrelated across securities. The standard deviation of the average performance measure is estimated on the basis of the standard deviation of the performance measure of each sample security in the $(-89, -11)$ period. For month '0', the test statistic is given by

$$\frac{\dfrac{1}{N} \sum_{i=1}^{N} A_{i0}}{\dfrac{1}{N} \left(\sum_{i=1}^{N} \left[\dfrac{1}{77} \sum_{t=-89}^{-11} \left(A_{it} - \left(\sum_{t=-89}^{-11} \dfrac{A_i}{79} \right) \right)^2 \right] \right)^{\frac{1}{2}}},$$ (A.11)

which is distributed Student-t with 78 degrees of freedom for the assumed normal and independent A_{it}s.

A.4. Fama–MacBeth residuals

For each security in the sample, we again use the market model to compute an estimate of its systematic risk over the period from -89 through -11. Using that estimate, we then compute a 'Fama–MacBeth' residual for each security for each month from -10 through $+10$,

$$A_{it} = R_{it} - \hat{\gamma}_1 - \hat{\gamma}_2 \hat{\beta}_i.$$ (A.12)

For a given month t, the Fama–MacBeth residual for security i, A_{it}, is the return on the security, net of the effect of marketwide factors captured by estimates of γ_1 and γ_2. We refer to the A_{it}s as 'Fama–MacBeth' residuals because the estimates of γ_1 and γ_2 which we use were derived by Fama and

MacBeth (1973).[50] For a given month, these coefficients reflect, respectively, the constant and the slope term in a cross-sectional regression of average portfolio return on average portfolio $\hat{\beta}$. The estimates $\hat{\gamma}_1$ and $\hat{\gamma}_2$ differ from calendar month to calendar month. However, for a given calendar month, they are the same for all securities, and should correspond to the return on the zero beta portfolio and the slope of the market line, respectively.[51]

The month '0' performance measure for a given security is its Fama–MacBeth residual. As with market model residuals, the performance measure for the *t*-test is the average Fama–MacBeth residual, and its statistical significance is assessed exactly as in that method. The test statistic is given in (A.11), unless otherwise stated.

A.5. Control portfolios

This method forms a portfolio of sample securities where the portfolio has approximately the same estimated systematic risk as the market index. The month '0' performance measure for this method is the difference between the return on that portfolio of sample securities and the average return on the market index in the months when securities experienced events.

The procedure we use to construct portfolios and estimate weights is as follows:

Portfolio Construction — Two portfolios are formed from the sample securities. Each portfolio is assigned half of those securities. The first portfolio consists of 'low-β' sample securities. The second portfolio consists of 'high-β' sample securities. The composition of each portfolio is determined by a market model regression for each of the securities in the sample for the months -89 through -50. The securities are ranked according to their estimated βs and, based on the rankings, securities are assigned to either the high-$\hat{\beta}$ or low-$\hat{\beta}$ portfolio.

Estimation of Weights — For each month in event-related time, we estimate the returns on each of two portfolios. The first is the equally weighted portfolio of high-β securities. The second is the equally weighted portfolio of low-β securities. For each equally weighted portfolio, we estimate its β, based on data from months -49 through -11. In this way, $\hat{\beta}$s used for forming portfolios and $\hat{\beta}$s used for estimating weights will be independent. Given the two estimates of β, we estimate a unique set of weights

---

[50]The estimates of γ_1 and γ_2 which we use are those reported in Fama (1976, pp. 357–360). The methodology for estimating those coefficients is discussed both there and in Fama and MacBeth (1973). In the original Fama–MacBeth article, γ_1 and γ_2 are referred to as γ_0 and γ_1, respectively.

[51]See Fama (1976, ch. 9). Brenner (1976) presents evidence that the Fama–MacBeth estimates of γ_1 are not uncorrelated with the market return.

summing to one which, when applied to the high- and low-β portfolios, yields a new portfolio with a β of 1 relative to the market index.

Since the βs of the high- and low-β security portfolios are estimates, the two weights derived are only an estimate of the correct weights which would be derived, given the true βs. The weights are constant over the estimation period, and may imply short-selling. For each event-related month, the return on a risk-adjusted portfolio of sample securities is estimated by applying the calculated weights to the return on the low- and high-β portfolios of sample securities. For each event-related month, we then estimate the difference between the return on the risk-adjusted portfolio of sample securities and the average return on the market index. The standard deviation of the difference is calculated on the basis of differences in returns from months -49 through -11. Thus, the significance tests involve Crude Dependence Adjustment. If the difference in returns on the portfolios is normal, independent, and identically distributed, then the test statistic is distributed Student-t with 38 degrees of freedom, and is given by

$$\frac{D_0}{\left[\frac{1}{38}\sum_{t=-49}^{-11}\left[D_t - \left(\frac{1}{39}\sum_{t=-49}^{-11} D_t\right)\right]^2\right]^{\frac{1}{2}}},\qquad\text{(A.13)}$$

where D_t is the difference in returns in event month t.

A.6. The Jaffe–Mandelker methodology[52]

For simulations where the Jaffe–Mandelker method of dependence adjustment is applied to the performance measures (residuals, deviations from mean return, etc.), sample security performance is examined in calendar rather than event time.

Measuring performance for a given event-related month

In order to examine security price performance for a given event-related month (say '0') this methodology forms portfolios in *calendar* time. For every month in calendar time, a portfolio is formed. For a given month, the portfolio consists of all securities which experience an event at that time. The portfolio for a given month may contain more than 1 security. This will happen whenever two or more securities have their event in the same calendar month. Conversely, the portfolio for a given month may contain no securities. This will be the case whenever it happens that no firms are experiencing an event in a particular calendar month. Thus, the number of

---

[52]See Jaffe (1974) and Mandelker (1974).

non-empty portfolios actually formed for investigating performance in event month '0' will be equal to the number of *different* calendar months in which firms experience events.

For each portfolio, the securities included in the portfolio (and their performance measures) are given equal weight, and a portfolio residual is calculated. The portfolio residual for a given calendar month is an un-weighted average of the residuals (or other performance measures) of the securities in the portfolio. This 'residual' is then standardized by dividing it by its estimated standard deviation.

The purpose of standardization is to insure that each portfolio residual will have the same variance. Standardization is accomplished by dividing each residual by its estimated standard deviation. In this way, each residual has an estimated variance of 1. If the standardization were not performed, the variance of the residual would not be constant: the variance would be low in months when many securities experienced events and were in the portfolio, and high in calendar months when few securities experienced events. A statistical test which assumed homogeneity of the variance would be inappropriate. Explicitly taking into account changes in the variance should lead to more precise tests; this will be true not only because portfolio size changes, but also because residual variance is not constant across securities.

The standardization procedure yields a vector of residuals, each of which is distributed t.[53] There will be one residual for every calendar month in which any sample firm had an event. The test for abnormal performance in month '0' is a test of the hypothesis that the mean standardized portfolio residual is equal to zero. Following Jaffe (1974, p. 418), the mean residual is assumed normally distributed.

References

Ball, Ray, 1978, Anomalies in relationships between securities' yields and yield-surrogates, Journal of Financial Economics 6, June/Sept., 103–126.
Ball, Ray and Philip Brown, 1968, An empirical evaluation of accounting numbers, Journal of Accounting Research 6, 159–178.
Ball, Ray, Philip Brown and Frank Finn, 1977, Share capitalization changes, information, and the Australian equity market, Australian Journal of Management 2, Oct., 105–117.
Bassett, Gilbert and Roger Koenker, 1978, Asymptotic theory of least absolute error regression, Journal of the American Statistical Association 73, Sept., 618–622.

[53]Details of the standardization procedure are given in Mandelker (1974, pp. 332–333). To compute the standard deviation of, say, the April 1969 residual, that portfolio must be reconstructed. For each month in the 49–month period prior to April 1969 (except the 10 calendar months immediately before April 1969), a residual for the securities which are in the April 1969 portfolio is calculated. The April 1969 portfolio residual is then standardized by dividing it by the standard deviation of that particular portfolio's residual calculated for this 39–month period. If we are dealing with, say, month '0', then for *each* portfolio the entire procedure must be repeated for each calendar month in which an event occurs.

Bawa. Vijay. Stephen Brown and Roger Klein, 1979, Estimation risk and optimal portfolio choice (North-Holland, New York).

Beaver, William H., 1979, Econometric properties of alternative security return metrics, Unpublished manuscript (Stanford University, Stanford, CA).

Black, Fischer, 1972, Capital market equilibrium with restricted borrowing, Journal of Business 45, July, 444–454.

Black, Fischer and Myron Scholes, 1973, The behavior of security returns around ex-dividend days, Unpublished manuscript (Massachusetts Institute of Technology, Cambridge, MA).

Black, Fischer, Michael Jensen and Myron Scholes, 1972, The capital asset pricing model: Some empirical tests, in: M. Jensen, ed., Studies in the theory of capital markets (Praeger, New York).

Brenner, Menachem, 1976, A note on risk, return, and equilibrium: Empirical tests, Journal of Political Economy 84, April, 407–409.

Brenner, Menachem, 1979, The sensitivity of the efficient market hypothesis to alternative specifications of the market model, Journal of Finance 34, Sept., 915–929.

Brown, R.L., J. Durbin and J.M. Evans, 1975, Techniques for testing the constancy of regression relationships over time, Journal of the Royal Statistical Society Series B 37, 149–192.

Charest, Guy, 1978, Split information, stock returns, and market efficiency, Journal of Financial Economics 6, June/Sept., 265–296.

Collins, Daniel W. and Warren T. Dent, 1978, Econometric testing procedures in market based accounting research, Unpublished manuscript (Michigan State University, East Lansing, MI).

Collins, Daniel W. and Warren T. Dent, 1979, The proposed elimination of full cost accounting in the extractive petroleum industry, Journal of Accounting and Economics 1, March, 3–44.

Cornell, Bradford and J. Kimball Dietrich, 1978, Mean-absolute-deviation versus least squares regression estimation of beta coefficients, Journal of Financial and Quantitative Analysis 13, March, 123–131.

Cowles, Alfred, 1933, Can stock market forecasters forecast?, Econometrica 1, 309–324.

Fama, Eugene F., 1976, Foundations of finance (Basic Books. New York).

Fama, Eugene F. and James D. MacBeth, 1973, Risk, return and equilibrium: Empirical tests. Journal of Political Economy 71, May/June, 607–636.

Fama, Eugene F., Lawrence Fisher, Michael Jensen and Richard Roll, 1969, The adjustment of stock prices of new information, International Economic Review 10, Feb., 1–21.

Foster, George, 1980, Accounting policy decisions and capital market research, Journal of Accounting and Economics, forthcoming.

Gonedes, Nicholas J., 1978, Corporate signaling, external accounting, and capital market equilibrium: Evidence on dividends, income and extraordinary items, Journal of Accounting Research 16, Spring, 26–79.

Gonedes, Nicholas J., Nicholas Dopuch and Stephen J. Penman, 1976, Disclosure rules, information-production, and capital market equilibrium: The case of forecast disclosure rules, Journal of Accounting Research 14, Spring, 89–137.

Jaffe, Jeffrey F., 1974, Special information and insider trading, Journal of Business 47, July, 410–428.

Kaplan, Robert S. and Richard Roll, 1972, Investor evaluation of accounting information: Some empirical evidence, Journal of Business 45, April, 225–257.

Langetieg, Terence C., 1978, An application of a three factor performance index to measure stockholder gains from merger, Journal of Financial Economics 6, Dec., 365–384.

Latane, Henry A. and Charles P. Jones, 1979, Standardized unexpected earnings — 1971–1977, Journal of Finance 34, 717–724.

Lehmann, E.L., 1975, Nonparametrics: Statistical methods based on ranks (Holden-Day, San Francisco, CA).

Mandelker, Gershon, 1974, Risk and return: The case of merging firms, Journal of Financial Economics 1, Dec., 303–335.

Marsaglia, G., K. Ananthanarayanan and N. Paul, 1973, Random number generator package — 'Super duper', Mimeo. (School of Computer Science, McGill University, Montreal).

Masulis, Ronald W., 1978, The effects of capital structure change on security prices, Unpublished Ph.D. dissertation (University of Chicago, Chicago, IL).

Mayers, David and Edward M. Rice, 1979, Measuring portfolio performance and the empirical content of asset pricing models, Journal of Financial Economics 7, March, 3–28.

Officer, Robert R., 1971, A time series examination of the market factor of the New York stock exchange, Ph.D. dissertation (University of Chicago, Chicago, IL).

Ohlson, James A., 1978, On the theory of residual analyses and abnormal performance metrics, Australian Journal of Management 3, Oct., 175–193.

Ohlson, James A., 1979, Residual (API) analysis and the private value of information, Journal of Accounting Research 17, Autumn, 506–527.

Patell, James M., 1976, Corporate forecasts of earnings per share and stock price behavior: Empirical tests, Journal of Accounting Research 14, Autumn, 246–276.

Patell, James M., 1979, The API and the design of experiments, Journal of Accounting Research 17, Autumn, 528–549.

Roll, Richard, 1977, A critique of the asset pricing theory's tests; Part I: On past and potential testability of the theory, Journal of Financial Economics 4, March 129–176.

Roll, Richard and Stephen A. Ross, 1979, An empirical investigation of the arbitrage pricing theory, Unpublished manuscript (University of California, Los Angeles, CA).

Scholes, Myron and Joseph Williams, 1977, Estimating betas from non-synchronous data, Journal of Financial Economics 5, Dec., 309–328.

Schwert, G. William, 1978, Measuring the effects of regulation: evidence from capital markets, Unpublished manuscript (University of Rochester, Rochester, NY).

Udinsky, Jerald and Daniel Kirshner, 1979, A comparison of relative predictive power for financial models of rates of return, Journal of Financial and Quantitative Analysis 14, June, 293–315.

Warner, Jerold B., 1977, Bankruptcy, absolute priority, and the pricing of risky debt claims, Journal of Financial Economics 4, May, 239–276.

Watts, Ross L., 1978, Systematic 'abnormal' returns after quarterly earnings announcements, Journal of Financial Economics 6, June/Sept., 127–150.

[3]

Conditional Methods in Event Studies and an Equilibrium Justification for Standard Event-Study Procedures

N. R. Prabhala
Yale University

The literature on conditional event-study methods criticizes standard event-study procedures as being misspecified if events are voluntary and investors are rational. We argue, however, that standard procedures (1) lead to statistically valid inferences, under conditions described in this article; and (2) are often a superior means of inference, even when event-study data are generated exactly as per a class of rational expectations specifications introduced by the conditional methods literature. Our results provide an equilibrium justification for traditional event-study methods, and we suggest how these simple procedures may be combined with conditional methods to improve statistical power in event studies.

I am grateful to Stephen Brown, my dissertation chairman, for stimulating my interest in the topic, his guidance, and numerous valuable suggestions. Thanks are also due to Franklin Allen (the executive editor), Yakov Amihud, Mitchell Berlin, Silverio Foresi, Robert Hansen, Kose John, L. Misra, Robert Whitelaw, and especially Bent Christensen, William Greene, Chester Spatt (the editor), and an anonymous referee whose extensive feedback has greatly improved the article. I have also benefitted from discussions with my colleagues at NYU, and from comments of seminar participants at various universities: British Columbia, Columbia, Cornell, Georgia Institute of Technology, Michigan, New York University, Purdue, Rutgers, Strathclyde, University of California, Los Angeles, Virginia Polytechnic Institute, and Yale. Any errors that remain are solely mine. Address correspondence to N. R. Prabhala, School of Management, Yale University, 135 Prospect Street, New Haven, CT 06520.

The Review of Financial Studies Spring 1997 Vol. 10, No. 1, pp. 1–38
© 1997 The Review of Financial Studies 0893-9454/97/$1.50

The Review of Financial Studies / v 10 n 1 1997

Event studies are widely used to study the information content of corporate events. Such studies typically have two purposes: (1) to test for the existence of an "information effect" (i.e., the impact of an event on the announcing firm's value) and to estimate its magnitude, and (2) to identify factors that explain changes in firm value on the event date.

To test for the existence of an information effect, empirical finance has primarily employed the technique developed in Fama, Fisher, Jensen, and Roll (1969) (referred to as FFJR hereafter). FFJR suggest that if an event has an information effect, there should be a nonzero stock-price reaction on the event date. Thus, inference is based on the statistical significance of the average announcement effect[1] for a sample of firms announcing the event in question. The FFJR test is usually followed by a linear regression of announcement effects on a set of firm-specific factors to identify those factors that explain the cross-section of announcement effects. Most event studies in the applied literature have been based on the above methods.[2]

However, recent literature on *conditional* event-study methods [Acharya (1988, 1993), Eckbo, Maksimovic, and Williams (1990)] argues that the traditional methods are misspecified in a rational expectations context. Briefly, the argument is that corporate events are voluntary choices of firms and are typically initiated when firms come to possess information not fully known to markets. The *unexpected* portion of such information should determine the stock-price reaction to the event.

When events are modeled in this manner within simple equilibrium settings, the resulting specifications are typically nonlinear cross-sectional regressions[3] that bear little resemblance to the simple models conventionally used in event studies. Hence, it has been suggested that the conventional methods are misspecified and lead to unreliable inferences, implying that such methods should not be used in practice. More generally, this debate does raise the important issue that though the standard event-study procedures have been widely used in empirical work, little is understood about their consistency and power

---

[1] Announcement effect (or abnormal return) denotes the excess of the actual event-date stock return over the unconditional expected return for the stock. The latter is usually estimated via the market model, calibrated on pre-event data [see Brown and Warner (1985) for a more complete discussion].

[2] A partial list of applications includes studies of (1) equity and debt issues [Asquith and Mullins (1986), Eckbo (1986)], (2) timing of equity issues [Korajczyk, Lucas, and McDonald (1991)], (3) takeovers [Asquith, Bruner, and Mullins (1983)], (4) dividends [Bajaj and Vijh (1990)], and (5) stock repurchases [Vermaelen (1984)].

[3] The nonlinearity stems from the endogeneity of events. Endogeneity truncates the statistical distribution of announcement effects.

in rational expectations settings, such as those underlying conditional methods.

This article has three purposes. First, we present a simple exposition of conditional methods that focuses on their economic content. We show that all conditional models have essentially the same economic intuition, and derive all received models within a common framework that reflects this perspective. This synthesis reconciles different specifications proposed in the literature, clarifies their shared intuition, and suggests how one might choose between or extend such models in practice.

Our second point is that while traditional event-study techniques are indeed misspecified in the conditional methods context, they still lead to valid inferences, under certain statistical conditions described in this article. Specifically, even when event-study data are generated *exactly* as per conditional models of the sort introduced by Acharya (1988), (1) the FFJR procedure remains a well-specified test for detecting the *existence* of information effects; and (2) the conventional cross-sectional procedure yields parameter estimates *proportional* to the true conditional model parameters, under the conditions mentioned before. The proportionality factor has a simple interpretation in terms of the informational parameters of the event. These results provide, for the first time, an equilibrium justification for the procedures conventionally used to conduct event studies.

Finally, if both traditional and conditional methods lead to equivalent inferences, how does one choose between the two in practice? Working in the context of the conditional model proposed by Acharya (1988), we develop simulation evidence on this issue. Our evidence suggests that one's choice would depend mainly on whether one has, besides the usual event-study data, an additional sample of "nonevent" firms, that is, firms that were partially anticipated to announce but did not announce the event in question. If such nonevent data are available, conditional methods are powerful means of conducting event studies and may be implemented effectively using a simple "two-step" estimator. Absent nonevent data, conditional methods appear to offer little value relative to traditional procedures.

This article is organized along the above lines. Section 1 presents conditional methods for event studies. Section 2 presents and discusses the main analytic results, regarding the equivalence of inferences via conditional and traditional event-study methods. Section 3 motivates the question of choosing between the two approaches, and Section 4 outlines the structure of the simulations conducted to address this question. Simulation results are presented in Section 5, and Section 6 offers concluding comments.

The Review of Financial Studies / v 10 n 1 1997

1. On Conditional Methods

Section 1 develops conditional models for event studies. The main point made here is that all conditional models have essentially the same economic intuition: they relate announcement effects to the unexpected information revealed in events. While the notion of relating announcement effects to unexpected information is not new, we show here that it is the common theme that underlies all conditional models. We demonstrate that all received models may be derived in terms of this framework, and that the models differ only because they make different assumptions about the information structure underlying events.

The exposition proceeds as follows. Section 1.1 opens with a discussion of the intuition underlying conditional methods. Section 1.2 discusses alternative ways of modeling the information structure in events, and Sections 1.3 through 1.5 develop econometric models for announcement effects for each of these information structures.

1.1 Intuition underlying conditional methods

To begin, note the potential dichotomy between the *fact* of an event and the *information* it reveals. For instance, the event "takeover" is plausibly less surprising for a bidder with announced acquisition programs than for a bidder with no history of acquisitions. Similarly, the event "dividend increase" is less surprising for a firm with an unusually good spell of earnings than for a firm with flat or declining earnings. Thus, a given event may convey less information for some firms and more for others. Further, it should be the *unexpected information* revealed in events that causes the stock-price changes around event dates.[4]

This discussion suggests the following empirical procedure for carrying out event studies: (1) estimate for each firm the unexpected information that the event reveals; (2) compute the cross-sectional correlation between information and abnormal return and test for its significance. A nonzero correlation would indicate that abnormal return is systematically related to information revealed in the event (i.e., there exists an information effect). Conversely, zero correlation implies lack of an information effect. This intuition underlies every conditional specification analyzed in this article.

Central to the conditional paradigm is the notion of "information revealed in events." Next, we discuss how this might be modeled in the event-study context.

---

[4] Malatesta and Thompson (1985), Thompson (1985), and Chaplinsky and Hansen (1993) also recognize the role of partial anticipation of events and examine its implications for event studies based on FFJR-style procedures.

4

1.2 Specifying the information structure

As argued before, events reveal the information that their announcement is conditioned on. Suppose that this information consists of a variable τ_i, which arrives at firm i on an *information arrival* date. Information τ_i is subsequently revealed to markets, via the event, on an *event date*.

What do markets learn from the revelation of τ_i? Clearly, this depends on what markets knew, prior to the actual event date, about the arrival of information τ_i at firm i. Here, we allow for three possibilities:

Assumption 1. *Markets know, prior to the event, that the event-related information τ_i has arrived at firm i (but not its exact content).*

Assumption 2. *Markets do not know, prior to the event, that information τ_i has arrived at firm i.*

Assumption 3. *Markets assess a probability $p \in (0, 1)$ that information τ_i has arrived at firm i.*

Under Assumption 1, information arrival is common knowledge prior to the event; under Assumption 2, markets do not know about information arrival prior to the event-date. Finally, Assumption 3 is the encompassing case that permits markets to make probabilistic assessments about information arrival.[5] Each assumption leads to a different econometric specification for announcement effects, as we show below.

For expositional ease and because previous work has been based on Assumptions 1 and 2, we first develop the methodology under Assumptions 1 and 2, in Sections 1.3 and 1.4. We then present an encompassing specification, based on Assumption 3, in Section 1.5.

1.3 Model I: information arrival known prior to event

We begin by making Assumption 1: that markets know, prior to the event, that the event-related information τ_i has arrived at firm i. In general, this leads markets to form expectations about τ_i. Suppose these expectations are given by

$$E_{-1}(\tau_i) = \underline{\theta}'\underline{x}_i = \sum_{j=1}^{n} \theta_j x_{ij} \tag{1}$$

---

[5] The following example illustrates the distinction between the three assumptions. Consider the event "takeover" and suppose takeovers occur if and only if the acquirer-bidder synergy (τ) is positive. Assumption 1 implies that markets always know, prior to each takeover announcement, that the bidder had identified the target in question. The only uncertainty is whether τ is positive or not. In contrast, Assumption 2 implies that markets do not know, prior to each announcement, that the target had been identified. Under Assumption 3, markets assign probability $p \varepsilon (0, 1)$ that the target had been identified.

The Review of Financial Studies / v 10 n 1 1997

where $\underline{x}_i$ denotes a vector of firm-specific variables in the pre-event market information set, and $\underline{\theta}$ is a vector of parameters. Given Equation (1), firm i's private information ψ_i is given by

$$\psi_i = \tau_i - E_{-1}(\tau_i), \tag{2}$$

where $E_{-1}(\psi_i) = 0$, with no loss of generality.

In what follows next, we model an *event* as an announcement that each firm chooses to make (or not to make), depending on the nature of its information τ_i. Our goal is to develop econometric models for the resultant announcement effect.

To fix matters, consider a situation in which each firm i must choose between two mutually exclusive and collectively exhaustive alternatives on the event date: either the firm must announce the *event* (E) or the *nonevent* (NE). Suppose that the firm's decision depends on its information τ_i, as follows:

$$E \Leftrightarrow \tau_i \geq 0 \Leftrightarrow \psi_i + \underline{\theta}'\underline{x}_i \geq 0 \tag{3}$$

$$NE \Leftrightarrow \tau_i < 0 \Leftrightarrow \psi_i + \underline{\theta}'\underline{x}_i < 0 \tag{4}$$

The choice model, Equations (3) and (4), reflects that the decision to announce an event is an endogenous choice of firms: here, event E is announced if and only if conditioning information τ is "large enough." Otherwise, the "nonevent" NE is announced.[6]

What do markets learn from firm i's announcement? Given Equations (3) and (4), firm i's choice between E and NE partially reveals its private information ψ_i, and thereby leads markets to form revised expectations about the value of ψ_i. The revised expectation, $E(\psi_i \mid C)$, $C \in \{E, NE\}$, constitutes the *unexpected information* on the event date.

If there is an information effect (i.e., the information revealed has a stock-price effect), we should find abnormal returns (say ϵ) to be related to unexpected information. This relationship is linear under the following (jointly sufficient) assumptions.

Assumption 4. *Risk Neutrality: Investors are risk-neutral towards the event risk.*

Assumption 5. *Linearity: Conditioning information is a linear signal of expected stock return. That is, $E(r_i \mid \psi_i) = \pi\psi_i$, where r_i stands for stock return, and ψ_i for conditioning information.*

---

[6] Conditioning on τ being "large enough," — equivalently, a *sample selection bias* — characterizes all voluntary corporate events. For instance, takeovers plausibly occur if and only if the personal or corporate gains (τ) from acquiring are positive; dividend increases are announced only when future earnings (τ) are "large enough" to sustain higher dividends, and so on. The fact that τ is a function of elements x in the pre-event information set captures the effect that some firms are more likely to announce the event than others.

Thus, if the event has an information effect, π should be significant in the nonlinear cross-sectional specifications:

$$E(\epsilon_i \mid E) = \pi E(\psi_i \mid E) = \pi E(\psi_i \mid \underline{\theta}' \underline{x}_i + \psi_i \geq 0), \qquad (5)$$

and

$$E(\epsilon \mid NE) = \pi E(\psi_i \mid NE) = \pi E(\psi_i \mid \underline{\theta}' \underline{x}_i + \psi_i < 0), \qquad (6)$$

where ϵ_i is the *event-date* abnormal return for firm i. Intuitively, when firm i makes an announcement C, it signals that the expected return, given its information, is $E(r_i \mid C) = \pi E(\psi_i \mid C)$ (via Assumption 5). Under risk neutrality, $E(r_i \mid C)$ also equals the expected *event-date* abnormal return $E(\epsilon_i \mid C)$.[7]

If private information ψ_i is distributed normally, $N(0, \sigma^2)$, the above models may be rewritten as

$$E(\epsilon_i \mid E) = \pi \sigma \frac{n(\underline{\theta}' x_i)/\sigma}{N(\underline{\theta}' x_i/\sigma)} = \pi \sigma \lambda_E(\underline{\theta}' \underline{x}_i/\sigma), \qquad (7)$$

and

$$E(\epsilon_i \mid NE) = \pi \sigma \frac{-n(\underline{\theta}' x_i/\sigma)}{1 - N(\underline{\theta}' x_i/\sigma)} = \pi \sigma \lambda_{NE}(\underline{\theta}' \underline{x}_i/\sigma), \qquad (8)$$

where $n(\cdot)$ and $N(\cdot)$ denote the normal density and distribution, respectively, and $\lambda_C(\cdot)$ denotes the updated expectation of private information ψ, given the firm's choice $C \epsilon \{E, NE\}$.

Equation (7), our first "conditional" specification for announcement effects, was introduced by Acharya (1988). The model admits to two sets of hypothesis tests:

1. *Test for existence of information effect*: A test for significance of π indicates whether announcement effects (ϵ) are related to the information revealed in the event [$\lambda_C(\cdot)$], that is, whether there exists an information effect.

2. *Factors explaining announcement effects*: A test for significance of coefficients θ_j ($j = 1, 2, \ldots, k$) identifies from the set x_j ($j = 1, 2, \ldots, k$) those factors that explain the cross-section of announcement effects.

---

[7] With risk aversion, we have two cases of potential interest. For firm-specific events of the sort analyzed here, announcement effects will be shifted upwards since (priced) uncertainty is resolved on the event date. In other words, $E_{-1}(\epsilon_i) > 0$. An interesting second case relates to events aggregate in character (such as federal interventions in fixed-income markets) and in which event risk is priced. Here $\lambda_C(\cdot)$, the "private information" is aggregate, and may be interpreted as a zero mean innovation in a priced APT factor. If the event risk is priced under a linear pricing operator, the risk-premium for the event could be estimated using cross-sectional and time-series data, much as in standard empirical APT studies [e.g., McElroy and Burmeister (1988)].

The Review of Financial Studies / v 10 n 1 1997

That the model is consistent with equilibrium follows from (1) risk neutrality towards event risk, and (2) the fact that the ex ante expected abnormal return is zero:

$$\Sigma_{k=E,NE} E(\epsilon_i \mid k) * Prob(k)$$
$$= \pi \sigma \{\lambda_E(\cdot) * N(\underline{\theta}'\underline{x}_i/\sigma) + \lambda_{NE}(\cdot) * [1 - N(\underline{\theta}'\underline{x}_i/\sigma)]\}$$
$$= 0. \tag{9}$$

With this discussion in hand, it is fairly straightforward to develop binary event models under the alternate information structures, Assumptions 2 and 3. We present these models next and close Section 1 with a discussion on how one might choose between the three specifications in practice.

1.4 Model II: information arrival not known prior to event

Equation (7) was based on Assumption 1, under which markets knew ex ante about the arrival of information τ. Suppose instead that the framework is Assumption 2: markets do not know ex ante about information arrival.[8] We now consider the conditional model for this situation.

Given Assumption 2, pre-event expectations about τ_i were not formed. Hence, τ_i itself (as opposed to ψ_i in the previous section) is firm i's private information. As before, the conditional expectation of private information (here τ_i), given event E, constitutes the information revealed by E. This variable must be related to announcement effects, linearly so under Assumptions 1 and 2, if the event has an information effect. That is, π should be significant in the model

$$E(\epsilon_i \mid E) = \pi E(\tau_i \mid E) = \pi E(\tau_i \mid \tau_i \geq 0)$$
$$= \pi \left[\underline{\theta}'\underline{x}_i + \lambda_E(\underline{\theta}'\underline{x}_i/\sigma)\right], \tag{10}$$

where the last equality is obtained by using $\tau_i = \underline{\theta}'\underline{x}_i + \psi_i$. Equation (10) — hereafter, the EMW model — was, in essence, introduced by Eckbo, Maksimovic, and Williams (1990).

For some intuition, compare the EMW model, Equation (10), with the Acharya model, Equation (7). The EMW model has the extra term $\underline{\theta}'\underline{x}_i$ — the unconditional expectation of τ_i. In the Acharya model, pre-event expectations of τ led to its unconditional expectation, $(\underline{\theta}'\underline{x}_i)$, being incorporated into the stock price *prior to the event*. Here, pre-event expectations were not formed (under Assumption 2); hence,

---

[8] This is the case, for instance, in takeover announcements involving bidders with no history of acquisitions or targets not previously in play. Here, markets plausibly do not know, prior to the actual takeover announcement, that the acquirer had identified the relevant target and that some announcement related to the acquisition was forthcoming.

the term $\underline{\theta}'\underline{x}_i$ appears in the expression for the abnormal return on the event date. Thus, contrary to a claim in Acharya (1993), we note that the EMW model is *not* nested within the Acharya model. The two models differ in their assumptions about the underlying information structure.

Both models are, in fact, limiting cases of a binary event model based upon Assumption 3. We derive this encompassing specification next and clarify the sense in which it nests the Acharya and EMW models.

1.5 Model III: information arrival partially known

Suppose now that the information structure is described by Assumption 3: markets assess a probability p that information τ_i has arrived at firm i. Given Equation (1), the stock-price reaction in light of the assessed probability p is given by

$$E_{-1}(\epsilon_i) = p\pi\underline{\theta}'\underline{x}_i.$$

Now, if event E does occur, it conveys two pieces of information. First, it confirms that information τ has arrived at firm i, that is, the probability of information arrival is raised from p to 1. Second, it conveys via choice model Equations (3) and (4) that $\underline{\theta}'\underline{x}_i + \psi > 0$. Together, the two pieces of information lead to an announcement effect given by

$$E(\epsilon_i \mid E) = \pi\left[(1-p)\underline{\theta}'\underline{x}_i + \sigma\lambda_E\left(\frac{\underline{\theta}'\underline{x}_i}{\sigma}\right)\right]. \tag{11}$$

It is easily seen that Equation (11) nests the EMW and Acharya models as the special cases $p = 0$ and $p = 1$, respectively. The traditional event-study methods never obtain as the appropriate specifications, for any value of p.

How does one choose between these conditional specifications in practice? The preceding discussion demonstrates that this choice is essentially a matter of picking the informational assumption appropriate to one's context. Specifically, the EMW model is probably a good approximation of Equation (11) for nonrepetitive announcements whose timing is not well-identified ex ante. On the other hand, when markets are reasonably certain that some event-related announcement is forthcoming, the Acharya model is appropriate. For intermediate situations, Equation (11) is appropriate. Its practical value is not known and awaits empirical applications, as all received work is based on the EMW and Acharya models.

For the discussion that follows, we focus on the Acharya model, Equation (7), (i.e., the case when $p \approx 1$) since the EMW model, Equa-

The Review of Financial Studies / v 10 n 1 1997

tion (10), a "truncated regression" specification [see Greene (1993) or
Maddala (1983)] has been treated fairly extensively in the econometric literature. By contrast, the properties of Equation (7) are not as
well-understood: they are related to, but differ in interesting ways
from, those of standard "selectivity" models. Hence, we focus on
the Acharya model, Equation (7), next and through the rest of this
article.

2. On Inferences Via Traditional Methods

The conditional specifications developed in Section 1 are quite different from traditional event-study procedures. How might one interpret
inferences via traditional methods in light of this difference?

Working in the context of the Acharya model, Equation (7), we
make two points. Specifically, we argue that even when event-study
data are generated exactly as per Equation (7), (1) the FFJR procedure
is well-specified as a test for *existence* of information effects (i.e., the
hypothesis $\pi = 0$), whether or not any of the factors $\underline{x}$ explain announcement effects; and (2) the traditional cross-sectional procedure
yields regression coefficients *proportional* to the true cross-sectional
parameters $\underline{\theta}$, under conditions to be described shortly. Thus, while
traditional techniques are indeed misspecified in the sense discussed
before, the implications of such misspecification are probably not as
serious as the previous literature [Acharya (1988, 1993), Eckbo, Maksimovic, and Williams (1990)] suggests. Conventional methods do allow one to conduct significance tests for both π and cross-sectional
parameters θ, despite these parameters being potentially estimated
inconsistently.

It is relatively straightforward to establish that the FFJR procedure
may be viewed as a test of the hypothesis $\pi = 0$.[9] The cross-sectional
results need some argument though, and we present these in what
follows next.

2.1 The conventional cross-sectional procedure
The conventional cross-sectional procedure may be written as a test
of significance of regression coefficients $(\beta_1, \ldots, \beta_k)$ in the linear

---

[9] Take expectations over conditioning factors x in Equation (7). The unconditional (over x) announcement effect, given event E, is given by $E_x(\epsilon_i \mid E) = \pi \sigma E_x[\lambda_E(\cdot)]$, which is nonzero if and
only if π is nonzero [since $\lambda_E(\cdot) > 0$]. Hence, detecting a nonzero unconditional announcement
effect, as in the FFJR procedure, is equivalent to an observation that π is nonzero. Variants of the
FFJR procedure, such as those introduced in Schipper and Thompson (1983), possess a similar
interpretation.

regression

$$E(\epsilon \mid E) = \beta_0 + \underline{\beta}'\underline{x} = \beta_0 + \beta_1 x_1 + \cdots + \beta_k x_k \tag{12}$$

estimated for a sample of firms announcing event E (firms announcing NE are not considered by the conventional procedure), where we have dropped firm-specific subscript i for notational ease. The linear model, Equation (12), is clearly misspecified, given the conditional model, Equation (7). What sort of inferences might it yield, if used anyway? That is, are regression coefficients β related in some way to the true cross-sectional parameters $\underline{\theta}$ of Equation (7)?

Such a relationship does exist and, under fairly weak conditions, it takes a simple form: each linear regression coefficient β_j is proportional to true coefficient θ_j. Additionally, every β_j is *biased towards zero*, relative to θ_j.

The underlying intuition is illustrated by the following observation: the true slope s_j of Equation (7) is *attenuated* relative to θ_j.[10] Formally,

$$s_j = \frac{\partial E(\epsilon \mid E)}{\partial x_j} = -\theta_j \pi \delta(y), \tag{13}$$

where $y = \underline{\theta}'\underline{x}/\sigma$ and $\delta(y) = \lambda_E(y)[\lambda_E(y) + y]$. Since (1) $\mid \pi \mid < 1$ (it is a correlation), and (2) $0 < \delta(y) < 1$,[11] it follows immediately from Equation (13) that $\mid s_j \mid < \mid \theta_j \mid$. One might conjecture on this basis that each regression coefficient β_j is biased towards zero, relative to θ_j, with the opposite sign if $\pi > 0$.[12] Further, Equation (13) also suggests that downward bias should be greater when

1. $\mid \pi \mid$ *is small.* Here, announcement effects are less sensitive to conditioning information. Hence, regression coefficients β_j should be smaller.

2. $\delta(y)$ *is small.* This happens when $y = \underline{\theta}'\underline{x}/\sigma$ is large [Goldberger (1983)], that is, for highly anticipated events. Here, little information is contained in firms' announcements of E or resultant abnormal returns. Once again, estimated regression coefficients β_j should be smaller.

Precisely these results obtain when regressors $\underline{x}$ are multivariate normally distributed. Proposition 1 contains the formal statement.

---

[10] In a different setting, Lanen and Thompson (1988) also suggest that slope s_j may be attenuated due to partial anticipation of the event.

[11] Interpreting π as a correlation involves the normalization $var(\epsilon) = \sigma$. The bounds on $\delta(y)$ follow from two properties of the standard normal variable z — (1) $E(z \mid z > -y) = \lambda_E(y)$ is decreasing in y, that is, $\lambda_E'(y) = -\delta(y) < 0$; and (2) $var(z \mid z > -y) = 1 - \delta(y) > 0$ [Greene (1993)].

[12] The linear regression itself does *not* necessarily estimate the slope of the nonlinear function [see, e.g., Stoker (1986), White (1980)].

The Review of Financial Studies / v 10 n 1 1997

Proposition 1. *Suppose (1) event E occurs if and only if $\theta_0 + \sum_{j=1}^{k} \theta_j x_j + \psi > 0$; and (2) information ψ and abnormal return ϵ are bivariate normal with correlation π and marginal distributions $N(0, 1)$; and regressors $(x_1, \ldots, x_k)$ are multivariate normal, independent of ψ.[13] Then, coefficients $(\beta_1, \ldots, \beta_k)$ in the linear model, Equation (12), estimated for a sample of firms announcing E are given by*

$$\beta_j = -\theta_j \pi \frac{(1 - R^2)(1 - t)}{t + (1 - R^2)(1 - t)} = -\theta_j \pi \mu, \qquad (14)$$

where

1. $t = var(\tau \mid E)/var(\tau)$, $\tau = \underline{\theta}' \underline{x} + \psi$.
2. R^2 = *coefficient of determination ("explained variance") in the population regression of τ on $(1, x_1, \ldots, x_k)$.*
3. $\mu = \frac{(1-R^2)(1-t)}{t+(1-R^2)(1-t)}$

See the Appendix for the proof.

To interpret the proportionality factor μ, observe that (1) the term $(1 - R^2)$ represents the variance of τ not explained by public information $\underline{x}$, that is, the *unexpected* component of information τ; and (2) term $(1 - t)$ proxies the information revealed by event E. Therefore, the product of the two — and hence the term μ — represents *the unexpected component of information τ revealed by event E.* Another way of viewing this is to consider the fraction of information τ that is lost by restricting oneself to event E. Part of information τ is lost to (1) pre-event expectations and (2) the nonevent NE. The constant μ represents the fraction of information τ that remains in event E. Thus, μ is small when the event reveals little information; conversely, μ is large for highly surprising events. This intuition is formalized in Lemma 1.

Lemma 1. *Let μ be as defined above. Then (1) $0 < \mu < 1$, and (2) μ is small when event E is, on average, highly anticipated.*

See the Appendix for the proof.

---

[13] In the choice model underlying Proposition 1, firms choose between E and NE based on latent information τ. Condition (2) specifies how the latent information maps into stock-return information since it is the latter that causes observed announcement effects. Multivariate normality of $(\underline{x}, \tau)$ is stronger than what is needed for Proposition 1 to obtain. All we need is that the conditional expectation $E(\underline{x} \mid \tau)$ be linear in τ. Multivariate normality is sufficient, though not necessary for this condition to hold. Finally, note that while firms have two choices (E or NE) in the event modeled here, Proposition 1 also applies to events in which each announcing firm has more than two choices — such as dividend announcements, wherein firms have three choices (increase, keep unchanged, or decrease dividends).

12

With these results in hand, one can readily establish useful comparative statics about regression coefficients β_j:

• *Downward bias in β_j's.* This is an immediate consequence of $0 < \mu < 1$ (Lemma 1), $|\pi| < 1$, and Equation (14); together, these imply that $|\beta_j| \leq |\theta_j|$.

• *Opposite Sign.* Each β_j is signed opposite to θ_j, provided $\pi > 0$, as seen from Equation (14). To understand this result, note that θ_j reflects the marginal impact of an increase in regressor x_j on the *probability* of event E, while β_j reflects the marginal impact on the *announcement effect* associated with E. Since an increase in the probability of event E decreases the expected announcement effect upon announcing E if $\pi > 0$, θ_j and β_j have the opposite sign when $\pi > 0$.

• *More attenuation when $|\pi|$ is small.* This follows directly from Equation (14).

• *More attenuation when events are highly anticipated.* For highly anticipated events, μ is small, from part 2 of Lemma 1. From Proposition 1, this implies that $|\beta_j|$ is small.

Summarizing, Proposition 1 has the interesting implication that the traditional cross-sectional procedure may be used for cross-sectional inferences in event studies. Specifically, a statistical test for significance of regression coefficient β_j, $(j = 1, \ldots, k)$, is equivalent to a test for significance of the corresponding cross-sectional parameter θ_j of the conditional model.

However, for practical purposes, two questions remain. One, while Proposition 1 provides an interpretation of the linear regression coefficients, are the usual OLS standard errors appropriate for use in significance tests? Second, how robust is Proposition 1 to the assumption that regressors $\underline{x}$ are multivariate normal? Simulation evidence needs to be developed on these issues.

3. Issues in Choosing Event-Study Methodology

Section 2 suggests that under certain conditions, both conditional and traditional methods are valid means of inference. How might one choose between the two approaches in practice? We address this issue in the context of cross-sectional inferences, as conditional methods are likely to be useful only when cross-sectional hypotheses are being tested.[14]

One's choice between the two approaches would depend primarily on the performance of each method (i.e., the likelihood of making

---

[14] Simulation evidence on the FFJR procedure (reported in earlier versions of this article) attest to this point. These results are available upon request.

The Review of Financial Studies / v 10 n 1 1997

correct inferences about the sign and significance of cross-sectional parameters $\underline{\theta}$), given typical event-study samples. We argue that the relative performance of the two approaches must be considered in two distinct cases:

1. *All assumptions satisfied*: To begin, suppose that event-study data are generated exactly as per Equation (7) and that the assumptions underlying Proposition 1 are satisfied, so that both conditional and traditional methods are equally valid means of inference. Even so, is there any reason why one method might be preferred over the other? Section 3.1 considers this question. We argue that even in this "ideal" case, one's choice should depend on what data one has — specifically, whether one has a sample of *nonevent* firms or not.

2. *Some assumptions not satisfied*: To motivate the second case, observe that the conditional model, Equation (7), places a fairly tight statistical structure on announcement effects. Not all of its econometric assumptions may be satisfied in practice. Hence, we also consider separately the question of methodological choice when some of the assumptions underlying the conditional model are not satisfied. This issue is addressed in Section 3.2.

One's choice would also depend, to some extent, on the computational burden involved in estimation, which is likely to be greater for the conditional model. Section 3.3 discusses these computational issues and presents a brief summary that motivates the empirical work to follow.

3.1 Choice when all assumptions are satisfied

With the identifying normalization $w = \pi\sigma$ and $\underline{\theta} = \frac{\theta}{\sigma}$ [equivalently, $var(\psi) = \sigma^2 = 1$], the conditional model, Equation (7), consists of a "probit" model governing firms' choices between event E and non-event NE:

$$C = \begin{cases} E & if \ \underline{\theta}'\underline{x}_i + \psi > 0 \\ NE & if \ \underline{\theta}'\underline{x}_i + \psi < 0 \end{cases} \tag{15}$$

coupled with a heteroskedastic cross-sectional regression for announcement effects,

$$\epsilon_i = w\lambda_C(\underline{\theta}'\underline{x}_i) + e_i, \tag{16}$$

and

$$var(e_i \mid C) = \sigma_\epsilon^2 - w^2\lambda_C(\underline{\theta}'\underline{x}_i)[\lambda_C(\underline{\theta}'\underline{x}_i) + \underline{\theta}'\underline{x}_i],$$

where $C \ \varepsilon \ \{E, NE\}$ is firm i's choice, $\sigma_\epsilon^2 = var(\epsilon_i)$, and e_i is an error term.

In this section, we argue that even if event-study data are generated exactly as above, and the results of Section 2 hold, conditional meth-

14

ods would be, a priori, one's preferred means of inference, under some conditions. Specifically, if one has, besides a sample of firms announcing event E, additional data on nonevent firms (those announcing NE), conditional methods are likely to be preferred over traditional methods.

To see why, observe that under the traditional approach, event studies are conducted using only data on firms that announced event E. However, Equations (15) and (16) point to the existence of a second category of firms: *nonevent* firms, that is, firms that were partially anticipated to announce but chose not to announce the event in question. Such firms are not used under the traditional procedure. On the other hand, nonevent information may be exploited in the conditional framework by estimating the conditional model with both event and nonevent data. Thus, when nonevent data are available, conditional methods should be more powerful relative to traditional methods.

In most practical situations though, nonevent data are not available. Nonevent data include (1) a set of firms that were anticipated to announce but chose not to announce the event in question; (2) the time when markets learn of the non-announcement; and (3) cross-sectional and announcement effect data on this date. Usually, such information cannot be obtained [Lanen and Thompson (1988) make a similar point], and one must work with only the firms that have announced event E. Here, both conditional and traditional procedures use the same data in estimation, and there is little to choose between the two procedures from an informational viewpoint, if Proposition 1 holds. However, Proposition 1 does not generalize for arbitrary distributions of regressors $\underline{x}$. Thus, if $\underline{x}$ does not satisfy the distributional assumptions of Proposition 1, conditional methods may be preferred since traditional procedures might give misleading inferences in this instance. We develop some Monte-Carlo simulation evidence on the seriousness of this issue.

Thus, in the benchmark case, one's choice of methodology depends on what data one has. If nonevent data are available, conditional methods are likely to be preferred; absent nonevent data, one's choice is less clear, and the issue warrants empirical investigation.

3.2 Choice when some assumptions are not satisfied

In the benchmark case, we assumed that event-study data are generated exactly as per the conditional model. However, some of the model's statistical assumptions may not be satisfied in practice. In this section, we discuss why such deviations might arise and examine the implications for one's choice of event-study methodology.

The first issue, raised in the econometric literature on "selectivity" models, relates to the sensitivity of Equations (15) and (16) to

The Review of Financial Studies / v 10 n 1 1997

nonnormality of private information ψ. Recollect that in developing Equations (16), ψ was assumed to be normally distributed. If ψ is in fact nonnormal, estimates based on the normality assumption are inconsistent.

There is little consensus on the seriousness of the nonnormality issue or on the value of alternate models robust to this distributional assumption. Received evidence has been essentially mixed on both scores [Arabmazar and Schmidt (1982); Goldberger (1983); Lee (1982, 1983); Newey, Powell, and Walker (1990)]. However, all reported evidence pertains to selectivity models that are quite different in focus[15] from that of event-study specification, Equation (16). Its relevance to the event-study situation is not clear, motivating the need to develop evidence more specific to our context.

A second concern relates to data problems that are endemic to the event-study situation [Brown and Warner (1985)]. Two issues are of particular relevance here:

1. *Noise in announcement effects*: Announcement effects are inevitably measured with noise, due to the need to estimate the calibrating market model. Additionally, noise may be induced by uncertainty about the true event date, non synchronous trading, or bid-ask spreads in prices, as well as any changes in sources of valuation not observable to the econometrician. Thus, it is difficult to isolate the portion of stock returns exclusively attributable to announcement of the event.

2. *Cross-sectional correlation*: Models such as Equation (16) are almost always estimated assuming that latent information ψ is cross-sectionally independent. However, in the event-study context, ψ is often cross-sectionally correlated, due to common macroeconomic or industry influences on firms' decisions to announce events, or due to clustering of event dates in calendar time.

While problems such as these do exist in practice, little is known about how they impact one's inferences via either event-study approach. In particular, are inferences via the conditional model affected more than those via the simpler traditional procedure? We develop some evidence along these lines in the work to follow.

---

[15] The prototype selectivity model is the regression $E(\epsilon_i \mid E) = \underline{\beta}'z + \pi\lambda_E(\underline{\theta}'x)$. This class of models focuses almost exclusively on consistent estimation of parameters $\underline{\beta}$ of the unconditional mean function $\underline{\beta}'z$. In contrast, our interest primarily centers on estimates of *selectivity* parameters $\underline{\theta}$, which is a subject of lesser interest in the selectivity literature (note that in the EMW model, Equation (10), $\underline{\beta} = \underline{\theta}$ since p is essentially zero). However, parameter $\underline{\beta}$ may also be of interest sometimes in the event-study context. For example, in the encompassing model, Equation (11), where $\underline{\beta} = \underline{\theta}(1-p)$, estimates of $\underline{\beta}$ might be of interest since they allow one to estimate parameter p and conduct related hypothesis tests. No such tests have been reported yet in the literature.

3.3 Computational considerations

The practical value of conditional specifications such as Equations (15) and (16) depends, to some extent, on the computational burden involved in estimation. Estimation turns out to be quite straightforward, provided one has both event and nonevent data. However, estimation is more demanding when one has only event data, as we discuss below.

To begin, consider the issue of estimating the conditional model when one has both event and nonevent data. In this setting, two natural estimation techniques are (1) maximum likelihood (ML) and (2) nonlinear least squares (NLS). However, consistent estimation may also be achieved through a simple two-step procedure [Heckman (1979)]. To motivate the two-step procedure, observe that in Equation (16), if one had consistent estimates of parameters $\underline{\theta}$ [and hence of $\lambda_C(\cdot)$], regression of ϵ on $\lambda_C(\cdot)$ would lead to consistent estimates of w. This suggests a computationally simple procedure for estimating the conditional model:

1. Estimate the "probit" choice model, Equation (15), to obtain consistent estimates of $\underline{\theta}$, say $\hat{\underline{\theta}}$.

2. Use $\hat{\underline{\theta}}$ to compute $\lambda_C(\cdot)$ for each observation and obtain w by OLS estimation of Equation (16), adjusting standard errors appropriately [see Greene (1981) and Heckman (1979)].

The two-step procedure offers two other advantages, relative to ML and NLS estimators, in the particular context of event studies. First, cross-sectional inferences under the two-step procedure do not require announcement-effect data. Hence, the abnormal return measurement problems discussed in Section 3.2 are no longer an issue in cross-sectional inferences. A more interesting consequence is that cross-sectional estimates via the two-step method are consistent not only for the Acharya model, Equation (16), but also for the EMW model, Equation (10), and the encompassing specification, Equation (11) as well, unlike ML and NLS estimates, which are model-specific.

Robustness, however, comes at a cost: the two-step procedure is not efficient precisely for the same reason it is robust, that is, the first step does not use announcement effect data. Announcement effects represent markets' assessments about the information conditioning the event and should add efficiency in cross-sectional parameter estimation. Nevertheless, our evidence indicates that such efficiency gains are typically small.[16] Hence, in the empirical work that follows, we

---

[16] The evidence was found in simulations with ML and NLS estimators. With large samples, or when w is known, additional information in announcement effects should clearly make cross-sectional parameter estimates more precise relative to those obtained via the two-step method. In finite

The Review of Financial Studies / v 10 n 1 1997

use the two-step estimator whenever both event and nonevent data are available.

Suppose, on the other hand, that one has only event data. In this setting, the two-step procedure is not available, and the conditional model must be estimated via ML or NLS. Estimation now involves optimization of a nonstandard maximand, and, as we describe later, successful convergence requires some experimentation with numerical procedures and parameters governing the optimization process. From a computational perspective, the conditional model is less attractive since estimation now involves greater effort. Whether such effort leads to more powerful inferences, relative to those via the much simpler traditional procedure, remains to be seen, and we explore this issue in the empirical work to follow.

To summarize, Section 3 has raised issues concerning one's choice of event-study methodology, and we address these issues via simulations. Our discussion also suggests how such simulation experiments should be organized. Specifically, simulations ought to be carried out for the case when all assumptions underlying the conditional model are met and, separately, when they are not met. In each instance, two sets of data should be used: one comprising event data only, and another comprising both event and nonevent data.

Section 4 details the broad structure of our simulation experiments, and Section 5 presents the simulation results.

4. Experiment Design

In broad terms, our experiment consists of three steps: (1) simulation of event-study data as per the conditional model; (2) introduction, where relevant, of problems such as nonnormality into the data; and (3) estimation of model parameters by alternative event-study techniques. Some remarks on our design choices are in order before moving to the details.

Two of our choices are different from ones made in related work by Acharya (1993). Acharya simulates regressors x from the normal distribution. We sample x from the uniform distribution. As analytic results (Section 2.1) are available for normally distributed regressors, a nonnormal alternative was desired, leading to our choice. Second, our sample sizes (100 or 250) are much smaller than the size (800) used in Acharya (1993). Our choice is governed by two considerations: (1) these represent sample sizes typically used in event studies

---

samples and when w must be estimated, the gains should be smaller. Indeed, under ML and NLS, the primary improvement relative to the two-step method was found to lie in the precision of estimates of w.

in corporate finance; (2) given the results of Section 2, both conditional and traditional procedures yield equivalent inferences in large samples. Thus, large sample comparisons of the two methods, the focus of previous work, are not relevant to the question of choosing between them in practice.

Our regressor and parameter choices give an adjusted R^2 of about 10% if the linear probability model is used to estimate the underlying choice model. The experiment design is similar to ones used previously in econometric literature [Nelson (1984), Paarsch (1984), Wales and Woodland (1980)].

We now describe in some detail the methodology used to (1) simulate the event and abnormal return data, and (2) construct the test statistics.

4.1 Broad design

1. *Event*: For $i = 1, 2, \ldots, n$ (the sample size), the event was simulated to occur as

$$\text{E} \quad \Leftrightarrow \quad \theta_0 + \theta_1 x_{1i} + \theta_2 x_{2i} + \psi_i \geq 0,$$

and

$$\text{NE} \quad \Leftrightarrow \quad \theta_0 + \theta_1 x_{1i} + \theta_2 x_{2i} + \psi_i < 0,$$

where

- $\theta_0 = 1$, $\theta_1 = -1$, $\theta_2 = 0.01$
- Regressor x_{2i}, $i = 1, 2, \ldots, n$, was drawn independently and identically distributed (i.i.d.) from a uniform distribution $U(0,100)$ once for each set of 400 simulations.
- Regressor x_{1i}, $i = 1, 2, \ldots, n$, was also drawn once for every set of 400 simulations, i.i.d. from a uniform distribution with support of unit length. The support location was varied, so as to get average event probabilities of 25% or 50%.[17]
- ψ_i was drawn i.i.d. from the normal distribution $N(0,1)$, except in experiments addressing nonnormality issues. Here, ψ_i was drawn from one of four nonnormal distributions: Laplace, Logistic, Chi-square or Student's t. We normalized the draw to unit variance/zero mean by (1) subtracting the mean, and (2) dividing by the standard deviation of the relevant distribution.

2. *Abnormal return*: Data for abnormal return were simulated as $\epsilon_i = w\psi_i + v_i$, where v_i is i.i.d. noise with (a) $E(v_i) = 0$, and (b) $var(v_i) = 1 - w^2$ (this normalization sets the unconditional variance

---

[17] When the average event probability was 50%, x_1 had support $(1, 2)$, except when ψ was χ^2 distributed, when it had support $(1.2, 2.2)$. For 25% average event probability, the support varied from $(1.5, 2.5)$ to $(1.75, 2.75)$, depending on the distribution.

The Review of Financial Studies / v 10 n 1 1997

of ϵ_i to unity) and the same distribution as ψ_i.[18] Each set of 400 simulations was repeated for three values of w — 0.30, 0.50, and 0.75 — going from less-informative (in terms of information contained in abnormal return) to more-informative events.

3. *Sample Size*: Each set of 400 simulations was repeated for two sample sizes — 100 and 250.

4. *Number of replications*: Statistics are based on 400 replications of each simulation.

4.2 Simulation methodology

A typical set of 400 simulations proceeds as follows:

1. Fix the desired average event probability, sample size, w, and distribution for ψ_i.

2. Draw a sample of regressors x_{2i} and x_{2i} to conform to the target average event probability fixed in step (1) above. This sample of $\underline{x}$'s is fixed for all 400 repetitions. We then repeat steps (3) through (5) 400 times.

3. Simulate ψ_i from the target distribution. Normalize ψ_i to zero mean/unit variance.

4. Simulate abnormal return data for each firm i, as in Section 4.1.

5. Estimate parameters $\underline{\theta}$, w, and $\underline{\beta}$ as appropriate and compute associated t-statistics.

Each set of 400 simulations is repeated for (1) three values of w — 0.30, 0.50, and 0.75; (2) two average event probabilities — 25% and 50%; and (3) two sample sizes — 100 and 250.

4.3 Reported statistics

Every set of 400 simulations yields 400 point estimates of w and $\underline{\theta}$, together with associated t-statistics. From these, we compute the following statistics.

• *Mean*: This denotes the average of the 400 point estimates of the relevant parameter.

• *Std. error*: This is the sample standard deviation of the 400 parameter estimates, from their simulated distribution. This should be equal to the standard error implied in the asymptotic t-statistics in individual simulations, provided the relevant estimator attains its asymptotic distribution.

• *Mean t-stat*: Every simulation produces a t-statistic for each model parameter. Mean t-stat denotes the average of the 400 t-statistics.

---

[18] There are no natural form representations for the implied bivariate distributions of (ψ, ϵ). Known bivariate forms corresponding to the univariate distributions used here (e.g., bivariate logistic, bivariate Student's t) have nonlinear conditional first moments, which is inconsistent with our Assumption 5.

20

Conditional Methods in Event Studies

Table 1
Performance of conditional model: base case

Model parameter	Truth	Sample size = 100			Sample size = 250		
		Mean	Std. error	Mean t-stat	Mean	Std. error	Mean t-stat
Average event probability = 25%							
w	0.30	0.31	0.13	2.30	0.30	0.09	4.27
w	0.50	0.50	0.13	3.81	0.50	0.08	6.01
w	0.75	0.74	0.11	6.38	0.75	0.08	10.13
θ_0	1.00	1.04	0.51	2.05	0.99	0.31	3.27
θ_1	−1.00	−1.04	0.52	−1.97	−0.98	0.32	−3.12
$100\theta_2$	1.00	1.02	0.52	1.99	0.96	0.31	3.08
Average event probability = 50%							
w	0.30	0.30	0.12	2.37	0.32	0.08	4.45
w	0.50	0.50	0.12	4.12	0.50	0.08	6.64
w	0.75	0.76	0.11	6.83	0.74	0.07	10.74
θ_0	1.00	0.99	0.75	1.36	0.97	0.46	2.08
θ_1	−1.00	−1.00	0.48	−2.15	−0.98	0.30	−3.36
$100\theta_2$	1.00	1.00	0.47	2.20	1.02	0.29	3.46

Table 1 presents statistics relating to the conditional model's performance when all underlying assumptions are satisfied.

We simulate event E to occur if and only if $\theta_0 + \theta_1 x_{1i} + \theta_2 x_{2i} + \psi_i > 0$, where $\theta_0 = 1$, $\theta_1 = -1$, and $\theta_2 = 0.01$. Information ψ_i, $i = 1, 2, \ldots, n$ (n is the sample size), is i.i.d. normal, N(0,1). Expected event-date abnormal return, conditional on ψ_i, is simulated as $E(\epsilon_i \mid \psi_i) = w\psi_i$.

In each simulation, we sample ψ_i and ϵ_i as above. We then apply the two-step method to estimate parameters w and θ. This process is repeated 400 times; each set of 400 simulations is carried out for (1) 3 values of w — (0.30, 0.50, and 0.75), (2) two sample sizes — (100 and 250), and (3) two average event probabilities (25% and 50%). From each set of 400 repetitions, we compute and report the following statistics: (1) *Mean*: mean parameter point estimate, averaged over the 400 repetitions; (2) *Std. error*: standard error of parameter estimate, computed as the sample standard deviation of the 400 point estimates; (3) *Mean t-stat*: Each repetition generates a t-statistic for the relevant parameter estimate. Mean t-stat refers to the mean of the 400 t-statistics. As estimates of θ are obtained independent of w, we report only one set of statistics for θ that applies to all three values of w.

5. Simulation Results

We present the simulation results in three parts. Section 5.1 discusses the conditional model's performance when both event and nonevent data are available. Here, we examine the model's sensitivity to non-normality and various event-study data problems mentioned before. Section 5.2 evaluates the traditional cross-sectional procedure, and finally, Section 5.3 discusses the conditional model's performance when only event data are available.

5.1 Conditional model: event and nonevent data
5.1.1 Base case.   Our first set of results concerns the conditional model's performance when all underlying assumptions are satisfied. These results are presented in Table 1. As first-step estimates of $\underline{\theta}$ are

21

The Review of Financial Studies / v 10 n 1 1997

independent of the true w, we report only one set of statistics for $\underline{\theta}$, which applies to all four values of w.

Discussion of results. It is useful to analyze our results in two parts, one pertaining to the Probit estimates of $\underline{\theta}$, and the other pertaining to second-step estimates of w.

Probit estimates of θ_1 and θ_2 (our main objects of interest) are close to truth on average, as expected. The average t-statistic for θ_1 (or θ_2) is about 2.0 for a sample size of 100 and about 3.0 for a sample size of 250. This corresponds to power of rejecting the hypothesis $\theta_1 = 0$ of about 50% and 86%, respectively (at 5% size).[19]

Next, consider the point estimates of w. Average estimates of w are close to truth. As true w increases, associated t-statistics get larger. For samples of size 100, the average t-statistic increases from about 1.4 for $w = 0.20$ to about 3.8 for $w = 0.50$, corresponding to power of 29% and 96%, respectively. Larger w are virtually certain to be picked up.

Finally, observe that standard errors used within simulations to construct the t-statistics are close to their true values. For instance, for 25% event probability and sample size of 100, the standard error implied in the probit t-statistic for θ_1 is 0.528 ($\frac{1.04}{1.97} = \frac{\theta_1}{t_{\theta_1}}$). This is almost exactly equal to the true standard error, 0.52 (see column Std. error), obtained from the simulated distribution of parameter estimates θ_1. Similar results are seen to hold for every other parameter, highlighting that the estimates do conform to their asymptotic distribution.

In the remainder of Section 5.1, we artificially introduce statistical and data problems into the data and report the conditional model's performance under these conditions.

5.1.2 Nonnormality. What sort of inferences does the procedure based on normality yield, when ψ_i is actually nonnormal? To address this issue, we simulate data as in Section 5.2, from the assumed nonnormal distribution, and estimate $\underline{\theta}$ and w using the two-step procedure based on normality. Four nonnormal distributions were considered, based on previous literature [Arabmazar and Schmidt (1982), Goldberger (1983), and Lee (1982, 1983)]: (1) logistic, (2) Student's t (5 degrees of freedom), (3) Chi-square (5 degrees of freedom), and (4) Laplace. The conditional moments and density functions of the four distributions are detailed in Goldberger (1983) and Lee (1982). The degrees of freedom in distributions (2) and (3) were kept small to maximize their departure from normality.

---

[19] Here, we define power as the probability of not committing a Type II error, that is, of rejecting the null hypothesis $H_0 : \theta_k = 0$. In practice, the test's power is obtained as the fraction of the 400 t-statistics for θ_1 exceeding $t_{critical} = 1.96$, the cutoff for a 5% significance level.

Conditional Methods in Event Studies

Table 2
Normality-based estimator when information is laplace distributed

Model parameter	Truth	Sample size = 100			Sample size = 250		
		Mean	Std. error	Mean t-stat	Mean	Std. error	Mean t-stat
Average event probability = 25%							
w	0.30	0.28	0.14	2.13	0.28	0.09	3.32
w	0.50	0.47	0.14	3.40	0.47	0.07	5.55
w	0.75	0.70	0.12	6.06	0.70	0.08	8.86
θ_0	1.00	1.26	0.59	2.22	1.24	0.36	3.46
θ_1	−1.00	−1.25	0.53	−2.41	−1.23	0.31	−3.85
$100\theta_2$	1.00	1.25	0.53	2.43	1.21	0.31	3.85
Average event probability = 50%							
w	0.30	0.27	0.13	2.10	0.28	0.08	3.50
w	0.50	0.46	0.12	3.73	0.45	0.07	5.77
w	0.75	0.69	0.12	6.40	0.69	0.07	9.76
θ_0	1.00	1.41	0.80	1.80	1.36	0.46	2.90
θ_1	−1.00	−1.41	0.50	−2.80	−1.36	0.30	4.54
$100\theta_2$	1.00	1.40	0.49	2.82	1.35	0.31	4.44

Table 2 presents statistics relating to the conditional model's performance, when conditioning information ψ_i is incorrectly assumed to be standard normal.

We simulate event E to occur if and only if $\theta_0 + \theta_1 x_{1i} + \theta_2 x_{2i} + \psi_i > 0$, where $\theta_0 = 1$, $\theta_1 = -1$, and $\theta_2 = 0.01$. Information ψ_i, $i = 1, 2, \ldots, n$ (n is the sample size), is i.i.d., sampled from the Laplace distribution (normalized to unit variance). Expected event-date abnormal return, conditional on ψ_i, is simulated as $E(\epsilon_i / \psi_i) = w\psi_i$.

In each simulation, we sample ψ_i and ϵ_i as above. We then apply the two-step method based on normality to estimate parameters w and $\underline{\theta}$. This process is repeated 400 times; each set of 400 repetitions is carried out for (1) 3 values of w (0.30, 0.50, and 0.75), (2) two sample sizes (100 and 250), and (3) two average event probabilities (25%, 50%). From each set of 400 simulations, we compute and report the following statistics: (1) *Mean*: mean parameter point estimate, averaged over the 400 repetitions; (2) *Std. error*: standard error of parameter estimate, computed as the sample standard deviation of the 400 point estimates; and (3) *Mean t-stat*: Each repetition generates a *t*-statistic for the relevant parameter estimate. Mean *t-stat* refers to the mean of this *t*-statistic, averaged over the 400 repetitions. As estimates of $\underline{\theta}$ are obtained independent of w, we report only one set of statistics for $\underline{\theta}$ for each average event probability/sample size. This applies to all three values of w.

Discussion of results. Table 2 presents results for the Laplace distribution. Qualitatively similar results obtain for other distributions and are not reported here.

Not surprisingly, point estimates of θ_1 and θ_2 in Table 2 are quite different from their true values. The difference reflects that the normality-based estimator is inconsistent when the true distribution of ψ is non-normal. However, note that the *sign* and order of these estimates are similar to those in Table 1, where data actually come from the normal distribution; the associated *t*-statistics are also of a similar magnitude. Thus, for the nonnormal distributions considered here, there seems to be little impact on one's inferences, reflecting the apparent robustness of inferences via the probit step.

Next, consider estimates of w. Point estimates of w are close to truth everywhere but are slightly attenuated. For example, when true

The Review of Financial Studies / v 10 n 1 1997

w = 0.75, average estimates range from 0.69 to 0.70. Nonnormality introduces a new source of noise into the second-step regressor $\lambda_k(\cdot)$, that of approximating it by its counterpart based on normality. This introduces "measurement error" into $\lambda_k(\cdot)$, which attenuates estimated w. In all instances though, the amount of attenuation is small, and the t-statistics for w are close to their corresponding values in Table 1.

As before, standard errors implied in t-statistics are roughly equal to their values from the empirical distribution of simulated parameter estimates, despite the misspecification engendered by nonnormality. Thus, nonnormality does lead to inconsistent parameter estimates but does not appear to impact one's inferences about the significance of model parameters.

5.1.3 Noise in announcement effects. As discussed in Section 3.2, announcement effects are always measured with noise in practice. In this section, we examine how such noise affects the conditional model's performance.

The experiment here involves simulating abnormal return data as in Section 4.2, and adding noise n_i, drawn i.i.d. $N(0, n^2)$, to the true abnormal returns. The two-step procedure is then applied to the data as usual, to estimate $\underline{\theta}$ and w. Simulations were carried out for four values of n^2 — 0.20, 0.40, 0.65, and 1.00 — corresponding to noise levels of 20%, 40%, 65% and 100%, respectively (since var[ϵ] = 1).

Qualitative discussion of results. For brevity, we do not report the complete simulation results but only provide a qualitative discussion instead.

Noise in announcement effects does not affect estimates of cross-sectional parameters $\underline{\theta}$ under the two-step procedure since the procedure does not use announcement-effect data in estimation of $\underline{\theta}$.[20] However, noise in estimated announcement effects does lead to larger error terms in the second-step regression. Hence, second-step estimates of w, while consistent, are now less precise and the average t-statistics for w are smaller as a result.

For moderate amounts of noise, there is little impact on one's inferences. For instance, when w = 0.30, we found that an increase in

---

[20] We also examined the effect of noise on other estimators of the conditional model that use announcement effects in estimating cross-sectional parameters. Simulation evidence (based on the maximum likelihood procedure for the case where there are both event and nonevent data) shows that noise in announcement effects makes estimates of w less precise. However, there was little effect on estimates of $\underline{\theta}$, whose distribution remained virtually unchanged for all levels of noise from 20% to 100%. Thus, in the context of Equation (7), most information relevant to cross-sectional estimation seems to be contained in whether firms announced an event or not, rather than the associated announcement effects.

noise from 0% to 40% reduces power (i.e., fraction of t-statistics exceeding 1.96) only from 64% to 52%. Thus, the two-step procedure does stand up to moderate amounts of noise at levels typical of event studies that use windows of a few days to measure announcement effects.

5.1.4 Cross-sectional correlation in information.

Thus far, we have assumed information ψ to be i.i.d. across firms. What effect does cross-sectional correlation have on the conditional model? Cross-sectional correlation does not affect consistency of probit estimates of $\underline{\theta}$, and by extension, second-step estimates of w. However, the t-statistics for tests of significance could be inappropriate. We develop some evidence on the direction of the potential bias.

Simulation methodology follows that of Section 4.2, with one change — information ψ_i is sampled differently to artificially introduce cross-sectional correlation into the data. This is accomplished by simulating ψ_i, $i = 1, 2, \ldots, n$ (n is the sample size), as

$$\psi_i = \alpha c + u_i \sqrt{1 - \alpha^2},$$

where (1) c is sampled from the normal distribution $N(0,1)$ once for each repetition; (2) u_i, $i = 1, 2, \ldots, n$, is sampled i.i.d. $N(0,1)$. This procedure effectively produces a sample with (a) $E(\psi_i)=0$, and (b) $\mathrm{var}(\psi_i)=1$ and correlation $E(\psi_i\psi_j) = \alpha^2$, $\forall i \neq j$. We carried out simulations for two values of α^2 — 0.25 and 0.50, corresponding to cross-sectional correlation of 25% and 50%, respectively. Apart from this change, simulations exactly follow the procedure outlined in Section 4.2.

Qualitative discussion of results. As in the previous section, we only provide a qualitative discussion of simulation results.

The simulation results had two features of interest. First, point estimates and standard errors of both $\underline{\theta}$ and w were quite close to the values reported in Table 1. Second, standard errors of estimates of w were 20% to 40% *smaller* than those reported in Table 1; that is, estimates of w appeared to be more precise in the presence of cross-sectional correlation. The standard errors were roughly equal to those computed via the empirical distribution of estimates of w. Hence, the lower standard error did reflect more-precise estimates of w.

To summarize the simulation results thus far, nonnormality and cross-sectional correlation in private information appear to matter less than imprecisely measured announcement effects. Noise in announcement effects somewhat degrades second-step estimates of w, though not significantly so for moderate amounts of noise.

The Review of Financial Studies / v 10 n 1 1997

5.2 The conventional cross-sectional procedure

How does the traditional cross-sectional procedure perform when data are generated as per the conditional model? We develop some evidence on this question here.

Simulation methodology is similar to that of Section 5.1, with one exception: here, we simulate only firms announcing event E. Abnormal returns are then regressed on a constant term and regressors x_1 and x_2 to obtain regression coefficients $\beta_0 - \beta_2$ of the linear model, Equation (12), and the associated t-statistics. Results are presented in Table 3, for average event probabilities of 25% and 50%.

5.2.1 Discussion of results.

Table 3 is best interpreted by comparing statistics for OLS regression coefficients β with corresponding statistics for probit estimates of $\underline{\theta}$ in Table 1.

To begin, observe that while regressors $\underline{x}$ do not satisfy the distributional assumptions of Proposition 1, our simulation results are consistent with its implied comparative statics:

- *Opposite sign*: Average point estimates of β_1 and β_2 are signed opposite to θ_1 and θ_2 everywhere.
- *Attenuation*: β_1 and β_2 are biased towards zero, relative to θ_1 and θ_2. For instance, $\theta_1 = -1$ everywhere, but average point estimates of β_1 range from 0.12 to 0.57.
- *More attenuation for smaller w*: Consider results of panel A, for instance. As w falls off from 0.75 to 0.30 (going upwards in the table), mean β_1 drops from 0.57 to 0.22.
- *More attenuation for highly anticipated events*: For instance, keeping w fixed at 0.30, estimates of β_1 drop from 0.21 to 0.12 as we go from panel A (25% event probability) to panel B (50% event probability).

Second, compare the empirically estimated standard errors (see column Std. error) with OLS standard errors implied in reported t-statistics. For instance, consider in panel A the evidence for $w = 0.30$ and sample size = 100. The t-statistic for β_1 is 0.62; the point estimate of β_1 is 0.21. Thus, the implied standard error produced by OLS is $\frac{0.21}{0.62} = 0.33$. This is equal to the empirical standard error, which is based on the actual distribution of the simulated parameter estimates. A similar correspondence is seen to hold for every regression coefficient in Tables 3. Consequently, the usual OLS standard errors seem to be appropriate for carrying out significance tests for cross-sectional parameters β_k.

Finally, how does the linear regression measure up in terms of power, compared to the conditional model? To judge the statistical power of the two procedures, compare the standard errors and t-

26

Conditional Methods in Event Studies

Table 3
Performance of conventional cross-sectional procedure

Panel A: Normally distributed information and 25% average event probability

True parameter	Estimated parameter	Sample size = 100			Sample size = 250		
		Mean	Std. error	Mean t-stat	Mean	Std. error	Mean t-stat
Correlation (w) = 0.30							
$\theta_0 = 1.00$	β_0	0.05	0.74	0.07	0.02	0.47	0.04
$\theta_1 = -1.00$	β_1	0.21	0.33	0.62	0.22	0.20	1.05
$100\theta_2 = 1.00$	$100\beta_2$	-0.22	0.33	-0.64	-0.23	0.20	-1.11
Correlation (w) = 0.50							
$\theta_0 = 1.00$	β_0	0.02	0.71	0.02	0.05	0.48	0.10
$\theta_1 = -1.00$	β_1	0.39	0.32	1.26	0.39	0.22	1.86
$100\theta_2 = 1.00$	$100\beta_2$	-0.38	0.29	-1.29	-0.38	0.19	-1.95
Correlation (w) = 0.75							
$\theta_0 = 1.00$	β_0	0.02	0.58	0.03	0.02	0.42	0.02
$\theta_1 = -1.00$	β_1	0.57	0.25	2.21	0.57	0.18	3.25
$100\theta_2 = 1.00$	$100\beta_2$	-0.57	0.26	-2.18	-0.56	0.18	-3.31

Panel B: Normally distributed information and 50% average event probability

True parameter	Estimated parameter	Sample size = 100			Sample size = 250		
		Mean	Std. error	Mean t-stat	Mean	Std. error	Mean t-stat
Correlation (w) = 0.30							
$\theta_0 = 1.00$	β_0	0.08	0.58	0.14	0.05	0.35	0.16
$\theta_1 = -1.00$	β_1	0.17	0.38	0.47	0.19	0.20	0.89
$100\theta_2 = 1.00$	$100\beta_2$	-0.19	0.32	-0.60	-0.18	0.23	-0.89
Correlation (w) = 0.50							
$\theta_0 = 1.00$	β_0	0.12	0.55	0.22	0.08	0.32	0.26
$\theta_1 = -1.00$	β_1	0.30	0.35	0.90	0.32	0.20	1.50
$100\theta_2 = 1.00$	$100\beta_2$	-0.30	0.33	-0.92	-0.31	0.22	-1.48
Correlation (w) = 0.75							
$\theta_0 = 1.00$	β_0	0.15	0.50	0.30	0.15	0.27	0.66
$\theta_1 = -1.00$	β_1	0.47	0.29	1.57	0.47	0.16	2.70
$100\theta_2 = 1.00$	$100\beta_2$	-0.47	0.28	-1.68	-0.48	0.17	-2.89

Table 3 presents statistics describing performance of the linear model when the true event/abnormal return data are generated by the conditional model, Equation (7), in the text.

Event E is simulated to occur if and only if $\theta_0 + \theta_1 x_{1i} + \theta_2 x_{2i} + \psi_i > 0$, where $\theta_0 = 1$, $\theta_1 = -1$, and $\theta_2 = 0.01$. Information ψ_i, $i = 1, 2, \ldots, n$ (n is the sample size), is sampled i.i.d. normal, N(0,1). Expected abnormal return, conditional on information ψ_i, is simulated as $E(\epsilon_i \mid \psi_i) = w\psi_i$.

In each simulation, we generate a sample of n firms announcing event E, and abnormal returns thereto. We then estimate β_0, β_1, and β_2 in the linear regression $E(\epsilon_i \mid E) = \beta_0 + \beta_1 x_{1i} + \beta_2 x_{2i}$ by OLS. This process is repeated 400 times, and each set of 400 repetitions is done for (1) two sample sizes (100 and 250) and (2) three values of w (0.30, 0.50, and 0.75). From each set of 400 simulations, we compute and report the following statistics: (1) *Mean*: the average parameter point estimate; (2) *Std. error*: the standard error of parameter estimate, computed as the sample standard deviation of the 400 point estimates; and (3) *Mean t-stat*: each simulation yields a t-statistic for β_j, $j = 1, \ldots, 3$. Mean t-stat refers to the average of the 400 t-statistics.

Based on Section 2.1, we expect regression coefficients β_i, $i = 1, 2$, to be (1) signed opposite to θ_i and (2) attenuated, relative to θ_i (i.e., $|\beta_i| < |\theta_i|$).

27

The Review of Financial Studies / v 10 n 1 1997

statistics for the β_j, $j = 1, 2$, with those for corresponding probit coefficients θ_j in Table 1.

On the one hand, the standard errors for the linear regression coefficients β_1 and β_2 are 30% to 40% smaller than those for the conditional model estimates of θ_1 and θ_2. Even so, the t-statistics for the linear regression coefficients are generally smaller. Thus, even though the linear model produces smaller standard errors, it is *less* powerful than the conditional model in picking up cross-sectional effects. In practice, the gap between the two procedures' performance is likely to be even wider than indicated above, since announcement effects are likely to be measured with error. With measurement error in announcement effects, t-statistics for cross-sectional parameters β_j of the linear model will be smaller, whereas those for the corresponding θ_j of the two-step procedure will remain unchanged since the procedure does not use announcement-effect data in cross-sectional parameter estimation.

Attenuation — equivalently, the information in nonevent firms, which is lost here — plays a central role in reducing the linear regression's power. As an illustration of this phenomenon, note that based on Proposition 1, we expect little attenuation and hence more power for the linear regression when w is large and the event is highly informative (i.e., has a low probability). The simulation results are consistent with this intuition: when the average event probability is small (25%) and w is large (0.75), regression coefficients have the largest t-statistics relative to all other parameter choices.

The lower power of the linear model suggests the following conjecture: the statistical significance of the linear regression coefficients β_j serves as a *lower bound* on significance of the θ_j. In other words, the linear regression is a conservative means of conducting cross-sectional inferences. Hence, if one rejects the hypothesis β_j at significance level α, one also rejects the hypothesis $\theta_j = 0$, at a significance level of at least α. The generality of this conjecture is unknown and warrants investigation in future work.

5.3 Conditional model without nonevent information

With both event and nonevent data, the conditional model is superior to the usual OLS procedure and appears to be fairly robust along several dimensions. Absent nonevent data, how does the model perform? We develop some evidence here.[21]

---

[21] Comments and suggestions of an anonymous referee have motivated and vastly improved much of this section.

We use the methodology described in Section 5.2 to simulate a sample of firms announcing the event and use this data to estimate the conditional model. However, estimation is a more delicate matter in this setting. We discuss some issues that arise, before presenting the simulation results.

With only event data, the conditional model may be estimated by nonlinear least squares (NLS), applied to regression Equation (16), or by maximum likelihood (ML). We began by experimenting with the NLS estimator. This estimator displayed poor statistical properties (it led to upward biased parameter estimates, and standard errors were overstated by a factor of 8 through 10), and was computationally as intensive as the (more-efficient) ML estimator. Accordingly, parameters were estimated via maximum likelihood. This involves maximization of the log-likelihood function

$$L(\underline{\theta}, w, \sigma_\epsilon) = -ln\, \sigma_\epsilon + ln\, n(\epsilon/\sigma_\epsilon) + ln\, N\left(\frac{\theta'x + w\epsilon/\sigma_\epsilon}{\sqrt{1-w^2}}\right)$$
$$-ln\, N(\underline{\theta}'x). \tag{17}$$

The optimization process requires choices along several dimensions. Below, we briefly describe the alternatives experimented with, as well as the decisions made in the final empirical work.

1. *Starting values*: Two sets of starting values were used to initialize the iterations. In the first "benchmark" set, starting values were set equal to the true parameter values. In the second set, all parameters were initialized to zero, except the parameter σ_ϵ, which was set to the sample standard deviation of announcement effects. Simulation results from the two sets were not appreciably different.

2. *Optimization algorithm*: We experimented with three algorithms: (1) Gauss-Newton, (2) Davidon-Fletcher-Powell (DFP), and (3) Broyden-Fletcher-Goldfarb-Shanno (BFGS) techniques. The first of these led to repeated problems of nonconvergence or noninvertibility of the Hessian, causing the optimization routine to abort. By contrast, the DFP and BFGS algorithms were better behaved, and the latter was chosen for empirical work.

3. *Gradient and Hessian*: Analytical (not numerical) gradients were employed in the iterations, as these improved computational and convergence properties. *T*-statistics are based on standard errors using the analytical Hessian.

4. *Convergence and exit criteria*: After some experimentation, we deemed the optimization routine to have converged when the relative change in all gradients was less than 10^{-4}. The maximum number of iterations was set at 175, beyond which there was no appreciable change in convergence behavior.

The Review of Financial Studies / v 10 n 1 1997

One final point deserves mention. Observe that the maximand, Equation (17), contains the term $\sqrt{1 - w^2}$. For the maximand to be computable, we require that $-1 < w < 1$, a constraint that must be imposed at all stages in the optimization. To get around this difficulty, we reparametrized the problem by setting $w_1 = \frac{w}{\sqrt{1-w^2}}$; equivalently $w = \frac{w_1}{\sqrt{1+w_1^2}}$. The advantage of this formulation is that unlike w, parameter w_1 is not constrained to lie in (-1,1), freeing the optimization process of this additional constraint. The best set of results obtained with these settings, and estimation was carried out using the OPTMUM routine in GAUSS.

Discussion of results. For both sets of starting values, our experience with regard to convergence was satisfactory for all but one set of parameter values.[22] Table 4 reports the results for the subsample of simulations that did converge, and we recognize the potential bias built in favor of conditional methods in interpreting these results.

Two facts emerge from the simulation results. First, the t-statistics reported in Table 4 are much smaller than those in Table 1. Thus, the absence of nonevent data has a severe negative impact on the conditional model's performance. Why are nonevent data so crucial to the conditional model's performance? We consider two explanations in this context. First, by using nonevent and event data rather than just event data only, one effectively increases the sample size, and this leads to greater statistical power. A second possibility is that the use of nonevent data expands the type of information being used in estimation. If the type of information represented by nonevent firms is useful in estimation, more powerful inferences should result. Indeed, our analysis supports the second conjecture. In all our simulations, the sample size, that is, the total number of firms (event *plus* nonevent firms) is fixed (at 100 or 250). Nevertheless, the conditional model's performance depends on the type of data within the sample: it performs better when there are both event and nonevent data rather than event data only.

The simulation results also indicate that the statistical properties of the ML estimator are somewhat unsatisfactory. Specifically, (1) parameter estimates are upward-biased, and (2) standard errors are slightly understated. The upshot is that the ML t-statistics appear to

---

[22] Aberrant behavior was displayed in only one instance, when w was small (0.30), and the sample was small (100). Here, only 60% of the iterations converged, and the reason for such behavior is intuitively straightforward. When $w = \mathrm{corr}(\epsilon, \psi)$ is small, little useful information is contained in announcement effects. Thus, the likelihood function becomes flat with respect to θ [this may be verified by allowing $w \to 0$ in Equation (17)], and location of extrema becomes difficult, especially in small samples.

Conditional Methods in Event Studies

Table 4
Performance of conditional model with truncated samples 50% average event probability

Parameter	Truth	Sample size = 100			Sample size = 250		
		Mean	Std. error	Mean t-stat	Mean	Std. error	Mean t-stat
$w = 0.30$							
$w_1 = \frac{w}{\sqrt{1-w^2}}$	0.31	0.93	1.19	1.39	0.67	0.79	1.91
θ_0	1.00	2.43	11.98	2.41	0.91	3.32	0.37
θ_1	−1.00	−2.24	6.09	−0.73	−1.19	2.39	−0.79
$100\theta_2$	1.00	2.46	4.96	0.69	1.90	2.99	0.99
$w = 0.50$							
$w_1 = \frac{w}{\sqrt{1-w^2}}$	0.58	1.12	1.39	1.69	0.89	0.81	2.37
θ_0	1.00	1.52	3.69	0.66	1.17	1.84	1.02
θ_1	−1.00	−1.56	2.15	−0.96	−1.37	1.34	−1.51
$100\theta_2$	1.00	1.60	2.06	0.99	1.17	1.08	1.40
$w = 0.75$							
$w_1 = \frac{w}{\sqrt{1-w^2}}$	1.13	1.45	1.07	1.91	1.17	0.54	2.77
θ_0	1.00	0.91	1.29	1.03	0.90	0.85	1.52
θ_1	−1.00	−1.20	0.82	−1.54	−1.16	0.63	−2.28
$100\theta_2$	1.00	1.53	1.00	1.45	1.17	0.54	2.21

Table 4 presents statistics describing performance of the conditional model, Equation (7), in the text, when data is available only for the firms announcing the event.
Event E is simulated to occur if and only if $\theta_0 + \theta_1 x_{1i} + \theta_2 x_{2i} + \psi_i > 0$, where $\theta_0 = 1$, $\theta_1 = -1$, and $\theta_2 = 0.01$. Information ψ_i, $i = 1, 2, \ldots, n$ (n is the sample size), is sampled i.i.d. normal, $N(0,1)$. Expected abnormal return, conditional on information ψ_i, is simulated as $E(\epsilon_i \mid \psi_i) = w\psi_i$.
In each simulation, we generate a sample of n firms announcing event E, and abnormal returns thereto. We then estimate parameters $w_1 = \frac{w}{\sqrt{1-w^2}}$, θ_0, and θ_1, θ_2 by maximum likelihood, the likelihood function being defined in Equation (17) in the text. This process is repeated 400 times, and each set of 400 repetitions is done for (1) two sample sizes (100 and 250) and (2) three values of w (0.30, 0.50, and 0.75). From each set of 400 simulations, we compute and report the following statistics: (1) *Mean*: the average parameter point estimate; (2) *Std. error*: the standard error of parameter estimate, computed as the sample standard deviation of the 400 point estimates; and (3) *Mean t-stat*: each simulation yields a t-statistic for parameters w_1 and θ_j, $j = 1, \ldots, 3$. Mean t-stat refers to the average of these t-statistics.

be somewhat larger than their true values. As an illustration of this phenomenon, consider the instance when the sample size is 100 and $w = 0.50$. Here, the average ML point estimate of θ_1 is -1.56, and the average t-statistic for θ_1 is -0.96, implying that the ML standard error is about $\frac{1.56}{0.96} = 1.62$. However, the true standard error (see column Std. error) is larger at 2.15. Thus, the reported ML t-statistic appears to be overstated. From Table 4, we see that this is more of an issue for small w and less so for larger w and sample sizes.

Despite this upward bias in the ML t-statistics, the t-statistics are no better than those produced by OLS (see Table 3, panel B). In this context, one situation — $w = 0.75$ and sample size = 250 — is somewhat interesting. For this parameter set, every one of the conditional model simulations converged; even so, ML t-statistics are 25% smaller

31

The Review of Financial Studies / v 10 n 1 1997

than the corresponding OLS counterparts! Thus, absent nonevent data, there is little evidence that the specification of the conditional model analyzed here has any practical value, relative to the much simpler OLS procedure.

6. Conclusions

Conditional methods offer an interesting perspective of event studies. Such methods are derived in the context of a well-defined economic equilibrium and have simple and appealing intuition: they relate announcement effects to the unexpected information revealed in events. Hence, conditional methods are potentially attractive means of conducting event studies.

The conditional model proposed by Acharya (1988) is a natural choice for many corporate events. When is it an empirically valuable tool? We find that it performs well only when one has, in addition to data on firms announcing the event, a set of nonevent firms, that is, firms that were partially anticipated to announce but chose not to announce the event in question. If such data are available, the conditional model is a valuable means of inference since it allows one to exploit nonevent information — which lies unused under traditional methods — in a straightforward manner.

In such settings, a simple two-step procedure appears to be an attractive method of estimating the conditional model. This estimator has three useful properties as a means of conducting cross-sectional tests in event studies. First, cross-sectional parameters are estimated without using abnormal return information. Thus, the usual data problems associated with event studies — event-date uncertainty, clustering of event dates, etc. — which are known to adversely afflict inferences via conventional procedures, do not affect cross-sectional inferences via the two-step procedure. Second, our evidence suggests cross-sectional inferences are not severely affected by incorrect distributional assumptions. Nevertheless, if this is a concern, there does exist a body of literature for distribution-free estimation that may be employed. Finally, cross-sectional inferences via the two-step procedure are also valid for other conditional models [e.g., that of Eckbo, Maksimovic, and Williams (1990)] discussed in this article. Thus, when nonevent data are available, the two-step procedure appears to be a desirable way of estimating the conditional model.

However, in most practical situations, nonevent data — a sample of firms that chose not to announce the event, the timing of this nonevent, and cross-sectional data and announcement effects at the time markets learn of the nonevent — are not available. One must then work only with firms that have announced the event in question. Here, we find that the conditional model becomes computationally burdensome and less powerful, even when efficiently estimated.

It is precisely under these circumstances that the results concerning traditional methods assume the greatest force, and we make two points in this context. First, regression coefficients obtained via the traditional linear regression are proportional to the true cross-sectional parameters, under weak conditions. Second, OLS standard errors appear to be appropriate for testing the significance of cross-sectional parameters. Together, the two results imply that the traditional OLS procedure may be used for carrying out cross-sectional inferences, though the coefficients are potentially inconsistently estimated. These results also provide an equilibrium justification for using the standard procedures in practice.

How useful are the results, from a practical perspective? Not surprisingly, OLS is less powerful than the conditional model when both event and nonevent data are available. However, when one has event data only, OLS appears to be a simple and effective substitute for the conditional model, even when the latter is efficiently estimated.

Thus, our results suggest that when the necessary nonevent data are available, inferences should be based on conditional methods. If not, we suggest that the traditional cross-sectional procedure be used and the associated *t*-statistics be interpreted as conservative lower bounds on the true significance level of the parameters.

Appendix

Proof of Proposition 1. Following Goldberger (1981) or Maddala (1983), we first reparametrize the selection equation so that $\underline{x}$ and τ have mean zero. With this reparametrization, event E occurs if and only if $\tau = \theta'\underline{x} + \psi > c$, where

$$c = -\theta_0 - \sum_{j=1}^{k} \theta_j E(x_j) \tag{18}$$

and $E(x_j)$ denotes the mean of the original regressor x_j. The proof simply consists of working through the normal equation defining the OLS estimator of β, for a sample of firms announcing E. We begin by stating some results that aid in this process.

The population regression of τ on $\underline{x}$ is given by

$$\underline{\theta} = \Sigma_x^{-1} cov(\underline{x}, \tau). \tag{19}$$

The Review of Financial Studies / v 10 n 1 1997

With $E(\tau)$ normalized to zero, the population mean of $\underline{x}$, conditional on τ, is given by

$$E(\underline{x} \mid \tau) = \underline{\alpha}\tau, \tag{20}$$

while the variance of $\underline{x}$, conditional on τ, is

$$V = Var(\underline{x} \mid \tau) = \Sigma_x - \underline{\alpha}\,\underline{\alpha}'s^2, \tag{21}$$

where α and s^2 are defined as

$$\underline{\alpha} = \frac{cov(\underline{x}, \tau)}{s^2} = \frac{\Sigma_x\underline{\theta}}{s^2}, \tag{22}$$

and

$$s^2 = var(\tau) = \underline{\theta}'\Sigma_x\underline{\theta} + 1. \tag{23}$$

Define R^2 and t as

$$R^2 = \frac{var(\underline{\theta}'\underline{x})}{s^2} = \frac{\underline{\theta}'\Sigma_x\underline{\theta}}{\underline{\theta}'\Sigma_x\underline{\theta} + 1}, \tag{24}$$

and

$$t = \frac{var(\tau \mid E)}{var(\tau)} = \frac{var(\tau^*)}{s^2}, \tag{25}$$

where the asterisk denotes the conditioning $\tau > c$. R^2 is the "explained variance" in the population regression of τ on $\underline{x}$.

The principal fact on which the proportionality result rests is as follows: Selection does not alter the conditional distribution of $\underline{x}$, given τ [Chung and Goldberger (1984)]. Hence, for the sample of firms announcing E, we have

$$E(\underline{x}^* \mid \tau) = \underline{\alpha}\tau, \tag{26}$$

and

$$var(\underline{x}^* \mid \tau) = V, \tag{27}$$

where $V, \underline{\alpha}$ are defined in Equations (21) and (22). With these results in hand, we can solve for the coefficients $\underline{\beta}$ in the regression of event-date abnormal returns on regressors $\underline{x}$. These coefficients are defined by the normal equation

$$\Sigma_x^*\underline{\beta} = cov(\underline{x}^*, \epsilon^*), \tag{28}$$

where ϵ^* is the event-date abnormal return, conditional on announce-

34

ment of E (i.e., $\tau > c$). Consider first the left-hand side of Equation (28). We have from the definition of Σ_x^*,

$$
\begin{aligned}
\Sigma_x^* &= var_\tau(E^*(\underline{x} \mid \tau)) + E_\tau(var^*(\underline{x} \mid \tau)), \\
&= var(\underline{\alpha}\tau^*) + V \quad \text{[from Equations (26) and (27)]}, \\
&= \underline{\alpha} var(\tau^*)\underline{\alpha}' + \Sigma_x - \underline{\alpha}\,\underline{\alpha}'s^2 \quad \text{[from Equation (21)]}, \\
&= \underline{\alpha}(ts^2)\underline{\alpha}' + \Sigma_x - \underline{\alpha}\,\underline{\alpha}'s^2 \quad \text{[from Equation (25)]}, \\
&= \Sigma_x - \underline{\alpha}\,\underline{\alpha}'(1 - t)s^2.
\end{aligned}
\tag{29}
$$

To simplify the right-hand side of Equation (28), use the bivariate normality of ψ and ϵ to get

$$
E(\epsilon \mid \psi) = \pi\psi = \pi(\tau - \underline{\theta}'\underline{x}),
$$

and

$$
E(\epsilon \mid E) = E(\epsilon^*) = \pi(\tau^* - \underline{\theta}'\underline{x}^*).
$$

Using this in the right-hand side of Equation (28), we have

$$
\begin{aligned}
cov(\underline{x}^*, \epsilon^*) &= cov(\underline{x}^*, \pi(\tau^* - \underline{\theta}'\underline{x}^*)), \\
&= \pi\,cov(\underline{x}^*, \tau^*) - \pi\,cov(\underline{x}^*, \underline{\theta}'\underline{x}^*), \\
&= \pi\underline{\alpha}ts^2 - \pi\Sigma_x^*\underline{\theta} \quad \text{[using Equation (26)]}, \\
&= \pi\underline{\alpha}ts^2 - \pi\left[\Sigma_x - \underline{\alpha}\,\underline{\alpha}'(1 - t)s^2\right]\underline{\theta} \quad \text{[using Equation (29)]}.
\end{aligned}
$$

Substituting for $\underline{\alpha}$ using Equation (22), we have

$$
\begin{aligned}
cov(\underline{x}^*, \epsilon^*) &= \pi\left(\frac{\Sigma_x\underline{\theta}}{s^2}\right)ts^2 - \pi\Sigma_x\underline{\theta} + \pi s^2\underline{\theta}\left(\frac{\Sigma_x\underline{\theta}}{s^2}\right)\left(\frac{\underline{\theta}'\Sigma_x}{s^2}\right)(1 - t), \\
&= \pi\Sigma_x\underline{\theta}\left[t - 1 + \left(\frac{\underline{\theta}'\Sigma_x\underline{\theta}}{s^2}\right)(1 - t)\right], \\
&= \pi\Sigma_x\underline{\theta}\left[t - 1 + R^2(1 - t)\right] \quad \text{[using Equation (24)]}, \\
&= -\pi(1 - R^2)(1 - t)\Sigma_x\underline{\theta}.
\end{aligned}
\tag{30}
$$

Finally, using Equations (29) and (30) in normal Equation (28), we have

$$
\underline{\beta}\left[\Sigma_x - \underline{\alpha}\,\underline{\alpha}'(1 - t)s^2\right] = \pi\Sigma_x\underline{\theta}(1 - R^2)(1 - t)
$$

and

$$
\underline{\beta}\left[\Sigma_x - \left(\frac{\Sigma_x\underline{\theta}}{s^2}\right)\left(\frac{\underline{\theta}'\Sigma_x}{s^2}\right)(1 - t)s^2\right] = -\pi\Sigma_x\underline{\theta}(1 - R^2)(1 - t),
\tag{31}
$$

where the last equation obtains by substituting for $\underline{\alpha}$ using Equation (22). Multiplying both sides of Equation (31) by $\underline{\theta}'$, we have, as

The Review of Financial Studies / v 10 n 1 1997

required,

$$(\underline{\theta}'\Sigma_x)\left\{\underline{\beta}\left[1 - \left(\frac{\theta'\Sigma_x\theta}{s^2}\right)(1-t)\right]\right\} = \underline{\theta}'\Sigma_x\left\{\left[-\pi\underline{\theta}(1-R^2)(1-t)\right]\right\},$$

$$\Rightarrow \underline{\beta} = -\pi\underline{\theta}\frac{(1-R^2)(1-t)}{t+(1-R^2)(1-t)},$$

$$= -\pi\underline{\theta}\mu. \tag{32}$$

Remark. *The intercept term β_0 can be computed as $E(\epsilon^* - \beta'\underline{x}^*)$. Using (1) Proposition 1 for $(\beta_1, \ldots, \beta_k)$ (2) $E(\tau^*) = \lambda_E(-c)$ and $E(x^*) = \underline{\alpha}\tau^*$, we obtain $\beta_0 = \pi\lambda_E(-c)(1 - \mu R^2)$, where c is defined in Equation (18). Also, while the proof pertains to conditional model defined by Equation (7), an analogous proportionality result may be obtained in similar fashion for encompassing specification, Equation (11), as well.*

Proof of Lemma 1: Result (1). The result $0 < \mu < 1$ is an immediate consequence of $0 < t, R^2 < 1$. The bounds on R^2 follow from its definition, Equation (24); those for T need some argument. From Equation (25), the definition of t, we have

$$t = \frac{var(\tau \mid E)}{var(\tau)} = \frac{var(\tau \mid \tau > c)}{s^2}, \tag{33}$$

$$= var\left(\frac{\tau}{s} \mid \frac{\tau}{s} > \frac{c}{s}\right) = var\left(z \mid z > \frac{c}{s}\right), \tag{34}$$

where $z = \frac{\tau}{s}$ is standard normal (multivariate normality of $\underline{x}$ is being invoked here). But if z is standard normal, $0 < var(z \mid z > \frac{c}{s}) < 1$, [see Greene (1993), and footnote 11 in the text]. Therefore, $0 < t < 1$.

Proof of Lemma 1: Result (2). For highly anticipated events, we show that t is large. As $\frac{\partial\mu}{\partial t} < 0$, it follows that μ is small for such events. Accordingly, consider the following facts:

Fact 1: Event E occurs if and only if $\theta_0 + \sum_{j=1}^k \theta_j x_j + \psi > c$, where c is defined in Equation (18). Hence, the smaller the value of c, the greater the average probability of E.

Fact 2: From Equation (34), if z is standard normal, $t = var(z \mid z > \frac{c}{s}) = var(z \mid z < -\frac{c}{s})$, where the last equality follows from symmetry. From Goldberger (1983), $\frac{\partial var(z\mid z < -\frac{c}{s})}{\partial c} = \frac{\partial t}{\partial c} < 0$.

From Facts 1 and 2, we have the following. For highly anticipated events, c is small (from Fact 1) and t is large (as $\frac{\partial t}{\partial c} < 0$ from Fact 2). But large t implies small μ since $\frac{\partial\mu}{\partial t} < 0$, using Equation (32). Thus, for highly anticipated events, μ is small, as claimed.

Conditional Methods in Event Studies

References

Acharya, S., 1988, "A Generalized Econometric Model and Tests of a Signalling Hypothesis with Two Discrete Signals," *Journal of Finance*, 43, 413–29.

Acharya, S., 1993, "Value of Latent Information: Alternative Event Study Methods", *Journal of Finance*, 48, 363–85.

Arabmazar, A., and P. Schmidt, 1982, "An Investigation into the Robustness of the Tobit Estimator to Nonnormality," *Econometrica*, 50, 1055–63.

Asquith, P., and D. Mullins, 1986, "Equity Issues and Offering Dilution," *Journal of Financial Economics*, 15, 61–89.

Asquith, P., R. Bruner, and D. Mullins, "The Gain to Bidding Firms from Merger," *Journal of Financial Economics*, 11, 121–39.

Bajaj, M., and A. Vijh, "Dividend Clienteles and the Information Content of Dividend Changes," *Journal of Financial Economics*, 26, 193–219.

Brown, S., and J. Warner, 1985, "Using Daily Stock Returns: The Case of Event Studies," *Journal of Financial Economics*, 14, 3–31.

Chaplinsky, S., and R. S. Hansen, 1993, "Partial Anticipation, the Flow of Information and the Economic Impact of Corporate Debt Sales," *Review of Financial Studies*, 6, 709–32.

Chung, C-F., and A. Goldberger, 1984, "Proportional Projections in Limited Dependent Variable Models," *Econometrica*, 52, 531–4.

Eckbo, E., 1986, "Valuation Effects of Corporate Debt Offerings," *Journal of Financial Economics*, 15, 119–51.

Eckbo, E., V. Maksimovic, and J. Williams, 1990, "Consistent Estimation of Cross-Sectional Models in Event-Studies," *Review of Financial Studies*, 3, 343–65.

Fama, E., L. Fisher, M. Jensen, and R. Roll, 1969, "The Adjustment of Stock Prices to New Information," *International Economic Review*, 10, 1–21.

Goldberger, A., 1981, "Linear Regression After Selection," *Journal of Econometrics*, 15, 357–66.

Goldberger, A., 1983, "Abnormal Selection Bias," in S. Karlin, T. Amemiya, and L. Goodman, (eds.), *Studies in Econometrics, Time Series and Multivariate Statistics*, Academic Press, Stamford.

Greene, W., 1981, "Sample Selection Bias as a Specification Error: Comment," *Econometrica*, 49, 795–8.

Greene, W., 1993, *Econometric Analysis*, Macmillan, New York.

Heckman, J., 1979, "Sample Selection Bias as a Specification Error," *Econometrica*, 47, 153–61.

Korajczyk, R., D. Lucas, and R. McDonald, 1991, "The Effect of Information Releases on the Pricing and Timing of Equity Issues," *Review of Financial Studies*, 4, 685–708.

Lanen, W., and R. Thompson, 1988, "Stock Price Reactions as Surrogates for the Net Cashflow Effects of Corporate Financial Decisions," *Journal of Accounting and Economics*, 10, 311–34.

Lee, L-F., 1982, "Some Approaches to the Correction of Selectivity Bias," *Review of Economic Studies*, 49, 355–72.

Lee, L-F., 1983, "Generalized Econometric Models with Selectivity," *Econometrica*, 51, 507–12.

The Review of Financial Studies / v 10 n 1 1997

Maddala, G. S., 1983, *Limited Dependent and Qualitative Variables in Econometrics*, Cambridge University Press, Cambridge, MA.

Malatesta, P., and R. Thompson, 1985, "Partially Anticipated Events: A Model of Stock Price Reactions with an Application to Corporate Acquisitions," *Journal of Financial Economics*, 14, 237–50.

McElroy, M., and E. Burmeister, 1988, "Arbitrage Pricing Theory as a Restricted Nonlinear Regression Model," *Journal of Business Economics and Statistics*, 6, 29–42.

Nelson, F., 1984, "Efficiency of the Two-Step Estimator with Endogenous Sample Selection," *Journal of Econometrics*, 24, 181–96.

Newey, W., J. Powell, and J. Walker, 1990, "Semiparametric Estimation of Selection Models: Some Empirical Results," *American Economic Review*, 80, 324–28.

Paarsch, H., 1984, "A Monte-Carlo Comparison of Estimators for Censored Regression Models," *Journal of Econometrics*, 24, 197–213.

Schipper, K., and R. Thompson, 1983, "Evidence on the Capitalized Value of Merger Activity for Acquiring Firms," *Journal of Financial Economics*, 11, 85–119.

Stoker, T., 1986, "Consistent Estimation of Scaled Coefficients," *Econometrica*, 54, 1461–81.

Thompson, R., 1985, "Conditioning the Return Generating Process on Firm-Specific Events: A Discussion of Event-Study Methods," *Journal of Financial and Quantitative Analysis*, 20, 151–68.

Vermaelen, T., 1984, "Repurchase Tender Offers, Signalling, and Managerial Incentives," *Journal of Financial and Quantitative Analysis*, 19, 163–81.

Wales, T., and A. Woodland, 1980, "Sample Selectivity and the Estimation of Labor Supply Functions," *International Economic Review*, 21, 437–68.

White, H., 1980, "Using Least Squares to Approximate Unknown Regression Functions," *International Economic Review*, 21, 149–70.

THE JOURNAL OF FINANCE • VOL. LIV, NO. 1 • FEBRUARY 1999

Improved Methods for Tests of Long-Run Abnormal Stock Returns

JOHN D. LYON, BRAD M. BARBER, and CHIH-LING TSAI*

ABSTRACT

We analyze tests for long-run abnormal returns and document that two approaches yield well-specified test statistics in random samples. The first uses a traditional event study framework and buy-and-hold abnormal returns calculated using carefully constructed reference portfolios. Inference is based on either a skewness-adjusted t-statistic or the empirically generated distribution of long-run abnormal returns. The second approach is based on calculation of mean monthly abnormal returns using calendar-time portfolios and a time-series t-statistic. Though both approaches perform well in random samples, misspecification in nonrandom samples is pervasive. Thus, analysis of long-run abnormal returns is treacherous.

COMMONLY USED METHODS TO TEST for long-run abnormal stock returns yield misspecified test statistics, as documented by Barber and Lyon (1997a) and Kothari and Warner (1997).[1] Simulations reveal that empirical rejection levels routinely exceed theoretical rejection levels in these tests. In combination, these papers highlight three causes for this misspecification. First, the *new listing* or *survivor bias* arises because in event studies of long-run abnormal returns, sampled firms are tracked for a long post-event period, but firms that constitute the index (or reference portfolio) typically include firms that begin trading subsequent to the event month. Second, the *rebalancing bias* arises because the compound returns of a reference portfolio, such as an equally weighted market index, are typically calculated assuming periodic (generally monthly) rebalancing, whereas the returns of sample firms are compounded without rebalancing. Third, the *skewness bias* arises because the distribution of long-run abnormal stock returns is positively skewed,

* Graduate School of Management, University of California, Davis. This paper was previously entitled "Holding Size while Improving Power in Tests of Long-Run Abnormal Stock Returns." We have benefited from the suggestions of John Affleck-Graves, Peter Bickel, Alon Brav, Sandra Chamberlain, Arnold Cowan, Masako Darrough, Eugene Fama, Ken French, Peter Hall, Inmoo Lee, Tim Loughran, Michael Maher, Terrance Odean, Stephen Penman, N. R. Prabhala, Raghu Rau, Jay Ritter, René Stulz, Brett Trueman, Ralph Walkling, two anonymous reviewers, and seminar participants at the Australian Graduate School of Management, State University of New York–Buffalo, Ohio State, University of California–Berkeley, University of California–Davis, the University of Washington, and 1997 Western Finance Association Meetings. Chih-Ling Tsai was supported by National Science Foundation grant DMS 95-10511. All errors are our own.

[1] Numerous recent studies analyze long-run abnormal stock returns in an event-study context. Citations to many of these studies can be found in Kothari and Warner (1997) and Barber and Lyon (1997a).

165

which also contributes to the misspecification of test statistics. Generally, the new listing bias creates a positive bias in test statistics, and the rebalancing and skewness biases create a negative bias.

In this research, we evaluate two general approaches for tests of long-run abnormal stock returns that control for these three sources of bias. The first approach is based on a traditional event study framework and buy-and-hold abnormal returns. In this approach we first carefully construct reference portfolios that are free of the new listing and rebalancing biases. Consequently, these reference portfolios yield a population mean abnormal return measure that is identically zero and, therefore, reduce the misspecification of test statistics. Then we control for the skewness bias in tests of long-run abnormal returns by applying standard statistical methods recommended for settings when the underlying distribution is positively skewed. Two statistical methods virtually eliminate the skewness bias in random samples: (1) a bootstrapped version of a skewness-adjusted t-statistic, and (2) empirical p values calculated from the simulated distribution of mean long-run abnormal returns estimated from pseudoportfolios. The first method is developed and analyzed based on a rich history of research in statistics that considers the properties of t-statistics in positively skewed distributions, which dates back at least to Neyman and Pearson (1928) and Pearson (1929a, 1929b). In the second method, based on the empirical methods of Brock, Lakonishok, and LeBaron (1992) and Ikenberry, Lakonishok, and Vermaelen (1995), we generate the empirical distribution of mean long-run abnormal stock returns under the null hypothesis. The statistical significance of the sample mean is evaluated based on this empirically generated distribution.[2] Kothari and Warner (1997) note that these methods "seem like a promising framework for alternative tests which can potentially reduce misspecification."

These two statistical methods yield well-specified test statistics in random samples, and in combination with carefully constructed reference portfolios, they control well for the new listing, rebalancing, and skewness biases. However, the methods are unable to control for two additional sources of misspecification: Cross-sectional dependence in sample observations, and a poorly specified asset pricing model. Brav (1997) argues that cross-sectional dependence in sample observations can lead to poorly specified test statistics in some sampling situations and we concur.

The second general approach that we consider is based on calendar-time portfolios, as discussed by Fama (1997) and implemented in recent work by Loughran and Ritter (1995), Brav and Gompers (1997), and Brav, Géczy, and Gompers (1995). Using this approach, calendar-time abnormal returns are calculated for sample firms. Inference is based on a t-statistic derived from the time-series of the monthly calendar-time portfolio abnormal returns. This approach eliminates the problem of cross-sectional dependence among sample firms but, unlike buy-and-hold abnormal returns, the abnormal return measure does not precisely measure investor experience.

---

[2] Research independently undertaken by Cowan and Sergeant (1996) considers the same general issues discussed here.

The most serious problem with inference in studies of long-run abnormal stock returns is the reliance on a model of asset pricing. All tests of the null hypothesis that long-run abnormal stock returns are zero are implicitly a joint test of (i) long-run abnormal returns are zero and (ii) the asset pricing model used to estimate abnormal returns is valid. In this research, we document that controlling for size and book-to-market alone is not sufficient to yield well-specified test statistics when samples are drawn from nonrandom samples, regardless of the approach used. In short, the rejection of the null hypothesis in tests of long-run abnormal returns is not a sufficient condition to reject the theoretical framework of market efficiency.

The remainder of this paper is organized as follows. We discuss the data and the construction of reference portfolios in Section I. We discuss the details of long-run abnormal return calculations in Section II. Our statistical tests and empirical methods are presented in Section III, followed by results in Section IV. We discuss the use of cumulative abnormal returns and calendar-time portfolio methods in Section V. We make concluding remarks in Section VI.

I. Data and the Construction of Reference Portfolios

Our analysis begins with all NYSE/AMEX/Nasdaq firms with available data on the monthly return files created by the Center for Research in Security Prices (CRSP). Our analysis covers the period July 1973 through December 1994 (we begin in 1973 because return data for Nasdaq firms are not available from CRSP prior to 1973). Since event studies of long-run abnormal returns focus on the common stock performance of corporations, we delete the firm-month returns on securities identified by CRSP as other than ordinary common shares (CRSP share codes 10 and 11). Thus, for example, we exclude from our analysis returns on American Depository Receipts, closed-end funds, foreign-domiciled firms, Primes and Scores, and real estate investment trusts.

A key feature of our analysis is the careful construction of reference portfolios, which alleviates the new listing and rebalancing biases (Barber and Lyon (1997a), Kothari and Warner (1997)). Our reference portfolios are formed on the basis of firm size and book-to-market ratios in July of each year, 1973 through 1993. Though we restrict our analysis to portfolios formed on the basis of these two variables, the method we employ to construct our reference portfolios can also be used to construct portfolios on the basis of other firm characteristics (e.g., prior return performance, sales growth, industry, or earnings yields).

We construct 14 size reference portfolios as follows:

1. We calculate firm size (market value of equity calculated as price per share multiplied by shares outstanding) in June of each year for all firms.
2. In June of year t, we rank all NYSE firms in our population on the basis of firm size and form size decile portfolios based on these rankings.

3. AMEX and Nasdaq firms are placed in the appropriate NYSE size decile based on their June market value of equity.
4. We further partition the smallest size decile, decile one, into quintiles on the basis of size rankings of all firms (without regard to exchange) in June of each year.
5. The returns of the size portfolios are tracked from July of year t for τ months.

Since Nasdaq is populated predominantly with smaller firms, this ranking procedure leaves many more firms in the smallest decile of firm size than in the other nine deciles (approximately 50 percent of all firms fall in the smallest size decile); therefore we further partition the smallest size decile into quintiles on the basis of size rankings without regard to exchange.

We construct ten book-to-market reference portfolios as follows:

1. We calculate a firm's book-to-market ratio using the book value of common equity (COMPUSTAT data item 60) reported on a firm's balance sheet in year $t - 1$ divided by the market value of common equity in December of year $t - 1$.[3]
2. In December of year $t - 1$, we rank all NYSE firms in our population on the basis of book-to-market ratios and form book-to-market decile portfolios based on these rankings.
3. AMEX and Nasdaq firms are placed in the appropriate NYSE book-to-market decile based on their book-to-market ratio in year $t - 1$.
4. The returns of the book-to-market portfolios are tracked from July of year t for τ months.

The extreme book-to-market deciles contain slightly more firms than deciles two through eight, but no book-to-market decile portfolio contains more than 20 percent of the firms.

We calculate one-, three-, and five-year returns for the size and book-to-market reference portfolios in two ways. First, in each month we calculate the mean return for each portfolio and then compound this mean return over τ months:

$$R_{ps\tau}^{\text{reb}} = \prod_{t=s}^{s+\tau} \left[1 + \frac{\sum_{i=1}^{n_t} R_{it}}{n_t} \right] - 1, \qquad (1)$$

where s is the beginning period, τ is the period of investment (in months), R_{it} is the return on security i in month t, and n_t is the number of securities in month t.

---

[3] Firms with negative book value of equity, though this is relatively rare, are excluded from the analysis.

Though research in financial economics commonly uses long-horizon reference portfolio returns calculated in this manner, for two reasons they do not
accurately reflect the returns earned on a passive buy-and-hold strategy of investing equally in the securities that constitute the reference portfolio. First,
this portfolio return assumes monthly rebalancing to maintain equal weights.
This rebalancing leads to an inflated long-horizon return on the reference portfolio, which can likely be attributed to bid-ask bounce and nonsynchronous trading.[4] We refer to this as the *rebalancing bias*. Second, this portfolio return
includes firms newly listed subsequent to portfolio formation (period s). Ritter (1991) documents that firms that go public underperform an equally weighted
market index, though Brav and Gompers (1997) document that this underperformance is confined to small, high-growth firms. Since it is likely that firms
that go public are a significant portion of newly listed firms, the result is a
downwardly biased estimate of the long-horizon return from investing in a *passive* (i.e., not rebalanced) reference portfolio in period s. We refer to this as the
new listing bias. In reference to the rebalanced nature of this return calculation, we denote the return calculated in this manner with the superscript "reb."

Our second method of calculating the long-horizon returns on a reference
portfolio involves first compounding the returns on securities constituting
the portfolio and then summing across securities:

$$R_{ps\tau}^{\text{bh}} = \sum_{i=1}^{n_s} \frac{\left[\prod_{t=s}^{s+\tau} (1 + R_{it}) \right] - 1}{n_s}, \tag{2}$$

where n_s is the number of securities traded in month s, the beginning period
for the return calculation. The return on this portfolio represents a passive
equally weighted investment in all securities constituting the reference portfolio in period s. There is no investment in firms newly listed subsequent to
period s, nor is there monthly rebalancing of the portfolio. Consequently, in
reference to the buy-and-hold nature of this return calculation, we denote
the return calculated in this manner with the superscript "bh."

An unresolved issue in the calculation of the buy-and-hold portfolio return
is where an investor places the proceeds of investments in firms delisted
subsequent to period s. In this research, we assume that the proceeds of
delisted firms are invested in an equally weighted reference portfolio, which
is rebalanced monthly. Thus, missing monthly returns are filled with the
mean monthly return of firms comprising the reference portfolio.[5]

---

[4] For a discussion of these issues, see Blume and Stambaugh (1983), Roll (1983), Conrad and
Kaul (1993), and Ball, Kothari, and Wasley (1995).

[5] As we document below, this leads to a small overstatement of the returns that can be
earned from investing in the portfolio of small firms (portfolio 1A). However, this would only
lead to biases in tests of long-run abnormal returns if sample firms are delisted significantly
more or less frequently than the firms comprising the benchmark portfolio.

In Table I, we present the annualized one-, three-, and five-year rebalanced and buy-and-hold returns on our fourteen size portfolios (Panel A) and ten book-to-market portfolios (Panel B) assuming investment in July of each year, 1973 through 1993.[6] The last three columns of this table present the difference between the rebalanced portfolio returns and the buy-and-hold portfolio returns. Examination of Panel A reveals the well-documented small firm effect. However, the returns from investing in unusually small firms (portfolio 1A) are overstated by more than 10 percent per year when calculated with monthly rebalancing.

The calculations in Table I, Panel A, are based on reinvestment of delisted firms in an equally weighted, monthly rebalanced portfolio of firms of similar size. If we assume reinvestment of delisted firms in a CRSP value-weighted market index (results not reported in the table), the returns on size portfolio 1A (1B) range from 26.1 percent (18.6 percent) at a one-year holding period to 21.8 percent (19.3 percent) at a five-year holding period. If we assume reinvestment of delisted firms in a firm from the same size class, the returns on size portfolio 1A (1B) range from 27.2 percent (18.4 percent) at a one-year holding period to 23.0 percent (19.3 percent) at a five-year holding period. Returns on the remaining size portfolios are affected by fewer than than 100 basis points, regardless of whether the reinvestment is in a similar size firm or a value-weighted market index.

Examination of Panel B reveals that the returns from investing in high book-to-market firms (portfolio 10) are overstated by 3 to 4 percent per year when calculated with monthly rebalancing. The calculations in Panel B are based on reinvestment of delisted firms in an equally–weighted, monthly rebalanced portfolio of firms of similar book-to-market ratios. If we assume reinvestment of delisted firms in a CRSP value-weighted market index (results not reported in the table), the returns on book-to-market portfolio 10 (9) range from 24.2 percent (23.0 percent) at a one-year holding period to 21.9 percent (22.2 percent) at a five-year holding period. If we assume reinvestment of delisted firms in a firm from the same book-to-market class, the returns on book-to-market portfolio 10 (9) range from 25.3 percent (23.4 percent) at a one-year holding period to 22.8 percent (23.3 percent) at a five-year holding period. The returns on the remaining book-to-market portfolios are affected by fewer than than 100 basis points, regardless of whether the reinvestment is in a firm with similar book-to-market ratio or a value-weighted market index.

Our results indicate that the use of compounded, equally weighted monthly returns also yields inflated returns on reference portfolios, particularly in reference portfolios composed of small firms or firms with high book-to-market ratios. Canina et al. (1998) document a similar bias when the daily returns of an equally weighted market index are used in lieu of monthly

---

[6] The three- and five-year return means include overlapping years, while the one-year return mean does not. The last one-, three-, and five-year return assumes initial investment in July 1993, July 1991, and July 1989, respectively.

Table I

Annualized Returns from Investing in Size or Book-to-Market Decile Portfolios with Monthly Rebalancing or Buy-and-Hold Strategy: July 1973 to June 1994

The rebalanced portfolio returns assume monthly rebalancing to maintain equal weights and include firms newly listed subsequent to July of each year. The buy-and-hold portfolio returns assume equal initial investments in each security traded in July of each year. If a firm is delisted or is missing return data, the return on the equally weighted size decile portfolio for that month is spliced into the return series for that firm.

Panel A reports size deciles created in July of each year based on rankings of NYSE firms with available size measures (price times shares outstanding) in June of that year. AMEX and Nasdaq firms are then place in the corresponding size decile portfolio. Size decile one (small firms) is further partitioned into quintiles based on size rankings for NYSE/AMEX/Nasdaq firms. Portfolio 1A (1E) contains the smallest (largest) 20 percent of firms in size decile one.

Panel B reports book-to-market deciles created in July of each year based on rankings of NYSE firms with available book-to-market data (book value of common equity divided by market value of common equity) in December of the preceding year. AMEX and Nasdaq firms are then placed in the corresponding book-to-market decile portfolio. Decile 1 contains growth firms (low book-to-market); decile 10 contains value firms (high book-to-market).

Decile	Rebalanced Returns (%)			Buy-and-Hold Returns (%)			Difference (%)		
	1 yr.	3 yrs.	5 yrs.	1 yr.	3 yrs.	5 yrs.	1 yr.	3 yrs.	5 yrs.
Panel A: Size Decile Portfolio Returns over Three Investment Periods									
1A	41.4	40.4	36.5	28.9	27.7	26.4	12.6	12.7	10.1
1B	24.1	23.8	23.8	19.3	20.0	20.7	4.8	3.9	3.1
1C	20.0	19.8	19.8	17.8	19.3	19.6	2.2	0.6	0.2
1D	17.8	17.5	18.0	17.1	17.7	18.5	0.7	−0.1	−0.6
1E	17.6	17.1	17.3	17.2	17.9	18.7	0.4	−0.8	−1.4
2	17.6	17.3	17.6	17.7	18.7	19.2	−0.1	−1.4	−1.6
3	18.1	18.0	18.2	18.1	19.1	19.3	0.0	−1.1	−1.0
4	18.2	18.0	18.2	18.1	18.6	19.1	0.1	−0.6	−0.8
5	18.9	18.8	18.7	19.1	18.1	18.3	−0.2	0.6	0.4
6	16.7	16.8	16.6	16.4	17.0	17.3	0.3	−0.2	−0.8
7	16.9	16.9	17.1	16.4	16.4	16.3	0.5	0.5	0.8
8	16.3	16.4	16.3	15.9	16.1	16.1	0.4	0.3	0.2
9	14.7	15.1	15.2	14.3	14.9	15.3	0.4	0.2	−0.1
10	12.8	13.4	14.0	12.4	13.2	13.9	0.4	0.2	0.1
Panel B: Book-to-Market Decile Portfolio Returns over Three Investment Periods									
1	10.6	9.6	9.9	8.3	9.4	11.1	2.2	0.2	−1.2
2	16.8	16.6	16.9	15.7	16.2	17.4	1.1	0.4	−0.5
3	18.2	18.2	18.4	16.8	17.4	17.4	1.4	0.8	1.0
4	19.7	19.0	19.0	18.2	17.9	18.3	1.5	1.1	0.7
5	21.1	20.7	20.8	19.4	19.0	19.3	1.7	1.7	1.5
6	20.6	20.4	20.1	19.7	19.6	19.7	0.9	0.8	0.3
7	21.3	21.6	21.7	21.0	20.9	21.2	0.4	0.6	0.5
8	23.0	23.5	23.2	21.0	22.4	22.3	2.0	1.0	0.9
9	25.2	25.4	25.0	23.4	23.6	23.6	1.9	1.7	1.4
10	29.3	28.4	26.9	25.1	24.5	23.8	4.2	3.9	3.1

returns on the same index. We later document that the use of our buy-and-hold reference portfolios significantly reduces much of the misspecification problems that plague tests of long-run abnormal returns.

II. Calculation of Abnormal Returns

We calculate long-horizon buy-and-hold abnormal returns as:

$$AR_{i\tau} = R_{i\tau} - E(R_{i\tau}), \tag{3}$$

where $AR_{i\tau}$ is the τ period buy-and-hold abnormal return for security i, $R_{i\tau}$ is the τ period buy-and-hold return, and $E(R_{i\tau})$ is the τ period expected return for security i. In this research, we use either: (i) the rebalanced return on a size/book-to-market reference portfolio ($R_{ps\tau}^{\text{reb}}$), (ii) the buy-and-hold return on a size/book-to-market reference portfolio ($R_{ps\tau}^{\text{bh}}$), or (iii) the return on a size and book-to-market matched control firm as a proxy for the expected return for each security.[7]

We use seventy size/book-to-market reference portfolios. These portfolios are formed as follows. Fourteen size reference portfolios are created as described in Section I. Each size portfolio is further partitioned into five book-to-market quintiles (without regard to exchange) in June of year t. We calculate the τ month rebalanced and buy-and-hold return on each of these seventy portfolios as described in Section I. Note that the population mean long-horizon abnormal return calculated using the buy-and-hold reference port-folios is guaranteed to be zero by construction of the abnormal return measure, regardless of the horizon of analysis. Thus, both the new listing and rebalancing biases, which plague tests of long-run abnormal stock returns, are eliminated.

To identify a size and book-to-market matched control firm, we first identify all firms with market value of equity between 70 percent and 130 percent of the market value of equity of the sample firm; from this set of firms we choose the firm with the book-to-market ratio closest to that of the sample firm.

It is well-documented that the common stocks of small firms and firms with high book-to-market ratios earn high rates of return (Fama and French (1992), Chan, Jegadeesh, and Lakonishok (1995), Davis (1994), Barber and Lyon (1997b), Fama and French (1997)). Consequently, we consider portfo-

---

[7] We only report results based on abnormal returns calculated in this manner. Research in financial economics often employs cumulative abnormal returns (summed monthly abnormal returns). However, Barber and Lyon (1997a) argue that cumulative abnormal returns can lead to incorrect inference regarding long-horizon return performance. Nonetheless, the alternative methods that we analyze in this research also work well for the analysis of cumulative abnormal returns when reference portfolios are constructed for each sample observation by averaging only the monthly returns of firms listed in the initial event month (period s). We discuss this issue in detail in Section V.

lios or control firms selected on the basis of firm size and book-to-market ratio. However, we later document that the use of these two characteristics alone can yield misspecified test statistics in certain sampling situations. Nonetheless, the methods that we analyze can be applied in straightforward ways to portfolios formed on alternative characteristics (for example, pre-event return performance, sales growth, industry, or earnings yields). In fact, one of our central messages is that controlling for firm size and book-to-market ratio alone does not guarantee well-specified test statistics.

III. Statistical Tests and Simulation Method

In this section, we describe the statistical tests that we analyze in tests of long-run abnormal returns. We close the section with a description of the simulation method used to evaluate the empirical specification of these tests.

A. Conventional t-statistic

To test the null hypothesis that the mean buy-and-hold abnormal return is equal to zero for a sample of n firms, we first employ a conventional t-statistic:

$$t = \frac{\overline{AR}_\tau}{\sigma(AR_\tau)/\sqrt{n}},\qquad(4)$$

where $\overline{AR}_\tau$ is the sample mean and $\sigma(AR_\tau)$ is the cross-sectional sample standard deviation of abnormal returns for the sample of n firms. We apply this conventional t-statistic to abnormal returns calculated using (i) 70 size/book-to-market rebalanced portfolios, (ii) 70 size/book-to-market buy-and-hold portfolios, and (iii) size/book-to-market matched control firms.

B. Bootstrapped Skewness-Adjusted t-statistic

Barber and Lyon (1997a) document that long-horizon buy-and-hold abnormal returns are positively skewed and that this positive skewness leads to negatively biased t-statistics. Their results are consistent with early investigations by Neyman and Pearson (1929a), and Pearson (1929a, 1929b), which indicate that skewness has a greater effect on the distribution of the t-statistic than does kurtosis and that positive skewness in the distribution from which observations arise results in the sampling distribution of t being negatively skewed. This leads to an inflated significance level for lower-tailed tests (i.e., reported p values will be smaller than they should be) and a loss of power for upper-tailed tests (i.e., reported p values will be too large).

Abnormal returns calculated using the control firm approach or buy-and-hold reference portfolios eliminate the new listing and rebalancing biases. Barber and Lyon (1997a) also document that the control firm approach eliminates the skewness bias. However, to eliminate the skewness bias when long-run abnormal returns are calculated using our buy-and-hold reference portfolios, we advocate the use of a bootstrapped skewness-adjusted t-statistic:

$$t_{sa} = \sqrt{n}\left(S + \frac{1}{3}\hat{\gamma}S^2 + \frac{1}{6n}\hat{\gamma}\right), \qquad (5)$$

where

$$S = \frac{\overline{AR}_\tau}{\sigma(AR_\tau)}, \quad \text{and} \quad \hat{\gamma} = \frac{\sum\limits_{i=1}^{n}(AR_{i\tau} - \overline{AR}_\tau)^3}{n\sigma(AR_\tau)^3}.$$

Note that $\hat{\gamma}$ is an estimate of the coefficient of skewness and $\sqrt{n}S$ is the conventional t-statistic of equation (4). This transformed test statistic, originally developed by Johnson (1978), is based on an Edgeworth Expansion and has been studied more recently by Hall (1992) and Sutton (1993). Sutton concludes that a bootstrapped application of Johnson's statistic "should be preferred to the t test when the parent distribution is asymmetrical, because it reduces the probability of type I error in cases where the t test has an inflated type I error rate and it is more powerful in other situations."

Though we evaluate the specification of the skewness-adjusted t-statistic, our results are consistent with Sutton's (1993) recommendation: Only the bootstrapped application of this skewness-adjusted test statistic yields well-specified test statistics. Bootstrapping the test statistic involves drawing b resamples of size n_b from the original sample. In general, the skewness-adjusted test statistic is calculated in each of these b bootstrapped resamples and the critical values for the transformed test statistic are calculated from the b values of the transformed statistic.

Specifically, the bootstrapping that we employ proceeds as follows: Draw 1,000 bootstrapped resamples from the original sample of size $n_b = n/4$.[8] In each resample, calculate the statistic:

$$t_{sa}^{b} = \sqrt{n_b}\left(S^b + \frac{1}{3}\hat{\gamma}^b S^{b2} + \frac{1}{6n_b}\hat{\gamma}^b\right), \qquad (6)$$

---

[8] Our choice of $n_b = n/4$ is based on empirical analysis. The skewness adjustment results in more conservative test statistics as the size of the bootstrap resample decreases. Bootstrap resample sizes of $n/2$ also yield well-specified inferences, while bootstrap resample sizes of n do not. An analysis of resampling fewer than n observations can be found in Bickel, Gotze, and van Zwet (1997) and Shao (1996).

where

$$S^b = \frac{\overline{AR_\tau^b} - \overline{AR_\tau}}{\sigma^b(AR_\tau)}, \quad \text{and} \quad \hat{\gamma}^b = \frac{\sum_{i=1}^{n_b}(AR_{i\tau}{}^b - \overline{AR_\tau^b})^3}{n_b\sigma^b(AR_\tau)^3}.$$

Thus, $t_{sa}{}^b$, S^b, and $\hat{\gamma}^b$ are the bootstrapped resample analogues of t_{sa}, S, and $\hat{\gamma}$ from the original sample for the $b = 1,\dots,1{,}000$ resamples. We reject the null hypothesis that the mean long-run abnormal return is zero if: $t_{sa} < x_l^*$ or $t_{sa} > x_u^*$. From the 1,000 resamples, we calculate the two critical values (x^*s) for the transformed test statistic (t_{sa}) required to reject the null hypothesis that the mean long-run abnormal return is zero at the α significance level by solving:

$$\Pr[t_{sa}{}^b \le x_l^*] = \Pr[t_{sa}{}^b \ge x_u^*] = \frac{\alpha}{2}.$$

C. Pseudoportfolios to Compute Empirical p value

The final method that we use to evaluate the statistical significance of long-run abnormal stock returns is a method employed by Brock et al. (1992), Ikenberry et al. (1995), Ikenberry, Rankine, and Stice (1996), Lee (1997), and Rau and Vermaelen (1996). In this approach, we generate the empirical distribution of long-run abnormal stock returns under the null hypothesis. Specifically, for each sample firm with an event month t, we randomly select with replacement a firm that is in the same size/book-to-market portfolio in event month t. This process continues until each firm in our original sample is represented by a control firm in this pseudoportfolio. This portfolio contains one randomly drawn firm for each sample firm, matched in time with similar size and book-to-market characteristics. After forming a single pseudoportfolio, we estimate long-run performance using the buy-and-hold size/book-to-market reference portfolios as was done for the original sample. This yields one observation of the abnormal performance obtained from randomly forming a portfolio with the same size and book-to-market characteristics as our original sample. This entire process is repeated until we have 1,000 pseudoportfolios, and thus 1,000 mean abnormal returns observations. These 1,000 mean abnormal return observations are used to approximate the empirical distribution of mean long-run abnormal returns.

Our results based on empirical p values are robust to abnormal returns calculated using the rebalanced reference portfolios. This is predictable because both the sample mean and pseudoportfolio sample means are calculated using the same reference portfolio. Nonetheless, we favor the use of the buy-and-hold reference portfolios, because the abnormal return measure more accurately reflects the excess return earned from investing in sample firms relative to an alternative executable trading strategy. Moreover, the population mean abnormal return is guaranteed to be zero when our buy-and-hold reference portfolios are employed, but the use of rebalanced reference portfolios does not guarantee a population mean abnormal return that is zero.

Unlike the conventional t-statistic or bootstrapped skewness-adjusted t-statistic, in which the null hypothesis is that the mean long-run abnormal return is zero, the null hypothesis tested by approximating the empirical distribution of mean long-run abnormal returns is that the mean long-run abnormal return equals the mean long-run abnormal return for the 1,000 pseudoportfolios. This hypothesis is rejected at the α significance level if: $\overline{AR}_\tau < y_l^*$ or $\overline{AR}_\tau > y_u^*$. The two y^* values are determined by solving

$$\Pr[\overline{AR}_\tau^p \le y_l^*] = \Pr[\overline{AR}_\tau^p \ge y_u^*] = \frac{\alpha}{2},$$

where $\overline{AR}_\tau^p$ are the $p = 1,\dots,1{,}000$ mean long-run abnormal returns generated from the pseudoportfolios.

In Table II we summarize the six statistical methods that we evaluate. The first two methods are the use of a conventional t-statistic when long-run abnormal returns are calculated using rebalanced size/book-to-market portfolios and a size/book-to-market matched control firm. Barber and Lyon (1997a) document that the former statistic is negatively biased in tests of long-run abnormal return, and the latter is well-specified. We report results for these two methods for purposes of comparison. The remaining four methods include: a conventional t-statistic, a skewness-adjusted t-statistic, a bootstrapped skewness-adjusted t-statistic, and empirical p values. All four methods rely on long-run abnormal returns calculated using our buy-and-hold reference portfolios.

D. Simulation Method

To test the specification of the test statistics based on our six statistical methods, we draw 1,000 random samples of n event months without replacement. For each of the 1,000 random samples, the test statistics are computed as described in Section III. If a test is well-specified, $1{,}000\alpha$ tests reject the null hypothesis. A test is conservative if fewer than $1{,}000\alpha$ null hypotheses are rejected and is anticonservative if more than $1{,}000\alpha$ null hypotheses are rejected. Based on this procedure we test the specification of each test statistic at the 1 percent, 5 percent, and 10 percent theoretical levels of significance. A well-specified null hypothesis rejects the null at the theoretical rejection level in favor of the alternative hypothesis of negative (positive) abnormal returns in $1{,}000\alpha/2$ samples. Thus, we separately document rejections of the null hypothesis in favor of the alternative hypothesis that long-run abnormal returns are positive or negative. For example, at the 1 percent theoretical significance level, we document the percentage of cal-

Table II
Summary of Statistical Methods

Method Description	Critical Values Based on	Statistic	Benchmark
Conventional *t*-statistic	Tabulated distribution of *t*-statistic	$t = \dfrac{\overline{AR_\tau}}{\sigma(AR_\tau)/\sqrt{n}}$	Rebalanced size/book-to-market portfolio
Conventional *t*-statistic	Tabulated distribution of *t*-statistic	$t = \dfrac{\overline{AR_\tau}}{\sigma(AR_\tau)/\sqrt{n}}$	Buy-and-hold size/book-to-market control firm
Conventional *t*-statistic	Tabulated distribution of *t*-statistic	$t = \dfrac{\overline{AR_\tau}}{\sigma(AR_\tau)/\sqrt{n}}$	Buy-and-hold size/book-to-market portfolios
Skewness-adjusted *t*-statistic	Tabulated distribution of *t*-statistic	$t_{sa} = \sqrt{n}\left(S + \dfrac{1}{3}\hat{\gamma}S^2 + \dfrac{1}{6n}\hat{\gamma}\right)$	Buy-and-hold size/book-to-market portfolios
Bootstrapped skewness-adjusted *t*-statistic	Empirical distribution of *t*-statistic from bootstrapped resamples	$t^b_{sa} = \sqrt{n_b}\left(S^b + \dfrac{1}{3}\hat{\gamma}^b S^{b2} + \dfrac{1}{6n_b}\hat{\gamma}^b\right)$	Buy-and-hold size/book-to-market portfolios
Empirical *p* value	Empirical distribution of sample means from pseudoportfolios	Not applicable	Buy-and-hold size/book-to-market portfolios

culated *t*-statistics that are less than the theoretical cumulative density function of the *t*-statistic at 0.5 percent and greater than the theoretical cumulative density function at 99.5 percent.

IV. Results

We begin with a discussion of the results in random samples, followed by a discussion of results in nonrandom samples. We consider nonrandom samples based on firm size, book-to-market ratio, pre-event return performance, calendar clustering of event dates, and industry clustering. We also discuss the impact of cross-sectional dependence on test statistics.

A. Random Samples

A.1. Specification

The first set of results is based on 1,000 random samples of 200 event months. The specification of the six statistical methods at one-, three-, and five-year horizons is presented in Table III. Two of our results are consistent with those reported in Barber and Lyon (1997a). First, *t*-statistics based on rebalanced size/book-to-market portfolios have a severe negative bias. Second, the *t*-statistics based on the buy-and-hold size/book-to-market reference portfolio are also negatively biased, though the magnitude of the bias is much less severe because the use of the buy-and-hold reference portfolios alleviates the new listing and rebalancing biases. The remaining negative bias can be attributed to the severe positive skewness of long-run abnormal returns. These two results indicate that the careful construction of our reference portfolios reduces much of the misspecification in test statistics. Left unresolved, however, is a means of controlling the skewness bias.

Though the skewness-adjusted *t*-statistic improves the specification of the test statistic, it too is negatively biased. However, when the critical values for rejection of the null hypothesis are determined using the bootstrapped procedure described in Section III, the misspecification is markedly reduced. Additionally, test statistics based on empirical *p* values derived from the distribution of mean long-run abnormal stock returns in pseudoportfolios also yield tests that are correctly specified in random samples. In sum, three of our six methods yield tests that are well-specified in random samples: a conventional *t*-statistic using size/book-to-market matched control firms, a bootstrapped skewness-adjusted test statistic using buy-and-hold size/book-to-market reference portfolios, and empirical *p* values derived from the distribution of mean long-run abnormal stock returns in pseudoportfolios.

The Central Limit Theorem guarantees that if the measures of abnormal returns in the cross section of firms are independent and identically distributed drawings from finite variance distributions, the distribution of the mean abnormal return measure converges to normality as the number of firms in the sample increases. Thus, we expect that the conventional *t*-statistic will

Table III
Specification (Size) of Alternative Test Statistics Using Buy-and-Hold Abnormal Returns (AR) in Random Samples

The numbers presented in this table represent the percentage of 1,000 random samples of 200 firms that reject the null hypothesis of no annual (Panel A), three-year (Panel B), and five-year (Panel C) buy-and-hold abnormal return (AR) at the theoretical significance levels of 1 percent, 5 percent, or 10 percent in favor of the alternative hypothesis of a significantly negative AR (i.e., calculated *p* value is less than 0.5 percent at the 1 percent significance level) or a significantly positive AR (calculated *p* value is greater than 99.5 percent at the 1 percent significance level). The alternative statistics and benchmarks are described in detail in the main text.

Statistic	Benchmark	Two-Tailed Theoretical Significance Level					
		1%		5%		10%	
		Theoretical Cumulative Density Function (%)					
		0.5	99.5	2.5	97.5	5.0	95.0
Panel A: Annual ARs							
t-statistic	Rebalanced size/book-to-market portfolio	3.6*	0.0	10.1*	0.1	16.3*	0.7
t-statistic	Buy-and-hold size/book-to-market portfolio	1.2*	0.0	4.9*	0.9	8.2*	2.4
Skewness-adjusted t-statistic	Buy-and-hold size/book-to-market portfolio	1.0	0.3	3.7*	2.2	7.1*	4.7
t-statistic	Size/book-to-market control firm	0.3	0.0	2.3	2.0	5.3	4.1
Bootstrapped skewness-adjusted t-statistic	Buy-and-hold size/book-to-market portfolio	0.2	0.6	2.1	2.7	5.3	4.6
Empirical p value	Buy-and-hold size/book-to-market portfolio	0.4	0.9	2.6	2.5	5.0	4.8
Panel B: Three-Year ARs							
t-statistic	Rebalanced size/book-to-market portfolio	10.6*	0.0	21.6*	0.0	30.5*	0.1
t-statistic	Buy-and-hold size/book-to-market portfolio	2.7*	0.0	6.8*	0.6	9.8*	2.6
Skewness-adjusted t-statistic	Buy-and-hold size/book-to-market portfolio	2.1*	0.3	5.3*	2.2	8.7*	5.2
t-statistic	Size/book-to-market control firm	0.3	0.2	3.2	1.2	5.5	3.0
Bootstrapped skewness-adjusted t-statistic	Buy-and-hold size/book-to-market portfolio	0.8	0.8	3.6	3.1	5.9	5.5
Empirical p value	Buy-and-hold size/book-to-market portfolio	0.8	0.9	3.4	3.1	6.8*	5.9
Panel C: Five-Year ARs							
t-statistic	Rebalanced size/book-to-market portfolio	11.7*	0.0	23.7*	0.0	33.2*	0.2
t-statistic	Buy-and-hold size/book-to-market portfolio	2.4*	0.0	6.1*	0.5	10.5*	1.6
Skewness-adjusted t-statistic	Buy-and-hold size/book-to-market portfolio	1.4*	0.4	4.4*	1.7	8.2*	4.8
t-statistic	Size/book-to-market control firm	0.1	0.1	3.0	1.9	5.4	3.9
Bootstrapped skewness-adjusted t-statistic	Buy-and-hold size/book-to-market portfolio	0.6	1.2*	2.2	3.1	5.0	5.7
Empirical p value	Buy-and-hold size/book-to-market portfolio	0.2	1.5*	2.7	3.7*	4.9	6.3

*Significantly different from the theoretical significance level at the 1 percent level, one-sided binomial test statistic.

be well specified if the sample under consideration is sufficiently large. We consider this issue by calculating the empirical rejection rates in 1,000 simulations of sample sizes ranging from 200 to 4,000. As predicted for a positively skewed distribution, the negative bias in the conventional t-statistic declines with sample size and is well specified in samples of size 4,000. In contrast the three alternative methods are well specified in all of the sample sizes considered.

A.2. Power

To evaluate the power of the three methods that yield reasonably well-specified test statistics in random samples, we conduct the following experiment. For each sampled firm in our 1,000 simulations, we add a constant level of abnormal return to the calculated abnormal return. We document the empirical rejection rates at the 5 percent theoretical significance level of the null hypothesis that the mean sample long-run abnormal return is zero across 1,000 simulations at induced levels of abnormal returns ranging from -20 percent to $+20$ percent in increments of 5 percent. The results of this experiment are depicted graphically in Figure 1. As anticipated, the bootstrapped skewness-adjusted t-statistic and empirical p values both yield improved power in random samples relative to the control firm approach

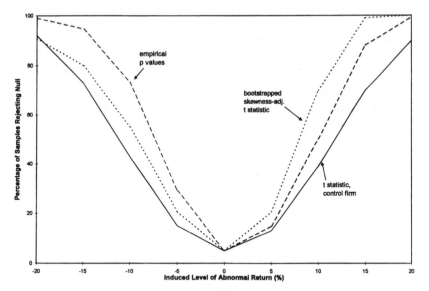

Figure 1. The power of test statistics in random samples. The percentage of 1,000 random samples of 200 firms rejecting the null hypothesis of no annual buy-and-hold abnormal return at various induced levels of abnormal return (horizontal axis) based on control firm method, bootstrapped skewness-adjusted t-statistic, and empirical p values.

advocated by Barber and Lyon (1997a). For example, in our 1,000 random samples of 200 firms, a +10 percent (-10 percent) abnormal return added to each of our sampled firms enables us to reject the null hypothesis in 43 percent (39 percent) when conventional *t*-statistics and the control firm method are used, 55 percent (70 percent) when the bootstrapped skewness-adjusted *t*-statistics and buy-and-hold reference portfolios are used, and 73 percent (50 percent) when empirical *p* values and buy-and-hold reference portfolios are used. The power advantage of the bootstrapped skewness-adjusted *t*-statistic and empirical *p* values is evident in all sampling situations that we analyze (differing sample size, horizons, and nonrandom samples).

B. Nonrandom Samples

Though our alternative methods are generally well specified and improve power for tests of long-run abnormal returns in random samples, we are also interested in how our proposed statistical methods work in nonrandom samples. Though we do not anticipate that our methods will work well in all sampling situations, a thorough understanding of the origin and magnitude of misspecification when sampling biases are present is important in developing a well-reasoned test statistic for a particular sample situation.

In general, to evaluate the impact of sampling biases we randomly draw 1,000 samples of 200 firms from a subset of our population. We then evaluate the empirical specification of four test statistics in these biased samples: (1) conventional *t*-statistic based on buy-and-hold reference portfolios, (2) conventional *t*-statistic based on size/book-to-market matched control firms, (3) bootstrapped skewness-adjusted *t*-statistic based on buy-and-hold reference portfolios, and (4) empirical *p* values based on buy-and-hold reference portfolios. We present results based on a conventional *t*-statistic in tables for purposes of illustration, though we know that it will be negatively biased in most sampling situations because of the severe positive skewness in the underlying distribution. In contrast, methods 2 through 4 are generally well-specified in random samples.

B.1. Firm Size

To assess the impact of size-based sampling biases on our statistical methods, we randomly draw 1,000 samples separately from the largest size decile (decile 10, Table I, Panel A) and smallest size decile (portfolios 1A to 1E in Table I, Panel A). The specifications of the four statistical methods in these samples are presented in Table IV. These results indicate that our three alternative methods are better specified than the conventional *t*-statistic based on buy-and-hold size/book-to-market reference portfolios.

B.2. Book-to-Market Ratio

To assess the impact of book-to-market based sampling biases on our statistical methods, we randomly draw 1,000 samples separately from the highest book-to-market decile (decile 10, Table I, Panel B) and smallest book-to-

Table IV
Specification (Size) of Alternative Test Statistics in Size-Based Samples

The numbers presented in this table represent the percentage of 1,000 random samples of 200 large (Panel A) or small (Panel B) firms that reject the null hypothesis of no one-, three-, and five-year buy-and-hold abnormal return (AR) at the theoretical significance level of 5 percent in favor of the alternative hypothesis of a significantly negative AR (i.e., calculated p value is less than 2.5 percent at the 5 percent significance level) or a significantly positive AR (calculated p value is greater than 97.5 percent at the 5 percent significance level). The statistics and benchmarks are described in detail in the main text.

Statistic	Benchmark	1 Year		3 Years		5 Years	
		2.5	97.5	2.5	97.5	2.5	97.5
		Theoretical Cumulative Density Function (%)					
		2.5	97.5	2.5	97.5	2.5	97.5
Panel A: Samples of Large Firms							
t-statistic	Buy-and-hold size/book-to-market portfolio	4.2*	1.2	3.8*	2.0	4.5*	1.6
t-statistic	Size/book-to-market control firm	3.9*	1.2	2.8	2.6	2.2	3.9*
Bootstrapped skewness-adjusted t-statistic	Buy-and-hold size/book-to-market portfolio	2.8	2.0	2.2	2.8	2.3	2.6
Empirical p value	Buy-and-hold size/book-to-market portfolio	3.5	3.6	2.5	3.3	3.6	2.1
Panel B: Samples of Small Firms							
t-statistic	Buy-and-hold size/book-to-market portfolio	5.7*	0.6	6.3*	0.3	8.0*	1.3
t-statistic	Size/book-to-market control firm	2.8	2.7	2.4	1.8	3.0	2.0
Bootstrapped skewness-adjusted t-statistic	Buy-and-hold size/book-to-market portfolio	2.5	2.8	2.4	2.8	2.8	3.3
Empirical p value	Buy-and-hold size/book-to-market portfolio	2.7	2.6	2.2	2.6	3.4	3.5

*Significantly different from the theoretical significance level at the 1 percent level, one-sided binomial test statistic.

market decile (decile 1, Table I, Panel B). The specifications of the four statistical methods in these samples are presented in Table V. Among firms with low book-to-market ratios, only the size/book-to-market matched control firm approach yields test statistics that are reasonably well specified.[9]

These results yield our first admonition regarding the use of reference portfolios to calculate long-run abnormal stock returns. Our methods assume that all firms constituting a particular portfolio have the same expected return. Recall that our reference portfolios are formed first by sorting firms into deciles on the basis of firm size and then by sorting these deciles into quintiles on the basis of book-to-market ratios. However, inspection of Table I, Panel B, reveals that there is a large difference between the returns on the bottom two book-to-market portfolios. Thus, when we sample from the lowest book-to-market *decile*, but (roughly) match these firms to the average return of firms from the lowest book-to-market *quintile*, the result is a negatively biased measure of mean abnormal returns and negatively biased test statistics.

This problem creates the negative bias in the methods that rely on the buy-and-hold reference portfolios (the bootstrapped skewness-adjusted *t*-statistic and empirical *p* values). However, the control firm approach alleviates this problem by matching sample firms reasonably well on book-to-market ratio. Reference portfolios formed based on a finer partition of book-to-market ratio could also alleviate the negative bias.

In contrast to the results in samples of firms with low book-to-market ratios, our three alternative methods yield reasonably well-specified test statistics among samples of firms with high book-to-market ratios. Unlike the bottom two deciles formed on the basis of book-to-market ratios, the top two deciles have similar rates of return.

B.3. Pre-Event Return Performance

A common characteristic of firms included in an event study is a period of unusually high or low stock returns preceding the event of interest. For example, equity issuance is generally preceded by a period of high stock returns, and share repurchases are generally preceded by a period of low stock returns. Moreover, Jegadeesh and Titman (1993) document persistence in stock returns, which Fama and French (1996) are unable to explain well using factors related to firm size and book-to-market ratio. Consequently, we anticipate an important factor to consider in long-run event studies to be the prior return performance of sample firms.

We calculate the preceding six-month buy-and-hold return on all firms in each month from July 1973 through December 1994. We then rank all firms on the basis of this six-month return and form deciles on the basis of the

---

[9] The negative bias at the five-year horizon is likely a result of random sampling variation. We do not observe this result at five-year horizons and the 1 percent and 10 percent theoretical significance levels.

Table V

Specification (Size) of Alternative Test Statistics in Book-to-Market Based Samples

The numbers presented in this table represent the percentage of 1,000 random samples of 200 firms with low (Panel A) or high (Panel B) book-to-market ratios that reject the null hypothesis of no one-, three-, and five-year buy-and-hold abnormal return (AR) at the theoretical significance level of 5 percent in favor of the alternative hypothesis of a significantly negative AR (i.e., calculated p value is less than 2.5 percent at the 5 percent significance level) or a significantly positive AR (calculated p value is greater than 97.5 percent at the 5 percent significance level). The statistics and benchmarks are described in detail in the main text.

		Horizon					
		1 Year		3 Years		5 Years	
		Theoretical Cumulative Density Function (%)					
Statistic	Benchmark	2.5	97.5	2.5	97.5	2.5	97.5
	Panel A: Samples of Firms with Low Book-to-Market Ratios						
t-statistic	Buy-and-hold size/book-to-market portfolio	7.7*	0.4	9.1*	0.2	11.2*	0.1
t-statistic	Size/book-to-market control firm	2.8	1.5	3.1	1.6	3.8*	2.3
Bootstrapped skewness-adjusted t-statistic	Buy-and-hold size/book-to-market portfolio	3.9*	2.7	3.8*	1.8	4.0*	1.2
Empirical p value	Buy-and-hold size/book-to-market portfolio	4.8*	2.1	5.9*	2.6	6.7*	1.3
	Panel B: Samples of Firms with High Book-to-Market Ratios						
t-statistic	Buy-and-hold size/book-to-market portfolio	5.8*	0.3	5.0*	0.4	5.7*	0.9
t-statistic	Size/book-to-market control firm	2.5	3.2	1.5	4.1*	1.7	2.1
Bootstrapped skewness-adjusted t-statistic	Buy-and-hold size/book-to-market portfolio	3.0	2.1	3.2	2.1	2.5	2.7
Empirical p value	Buy-and-hold size/book-to-market portfolio	3.6	1.9	2.8	2.0	2.9	2.6

*Significantly different from the theoretical significance level at the 1 percent level, one-sided binomial test statistic.

rankings in each month. Finally, we separately draw 1,000 samples of 200 firms from the high-return decile and the low-return decile.

The results of this analysis are presented in Table VI. For firms with high six-month pre-event returns, all test statistics are positively biased at an annual horizon, but negatively biased at a three- or five-year horizon. The annual results are consistent with those of Jegadeesh and Titman (1993), who document return persistence for up to one year followed by significant reversals. These reversals are sufficiently large to render test statistics at three- and five-year horizons negatively biased. For firms with low six-month pre-event returns, all test statistics are negatively biased at an annual horizon. The magnitude of the negative bias declines at a three-year horizon and is virtually nonexistent at a five-year horizon.

These results indicate that an important dimension to consider, one that is commonly overlooked in tests of long-run abnormal returns, is the pre-event return performance. Though we do not analyze reference portfolios formed on the basis of prior return performance, the methods used to construct our size/book-to-market portfolios could be applied to create portfolios formed on the basis of recent return performance. Similarly, we anticipate that matching sample firms to firms of similar pre-event return performance would also control well for the misspecification documented here. Lee (1997) and Ikenberry et al. (1996) employ sensible variations of the empirical *p*-value approach which control for pre-event returns.

B.4. Industry Clustering

Assume that expected returns vary by industry and we have an imprecise asset pricing model. We would reject the null hypothesis of zero long-run abnormal returns in favor of both positive and negative long-run abnormal returns too often. We assess the impact of industry clustering of sample firms by drawing 1,000 samples of 200 firms such that each of the 200 firms in a particular sample has the same two-digit SIC code. This sampling procedure involves two steps. First, we randomly select a two-digit SIC code; second, we draw a sample of 200 firms from this two-digit SIC code. If the two-digit SIC code contains fewer than 200 firms over our period of analysis, we complete the sample with firms from a second, randomly selected, two-digit SIC code.[10] The results of this analysis are presented in Table VII.

---

[10] The same firm is allowed to appear more than once within a particular sample of 200 firms. However, multiple occurrences of the same firm are not allowed to have overlapping periods for the calculation of returns. For example, if an event date of January 1981 were selected for IBM in our analysis of annual abnormal returns, subsequent randomly selected observations would preclude the sampling of IBM from February 1980 through November 1982. Thus, our analysis isolates the impact of sampling from one industry rather than the impact of overlapping returns, which we discuss in the next section.

Table VI
Specification (Size) of Alternative Test Statistics in Samples Based on Pre-Event Return Performance

The numbers presented in this table represent the percentage of 1,000 random samples of 200 firms with high six-month pre-event returns (Panel A) or low six-month pre-event returns (Panel B) that reject the null hypothesis of no one-, three-, and five-year buy-and-hold abnormal return (AR) at the theoretical significance level of 5 percent in favor of the alternative hypothesis of a significantly negative AR (i.e., calculated p value is less than 2.5 percent at the 5 percent significance level) or a significantly positive AR (calculated p value is greater than 97.5 percent at the 5 percent significance level). The statistics and benchmarks are described in detail in the main text.

Statistic	Benchmark	Horizon					
		1 Year		3 Years		5 Years	
		Theoretical Cumulative Density Function (%)					
		2.5	97.5	2.5	97.5	2.5	97.5
Panel A: Samples of Firms with High Six-Month Pre-Event Returns							
t-statistic	Buy-and-hold size/book-to-market portfolio	1.1	3.8*	14.4*	0.1	20.8*	0.1
t-statistic	Size/book-to-market control firm	0.4	6.3*	4.5*	1.3	7.3*	0.6
Bootstrapped skewness-adjusted t-statistic	Buy-and-hold size/book-to-market port.	0.4	6.8*	7.4*	0.4	9.1*	0.4
Empirical p value	Buy-and-hold size/book-to-market portfolio	0.4	5.2*	10.4*	0.6	14.8*	0.3
Panel B: Samples of Firms with Low Six-Month Pre-Event Returns							
t-statistic	Buy-and-hold size/book-to-market portfolio	21.0*	0.1	8.5*	0.3	5.2*	0.4
t-statistic	Size/book-to-market control firm	11.0*	0.3	5.0*	0.8	3.1	1.2
Bootstrapped skewness-adjusted t-statistic	Buy-and-hold size/book-to-market portfolio	10.3*	0.9	3.0	2.6	1.6	3.0
Empirical p value	Buy-and-hold size/book-to-market portfolio	22.1*	2.3	6.2*	4.3*	3.4	3.8*

*Significantly different from the theoretical significance level at the 1 percent level, one-sided binomial test statistic.

Table VII

Specification (Size) of Alternative Test Statistics in Samples with Industry Clustering

The numbers presented in this table represent the percentage of 1,000 random samples of 200 firms with a common two-digit SIC code that reject the null hypothesis of no one-, three-, and five-year buy-and-hold abnormal return (AR) at the theoretical significance level of 5 percent in favor of the alternative hypothesis of a significantly negative AR (i.e., calculated p value is less than 2.5 percent at the 5 percent significance level) or a significantly positive AR (calculated p value is greater than 97.5 percent at the 5 percent significance level). If 200 firms cannot be drawn from the same two-digit SIC code, a second two-digit SIC code is used to fill the sample of 200 firms. The statistics and benchmarks are described in detail in the main text.

		Horizon					
		1 Year		3 Years		5 Years	
Statistic	Benchmark	2.5	97.5	2.5	97.5	2.5	97.5
		Theoretical Cumulative Density Function (%)					
t-statistic	Buy-and-hold size/book-to-market portfolio	9.5*	3.3	13.2*	8.2*	20.4*	11.0*
t-statistic	Size/book-to-market control firm	2.8	4.7*	6.1*	7.6*	7.8*	10.6*
Bootstrapped skewness-adjusted t-statistic	Buy-and-hold size/book-to-market portfolio	6.4*	6.0*	7.7*	10.7*	10.5*	15.9*
Empirical p value	Buy-and-hold size/book-to-market portfolio	6.9*	5.1*	9.4*	9.4*	14.2*	12.9*

*Significantly different from the theoretical significance level at the 1 percent level, one-sided binomial test statistic.

Our analysis reveals that controlling for size and book-to-market alone is not sufficient when samples are drawn from a single two-digit SIC code. All of the empirical methods analyzed yield empirical rejection levels that exceed theoretical rejection levels. Auxiliary analyses (not reported in a table) reveal that this misspecification disappears when samples are evenly distributed among four or more two-digit SIC codes. Thus, only extreme industry clustering leads to the misspecification that we document.

C. Cross-Sectional Dependence of Sample Observations

Brav (1997) argues that cross-sectional dependence in sample observations can lead to misspecified test statistics. Cross-sectional dependence inflates test statistics because the number of sample firms overstates the number of independent observations. To assess the magnitude of the problem of cross-sectional dependence we consider two extreme sample situations: (1) calendar clustering and (2) overlapping return calculations.

C.1. Calendar Clustering

We make the reasonable assumption that the contemporaneous returns of firms are more likely to be cross-sectionally related than returns from different periods. If true, the problem of cross-sectional dependence will be most severe when all sample firms share the same event date. We assess the impact of calendar clustering of event dates by drawing 1,000 samples of 200 firms such that all of the 200 firms in a particular sample have the same event date. The results of this analysis, presented in Table VIII, indicate that the three alternative methods we analyze control well for calendar clustering of event dates, though there is some evidence of a positive bias when the size/book-to-market matched control firm method is used at an annual horizon.

Auxiliary analyses (not reported in a table) indicate that when samples are composed of small firms, large firms, low book-to-market firms, or high book-to-market firms the three alternative methods yield test statistics with rejection levels similar to those reported in Table IV and Table V, even when all sample firms share a common event date. When samples are composed of firms from a single industry or of firms with unusually high or low pre-event returns, the empirical rejection rates of the three alternative methods are approximately 50 percent greater than those reported in Table VI and Table VII. In sum, the three alternative methods that we analyze control reasonably well for cross-sectional dependence that arises from the relation between firm size, book-to-market ratios, and returns. However, when samples are calendar clustered and exhibit unusual pre-event return performance or industry clustering, these methods yield misspecified test statistics. This misspecification can be attributed to cross-sectional dependence and/or the use of a poor asset pricing model—an issue that we discuss in more detail in the conclusion.

Table VIII

Specification (Size) of Alternative Test Statistics in Samples with a Common Event Month (Calendar Clustering)

The numbers presented in this table represent the percentage of 1,000 random samples of 200 firms with a common event month that reject the null hypothesis of no one-, three-, and five-year buy-and-hold abnormal return (AR) at the theoretical significance level of 5 percent in favor of the alternative hypothesis of a significantly negative AR (i.e., calculated p value is less than 2.5 percent at the 5 percent significance level) or a significantly positive AR (calculated p value is greater than 97.5 percent at the 5 percent significance level). The statistics and benchmarks are described in detail in the main text.

		Horizon					
		1 Year		3 Years		5 Years	
		Theoretical Cumulative Density Function (%)					
Statistic	Benchmark	2.5	97.5	2.5	97.5	2.5	97.5
t-statistic	Buy-and-hold size/book-to-market portfolio	4.5*	1.3	3.8*	0.9	7.2*	0.6
t-statistic	Size/book-to-market control firm	2.8	5.9*	2.5	1.9	2.0	1.4
Bootstrapped skewness-adjusted t-statistic	Buy-and-hold size/book-to-market portfolio	3.0	3.4	1.8	2.7	3.1	2.5
Empirical p value	Buy-and-hold size/book-to-market portfolio	3.1	3.3	1.9	2.2	2.8	2.8

*Significantly different from the theoretical significance level at the 1 percent level, one-sided binomial test statistic.

C.2. Overlapping Return Calculations

A common problem in event studies that analyze long-run abnormal returns is overlapping periods of return calculation for the same firm—for example, Microsoft's common stock split in April 1990, June 1991, and June 1992. Clearly, the three- or five-year returns calculated relative to each of these event months are not independent because these returns share several months of overlapping returns. This is the most severe form of cross-sectional dependence that a researcher could encounter in an event study of long-run abnormal stock returns.

To assess the impact of overlapping return calculations on tests of long-run abnormal stock returns, we proceed in two steps. First, we randomly sample 100 firms from our population. Second, for these *same* 100 firms, we randomly select a second event month that is within $\tau - 1$ periods of the original event month (either before or after), where τ is the period over which returns are compounded (12, 36, or 60 months). Combining these two sets of 100 observations yields one sample of 200 event months for the 100 firms. We repeat this procedure 1,000 times. The results of this analysis are reported in Table IX.

As anticipated, the lack of independence generated by overlapping returns yields misspecified test statistics. Note that these samples are random with respect to firm size, book-to-market ratio, pre-event return performance, and industry. Thus, this experiment best demonstrates the problem of cross-sectional dependence discussed in Brav (1997), since it is unlikely that a poor model of asset pricing is leading to overrejection in these samples. Cowan and Sergeant (1996) also document that overlapping return calculations yield misspecified test statistics in random samples when the horizon of analysis is long (three or five years) and sample sizes are large, since the probability of samples containing overlapping return calculations in these sampling situations is large. The only ready solution to this source of bias in event studies of long-run buy-and-hold abnormal stock returns is to purge the sample of observations of overlapping returns. For example, in their analysis of seasoned equity offerings, Loughran and Ritter (1995) and Speiss and Affleck-Graves (1995) require sample firms to have a five-year pre-event period with no equity issuance. Speiss and Affleck-Graves (1996) impose an analogous requirement in their analysis of debt issuance. This pre-event screen would solve the overlapping return problem that we document here.

C.3. Adjustments to the Variance-Covariance Matrix

Conceptually, a researcher could adjust test statistics for cross-sectional dependence if for a sample of n firms an appropriate $n \times n$ variance-covariance matrix could be estimated. We investigated several possible methods for estimating the variance-covariance matrix of event-time abnormal returns, which we discuss in the Appendix. In short, though these methods reduce the misspecification in samples with overlapping return calculations, they do not eliminate the problem of cross-sectional dependence.

Table IX
Specification (Size) of Alternative Test Statistics in Samples with Overlapping Returns

The analysis is this table is based on 1,000 random samples of 200 event month for 100 firms. The sampling is conducted in two steps. First, 100 event months are randomly selected. For each of these 100 event month, a second event month is randomly selected within τ periods of the original event month (either before or after) to guarantee the presence of overlapping returns. The numbers presented in this table represent the percentage of the 1,000 random samples that reject the null hypothesis of no one-, three-, and five-year buy-and-hold abnormal return (AR) at the theoretical significance level of 5 percent in favor of the alternative hypothesis of a significantly negative AR (i.e., calculated p value is less than 2.5 percent at the 5 percent significance level) or a significantly positive AR (calculated p value is greater than 97.5 percent at the 5 percent significance level). The statistics and benchmarks are described in detail in the main text.

Statistic	Benchmark	Horizon					
		1 Year		3 Years		5 Years	
		2.5	97.5	2.5	97.5	2.5	97.5
		Theoretical Cumulative Density Function (%)					
t-statistic	Buy-and-hold size/book-to-market portfolio	8.8*	3.4	9.5*	2.4	10.6*	1.9
t-statistic	Size/book-to-market control firm	4.5*	5.2*	4.5*	3.4	4.3*	4.1*
Bootstrapped skewness-adjusted t-statistic	Buy-and-hold size/book-to-market portfolio	5.7*	6.3*	5.5*	5.2*	6.1*	6.7*
Empirical p value	Buy-and-hold size/book-to-market portfolio	6.5*	5.1*	6.1*	5.3*	5.1*	4.8*

*Significantly different from the theoretical significance level at the 1 percent level, one-sided binomial test statistic.

V. The Use of Cumulative Abnormal Returns and Calendar-Time Portfolio Methods

The analysis to this point has focused on buy-and-hold abnormal returns. The analysis of buy-and-hold abnormal returns is warranted if a researcher is interested in answering the question of whether sample firms earned abnormal stock returns over a particular horizon of analysis. A related, but slightly different question, can be answered by analyzing cumulative abnormal returns or mean monthly abnormal returns over a long-horizon (or, equivalently, mean monthly returns): Do sample firms persistently earn abnormal monthly returns? Though correlated, cumulative abnormal returns are a biased predictor of buy-and-hold abnormal returns (Barber and Lyon (1997a)). Nonetheless, cumulative or mean monthly abnormal returns might be employed because they are less skewed and therefore less problematic statistically.

A. Cumulative Abnormal Returns

We reestimate many of our results using cumulative abnormal returns, but in the interest of parsimony summarize the major results of the analysis here. First, in random samples all of the methods that yield well-specified test statistics for buy-and-hold abnormal returns also yield well-specified test statistics for cumulative abnormal returns: the control firm approach, the bootstrapped skewness-adjusted t-statistic, and the pseudoportfolio approach.

Second, since cumulative abnormal returns are less skewed than buy-and-hold abnormal returns, conventional t-statistics also yield well-specified test statistics. It is important to note that conventional t-statistics are only well specified when reference portfolios are purged of the new listing or survivor bias. Thus, the τ-period cumulative abnormal return ($CAR_{i\tau}$) for firm i beginning in period s is calculated as:

$$CAR_{i\tau} = \sum_{t=s}^{s+\tau} \left[R_{it} - \frac{1}{n_t^s} \sum_{j=1}^{n_t^s} R_{jt} \right], \tag{7}$$

where R_{it} is the simple monthly return for sample firm i, R_{jt} is the simple monthly return for the $j = 1,\ldots,n_t^s$ firms that are in the same size/book-to-market reference portfolio as firm i, which are also publicly traded in *both* period s and t. Cumulative abnormal returns based on conventional rebalanced size/book-to-market portfolios yield positively biased test statistics (Kothari and Warner (1997), Barber and Lyon (1997a)).

Third, cumulative abnormal returns are affected by sampling biases (size, book-to-market, pre-event returns, calendar clustering, industry clustering, and overlapping returns) in an analogous fashion to buy-and-hold abnormal returns.

B. Calendar-Time Portfolio Methods

Loughran and Ritter (1995), Brav and Gompers (1997), and Brav et al. (1995) employ the Fama–French three-factor model to analyze returns on calendar-time portfolios of firms that issue equity. Jaffe (1974) and Mandelker (1974) use variations of this calendar-time portfolio method. We consider two variations of calendar-time portfolio methods: one based on the use of the three-factor model developed by Fama and French (1993) and one based on the use of mean monthly calendar-time abnormal returns.

The calendar-time portfolio methods offer some advantages over tests that employ either cumulative or buy-and-hold abnormal returns. First, this approach eliminates the problem of cross-sectional dependence among sample firms because the returns on sample firms are aggregated into a single portfolio. Second, the calendar-time portfolio methods yield more robust test statistics in nonrandom samples. Nonetheless, in nonrandom samples, the calendar-time portfolio methods often yield misspecified test statistics.

B.1. The Fama–French Three-Factor Model and Calendar-Time Portfolios

Assume the event period of interest is five years. For each calendar month, calculate the return on a portfolio composed of firms that had an event (e.g., issued equity) within the last five years of the calendar month. The calendar-time return on this portfolio is used to estimate the following regression:

$$R_{pt} - R_{ft} = \alpha_i + \beta_i(R_{mt} - R_{ft}) + s_i SMB_t + h_i HML_t + \epsilon_{it}, \tag{8}$$

where R_{pt} is the simple monthly return on the calendar-time portfolio (either equally weighted or value-weighted), R_{ft} is the monthly return on three-month Treasury bills, R_{mt} is the return on a value-weighted market index, SMB_t is the difference in the returns of value-weighted portfolios of small stocks and big stocks, HML_t is the difference in the returns of value-weighted portfolios of high book-to-market stocks and low book-to-market stocks.[11] The regression yields parameter estimates of α_i, β_i, s_i, and h_i. The error term in the regression is denoted by ϵ_{it}. The estimate of the intercept term (α_i) provides a test of the null hypothesis that the mean monthly excess return on the calendar-time portfolio is zero.[12]

---

[11] The construction of these factors is discussed in detail in Fama and French (1993). We thank Kenneth French for providing us with these data.

[12] The error term in this regression may be heteroskedastic, since the number of securities in the calendar-time portfolio varies from one month to the next. We find that this heteroskedasticity does not significantly affect the specification of the intercept test in random samples. However, a correction for heteroskedasticity can be performed using weighted least squares estimation, where the weighting factor is based on the number of securities in the portfolio in each calendar month.

We evaluate the empirical specification of the calendar-time portfolio approach by randomly drawing 1,000 samples of 200 event months. For each sample, we estimate an equally weighted and value-weighted (by market capitalization) calendar-time portfolio return, which assumes sample firms are held in the portfolio for either 12, 36, or 60 months after the randomly selected event month. The number of firms in the calendar-time portfolio varies from month to month. If in a particular calendar month there are no firms in the portfolio, that month is dropped when estimating equation (8). We also analyze the specification of the calendar-time portfolio approach in nonrandom samples. The results of these analyses are presented in Table X.

The calendar-time portfolio methods are well specified in random samples. However, the calendar-time portfolio methods are generally misspecified in nonrandom samples. For example, the calendar-time portfolio method does not perform as well as test statistics based on reference portfolios in samples with size-based or book-to-market-based biases. On the other hand, the calendar-time portfolio method performs well when cross-sectional dependence is severe (e.g., when return calculations are overlapping). Note also that the calendar-time portfolio approach reduces, but does not eliminate, misspecification when samples are drawn from a single industry. This result indicates that the misspecification that results from industry clustering is at least partially attributable to the bad model problem. In sum, the calendar-time portfolio method controls well for the problem of cross-sectional dependence, but remains sensitive to the bad model problem.

B.2. Mean Monthly Calendar-Time Abnormal Returns

Assume the event period of interest is five years. For each calendar month, calculate the abnormal return (AR_{it}) for each security using the returns on the seventy size/book-to-market reference portfolios (R_{pt}):

$$AR_{it} = R_{it} - R_{pt}.$$

In each calendar month t, calculate a mean abnormal return (MAR_t) across firms in the portfolio:

$$MAR_t = \sum_{i=1}^{n_t} x_{it} AR_{it},$$

where n_t is the number of firms in the portfolio in month t. The weight, x_{it}, is $1/n_t$ when abnormal returns are equally weighted and $MV_{it}/\Sigma MV_{it}$ when abnormal returns are value-weighted. A grand mean monthly abnormal returns ($MMAR$) is calculated:

$$MMAR = \frac{1}{T} \sum_{t=1}^{T} MAR_t,$$

Table X

Specification (Size) of Intercept Tests from Regressions of Monthly Calendar-Time Portfolio Returns on Market, Size, and Book-to-Market Factors

The analysis is this table is based on 1,000 random samples of 200 event months. Each of the 200 securities is included in the calendar-time portfolio for 12, 36, or 60 months following the randomly selected event month. The following regression is estimated:

$$R_{pt} - R_{ft} = \alpha_i + \beta_i(R_{mt} - R_{ft}) + s_i SMB_t + h_i HML_t + \epsilon_{it},$$

where R_{pt} is the simple return on the calendar-time portfolio (either equally weighted or value-weighted, R_{ft} is the return on three-month Treasury bills, R_{mt} is the return on a value-weighted market index, SMB_t is the difference in the returns of a value-weighted portfolio of small stocks and big stocks, HML_t is the difference in the returns of a value-weighted portfolio of high book-to-market stocks and low book-to-market stocks. The estimate of the intercept term (α_i) provides a test of the null hypothesis that the mean monthly excess return on the calendar-time portfolio is zero. The numbers presented in the first row of each panel represent the percentage of the 1,000 random samples that reject the null hypothesis of no mean monthly excess return when the holding period is one, three, or five years at the theoretical significance level of 5 percent in favor of the alternative hypothesis of a significantly negative intercept (i.e., calculated p value is less than 2.5 percent at the 5 percent significance level) or a significantly positive intercept (calculated p value is greater than 97.5 percent at the 5 percent significance level). The remaining rows of each panel represent the rejection levels in nonrandom samples, which are described in detail in Section IV.B and IV.C and Tables IV through Table IX.

	Holding Period					
	12 Months		36 Months		60 Months .	
	Theoretical Cumulative Density Function (%)					
Sample Characteristics	2.5	97.5	2.5	97.5	2.5	97.5
Panel A: Equally-Weighted Calendar-Time Portfolios						
Random samples	2.1	1.7	1.5	2.1	0.9	1.8
Small firms	1.4	2.4	0.5	2.1	0.2	3.1
Large firms	1.9	2.0	1.3	3.2	0.7	2.9
Low book-to-market ratio	22.8*	0.0	22.5*	0.0	16.8*	0.0
High book-to-market ratio	0.0	7.2*	0.0	17.1*	0.0	15.0*
Poor pre-event returns	5.2*	0.0	1.2	0.2	1.2	0.2
Good pre-event returns	0.5	5.1*	2.2	1.0	1.0	1.0
Industry clustering	3.3	3.6	3.5	6.0*	3.9*	7.5*
Overlapping returns	2.3	1.4	1.3	1.0	0.2	2.2
Calendar clustering	5.6*	3.4	3.7*	6.7*	3.1	7.8*
Panel B: Value-Weighted Calendar-Time Portfolios						
Random samples	2.7	1.3	2.6	1.1	3.3	1.2
Small firms	5.3*	0.9	3.8*	0.7	2.9	1.0
Large firms	2.1	1.9	2.1	3.3	1.7	2.7
Low book-to-market ratio	10.8*	0.1	9.6*	0.2	9.9*	0.4
High book-to-market ratio	1.9	1.6	0.9	4.6*	1.6	4.1*
Poor pre-event returns	24.9*	0.0	12.0*	0.1	10.1*	0.2
Good pre-event returns	1.0	4.3*	2.9	1.7	4.0*	1.3
Industry clustering	5.0*	2.2	4.4*	2.7	4.9*	3.9*
Overlapping returns	3.7*	1.2	2.8	2.3	3.6	1.4
Calendar clustering	2.8	3.2	3.2	3.4	2.0	3.2

*Significantly different from the theoretical significance level at the 1 percent level, one-sided binomial test statistic.

The Journal of Finance

Table XI
Specification (Size) of Monthly Calendar-Time Portfolio Abnormal Returns

The analysis is this table is based on 1,000 random samples of 200 event months. Each of the 200 securities is included in the calendar-time portfolio for 12, 36, or 60 months following the randomly selected event month. Monthly abnormal returns (AR_{it}) for each security are calculated using the returns on the seventy size/book-to-market reference portfolios (R_{pt}): $AR_{it} = R_{it} - R_{pt}$. In each calendar month, a mean abnormal return of firms in the portfolio is calculated as $MAR_t = \sum_{i=1}^{n_t} x_{it} AR_{it}$. For the analysis of equally weighted abnormal returns, $x_{it} = 1/n_t$; for the value-weighted analysis, $x_{it} = MV_{it}/\sum_{i=1}^{n_t} MV_{it}$. A grand mean monthly abnormal return is calculated as $MMAR = (1/T)\sum_{t=1}^{T} MAR_t$. To test the null hypothesis of zero mean monthly abnormal returns, a t-statistic is calculated using the time-series standard deviation of the mean monthly abnormal returns: $t(MMAR) = MMAR/[\sigma(MAR_t)/\sqrt{T}]$. The numbers presented in the first row of each panel represent the percentage of the 1,000 random samples that reject the null hypothesis of no mean monthly excess return when the holding period is one, three, or five years at the theoretical significance level of 5 percent in favor of the alternative hypothesis of a significantly negative intercept (i.e., calculated p value is less than 2.5 percent at the 5 percent significance level) or a significantly positive intercept (calculated p value is greater than 97.5 percent at the 5 percent significance level). The remaining rows of each panel represent the rejection levels in nonrandom samples, which are described in detail in Section IV.B and IV.C and Table IV through Table IX.

	Holding Period					
	12 Months		36 Months		60 Months	
	Theoretical Cumulative Density Function (%)					
Sample Characteristics	2.5	97.5	2.5	97.5	2.5	97.5
Panel A: Equally-Weighted Calendar-Time Portfolios						
Random samples	2.2	1.8	0.9	1.6	1.3	2.3
Small firms	1.9	1.8	1.1	1.3	1.1	1.9
Large firms	1.6	1.4	0.7	2.8	0.0	2.1
Low book-to-market ratio	4.0*	1.1	2.4	0.6	1.0	1.2
High book-to-market ratio	1.5	1.2	1.1	1.3	1.9	0.4
Poor pre-event returns	2.7	0.7	0.3	1.2	0.5	2.2
Good pre-event returns	0.6	2.8	2.3	1.0	1.6	0.9
Industry clustering	2.6	3.9*	3.0	5.2*	2.8	6.9*
Overlapping returns	1.9	1.3	1.8	0.9	1.1	1.4
Calendar clustering	2.5	2.2	0.9	2.4	1.1	3.5
Panel B: Value-Weighted Calendar-Time Portfolios						
Random samples	2.4	1.2	3.3	1.5	3.4	1.0
Small firms	3.4	0.9	4.5*	0.7	2.2	1.4
Large firms	2.4	1.8	2.1	1.1	1.1	0.8
Low book-to-market ratio	4.9*	0.8	4.4*	1.0	4.0*	1.8
High book-to-market ratio	3.4	0.7	2.6	1.2	2.8	0.7
Poor pre-event returns	10.3*	0.2	5.3*	0.3	4.5*	0.7
Good pre-event returns	1.0	4.0*	3.9*	1.1	4.7*	0.9
Industry clustering	3.3	1.7	2.6	1.9	1.9	2.1
Overlapping returns	2.5	0.9	2.9	1.0	3.0	1.2
Calendar clustering	3.7*	2.7	2.3	1.6	2.7	2.0

*Significantly different from the theoretical significance level at the 1 percent level, one-sided binomial test statistic.

where T is the total number of calendar months. To test the null hypothesis of zero mean monthly abnormal returns, a t-statistic is calculated using the time-series standard deviation of the mean monthly abnormal returns:

$$t(MMAR) = \frac{MMAR}{\sigma(MAR_t)/\sqrt{T}}.$$

Our analysis of the empirical specification of the calendar-time portfolio methods based on reference portfolios is reported in Table XI. When contrasted with the results based on the Fama–French three-factor model (Table X), the empirical rejection levels for test statistics based on calendar-time abnormal returns calculated using reference portfolios are generally more conservative. For example, in samples of firms with extreme book-to-market or pre-event return characteristics, the empirical rejection levels reported in Table XI (calendar-time abnormal returns based on reference portfolios) are uniformly lower than those based on the Fama–French three-factor model. Though the issues involved are complex, we suspect that the calendar-time portfolio methods based on reference-portfolio abnormal returns generally dominate those based on the Fama–French three-factor model for two reasons. First, the latter implicitly assumes linearity in the constructed market, size, and book-to-market factors. Inspection of Table I reveals that this assumption is unlikely to be the case for the size and book-to-market factors, at least during our period of analysis. Second, the Fama–French three-factor model assumes there is no interaction between the three factors. During our period of analysis, this assumption is also likely violated because the relation between book-to-market ratio and returns is most pronounced for small firms (Loughran (1997)).[13]

VI. Conclusion

In this research, we analyze various methods to test for long-run abnormal stock returns. Generally, misspecification of test statistics can be traced to (1) the new listing bias, (2) the rebalancing bias, (3) the skewness bias, (4) cross-sectional dependence, and/or (5) a bad model of asset pricing. How and whether these factors affect the misspecification of test statistics depend on the methods used to calculate abnormal returns.

To recommend a particular approach to test for long-run abnormal returns, we consider it a necessary condition that the method yield well-specified test statistics in random samples. Ultimately, we identify two general

---

[13] There is a tendency for negative rejection when the abnormal returns are value-weighted (Panel B, Table XI). We suspect that this results from the fact that the benchmark portfolios are equally weighted, giving more weight to the relatively high returns of small firms. Thus, large firms, which receive more weight in the calculation of a value-weighted mean, likely have negative abnormal returns.

approaches that satisfy this condition. Though both offer advantages and disadvantages, a pragmatic solution for a researcher who is analyzing long-run abnormal returns would be to use both.

The first approach relies on a traditional event study framework and the calculation of buy-and-hold abnormal returns using a carefully constructed reference portfolio, such that the population mean abnormal return is guaranteed to be zero. Inference is based on either a bootstrapped skewness-adjusted t-statistic or the empirically generated distribution of mean long-run abnormal stock returns from pseudoportfolios. The advantage of this approach is that it yields an abnormal return measure that accurately represents investor experience. The disadvantage of this approach is that it is more sensitive to the problem of cross-sectional dependence among sample firms and a poorly specified asset pricing model.

The second method relies on the calculation of calendar-time portfolio abnormal returns (either equally weighted or value-weighted). The advantage of this approach is that it controls well for cross-sectional dependence among sample firms and is generally less sensitive to a poorly specified asset pricing model. The disadvantage of this approach is that it yields an abnormal return measure that does not precisely measure investor experience.

Even these two methods, which yield well-specified test statistics in random samples, often yield misspecified test statistics in nonrandom samples (e.g., in samples with unusual pre-event returns or samples concentrated in one industry). Though we are able to control for many sources of misspecification, ultimately, the misspecification that remains can be attributed to the inability of firm size and book-to-market ratio to capture all of the misspecifications of the Capital Asset Pricing Model. Though firm size and book-to-market ratio have received considerable attention in the recent research in financial economics, some would argue that other variables explain the cross section of stock returns (e.g., recent return performance, recent quarterly earnings surprises, price-to-earnings ratios). To address this issue, we recommend that researchers compare sample firms to the general population on the basis of these (and perhaps other) characteristics. A thoughtful descriptive analysis should provide insights regarding the important dimensions on which researchers should develop a performance benchmark.

Our central message is that the analysis of long-run abnormal returns is treacherous. As such, we recommend that the study of long-run abnormal returns be subjected to stringent out-of-sample testing, for example in different time periods or across many financial markets. Furthermore, we recommend that such studies be strongly rooted in theory, which might, for example, emanate from traditional models of asset pricing or from the systematic cognitive biases of market participants.

Appendix

This appendix documents methods that we considered for estimating the variance-covariance matrix of event-time abnormal returns. The results presented in Table III through Table IX assume cross-sectional independence of sample observations. Thus, it is assumed that the variance-covariance matrix of event-time abnormal returns (Σ) is diagonal, where the cross-sectional standard deviation of sample observations is the estimate of the n diagonal elements of this matrix. In matrix form, the conventional t-statistic is estimated as $\overline{AR}_\tau [\mathbf{1}'\hat{\Sigma}\mathbf{1}/n^2]^{-1/2}$, where $\mathbf{1}$ is a $n \times 1$ vector of ones and $\overline{AR}_\tau$ is the mean abnormal return for the sample.

A.I. Buy-and-Hold Abnormal Returns

When abnormal returns are calculated using either a single control firm or the bootstrapped skewness-adjusted test statistic, in principle a researcher could calculate test statistics assuming a variance-covariance matrix that is not diagonal (i.e., sample observations are not assumed independent). We estimate the variance-covariance matrix (Σ) as follows. Consider two firms: firm i has an abnormal return calculated from period s to $s + \tau$, firm j has an abnormal return calculated from period $s + a$ to $s + \tau + a$. If $a \geq \tau$, we assume the covariance between the abnormal returns is zero. If $a < \tau$, we estimate the i,jth element of the variance-covariance matrix (σ_{ij}) as:

$$\frac{1}{\tau - a - 1} \sum_{t=s+a}^{s+\tau} (AR_{it} - \overline{AR}_i)(AR_{jt} - \overline{AR}_j),$$

where AR_{it} is the monthly abnormal return for firm i. The mean abnormal returns used in the estimate of the covariance are the means for the $\tau - a$ overlap periods.

We test the specification of test statistics in samples with overlapping returns calculations (see Table IX) based on (1) a conventional t-statistic and the use of a single control firm and (2) a bootstrapped skewness-adjusted t-statistic using the buy-and-hold reference portfolios. We focus on the samples with overlapping returns because that situation is where cross-sectional dependence is most severe. The details of the bootstrap procedure are available on request. The empirical p value approach cannot be adjusted using the estimated variance-covariance matrix. The method described here reduces, but does not eliminate, the misspecification in samples with overlapping return calculations.

A.II. Cumulative Abnormal Returns

We also apply the method described in the preceding section to the calculation of test statistics based on cumulative abnormal returns calculated using conventional t-statistics and abnormal returns calculated using (1) a single control firm and (2) reference portfolios free of the new listing bias (see Section VI.A). Thus, the diagonal elements of the variance-covariance matrix are estimated using the cross-sectional standard deviation of sample observations and the off-diagonal covariance elements are estimated as described before. This adjustment for cross-sectional dependence again reduces but does not eliminate the bias documented in Table IX.

Finally, we estimate the n diagonal elements of the variance-covariance matrix separately using the time-series standard deviation of monthly abnormal returns for each sample firm during the event period. The covariance elements are estimated as before. This adjustment again reduces, but does not eliminate, the bias that results from cross-sectional dependence.

In summary, severe cross-sectional dependence can lead to overrejection of the null hypothesis. When researchers are faced with a sample where cross-sectional dependence is likely to be a problem (e.g., when return calculations involve overlapping periods or there is severe industry clustering), the calendar-time portfolio methods described in Section VI.B would be preferred.

REFERENCES

Ball, Ray, S. P. Kothari, and Charles E. Wasley, 1995, Can we implement research on stock trading rules?, *Journal of Portfolio Management* 21, 54–63.

Barber, Brad M., and John D. Lyon, 1997a, Detecting long-run abnormal stock returns: The empirical power and specification of test statistics, *Journal of Financial Economics* 43, 341–372.

Barber, Brad M., and John D. Lyon, 1997b, Firm size, book-to-market ratio, and security returns: A holdout sample of financial firms, *Journal of Finance* 52, 875–884.

Bickel, Peter J., Friedrich Götze, and Willem R. van Zwet, 1997, Resampling fewer than n observations: Gains, losses, and remedies for losses, *Statistica Sinica* 7, 1–31.

Blume, Marshall E., and Robert F. Stambaugh, 1983, Biases in computed returns: An application to the size effect, *Journal of Financial Economics* 12, 387–404.

Brav, Alon, 1997, Inference in long-horizon event studies: A Bayesian approach with application to initial public offerings, Working paper, University of Chicago.

Brav, Alon, Chris Géczy, and Paul A. Gompers, 1995, Underperformance of seasoned equity offerings revisited, Working paper, Harvard University.

Brav, Alon, and Paul A. Gompers, 1997, Myth or reality? The long-run underperformance of initial public offerings: Evidence from venture and nonventure capital-backed companies, *Journal of Finance* 52, 1791–1821.

Brock, William, Josef Lakonishok, and Blake LeBaron, 1992, Simple technical trading rules and the stochastic properties of stock returns, *Journal of Finance* 47, 1731–1764.

Canina, Linda, Roni Michaely, Richard Thaler, and Kent Womack, 1998, Caveat compounder: A warning about using the daily CRSP equally-weighted index to compute long-run excess returns, *Journal of Finance* 53, 403–416.

Chan, Louis K. C., Narasimhin Jegadeesh, and Josef Lakonishok, 1995, Evaluating the performance of value versus glamour stocks: The impact of selection bias, *Journal of Financial Economics* 38, 269–296.

Conrad, Jennifer, and Gautum Kaul, 1993, Long-term market overreaction or biases in computed returns?, *Journal of Finance* 48, 39–64.

Cowan, Arnold R., and Anne M. A. Sergeant, 1996, Interacting biases, non-normal return distributions and the performance of parametric and bootstrap tests of long-horizon event studies, Working paper, Iowa State University.

Davis, James L., 1994, The cross-section of realized stock returns: The pre-Compustat evidence, *Journal of Finance* 49, 1579–1593.

Fama, Eugene F., 1998, Market efficiency, long-term returns and behavioral finance, *Journal of Financial Economics* 49, 283–306.

Fama, Eugene F., and Kenneth R. French, 1992, The cross-section of expected stock returns, *Journal of Finance* 47, 427–465.

Improved Tests of Long-Run Abnormal Stock Returns   201

Fama, Eugene F., and Kenneth R. French, 1993, Common risk factors in returns on stocks and bonds, *Journal of Financial Economics* 33, 3–56.

Fama, Eugene F., and Kenneth R. French, 1996, Multifactor explanations of asset pricing anomalies, *Journal of Finance* 51, 55–84.

Fama, Eugene F., and Kenneth R. French, 1998, Value versus growth: The international evidence, *Journal of Finance* 53, 1975–1999.

Hall, Peter, 1992, On the removal of skewness by transformation, *Journal of the Royal Statistical Society*, Series B 54, 221–228.

Ikenberry, David, Josef Lakonishok, and Theo Vermaelen, 1995, Market underreaction to open market share repurchases, *Journal of Financial Economics* 39, 181–208.

Ikenberry, David, Graeme Rankine, and Earl Stice, 1996, What do stock splits really signal?, *Journal of Financial and Quantitative Analysis* 31, 357–376.

Jaffe, Jeffrey F., 1974, Special information and insider trading, *Journal of Business* 47, 410–428.

Jegadeesh, Narasimhan, and Sheridan Titman, 1993, Returns to buying winners and selling losers: Implications for stock market efficiency, *Journal of Finance* 48, 65–91.

Johnson, Norman J., 1978, Modified t tests and confidence intervals for asymmetrical populations, *Journal of the American Statistical Association* 73, 536–544.

Kothari, S. P., and Jerold B. Warner, 1997, Measuring long-horizon security price performance, *Journal of Financial Economics* 43, 301–340.

Lee, Inmoo, 1997, Do firms knowingly sell overvalued equity?, *Journal of Finance* 52, 1439–1466.

Loughran, Tim, 1997, Book-to-market across firm size, exchange, and seasonality: Is there an effect?, *Journal of Financial and Quantitative Analysis* 32, 249–268.

Loughran, Tim, and Jay Ritter, 1995, The new issues puzzle, *Journal of Finance* 50, 23–52.

Mandelker, Gershon, 1974, Risk and return: the case of merging firms, *Journal of Financial Economics* 1, 303–336.

Neyman, Jerzy, and Egon S. Pearson, 1928, On the use and interpretation of certain test criteria for purposes of statistical inference, part I, *Biometrika* 20A, 175–240.

Pearson, Egon S., 1929a, The distribution of frequency constants in small samples from symmetrical distributions, *Biometrika* 21, 356–360.

Pearson, Egon S., 1929b, The distribution of frequency constants in small samples from nonnormal symmetrical and skew populations, *Biometrika* 21, 259–286.

Rau, P. Rahavendra, and Theo Vermaelen, 1996, Glamour, value and the post-acquisition performance of acquiring firms, Working paper, INSEAD.

Ritter, Jay R., 1991, The long-run performance of initial public offerings, *Journal of Finance* 46, 3–27.

Roll, Richard, 1983, On computing mean returns and the small firm premium, *Journal of Financial Economics* 12, 371–386.

Shao, Jun, 1996, Bootstrap model selection, *Journal of the American Statistical Association* 91, 655–665.

Speiss, D. Katherine, and John Affleck-Graves, 1995, Underperformance in long-run stock returns following seasoned equity offerings, *Journal of Financial Economics* 28, 243–268.

Speiss, D. Katherine, and John Affleck-Graves, 1996, The long-run performance of stock returns following debt offers, Working paper, University of Notre Dame.

Sutton, Clifton D., 1993, Computer-intensive methods for tests about the mean of an asymmetrical distribution, *Journal of the American Statistical Association* 88, 802–808.

Part II
Venture Capital and Initial Public Offerings

[5]

Journal of Financial Economics 47 (1998) 243–277 OECD

Venture capital and the structure of capital markets: banks versus stock markets[1]

Bernard S. Black[a],*, Ronald J. Gilson[a],[b]

[a] Columbia University School of Law, New York, NY 10027, USA
[b] Stanford University School of Law, Stanford, California 94305, USA

Received 18 July 1996; accepted 29 August 1997

Abstract

The United States has many banks that are small relative to large corporations and play a limited role in corporate governance, and a well developed stock market with an associated market for corporate control. In contrast, Japanese and German banks are fewer in number but larger in relative size and are said to play a central governance role. Neither country has an active market for corporate control. We extend the debate on the relative efficiency of bank- and stock market-centered capital markets by developing a further systematic difference between the two systems: the greater vitality of venture capital in stock market-centered systems. Understanding the link between the stock market and the venture capital market requires understanding the contractual arrangements between entrepreneurs and venture capital providers; especially, the importance of the opportunity to enter into an implicit contract over control, which gives a successful entrepreneur the option to reacquire control from the venture capitalist by using an initial public offering as the means by which the venture capitalist exits from a portfolio investment. We also extend the literature on venture capital contracting by offering an explanation for two central characteristics of the U.S. venture capital market: relatively rapid exit by venture capital providers from investments in portfolio companies; and the

* Corresponding author. Tel.: 212/854-8079; fax:212/854-7946; e-mail: bblack@law.columbia.edu.

[1] The authors are grateful for helpful suggestions from the editor and an anonymous referee, and from Anant Admati, Erik Berglof, Stephen Choi, Kevin Davis, Uri Geiger, Victor Goldberg, Paul Gompers, Joseph Grundfest, Ehud Kamar, Michael Klausner, Joshua Lerner, Ronald Mann, Paul Pfleiderer, Mark Ramsayer, Charles Sabel, Allen Schwartz, and Omri Yadlin, and from participants in workshops at Columbia Law School, Harvard Law School, Stanford Law School, the Max Planck Institute (Hamburg, Germany), and the American Law and Economics Association. Research support was provided by Columbia Law School and the Roberts Program in Law and Business, Stanford Law School. We thank Laura Menninger, Nishani Naidoo, Annette Schuller, and Ram Vasudevan for research assistance.

244   *B.S. Black, R.J. Gilson/Journal of Financial Economics 47 (1998) 243–277*

common practice of exit through an initial public offering. © 1998 Elsevier Science S.A. All rights reserved.

JEL classification: G23; G32

Keywords: Venture Capital; Exit Strategy; IPO; Comparative corporate governance

1. Introduction

Contrasting capital markets in the United States with those of Japan and Germany has become a commonplace activity. The United States has a large number of comparatively small banks that play a limited role in the governance of large corporations, and a well developed stock market with an associated market for corporate control that figures prominently in corporate governance. In contrast, Japanese main banks and German universal banks are few in number but larger in size, relative to Japanese and German firms, and are said to play a central corporate governance role in monitoring management (e.g., Aoki, 1994; Roe, 1994). Neither country has an active market for corporate control.

Advocates of bank-centered capital markets claim that this structure fosters patient capital markets and long-term planning, while a stock market-centered capital market is said to encourage short-term expectations by investors and responsive short-term strategies by managers (e.g., Edwards and Fischer, 1994; Porter, 1992). Advocates of stock market-centered systems (e.g., Gilson, 1996) stress the adaptive features of a market for corporate control which are lacking in bank-centered systems, and the lack of empirical evidence of short-termism.

Paralleling the assessment of the comparative merits of stock market and bank-centered capital markets, scholars have also sought to explain how the United States, Germany, and Japan developed such different capital markets. Recent work has stressed that the characteristics of the three capital markets do not reflect simply the efficient outcome of competition between institutions, in which the most efficient institutions survive. The nature of the American capital market – a strong stock market, weak financial intermediaries, and the absence of the close links between banks and nonfinancial firms said to characterize the Japanese and German capital markets – reflects, at least in part, politics, history and path-dependent evolution, rather than economic inevitability (e.g., Black, 1990; Gilson, 1996; Roe, 1994). Much the same seems to be true of Germany and Japan (Hoshi, 1993; Roe, 1994). To be sure, competitively driven evolution hones efficiency, but institutions that emerge are shaped at critical stages by the random hand of events and the instrumental hand of politics.

In this article, we seek to contribute to two literatures. First, we extend the debate about the relative efficiency of bank- and stock market-centered capital markets by documenting and explaining a second systematic difference between the two systems: the existence of a much stronger venture capital industry in stock market-centered systems.

We define 'venture capital', consistent with American understanding, as investment by specialized venture capital organizations (which we call 'venture capital funds') in high-growth, high-risk, often high-technology firms that need capital to finance product development or growth and must, by the nature of their business, obtain this capital largely in the form of equity rather than debt. We exclude 'buyout' financing that enables a mature firm's managers to acquire the firm from its current owners, even though in Europe, so-called 'venture capital' firms often provide such financing – more often, in many cases, than the financing that we call venture capital.

Other countries have openly envied the U.S. venture capital market and have actively, but unsuccessfully, sought to replicate it. We offer an explanation for this failure: We argue that a well developed stock market that permits venture capitalists to exit through an initial public offering (IPO) is critical to the existence of a vibrant venture capital market.

Understanding this critical link between the stock market and the venture capital market requires that we understand the implicit and explicit contractual arrangements between venture capital funds and their investors, and between venture capital funds and entrepreneurs. This brings us to our second contribution: We extend the literature on venture capital contracting by offering an explanation for two characteristics of the United States venture capital market. First, we explain the importance of exit – why venture capital providers seek to liquidate their portfolio company investments in the near to moderate term, rather than investing for the long-term like Japanese or German banks. Second, we explain the importance of the form of exit: why the potential for the venture capital provider to exit from a successful start-up *through an IPO*, available only through a stock market, allows venture capital providers to enter into implicit contracts with entrepreneurs concerning future control of startup firms, in a way not available in a bank-centered capital market. Thus, we make explicit a functional link between private and public equity markets: The implicit contract over future control that is permitted by the availability of exit through an IPO helps to explain the greater success of venture capital as an organizational form in stock market-centered systems.

Section 2 of this article motivates the theoretical analysis by contrasting the venture capital markets in the United States and Germany. Section 3 develops the importance of exit from venture capital investments to the viability and structure of the venture capital industry. Exit serves two key functions. First, venture capital investors specialize in providing portfolio companies with a combination of financial capital, monitoring and advisory services, and reputational capital. The combination of financial and nonfinancial services loses its efficiency advantages as the portfolio company matures. Thus, recycling venture capital investors' capital through exit and reinvestment is jointly efficient for the

246   *B.S. Black, R.J. Gilson/Journal of Financial Economics 47 (1998) 243–277*

provider and the portfolio company. Second, exit facilitates contracting between venture capital managers (persons with expertise in identifying and developing promising new businesses) and providers of capital to venture capital managers. The exit price gives capital providers a reliable measure of the venture capital manager's skill. The exit and reinvestment cycle also lets capital providers withdraw capital from less skilled venture capital managers or managers whose industry-specific expertise no longer matches the nature of promising start-up firms. It supports an implicit contract under which capital providers reinvest in the future limited partnerships of successful venture capital managers.

Section 4 focuses on the implicit contract over control between the entrepreneur and the venture capital fund. The potential to exit through an IPO allows the entrepreneur and the venture capital fund to enter into a self-enforcing implicit contract over control, in which the venture capital fund agrees to return control to a successful entrepreneur by exiting through an IPO. This implicit contract cannot readily be duplicated in a bank-centered capital market. Section 5 compares the predictions from our informal model to evidence about the success of venture capital in other countries, including Canada, Great Britain, Israel, and Japan. Section 6 considers alternative explanations for the observed international patterns of venture capital development, especially differences in legal rules. Some of these reasons may have predictive power, but none has enough power to displace our theory as an explanation for a substantial portion of the observed intercountry variation. Section 7 considers the implications of the symbiosis between stock markets and venture capital markets for efforts by other countries to expand their venture capital markets. Section 8 concludes.

2. The venture capital industry in the United States and Germany

In this section, we compare the venture capital industries in the United States and Germany in order to motivate the theory developed in Sections 3 and 4, in which a stock market-centered capital market (present in the United States but absent in Germany) is a precondition to a substantial venture capital industry.

The United States has a much more fully developed venture capital market than Germany. The differences are of both size and substance. The United States has a larger number of funds and the funds themselves are larger relative to each country's economy. Substantively, United States funds are more heavily invested in early-stage ventures and high-technology industries, while German venture capital provides primarily later-stage financing in lower-technology industries.

The United States venture capital market is quite large. As of the end of 1994, 591 U.S. venture capital funds had total investments (from which the fund had not yet exited or written off) of around $34 billion (Venture Capital Yearbook, 1995). New investment in venture capital funds in 1996 was $6.5 billion (Fig. 1). In recent years, venture capital-backed firms have raised several billion dollars

B.S. Black, R.J. Gilson/Journal of Financial Economics 47 (1998) 243–277 247

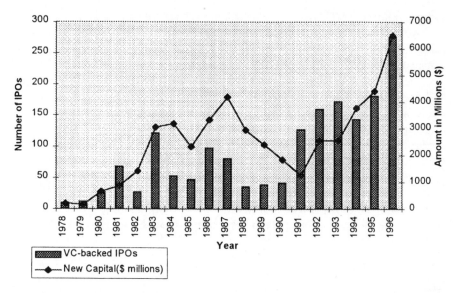

Fig. 1. Venture capital-backed IPOs and new venture capital commitments. Number of initial public offerings of venture-capital-backed companies (left-hand scale), and amount of new capital commitments to venture capital funds (right-hand scale), between 1978 and 1996. Source: Venture Capital Journal and Venture Capital Yearbook (various dates); Economist, Mar. 29, 1997 (survey of Silicon Valley)

annually through IPOs, including a 1996 total of $12 billion; they form a significant portion of the total IPO market (Venture Capital Yearbook, various years through 1997; Brav and Gompers, 1997).[2] Between 1991 and 1996, there were 1059 venture capital-backed IPOs, an average of over 175 per year (see Table 1), as well as 466 exits through acquisition of the venture-capital-backed firm.

Fig. 1 shows the annual variation in the number of venture-capital-backed IPOs, as well as the amount of new capital committed to venture capital funds. Inspection of Fig. 1 suggests a correlation between the availability of exit through IPO (proxied by the number of venture-capital-backed IPOs) and investor willingness to invest in venture capital funds (measured by new capital commitments), with perhaps a one-year lag between a change in the number of IPOs and a resulting change in the amount of capital committed. This correlation is consistent with the theory developed below on the link between the stock market and the venture capital market.

---

[2] An alternate way to measure the importance of venture-capital-backed IPOs is to measure the firms' market capitalization rather than the amount of funds raised in the IPO. The 276 venture-capital-backed firms taken public in 1996 had a mean market capitalization of $209 million and total market capitalization of $58 billion (Venture Capital Journal, April, 1997).

248   *B.S. Black, R.J. Gilson/Journal of Financial Economics 47 (1998) 243–277*

Table 1
VC-backed IPOs, public acquisitions, and private acquisitions

Number of initial public offerings of venture-capital-backed companies and number of sales of venture-capital-backed companies, between 1984 and 1996.

| Year | VC-backed IPOs | Exits via acquisitions | | |
		Of private companies	Of already public companies	Total
1984	53	59	27	86
1985	47	83	18	101
1986	98	90	30	120
1987	81	113	27	140
1988	36	106	29	135
1989	39	101	45	146
1990	42	76	33	109
1991	127	65	19	84
1992	160	90	4	94
1993	172	78	14	92
1994	143	99	no data	no data
1995	183	98	no data	no data
1996	276	94	no data	no data

Source: Venture Capital Journal (various dates) (data for acquisitions of already public companies was available only through 1993)

The visual impression of a correlation between venture-capital-backed IPOs and new capital commitments to venture capital funds is confirmed by a simple regression of capital contributions in year $X + 1$ (as a dependent variable) against number of venture-capital-backed IPOs in year X (Table 2). Regression 1 below shows that the number of IPOs in year X correlates strongly with new capital contributions in year $X + 1$. Regression 2 adds year as an additional possible explanatory variable. The correlation between number of IPOs in year X and new capital commitments in the following year remains statistically significant as a predictor of new capital commitments in the following year. These regressions are not intended to fully capture the factors that affect capital commitments to venture capital funds, but do confirm the visual correlation evident from Fig. 1.

United States venture capital funds obtain capital from a range of sources, but pension funds are the largest contributor. Pension funds have provided roughly 40% of the capital raised by venture capital funds over the last 10 years or so (Table 3). In Germany, on the other hand, banks supply the majority of venture capital commitments.

Seed, startup and other early stage investments that take a company through development of a prototype and initial product shipments to customers

B.S. Black, R.J. Gilson/Journal of Financial Economics 47 (1998) 243–277   249

Table 2

Correlation between venture capital backed IPOs and new capital commitments to venture capital funds

Least-squares regression of capital contributed to venture capital funds ($ millions) in year $X + 1$ against number of initial public offerings of venture-capital backed companies in year X. Based on data from 1978–1996 as shown in Fig. 1. t-statistics in parentheses. *** (**) (*) = significant at 0.001 (0.01) (0.05) level.

Dependent variable	Independent variable(s)			R^2	Number of observations
	Intercept	VC-backed IPOs in year X	Year		
1 Capital contribution in year $X + 1$	1015 $(t = 2.35)$*	20.2 $(t = 4.54)$***		0.56	18
2 Capital contribution in year $X + 1$	− 137846 $(t = -0.93)$	15.1 $(t = 2.17)$*	70.1 $(t = 0.94)$	0.59	18

Table 3

United States and Germany capital raised by venture capital funds by type of investor

Percentage of capital raised by venture capital funds in the United States and Germany, by type of investor, for 1992–1995.

	1992	1993	1994	1995
United States				
Corporations	3%	8%	9%	2%
Private individuals & families	11	8	9	17
Government agencies	—	—	—	—
Pension funds	42	59	46	38
Banks and insurance companies	15	11	9	18
Endowments and foundations	18	11	21	22
Other	11	4	2	3
Total	100%	100%	100%	100%
Germany				
Corporations	7%	9%	8%	10%
Private individuals & families	6	7	8	5
Government agencies	4	6	7	8
Pension funds	—	—	—	9
Banks	53	52	55	59
Insurance companies	10	12	12	6
Endowments and foundations	—	—	—	—
Other	17	14	10	2
Total	100%	100%	100%	100%

Sources: European Venture Capital Association Yearbook (1995); Bundesverband Deutsche Kapitalbeteiligungsgesellschaften Jahrbuch [German Venture Capital Association Yearbook] (various years through 1996); Venture Capital Yearbook (various years through 1997).

Table 4
United States and Germany venture capital disbursements by stage of financing

Percentage of capital disbursed by venture capital funds in the United States and Germany, by nature of investment, for 1992–1995.

	1992	1993	1994	1995
United States				
Seed	3%	7%	4%	
Startup	8	7	15	
Other early stage	13	10	18	
Expansion	55	54	45	
LBO/Acquisition	7	6	6	
Other	14	16	12	
Total	100%	100%	100%	
Germany				
Seed	1%	1%	2%	2%
Startup	6	7	8	6
Expansion	45	66	54	65
LBO/Acquisition	24	25	36	18
Other	25	—	—	8
Total	100%	100%	100%	100%

Sources: European Venture Capital Association Yearbook (1995); Bundesverband Deutsche Kapitalbeteiligungsgesellschaften (BVK) Jahrbuch [German Venture Capital Association Yearbook] (various years through 1996); Venture Capital Yearbook (various years through 1997).

accounted for about 37% of new capital invested by venture capital funds in 1994 (Table 4). Later-stage expansion financing represented another 45% of 1994 investments. Because venture capitalists usually stage their investments (Sahlman, 1990; Gompers, 1995), most expansion financing goes to companies that received early-stage financing. Thus, the bulk of venture capital investments go to firms that receive venture capital financing very early in their life. Moreover, most investments go to technology-based companies; in 1994, 68% of new investments went to these companies (Venture Economics, 1995).

   Lest venture capital be dismissed as trivial in amount, and therefore not an important factor in comparing corporate governance systems, we note that mature firms which began with venture capital backing assume macroeconomic significance in the U.S. economy. They play a major, often dominant role in several important and rapidly growing sectors where the United States is recognized as a world leader, including biotechnology (for example, Genentech and Biogen); personal computers and workstations (for example, Apple, Compaq, and Sun Microsystems); many personal computer components and related devices such as hard drives and routers (for example, Seagate Technologies, Connor Peripherals, and Cisco Systems); personal computer software (for example, Lotus Development and Harvard Graphics); and semiconductors (for example, Intel and Advanced Micro Devices).

B.S. Black, R.J. Gilson / Journal of Financial Economics 47 (1998) 243–277 251

The German venture capital industry is a fraction of the size of the United States industry. Only 85 venture capital organizations existed at the end of 1994, with DM 8.3 billion ($5.5 billion) in cumulative capital commitments (European Venture Capital Yearbook, 1995) and annual investments of under $400 million. Venture capital investments were 0.01% of German GDP in 1994; only one-sixth of the U.S. level. This comparison understates the difference in venture capital activity between the two countries because the European definition of venture capital is broader than the American definition. These organizations received the majority of their capital from banks (55%) and insurance companies (12%). Pension funds are not a factor in the German market because German corporate and government pension obligations are largely unfunded.

The German venture capital industry also differs from the United States in its aversion both to early-stage investment (Table 4) and to investment in high-technology industries (Harrison, 1990). In 1994, only 8% of the venture capital invested went to startup companies, and only 2% to seed financing. Technology-related investments comprised only 11% of all new investments.

In Germany, as in the United States, exit by the venture capital fund is the norm, but the form of exit differs. Exit through the stock market is largely unavailable, although a handful of German venture capital-backed firms have gone public on Britain's AIM (Alternative Investment Market). The venture capital fund's exit therefore comes principally through the company's repurchase of the venture fund's stake (a strategy not available to the rapidly growing firms that are the predominant recipients of venture capital financing in the United States), or through selling the company. Table 5 shows the exit strategies employed by German venture capital funds for 1995. Of the 12 exits through IPO, only one was in Germany; the rest were on foreign markets.

This section has only sketched the United States and German venture capital markets. But it demonstrates the pattern we seek to explain: the existence in the

Table 5
Exits by German venture capital funds, 1995

Type of exit from portfolio companies by German venture capital funds for 1995.

Exit type	Number of firms
Buyback by portfolio company	166
Sale of portfolio company	74
Block sale of venture capital fund's stake	8
Initial Public Offering	12
(IPOs on foreign stock markets)	(11)
Other	4
Total	264

Source: Bundesverband Deutsche Kapitalbeteiligungsgesellschaften Jahrbuch [German Venture Capital Association Yearbook] (1996)

United States of a dynamic venture capital industry centered on early stage investments in high-technology companies and the absence of a comparable industry in Germany.

3. The importance of exit by the venture capital fund

The first step in understanding the link between the stock market and the venture capital market involves the importance of exit by the venture capital fund from its investments. We develop below an informal theory for why exit by venture capital providers from their successful investments is critical to the operation of the venture capital market, both for the relationship between a venture capital fund and its portfolio companies, and for the relationship between the fund and its capital providers. Florida and Kenney (1990) argue that U.S. venture investors' refusal to act as long-term investors in portfolio companies weakens United States competitiveness. Our analysis provides an efficiency justification for exit.

The need for an exit strategy does not itself explain the distinctive properties of exit through an IPO and, therefore, the special role of an active IPO market. We develop that relationship in Section 4.

3.1. Exit from the venture capital fund – portfolio company relationship

Venture capitalists provide more than just money to their portfolio companies. Three additional contributions loom large (Bygrave and Timmons, 1992; Barry, 1994; Lerner, 1995; Gorman and Sahlman, 1989): management assistance to the portfolio company, analogous to that provided by a management consulting firm; intensive monitoring of performance, reflecting the incentives to monitor arising from equity ownership and the power to act using the venture capitalist's levers of control; and reputational capital, that is, the venture capitalist's ability to give the portfolio company credibility with third parties, similar to the role played by other reputational intermediaries such as investment bankers.

3.1.1. Management assistance
The typical venture capital fund is a limited partnership run by general partners who are experienced at moving companies up the development path from the startup stage and market knowledge based on other investments in the portfolio company's industry and related industries (Sahlman, 1990; Gompers and Lerner, 1996). With this experience, the venture capitalist can assist a management-thin early-stage company in locating and recruiting the management and technical personnel it needs as its business grows, and can help the company through the predictable problems that high-technology firms face in moving

B.S. Black, R.J. Gilson/Journal of Financial Economics 47 (1998) 243–277 253

from prototype development to production, marketing, and distribution. The venture capital fund's industry knowledge and experience with prior startup firms helps it locate managers for new startups (Carvalho, 1996).

3.1.2. Intensive monitoring and control

Venture capital funds have both strong incentives to monitor entrepreneurs' performance, deriving from equity ownership. They also receive strong control levers, disproportionate to the size of their equity investment. One control lever results from the staged timing of venture capital investment. The initial investment is typically insufficient to allow the portfolio company to carry out its business plan (Gompers, 1995; Sahlman, 1990). The venture capitalist will decide later whether to provide the additional funding that the portfolio company needs. The company's need for additional funds gives its management a performance incentive in the form of a hard constraint, analogous to the use of debt in leveraged buyouts.[3]

The typical contractual arrangements between a venture capital fund and a portfolio company provide other control levers. The venture capitalist typically receives convertible debt or convertible preferred stock that carries the same voting rights as if it had already been converted into common stock (Benton and Gunderson, 1993; Gompers, 1997).[4] The venture capital fund commonly receives greater board representation – often an absolute majority of the board – than it could elect if board representation were proportional to overall voting power. Board control lets the venture capital provider replace the entrepreneur as chief executive officer if performance lags.[5] Even where the venture capitalist lacks board control, the investor rights agreement gives the venture capital provider veto power over significant operating decisions by the portfolio company.

---

[3] Gompers (1995) explains the extra control rights given to the venture capital fund as a response to adverse selection problems in early-stage financing, where information asymmetries between the entrepreneur and the venture capital fund are greatest.

[4] The standard contractual package for an early-stage venture capital investment consists of a convertible preferred stock purchase agreement; the portfolio company's certificate of incorporation; and an investor rights agreement. The purchase agreement, through detailed representations and warranties, documents the portfolio company's condition at the time of the venture capital investment. The certificate of incorporation sets out the voting and other rights of the venture capital fund's convertible debt or preferred stock. The investor rights agreement contains the portfolio company's ongoing obligations to the venture capital fund, including detailed negative covenants and such things as registration rights.

[5] Hellman (1995a) explains why an entrepreneur would give the venture capitalist this right: to reduce the cost of capital, thereby increasing the share of the equity the entrepreneur retains. We discuss the reputation market necessary to prevent the venture capitalist from misusing this power in Section 4.

3.1.3. Reputational capital

Much like an investment bank underwriting an initial public offering (Gilson and Kraakman, 1984; Booth and Smith, 1986), the venture capital fund acts as a reputational intermediary. Venture capital financing enhances the portfolio company's credibility with third parties whose contributions will be crucial to the company's success. Talented managers are more likely to invest their human capital in a company financed by a respected venture capital fund, because the venture capitalist's participation provides a credible signal about the company's likelihood of success. Suppliers will be more willing to risk committing capacity and extending trade credit to a company with respected venture capital backers. Customers will take more seriously the company's promise of future product delivery if a venture capitalist both vouches for and monitors its management and technical progress. Moukheiber (1996) provides an account of the reputational power of Kleiner, Perkins, Caufield and Byers, a leading venture capital fund. Later on, the venture capitalist's reputation helps to attract a high quality underwriter for an initial public offering of the portfolio company's stock (Lerner, 1994a; Megginson and Weiss, 1991).

The venture capital fund's proffer of its reputation to third parties who have dealings with a portfolio company is credible because the fund is a repeat player, and has put its money where its mouth is by investing in the portfolio company. The fund's reputation is crucial for its own dealings with investors in its existing and future limited partnerships, with other venture capitalists in syndicating investments in portfolio companies and in negotiating with entrepreneurs concerning new portfolio investments (Sahlman, 1990; Lerner, 1994b). Consistent with a reputational analysis, Brav and Gompers (1997) report that venture-capital-backed IPOs do not suffer the long-run underperformance reported for IPOs in general.

Like a venture capitalist's provision of financial capital, its non-financial contributions are also staged, albeit informally. A venture capitalist can choose not to make or return telephone calls to or from a portfolio company or its suppliers, customers, or prospective employees. The fund's power to withhold its management assistance and reputational capital reinforces its incentive and power to monitor.

The management assistance, monitoring, and service as a reputational intermediary that a venture capitalist provides share a significant economy of scope with its provision of capital. This scope economy arises from a number of sources. The portfolio company must evaluate the quality of the venture capital fund's proffered management assistance and monitoring. Similarly, potential employees, suppliers, and customers must evaluate the credibility of the fund's explicit and implicit representations concerning the portfolio company's future. Combining financial and nonfinancial contributions both enhances the credibility of the information that the venture capitalist provides to third parties and bonds the venture capitalist's promise to the portfolio company to provide

B.S. Black, R.J. Gilson/Journal of Financial Economics 47 (1998) 243–277 255

nonfinancial assistance. The venture capitalist will suffer financial loss if it reneges on its promise of nonfinancial support. Combining financial and non-financial contributions also lets investors in venture capital funds evaluate a fund's nonfinancial contributions by measuring its return on investment. Lin and Smith (1995) also link the venture capitalist's financial and nonfinancial investments. Finally, there is the customary role of monitoring in ensuring that the portfolio company's managers do not divert to themselves some of the company's income stream.

The non-capital inputs supplied by venture capital providers have special value to early-stage companies. As the portfolio company's management gains its own experience, proves its skill, and establishes its own reputation, the relative value of the venture capital provider's management experience, monitoring, and service as a reputational intermediary declines.[6] Thus, by the time the portfolio company succeeds, the venture capital provider's nonfinancial contributions can be more profitably invested in a new round of early-stage companies. But because the economies of scope discussed above link financial and nonfinancial contributions, recycling the venture capitalist's nonfinancial contributions also requires the venture capitalist to exit – to recycle its financial contribution from successful companies to early-stage companies.

3.2. The exit and reinvestment cycle for venture capital funds and capital providers

The efficiency of exit for the venture capitalist-portfolio company relationship complements a similar efficiency arising from the relationship between the venture capitalist and the investors in its limited partnerships. The cycle of financial commitment to early-stage firms, followed by exit from these invest-ments, responds to three contracting problems in the venture capitalist – capital provider relationship. First, capital providers need a way to evaluate venture capitalists' skill, in order to decide to which managers to commit new funds. Second, capital providers need to evaluate the risks and returns on venture capital investments relative to other investments, in order to decide whether to invest in venture capital, and how much to invest. Third, capital providers need to be able to withdraw funds from less successful managers, or from managers whose industry-specific expertise no longer matches current investment oppor-tunities. Yet the very specialization that explains why capital providers hire venture capitalists rather than invest directly ensures that capital providers

---

[6] Compare Rajan's (1992) analysis of the trade-off between a bank-like lender who has the ability to monitor the borrower's on-going performance and public investors who cannot monitor. As the borrower's quality improves, the returns to monitoring decrease, and the most efficient capital provider shifts from a monitoring bank-like lender to a non-monitoring investor. Diamond (1991) discusses a similar generational theory in which optimal investor type depends on a firm's stage in its life-cycle.

cannot easily assess whether a venture capital fund's ongoing investments are or are likely to become successful, or how successful they are likely to be.

Exit by the venture capital manager from specific portfolio investments provides a benchmark that lets capital providers evaluate both the relative skill of venture capital managers and the profitability of venture capital relative to other investments (Gompers, 1996). At the same time, payment of the exit proceeds to capital providers lets the capital providers recycle funds from less successful to more successful venture capital managers.

Conventional limited partnership agreements between venture capital funds and capital providers reflect the efficiency of exit for this relationship. The limited partnership agreement typically sets a maximum term for the partnership of 7–10 years, after which the partnership must be liquidated and the proceeds distributed to the limited partners (Sahlman, 1990). During the term of the limited partnership agreement, the proceeds from investments in particular firms are distributed to limited partners as realized. Moreover, venture capital funds have strong incentives to exit from their investments, when feasible, well before the end of the partnership period. A fund's performance record, based on completed investments, is the fund's principal tool for soliciting capital providers to invest additional funds in new limited partnerships.

The explicit contract between capital providers and the venture capitalist, requiring liquidation of each limited partnership, is complemented by an implicit contract in which capital providers are expected to reinvest in future limited partnerships sponsored by successful venture capital funds. The expectation of reinvestment makes it feasible for venture capital funds to invest in developing infrastructure and expertise that will outlive the term of any one limited partnership, and could not be justified by the returns on the modest amount of capital that a venture capitalist without a track record can expect to raise. Fig. 2

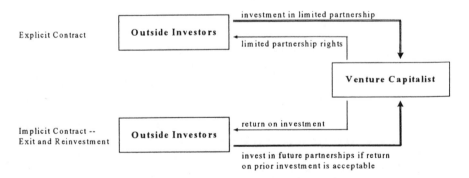

Fig. 2. Implicit and explicit contracts between venture capitalists and outside investors.

B.S. Black, R.J. Gilson/Journal of Financial Economics 47 (1998) 243–277   257

illustrates the explicit and implicit contracts between venture capitalists and their investors.

In sum, exit is central to the venture capital manager's accountability to capital providers. The efficiency of exit for the venture capital fund – capital provider relationship complements its efficiency properties for the portfolio firm – venture capital fund relationship. Taken together, they provide a strong rationale for exit from individual portfolio investments as a critical component of a viable venture capital industry.

4. The availability of exit by IPO: Implicit contracting over future control

The analysis in part 3 establishes the importance of an exit strategy to the venture capital market. But it does not differentiate between stock market-centered and bank-centered capital markets. A stock market makes available one special type of exit – an initial public offering. But another exit strategy is available to venture capital funds in both bank-centered and stock-market centered capital markets: the fund can cause the portfolio company to be sold to a larger company. Indeed, even in the United States, venture capitalists frequently exit through sale of the portfolio company rather than through an IPO (Table 1). A third exit option – leveraging the portfolio company so it can repurchase the venture capitalist's stake – is generally not feasible for the fast-growing, capital-consuming companies that are the typical focus for venture capital investing in the U.S.

Exit through sale of the portfolio company is likely to be the most efficient form of exit in some cases. For example, innovation may be better accomplished in small firms while production and marketing may be better accomplished in large firms. In this circumstance, selling a startup company to another firm with manufacturing or marketing expertise can produce synergy gains. These gains can be partly captured by the startup firm through a higher exit price (Bygrave and Timmons, 1992).

In other cases, an IPO may be the most efficient form of exit. The potential for an IPO to provide a higher-valued exit than sale of the company must be considered plausible, given the frequency with which this exit option is used in the United States. Viewed ex ante, venture capital financing of firms for which exit through IPO will (or might turn out to) maximize exit price could be a positive net present investment in a stock-market-centered capital market, but not in a bank-centered capital market. But this difference should affect investment decisions only at the margin. Thus, it cannot easily explain the dramatic differences between the venture capital industries in the United States and Germany, both in size and in type of investment.

Thus, we are only part of the way towards a theory that explains the observed link between venture capital markets and stock markets. We have shown why venture capital providers need an exit strategy. What remains to be shown is that the potential for exit through IPO, *even if exit often occurs through the portfolio company's sale*, is critical to the development of an active venture capital market. This part shows that the potential for exit through IPO allows the venture capital provider and the entrepreneur to enter into an implicit contract over future control of the portfolio company in a manner that is not readily duplicable in a bank-centered system.

4.1. The contracting framework

In a contracting framework, the relevant time to assess the influence of an IPO's availability (and therefore the importance of a stock market) on the operation of the venture capital market is when the entrepreneur and venture capital provider contract over the initial investment, not when exit actually occurs. A number of authors have modeled aspects of this contract, including the staging of the venture capitalist's funding, which vests in the venture capital provider the decision whether to continue the portfolio company's projects (Admati and Pfleiderer, 1994; Gompers, 1995), and the venture capital fund's purchase of a convertible security both to mitigate distributional conflicts between the entrepreneur and the venture capitalist associated with a future sale of the firm (Bergloff, 1994), and to solve an adverse selection problem among prospective entrepreneurs (Marx, 1994; Gompers, 1997). Our informal model seeks to explain three additional characteristics of venture capital contracting: (1) the parties' ex ante joint preference that the venture capital fund exit through an IPO; (2) how the entrepreneur's preference that the fund use this exit strategy if it becomes available ex post is expressed through a self-enforcing implicit contract over future control; and (3) how this implicit contract provides the entrepreneur with incentives that are not easily duplicated if sale of the portfolio company is the only exit option. Because the incentive properties of this contract go to the heart of the entrepreneurial process, its availability in a stock-market-centered capital market links the venture capital market and the stock market and can explain the absence of vigorous venture capital in countries with bank-centered capital markets.

Our IPO exit model requires three noncontroversial assumptions: (i) the entrepreneur places substantial private value on control over the company she starts; (ii) it is not feasible for an untested entrepreneur to retain control at the time of the initial venture capital financing; and (iii) it is feasible for a successful entrepreneur to reacquire control from the venture capitalist when the venture capitalist exits. We discuss each assumption below.

A private value for control is a standard feature in venture capital models and, more generally, in models that seek to explain the incentive properties of capital structure (Holmstrom and Tirole, 1989; Grossman and Hart, 1988; Harris and Raviv, 1988). Moreover, for entrepreneurs, the assumption appears to be

B.S. Black, R.J. Gilson/Journal of Financial Economics 47 (1998) 243–277 259

descriptively accurate. The failure rate for startup companies is high enough[7] so that, without a large private value for control, many potential entrepreneurs would decide not to leave a secure job to start a new company. It is also apparent that ceding to the venture capital provider the power, frequently exercised, to remove the entrepreneur from management is a significant cost to the entrepreneur (Hellman, 1995a).

Even if entrepreneurs value control highly, they cannot demand its retention at the time that they are seeking venture financing. The typical entrepreneur has not previously run a startup company. Venture capitalists rationally insist on retaining control to protect themselves against the risk that the entrepreneur would not run the firm successfully or will extract private benefits from the firm instead of maximizing its value to all investors.

The situation changes once a startup firm has succeeded. The entrepreneur has proved her management skill and provided some evidence that she can be trusted with other peoples' money. Returning control to the entrepreneur could now maximize firm value. Even if not, the value lost may be less than the entrepreneur's private value of control. The opportunity to regain control also provides an incentive, beyond mere wealth, for the entrepreneur to devote the effort needed for success. This possibility squarely raises the contracting problem that we address below: How can the venture capitalist commit, ex ante, to transfer control back to the entrepreneur, contingent on a concept as nebulous as 'success'?

4.2. The entrepreneur's incentive contract

When the entrepreneur sells an interest in her company to a venture capital fund, the venture capitalist receives both a residual interest in the firm's value, typically in the form of convertible preferred stock or debt and significant control rights, both explicit (for example, the right to remove the chief executive officer) and implicit (for example, the right to decide whether the firm can continue in business through staged funding). In return, the company and the entrepreneur get three things. The portfolio company receives capital plus nonfinancial contributions including information, monitoring, and enhanced credibility with third parties. This explicit contract is illustrated in Fig. 3. In addition, the entrepreneur receives an implicit incentive contract denominated in control. The structure of this incentive contract depends on the availability of an IPO exit strategy.

---

[7] See Gompers (1995) (16% of portfolio companies are liquidated or go bankrupt), Barry (1994) (one-third of venture capital investments result in losses), Sahlman (1990) (one-third of venture capital investments result in losses). Additionally, a significant percentage of would be entrepreneurs never secure venture funding at all.

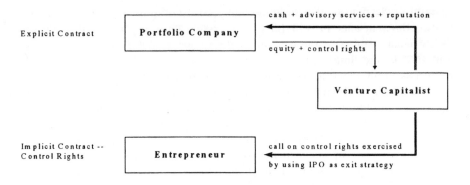

Fig. 3. Implicit and explicit contracts between venture capitalist and entrepreneur.

To begin with, an IPO is available to the portfolio company only when the company is successful. Indeed, the frequency with which a venture capital fund's portfolio companies go public is a central measure of the venture capitalist's success in the eyes of investors in venture capital funds (Gompers, 1996). When an IPO occurs, the entrepreneur receives two things. Like the venture capital provider, the entrepreneur gets cash to the extent that she sells some of her shares in the offering, plus increased value and liquidity for unsold shares. In addition, the entrepreneur reassumes much of the control originally ceded to the venture capitalist. The venture capitalist's percentage stake is reduced by its direct sale of shares,[8] by the venture capitalist's in-kind distribution of shares to its investors (Gompers and Lerner, 1997), and by the company's sale of new shares in the IPO to dispersed shareholders. The now-public firm also no longer depends on the venture capitalist for continuation decisions through staged funding; the public equity market is available. The greater liquidity of the venture capitalist's remaining investment after the IPO also reduces the venture capitalists' incentive to monitor (Coffee, 1991 discusses the tradeoff between monitoring and liquidity).[9] The venture capitalist's need to monitor the portfolio company intensively is further reduced because some of the monitoring task will now be undertaken by stock market analysts. On average, venture

---

[8] Over the years 1979–1990, lead venture capitalists sold shares in some 27% of IPOs of venture capital backed companies. The incidence of venture capitalist sales increased to 37% in the last three years of that period. (Lin and Smith, 1995).

[9] The increased liquidity and the venture capitalist's ability to sell off its investment gradually after the initial public offering is critical because the underwriter will typically limit the amount that the venture capitalist can sell in the IPO and over the following six months lest the market draw an unfavorable inference about the portfolio company's future value from the venture capitalist's sales (Benton and Gunderson 1993).

B.S. Black, R.J. Gilson/Journal of Financial Economics 47 (1998) 243–277 261

capital funds reduce their holdings of a portfolio company's shares by 28% within one year after an IPO (Barry et al., 1990). Three years after the IPO, only 12% of lead venture capitalists retain 5% or more of the portfolio company's shares (Lin and Smith, 1995).

Finally, and most significantly, the explicit contract between the venture capital fund and the portfolio company ensures that important control rights that were initially given to the fund, including guaranteed board membership and veto power over business decisions, disappear on an initial public offering whether or not the fund sells any shares at all in the IPO. Typically, the terms of the convertible securities held by the venture capital fund require conversion into common stock at the time of the IPO (Gompers, 1997); the negative covenants contained in the investor rights agreement also terminate on an IPO (Benton and Gunderson, 1993). In short, the venture capital fund's special control rights end at the time of an IPO, leaving the fund with only the weaker control rights attendant to substantial stock ownership. Even this control will diminish over time as the venture capital fund reduces its remaining stock position. Control becomes vested in the entrepreneur, who often retains a controlling stock interest and, even if not, retains the usual broad discretion enjoyed by chief executives of companies without a controlling shareholder.

The opportunity to acquire control through an IPO exit if the company is successful gives the entrepreneur a powerful incentive beyond the purely financial gains from the increased value of her shares in the firm. In effect, the prospect of an IPO exit gives the entrepreneur something of a call option on control, contingent on the firm's success.

Contrast this outcome with what the entrepreneur receives when the venture capital provider exits through sale of the portfolio company to an established company. As in an IPO, the entrepreneur receives cash or the more liquid securities of a publicly traded acquirer. Control, however, passes to the acquirer, even if the entrepreneur remains in charge of day-to-day management. Thus, if an IPO exit is not available, the entrepreneur cannot be given the incentive of a call option on control exercisable in the event of success. Exit through an IPO is possible only in the presence of a stock market; its role in the contract between the venture capitalist and the entrepreneur links the venture capital market and the stock market.

4.3. Feasibility of the implicit contract over control

It remains to demonstrate the feasibility of the implicit incentive contract over control and its superiority to an explicit contract. We undertake these tasks in this and the next subsection. The difficulty of defining success and the potential advantages of an implicit contract are suggested by the parties' use of an implicit contract involving staged funding to handle the pre-IPO decision as to whether and on what terms the venture capitalist will provide additional financing.

B.S. Black, R.J. Gilson/Journal of Financial Economics 47 (1998) 243–277

The feasibility problem is to specify a self-enforcing implicit contract: (i) whose terms are clear; (ii) whose satisfaction by the entrepreneur is observable; and (iii) whose breach by the venture capital provider would be observable and punished by the market. Consider the following stylized implicit contract: The entrepreneur will be deemed sufficiently successful to exercise her call option on control and the venture capital provider will exit through an IPO, so long as a reputable investment banker will underwrite a firm commitment offering. The need to clearly specify the conditions under which the entrepreneur can exercise the call option on control is met, not by defining numerical performance standards that the portfolio company must meet, but by delegating the performance assessment to a third party. Investment bankers have an incentive to seek out (or respond to inquiries from) portfolio companies whose performance has been strong enough to allow a successful public offering. A central feature of the investment banker's role in a public offering is as an information intermediary who proffers its reputation on behalf of the portfolio company much as the venture capitalist provides credibility to the portfolio company at an earlier stage in its development. The investment banker's internal standards for companies it is willing to take public, made credible by its willingness to commit its own capital and reputation to the offering, provide a self-enforcing statement of the conditions for exercise of the entrepreneur's call option.

The second requirement, that the entrepreneur's satisfaction of the exercise conditions be observable, is met in the same way. The investment banker's offer to take the portfolio company public is directly observable by the venture capital provider and the entrepreneur and is credible because the investment banker has the right incentives to honestly evaluate a portfolio company's performance.

The final requirement, that the venture capitalist's breach of the implicit contract be observable and punishable by the market, is also met. Observability results from the character of the venture capital market. The universe of portfolio companies sufficiently successful to merit a public offering is limited, as is the number of venture capital providers. Both sides of the market are relatively concentrated, with a significant number of portfolio companies geographically concentrated and the offices of a significant percentage of U.S. venture capital providers found along a short strip of Sand Hill Road in Silicon Valley (Saxanian, 1994). Moreover, venture capital funds typically specialize in portfolio companies geographically proximate to the fund's office.[10] While

---

[10] Lerner (1994a) reports that venture capital providers located within five miles of a portfolio company are twice as likely to have a board representative than providers located more than 500 miles distant. The fact that in 1996, 40% of total venture capital disbursements were to portfolio companies in California (Venture Capital Yearbook, 1997) provides further evidence of venture capital provider concentration sufficient to support a reputation market.

proximity facilitates monitoring, it also facilitates the emergence and mainten-ance of a reputation market. A claim by an entrepreneur that a venture capital provider declined to allow a portfolio company to go public when a reputable investment banker was available would quickly circulate through the commun-ity. Finally, venture capital providers are repeat players, who typically seek at regular intervals to raise funds for new limited partnerships, which must then invest in new portfolio companies, before prior limited partnerships are com-pleted (Sahlman, 1990). In the competition to be lead venture investor in the most attractive companies, a reputation for breaching the implicit contract for control is hardly an advantage.

The viability of reputation market constraints on venture capitalist behavior is confirmed by another aspect of the overall venture capitalist-entrepreneur relationship. The venture capitalist's staged capital commitment gives the ven-ture capitalist the option to abandon short of providing the portfolio company sufficient funds to complete its business plan. This gives the entrepreneur incentive to perform, gives the venture capitalist incentives to monitor, and reduces agency costs by shifting the continuation decision from the entrepreneur to the venture capitalist. However, this pattern, coupled with the right of first refusal with respect to future financing typically given to the venture capitalist (Sahlman, 1990), also permits the venture capitalist to act opportunistically. What can the entrepreneur do if the venture capitalist opportunistically offers to provide the second-stage financing necessary for the entrepreneur to continue at an unfair price? The entrepreneur could seek financing from other sources, but the original venture capitalist's right of first refusal presents a serious barrier: who would incur the costs of making a bid when potential bidders know that a bid will succeed only when a better informed party – the original investor – believes the price is too high? A reputation market can police this potential for opportunism.[11]

4.4. Superiority of the implicit contract over control

An explicit contract that specifies the operating performance necessary to entitle the entrepreneur to reacquire control is a difficult undertaking. Creating a state-contingent contract that specifies the control consequences of the full range of possible states of the world over the four- to ten-year average term of a venture investment, without creating perverse incentives, is a severe challenge both to the parties' predictive powers and their drafting capabilities. It is in precisely these circumstances that an implicit contract is likely to have a com-parative advantage over an explicit contract.

---

[11] Admati and Pfleiderer (1994), who model the shift of the continuation decision to the venture capitalist, do not address this problem.

Moreover, the venture capitalist will be willing to cede control only at the time of exit, not before. Yet a mechanical formula cannot ensure that a reputable underwriter will be willing to take the portfolio company public. In addition, the venture capitalist must actively cooperate for an IPO to succeed. At the same time, the venture capitalist cannot unduly 'puff' the portfolio company's prospects, because the capital markets will punish this behavior through reduced marketability of IPOs of other portfolio companies. Thus, a supposedly explicit contract, defining when the entrepreneur and the venture capital fund have the right to take the portfolio company public, cannot easily be enforced. Such a contract would be substantially implicit in fact, even if explicit in form. Thus, it is not surprising that entrepreneurs and venture capitalists, for the most part, do not seek to contract explicitly over control.

Finally, the implicit/explicit dichotomy presented above oversimplifies the real world. In fact, some elements of the contract over control are explicit, while others are left implicit. For example, cessation of the venture capital fund's special control rights at the time of an IPO is explicitly required, while the timing of the triggering event – the IPO – is left implicit. Conversion of the venture capitalist's convertible securities into common stock special rights is sometimes explicitly required if the portfolio company achieves defined financial milestones, even without an IPO (Benton and Gunderson, 1993; Gompers, 1997). Also, consistent with the greater importance of control earlier in a firm's life, the venture capitalist's explicit control rights are generally stronger, the earlier the stage of the investment (Gompers, 1997).

4.5. Consistency with empirical evidence

In our model, successful entrepreneurs often prefer exit by IPO, and have the implicit contractual right to demand this form of exit not only when it maximizes firm value compared to the alternative of sale of the firm, but also when the entrepreneur's private value of control outweighs the entrepreneur's loss in share value. Our model predicts that the venture capitalist's successful exits will take place disproportionately through IPO. If so, IPO exits will be more profitable than exits through sale of the portfolio company, by more than can plausibly be explained by the different values available through these different forms of exit.

This prediction is confirmed. Gompers (1995) reports that venture capital funds earn an average 60% annual return on investment in IPO exits, compared to 15% in acquisition exits; see also Petty et al. (1994); Sagari and Guidotti (1993). MacIntosh (1996) reports that IPO exits are more profitable in Canada as well. It is not plausible that these large differences could arise if the venture capitalist chose in each case the exit that maximized return on investment.

B.S. Black, R.J. Gilson/Journal of Financial Economics 47 (1998) 243–277 265

5. Evidence from other countries

We have developed an informal theory in which the success of early stage venture capital financing of high-growth, often high-technology firms, is linked to the availability of exit through an initial public offering. The weak form of the theory is that IPO exit is preferred by entrepreneurs. This preference leads to an implicit contract over control between the entrepreneur and the venture capitalist, in which the entrepreneur's success is rewarded by giving the entrepreneur the option to reacquire control through an IPO exit. This theory is consistent with the evidence discussed in part 2 of a correlation between frequency of IPO exit and amount of new capital contributed to venture capital funds, and the evidence in Section 4.5 that successful exits occur disproportionately through IPO.

The strong form of our theory is that the entrepreneur's preference for control is strong enough to significantly impair the development of a venture capital market in countries where exit by acquisition is the only viable option. This section offers an informal test of the strong form of our theory: Does the theory predict the observed success of venture capital in different countries with different types of capital markets? We provide data on Germany and the United States in part 2; we survey several other countries below.

5.1. Japan

We have only limited quantitative data on the size of the venture capital industry in Japan. However, the quantitative and qualitative data that we have (primarily from Milhaupt, 1997) is consistent with our theory: Japan, with its bank-centered capital market, has relatively little venture capital. In 1995, there were only 121 venture capital funds, of which more than half were affiliated with banks and run by the parent bank's employees. The employees of bank-affiliated funds commonly rotate through jobs in the bank's venture capital affiliate and then return to the parent bank. Thus, they are unlikely to develop the special skills needed to evaluate high-technology investments. Another 25 Japanese venture capital funds were run by securities firms or insurance companies.

Unlike American venture capital funds, which primarily provide equity financing, Japanese funds, perhaps reflecting their parentage, provide funds mostly through loans. Where American venture capital funds concentrate on high-tech businesses, and are the principal capital source for many startup high-tech firms, Japanese venture capital firms rarely invest in high-technology firms. Instead, they concentrate on manufacturing and services, including such mundane investments as small shops and restaurants. As of 1995, Japanese venture capital funds owned more than 10% of the stock of only one biotechnology company, two new materials firms, and 12 electronics firms.

Empirical Corporate Finance I

5.2. Great Britain and Other European Countries

The similarity between Germany and Japan in the weakness of their venture capital industries strengthens the empirical support for the claim that bank-centered capital markets do not develop a strong venture capital industry. The converse claim is that stock-market centered capital markets can develop a strong venture capital industry. In particular, our theory predicts that Great Britain, with its active stock market, should have comparatively strong venture capital industries. This prediction is also supported by the evidence. British GDP is only about two-thirds of Germany's, yet its venture capital industry is almost five times larger, measured by cumulative capital committed (Economist, 1996); new capital commitments are comparable to the United States as a percentage of GDP. Ireland, with its easy access to the London stock market, also has relatively high venture capital as a percentage of GDP. Britain and Ireland are the clear European leaders in venture capital, with everyone else far behind.

Table 6 shows new funds raised by venture capital funds in 1993 and 1994 as a percentage of GDP. Great Britain's lead over everyone else would be greater still if the data were classified by the venture capital fund's home country,

Table 6
New capital committed to venture capital funds, 1993–1994 (percent of GDP)

New capital commitments to venture capital funds, as percent of national GNP, for various countries between 1993 and 1994.

Country	Year		Average: 1993–1994
	1993	1994	
United States	0.03%	0.06%	0.05%
Great Britain	0.09	0.27	0.18
France	0.06	0.07	0.06
Italy	0.02	0.02	0.02
Germany	0.01	0.01	0.01
Netherlands	0.04	0.07	0.05
Spain	0.03	0.01	0.02
Sweden	0.06	0.06	0.06
Ireland	0.04	0.25	0.15
Portugal	0.06	0.07	0.06
Belgium	0.04	0.03	0.04
Denmark	0.01	0.08	0.04
Switzerland	0.03	0.02	0.03
Norway	0.05	0.03	0.04
Finland	0.01	0.04	0.02
Iceland	0.06	0	0.03
Austria	0	0	0

Source: European Venture Capital Association, 1995.

B.S. Black, R.J. Gilson/Journal of Financial Economics 47 (1998) 243–277   267

because British-based venture capital funds invest substantial amounts through affiliates in other European countries.

These data understate the relative size of the U.S. venture capital industry. European venture capital firms are less specialized than their American counterparts and are often affiliated with commercial banks. The European Venture Capital Association defines 'venture capital' to include leveraged buyouts and buyins, and replacement of a firm's existing financing. In contrast, leveraged buyout firms in the United States are a distinct industry from venture capital firms; venture capital is also distinct from non-venture private equity financing. Non-venture uses of funds by European 'venture capital' firms are substantial. For example, in Great Britain, 47% of capital commitments in 1994 went to buyins and buyouts, and only 8% to early stage financing. In France, 40% of venture capital comes from banks, and in 1994, 51% of funds committed went to buyouts, buyins, and replacement financing, while only 9% went to early stage financing.

5.3. Canada

Our evidence on Canada is drawn primarily from the recent survey by MacIntosh (1996). Canada has a relatively open IPO market – both domestic IPOs and access to the U.S. IPO market. Thus, our theory predicts that Canada should have a relatively active venture capital industry. The Canadian data are difficult to interpret because of heavy government intervention in the venture capital industry. Labor Sponsored Venture Capital Corporations (LSVCCs), which must be formed by a labor union, receive substantial tax benefits. As a result, they dominate the Canadian venture capital industry. These funds tend to invest more conservatively than other venture capital funds. The largest single LSVCC fund, the Solidarite fund, is owned by the government of Quebec.

Still, there is substantial evidence that Canadian venture capital funds, especially private funds, play a large role in early-stage financing of high-technology Canadian firms. In 1994, private independent funds had C$1.8 billion under management, and all Canadian venture capital firms had C$4.5 billion under management. The latter figure is comparable to the United States after adjusting for the size of the economy. Moreover, 25% of new capital went to early-stage financing – a figure similar to that for the United States, and much higher than for European and Japanese venture capital firms. The percentage of early-stage investments is likely higher than this for non-LSVCC funds. In Canada, as in the United States, IPO exit is common and the highest-return exits are through IPOs.

5.4. Israel

Israel offers an interesting case study of how an existing venture capital industry can adapt when the option of a domestic IPO is taken away through regulation. The Israeli economy has grown rapidly during the 1990s, partly in response to deregulation of a formerly heavily government-controlled economy. High-technology startups, often financed by venture capital funds, have been an important element in this growth (Gourlay, 1996). Multiple elements have contributed to the Israeli high-technology and venture capital industries, including government guarantees against large losses by publicly traded venture capital funds in the form of a put option on the fund's shares, government creation of incubator facilities for startup firms, and a substantial influx in the early 1990s of immigrant scientists from Russia.

In the early 1990s, Israeli high-technology firms often went public on the Tel Aviv Stock Exchange at a very early stage. After a stock price crash in early 1994, the Tel Aviv Stock Exchange adopted listing rules that limited IPOs by early-stage companies. Israeli venture capital funds have nonetheless continued to flourish by shifting their IPOs from the Tel Aviv Stock Exchange to the NASDAQ market. Giza Group (1996) reports the results of 16 IPOs of venture capital-backed Israeli companies from 1993 through early 1996, of which 14 were on NASDAQ, one on the British 'AIM' small-firm market, and one on the Tel Aviv Stock Exchange. As of March 31, 1997, 62 Israeli companies had listed securities on NASDAQ, including 22 in 1996 alone; most were high-tech companies. The cumulative total exceeds any other country's except Canada's, and far exceeds any other country's relative to GDP.

6. Alternative explanations for intercountry variations in venture capital

We have developed in this paper an informal theory, based on the stock market's role in providing contracting options not available in a bank-centered capital market, that may partially explain cross-country variations in venture capital. In this section, we evaluate briefly several alternative explanations for the different levels of venture capital financing in stock market-centered and bank-centered capital markets. We first consider a claim of functional irrelevance: institutional differences between stock market-centered and bank-centered systems do not affect economic outcomes because bank-centered systems have developed functionally equivalent means for financing early-stage entrepreneurial activities. We then turn to explanations that acknowledge differences between countries in their ability to provide financing for high-technology ventures, but assign causation differently than we do.

While our analysis here is only suggestive, differential performance between the United States and Germany in industries where venture capital plays a significant role in the U.S. suggests that Germany has not yet developed a functional substitute for venture capital. Alternative explanations may account for some of this functional difference, but none appears able to fully displace the account of cross-national differences offered here.

B.S. Black, R.J. Gilson/Journal of Financial Economics 47 (1998) 243–277 269

6.1. Institutional but not functional differences

Different methods of organizing capital markets do not necessarily dictate corresponding functional or performance differences. For example, empirical research by Kaplan (1994a,b) and Kaplan and Minton (1994) suggests that Japanese and German companies change top management in response to poor earnings and stock price performance about as often and as quickly as United States companies, despite the three countries' quite different corporate governance institutions. The similar outcomes could reflect the impact of selection on path-dependent corporate governance systems. That three leading industrial economies change senior management under roughly the same circumstances may reflect a selection bias. By limiting the sample to these successful systems, we observe only systems that, within the constraints established by their particular institutions, have solved reasonably well the central corporate governance problem of replacing poorly performing managers (Gilson, 1996; Kaplan and Ramseyer, 1996).

The same functional equivalence argument can be made with respect to differences in how successful economies finance entrepreneurial activities. If other financing methods, such as bank financing of startup companies or internalization of the entrepreneurial process by large companies, yields the same performance as the United States' venture capital market, then the institutional differences are historically interesting but not functionally significant.

The empirical evidence needed to assess the functional equivalence argument for venture-capital financed industries is not available, but anecdotal evidence makes us skeptical about functional equivalence. The United States has become a world leader in precisely those industries, notably biotechnology and computer-related high technology, in which the venture capital market figures centrally (Powell, 1996). Moreover, in both Europe and the United States, large pharmaceutical companies are responding to biotechnology entrepreneurship not by funding the entrepreneurs directly, but instead by providing later-stage financing and partnering arrangements to entrepreneurial companies, mostly U.S.-based and originally financed through U.S. venture capital (Powell, 1996; Hellman, 1995b; Lerner and Merges, 1997). The result is not functional equivalence but specialization: Different activities are allocated to different countries on the basis of differences in their venture capital markets.

6.2. The role of pension fund financing of venture capital

In both Japan and Germany, pension funds do not invest in venture capital. In Germany, corporate pension obligations are typically unfunded, so large private pension plans do not exist. Japan has moderate sized corporate pension plans, but these plans are barred by law from investing in venture capital (Milhaupt, 1997). In the United States, in contrast, the Department of Labor in

1979 explicitly sanctioned pension fund investment in venture capital. As shown in Table 3, pension plans now provide over 40% of total investment in U.S. venture capital funds.

Differences in pension fund size and regulation can explain part, but in our judgment only part, of the cross-national differences in the size of the venture capital industry. Funded pension obligations, as in the United States, as opposed to unfunded pension obligations in Germany, dictate only who makes employee pension investments, not the investments themselves. A company with an unfunded pension plan, in effect, incurs an unsecured debt – its promise to pay pensions when workers retire. The company can invest the funds thus made available in any way it chooses, including in venture capital. German firms could also voluntarily fund their pension obligations, as many American firms did even before ERISA established minimum funding requirements in 1973. The pension plan could then invest in venture capital, if it so chose.

In the U.S., the unclear legality of pension fund investments in venture capital between 1973 and 1979 sterilized this pool of investable funds. Not surprisingly, the 1979 regulatory change resulted in a flow of funds into the previously restricted area. German firms have never been subject to an investment restriction similar to 1973–1979 U.S. regulation.

More generally, money is the ultimate fungible commodity, and venture capital commitments are a tiny fraction of total business investment – in the U.S., around $5 billion annually compared to gross investment of over $1 trillion. If there were attractive profits to be made from venture capital investing, it seems likely that funds would be available from other sources, even if not from pension plans. After all, the Germans and the Japanese save more than Americans as a percentage of GDP, merely in different forms.

6.3. Differences in labor market regulation

Germany and a number of other Western European countries impose substantial restrictions on layoffs, especially severance payment obligations. These rules impose costs on startup businesses and thus could discourage their formation. Variations in labor market restrictions correlate with observed national variations in venture capital. Germany has strong layoff protections and little venture capital. Japan has few formal restrictions on layoffs, but the common practice by large companies of hiring only recent college graduates and promising them lifetime employment reduces labor market mobility (Gilson and Roe, 1997). In contrast, the United States and Britain have more flexible labor markets and more active venture capital markets.

Labor market regulation and practices could well affect the vitality of venture capital. For example, Gilson (1997) argues that weak enforcement of covenants not to compete is a factor in the strength of venture capital in California; Hyde (1997) argues that the concentration of venture-capital-backed firms in Silicon

B.S. Black, R.J. Gilson/Journal of Financial Economics 47 (1998) 243–277 271

Valley both supports and depends on what he calls 'high velocity' labor markets. But labor market regulation, as a partial explanation for the vitality of venture capital markets, seems unlikely to fully displace our explanation, based on differences in capital markets.

Consider Germany as an example. Severance obligations build over time; they are much less burdensome for a startup firm that fails after a few years of operation than for a mature firm that closes a plant that has operated for decades. Moreover, unpaid severance obligations are of little significance if a firm goes bankrupt – they merely expand the pool of unsecured claims on the firm's assets.

Moreover, labor market restrictions do not map perfectly onto national patterns in venture capital activity. Canada has moderately strong labor market restrictions; Ireland and Israel have strong restrictions comparable to West Germany's. Yet these countries also have strong venture capital. This pattern is consistent with their access to stock markets: the London market for Ireland; the U.S. market for Israel; and U.S. and domestic stock markets for Canada.

6.4. Cultural differences in entrepreneurship

A final explanation is cultural. Germans and Japanese could be less entrepreneurial and less willing to risk failure than Americans, leading to lesser demand for venture capital services (Milhaupt, 1997, discusses Japanese culture). Cultural explanations for different patterns of economic activity are hard to evaluate. They can be partly tautological. In economically successful countries like Germany and Japan, the forces of economic selection will cause culture and economic institutions to become mutually supportive. Because both are endogenously determined, observing that cultural institutions support existing economic patterns tells us nothing about causation. For present purposes, the more interesting issue is not a static inquiry into the current equilibrium of culture and economic institutions, but a dynamic one: how can culture and institutions change in response to exogenous changes in the economic environment (North, 1990, 1994). We briefly consider this issue from an instrumental perspective in Section 7.

However, there is some reason for skepticism about claims of large cultural differences in willingness to take risks. People in all countries found large numbers of businesses, most of which fail. The empirical regularity to be explained is *not* why the Germans and Japanese do not start risky new businesses, but why they do not start many *high-technology* businesses, with few tangible assets on which a bank can rely for partial return of its investment. The success of immigrant entrepreneurs in countries with strong venture capital (for example, Russian immigrants in Israel and Asian immigrants in the United States) suggests that entrepreneurs will emerge if the institutional infrastructure needed to support them is available. After all, Russia and India are also not

272   B.S. Black, R.J. Gilson/Journal of Financial Economics 47 (1998) 243–277

known for their cultural support of entrepreneurship. Moreover, efforts to find large cross-cultural differences in entrepreneurship between the U.S. and Russia at the close of the Communist period have failed, even though these two countries ought to exhibit much larger differences than the United States, Germany, and Japan (Shiller et al., 1991, 1992).

7. Implications for venture capital in bank-centered capital markets

Exploring the implications of the link between venture capital markets and stock markets is more complicated than the simple admonition that bank-centered capital markets should create a stock market. That straightforward approach has been tried before and failed. For example, France and Germany created special stock exchange segments for newer, smaller companies during the 1980s that, by the mid-1990s, had been shuttered or marginalized (Rasch, 1994). Nonetheless, the financial press still stresses the absence of a venture capital market as being at the root of the European high technology sector's poor performance, particularly with respect to Germany (e.g., Fisher, 1996a,b), and three efforts are underway to try again to create stock markets that cater to small high-technology companies. The Alternative Investment Market of the London Stock Exchange began trading in June 1995 and now lists over 200 firms (Price, 1996). Euro NM, a consortium of the French Le Nouveau Marche', which began trading in February, 1996, the German Neur Market, and the Belgian New Market, is scheduled to begin full operation in 1997. Finally, EASDAQ, an exchange explicitly patterned after the U.S. NASDAQ and of which the NASD is a part owner, opened on September 30, 1996 (Pickles, 1996). This flurry of stock market creation, taken with the explicit goal of enhancing the European venture capital market, suggests that there may be value in exploring the normative implications of the stock market-venture capital market link.

We begin our analysis of this link by stressing the path dependency of national capital markets. It is not merely a stock market that is missing in bank-centered systems. The secondary institutions that have developed in bank-centered systems, including the banks' conservative approach to lending and investing, and social and financial incentives that less richly reward entrepreneurial zeal and more severely penalize failure (See Harrison, 1990 (Germany); Milhaupt, 1997 (Japan)), are less conducive to entrepreneurial activity than the secondary institutions of stock market-centered capital markets. More critically, experienced venture capitalists, able to assess the prospects of new venture and to provide the nonfinancial contributions that venture capitalists supply in the United States are absent, as are investment bankers experienced in taking early-stage companies public. Neither institution will develop quickly. A strong venture capital market thus reflects an equilibrium of a

B.S. Black, R.J. Gilson/Journal of Financial Economics 47 (1998) 243–277   273

number of interdependent factors, only one of which is the presence of a stock market.

For example, Germany today faces a chicken and egg problem: a venture capital market requires a stock market, but a stock market requires a supply of entrepreneurs and deals which, in turn, require a venture capital market. In addition, German entrepreneurs who care about future control of their company must trust venture capitalists to return control to them some years hence and must further trust that the stock market window will be open when they are ready to go public. The institutional design issue is how to simultaneously create both a set of mutually dependent institutions and the trust that these institutions will work as expected when called upon.

In such a path-dependent equilibrium, the cost of change is the guard rail that keeps us on the path. We remain in an equilibrium less efficient than would be possible without the transaction costs of creating the institutions needed to support alternatives (Kohn, 1995). While we do not aspire to offer a solution here, our analysis suggests an approach to creating the conditions conducive to a vigorous venture capital market: avoid the problem of creating multiple new institutions by piggybacking on another country's institutions. If this is successful, a profit opportunity and corresponding potential for the development of local institutions will be created.

Most obviously, in the increasingly global capital market, the German venture capital market could follow Israel's lead in relying on the United States stock market and its supporting infrastructure. A German company that maintains accounting records in a fashion consistent with U.S. standards – arguably much less of a burden when done from the beginning than if implemented by a conversion, as when Daimler-Benz listed its shares on the New York Stock Exchange – confronts no regulatory barrier to listing on NASDAQ, the exchange most suitable to venture-capital-backed IPOs. At present, over 100 European companies, including one German company, list their shares on NASDAQ. Many of these listings represent the initial public offering of the company's stock. With NASDAQ comes its institutional infrastructure. For example, both Hambrecht and Quist and Robertson, Stephens and Co., leading investment bankers for venture-capital-backed IPOs in the United States, are opening European offices and holding conferences to introduce American venture capital funds to European entrepreneurs (Lavin, 1996). Silicon Valley law firms are also actively recruiting European IPO candidates.

The availability of this institutional infrastructure, without the costs of establishing it from scratch, can shorten the shadow of the past and, in the medium term, induce the development of competing local institutions. For example, in the near term, foreign venture capitalists will likely find it profitable to hire and train locals to help them find profitable investment opportunities. In the medium term, some of these people, once trained, will form their own firms and compete with their former employers.

274 *B.S. Black, R.J. Gilson/Journal of Financial Economics 47 (1998) 243–277*

8. Conclusion

In this paper. we have examined one of the path-dependent consequences of the difference between stock market-centered and bank-centered capital markets: the link between an active stock market and a strong venture capital market. We have shown that economies of scope among financial and nonfinancial contributions by venture capital providers, plus venture capital investors' need for a quantitative measure of venture capital funds' skill, can explain the importance of an exit strategy. Moreover, the potential for exit through an IPO, possible in a stock-market-centered capital market, allows the venture capitalist and the entrepreneur to contract implicitly over control, in a manner that is not easily duplicable in a bank-centered capital market. Finally, we have suggested that the best strategy for overcoming path dependent barriers to a venture capital market in bank-centered systems is to piggyback on the institutional infrastructure of stock-market-centered systems.

Our model seeks to explain the importance of a possible IPO exit for a high-growth firm financed by a venture capital fund, for which exit by the fund is desirable at a stage in the firm's life when it is still consuming rather than generating capital. For a mature, cash-generating firm, another exit strategy that preserves the entrepreneur's control is possible: the firm itself can buy back the venture capital fund's stake, perhaps by borrowing the needed funds. This strategy permits a somewhat different implicit contract over control between the fund and an entrepreneur: if the firm is successful enough to buy out the fund, the fund will acquiesce in this strategy even if this form of exit does not maximize the fund's return on an individual investment. In the United States, this form of exit is associated not with venture capital funds but with 'leveraged buyout' funds. In Europe, which has a less clear distinction between venture capital and leveraged buyouts, this form of exit is common when venture capital funds invest in management buyouts of mature firms. We plan to explore in future work the possible extension of our model to the leveraged buyout industry.

References

Admati, A., Pfleiderer, P., 1994. Robust financial contracting and the role of venture capitalists. Journal of Finance 49, 371–402.

Aoki, M., 1994. Monitoring characteristics of the main bank system: an analytical and developmental view. In: Aoki, M., Patrick, H. (Eds.), The Japanese Main Bank System: Its Relevance for Developing and Transforming Economies. Oxford University Press, Oxford.

Barry, C., 1994. New directions in venture capital research. Journal of Financial Management 23, 3–15.

Barry, C., Muscarella, C., Peavy J., III, Vetsuypens, M., 1990. The role of venture capitalists in the creation of a public company. Journal of Financial Economics 27, 447–471.

B.S. Black, R.J. Gilson/Journal of Financial Economics 47 (1998) 243–277   275

Benton, L., Gunderson, R.,Jr., 1993. Portfolio company investments: hi-tech corporation, venture capital and public offering negotiation. In: Halloran, M., Benton, L., Gunderson, R., Jr., Kearney, K., del Calvo, J. (Eds.), Law and Business, Inc. Harcourt Brace Jovanovich, New York.

Bergloff, E., 1994. A control theory of venture capital finance. Journal of Law, Economics and Organization 10, 247–267.

Black, B., 1990. Shareholder passivity reexamined. Michigan Law Review 89, 520–608.

Booth, J., Smith, R., 1986. Capital raising, underwriting and the certification hypothesis. Journal of Financial Economics 15, 261–281.

Brav, A., Gompers, P., 1997. Myth or reality? The long-run underperformance of initial public offerings: evidence from venture and nonventure capital-backed companies. Journal of Finance, forthcoming.

Bundesverband Deutsche Kapitalbeteiligungsgesellschaften (BVK) Jahrbuch [German Venture Capital Association Yearbook], various years through 1996 (BVK, Berlin, Germany).

Bygrave, W., Timmons, J., 1992. Venture capital at the crossroads. Harvard Business School Press, Cambridge, MA.

Carvalho, A., 1996. Venture capital as a network for human resources allocation. Unpublished working paper. University of Illinois.

Coffee, J., 1991. Liquidity versus control: The institutional investor as corporate monitor. Columbia Law Review 91, 1277–1368.

Diamond, D., 1991. Monitoring and reputation: the choice between bank loans and directly placed debt. Journal of Political Economy 99, 689–721.

Economist, 1996. Going for the golden egg. Sept. 28, 1996, at 89.

Edwards, J., Fischer, K., 1994. Banks, finance and investment in Germany. Cambridge University Press, Cambridge.

European Venture Capital Association, 1995. EVCA Yearbook 1995. Ernst and Young, London, England.

Fisher, A., 1996a. A venture across the pond. Financial Times, July 24, 1996, 12.

Fisher, A., 1996b. Germans urged to take a risk for jobs. Financial Times, July 16, 1996, 2.

Florida, R., Martin, K., 1990. The Breakthrough Illusion: Corporate America's Failure to Move from Innovation to Mass Production. BasicBooks, New York.

Gilson, R., Kraakman, R., 1984. The mechanisms of market efficiency. Virginia Law Review 70, 549–644.

Gilson, R., Roe, M., 1997. Lifetime employment: Labor peace and the evolution of Japanese corporate governance. Unpublished working paper. Columbia Law School.

Gilson, R., 1996. Corporate governance and economic efficiency. Washington University Law Quarterly 74, 327–345.

Gilson, R., 1997. The legal infrastructure of high-technology industrial districts: Silicon Valley and covenants not to compete. Unpublished working paper. Stanford Law School.

Giza Group, 1996. Survey of venture capital and investment funds in Israel: August 1996 Update. Giza Group, Tel Aviv, Israel.

Gompers, P., 1997. An examination of convertible securities in venture capital. Journal of Law and Economics, forthcoming.

Gompers, P., 1996. Grandstanding in the venture capital industry. Journal of Financial Economics 42, 133–156.

Gompers, P., 1995. Optimal investment, monitoring, and the staging of venture capital. Journal of Financial Economics 50, 1461–1489.

Gompers, P., Lerner, J., 1996. The use of covenants: an empirical analysis of venture partnership agreements. Journal of Law and Economics 39, 463–498.

Gompers, P., Lerner, J., 1997. Venture capital distributions: short-run and long-run reactions. Unpublished working paper. Harvard Business School.

Gorman, M., Sahlman, W., 1989. What do venture capitalists do? Journal of Business Venturing 4, 231–248.

Gourlay, R., 1996. The development of a venture capital industry lies behind the economic success of a new breed of high-tech Israeli company. Financial Times, April 30, 1996, 14.

Grossman, S., Hart, O., 1988. One share-one vote and the market for corporate control. Journal of Financial Economics 20, 175–202.

Harris, M., Raviv, A., 1988. Corporate governance: voting rights and majority rules. Journal of Financial Economics 20, 203–235.

Harrison, E., 1990. The West German venture capital market. Peter Lang, Frankfurt am Main, Frankfurt, Germany.

Hellman, T., 1995a. The allocation of control rights in venture capital contracts. Research Paper No. 1362. Stanford Business School, Stanford.

Hellman, T., 1995b. Competition and cooperation between entrepreneurial an established companies: the viability of corporate venture investments. Unpublished working paper. Stanford Business School, Stanford.

Hyde, A., 1997. High-velocity labor markets. Unpublished working paper. Rutgers Law School.

Hoshi, T., 1993. Evolution of the main bank system in Japan. Unpublished working paper. University of California at San Diego.

Kaplan, S., 1994a. Top executive rewards and firm performance: a comparison of Japan and the United States. Journal of Political Economy 102, 510–546.

Kaplan, S., 1994b. Top executives, turnover, and firm performance in Germany. Journal of Law, Economics and Organization 10, 142–159.

Kaplan, S., Minton, B., 1994. Appointments of outsiders to Japanese boards: determinants and implications for managers. Journal of Financial Economics 36, 225–258.

Kaplan, S., Ramseyer, J., 1996. Those Japanese firms with their disdain for shareholders: another fable for the academy. Washington University Law Quarterly 74, 403–418.

Kohn, M., 1995. Economics as a theory of exchange. Unpublished working paper. Dartmouth College Department of Economics, Dartmouth, NH.

Lavin, D., 1996. The sky's the limit. Convergence 2, 8.

Lerner, J., 1995. Venture capitalists and the oversight of private firms. Journal of Finance 50, 301–318.

Lerner, J., 1994a. The syndication of venture capital investments. Financial Management 23, 16–27.

Lerner, J., 1994b. Venture capitalists and the decision to go public. Journal of Financial Economics 35, 293–316.

Lerner, J., Merges, R., 1997. The control of strategic alliance: an empirical analysis of biotechnology collaborations. Working paper No. 6014. National Bureau of Economic Research.

Lin, T., Smith, R., 1995. Insider reputation and selling decisions: the unwinding of venture capital investments during equity IPOs. Unpublished working paper. Claremont Graduate School.

MacIntosh, J., 1996. Venture capital exits in Canada and the U.S. Unpublished working paper. University of Toronto Faculty of Law.

Marx, L., 1994. Negotiation of venture capital contracts. Unpublished working paper. University of Rochester.

Megginson, W., Weiss, K., 1991. Venture capital certification in initial public offerings. Journal of Finance 46, 879–903.

Milhaupt, C., 1997. The market for innovation in the United States and Japan: Venture capital and the comparative corporate governance debate. Northwestern University Law Review 91, 865–898.

Moukheiber, Z., March 25, 1996, Kleiner's web. Forbes, 40–42.

North, D., 1994. Economic performance through time. American Economic Review 84, 359–368.

North, D., 1990. Institutions, institutional change, and economic performance. Cambridge University Press, Cambridge, England.

Petty, W., Bygrave, W. Shulman, J., 1994. Harvesting the entrepreneurial venture: a time for creating value. Journal of Applied Corporate Finance. Spring, 48–58.

Pickles, C., 1996. One answer to Europe's capital needs. Wall Street Journal, Europe, October 23, 1996.

Porter, M., 1992. Capital disadvantages: America's failing investment system. Harvard Business Review, Sept.–Oct, 65–82.

Powell, W., 1996. Inter-organizational collaboration in the biotechnology industry. Journal of Institutional and Theoretical Economics 152, 197–215.

Price, C., 1996. EASDAQ pins hopes on NASDAQ. Financial Times, Sept. 30, 1996, 23.

Rajan, R., 1992. Insiders and outsiders: the choice between informed and arm's length debt. Journal of Finance 47, 1367–1400.

Rasch, S., 1994. Special stock market segments for small company shares in Europe – what went wrong? Discussion Paper No. 93-13. Center for European Economic Research.

Roe, M., 1994. Strong managers, weak owners: the political roots of American corporate finance. Princeton University Press, Princeton.

Sahlman, W., 1990. The structure and governance of venture capital organizations. Journal of Financial Economics 27, 473–522.

Sagari, S., Guidotti, G., 1993. Venture capital: the lessons from the developing world for the developing world. Financial Markets. Instruments and Investments 1, 31–42.

Saxanian, A., 1994. Regional Advantage: Culture and Competition in Silicon Valley and Route 128. Harvard University Press, Cambridge, MA.

Shiller, R., Boycko, M., Korobov, V., 1991. Popular attitudes toward free markets: the Soviet Union and the United States compared. American Economic Review 81, 385–400.

Shiller, R., Boycko, M., Korobov, V., 1992. Hunting for homo sovieticus: situational versus attitudinal factors in economic behavior. Brookings Papers on Economic Activity, 127–181.

Venture Capital Yearbook, various years through 1997. Venture Economics Publishing, New York.

[6]

Journal of Financial Economics 27 (1990) 473–521. North-Holland

The structure and governance of venture-capital organizations

William A. Sahlman*

Harvard Business School, Boston, MA 02163, USA

Received August 1989, final version received December 1990

Venture-capital organizations raise money from individuals and institutions for investment in early-stage businesses that offer high potential but high risk. This paper describes and analyzes the structure of venture-capital organizations, focusing on the relationship between investors and venture capitalists and between venture-capital firms and the ventures in which they invest. The agency problems in these organizations and to the contracts and operating procedures that have evolved in response are emphasized. Venture-capital organizations are contrasted with large, publicly traded corporations and with leveraged buyout organizations.

1. Introduction

The venture-capital industry has evolved operating procedures and contracting practices that are well adapted to environments characterized by uncertainty and information asymmetries between principals and agents. By venture capital I mean a professionally managed pool of capital that is invested in equity-linked securities of private ventures at various stages in their development. Venture capitalists are actively involved in the management of the ventures they fund, typically becoming members of the board of directors and retaining important economic rights in addition to their ownership rights. The prevailing organizational form in the industry is the limited partnership, with the venture capitalists acting as general partners and the outside investors as limited partners.

Venture-capital partnerships enter into contracts with both the outside investors who supply their funds and the entrepreneurial ventures in which

*The author gratefully acknowledges the useful comments of Bruce Greenwald, Michael Jensen, Christopher Barry, Clifford Smith, Kenneth French, Richard Ruback, two anonymous referees, Geoff Barss, Howard Stevenson, Jeffry Timmons, Regina Herzlinger, Andre Perold, Peter Wendell, Tench Coxe, and Christina Darwall. All errors and omissions remain the responsibility of the author.

they invest. The contracts share certain characteristics, notably:

(1) staging the commitment of capital and preserving the option to abandon,
(2) using compensation systems directly linked to value creation,
(3) preserving ways to force management to distribute investment proceeds.

These elements of the contracts address three fundamental problems:

(1) the sorting problem: how to select the best venture capital organizations and the best entrepreneurial ventures,
(2) the agency problem:[1] how to minimize the present value of agency costs,
(3) the operating-cost problem: how to minimize the present value of operating costs, including taxes.

From one perspective, venture capital can be viewed as an alternative model for organizing capital investments. Like corporations, venture-capital firms raise money to invest in projects. Many projects funded by venture capitalists (for example, the development of a new computer hardware peripheral) are similar to projects funded within traditional corporations. But the governance systems used by venture-capital organizations and traditional corporations are very different. This paper addresses some of the differences.

The information and analysis in the paper comes from two basic sources. Most of the data cited come from Venture Economics, the leading information source on the venture-capital industry. Venture Economics publishes the *Venture Capital Journal* (VCJ), a monthly magazine on trends in the industry, as well a number of specialized studies. The second major source is extensive field research I have done over the past eight years. This effort has resulted in 20 Harvard Business School cases based on decisions in venture-capital firms or in the companies they fund [e.g., Sahlman (1986c), Knights and Sahlman (1986d)], four technical and industry notes [e.g., Sahlman and Scherlis (1988)], and several articles [e.g., Sahlman and Stevenson (1985)]. The field research embodied in the cases and notes has been supplemented with on-site interviews with 25 venture-capital-firm management teams, over 150 venture capitalists, and approximately 50 venture-capital-backed entrepreneurial management teams.

Section 2 provides background information on the venture-capital industry, emphasizing the great uncertainty about returns on individual venture-capital projects. Sections 3, 4, and 5 discuss the general structure of a venture-capital firm and the contracts between external investors and venture capitalists. Sections 6 and 7 examine the contractual relationship between the venture-

---

[1]See Jensen and Meckling (1976), Fama (1980), and Fama and Jensen (1985) for background on the theory of agency costs. See also Williamson (1975, 1988) for background on transaction-cost theory. For related articles using the same basic framework to analyze organizational forms, see Wolfson (1985) on oil and gas limited partnerships and Brickley and Dark (1987) on franchises. Smith and Warner (1979) provide a similar analysis of financial contracts.

capital firm and the companies in which it invests. Venture-capital organizations are compared with other organizational forms for corporate or project governance in section 8. Section 9 summarizes the paper.

2. General industry background

Table 1 presents historical data on the venture-capital industry from 1980 to 1988. In 1988 an estimated 658 venture-capital firms in the U.S. managed slightly over $31 billion in capital and employed 2,500 professionals (panel A, table 1).[2] Industry resources were concentrated: the largest 89 firms controlled approximately 58% of the total capital. The average amount controlled by these 89 firms was just under $200 million [VCJ April 1990, p. 13)].

In each of the last several years, venture capitalists disbursed approximately $3 billion to fewer than 2,000 companies, most in high-technology industries (panel C, table 1). Although a typical large venture-capital firm receives up to 1,000 proposals each year, it invests in only a dozen or so new companies.

Venture capitalists invest at reasonably well-defined stages (panel C, table 1). The seed stage typically precedes formation of a complete management team or completion of a product or service design. Each successive stage is generally tied to a significant development in the company, such as completion of design, pilot production, first profitability, introduction of a second product, or an initial public offering [Plummer (1987), Kozmetsky et al. (1985)]. The stages of investment are described more completely in table 2.

Approximately 15% of the capital disbursed in each of the last three years went to ventures in early stages, whereas 65% was invested in later-stage companies, typically still privately held. The remaining 20% was invested in leveraged buyout or acquisition deals. In recent years venture capitalists have channeled roughly two-thirds of the capital invested each year into companies already in their portfolios, and one-third into new investments. Venture capitalists often participate in several rounds of financing with the same portfolio company, as illustrated in table 3.

Venture-capital investing plays a small role in overall new-business formation. According to Dun & Bradstreet, approximately 600,000 to 700,000 new businesses are incorporated in the United States each year [Council of Economic Advisors (1990)]. The vast majority of those that seek external funding do so from sources other than venture capitalists. Some analysts

---

[2] Venture Economic's estimate of total industry capital is based on commitments of capital and is measured at cost rather than market value: thus, the $31.1 billion cited in table 1 consists of capital that has been committed to venture-capital funds but not yet invested, some cash, and portfolio investments in individual ventures by venture-capital funds. The market value of the assets under management in the industry probably exceeds book value.

Table 1

Selected data on the United States venture-capital industry, 1980–1988.[a]

	1980	1981	1982	1983	1984	1985	1986	1987	1988
Panel A: Aggregate venture-capital industry statistics									
1 Total venture-capital pool ($M)	$4,500	$5,800	$7,600	$12,100	$16,300	$19,600	$24,100	$29,000	$31,100
2 Number of venture-capital firms	NA	NA	331	448	509	532	587	627	658
3 Number of industry professionals	NA	NA	1,031	1,494	1,760	1,899	2,187	2,378	2,474
4 Net new commitments to the venture-capital industry ($M)	$700	$1,300	$1,800	$4,500	$4,200	$3,300	$4,500	$4,900	$2,900
Panel B: Data on the independent private sector (noncorporate and non-SBIC venture capital organizations)									
1 Net new commitments to the independent private sector ($M)	$661	$867	$1,400	$3,400	$3,200	$2,300	$3,300	$4,200	$2,100
Sectoral analysis (% of total capital)									
2 Independent private	40.0%	44.0%	58.0%	68.7%	72.0%	73.0%	75.0%	78.0%	80.0%
3 Corporate	31.1%	28.0%	25.0%	21.0%	18.0%	17.0%	16.0%	14.0%	13.0%
4 SBIC	28.9%	28.0%	17.0%	11.0%	10.0%	10.0%	9.0%	8.0%	7.0%
Sectoral analysis – Average capital per firm ($M)									
5 Independent private	NA	NA	$27	$36	$45	$52	$57	$65	$65
6 Corporate	NA	NA	$30	$37	$36	$37	$34	$32	$29
7 SBIC	NA	NA	$6	$5	$5	$5	$5	$6	$5
8 Median size of independent private firms ($M)	NA	NA	$22	$18	$21	$25	$30	$30	$30

W. A. Sahlman, Structure of venture-capital organizations   477

Independent private-sector partnership formation									
9 Total # of funds raising capital	22	37	54	89	101	77	77	110	84
10 Total capital raised ($M)	$661	$866	$1,423	$3,460	$3,300	$2,327	$3,320	$4,184	$2,810
11 # of follow-on funds	12	13	18	47	58	40	44	66	59
12 Capital raised by follow-on funds ($M)	$418	$477	$628	$2,383	$2,300	$1,396	$2,800	$3,347	$2,422
13 # of new funds	10	24	36	42	43	37	33	44	25
14 Capital raised by new funds ($M)	$243	$389	$795	$1,077	$1,000	$931	$520	$837	$388
Sources of capital to the independent private sector (%)									
15 Corporations	19.0%	17.0%	12.0%	12.0%	14.0%	12.0%	11.0%	10.0%	12.0%
16 Individuals	16.0%	23.0%	21.0%	21.0%	15.0%	13.0%	12.0%	12.0%	8.0%
17 Pension funds	30.0%	23.0%	33.0%	31.0%	34.0%	33.0%	50.0%	39.0%	47.0%
18 Foreign	8.0%	10.0%	13.0%	16.0%	18.0%	23.0%	11.0%	14.0%	13.0%
19 Endowments	14.0%	12.0%	7.0%	8.0%	6.0%	8.0%	6.0%	10.0%	11.0%
20 Insurance companies	13.0%	15.0%	14.0%	12.0%	13.0%	11.0%	10.0%	15.0%	9.0%
Panel C: Investment activity of venture capitalists									
Disbursements									
1 Estimated value of disbursements ($M)	$610	$1,160	$1,450	$2,580	$2,760	$2,670	$3,230	$3,940	$3,650
2 Number of companies financed	504	797	918	1,320	1,469	1,377	1,504	1,729	1,474
3 Average investment per company	$1.21	$1.46	$1.58	$1.95	$1.88	$1.94	$2.15	$2.28	$2.48
Allocation of investments									
4 New company commitments as a % of total	58.0%	55.0%	39.0%	34.0%	31.0%	23.0%	37.0%	39.0%	33.0%
5 Follow-on financings as a % of total	42.0%	45.0%	61.0%	66.0%	69.0%	77.0%	63.0%	61.0%	67.0%
Stages of financing									
6 Seed and startup as a % of total	25.0%	22.6%	20.0%	17.2%	21.0%	15.0%	19.0%	13.0%	12.5%
7 Expansion and later-stage as a % of total	75.0%	77.4%	68.0%	70.8%	67.0%	69.0%	58.0%	69.0%	67.5%
8 Leveraged buyouts as a % of total	NA	NA	12.0%	12.0%	12.0%	16.0%	23.0%	18.0%	20.0%

Table 1 (continued)

	1980	1981	1982	1983	1984	1985	1986	1987	1988
Panel D: Exiting venture-capital investments									
1 # of venture-capital-backed companies that are acquired	28	32	40	49	86	101	120	147	106
Venture-capital-backed initial public offerings (IPOs)									
2 # of companies	27	68	27	121	53	46	97	81	35
3 Total amount raised ($M)	$420	$770	$549	$3,031	$743	$838	$2,118	$1,840	$756
4 Total market value of companies with IPO in each year ($M)	$2,626	$3,610	$2,374	$14,035	$3,495	$3,258	$8,434	$6,893	$3,122
All IPOs									
5 # of companies	95	227	100	504	213	195	417	259	96
6 Total amount raised ($M)	$1,089	$2,723	$1,213	$9,580	$2,545	$3,166	$8,190	$5,220	$2,392
7 Total market value of companies ($M)	$5,717	$10,922	$5,466	$40,473	$10,792	$11,618	$31,616	$23,813	$11,759
Venture capital backed IPOs as % of total IPOs									
8 # of companies	28.4%	30.0%	27.0%	24.0%	24.9%	23.6%	23.3%	31.3%	36.5%
9 Total amount raised	38.6%	28.3%	45.2%	31.6%	29.2%	26.5%	25.9%	35.2%	31.6%
10 Total market value of companies	45.9%	33.1%	43.4%	34.7%	32.4%	28.0%	26.7%	28.9%	26.5%

[a]*Source:* Various publications of Venture Economics (Needham, MA).
NA: not available.
Total capital (for example, panel A, row 1) is the book value of all commitments to professional venture-capital firms (net of fund liquidations). See also footnote 2 in text.
Data on initial public offerings in panel D, rows 5–7, come from Securities Data Corporation (see footnote 3 in the text).

Table 2

The stages of venture-capital investing.[a]

1. *Seed investments*

   Although the term is sometimes used more broadly, the strict meaning of 'seed investment' is a small amount of capital provided to an inventor or entrepreneur to determine whether an idea deserves of further consideration and further investment. The idea may involve a technology, or it may be an idea for a new marketing approach. If it is a technology, this stage may involve building a small prototype. This stage does not involve production for sale.

2. *Startup*

   Startup investments usually go to companies that are less than one year old. The company uses the money for product development, prototype testing, and test marketing (in experimental quantities to selected customers). This stage involves further study of market-penetration potential, bringing together a management team, and refining the business plan.

3. *First stage – early development*

   Investment proceeds through the first stage only if the prototypes look good enough that further technical risk is considered minimal. Likewise, the market studies must look good enough so that management is comfortable setting up a modest manufacturing process and shipping in commercial quantities. First-stage companies are unlikely to be profitable.

4. *Second stage – expansion*

   A company in the second stage has shipped enough product to enough customers so that it has real feedback from the market. It may not know quantitatively what speed of market penetration will occur later, or what the ultimate penetration will be, but it may know the qualitative factors that will determine the speed and limits of penetration. The company is probably still unprofitable, or only marginally profitable. It probably needs more capital for equipment purchases, inventory, and receivable financing.

5. *Third stage – profitable but cash poor*

   For third-stage companies, sales growth is probably fast, and positive profit margins have taken away most of the downside investment risk. But, the rapid expansion requires more working capital than can be generated from internal cash flow. New VC capital may be used for further expansion of manufacturing facilities, expanded marketing, or product enhancements. At this stage, banks may be willing to supply some credit if it can be secured by fixed assets or receivables.

6. *Fourth stage – rapid growth toward liquidity point*

   Companies at the fourth stage of development may still need outside cash to sustain growth, but they are successful and stable enough so that the risk to outside investors is much reduced. The company may prefer to use more debt financing to limit equity dilution. Commercial bank credit can play a more important role. Although the cash-out point for VC investors is thought to be within a couple of years, the form (IPO, acquisition, or LBO) and timing of cash-out are still uncertain.

7. *Bridge stage – mezzanine investment*

   In bridge or mezzanine investment situations, the company may have some idea which form of exit is most likely, and even know the approximate timing, but it still needs more capital to sustain rapid growth in the interim. Depending on how the general stock market is doing, and how given types of high tech stocks are doing within the stock market, 'IPO windows' can open and close in very unpredictable ways. Likewise, the level of interest rates and the availability of commercial credit can influence the timing and feasibility of acquisitions or leveraged buyouts. A bridge financing may also correspond to a limited cash-out of early investors or management, or a restructuring of positions among VC investors.

8. *Liquidity stage – cash-out or exit*

   A literal interpretation of 'cash-out' would seem to imply trading the VC-held shares in a portfolio company for cash. In practice, it has come to mean the point at which the VC investors can gain liquidity for a substantial portion of their holdings in a company. The liquidity may come in the form of an initial public offering. If it does, liquidity is still restricted by the holding periods and other restrictions that are part of SEC Rule 144, or by 'stand-off' commitments made to the IPO underwriter, in which the insiders agree not to sell their shares for some period of time after the offering (for example, 90 or 180 days). If acquisition is the form of cash-out, the liquidity may be in the form of cash, shares in a publicly traded company, or short-term debt. If the acquisition is paid for in shares of a nonpublic company, such shares may be no more liquid than the shares in the original company. Likewise, if the sellers take back debt in a leveraged buyout, they may wind up in a less liquid position than before, depending on the liquidity features of the debt.

---

[a]This table is drawn from Plummer (1987, pp. I-11 to I-13).

Table 3

Participation in multiple financing rounds by a venture-capital fund.[a,b]

Company/ Date of purchase	Security purchased	Price per share	Number of shares	Total cost
Company 1				
5/1/85	Convertible preferred series B	$0.68	525,145	$354,473
8/1/85	Convertible preferred series B	$0.68	972,531	$656,458
3/1/86	Convertible preferred series C	$2.25	444,445	$1,000,001
4/1/87	Convertible preferred series D	$4.50	66,667	$300,002
	Totals (average price per share)	$1.15	2,008,788	$2,310,934
7/24/90	Estimated value	$23.00		$46,202,124
Company 2				
6/1/85	Convertible preferred series A	$15.00	20,833	$312,500
11/1/85	Convertible preferred series A	$15.00	20,833	$312,495
4/1/86	Convertible preferred series A	$15.00	25,000	$375,000
5/2/88	Convertible preferred series B	$8.60	28,588	$245,857
	Totals (average price per share)	$13.08	95,254	$1,245,852
	Note: Loans totalling $206,500 were made in 1987 and these were converted to series B preferred on 5/2/88			
7/24/90	Estimated value	$3.27		$311,463
Company 3				
2/1/87	Convertible preferred series B	$1.15	347,827	$400,001
7/1/87	Convertible preferred series C	$1.90	131,579	$250,000
3/16/88	Convertible preferred series D	$1.60	283,326	$453,322
	Totals (average price per share)	$1.45	762,732	$1,103,323
	Note: Loans totalling $200,000 were made in 1987 and these were converted to series D preferred on 3/16/88			
7/24/90	Estimated total value	$1.45		$1,103,323

Company 4

2/1/86	Convertible preferred series B	$0.95	1,473,684	$1,400,000
12/1/86	Convertible preferred series D	$1.85	461,808	$854,345
7/22/87	Convertible preferred series D	$1.85	141,829	$262,384
	Totals (average price per share)	$1.21	2,077,321	$2,516,728
7/24/90	Estimated value	$4.34		$9,005,259

Company 5

11/1/85	Convertible preferred series A	$0.34	1,470,588	$500,000
3/1/86	Convertible preferred series B	$0.45	2,083,333	$937,500
3/1/87	Convertible preferred series C	$0.75	1,333,333	$1,000,000
	Totals (average price per share)	$0.50	4,887,254	$2,437,500
7/24/90	Estimated value	$0.00		$0

Total cost for 5 companies	$9,614,336
Total estimated value for 5 companies	$56,622,169
Total gain for 5 companies	$47,007,832

[a] *Source:* An interim report to the limited partners of a venture-capital fund with more than $20 million in capital.
[b] The amounts listed do not include investments made by others at the same time or at other times.

estimate that the amount invested by so-called angels is an order of magnitude larger than the amount invested by professional venture capitalists [see, for example, Wetzel (1983) and Freear and Wetzel (1990)].

Venture-capital investing is also modest in comparison with the level of capital investment in the domestic corporate sector: total capital expenditures in 1988 by the nonfinancial, nonfarm sector exceeded $380 billion [Economic Report of the President (1990)]. Total expenditures on research and development in the U.S. each year are estimated to top $150 billion, of which $74 billion is invested by private industrial concerns [Studt (1990)]. Finally, the $3 billion disbursed by all professional venture capitalists in 1988 was only slightly less than one-third the amount invested by IBM in capital expenditures and R & D in the same year, and 25% of the amount invested by General Motors.

Despite its modest scope, the industry has helped create many successful enterprises, including Apple Computer, Intel, Federal Express, People Express, Businessland, Lotus Development, Microsoft, Sun Microsystems, Digital Equipment, Compaq Computer, Teledyne, Tandem, Tandon, Hybritech, and Genentech. Each of these companies received venture capital early in its development and later went public. In aggregate, 579 venture-capital-backed companies went public during the 11 years ending in 1988. Their total market value exceeded 30% of the total market value of all comparable companies going public during the same period (panel D, table 1).[3]

The payoff to venture capitalists has been handsome in some cases. During 1978 and 1979, for example, slightly more than $3.5 million in venture capital was invested in Apple Computer. When Apple went public in December 1980, the approximate value of the venture capitalists' investment was $271 million, and the total market capitalization of Apple's equity exceeded $1.4 billion. Similarly, several venture capitalists invested slightly over $4.7 million in Lotus Development Corporation in two rounds of financing in 1982: their equity was assigned a market value of almost $130 million in October 1983. The lead venture capitalist, Ben Rosen of Sevin-Rosen Partners, played a very important role in the formation and evolution of the company [see Sahlman (1985e) for background on the Sevin-Rosen investment in Lotus].

The industry has also been involved in some spectacular failures. Well-known examples include Ovation Technologies, Osborne Computer, Ztel, and Gavilan. In each case, venture capitalists lost their entire investment. In late 1983 Ovation Technologies raised almost $6 million in venture capital to compete with Lotus Development in microcomputer software. The product proved far more difficult and costly to complete than anticipated, however,

---

[3]Venture Economics provides the data on the venture-capital-backed companies. Data on all initial public offerings (IPOs) during the period come from Securities Data Corporation. The specific comparison sample excludes all closed-end investment companies, savings and loan conversions, and companies with an offering price under $5.00 per share.

and the venture-capital firms chose to liquidate the company rather than continue funding development. Ovation closed its doors in late 1984 without having generated one dollar of revenues. [For further information on Ovation, see Knights and Sahlman (1986a).]

Although comprehensive data are difficult to obtain, the overall rate of return on venture capital seems to have been high from the mid-1960s through the mid-1980s, the only period for which reliable data are currently available. Between 1965 and 1984, for example, the median realized compound rate of return on 29 venture-capital partnerships over the life of each partnership (an average of 8.6 years) exceeded 26% per year [Venture Economics (1985, p. 69)]. The minimum compound annual rate of return for the 29 funds was 6%.[4]

A more recent and comprehensive study [Venture Economics (1988c)] suggests that funds started before 1981 experienced generally positive returns through 1987. For example, the average annual rate of return (weighted by initial investment) on the 13 funds started in 1980 was 20.6% for the period ending December 31, 1987, compared with 16% for the Standard & Poor's 500 and 16% for smaller capitalization stocks during the same period [Ibbotson Associates (1988)]. These 13 funds represented 50% of the total funds raising money in 1980 and 66% of the capital raised that year. This study also reveals that rates of return have declined since 1983, particularly for funds started later in the period. It is extremely difficult to estimate the extent to which returns have declined, however, because accounting practices in the industry typically reflect a downward bias. [See also VCJ (August 1989) and Sahlman (1989).]

Returns on individual investments in a venture-capital portfolio vary widely. According to Huntsman and Homan (1980), slightly more than half of the 110 investments made by three venture-capital firms from 1960 to 1975 resulted in a realized rate of return of less than 10%; over one-quarter resulted in an absolute loss. According to Venture Economics (1988c), more than one-third of 383 investments made by 13 firms between 1969 and 1985 resulted in an absolute loss. More than two-thirds of the individual investments made by these same firms resulted in capital returns of less than double the original cost.

Nevertheless, the returns on a few investments have more than offset these disappointments. Venture Economics (1988c) reports, for example, that 6.8% of the investments resulted in payoffs greater than ten times cost and yielded 49.4% of the ending value of the aggregate portfolio (61.4% of the profits).

---

[4]The findings reported in Venture Economics (1985) are supported by Huntsman and Homan (1980), Chiampou and Kellet (1989), Bygrave et al. (1987), Horsley Keogh (1988), and analysis of the returns reported by 20 venture-capital funds in offering memoranda used to raise new capital. No attempt was made in these studies to adjust for the systematic risk incurred in venture-capital investing.

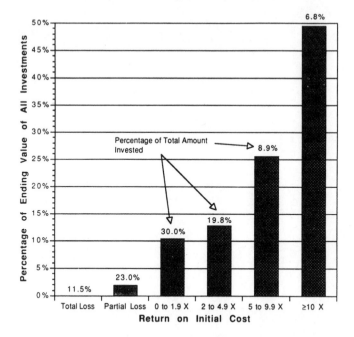

Fig. 1. Payoffs from venture-capital investing.

This graph shows the distribution of gains and losses on a group of investments made by venture-capital firms. The data are taken from Venture Economics (1988c) and cover investments by 13 venture-capital partnerships in 383 companies from 1969 to 1985. In total, $245 million was invested, which resulted in total value of $1.049 billion (4.3 times cost). The vertical axis shows the percentage of total ending value (that is, the $1.049 billion) resulting from six groups of investments, comprising investments with differing returns on capital invested (from total loss to more than 10 times capital invested). At the top of each bar the percentage of total cost represented by each group is shown. Thus, 6.8% of the capital invested resulted in payoffs of more than 10 to 1 and contributed almost 50% of the total ending value. Similarly, 11.5% of the cost was invested in companies that experienced a total loss.

Fig. 1 shows the distribution of outcomes analyzed in Venture Economics (1988c). An earlier Venture Economics report (1985) reached similar conclusions: investments in 22 of 216 companies yielded more than ten times cost, and the profits realized were more than 40 times larger than the losses incurred on the 70 companies that failed to return the amount invested. The same basic patterns are found by Keeley (1986) and Horsley Keogh (1988). See also Stevenson et al. (1987) and Sahlman and Soussou (1985a).

Even companies that are successful in the long run sometimes flirt with failure. For example, an analysis of various documents filed with the Securities and Exchange Commission (SEC) reveals that Federal Express raised

W. A. Sahlman, Structure of venture-capital organizations

Table 4

Multiple financing rounds for selected venture-capital-backed firms.[a]

Company (business)	Investor[b]	Date	Amount raised ($000)	Cumulative funding ($000)	Stock received (000)	Total shares outstanding (000)	% ownership acquired	Fully diluted valuation ($000)	Price per share ($)	Estimated ending ownership %[c]
Apple Computer (computer)	Founders	Mar-77	1	1	16,640	16,640	100.0%	1	0.00	30.7%
	Founders	Nov-77	115	116	10,480	27,120	38.6%	298	0.01	19.3%
	Venture 1	Jan-78	518	634	5,520	32,640	16.9%	3,063	0.09	10.2%
	Founders	Jul-78	426	1,060	4,736	37,376	12.7%	3,362	0.09	8.7%
	Venture 2	Sep-78	704	1,764	2,503	39,879	6.3%	11,216	0.28	4.6%
	Venture 3	Dec-80	2,331	4,095	2,400	43,306	5.5%	42,061	0.97	4.4%
	IPO	Dec-80	101,200	105,295	4,600	54,215	8.5%	1,192,730	22.00	8.5%
Cray Research (computer)	Founders	Aug-72	2,550	2,550	2,869	2,794	102.7%	2,483	0.89	24.3%
	Venture 1	Jan-74	2,675	5,225	2,006	4,875	41.1%	6,501	1.33	17.0%
	Venture 2	Jan-75	642	5,867	387	5,302	7.3%	8,796	1.66	3.3%
	Venture 3	Apr-75	2,720	8,587	1,530	6,832	22.4%	12,146	1.78	13.0%
	IPO	Mar-76	10,890	19,477	4,950	11,783	42.0%	25,923	2.20	42.0%
Federal Express (transportation)	Founders	Jan-72	4,745	4,745	100	100	100.0%	4,745	47.45	0.7%
	Venture 1	Sep-73	12,250	16,995	60	160	37.5%	32,667	204.17	0.4%
	Venture 2	Mar-74	6,400	23,395	872	1,032	84.5%	7,574	7.34	6.4%
	Venture 3	Sep-74	3,876	27,271	6,200	7,232	85.7%	4,521	0.63	45.8%
	IPO	Apr-78	25,800	53,071	4,300	13,535	31.8%	81,210	6.00	31.8%
Genentech (biotechnology)	Founders	Jan-76	126	126	3,200	3,200	100.0%	126	0.04	41.4%
	Venture 1	Apr-76	850	976	1,180	4,280	27.6%	3,083	0.72	15.3%
	Venture 2	May-78	950	1,926	475	4,945	9.6%	9,890	2.00	6.1%
	Corporate	Sep-79	10,000	11,926	1,000	6,348	15.8%	63,480	10.00	12.9%
	IPO	Oct-80	38,500	50,426	1,100	7,724	14.2%	270,340	35.00	14.2%

Table 4 (continued)

Company (business)	Investor[b]	Date	Amount raised ($000)	Cumulative funding ($000)	Stock received (000)	Total shares outstanding (000)	% ownership acquired	Fully diluted valuation ($000)	Price per share ($)	Estimated ending ownership %[c]
Lotus Development (software)	Founders	Apr-82	13	13	4,410	4,410	100.0%	13	0.00	30.9%
	Venture 1	Apr-82	1,000	1,013	3,500	7,910	44.2%	2,260	0.29	24.5%
	Venture 2	Dec-82	3,755	4,768	3,767	11,677	32.3%	12,044	1.03	26.4%
	IPO	Oct-83	46,800	51,568	2,600	14,277	18.2%	256,988	18.00	18.2%
Midway Airlines (transportation)	Founders	Jun-76	7	7	700	700	100.0%	7	0.01	19.2%
	Venture 1	Jul-79	5,739	5,746	1,380	2,080	66.3%	8,650	4.16	37.9%
	Venture 2	Sep-80	6,000	11,746	789	2,789	28.3%	23,620	7.60	21.7%
	IPO	Dec-80	11,475	23,221	850	3,639	23.4%	53,433	13.50	23.4%
Seagate (disk drives)	Founders	Oct-79	161	161	11,723	11,723	100.0%	161	0.01	64.1%
	Venture 1	Jun-80	1,000	1,161	3,125	14,848	21.0%	4,751	0.32	17.1%
	IPO	Sep-81	25,000	26,161	2,500	18,277	13.7%	182,770	10.00	13.7%
Staples (retailing)	Founders/ Venture 1	Jan-86	4,425	4,425	1,844	1,844	100.0%	4,425	2.40	20.2%
	Venture 2	Jan-87	13,927	18,352	2,211	4,054	54.5%	25,543	6.30	24.2%
	Venture 3	Dec-87	13,597	31,950	1,563	5,617	27.8%	48,871	8.70	17.1%
	Venture 4	Sep-88	2,800	34,750	267	5,884	4.5%	61,782	10.50	2.9%
	IPO	Apr-89	61,750	96,500	3,250	9,134	35.6%	173,546	19.00	35.6%

Sources: Annual reports, prospectuses.

[b]Venture 1, etc., represent rounds of financing from venture capitalists; IPO = Initial Public Offering.

[c]Ending ownership is based on final total shares outstanding. The figures do not always add exactly to 100%, which reflects stock options issued and other capital structure changes, including share repurchases, warrants issued, and debt conversions.

three rounds of venture capital in 1973 and 1974. With the company behind plan and over budget, the price paid per share in the third round was $0.63, compared with the adjusted price of more than $200 in the first round and just over $7 per share in the second round. By 1976, when the company made its first public offering of shares, the adjusted price per share was $6; by 1981, it was $47.45. Table 4 shows the prices paid and capital raised in Federal Express and seven other ventures.

Conversely, companies that give venture capitalists and their investors high rates of return do not always succeed in the long run. Priam Corporation, a disk-drive manufacturer, received five rounds of venture capital before it went public. In the initial round of financing in 1978 the price per share was less than $1, whereas the per-share value assigned soon after the company went public in 1983 was $23. Every intervening round had taken place at a higher price per share, but although it raised more than $70 million in its IPO, Priam filed for bankruptcy in 1989. [See Sahlman (1984), Knights and Sahlman (1986c, 1986d), and Sahlman and Stevenson (1985) for details on Priam and other disk-drive manufacturers.]

An important variable in venture-capital investments is the time that elapses between the initial investment and the return of capital. According to Venture Economics (1988c), the average holding period for an investment is 4.9 years. Roughly one-third of the individual investments studied are held for more than six years. Investments with payoffs greater than five times the invested capital are held significantly longer than investments that fail completely. The average investment in companies with high payoffs is approximately $1 million, versus $366,000 for the losers.

3. The most common structure of venture-capital firms[5]

By 1988 the typical venture-capital firm was organized as a limited partnership, with the venture capitalists serving as general partners and the investors as limited partners. According to Venture Economics (1987), 500 firms with $20 billion in capital in 1987 were structured as limited partnerships. The remaining one-third of industry capital was invested in independent private venture-capital firms not organized as limited partnerships (for example, incorporated venture-capital companies and publicly traded closed-end funds) (9% in 1987); in venture-capital subsidiaries of industrial and financial corporations (14%); and in independent small-business investment companies (SBICs) (8%), which had access to government-guaranteed debt to

---

[5]For background information on the venture-capital industry and the structure of venture-capital firms, see Gorman and Sahlman (1989), Sahlman and Stevenson (1985), Sahlman (1988, 1989), Wilson (1985), Morris (1988a), Bartlett (1988), and Venture Economics (1985, 1987, 1988a, 1988b, 1988c).

leverage their equity capital (panel B, table 1). The share of total industry capital managed by the independent private sector, which comprises mostly limited partnerships, increased dramatically over the nine years ending in 1988.

Table 1 (panel B) also reveals that in 1988 12% of the new capital committed to the private independent sector (i.e., noncorporate subsidiaries and non-SBICs) came from individuals, whereas 64% came from pension funds, endowments, and insurance companies. Typically, the general partners provide only a small proportion (about 1%) of the capital raised by a given fund. Most venture-capital firms are structured as management companies responsible for managing several pools of capital, each representing a legally separate limited partnership.

In each new fund, the capital is invested in new ventures during the first three to five years of the fund. Thereafter few if any investments are made in companies not already in the portfolio, and the goal is to begin converting existing investments to cash. As investments yield cash or marketable securities, distributions are made to the partners rather than reinvested in new ventures.

Typically, well before all of the capital from a venture-capital pool is distributed to the partners, a new fund is raised and invested in new ventures. For example, Institutional Venture Partners (IVP), a California-based venture-capital firm, raised $16.5 million in 1980, the year it was formed. In 1982 the IVP management company raised $40 million in a fund called IVP II. The group raised $96 million in 1985, launching IVP III, which was followed in 1988 by IVP IV, a $115 million fund [VCJ (May 1989, pp. 26–29)]. Thus investment and distribution periods overlap. Approximately 72% of the increase in capital controlled by the private independent sector from 1977 to 1988 was attributable to so-called follow-on funds, new venture-capital pools raised by existing firms.

The average firm in 1988 had $65 million in committed capital (measured at cost rather than market value). The largest 89 firms, as noted earlier, had average committed capital of almost $200 million and controlled almost 60% of the industry's assets. A fund with $200 million in committed capital is typically managed by a professional staff of between 6 and 12, who invest approximately $15 to $35 million each year in new companies and companies already in the portfolio.

Most venture-capital firms have several general partners and a staff of associates and administrative support personnel. Associates function as apprentices to the general partners and often become general partners themselves in later funds. In 1988, the average capital managed per professional (partner or associate) was $12.6 million. For the independent private sector, the figure was $15 million per professional [Venture Economics (1989)]. The capital managed by each professional is a function of total capital under management. For independent private firms with total committed capital of more than $200 million, each professional was responsible for managing $34 million.

Institutional Venture Partners, for example, had six general partners and two associates responsible for managing the various active funds. In 1988 IVP invested $11.2 million in 11 new companies not already in one of the fund portfolios and $19.2 million in 27 follow-on deals.

By 1988 roughly one-third of all venture-capital firms had at least one partner with more than 10 years of experience, and these firms managed almost 60% of total industry capital. In the independent private sector, which was characterized by more experience, roughly 68% of the firms (managing 89% of the capital) had one partner with at least five years of experience in the industry [Venture Economics (1989)].

Venture-capital firms tend to specialize by industry or stage of investment. Some firms focus on computer-related companies, others on biotechnology or specialty retailers. Some will invest only in early-stage deals, whereas others concentrate on later-stage financings. Many firms also limit their geographic scope.

4. The contract between the investors and the venture-capital firm

The relationship between investors and managers of the venture funds is governed by a partnership agreement that spells out the rights and obligations of each group. Key elements of the contract are described in this section, and an economic analysis follows in section 5. The description of the legal structure of a venture-capital firm is based primarily on Venture Economics (1987), which studied contracts for 76 funds raised between January 1986 and August 1987. These funds represented 76% of all venture-capital funds raised during this period. Of the 76, 40 were initial funds and 36 were follow-on funds started by firms already managing other pools. The findings in that report were checked against primary-source documents from 25 venture capital firms. See also Bartlett (1988).

4.1. Legal structure

The limited-partnership organizational form has important tax and legal considerations. Limited-partnership income is not subject to corporate taxation; instead income is taxable to the individual partners. Also, partnerships can distribute securities without triggering immediate recognition of taxable income: the gain or loss on the underlying asset is recognized only when the asset is sold. To qualify for this form of tax treatment, partnerships must meet several conditions:[6]

(1) A fund's life must have an agreed-upon date of termination, which is established before the partnership agreement is signed.
(2) The transfer of limited partnership units is restricted; unlike most registered securities, they cannot be easily bought and sold.
(3) Withdrawal from the partnership before the termination date is prohibited.
(4) Limited partners cannot participate in the active management of a fund if their liability is to be limited to the amount of their commitment.

General partners, in contrast, bear unlimited liability, so they can conceivably lose much more than they commit in capital. The consequences of unlimited liability are minor, however, because venture-capital partnerships typically do not borrow, nor are they exposed to the risk of having liabilities in excess of assets.

Despite restrictions on their managerial rights, limited partners are almost always permitted to vote on key issues such as amendment of the limited-partnership agreement, dissolution of the partnership before the termination date, extension of the fund's life, removal of any general partner, and valuation of the portfolio. Contracts vary, but typically a two-thirds majority of limited-partnership votes is required to effect change.

4.2. General-partner contribution

Of the 76 partnerships surveyed in Venture Economics (1987), 61% report general-partner contributions of exactly 1% of committed capital. This contribution can be, and often is, in the form of a promissory note rather than cash. Some tax advisors counsel those forming venture-capital partnerships to have the general partners contribute at least 1% in order to be assured of favorable tax treatment.

4.3. Economic life

For the Venture Economics (1987) sample, the economic life of 72% of the funds is set at ten years. All of the partnerships include provisions to extend the life of the funds, with 52% requiring some level of consent by the limited partners and 48% leaving the decision up to the general partners. The most frequent extension period is three years maximum in one-year increments. At the end of a fund's legal existence, all cash and securities are distributed and a final accounting is rendered.

---

[6]The list below is replicated from Venture Economics (1987, p. 7). See also Wolfson (1985), who describes the use of the limited-partnership organization form in the oil and gas industry, which is driven primarily by tax considerations.

4.4. Takedown schedules

In the survey sample the limited partners typically are required to invest a certain amount at the outset, but can phase in the remainder of their investment over time. Most fund agreements call for a cash commitment of between 25% and 33% at the close, with additional capital to be invested at some future date or dates (for example, 25% each year). The venture capitalists exercise considerable control over the timing of capital infusions by the limited partners.

If limited partners renege on a funding commitment, severe penalties are imposed on the ownership percentages associated with the partners' earlier investments and their ability to withdraw already invested funds. The kinds of penalties imposed vary considerably, though a common clause calls for the limited partner to forfeit one-half of the partner's capital account in the partnership and therefore one-half of the profits to which the partner would have been entitled.

4.5. Compensation

Venture-capital management companies typically receive compensation from two sources for managing the investments in each limited partnership. They are entitled to a management fee, and they receive some percentage of the profits over the life of each fund. More than 50% of the contracts surveyed by Venture Economics call for an annual management fee equal to 2.5% of committed capital through the life of the fund. Most of the remaining partnerships base the management fee on capital committed, though the formula varies. Only seven of the funds base the fee directly on the estimated value of the portfolio. Typically the base management fee increases annually by the rate of consumer price inflation. The survey finds little evidence that the percentage fee declines with the amount of capital under management.

In 88% of the funds surveyed, venture capitalists are entitled to 20% of the realized gains on the fund. In the remaining partnerships, the general partner's share of realized gains ranges from 15% to 30%. Given the diversity of fund organizers and their differing stated purposes, this seems remarkably consistent, in sharp contrast to the widely varying contract terms found in oil and gas partnerships [Wolfson (1985)].

4.6. Distributions

Half of the partnership agreements studied by Venture Economics require annual distributions from realized profits. In 18% of the agreements, the general partners state their intentions to make annual distributions, whereas the remaining partnerships leave the issue of distribution to the discretion of the general partners.

In 29% of the contracts studied, the general partners are entitled to take their profit participation (called the 'carried interest') – in income or gains without restriction. In the other partnerships the general partners are not entitled to take the carried interest until the limited partners have received an amount at least equal to their cumulative capital contribution.

General partners generally have the option to make distributions in the form of securities, cash, or both. Often when a portfolio company becomes successful, its shares are registered with the SEC and a public offering takes place [see Barry et al. (1990)]. Typically, the venture-capital firm does not or cannot liquidate its shareholdings on the offering. The shares can be distributed to the limited partners in proportion to their ownership of the fund, or the fund can continue to hold the shares, taking responsibility for distributing them at some future date, or converting them to cash through a transaction such as a secondary offering. If the shares are distributed to the limited partners, the value assigned is the last price in the stock market before the distribution.

4.7. Reporting and accounting policies

All venture-capital firms surveyed agree to provide the limited partners with periodic reports on the value and progress of portfolio companies, including an annual meeting with the general partners and selected portfolio-company management teams. Because most investments are made in private companies with highly uncertain prospects, assigning values is very difficult. Often the partners agree to recognize losses quickly and to write up the value of an investment only if there is a significant arms-length transaction at a higher value. If no such transactions have occurred and no loss seems likely, cost is used as a basis for reporting. As a result of these policies, most venture-capital firms report negative rates of return during the first few years of the fund [see also Venture Economics (1988c)].

4.8. Specific conflicts of interest

Most contracts specify the percentage of time the venture capitalists propose to devote to the management of the fund being raised. A small number of partnership agreements restrict the ability of general partners to coinvest or receive securities from portfolio companies. Some partnerships restrict follow-on funds from investing in securities held by a previous fund managed by the same venture capitalists. Other fund agreements prevent the general partner from raising a new fund until some percentage (for example,

50%) of the capital raised in the existing fund has been invested in portfolio companies.

4.9. Special advisory committees

Of the 76 funds studied by Venture Economics (1987), 41 establish formal advisory boards; another 17 create informal advisory boards. Of those with formal advisory boards, 19 require limited-partner representation. An additional 18 funds establish boards composed solely of representatives of the limited partners; these boards are separate and distinct from the advisory board.

Advisory boards and boards composed of limited partners are often designed to provide access to deals or technical expertise. Some boards are structured like traditional boards of directors, providing guidance and oversight for the operation of the venture-capital fund. Still other advisory committees are assigned specific responsibilities, the most important of which is determining the value of the portfolio.

5. Analyzing the relationship between external investors and venture capitalists

Venture capitalists act as agents for the limited partners, who choose to invest in entrepreneurial ventures through an intermediary rather than directly. In such situations, conflicts arise between the agent and the principal, which must be addressed in the contracts and other mechanisms that govern their relationship.

In the venture-capital industry, the agency problem is likely to be particularly difficult. There is inevitably a high degree of information asymmetry between the venture capitalists, who play an active role in the portfolio companies, and the limited partners, who cannot monitor the prospects of each individual investment as closely.

The contractual provisions outlined in section 4 can be explained as attempts to resolve the agency problem, the operating cost problem, and the sorting problem simultaneously.

5.1. Agency costs

Venture capitalists have many opportunities to take advantage of the people who invest with them. To a degree, the agency problem is exacerbated by the legal structure of limited partnerships, which prevents limited partners from playing a role in the management of the venture-capital partnership.

Contracts are designed with several key provisions to protect the limited partners from the possibility that the venture capitalists will make decisions against their interests. First, the life of a venture-capital fund is limited; the venture capitalist cannot keep the money forever. Organizational models like mutual funds or corporations, in contrast, have indefinite life spans. Implicitly, the investors also preserve the right not to invest in any later fund managed by the same venture capitalists.

Second, the limited partners preserve the right to withdraw from funding the partnership by reneging on their commitments to invest beyond the initial capital infusion as described in section 4.4. Third, the compensation system is structured to give the venture capitalists the appropriate incentives. The fund managers are typically entitled to receive 20% of the profits generated by the fund. For reasons which will be explored more fully below, the profit participation and other aspects of the contract encourage the venture capitalist to allocate the management fee to activities that will increase the total value of the portfolio.

Fourth, the mandatory distribution policy defuses potential differences of opinion about what to do with the proceeds from the sale of assets in the portfolio. The general partners cannot choose to invest in securities that serve their own private interests at the expense of the limited partners.

Finally, the contract addresses obvious areas of conflict between the venture capitalist and the limited partner. Thus, the venture capitalist is often explicitly prohibited from self-dealing (for example, being able to buy stock in the portfolio on preferential terms or receiving distributions different from those given to the limited partner). Also, the venture capitalists are contractually required to commit a certain percentage of their effort to the activities of the fund. Although this requirement is difficult to monitor, egregious violations can be the subject of litigation if fund performance is poor.

5.2. Further analysis of the compensation system

The compensation system plays a critical role in aligning the interests of the venture capitalists and the limited partners. To understand the implicit incentives, consider a $200 million fund with eight general partners that receives a management fee of 2.5% of total capital committed. Annual revenues are $5 million and revenues per partner are $625,000. Various expenses must be subtracted, including partner base salaries, office expenses, travel, insurance, and support staff. A reasonable estimate of the partners' base pay is $250,000 per year per partner, equivalent to 40% of total revenues. An informal survey of five venture-capital firms with this amount of capital under management revealed that the firm can be expected to clear a profit each year. If total expenses are 2.1% of the capital committed (the average reported in the informal survey), the annual operating profit is $800,000, or $100,000 per partner. Such profits are typically distributed to partners at the end of the year as a bonus.

If this hypothetical $200 million fund is successful and achieves a 20% rate of return on committed capital over its five-year duration (before consideration of the profit participation but after taking into account the management fee), the ending value will be approximately $498 million. The general partners will be entitled to 20% of the $298 million profit, or $59 million, equivalent to $7.4 million per partner. This figure translates to a $4.2 million present value per partner, assuming payment at the end of the last year and a 10% discount rate, or roughly $1.2 million per year per partner on a comparable annuity basis (also assuming a 10% discount rate). This figure far outweighs each general partner's combined base salary and annual bonus, estimated at $350,000 per year. An extra 1% in compound rate of return increases the present value of the carried interest from $4.2 million to $4.5 million, based on the assumptions used earlier. As long as the compound annual rate of return on the fund is positive, the percentage increase in the venture capitalists' share exceeds the percentage increase in the total value of the portfolio.[7]

Gathering hard data on venture-capital compensation is very difficult: many firms do not reveal key statistics about their business. According to a survey of 63 private independent venture-capital firms with over $5 billion in total committed capital in 1988 [Hay Management Consultants (1988)], however, the average 1987 base pay of a managing partner of a private, independent venture-capital firm was $223,000. The annual operating bonus was $51,000 and the average realized profits distribution was $163,000, resulting in total compensation of $437,000. These figures are not as dramatic as the simple numerical calculation used above, which accurately reflects the data provided by the four venture firms interviewed specifically about compensation. Also, the Hay Management Consultants data are difficult to interpret in light of the poor overall returns for most venture-capital funds in 1987 and the tendency for general partners to defer as long as possible the recognition of income for tax purposes. Nevertheless, the carried interest component of compensation is large in relation to the other components.[8] The implication is that the venture capitalists have incentives to engage in activities that increase the value of the carried interest, which is precisely what benefits the limited partners.

---

[7]These calculations ignore the return the venture capitalists receive on their direct investments in the partnership (for example, on the 1% investment described in section 4.2).

[8]The informal survey cited earlier also revealed that a number of successful venture-capital firms operate on an annual budget, which is negotiated each year with the limited partners. Examples include Greylock, Sutter Hill, and Charles River Partners. In these firms, the partners receive modest cash salaries and the venture-capital management company does not realize an annual profit. The partners are dependent on the carried interest to supplement current salaries. It is difficult to find evidence of a correlation between compensation structures and performance, however. For example, one highly regarded firm, Kleiner Perkins, receives a management fee of 3% and a carried interest percentage of 30%.

Although the compensation system seems to provide appropriate incentives, there are some difficult issues. One area of potential conflict between the limited and general partners relates to risk. The venture capitalist's equity participation may be thought of as an option that entitles the venture-capital management firm to 20% of the increase in value of the underlying fund. The exercise price of the option is the cost basis of the fund, and the life of the option equals the life of the fund.

Numerical analyses, based on a simple Black–Scholes model, suggest that the ex ante value of the venture-capital contract might be as high as 10% of the initial total capital of the fund. Thus the value of the contract on a $100 million fund might be $10 million at the time of signing. Table 5 presents estimates of the value of the contract (as a fraction of the original cost of the fund assets) based on different assumptions about the volatility of returns, current fund value, the carried interest percentage, and the life of the fund.

The fact that the management contract can be viewed as an option suggests the inherent agency problem: if one party has a contingent claim on value, there is an implicit incentive to increase risk [Myers (1986)]. The value of the contingent claim increases as risk increases. In the example above, the value of the contract would rise from approximately $13.2 million to $16 million if the assumed annual volatility were increased from 50% to 80%. In some situations, it will pay a venture capitalist to make negative-net-present-value investments because doing so increases the value of the option by more than the loss in value on his portion of the equity claim.

Partnership agreements respond in several ways to the possibility that the venture capitalist will take undue risks. Since the contract can be cancelled by the limited partners at any point in the life of the fund, the venture capitalist's incentive to incur such uncompensated risks is reduced. Although this solution helps resolve the agency problem from the limited partners' perspective, however, it can be abused. In one situation [Sahlman (1988c)], for example, a contract was cancelled by the sole limited partner after three years of a ten-year term. At the time of cancellation, the estimated value of the fund's underlying assets was close to the cost of those assets. The contract stipulated that the only payment due the venture-capital management company by the limited partner upon cancellation was the 20% share of estimated realized and unrealized gains on the portfolio. The limited partner was not contractually required to pay anything to the venture-capital management company for canceling the contract per se, even though from an option-valuation perspective the contract was clearly valuable. Most contracts, however, make cancellation more difficult than this (for example, by defining a narrow set of circumstances – such as fraud – under which the general partner can be fired).

Other mechanisms are also used to manage the perverse incentives of the contract. For example, the partnership agreement usually limits the amount

Table 5

Sensitivity of the present value of the carried interest of a venture-capital fund (as a fraction of original cost) to changes in volatility, current market value of fund assets, carried interest percentage, and life of the fund.

Assumptions:

Total original capital of the fund (cost)	$100,000,000
Current market value of fund assets	$100,000,000
Profit participation % – Carried interest	20%
Time to maturity – Economic life in years	7
Risk-free interest rate	10.0%
Volatility – Standard deviation of annual returns	50.0%

Results:

Estimated present value of carried interest	13,212,516
Estimated value of carried interest as a % of original capital (cost)	13.2%

Present value of the carried interest as a fraction of the original capital of the fund as a function of volatility and the current market value of the fund assets

Volatility	Current market value of fund (millions)						
	$70.00	$80.00	$90.00	$100.00	$110.00	$120.00	$130.00
10.0%	4.2%	6.1%	8.1%	10.1%	12.1%	14.1%	16.1%
20.0%	5.0%	6.7%	8.5%	10.4%	12.3%	14.2%	16.2%
30.0%	6.0%	7.7%	9.4%	11.2%	13.0%	14.9%	16.7%
40.0%	7.1%	8.7%	10.4%	12.2%	14.0%	15.8%	17.6%
50.0%	8.1%	9.8%	11.5%	13.2%	15.0%	16.8%	18.6%
60.0%	9.0%	10.7%	12.5%	14.2%	16.0%	17.8%	19.7%
70.0%	9.9%	11.6%	13.4%	15.2%	17.0%	18.8%	20.7%
80.0%	10.6%	12.4%	14.2%	16.0%	17.9%	19.7%	21.6%
90.0%	11.3%	13.1%	14.9%	16.8%	18.7%	20.5%	22.4%

Table 5 (continued)

Present value of the carried interest as a fraction of the original capital of the fund as a function of volatility and the profit participation – Carried interest (%)

Volatility	Profit participation – Carried interest (%)						
	5.0%	10.0%	15.0%	20.0%	25.0%	30.0%	35.0%
10.0%	2.5%	5.0%	7.6%	10.1%	12.6%	15.1%	17.6%
20.0%	2.6%	5.2%	7.8%	10.4%	13.0%	15.6%	18.2%
30.0%	2.8%	5.6%	8.4%	11.2%	14.0%	16.8%	19.5%
40.0%	3.0%	6.1%	9.1%	12.2%	15.2%	18.3%	21.3%
50.0%	3.3%	6.6%	9.9%	13.2%	16.5%	19.8%	23.1%
60.0%	3.6%	7.1%	10.7%	14.2%	17.8%	21.3%	24.9%
70.0%	3.8%	7.6%	11.4%	15.2%	19.0%	22.8%	26.6%
80.0%	4.0%	8.0%	12.0%	16.0%	20.0%	24.0%	28.1%
90.0%	4.2%	8.4%	12.6%	16.8%	21.0%	25.2%	29.4%

Present value of the carried interest as a fraction of the original capital of the fund as a function of volatility and the time to maturity (life) of the fund

Volatility	Time to maturity – Life (years)						
	2.5	4.0	5.5	7.0	8.5	10.0	11.5
10.0%	4.5%	6.6%	8.5%	10.1%	11.5%	12.6%	13.7%
20.0%	5.1%	7.1%	8.9%	10.4%	11.7%	12.8%	13.8%
30.0%	6.0%	8.0%	9.7%	11.2%	12.4%	13.4%	14.3%
40.0%	7.0%	9.1%	10.8%	12.2%	13.3%	14.3%	15.1%
50.0%	7.9%	10.1%	11.8%	13.2%	14.3%	15.2%	16.0%
60.0%	8.9%	11.2%	12.9%	14.2%	15.3%	16.1%	16.8%
70.0%	9.9%	12.2%	13.9%	15.2%	16.2%	16.9%	17.5%
80.0%	10.8%	13.2%	14.8%	16.0%	16.9%	17.6%	18.1%
90.0%	11.6%	14.0%	15.7%	16.8%	17.6%	18.2%	18.6%

of capital that can be invested in a single venture, which prevents excessive investments in high-risk ventures with inadequate rewards. As mentioned earlier, many contracts call for mandatory distributions of realized gains. If venture capitalists were allowed to invest realized gains in new ventures, they might increase the risk to the fund without a commensurate increase in return. Mandatory distributions also protect the principals against activities not consistent with the goals of the fund.

One final contractual response to the problem of risk is to force the general partner to invest more in the fund than the customary small amounts mentioned earlier. Then the venture capitalists bear a greater share of the costs of investing in ventures that perform poorly. On the other hand, the risk problem will be intensified if the venture capitalist is required to pay a fee up front for the right to manage the funds of the limited partners.[9] This has the effect of making the excise price on the option higher. The same basic problem arises if there is a rate-of-return hurdle that has to be exceeded before the venture capitalist is entitled to a carried interest. In this case, the exercise price of the option rises each year, which means that an increase in risk has a significant payoff to the option holder.

One other area of concern in the compensation system used in the venture-capital organization relates to incentives to increase the amount of capital under management and/or to manage multiple pools of capital over time. The basic issues are discussed in the next section.

5.3. Operating costs

Two kinds of operating costs deserve analysis when discussing venture capital, taxes, and continuing operating costs. With respect to taxes, partnership gains are not subject to partnership-level taxation. The limited and general partners report the realized gains and losses on their individual tax returns. Second, securities can be distributed without triggering immediate taxable income for the recipient. Thus a limited partner who receives stock in a portfolio company can defer recognizing the gain (or loss) until that security is sold. Third, the venture capitalists do not incur taxable income when they receive their carried interest in the partnership: they report taxable income only as gains and losses are realized on the underlying securities.

Finally, the partnership's compensation scheme can be structured to allocate losses to those who can make best use of them. This feature of partnerships has been used widely in structuring oil-and-gas partnerships [Wolfson (1985)] and research-and-development limited partnerships. Tax

---

[9]In a number of cases, venture-capital management firms have been purchased. Examples include Ampersand Ventures, TA Associates, and Brinson Partners.

incentives in venture capital are less important, however, because many of the investors in venture funds are tax-exempt. More importantly, there are no significant tax losses to be allocated because a fund's unrealized losses are not recognized by the IRS for tax purposes unless the underlying securities are transferred to another party in an arms-length transaction. Often partnerships do allocate these losses to the limited partners, but the economic impact is minimal.

With respect to operating costs, scale economies, scope economies, and learning-curve effects are often very significant to a venture-capital management company that manages one or more funds. Scale economies exist if the unit cost of production and distribution of a product or service declines as volume increases. In the venture-capital organization, production and distribution encompass raising capital, finding and structuring deals, monitoring the investments, and distributing the proceeds. Scope economies exist if unit costs decline if multiple products or services are produced simultaneously (for example, if more than one fund is managed at a time). Learning-curve effects exist if the unit cost of a process declines over time with accumulated volume.

With respect to scale economies, it seems likely that unit costs decline with the absolute size of the venture-capital pool under management because there are a number of fixed (or near-fixed) costs, including items in the overhead budget such as rent, information acquisition, accounting, and certain legal costs. Economies of scope are also likely because the cost of managing multiple pools of capital does not rise linearly with the number of such pools.

Finally, with respect to learning-curve effects, venture-capital firms become repositories of useful institutional knowledge. Venture capitalists and their support staffs benefit from learning-curve effects as they become adept in dealing with each other and with other resource suppliers, such as law firms, accounting firms, investment bankers, and management recruiting firms. They cultivate a deal flow based on networks of contacts and relationships. The venture-capital organization develops a reputation that has economic value. The ultimate effect is to make the firm more efficient as time passes and experience accumulates.

Compensation practices give evidence of scale and/or scope economies as well as experience effects. According to the Hay Management Consultants (1988) survey, the total compensation for the managing partner of a venture-capital fund with less than $25 million in capital averages $163,000. The comparable figure for a managing partner of a fund with more than $200 million under management is $581,000. The annual bonus, which is based on the operating profit of the management company rather than the investment performance of the fund, constitutes 28% of total compensation in the larger funds, compared with 17% in the small funds. These differences suggest that venture capitalists have an incentive to increase the size of the firm. One driving factor in this regard is the fact that the percentage fee charged to manage a venture-capital fund does not appear to decline with the size of the fund [see Venture Economics (1987)].

There can also be incentives to create multiple funds over time, all managed by the same venture capitalists. Doing so accomplishes two goals. First, keeping the venture-capital management company in existence preserves the learning that has taken place. Second, managing multiple funds takes advantage of any scale or scope economies. From 1977 to 1988, new funds averaged less than one-half the size of follow-on funds (panel B, table 1).

Even though unit costs decline as the size of the venture-capital management firm (or number of funds under management) increases, the limited partners and general partners will not necessarily agree about the optimal size and structure of the firm. This is because the unit costs and risk-adjusted rates of return to the limited partners may be negatively correlated, and because the limited and general partners do not have equal stakes in all the income streams generated by the fund. There could easily be situations in which the venture capitalists find it more profitable to have a large firm, one effect of which is lower returns to the limited partners. This would be true if there were diseconomies of scale or scope in the investment-return-generating process.

The possibility that the interests of the general and limited partners will diverge over time is addressed directly by limiting the lifespan of the venture-capital partnership. If the venture capitalists make decisions that aren't in the best interests of the limited partners, they can be denied access to capital. Any learning, scale, or scope economies will then go to waste. The ability to withdraw funding support is the ultimate tool for aligning the interests of the agent and principal in this organizational form, and is reinforced by the existence of the scale or scope economies and learning-curve effects.

5.4. The sorting problem

The final component of this analysis of the economic relationship between the limited partners and the venture capitalists is an examination of how limited partners decide which venture capitalists to back. For obvious reasons, filtering out the 'good' from the 'bad' venture capitalists is extremely important. 'Good' venture capitalists have the skill and intention to generate high risk-adjusted rates of return for the limited partners. Actual rates of return will also depend, of course, on such factors as the capital markets, competition among venture capitalists, and the market for innovation.

Limited partners in venture-capital firms typically invest at least $1 million in each fund. Before committing this amount of capital, the investors spend resources on due diligence. They read the offering memoranda prepared by the venture capitalists in accordance with SEC regulations, and they often check the venture capitalists' credentials. This investigation acts as a preliminary screen on potential investments.

The governance structure also helps potential investors distinguish between good venture capitalists and weak ones. The basic argument is simple: good venture capitalists are more likely than weak venture capitalists to accept a finite life for each new partnership and a compensation system heavily dependent on investment returns. By doing so, they agree explicitly to have their performance reviewed at least every few years: if they engage in opportunistic acts or are incompetent, they will be denied access to funds. In addition, most of their expected compensation comes from a share in the fund's profits. If they perform well, they will participate handsomely in the fund's success. They will also be rewarded by being able to raise additional capital and, most likely, benefit from the various economies characteristic of the business. If they are not confident of performing well, or if they intend to neglect the interests of the limited partners, they will probably not agree to the basic terms of the contract.[10]

5.5. The overall incentives

In sum, the relationship between the limited and general partners in a venture-capital fund is fraught with agency problems. The limited partners structure a contract that creates incentives for mutual gain, and they specifically forbid certain obvious acts of self-interest like buying stock in portfolio companies at prices less than those paid by the fund. The limited partners then expend resources to monitor the fund's progress, often through special committees. At the same time the venture capitalists agree to forego certain self-interested acts and to supply information to the limited partners. The venture capitalists willingly enter into an agreement with a finite life, exposing the contract to renewal. In effect, the limited partners stage the commitment of capital to the venture capitalists while preserving mechanisms to ensure that the profits will be distributed rather than kept inside the venture-capital fund. And the terms of the contract both communicate the

[10]This description of the incentives of the venture capitalists is drawn from the signaling literature [Spence (1973), Ross (1977), Leland and Pyle (1977), and Bhattacharya (1979)]. The implicit condition for the sorting process to work is that the short-term payoff (in present-value terms) to the venture capitalist must be less than the opportunity cost for a 'bad' venture capitalist. Note also that each limited partner spends time and resources researching venture capitalists seeking to raise funds, which helps guard against false signaling. From another perspective, accepting these terms may be viewed as a bonding commitment by the venture capitalist, who implicitly agrees not to divert money from the fund.

expectations of the limited partners to the venture capitalists, and filter out those who are unable or unwilling to meet those expectations.

The contracts and operating procedures that have evolved in the venture-capital industry address three issues simultaneously: sorting good from bad venture capitalists, minimizing the present value of agency costs, and minimizing the present value of operating costs. The same basic issues confront the venture capitalists when they invest in entrepreneurial ventures. In this case, the venture capitalists become the principals and the entrepreneurs the agents. Analogous contractual and operating responses to these issues are made by the venture-capital fund.

6. The venture-capital investment process

Once a venture-capital fund is raised, the venture capitalists must identify investment opportunities, structure and execute deals with entrepreneurial teams, monitor investments, and ultimately achieve some return on their capital. For the purposes of this paper, I focus on structuring deals.

Just as venture-capital partnerships have many elements in common, the contracts between the venture capitalists and the companies they invest in are similar in many ways. The basic document that governs the relationship between the venture-capital firm and the venture is the stock-purchase agreement, which is described below.[11] The economic rationale for the terms and conditions of this document and other aspects of the venture-capital process are explored in section 7.

6.1. Amount and timing

Each stock-purchase agreement fixes the amount and timing of the investment. Venture capitalists typically invest more than once during the life of a company, and the amount invested often increases with each round (see tables 3 and 4). They expect the capital invested at each point to be sufficient to take the company to the next stage of development, when it will require additional capital to make further progress.

---

[11]This account of stock-purchase agreements is drawn from a number of sources. First, I have gathered approximately 40 such agreements from a broad range of venture-capital partnerships. Venture capitalists tend to use the same deal structure in all of their deals so that knowing how one deal is structured sheds light on many investments made by the same fund. Some of these materials have formed the basis for case studies used at Harvard Business School, including Knights and Sahlman (1986a, 1986b, 1986c, 1986d), Sahlman (1983a, 1983b, 1984, 1985a, 1985b, 1985c, 1985d, 1985e, 1986a, 1986b, 1986c, 1986d, 1988c, 1989b), Sahlman and Knights (1986), Sahlman and Scherlis (1988), Sahlman and Soussou (1985a, 1985b), and Soussou and Sahlman (1986). See also Sahlman (1988). A broad survey of the characteristics of deals struck by venture-capital firms is included in Plummer (1987). Finally, a number of texts describe standard operating procedures in the industry, including Bartlett (1988) and Morris (1988a).

6.2. Form and terms of investment

Many venture-capital investments are made as purchases of convertible preferred stock. Specific terms concern:

(1) conversion price, which can vary according to the performance of the company;
(2) liquidation preference, including a description of the events that trigger liquidation (for example, a merger or reorganization with a total value less than some predetermined amount);
(3) dividend rate, payment terms, and voting rights (typically on an as-if-converted basis).

Typically, the convertible preferred stock does not pay a dividend on a current basis, but at the discretion of the board of directors. Some preferreds have provisions that call for accruing dividends but deferring the payment of cash. The liquidation preference amount is equal in most cases to the face amount of the convertible preferred issue and all accrued but unpaid dividends.

6.3. Puts and calls

Agreements typically give the venture capitalists the right to put the security by calling for redemption of the preferred stock. Less frequently, contracts give portfolio-company management the right to call the security away from the venture capitalists at some point.

6.4. Registration rights

Most agreements give the venture capitalists the right to register their shares at some point or points in the future. This enables the venture capitalists to demand registration at any two dates in the future, with the expenses of registration paid by the company. Venture capitalists also insist on piggyback registration rights that entitle them to register shares at the same time as the company, subject to limitations imposed by the SEC and the underwriters.

6.5. Go-along rights

Many agreements specify that the venture capitalists can sell shares after conversion at the same time and on the same terms as the key employees.

6.6. Preemptive rights and rights of first refusal

Many agreements entitle the venture-capital investors to participate in new financings by buying newly issued shares from the company, often in proportion to their common-stock-equivalent holdings before the issuance of new equity-equivalent shares. The terms of such financing rounds are not typically negotiated in advance; they reflect the then-current conditions in the capital markets and the performance and prospects of the firm.

6.7. Option pool

Most agreements fix the number of shares outstanding and the size of the pool of shares that can be granted or sold to current and future employees. Provisions for modifying the option pool are also included in the stock-purchase agreement.

6.8. Employment contracts

Most agreements require that key employees execute employment contracts and agree to noncompete clauses. Such contracts usually specify compensation, benefits, and, most important, the conditions under which the contract can be terminated and the consequences of termination.

6.9. Vesting schedules and buy-back provisions

Employees of venture-capital-backed companies often accept modest cash salaries in return for equity ownership. Many agreements set explicit vesting schedules for management shares and also grant the company being financed the right to repurchase shares in the event of an employee's voluntary or involuntary departure. When shares are repurchased under these agreements, the price paid by the company to the departing entrepreneur is often based on book value, which may be below market value.

6.10. Information rights

Most agreements call for regular transmission of information, including financial statements and budgets, and permit the venture capitalists to inspect the company's financial accounts at will. Venture capitalists insist on timely access to such information. They typically receive detailed monthly financial statements and more frequent operating statements. They evaluate this information to anticipate problems and respond expeditiously when performance falls short.

6.11. Board structure

Most agreements call for venture capitalist representation on the company's board of directors [see Barry et al. (1990) for information on venture-capitalist board representation of companies going public]. Often, the agreement calls for other mutually acceptable people to be elected to the board. The venture capitalists typically receive no cash compensation for board duties; if any cash is received for board membership, it is paid into the partnership. Outside members recruited to join the board usually receive inexpensive common stock or warrants to acquire shares, and little or no cash compensation.

7. The relationship between the venture capitalists and the entrepreneurial ventures

Each year venture capitalists screen hundreds of investment proposals before deciding which ideas and teams to support. The success or failure of any given venture depends on the effort and skill of the people involved as well as on certain factors outside their control (for example, the economy), but the capabilities of the individuals involved are difficult to gauge up front.

Once investment decisions are made and deals consummated, it is difficult to monitor progress. The probability of failure is high (see fig. 1, which shows that 34.5% of the capital invested in the survey resulted in a loss). The venture capitalist and the entrepreneur are also likely to have different information. Even with the same information, they are likely to disagree on certain issues, including if and when to abandon a venture and how and when to cash in on investments.

Venture capitalists attack these problems in several ways. First, they structure their investments so they can keep firm control. The most important mechanism for controlling the venture is staging the infusion of capital. Second, they devise compensation schemes that provide venture managers with appropriate incentives. Third, they become actively involved in managing the companies they fund, in effect functioning as consultants. Finally, venture capitalists preserve mechanisms to make their investments liquid.

7.1. Staging the commitment of capital and other control mechanisms

Venture capitalists rarely, if ever, invest all the external capital that a company will require to accomplish its business plan: instead, they invest in companies at distinct stages in their development. As a result, each company begins life knowing that it has only enough capital to reach the next stage. By staging capital the venture capitalists preserve the right to abandon a project whose prospects look dim. The right to abandon is essential because an entrepreneur will almost never stop investing in a failing project as long as others are providing capital.

Staging the capital also provides incentives to the entrepreneurial team. Capital is a scarce and expensive resource for individual ventures. Misuse of capital is very costly to venture capitalists but not necessarily to management. To encourage managers to conserve capital, venture-capital firms apply strong sanctions if it is misused. These sanctions ordinarily take two basic forms. First, increased capital requirements invariably dilute management's equity share at an increasingly punitive rate. (This was the case with Federal Express). Second, the staged investment process enables venture-capital firms to shut down operations completely. The credible threat to abandon a venture, even when the firm might be economically viable, is the key to the relationship between the entrepreneur and the venture capitalist [see also Stiglitz and Weiss (1983) for a similar argument in the banking industry].[12] By denying capital, the venture capitalist also signals other capital suppliers that the company in question is a bad investment risk.

Short of denying the company capital, venture capitalists can discipline wayward managers by firing or demoting them. Other elements of the stock-purchase agreement then come into play. For example, the company typically has the right to repurchase shares from departing managers, often at prices below market value (for example, at book value). The use of vesting schedules limits the number of shares employees are entitled to if they leave prematurely. Finally, noncompete clauses can impose strong penalties on those who leave, particularly if their human capital is closely linked to the industry in which the venture is active.

Entrepreneurs accept the staged capital process because they usually have great confidence in their own abilities to meet targets. They understand that if they meet those goals, they will end up owning a significantly larger share of the company than if they had insisted on receiving all of the capital up front. As discussed below, entrepreneurs also must make conscious choices about who provides capital and what value they can add in addition to capital.

Finally, whereas venture capitalists insist on retaining the option to abandon a particular venture, they also want to be able to invest more if the company requires and warrants additional capital. This option is preserved by insisting on rights of first refusal or pre-emptive rights.

---

[12] The seemingly irrational act of shutting down an economically viable entity is rational when viewed from the perspective of the venture capitalist confronted with allocating time and capital among various projects. Although the individual company may be economically viable, the return on time and capital to the individual venture capitalist is less than the opportunity cost, which is why the venture is terminated.

7.2. *The compensation scheme*

Entrepreneurs who accept venture capital typically take smaller cash salaries than they could earn in the labor market. The shortfall in current income is offset by stock ownership in the ventures they start. Common stock and any subsequent stock options received will not pay off, however, unless the company creates value and affords an opportunity to convert illiquid holdings to cash. In this regard, the interests of the venture-capital investor and entrepreneur are aligned.

This compensation system penalizes poor performance by an employee. If the employee is terminated, all unvested shares or options are returned to the company. In almost all cases, the company retains the right to repurchase shares from the employee at predetermined prices.

Without sanctions, entrepreneurs might sometimes have an incentive to increase risk without an adequate increase in return. An entrepreneur's compensation package can be viewed as a contingent claim, whose value increases with volatility. The sanctions, combined with the venture capitalists' active role in the management of the venture, helps to mitigate the incentive to increase risk.

7.3. *Active involvement of venture capitalists in portfolio companies*

No contract between an entrepreneur and venture capitalist can anticipate every possible disagreement or conflict. Partly for this reason, the venture capitalist typically plays a role in the operation of the company.

Venture capitalists sit on boards of directors, help recruit and compensate key individuals, work with suppliers and customers, help establish tactics and strategy, play a major role in raising capital, and help structure transactions such as mergers and acquisitions. They often assume more direct control by changing management and are sometimes willing to take over day-to-day operations themselves. All of these activities are designed to increase the likelihood of success and improve return on investment: they also protect the interests of the venture capitalist and ameliorate the information asymmetry.

According to one survey [Gorman and Sahlman (1989)], lead venture investors visit each portfolio company an average of 19 times per year, and spend 100 hours in direct contact (on site or by phone) with the company. Since each venture capitalist in the survey is responsible for almost nine investments and sits on five boards of directors, the allocation of time to each portfolio company is considerable [see also MacMillan et al. (1989) and Timmons (1987)]. In addition to devoting time to companies already in the portfolio, a venture capitalist must allocate time to raising capital for the venture-capital firm, finding new deals, managing the venture-capital firm, and meeting with various resource suppliers, such as bankers and accountants.

Successful venture capitalists bring instant credibility associated with their capital, their contacts, and their range of projects. A venture-capital-backed company can often gain access to more capital from the fund itself, and the venture capitalist's contacts in the financial community can make it easier to raise new capital from other sources. In addition, resource suppliers form implicit and explicit relationships with venture capitalists in an attempt to piggyback on the data-gathering and monitoring process [see the HBS cases Sahlman (1986d, 1985e) and Knights and Sahlman (1986b)]. Venture capitalists have incentives not to exploit a resource supplier on any individual deal, since the repercussions can affect other deals. At the same time, the resource suppliers have incentives to preserve their relationship with venture-capital firms by avoiding opportunistic behavior on individual deals.

Finally, venture capitalists maintain close ties to investment bankers who can assist companies going public or merging with other companies [Barry et al. (1990)]. Venture capitalists also often have contacts in large companies to which entrepreneurial ventures might be sold.

7.4. Mechanisms related to liquidity

Both venture capitalists and entrepreneurs want eventually to convert their illiquid holdings into cash or cash equivalents, but they can disagree on the timing or the method. The standard stock-purchase agreement has a number of features that control the process by which the venture capitalists and the entrepreneurs achieve their goals. Chief among these is the decision to invest in the form of a convertible preferred.

Using preferred stock with a dividend creates a mechanism for deriving some income from an investment if the company is only marginally successful. Most deals defer payment of the dividend until the board allows it, but because venture capitalists often control the board, they can make the decision. Since the dividends are not tax-deductible, the burden of paying dividends is often onerous, which often leads the entrepreneurs to try to buy out the preferred.

Many agreements also give the venture capitalists the right to force redemption of a preferred stock or the right to put the stock to the company, to achieve liquidity. This option may be exercised if the company is financially viable but too small to go public. Some contracts give entrepreneurs the right to sell stock back to the venture capitalist, as might happen if the venture capitalists terminate the entrepreneur's employment without cause.

Finally, venture capitalists are concerned about situations where the entrepreneurs have an opportunity to sell their shares before the venture capitalists sell theirs. Therefore, the contract typically specifies that the venture capitalists can sell their shares at the same time and on the same terms as the entrepreneur.

7.5. Additional implications of using convertible preferred stock

Using a convertible preferred also provides flexibility in setting the conversion terms. The venture capitalist often can base the conversion ratio for the preferred stock on the company's performance. If the company does well, the conversion price might be higher, with lower dilution for the management team. A similar tool is the 'ratchet', which ensures that the effective price per share paid by the venture capitalist is at least as low as any price paid in the future.

Flexible conversion terms alter the risk-and-reward-sharing scheme. One intent is to discourage entrepreneurs from overstating their projections to increase the initial valuation, and to encourage them to build value. Incorporating these provisions into contracts also serves as a negotiating tool to account for differences of opinion about future prospects.[13]

One final consequence of having preferred stock in the capital structure relates to taxation: using a preferred creates two kinds of securities, one with superior rights. A security that is senior in rights to common stock in effect lowers the economic value of the common. Members of the management team can therefore buy the common stock at low prices without incurring taxable income. Common-stock value is frequently set at 10% of the conversion price of the preferred. If the common stock had the same rights as the preferred, the managers would have to report taxable income on the difference between the price they paid and the price paid by the venture capitalists. There is no immediate tax disadvantage to using preferred stock, however, because the dividend is deferred and many of the ultimate recipients are tax exempt.

7.6. Using the contract to sort out entrepreneurs

A key feature of the contracts and operating procedures is that risk is shifted from the venture capitalists to the entrepreneur. The entrepreneur's response to these terms enables the venture capitalist to make informed evaluations and judgments. It would be foolish for entrepreneurs to accept such contract terms if they were not truly confident of their own abilities and deeply committed to the venture.

For example, by substituting stock ownership for higher current income, the contract shifts the risks of poor performance to the entrepreneur. Similarly, the convertible preferred security shifts some of the costs of poor performance to the entrepreneurial team. Given the liquidation preference

---

[13]See Knights and Sahlman (1986b) for a description of a conditional conversion price. In that situation, the venture capitalists agreed to increase the conversion price (from $0.45 to $0.67) if the company met its business-plan sales-and-profit targets.

Table 6[a]

Stage	Discount rate range (%)
Startup	50 to 70
First stage	40 to 60
Second stage	35 to 50
Third stage	35 to 50
Fourth stage	30 to 40
IPO	25 to 35

[a]*Source:* Plummer (1987, p. I-18).

embodied in the security, the venture capitalists will be entitled to a larger share of total value if total value is low.

Moreover, the entrepreneurs typically hold undiversified portfolios. Much of their wealth is invested in the securities of the company they manage. The entrepreneur's willingness to bear diversifiable risk also conveys useful information to the venture capitalists.

7.7. Evaluation techniques

The methods venture capitalists use to judge the prospects of individual projects are also used to sort out entrepreneurs. In screening potential ventures, venture capitalists use certain standard evaluation techniques, including this simple method for determining the value of the companies[14]:

(a) A forecast is made reflecting successful attainment of achievable long-term goals.
(b) The venture capitalist estimates a possible terminal value that would obtain if the investment in the company were harvested at that point.
(c) The terminal value is converted to a present value by applying a high discount rate, usually between 40% and 60%.
(d) The proportion of company stock to be owned by the venture-capital firm is then calculated by dividing the required investment by the total present value.

The most important element of this process is determining the discount rate. According to Plummer (1987), the discount rates used by venture capitalists vary by the company's stage of development. The results of that study are summarized in table 6 (the stages are defined in table 2):

These discount rates seem high compared with other rates of return in the economy [for example, the returns on publicly traded stocks and bonds as reported in Ibbotson (1988)] or even the actual returns reported by profes-

---

[14]See Plummer (1987), Morris (1988b), and Sahlman and Scherlis (1988) for more detailed descriptions of the method.

sional venture-capital funds [Venture Economics (1985, 1988c)]. In theory the required rate of return on an entrepreneurial investment reflects the risk-free interest rates in the economy, the systematic risk of the particular asset and the market risk premium, the liquidity of the asset,[15] and compensation for the value added by the supplier of capital (including favored access to other resources). This last adjustment is required to compensate venture capitalists for monitoring the company and playing an active role in management, while leaving the limited partner with the appropriate rate of return after taking into account the venture-capital fund's management fees and profit participation.

In practice, the use of high discount rates also reflects a well-known bias in financial projections made by entrepreneurs. Because few companies ever do as well as their founders believe they will, the numerator used in the calculation described above is typically higher than the expected value, though it may be an unbiased estimate conditional on success. To adjust for the bias, projections can be lowered or a higher discount rate can be used. The latter mechanism seems to dominate in the venture-capital industry [Keeley (1986)].

The use of high discount rates, however, means that few projects are feasible. Suppose a venture requires a $2 million capital infusion (the average invested in recent years in each venture) and that in five years the company will be worth $12 million. If the required rate of return is 50% per year, the $2 million investment must be worth approximately $15.2 million by the end of the fifth year, an amount exceeding the likely value of the entire company. Accordingly, venture capitalists are reluctant to back any company that cannot reasonably be expected to generate at least $25 to $50 million in total value in five years [MacMillan et al. (1985)]. The entrepreneurs' willingness to accept high discount rates indicates belief in the prospects of the company.

The use of high discount rates in venture-capital investing seems to fly in the face of conventional wisdom. One often reads that high discount rates discourage investments in highly uncertain, long-term projects [Hayes and Garvin (1982)], but in venture capital high discount rates are part of a more complex process of investing and managing the agency problem.

7.8. Adverse selection

Using very high discount rates might have the unintended effect of driving the most competent entrepreneurs to seek alternative sources of capital, leaving only those with no other financing options.

---

[15] Venture-capital investments are illiquid for a number of reasons, including the existence of information asymmetries and restrictions imposed by regulatory authorities on transfers of unregistered securities.

The adverse-selection problem is a difficult one in venture capital. Venture capitalists argue that by playing a positive role in the venture, they can increase total value by enough to offset the high cost of the capital they provide. To the extent that venture capitalists make good on this claim, the adverse-selection issue is effectively mitigated. In addition, the due diligence conducted before an investment is made is intended partly to make sure the entrepreneurs are qualified.

Although it seems that venture capitalists retain much of the power in the relationship with entrepreneurial ventures, there are checks and balances in the system. Venture capitalists who abuse their power will find it hard to attract the best entrepreneurs, who have the option of approaching other venture capitalists or sources other than venture capital. In this regard, the decision to accept money from a venture capitalist can be seen as a conscious present-value-maximizing choice by the entrepreneur.

7.9. Comparing the venture-capital fund – limited partner and venture capitalist – entrepreneur relationships

The relationship between the limited partners and the venture capitalists shares several elements with that between the venture capitalists and the entrepreneurs. First, each relationship entails staging the commitment of capital and preserving the option to abandon. The limited partners insist on a limited life for the fund, and the venture capitalists invest in stages related to the attainment of specific goals by the venture.

The compensation schemes are similar as well. The venture capitalists have strong incentives to create value because they share in the profits of the fund. The entrepreneurs receive a significant share of the value they help create (see table 4 for evidence about the share held by founders).

Also, in both cases, there are defined mechanisms in place to achieve liquidity. The limited partners insist on distributions of investment returns. The venture capitalists build into their stock-purchase agreements a number of mechanisms for achieving liquidity, such as the right to demand redemption of their convertible preferred stock.

Finally, the venture capitalist and entrepreneur alike face serious consequences if they fail. Entrepreneurs will be denied access to capital, their equity participation will be retracted, and their reputations damaged. Similarly, venture capitalists will find capital more difficult and costly to raise and their reputations will suffer as well, though their penalties are modest in comparison with those confronting entrepreneurs. In both cases, however, the multiperiod nature of the game creates strong incentives to perform well and to forego opportunistic behavior.

These common elements reinforce each other. For example, because venture capitalists capture 20% of their funds' profits, they structure incentives for the entrepreneurs that reward value creation. Similarly, because venture capitalists are legally required to liquidate the fund in ten years or so, they build mechanisms into their contracts with the entrepreneurs to make that feasible.

8. Other organizational forms

The venture-capital organization has evolved in response to the demanding investment environment in which new businesses are built. But, sorting, agency, and transactions cost problems are present in other settings as well.

A venture-capital firm performs economic functions similar to those of a corporation. Both raise capital from outsiders and invest in projects on behalf of the outside investors. The outside investors in both cases create a governance structure for monitoring the decisions made by the agents. When investments are made in individual projects, the managers within the venture-capital fund or within the corporation must monitor performance. Ultimately, the outside investors insist that they receive some return on their capital.

A venture-capital firm is also similar to a leveraged buyout fund. Each organization raises capital to invest in individual projects. In the venture-capital example, the projects tend to be early-stage ventures: in the leveraged-buyout example, the projects are more mature businesses with substantial debt capacity. The following sections compare the venture-capital organization, the corporate organization, and the leveraged-buyout-fund organization.

8.1. Capital budgeting

Corporate managers confront issues similar to those facing venture capitalists, yet their responses are very different. For example, consider an opportunity to invest in a new computer technology that could be funded inside a large company or as a separate business by venture capitalists.

If the project is funded within a corporation, the project initiation and management team probably will not receive a significant share of the value it creates. More likely, if the project is successful, their rank in the company and current compensation will increase [see Baker (1987)]. Team members often own or receive some stock options in the company, but the value of these options does not necessarily reflect the success of the project they undertook.[16] If the project is not successful, on the other hand, team members probably will find other tasks within the corporation, provided they

---

[16]See Jensen and Murphy (1990) for information on the relationship between compensation and value changes for American managers.

were not guilty of gross incompetence or malfeasance. Though the pecuniary rewards for success are modest, so too are the consequences of failure.

During development of the technology, the in-house team receives assistance from other members of company management, who monitor performance and try to increase the chances that the project will succeed. The specific team generally does not need to compensate these advisors. To the extent that the project is charged with the costs of monitoring, the costs reflect standard overhead-absorption charges rather than the amount of assistance provided or its perceived value, and the compensation of the advisors will probably not be dramatically affected by the project's outcome.

In contrast, if the project is financed by a venture-capital fund, the initiators and key members of the team own part of the venture, and they probably receive lower salaries than an in-house management team. If the project succeeds, management participates directly in the value it helped create. The team is not broken up as often occurs in large companies when individual managers in a team are promoted or transferred after a successful venture.[17] If the project fails, management suffers the consequences directly. If the project falters in midstream, entrepreneurial managers stand a good chance of being fired, often losing equity shares because of the vesting schedules used by venture capitalists. Further, the compensation of the venture capitalists (and the other outside directors) mirrors that of the entrepreneurial team: they will benefit only if the company succeeds, and they will suffer the consequences if the venture fails.

There is often one other substantive difference between the two approaches. In the corporate setting, projects are often funded all at once. In the venture-capital situation, the capital is meted out according to perceived performance at each successive project stage. Although in either situation managers will not purposefully pour good money after bad, team managers inside the company feel more secure about access to future capital than managers do in the venture-capital scenario.

If the typical American corporation were organized like a venture-capital fund, its discrete business units would be separated into individual business entities, equity shares in those entities would be awarded to their managers, capital would be meted out according to the attainment of specific business goals, a separate board of directors would be constituted for each business entity, and each board would be compensated according to the value created in each unit. The board would have the right to demand that funds be returned from the operating units to the holding company, and the ultimate

---

[17]The venture capitalists ultimately do leave the team, often when the company goes public, and always when the company is sold. In these instances, however, new directors are recruited who bring skills and resources appropriate to the issues confronting the company as it matures. Also, in many instances (for example, Teradyne, Thermo Electron, New England Business Services, Apple Computer), the venture capitalists remain on the board long after the limited partners have received distributions of shares in the company.

owners of the holding company would also have the right to demand distribution of the rewards of investing (for example, by imposing a finite life on the organization). In contrast to a traditional corporation, the new organization would be structured as a limited partnership, which would eliminate the possibility of adverse tax consequences in distributing the rewards of investing to the ultimate owners. In effect, the entire incentive system for directors and unit managers would be radically altered, as would the process of allocating capital. This model is similar to the leveraged-buyout fund, described in the following section.

8.2. Leveraged-buyout funds

Separation of ownership and management has become a pressing problem in American business [Jensen and Ruback (1983), Jensen (1986, 1988)]. Evidence from the capital markets suggests that corporate managers do not always make value-maximizing decisions. One response to this problem has been the leveraged buyout (LBO). In an LBO, a company or business unit is acquired by a group of managers and financiers who end up owning the equity in the new organization. Most of the capital required to finance the acquisition is raised as debt rather than equity.

The reallocation of equity to management and the imposition of heavy debt burdens (interest and amortization) can be interpreted as a direct response to the agency problems inherent in corporations [Jensen (1989)]. After an LBO, managers have greater incentives to create value than they did when they had little or no equity stake in the outcome. Because of the substantial debt burdens, there is little or no discretionary cash flow that can be dissipated on negative-net-present-value investments, including perquisites.

In LBO organizations the relationships among the company, its management, and financiers are similar to the deal struck between venture capitalists and management teams in entrepreneurial ventures. The compensation scheme is oriented toward equity, whose value depends on the efforts and skills of the managers involved. There are severe penalties for underperformance: for example, managers' equity shares are often vested over time so that, if they are fired before full vesting has occurred, they lose the unvested portion of their claim. The debt used in LBOs is similar in function to the staged-capital-commitment process used in venture-capital deals; in neither is there much discretionary cash flow. The critical characteristic of the debt is really the contractual right to take control of the project by denying access to new funds or changing the terms of that access if the company's performance falters.[18]

---

[18]See Hart and Moore (1989) for a discussion of the nature of control in a firm and the somewhat arbitrary distinction between debt and equity.

Venture-capital funds and LBO funds are also similar in structure; indeed, many venture-capital firms also invest in leveraged buyouts. LBO funds are typically organized as private limited partnerships with the LBO fund managers acting as general partners: each partnership has a finite life, typically ten years. These funds raise capital from larger financial institutions such as pension funds and endowments, and they invest in diversified portfolios of companies. LBO fund managers also raise multiple funds over time; as investment activities wind down in one fund, a new one is raised, often from the same investors. LBO fund managers are active in the operation of the companies in which they invest, typically assuming control of the board of directors, but they are generally less likely than venture capitalists to assume operational control. They bring a great deal of process knowledge to bear, particularly in the area of financing, and they have close contacts with financial institutions and investment bankers. Their compensation is highly sensitive to value creation; like general partners in venture-capital deals, general partners of LBO funds typically receive a 20% share of the value created in addition to a periodic management fee. Most importantly, LBO fund managers are skilled and active monitors of the decisions being made by the company managers. They are the antithesis of the passive institutional investors who have come to dominate ownership of American companies.

Both the venture-capital fund and the LBO fund invest capital on behalf of institutions that could conceivably invest directly rather than through intermediaries. The LBO-fund model is interesting because the same institutions that invest in publicly traded residual claims also choose to participate through the LBO limited partnership in the new structure. Investing through the LBO fund addresses some of the inherent agency problems in publicly traded securities while also minimizing the present value of tax burdens.

There are also some significant differences between the venture-capital model and the leveraged-buyout firm. First, leveraged buyouts are typically restricted to companies that have modest growth rates and stable cash flows, firms in which management would otherwise have significant control over discretionary cash flows. After the LBO, management has an incentive to use its cash flow to pay down debt, thus increasing the value of its equity. In the traditional venture-capital model, there is little discretionary cash flow to begin with. Value is created by building the company to gain access to more resources, which in turn facilitates more growth. A final distinction to be drawn is that leveraged-buyout funds often charge up-front investment banking fees and continuing management fees to the companies in which they invest: venture capitalists rarely if ever charge fees to portfolio companies.

9. Conclusions

The venture-capital industry is a productive place to study organizational responses to agency and other problems. The environment is characterized by substantial uncertainty about payoffs on individual investments and a high degree of information asymmetry between principals and agents. To cope with the challenges posed by such an environment, certain standard operating procedures and contracts have evolved, including staging the commitment of capital, basing compensation on value created, and preserving mechanisms to force agents to distribute capital and profits. These procedures and contracts help sort out the skills and intentions of the participants while simultaneously addressing cost and taxation issues.

The venture-capital organizational form may be applicable in other settings, particularly corporate and project governance. At the corporate level, adopting some aspects of the venture-capital organization, such as the compensation system and the finite-life form of organization, might solve some of the problems that lead to leveraged-buyout transactions in the first place. Then the goals of shareholders, monitors, and managers would be better aligned [see Sahlman (1990) for a description of the specific issue of compensating corporate boards of directors].

At the project level, there are also important insights from studying the organization of venture-capital firms. For example, establishing project boards of directors, with skills and resources specifically tailored to the project, seems to make sense. Also, implementing value-sensitive compensation systems and staging the commitment of capital has potential advantages, particularly for projects designed to exploit new business opportunities.

Much research remains to be done on the venture-capital organization. Though the economic resources under management are modest, the model seems to have been effective. Understanding why it works is in the interests of academics and practitioners alike.

References

Baker, George P., 1987, Incentives in hierarchies: Promotions, bonuses and monitoring, Working paper no. 88-023 (Harvard Business School, Boston, MA).

Barry, Christopher B., Chris J. Muscarella, John W. Peavy III, and Michael R. Vetsuypens, 1990, The role of venture capital in the creation of public companies: Evidence from the going-public process, Journal of Financial Economics, this volume.

Bartlett, Joseph W., 1988, Venture capital law, business strategies, and investment planning (Wiley, New York, NY).

Bhattacharya, Sudipto, 1979, Imperfect information, dividend policy and the 'bird in the hand' fallacy, Bell Journal of Economics 10, 259–270.

Brickley, James A. and Frederick H. Dark, 1987, The choice of organizational form: The case of franchising, Journal of Financial Economics 18, 401–420.

Bygrave, William, Norman Fast, Roubina Khoylian, Linda Vincent, and William Yue, 1987, Early rates of return of 131 venture capital funds started 1978–1984, Journal of Business Venturing 4, 93–106.

Chiampou, Gregory F. and Joel J. Kellet, 1989, Risk/return profile of venture capital, Journal of Business Venturing 4, 1–10.

Council of Economic Advisors, 1990, Economic report of the President (U.S. Government Printing Office, Washington, DC).

Fama, Eugene F., 1980, Agency problems and the theory of the firm, Journal of Political Economy 88, 288–307.

Fama, Eugene F. and Michael C. Jensen, 1985, Organization forms and investment decisions, Journal of Financial Economics 14, 101–119.

Freear, John and William E. Wetzel, Jr., 1990, Who bankrolls high-tech entrepreneurs?, Journal of Business Venturing 5, 77–90.

Gorman, Michael and William A. Sahlman, 1989, What do venture capitalists do?, Journal of Business Venturing 4, 231–248.

Hart, Oliver and John Moore, 1989, Default and renegotiation: A dynamic model of debt, Working paper no. 89-069 (Harvard Business School, Boston, MA).

Hay Management Consultants, 1988, Survey of compensation among venture capital/leveraged buy-out firms (Hay Group, New York, NY).

Hayes, Robert H. and David Garvin, 1982, Managing as if tomorrow mattered, Harvard Business Review, May–June, 70–79.

Horsley Keogh & Associates, 1988, Horsley Keogh venture study (Horsley Keogh & Associates, Pittsford, NY).

Huntsman, Blaine and James P. Homan, Jr., 1980, Investment in new enterprise: Some empirical observations on risk, return, and market structure, Financial Management 9, 44–51.

Ibbotson Associates, 1988, Stocks, bonds, bills, and inflation, 1988 yearbook (Ibbotson Associates, Chicago, IL).

Jensen, Michael C., 1986, The agency costs of free cash flow: Corporate finance and takeovers, American Economic Review 76, 323–329.

Jensen, Michael C., 1988, Takeovers: Their causes and consequences, Journal of Economic Perspectives 2, 21–38.

Jensen, Michael C., 1989, Active investors, LBOs, and the privatization of bankruptcy, Journal of Applied Corporate Finance 2, 35–49.

Jensen, Michael C. and William H. Meckling, 1976, Theory of the firm: Managerial behavior, agency costs and ownership structure, Journal of Financial Economics 3, 305–360.

Jensen, Michael C. and Kevin J. Murphy, 1990, Performance pay and top management incentives, Journal of Political Economy 98, 225–264.

Jensen, Michael C. and R. Ruback, 1983, The market for corporate control: The scientific evidence, Journal of Financial Economics 11, 5–50.

Keeley, Robert, 1986, Risk (over)adjusted discount rates: The venture capitalist's method, Unpublished working paper.

Knights, David H. and William A. Sahlman, 1986a, Horizon Group, 286-058 Rev. 9/86 (Publishing Division, Harvard Business School, Boston, MA).

Knights, David H. and William A. Sahlman, 1986b, Centex Telemanagement, Inc., 286-059 Rev. 9/88 (Publishing Division, Harvard Business School, Boston, MA).

Knights, David H. and William A. Sahlman, 1986c, Vertex Peripherals, 286-069 Rev. 12/87 (Publishing Division, Harvard Business School, Boston, MA).

Knights, David H. and William A. Sahlman, 1986d, Priam Corporation – Vertex Peripherals, 286-103 Rev. 9/86 (Publishing Division, Harvard Business School, Boston, MA).

Kozmetsky, George, Michael D. Gill, Jr., and Raymond W. Smilor, 1985, Financing and managing fast-growth companies: The venture capital process (Lexington Books, Lexington, MA).

Leland, Hayne and David Pyle, 1977, Information asymmetries, financial structure and financial intermediation, Journal of Finance 32, 371–387.

MacMillan, Ian C., David M. Kulow, and Roubina Khoylian, 1989, Venture capitalists' involvement in their investments: Extent and performance, Journal of Business Venturing 4, 27–34.

MacMillan, Ian C., Robin Siegel, and P.N. Subba Narisimha, 1985, Criteria used by venture capitalists to evaluate new venture proposals, Journal of Business Venturing 1, 119–128.

Morris, Jane K., ed., 1988a, Pratt's guide to venture capital sources, 12th ed. (Venture Economics, Inc., Needham, MA).

Morris, Jane K., 1988b, The pricing of a venture capital investment, in: Pratt's guide to venture capital sources, 12th ed. (Venture Economics, Inc., Needham, MA) 55–61.

Myers, Stewart C., 1977, Determinants of corporate borrowing, Journal of Financial Economics 5, 147–176.

Plummer, James L., 1987, QED report on venture capital financial analysis (QED Research, Inc., Palo Alto, CA).

Ross, Stephen, 1977, The determination of financial structure: The incentive signalling approach, Bell Journal of Economics 8, 23–40.

Sahlman, William A., 1983a, Technical Data Corporation, 283-072 Rev. 12/87 (Publishing Division, Harvard Business School, Boston, MA).

Sahlman, William A., 1983b, Technical Data Corporation Business Plan, 283-073 Rev. 11/87 (Publishing Division, Harvard Business School, Boston, MA).

Sahlman, William A., 1984, Priam Corporation, 284-043 Rev. 9/84 (Publishing Division, Harvard Business School, Boston, MA).

Sahlman, William A., 1985a, CML Group, Inc. – Going public (A), 285-003 Rev. 9/86 (Publishing Division, Harvard Business School, Boston, MA).

Sahlman, William A., 1985b, Business Research Corporation (A), 285-089 (Publishing Division, Harvard Business School, Boston, MA).

Sahlman, William A., 1985c, Business Research Corporation (B), 285-090 (Publishing Division, Harvard Business School, Boston, MA).

Sahlman, William A., 1985d, CML Group, Inc. – Going public (B), 285-092 Rev. 9/86 (Publishing Division, Harvard Business School, Boston, MA).

Sahlman, William A., 1985e, Lotus Development Corporation, 285-094 Rev. 11/87 (Publishing Division, Harvard Business School, Boston, MA).

Sahlman, William A., 1986a, CML Group, Inc. – Going public (C), 286-009 (Publishing Division, Harvard Business School, Boston, MA).

Sahlman, William A., 1986b, Note on the venture capital industry – update (1985), 286-060 (Publishing Division, Harvard Business School, Boston, MA).

Sahlman, William A., 1986c, Palladian Software, 286-065 Rev. 11/87 (Publishing Division, Harvard Business School, Boston, MA).

Sahlman, William A., 1986d, Bank of Boston New Ventures Group, 286-070 Rev. 9/86 (Publishing Division, Harvard Business School, Boston, MA).

Sahlman, William A., 1988a, Aspects of financial contracting in venture capital, Journal of Applied Corporate Finance 1, 23–36.

Sahlman, William A., 1988b, Note on financial contracting: 'Deals', 288-014 Rev. 6/89 (Publishing Division, Harvard Business School, Boston, MA).

Sahlman, William A., 1988c, Sarah Jenks-Daly, 288-008 Rev. 9/88 (Publishing Division, Harvard Business School, Boston, MA).

Sahlman, William A., 1989a, Report on the Harvard Business School venture capital conference: September 23–24, 1988, Unpublished manuscript (Harvard Business School, Boston, MA).

Sahlman, William A., 1989b, Tom Volpe, 289-025 Rev. 2/89 (Publishing Division, Harvard Business School, Boston, MA).

Sahlman, William A., 1990, Why sane people shouldn't serve on public boards, Harvard Business Review 90-3, 28–37.

Sahlman, William A. and Howard H. Stevenson, 1985, Capital market myopia, Journal of Business Venturing 1, 7–30.

Sahlman, William A. and David H. Knights, 1986, Analog Devices – Bipolar Integrated Technology, 286-117 Rev. 12/88 (Publishing Division, Harvard Business School, Boston, MA).

Sahlman, William A. and Dan Scherlis, 1988, A method for valuing high-risk long-term investments, 288-006 Rev. 6/89 (Publishing Division, Harvard Business School, Boston, MA).

Sahlman, William A. and Helen Soussou, 1985a, Note on the venture capital industry (1981), 285-096 Rev. 11/85 (Publishing Division, Harvard Business School, Boston, MA).

Sahlman, William A. and Helen Soussou, 1985b, Precision Parts, Inc. (A), 285-131 (Publishing Division, Harvard Business School, Boston, MA).

Smith, Clifford W., Jr. and Jerold B. Warner, 1979, On financial contracting: An analysis of bond convenants, Journal of Financial Economics 7, 117–161.

Soussou, Helen and William A. Sahlman, 1986, Peter Wendell, 286-008 Rev. 1/86 (Publishing Division, Harvard Business School, Boston, MA).

Spence, A. Michael, 1973, Job market signalling, Quarterly Journal of Economics 3, 355–379.

Stevenson, Howard H., Daniel F. Muzyka, and Jeffry A. Timmons, 1987, Venture capital in transition: A Monte Carlo simulation of changes in investment patterns, Journal of Business Venturing 2, 103–122.

Stiglitz, Joseph E. and Andrew Weiss, 1983, Incentive effects of terminations: Applications to the credit and labor markets, American Economic Review 73, 912–927.

Studt, Tim A., 1990, There's no joy in this year's $150 billion for R&D, Research & Development, Jan., 41–44.

Testa, Richard J., 1988, The legal process of venture capital investment, in: Pratt's guide to venture capital sources, 12th ed. (Venture Economics, Inc., Needham, MA).

Timmons, Jeffry A., 1987, Venture capital: More than money, in: Pratt's guide to venture capital sources, 12th ed. (Venture Economics, Inc., Needham, MA).

Venture Economics, 1985, The venture capital industry: Opportunities and considerations for investors (Venture Economics, Inc., Needham, MA).

Venture Economics, 1987, Terms and conditions of venture capital partnerships (Venture Economics, Inc., Needham, MA).

Venture Economics, 1988a, Exiting venture capital investments (Venture Economics, Inc., Needham, MA).

Venture Economics, 1988b, Trends in venture capital – 1988 edition (Venture Economics, Inc., Needham, MA).

Venture Economics, 1988c, Venture capital performance: Review of the financial performance of venture capital partnerships (Venture Economics, Inc., Needham, MA).

Venture Economics, 1989, Venture capital yearbook 1989 (Venture Economics, Inc., Needham, MA).

Wetzel, William E., 1983, Angels and informal risk capital, Sloan Management Review 24, 23–34.

Williamson, Oliver E., 1975, Markets and hierarchies (Free Press, New York, NY).

Williamson, Oliver E., 1988, Corporate finance and corporate governance, Journal of Finance XLII, 567–591.

Wilson, John, 1985, The new venturers: Inside the high stakes world of venture capital (Addison-Wesley, Reading, MA).

Wolfson, Mark A., 1985, Empirical evidence of incentive problems and their mitigation in oil and gas tax shelter programs, in: John W. Pratt and Richard J. Zeckhauser, eds., Principals and agents; The structure of business, (Harvard Business School Press, Boston, MA) 101–126.

Journal of Financial Economics 35 (1994) 293–316. North-Holland

[7]

Venture capitalists and the decision to go public*

Joshua Lerner

Harvard Business School, Boston, MA 02163, USA

Received September 1992, final version received August 1993

This paper examines the timing of initial public offerings and private financings by venture capitalists. Using a sample of 350 privately held venture-backed biotechnology firms between 1978 and 1992, I show that these companies go public when equity valuations are high and employ private financings when values are lower. Seasoned venture capitalists appear to be particularly proficient at taking companies public near market peaks. The results are robust to a variety of controls and alternative explanations.

Key words: Venture capital; Initial public offerings; Financing strategy
JEL classification: G24; G32

1. Introduction

This paper examines the ability of venture capitalists to time initial public offerings (IPOs) by going public when equity values are high and using private financings when values are lower. Venture capitalists, who specialize in providing funds to privately held firms, generate the bulk of their profits from firms that go public. A Venture Economics study (1988a) finds that a $1 investment in a firm that goes public provides an average cash return of $1.95 beyond the initial investment with an average holding period of 4.2 years. The next best

Correspondence to: Joshua Lerner, Graduate School of Business Administration, Harvard University, Morgan Hall, Soldiers Field, Boston, MA 02163, USA.

*I thank for their suggestions Carliss Baldwin, Gary Chamberlain, Richard Caves, Joetta Forsyth, Stuart Gilson, Paul Gompers, Zvi Griliches (my dissertation chair), Michael Jensen (the editor), Steven Kaplan, Lisa Meulbroek, Jay Ritter (the referee), Richard Ruback, William Sahlman, Andrei Shleifer, Erik Sirri, Howard Stevenson, Peter Tufano, Michael Vetsuypens, and Karen Wruck. Assistance in obtaining data was provided by Jesse Reyes of Venture Economics, Mark Edwards of Recombinant Capital, and Mark Dibner of the North Carolina Biotechnology Center, and is gratefully acknowledged. Financial support was provided by the Consortium on Competitiveness and Cooperation; the Center for Science and International Affairs, John F. Kennedy School of Government, Harvard University; and the Division of Research, Harvard Business School. All errors and omissions are my own.

alternative, an investment in an acquired firm, yields a cash return of only 40 cents over a 3.7-year mean holding period.

I use a sample of 350 privately held biotechnology firms financed by venture capitalists between January 1978 and September 1992. I examine not only the timing of their IPOs, but also their private financings. I show that venture capitalists successfully time IPOs by being more likely to take companies public when their valuations are at their absolute and short-run peaks. I also show that experienced venture capitalists appear to be more proficient in timing IPOs than their less experienced counterparts.

I focus on the biotechnology industry because the development of a bioengineered pharmaceutical or agricultural product typically takes more than a decade. Biotechnology firms remain in a research-and-development phase until well after going public. These firms mature slowly, and do not incur large up-front costs in building manufacturing facilities. Venture capitalists provide funds in stages, with each financing round accompanied by a formal review of the firm's status. Each round involves an explicit decision to go public or remain private. Therefore, venture investors in biotechnology firms have the flexibility to try to time their IPOs according to market conditions. For IPOs in other industries, the demand for capital and the changing need for oversight by active investors may be more important to the decision to go public than market conditions. Thus, my sample provides an opportunity for a more precise test of the ability to time IPOs.[1] The analysis suggests that the positive correlation between IPO volume and public equity market valuations is due not only to greater financing activity when investment opportunities are good, but also to the substitution of public for private equity.

Successful timing of the IPO market provides significant benefits to venture capitalists, even through they rarely sell shares at the time of the offering [Barry, Muscarella, Peavy, and Vetsuypens (1990)]. Taking companies public when equity values are high minimizes the dilution of the venture investors' ownership stake. Models of sequential stock sales [Allen and Faulhaber (1989), Grinblatt and Hwang (1989), Welch (1989)] suggest a second rationale for timing the IPO. The deliberate underpricing of a new issue, which may be easier to accomplish in a hot market, 'leaves a good taste' with investors. These investors are then more willing to purchase shares in follow-on offerings.

Venture capitalists have several mechanisms to insure that firms go public at times that they perceive as optimal. Venture investors usually have several board seats and powerful control rights, including the right to put their shares to the firm's management [Barry, Peavy, Muscarella, and Vetsuypens (1990),

---

[1] Ibbotson and Jaffe (1975) and Ritter (1984) document 'hot issue' markets, while Ritter (1991) and Loughran and Ritter (1993) show that the poor long-run returns from investments in IPOs are due both to their poor performance relative to the market and their concentration around equity market peaks. The 'impresario hypothesis' of Shiller (1990) and Shiller and Pound (1989) suggests that IPOs are subject to fads, which underwriters exploit by rushing firms to the market.

Sahlman (1990)]. Probably more important is their activity as informal advisors to managers. Since 30% of the firms backed by venture capitalists over the past two decades have gone public (the remainder are liquidated or acquired in roughly equal proportions [Venture Economics (1988a)]), the venture investors have usually experienced many more IPOs than the firm's managers. Consequently, the venture capitalists may take the lead in deciding when and how a firm should go public.

The sample also enables me to isolate the impact of investor characteristics on IPO timing. The 1978–1992 period was characterized by diverse venture investors. Freed by a 1979 Department of Labor policy statement to enter into venture partnerships, pension funds invested heavily during the sample period. This led to extensive entry on the part of new venture partnerships. The pool of venture capital under management increased sixfold from 1978 to 1990 (adjusted by the Gross Domestic Product deflator). The wide range of experience among venture capitalists during the sample period makes it easier to identify the influence of venture experience.

The structure of this article is as follows: section 2 describes the construction of the data set. In section 3, I present the empirical results and check their robustness. In section 4, I examine two alternative hypotheses. Section 5 concludes the paper.

2. The sample

2.1. The financing data set

In contrast to earlier studies of IPO timing and performance, I examine both public and private financings. Information on venture capital investments is difficult to gather from public sources. Unlike mutual funds, venture capitalists need not reveal in public filings all their investments. Thus, the primary sources of public information are the companies in which they invest. For the subset of venture-backed firms that eventually go public, information is available in IPO prospectuses and S-1 registration statements. Investments in firms that do not go public are more difficult to uncover, since these investments are not usually publicized.

The relative performance of venture funds is an important issue for investors. Venture capitalists typically raise funds every few years; limited partners (wealthy individuals, endowments, and institutional investors) provide the bulk of the capital. An investment in a venture fund is almost always for at least a ten-year period, and funds may only be withdrawn under extreme circumstances. Thus, potential investors scrutinize the performance of venture capitalists' past funds. While venture partnerships present historical performance data in offering documents, the methodology of these calculations is frequently idiosyncratic. Furthermore, because the IPO market is so variable, potential investors usually look for a measure of relative, rather than absolute, performance.

Venture Economics (1991) addresses the need for information on performance by confidentially gathering data from venture funds and institutional investors. The organization, formed in 1961 to track the venture capital industry, has compiled two databases since 1977. One reports on the performance of venture funds, the other on venture investments. I use the investment database as the source for this analysis. It includes the dates of venture financings, the investors in each round, and the amount of funds disbursed. It includes firms that did and did not go public.[2] In a companion paper to this [Lerner (1993)], I analyze the completeness and accuracy of the Venture Economics database. I conclude that the database is comprehensive, and accurately depicts the amount of funds disbursed. In the case of older firms with many venture investors, however, there is a tendency to include multiple entries for a single venture round.

I confirm – and, if necessary, correct – the information in the Venture Economics database, using the following procedure:

• *Firms included in Recombinant Capital database.* Recombinant Capital (1991, 1992) is a San Francisco-based firm that specializes in collecting information on the biotechnology industry. The firm compiles data on venture financings from Securities and Exchange Commission (SEC) filings by public firms and state filings by private firms. In many states, privately held firms must provide detailed financial data to state authorities that becomes a part of the public record. The firm publishes round-by-round summaries of venture investments in biotechnology companies. I compare the Venture Economics records to those of Recombinant Capital. If they are the same, I consider the Venture Economics records as corroborated. If they conflict, and SEC filings are available, I use these filings to resolve the conflict. If the databases conflict, and SEC filings are not available, I rely on company and venture capitalist contacts. If I am unable to make any contacts, I use the Venture Economics data. I do not include as external financing rounds situations where founders contributed a small amount of funds (typically under $20,000) in exchange for common stock, or bridge loans by venture capital providers in the six months prior to the IPO, due immediately after the offering. These entries are relatively infrequent in the Venture Economics data set.

Firms with SEC filings not included in Recombinant Capital database. A firm going public discloses its investors in its prospectus (the 'Certain Transactions' and 'Financial Statements' sections) and the accompanying S-1 registration

---

[2]For firms that went public, Barry, Muscarella, Peavy, and Vetsuypens (1990) and Megginson and Weiss (1991) used information from the database published in Venture Economics' Venture Capital Journal.

statement (the 'Recent Sales of Non-Registered Securities' section and exhibits). Detailed financial information is often available about private firms
that have been acquired by public firms in the acquirers' proxy, 10-K, or 10-Q
statements. Information on firms that file for an aborted IPO is available in
the ultimately withdrawn registration statements. Using these records, I compare the Venture Economics records to the SEC filings. If they conflict, I use
the SEC filings.
• *Firms without SEC filings not included in Recombinant Capital database.* I rely
on company and venture capitalist contacts to confirm the Venture Economics data. I can frequently identify venture capitalists through Pratt's Guide
to Venture Capital Sources [Venture Economics (1992)]. This guide is in-
dexed by both individual and fund, so I can locate those venture capitalists
associated with terminated partnerships who are still employed in the industry. I identify companies by using industry directories [Corporate (1992),
Mega-Type (1992), NCBC (1990a), Ornx (1992)]. Some of the firms most
difficult to obtain information about are those that failed before going public.
I follow a methodology that I developed earlier [USGAO (1989)] to locate
managers of failed high technology businesses. If I am unable to make any
contacts, I use the Venture Economics data.

The resulting sample, summarized in table 1, consists of 750 financings by
privately held firms that had already received venture capital. These include 136
IPOs and 614 private financings. The public financings raised a total of $3.6
billion in 1992 dollars; the private financings raised $3.1 billion. (Both figures are
gross amounts, before deducting expenses associated with the equity sales.)

The firms in this sample went public after as few as one venture financing
round or as many as eight. The median for the 136 IPOs in the sample is three
prior venture rounds; the mean is 3.2. The mean firm went public 4.8 years after
being established; the median after 4.3 years. This can be contrasted with
Megginson and Weiss's sample of 320 venture-backed IPOs between 1983 and
1987, where the mean age was 8.6 years and the median 5.3 years.

2.2. The biotechnology equity index

To assess the ability of venture capitalists to time public and private financings, I examine the equity values around these transactions. I employ an index
of publicly traded biotechnology firms. This section describes the construction
of the index.

Ideally, I would use publicly traded biotechnology companies as a benchmark
throughout this period. Because companies dedicated to biotechnology did not
begin going public until the late 1970s, however, I must rely on 'comparable'
companies in the early years. For the 1978–1982 period, I use thirteen companies identified in the 1977 business press (primarily the analyst reports

Table 1

Distribution of the sample. The table indicates by year the number and cumulative size (in millions of 1992 dollars) of public and private financings by privately held biotechnology firms which had already received venture capital. The gross amount raised is reported for both public and private financings, before any deductions for offering cost.

Year	Public financings (IPOs) by private venture-backed firms		Private financings by private venture-backed firms	
	Number of IPOs	Total $ raised	Number of rounds	Total $ raised
1978	0	0	4	10
1979	1	6	4	31
1980	1	59	8	93
1981	4	219	9	58
1982	4	88	18	136
1983	18	365	40	218
1984	2	35	30	129
1985	2	8	36	122
1986	17	457	52	247
1987	12	204	61	337
1988	1	23	68	334
1989	6	57	75	364
1990	4	65	87	443
1991	34	1103	86	404
1992[a]	30	875	36	177
Total	136	3,564	614	3,103

[a]Through September 30 only.

summarized in Wall Street Transcript, but also the Wall Street Journal, Business Week, and Fortune) as well-positioned to capitalize on the then-current developments in biological science. Beginning January 1, 1983, I use thirteen 'dedicated' biotechnology firms that went public between 1979 and 1982. The pre-1983 sample has the same distribution as the dedicated biotechnology firms: seven firms specialized in human pharmaceuticals or diagnostics, three firms whose products relate to agricultural or animal science, two producers of research equipment, and one specialty chemical producer.

I invest equally in the comparable firms on January 1, 1978. At the end of each year, I rebalance the portfolio so I hold equal dollar amounts of each security. I do not rebalance the portfolio daily, because for many securities the spread between the bid and ask prices is significant relative to the share price. An index with daily rebalancing would be biased upward because of the 'bid–ask bounce' documented by Blume and Stambaugh (1983). On January 1, 1983, I liquidate the investment in the comparable portfolio, and use the proceeds to buy equal dollar amounts of the dedicated portfolio. As companies are acquired or delisted, I add the most seasoned, publicly traded dedicated biotechnology company to the index. The indices constructed using the comparable and dedicated

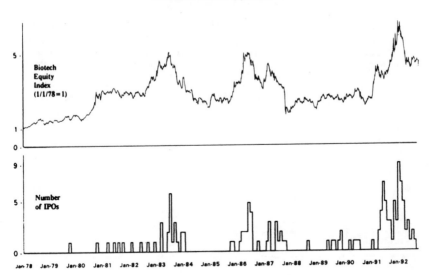

Fig. 1. The timing of initial public offerings by privately held venture-backed biotechnology companies, January 1978 through September 1992. The top graph depicts an index of biotechnology
equity, computed using the value of an investment in (between 1978 and 1982) thirteen companies
identified in the 1977 business press as well-positioned to capitalize on biotechnology developments
and (from 1983 onwards) thirteen biotechnology companies. Acquired or delisted firms are replaced
with the most seasoned, publicly traded biotechnology firm. January 1, 1978 is normalized as one.
The lower plot represents the *number* of biotechnology IPOs in each month. The data are compiled
from Venture Economics, Recombinant Capital, SEC filings, and company contacts, as well as
CRSP.

portfolios are highly correlated. During 1982 and 1983 (the year before and after
the switch), the correlation coefficient of the daily returns is over 0.96.

Figs. 1 and 2 display the number of IPOs and private financings in each
month and the biotechnology equity index. The IPOs coincide with the peaks in
equity valuations, while no clear pattern appears in the private financings. In
particular, the high valuations of 1983, 1986, and 1991–92 were accompanied by
intense IPO activity. The level of private financing activity, however, changed
little. These patterns suggest that venture capitalists are able to time the market,
taking companies public at times when industry valuations are highest.

3. Empirical analysis

In this section, I examine the timing of financings by these firms. First, I look
at financings in the entire sample. Then I compare more- with less-experienced
venture capitalists. Finally, I check the robustness of the results through a series
of diagnostic tests.

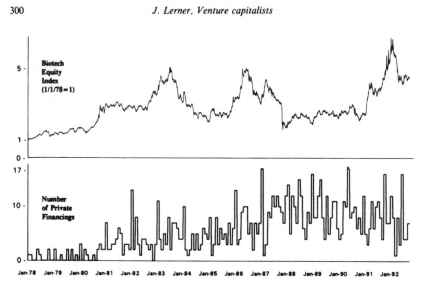

Fig. 2. The timing of private financings by privately held venture-backed biotechnology companies, January 1978 through September 1992. The top graph depicts an index of biotechnology equity, computed using the value of an investment in (between 1978 and 1982) thirteen companies identified in the 1977 business press as well-positioned to capitalize on biotechnology developments and (from 1983 onwards) thirteen biotechnology companies. Acquired or delisted firms are replaced with the most seasoned, publicly traded biotechnology firm. January 1, 1978 is normalized as one. The lower plot represents the *number* of biotechnology private financings in each month. The data are compiled from Venture Economics, Recombinant Capital, SEC filings, and company contacts, as well as CRSP.

3.1. The timing of financings

I first examine the timing of all external financings in the sample. Panel A of table 2 presents the main results. As figs. 1 and 2 suggest, IPOs are far more likely to occur when the equity values are high. The mean equity index at the time of IPOs is 4.05, as opposed to 3.05 at the time of private financings. (The index is normalized as one on January 1, 1978.) Using a nonparametric Wilcoxon test, panel B of table 2 shows that the difference is statistically significant at the 1% level of confidence.

I repeat this test, as well as the other shown below, adjusting the index in two ways. The increase in the equity index is partially due to inflation, and also to the need to provide a return to investors in excess of inflation. I detrend the index by the Gross Domestic Product deflator and by inflation plus a 5% annual premium. The differences in the index around IPOs and private financings remain significant. In the case of the inflation-adjusted series, the mean index at the time of the IPOs is 2.10; the mean index at the time of private financings is 1.69. (January 1, 1978, is once again normalized as one.) In the case of the inflation-adjusted series with the 5% annual premium, the mean index at

Table 2

Biotechnology equity prices around public and private financings by privately held venture-backed biotechnology companies. The sample consists of 750 IPOs and private financings between January 1978 and September 1992 by firms that had already received venture capital. The table presents the level of a biotechnology equity index[a] and the mean return from biotechnology equities in the three months before and after the financing. The table also compares the means and medians of these variables.

Panel A: Biotechnology equity prices

		Mean raw 'buy-and-hold' return from biotech equities around financing date	
Type of financing	Mean level of biotechnology index	Trading days − 60 to − 1	Trading days 0 to 59
136 initial public offerings	4.05	9.9%	− 4.6%
614 private financings	3.05	4.6%	6.1%

Panel B: Tests of differences in means and medians

Test	*p*-value
Wilcoxon test, median equity index on date of IPO = median equity index on date of private financing	0.00
t-test, mean return in [− 60, − 1] window before IPO = mean return in [− 60, − 1] window before private financing	0.00
t-test, mean return in [0, 59] window after IPO = mean return in [0, 59] window after private financing	0.00
t-test, mean return in [− 60, − 1] window before IPO = mean return in [0, 59] window after IPO	0.00
t-test, mean return in [− 60, − 1] window before private financing = mean return in [0, 59] window after private financing	0.27

[a]The index and change in equity values are computed for the period 1978 to 1982 using thirteen companies identified in the 1977 business press as well-positioned to capitalize on biotechnology developments and (from 1983 onwards) thirteen biotechnology companies. Acquired or delisted firms are replaced with the most seasoned, publicly traded biotechnology firm. The index is normalized to one on January 1, 1978. For the private financings where I know only the month and year of the transaction, I use the twelfth trading day of the month.

the time of the IPOs is 1.26; the mean index at the time of private financings is 1.03. Nonparametric Wilcoxon tests reject in both cases the null hypotheses of the equality of the distributions at the 1% level of confidence. The modified indices remain significant at the 1% level of confidence when used in probit regressions akin to that reported in table 3.

An IPO is also likely to coincide with a short-term maximum in equity values. I examine the buy-and-hold returns from an equal-weighted investment in thirteen biotechnology securities in the three months before and after the financing. I use thirteen comparable securities prior to 1983, and thirteen publicly traded dedicated firms thereafter. I extend the index back into late 1977 and forward to the end of 1992 in order to be able to use observations that are near the beginning and the end of the sample period. If a firm is acquired or delisted during the period, I roll over the investment into the most seasoned, publicly traded dedicated biotechnology firm.

Such an investment gains an average of 9.9% in the event window (− 60, − 1) before an IPO. [I choose an event window of sixty trading days so I can be consistent with Mikkelson and Partch (1988) and several other studies.] An identical investment made at the close of the IPO date has lost 4.6% of its value by day 59. Panel B indicates that the mean returns differ significantly at the 1% level of confidence.

Private financings display no such differences in the months before (+ 4.6%) and after (+ 6.1%) the transaction. Panel B shows that the mean returns in the three months prior to the IPOs are significantly greater than in the three months prior to the private financings. The mean returns are also significantly lower in the three months after IPOs. In some older entries in the database where the firm did not subsequently go public, I know only the month and year of the private financings. In these cases, I use the twelfth trading day of the month. The results are robust to alternative approaches, including assuming that the un-dated private financings took place on the first or last trading date of the month. They also are robust to using the changes in the index in the three months before and after the public and private financings, but not including the returns from the month of the financing.

I have one concern with the tests of the equality of means: their assumption of independence. The bunching of the IPOs and private financings implies that many of the sixty-trading-day windows over which returns are calculated overlap. To address concerns about whether the bunching of returns may lead to an overstating of significance levels, I undertake analyses that repeat the t-tests in table 2 in a regression framework. I regress the return on a constant and a dummy variable to indicate if the observation is from one of the two classes being compared: e.g., if this is an observation of the returns in the sixty trading days prior to a private financing. Instead of assuming independence, however, I use a Generalized Least Squares (GLS) approach akin to that used by Hansen and Hodrick (1980) and Meulbroek (1992). These authors employ in their analyses monthly observations of forward and futures prices several months ahead. Through the use of GLS estimation, they correct their standard errors for the degree of overlap in the observations. Though the overlap here arises from the clustering of observations rather than the sampling procedure, I use a similar approach to examine the robustness of the results. I create a variance–covariance matrix Ω, and compute standard errors from the matrix $(X'\Omega^{-1}X)^{-1}$. I constrain the off-diagonal elements of the variance–covariance matrix Ω to be zero if the sixty-trading-day windows over which the equity index is calculated do not overlap, and to be proportional to the extent of the overlap otherwise. In this way, nearby observations are assigned less weight in the analysis. Returns in the sixty trading days before and after IPOs remain significantly different at the 1% level of confidence. Returns in the sixty trading

Table 3

Estimated probit regressions of the decision of privately held venture-backed biotechnology firms to employ public or private financing. The sample consists of 750 IPOs and private financings between January 1978 and September 1992 by firms that had already received venture capital. The dependent variable is 1 for firms that went public and 0 for firms that employed private financings. Independent variables include three alternative measures of market timing: the level of a biotechnology equity index[a] at the time of the financing, and the changes in equity prices in the three months before and after the financing (absolute *t*-statistics in brackets).

| | Dependent variable: did firm go public? | | |
	Regressions use alternative measures of market timing		
Level of biotechnology index	0.50 [9.33]		
Raw return from biotech equities in [−60, −1] window		0.74 [2.80]	
Raw return from biotech equities in [0, 59] widow			−0.65 [3.64]
Constant	−2.65 [13.16]	−0.96 [16.78]	−0.90 [16.71]
Log-likelihood	−307.55	−351.14	−348.23
χ^2-statistic	95.00	7.83	13.66
p-value	0.00	0.00	0.00
Number of observations	750	750	750

[a]The index and change in equity values are computed for the period 1978 to 1982 using thirteen companies identified in the 1977 business press as well-positioned to capitalize on biotechnology developments and (from 1983 onwards) thirteen biotechnology companies. Acquired or delisted firms are replaced with the most seasoned, publicly traded biotechnology firm. The index is normalized to one on January 1, 1978. For the private financings where I know only the month and year of the transaction, I use the twelfth trading day of the month.

days prior to public and private financings do not differ at conventional confidence levels. Returns in the sixty trading days after public and private financings differ at the 5% level of confidence. In another analysis, I detrend the sixty-trading-day returns for inflation and inflation plus a 5% annual premium. I find these corrections make little difference.

I examine these patterns using the probit regression shown in table 3. I employ as observations each financing by a privately held firm that has already received venture capital. The dependent variable is a dummy indicating whether the firm received public or private financing (where 1 denotes an IPO and 0 a private financing):

$$IPO_{it} = \alpha_0 + \alpha_{1j} TIMING_{ijt} + \varepsilon_{it}. \tag{1}$$

The three measures of timing are the value of the biotechnology index at the time of the financing, the raw returns from an investment in biotechnology securities in the three months before the financing, and the raw returns in the three months after the financing.

Each of the variables is significant in explaining the decision to go public. As the coefficient of 0.50 suggests, a higher level of the equity index increases the probability of a public financing. I assess the magnitude of this coefficient by examining the effect of a 10% increase in the level of the equity index on the predicted probability that a public financing is employed. At the mean of all independent variables, the regression coefficients imply that the probability of an IPO is 15%. A 10% increase in the level of the equity index (i.e., from the mean of 3.23 to 3.56) boosts the probability of an IPO to 19%, or an increase of 27%. Increases in biotechnology equity values in the three months prior to the financing boost the chance of an IPO (the coefficient of 0.74), as do decreases in the three months after an IPO (− 0.65).

3.2. The impact of venture capitalist experience

I next examine whether seasoned and inexperienced venture capitalists differ in their proficiency in taking firms public at market peaks. To examine this, I repeat the analyses in tables 2 and 3. I divide up the firms into those financed by more or less seasoned venture capitalists.

I use as a proxy for venture capitalist experience the age of the oldest venture capital partnership having financed the firm. My approach differs slightly from Barry, Muscarella, Peavy, and Vetsuypens (1990). Those authors used the venture capitalist with the largest equity stake in the firm at the time of the IPO to characterize the venture investors. Since I do not always know the relative valuation of each round, however, I cannot always determine the largest shareholder. In section 3.3 below, I consider the use of alternative measures of venture capital experience. In point of fact, these measures show little difference. Venture capitalists tend to syndicate investments either to their peers or to their less experienced counterparts. They are not likely to invest in deals begun by their less seasoned counterparts [Lerner (1994)]. The lead venture capitalist is usually the oldest one.

To establish that this is an economically meaningful partition of firms, I divide the 136 IPOs in the sample by the age of the oldest venture capital organization investing in the firm. I characterize venture capital organizations by using several reference volumes [Clay (1987), National Register (1992), Venture Economics (1988b, 1992)]. If the name of the venture capital fund recorded in the Venture Economics database does not match an entry in these directories of venture organizations, then to establish a match I use an unpublished database from Venture Economics which lists venture capital funds and organizations. I collect data about the IPOs from prospectuses, S-1 registration statements, and the SDC corporate new issues database (1992).

IPOs divided in this manner differ in several respects. Table 4 shows that the reputation of the underwriter differs significantly at the 1% level of confidence. I use the Carter–Manaster (1990) rankings of underwriter prestige. In this

Table 4

Characteristics of IPOs by venture-backed biotechnology firms, divided by the age of the oldest venture investor in the firm. The sample consists of 136 IPOs between January 1978 and September 1992. The table compares the underwriter ranking,[a] the presence of a 'Big Six' accounting firm as the firm's auditor, and the most frequently represented underwriters, law firms, and accounting firms. The remaining columns describe these offerings: the share of equity retained by employees and management after the IPO,[b] the mean inflation-adjusted offering size,[c] the percentage of offerings in which units rather than common stock were sold, and the percentage change from the offering price to the first-day close.[d] The table also compares the means of these variables for firms whose oldest venture capitalist is above and below the median age.

Characteristics	Firms divided by age of oldest venture capital provider		p-value, t-test of difference of means
	Above median	Below or equal to median	
Underwriter characteristics			
Carter–Manaster ranking	6.6	4.8	0.00
Most frequent firm (number)	Hambrecht and Quist (6)	D.H. Blair (14)	
Auditor characteristics			
% of firms in 'Big Six'	98.5%	96.1%	0.56
Most frequent firm (number)	Ernst and Young (26)[e]	Ernst and Young (21)[e]	
Issuer's law firm characteristics			
Most frequent firm (number)	Cooley, Godward, Castro, Huddleston, and Tatum (11)	Bachner, Tally, Polevoy, and Misher (5)	
Offering characteristics			
% of equity retained by employees and management	7.2%	11.8%	0.00
Funds raised (millions of 1992 dollars)	29.7	22.6	0.08
% of IPOs which are unit offerings	4.4%	25.0%	0.00
Initial return	10.3%	15.4%	0.31

[a]Carter and Manaster's (1990) ranking of lead underwriter prestige is employed, with 9 representing the most prestigious underwriters and 0 the least. If the book underwriter is not included in the Carter–Manaster ratings, I use the ranking of the co-managing underwriter. If there is no co-managing underwriter, or it is also not ranked, I assign these underwriters a rank of 0.

[b]This measure includes all shareholdings by full-time managers and employees, but not venture capitalists or other financiers working as consultants at the firm.

[c]This is the gross amount paid by the public, before allowance for direct and indirect underwriting fees. The Gross Domestic Product deflator is used.

[d]The closing price, when not available, is calculated as the mean of the bid and ask.

[e]Includes predecessor entities Ernst and Whinney and Arthur Young.

scheme, 9 denotes the most prestigious underwriters and 0 the least prestigious. They determine these rankings through the positioning of companies in 'tombstones', the advertisements that underwriters use to publicize offerings. If the book underwriter is not included in the Carter–Manaster ratings, I use the ranking of the co-managing underwriter. For twelve cases, there is no co-managing underwriter, or else it is not ranked. (These are all small regional investment banks with limited underwriting experience [National (1992)].) I assign these underwriters a rank of 0. While Hambrecht and Quist is the most frequent underwriter for firms backed by experienced venture capitalists, D.H. Blair dominates the less experienced group.

I also examine other intermediaries involved in the offering. A partition frequently used to divide accounting firms in underpricing studies is the 'Big Six' (previously the 'Big Eight'), the largest U.S. accounting firms as measured by revenue [Balvers, McDonald, and Miller (1988), Beatty (1989)]. While the firms backed by more experienced venture capitalists are more likely to have a 'Big Six' accounting firm, the difference is not significant. I also report the most frequently used accountants and law firms.

The offerings also differ in magnitude. The equity stake retained by managers and employees after the offering is significantly larger for firms backed by the less experienced venture capitalists. In addition, the dollars raised in the IPOs by firms with seasoned venture investors is larger (though only at the 10% level of confidence). Both results are consistent with Leland and Pyle (1977), who argue that lower-quality managers must retain larger equity stakes and raise less money to obtain any external financing.

Firms backed by seasoned venture capitalists are significantly less likely to employ a unit offering. These bundled offerings include at least one share of stock and one warrant. Schultz (1993) shows that unit offerings are usually employed by small firms with uncertain prospects. He suggests that by providing only some of the funding up front, unit offerings limit the danger of managers squandering invested capital. The remaining funds are provided only if the warrants are exercised. Because the warrants are typically 'out-of-the-money' at the time of the IPO (i.e., they can be exercised at a price higher than the per-share price of the IPO), the exercise of the warrants is usually conditional on the stock price rising. The first-day returns from the IPOs are lower for the firms backed by experienced venture capitalists, consistent with Barry, Peavy, Muscarella, and Vetsuypens (1990), but the difference is not significant.

After separating firms by whose oldest venture investor is above or below the median age, I repeat the analysis in table 2. Panel A of table 5 examines the choice between private and public equity. Both classes of firms appear to time IPOs. The effectiveness of this timing, however, appears greater for the more experienced venture capitalists, as the tests in panel B confirm. The average firm backed by experienced venture capitalists went public when the index was at 4.31; for the firms below the median, the level was 3.80. Similarly, the index run-up in the three months before the IPO and the run-down in the three months after are both larger.

Table 6 repeats the probit regression estimation of the decision to go public. I separate firms by venture capitalists above or below the median age. Again, I examine the probability of the firm going public, using the three measures of

Table 5

Biotechnology equity prices around public and private financings for privately held venture-backed biotechnology companies, divided by the age of the oldest venture investor in the firm. The sample consists of 750 IPOs and private financings between January 1978 and September 1992 by firms that had already received venture capital. The table presents the level of a biotechnology equity index,[a] and the changes in equity prices in the three months before and after the financing. The table also compares the means and medians of these variables for firms whose oldest venture capitalist is above and below the median age.

Panel A: Biotechnology equity prices

Type of financing	Mean level of biotechnology index	Mean raw 'buy-and-hold' returns from biotech equities around financing date	
		Trading days −60 to −1	Trading days 0 to 59
136 initial public offerings			
Firms whose oldest venture investor is above the median age	4.31	12.5%	−6.8%
Firms whose oldest venture investor is below the median age	3.80	7.4%	−2.4%
614 private financings			
Firms whose oldest venture investor is above the median age	3.08	5.1%	6.6%
Firms whose oldest venture investor is below the median age	3.03	4.0%	5.1%

Panel B: Tests of differences in means and medians

	p-value
Tests using firms whose oldest venture investor is above the median age	
Wilcoxon test, median equity index on date of IPO = median equity index on date of private financing	0.00
t-test, mean return in [−60, −1] window prior to IPO = mean return in [−60, −1] window prior to private financing	0.00
t-test, mean return in [0,59] window after IPO = mean return in [0,59] window after private financing	0.00
Tests using firms whose oldest venture investor is below the median age	
Wilcoxon test, median equity index on date of IPO = median equity index on date of private financing	0.00
t-test, mean return in [−60, −1] window prior to IPO = mean return in [−60, −1] window prior to private financing	0.20
t-test, mean return in [0,59] window after IPO = mean return in [0,59] window after private financing	0.01
Tests comparing firms whose oldest venture investor is above and below the median age	
Wilcoxon test, median equity index on date of IPO is same for both sets of firms	0.00
t-test, mean return in [−60, −1] window prior to IPO is same for both sets of firms	0.03
t-test, mean return in [0, 59] window after IPO is same for both sets of firms	0.07

[a] The index and change in equity values are computed for the period 1978 to 1982 using thirteen companies identified in the 1977 business press as well-positioned to capitalize on biotechnology developments and (from 1983 onwards) thirteen biotechnology companies. Acquired or delisted firms are replaced with the most seasoned publicly traded biotechnology firm. The index is normalized to one on January 1, 1978. For the private financings where I know only the month and year of the transaction, I use the twelfth trading day of the month.

Table 6

Estimated probit regressions of the decision of privately held venture-backed biotechnology firms to employ public or private financing, with observations are divided by the age of the oldest venture investor in the firm. The sample consists of 750 financing rounds between January 1978 and September 1992 by firms that had already received venture capital. The dependent variable is 1 for firms that went public and 0 for firms that employed private financings. Independent variables include three alternative measures of market timing: the level of a biotechnology equity index[a] at the time of the financing, and the changes in equity prices in the three months before and after the financing (absolute t-statistics in brackets). The table also compares the regression coefficients for firms whose oldest venture capitalist is above and below the median age.

Panel A: Estimated probit regressions using firms whose oldest venture investor is above the median age

Dependent variable: did firm go public?

Regressions use alternative measures of market timing

Level of a biotechnology index	0.65 [7.75]		
Raw return from biotech equities in [− 60, − 1] window		0.93 [2.53]	
Raw return from biotech equities in [0, 59] window			− 1.44 [3.94]
Constant	− 2.79 [10.10]	− 0.87 [10.89]	− 1.04 [12.90]
Log-likelihood	− 160.40	− 191.14	− 187.52
χ^2-statistic	67.95	6.48	9.11
p-value	0.00	0.01	0.00
Number of observations	375	375	375

Panel B: Estimated probit regressions using firms whose oldest venture investor is below the median age

Dependent variable: did firm go public?

Regressions use alternative measures of market timing

Level of biotechnology index	0.31 [4.92]		
Raw return from biotech equities in [− 60, − 1] window		0.48 [1.23]	
Raw return from biotech equities in [0, 59] window			− 0.54 [2.32]
Constant	− 2.39 [8.09]	− 1.07 [12.84]	− 0.78 [10.65]
Log-likelihood	− 145.46	− 157.32	− 155.58
χ^2-statistic	25.33	1.52	5.60
p-value	0.00	0.29	0.02
Number of observations	375	375	375

Panel C: χ^2-tests of differences in regression coefficients

Tests comparing firms whose oldest venture investor is above and below the median age	p-value
Coefficient of 'level of biotechnology index' variable is identical in both regressions	0.01
Coefficient of 'raw return from biotech equities in [− 60, − 1] window' variable is identical in both regressions	0.21
Coefficient of 'raw return from biotech equities in [0, 59] window' variable is identical in both regressions	0.03

[a]The index and change in equity values are computed for the period 1978 to 1982 using thirteen companies identified in the 1977 business press as well-positioned to capitalize on biotechnology developments and (from 1983 onwards) thirteen biotechnology companies. Acquired or delisted firms are replaced with the most seasoned, publicly traded biotechnology firm. The index is normalized to one on January 1, 1978. For the private financings where I know only the month and year of the transaction, I use the twelfth trading day of the month.

market timing as independent variables. In each of the three pairs of regressions, the timing variable is greater in magnitude and significance in the seasoned venture capital regression.

In panel C, I examine whether the regression coefficients differ significantly. First I estimate a pooled regression, allowing firms above and below the median to have distinct coefficients for the timing variable and constant. I then constrain the coefficient of the timing variable to be the same in both regressions. The table presents the *p*-values from χ^2-tests of this constraint. In two of the three cases, I reject the null hypothesis of no difference at the 5% level of confidence. These findings suggest that firms backed by established venture capitalists are more successful at timing their IPOs.

3.3. Robustness to alternative measures and control variables

I undertake several analyses to assess the robustness of the results to alternative measures of venture experience and the presence of control variables. They have little effect on the qualitative and quantitative results.

First, I examine whether the results are an artifact of the criteria that I used to divide the venture capitalists. As an alternative, I use size to divide venture capitalists into experienced and inexperienced investors. In this way, I count as seasoned investors experienced venture capitalists who raise new (but large) partnerships. I compute the ratio of funds under management by the partnership to the total pool of venture capital under management in the year of the investment. I use the annual values reported in Pratt's Guide [Venture Economics (1992)]. When this information is incomplete, I use the unpublished Venture Economics database. The results using this partition are consistent with the ones reported earlier.[3]

I use a related set of regressions to divide firms by relative, rather than absolute, age and size. The mean age and size of the venture partnerships that financed biotechnology firms dipped in the mid-1980s, reflecting the extensive entry into venture capital. I examine the age of the oldest venture capitalist providing funds to each biotechnology firm in each year. I then divide the firms by whether their oldest investor was older or younger than the oldest investor in the median firm in that year. (The procedure for size is similar.) There appears to be little difference between these results and those in tables 5 and 6. These tests are not independent: relatively older venture partnerships are often the older ones on an absolute scale as well. The analysis shows, however, that these results are not an artifact of a particular approach to dividing firms.

I also recast my independent variables, using the change in the market index over two- and four-month windows. Using the longer window tends to slightly strengthen the results; the shorter window tends to weaken them. While there

---

[3] I do not report the results in the tables, but would be glad to send them to any interested reader.

are only a small number of cases in the sample where venture capitalists exited viable firms through mergers or sales, nevertheless I examine the impact of including these cases. I recast the dependent variable to measure IPOs and acquisitions of firms at prices higher than that of the last venture round. This change has little impact.

Finally, I control for the quality of the firms going public. More experienced venture capitalists are likely to fund higher-quality firms, which may bias the results. I use three sets of control variables for firm quality:

(1) *The age of the firm.* I use, in order of preference, the incorporation date reported in SEC filings, the self-reported founding date in industry directories [Corporate (1992), Mega-Type (1992), NCBC (1990a), Ornx (1992)], a questionnaire response [NCBC (1990b)], or the date reported by Venture Economics.

(2) *A private placement from a corporation with a related line of business.* Strategic investments are frequently used in high-technology industries, particularly biotechnology, to cement long-run agreements [Pisano (1989)]. I define corporations with related lines of business as those with any of the following Standard Industrial Code identifiers in the Million Dollar Directory [Dun's (1992)] in the year of the transaction: SIC 283, Drugs; SIC 287, Agricultural Chemicals; and SIC 384, Medical Instruments and Supplies.

(3) *The firm's intellectual property position.* Intellectual property protection was a critical focus of biotechnology firms in the 1980s. [See Kenney (1986) and USOTA (1989) for an overview.] Product market competition was embryonic, and the alternative methods of protecting intellectual property ineffective. The disposition of a single patent could shift the valuation of a biotechnology firm by as much as 50%. I identify the patents associated with these 350 firms using U.S. Patent Office databases [USPTO/OPDLP (1989, 1990)]. I identify not only patents assigned to these firms, but also those assigned to their wholly owned subsidiaries and their research-and-development limited partnerships. I count awards to joint ventures and spin-offs to the extent that the firm had an interest in the venture. I construct two alternative variables. The first indicates the number of the patents awarded at the time of the financing round. The second indicates the number of successful patent applications awarded and in progress at the time. Because patent applications are held confidential by USPTO until the time of award, I use only observations made prior to 1990 in the second analysis.

I find in unreported regressions that, while the age and patents variables have significant explanatory power, the timing variables remain significantly larger in the regressions employing the firms backed by seasoned venture capitalists.

Table 7

Time from the filing of the original S-1 statement to the effective date of initial public offering, divided by the age of the oldest venture provider. The sample consists of 136 IPOs by venture-backed biotechnology firms between January 1978 and September 1992. The table also compares the mean and median time for firms whose oldest venture capitalist was above and below the median age.

Panel A: Months from S-1 filing to IPO effective date		
	Mean	Median
Firms whose oldest venture investor is above the median age	2.0	1.6
Firms whose oldest venture investor is below the median age	1.9	1.7

Panel B: Tests of differences in means and medians	
Tests comparing firms whose oldest venture investor is above and below the median age	p-value
t-test, mean months from S-1 filing to IPO effective date is same for both sets of firms	0.52
Wilcoxon test, median months from S-1 filing to IPO effective date is same for both sets of firms	0.54

4. Alternative explanations

4.1. Speed of IPO execution

One alternative explanation for established venture capitalists' apparent superiority in timing IPOs is better execution. The failure of less experienced venture capitalists to take their firms public at market peaks may reflect their limited skill in planning and executing an offering, not their inability to perceive when the market is hot. In particular, SEC reviews of proposed IPOs can be protracted. Similarly, organizing a selling syndicate and assuring demand for the offering may be time-consuming.

I test this claim by examining the time from the receipt of the original S-1 statement by the SEC to the effective date of the IPO. I identify the filing date from SDC's corporate new issues database (1992). When it is not available from this source, I use the date of the 'Received' stamp on the original S-1 filing.

Table 7 summarizes the results. The mean time from filing to offering does not differ significantly for the firms financed by seasoned or inexperienced venture capitalists (2.0 months for more experienced, 1.9 months for the less experienced). Nor do the medians differ appreciably. The results provide no support for the claim that the superior timing of the IPO market by seasoned firms is due to better execution.

4.2. Willingness to withdraw offerings

A second explanation relates to withdrawn offerings. The legal procedure in canceling a proposed IPO is straightforward. Firms may use a letter to SEC to withdraw proposed security offerings before their effective date. Often firms do not withdraw failed IPOs. When a registration statement has been on file at the SEC for nine months, the SEC writes a letter to the firm, and then declares the offering abandoned (17 CFR § 230.479).

While the formalities associated with an IPO withdrawal are few, the repercussions may be severe. A firm that withdraws its IPO may later find it difficult to access the public marketplace. Even if the stated reason for the withdrawal is poor market conditions, the firm may be lumped with other businesses whose offerings did not sell because of questionable accounting practices or gross mispricing. These reputational considerations may be less severe for a firm associated with a major venture capitalist. A greater willingness to withdraw IPOs in the face of deteriorating market conditions may explain the apparent superiority of experienced venture capitalists in timing offerings.

To examine these claims, I identify withdrawn or abandoned IPO filings by these firms. I identify these offerings using the SDC corporate new issues database. [SDC employs a data collection procedure similar to the Investment Dealers' Digest listings used by Mikkelson and Partch (1988) to identify withdrawn seasoned security offerings.] Because the coverage of abandoned IPOs is less than comprehensive, I supplement these records with the 'No Go IPOs' section of Going Public [Howard (1992)] and a database of failed IPOs compiled by a federal agency. (The official responsible for the creation of this database has requested anonymity.) I identify fourteen withdrawn or abandoned IPOs by these firms in this period.

In table 8, I examine the probability that an IPO filing is completed successfully. I use as observations all filings of S-1 registration statements by privately held firms in the Venture Economics sample. (These include the 136 successful IPOs and the fourteen withdrawn offerings.) I estimate in a probit regression:

$$COMPLETE_{it} = \beta_0 + \beta_1 MAXAGE_{it} + \varepsilon_{it}. \tag{2}$$

The dependent variable is a dummy, which takes on the value of 1 if the offering was successfully completed. The independent variable measures the age (in years) of the oldest venture capitalist to have financed the firm. I find no evidence that older venture capitalists are more willing to withdraw IPOs: the coefficient, 0.01, is of the opposite sign and insignificant.

The right-hand column reports the results when I rerun the regression, controlling for the quality of the firm. Superior-quality offerings may be less likely to be withdrawn, no matter who the venture investor. I use the same independent variables discussed in section 3.3: the age of the firm, the presence of a private placement from a related corporation, and the number of patent awards at the time of the financing. I can find no evidence that firms backed by seasoned venture capitalists are more likely to withdraw offerings, even after controlling for quality.

Table 8

Estimated probit regressions of the successful completion of an IPO by privately held venture-backed biotechnology firms who filed S-1 registration statements. The sample consists of 150 filings between January 1978 and September 1992. The dependent variable is 1.0 for firms that went public and 0.0 for firms that withdrew or abandoned their offerings. Independent variables include the age of the oldest venture investor, the age of the firm at the time of the filing, the number of patents awarded to the firm at the time of the filing,[a] and a dummy variable indicating whether the firm had previously received a private placement from a corporation with a related line of business at the time of the filing[b] (absolute *t*-statistics in brackets).

	Dependent variable: did firm go public?	
Age of oldest venture investor (in years)	0.01 [0.46]	0.01 [0.76]
Age of firm at time of filing (in years)		− 0.08 [1.48]
Patents awarded at time of filing		0.10 [1.04]
Did firm receive private placement from related corporation?		− 0.32 [1.08]
Constant	1.22 [4.63]	1.58 [4.44]
Log-likelihood	− 46.62	− 44.67
χ^2-statistic	0.21	3.71
p-value	0.64	0.44
Number of observations	150	150

[a]All patents assigned to firms, their wholly owned subsidiaries, and their research and development limited partnerships are included. Awards to joint ventures and spin-offs are counted to the extent that a firm had an interest in the venture.

[b]Corporations with related lines of business are defined as those with any of the following Standard Industrial Code identifiers in the Million Dollar Directory [Dun's (1992)] in the year of the transaction: SIC 283, Drugs; SIC 287, Agricultural Chemicals; and SIC 384, Medical Instruments and Supplies.

I also examine equity valuations after the filing of S-1 statements. Mikkelson and Partch (1988) examine stock prices after the announcement of seasoned security issues. In the weeks after the announcement of an ultimately withdrawn seasoned issue, both the market returns and the issuer's net-of-market returns are negative. No such pattern appears after the filing of successful offerings. I examine the returns from an equally-weighted investment in thirteen biotechnology securities between the close of the S-1 filing date and the close of the twentieth trading day thereafter. (I use the same procedure as above.) The index rises by 2% after the filing of successful offerings, and declines by 9% after the filing of ultimately withdrawn offerings. The difference is significant at the 1% level of confidence, as are those computed using other windows.

5. Conclusions

In this paper, I explore the choice between private and public equity. Using a sample of 350 privately held venture-backed firms, I examine both the private and public financings. I show that venture capitalists take firms public at market

Empirical Corporate Finance I

peaks, relying on private financings when valuations are lower. Seasoned venture capitalists appear more proficient at timing IPOs. The results are robust to the use of alternative criteria to separate firms and controls for firms' quality. The results are not caused by differences in the speed of executing the IPOs, or in the willingness to withdraw the proposed IPOs.

Two limitations deserve further discussion. The first reflects the design of this study, which examined a setting particularly conducive to the empirical identification of market timing. In other industries, the need for oversight, or lumpy demands for capital, as the firm matures may affect the going-public decision more dramatically. In other periods, the heterogeneity between new and seasoned venture capitalists may not be as pronounced. Practitioner accounts, however, underscore the importance of IPO timing across industries and time. As an example, I cite an investment manager's discussion [McNamee (1991)] of market conditions around peak periods for computer and electronics IPOs:

> The whole problem can be summed up in the phrase 'IPO window'. The IPO window occurs when sellers try to bail out and buyers try to get rich without doing any work.... It is when the AEA (American Electronics Association) puts up a billboard on Highway 101 near Great America that says, 'The buy side has lost its mind, let's bag them quick, before they catch on.' Sometime late in the IPO window, we get to watch venture capitalists behave like Keystone Kops.

Nor are such narratives confined to the 1980s and 1990s. For instance, Jeffery (1961) describes similar patterns in the market for new securities of high-technology firms in the 1950s. In the business press, Stern and Pouschine (1992) discuss the timing of 'reverse LBOs' (IPOs of firms that have previously undergone leveraged buy-outs) by LBO funds. Venture capitalists may also time the market when they sell or distribute shares in firms which have gone public. In an ongoing project on the contractual arrangements between venture partnerships and their limited partners, Paul Gompers and I are examining this issue.

A second concern relates to the results' interpretation. The seasoned venture capitalists' more effective timing of IPOs may reflect their superior proficiency. They may be better at recognizing when valuations are at a peak. There remain, however, several alternative interpretations. Less experienced venture capitalists may also wish to take firms public at market peaks, but may be unable to command the attention of investment bankers. This assertion may be plausible if underwriting services are rationed in key periods. Alternatively, Gompers' (1993) 'grandstanding' model suggests that inexperienced venture capitalists may not wait until the market is optimal to take firms public, because they need to signal *their* quality to potential investors in follow-on funds. The mechanisms through which managers and venture capitalists decide to go public and obtain access to investment bankers deserve further study.

A second opportunity for further research relates to the implications of the timing of the going-public decision. IPOs have been shown to coincide with declines in operating performance [Jain and Kini (1992)] and broad shifts in the incentives offered managers [Beatty and Zajak (1992)]. Do early initial public offerings affect the subsequent performance of the firm? To what extent are these factors related to the maturity of the firm and the market conditions at the time of the IPO? The interactions between these financing choices and operational performance deserve further scrutiny.

References

Allen, Franklin and Gerald Faulhaber, 1989, Signaling by underpricing in the IPO market, Journal of Financial Economics 23, 303–323.

Balvers, Ronald J., Bill McDonald, and Robert E. Miller, 1988, Underpricing of new issues and the choice of auditor as a signal of investment banker reputation, Accounting Review 63, 605–622.

Barry, Christopher B., Chris J. Muscarella, John W. Peavy III, and Michael R. Vetsuypens, 1990, The role of venture capital in the creation of public companies: Evidence from the going public process, Journal of Financial Economics 27, 447–471.

Beatty, Randolph A., 1989, Auditor reputation and the pricing of initial public offerings, The Accounting Review 64, 693–709.

Beatty, Randolph A. and Edward Zajak, 1992, Firm risk and alternative mechanisms for internal corporate control: Evidence from initial public offerings, Unpublished working paper (Southern Methodist University, Dallas, TX and Northwestern University, Evanston, IL).

Blume, Marshall E. and Robert F. Stambaugh, 1983, Biases in computed returns: An application to the size effect, Journal of Financial Economics 12, 387–404.

BRS Information Technologies, 1986, PATDATA, Mimeo.

Carter, Richard and Steven Manaster, 1990, Initial public offerings and underwriter reputation, Journal of Finance 45, 1045–1067.

Clay, Lucius, 1987 and earlier years, The venture capital report guide to venture capital in the U.K. 3rd ed. (Venture Capital, Bristol).

Corporate Technology Information Services, 1992 and earlier years, Corporate technology directory (CorpTech, Woburn, MA).

Dun's Marketing Services, 1992 and earlier years, Million dollar directory (Dun and Bradstreet, Parsippany, NJ).

Gompers, Paul A., 1993, Grandstanding in the venture capital industry, Unpublished working paper (University of Chicago, Chicago, IL).

Grinblatt, Mark and Chuan Y. Hwang, 1989, Signaling and the pricing of new issues, Journal of Finance 44, 383–420.

Hansen, Lars P. and Robert J. Hodrick, 1980, Forward exchange rates as optimal predictors of future spot rates: An econometric analysis, Journal of Political Economy 88, 829–853.

Howard and Company, 1992 and earlier years, Going public: The IPO reporter (Howard and Co., Philadelphia, PA).

Ibbotson, Roger G. and J.F. Jaffe, 1975, 'Hot' issue markets, Journal of Finance 30, 1027–1042.

Jain, Bharat A. and Omesh Kini, 1992, Information asymmetry, agency costs and the operating performance of IPOs, Unpublished working paper (Pennsylvania State University, University Park, PA).

Jeffery, Grant, 1961, Science and technology stocks: A guide for investors (Meridian, New York, NY).

Leland, Hayne E. and David H. Pyle, 1977, Informational asymmetries, financial structure and financial intermediation, Journal of Finance 33, 371–387.

Lerner, Joshua, 1993, Venture capitalists and the oversight of private firms, Unpublished working paper (Harvard University, Cambridge, MA).

Lerner, Joshua, 1994, The syndication of venture capital investments, Financial Management, forthcoming.

Loughran, Tim and Jay R. Ritter, 1993, The timing and subsequent performance of IPOs: The U.S. and international evidence, Unpublished working paper (University of Illinois, Urbana-Champaign, IL).

McNamee, Roger, 1991, How to fix the IPO market, Upside 3, Jan., 24–27.

Mega-Type Publishing, 1991, Genetic engineering and biotechnology-related firms – Worldwide directory (Mega-Type, Princeton Junction, NJ).

Megginson, William C. and Kathleen A. Weiss, 1991, Venture capital certification in initial public offerings, Journal of Finance 46, 879–893.

Meulbroek, Lisa, 1992, Comparison of forward and futures prices of an interest rate-sensitive financial asset, Journal of Finance 47, 381–396.

Mikkelson, Wayne H. and M. Megan Partch, 1988, Withdrawn security offerings, Journal of Financial and Quantitative Analysis 23, 119–133.

National Register Publishing Company, 1992 and earlier years, Corporate finance sourcebook, (National Register Publishing Co., Wilmette, IL).

North Carolina Biotechnology Center, Biotechnology Information Division (NCBC), 1990a, North Carolina Biotechnology Center documentation for companies database (NCBC, Research Triangle Park, NC).

North Carolina Biotechnology Center, Biotechnology Information Division (NCBC), 1990b, Survey of U.S. biotechnology firms, Unpublished report (NCBC, Research Traingle Park, NC).

Ornx Press, 1991 and earlier editions, BioScan: The worldwide biotech industry reporting service (Ornx Press, Phoenix, AZ).

Pisano, Gary P., 1989, Using equity participation to support exchange: Evidence from the biotechnology industry, Journal of Law, Economics and Organization 5, 109–126.

Recombinant Capital, 1991, Valuation histories for private biotechnology companies (Recombinant Capital, San Francisco, CA).

Recombinant Capital, 1992, Valuation histories for public and acquired biotechnology companies (Recombinant Capital, San Francisco, CA).

Ritter, Jay R., 1984, The 'hot issue' market of 1980, Journal of Business 57, 215–240.

Ritter, Jay R., 1991, The long–run performance of initial public offerings, Journal of Finance 46, 3–27.

Sahlman, William A., 1990, The structure and governance of venture capital organizations, Journal of Financial Economics 27, 473–521.

Schultz, Paul, 1993, Unit initial public offerings: A form of staged financing, Journal of Financial Economics 34, 199–129.

Securities Data Company (SDC), 1992, Corporate new issues database: A tutorial (SDC, Newark, NY).

Shiller, Robert J., 1990, Speculative prices and popular models, Journal of Economic Perspectives 4, 55–65.

Shiller, Robert J. and John Pound, 1989, Survey evidence of diffusions of interest and information among investors, Journal of Economic Behavior and Organization 12, 47–66.

Stern, Richard L. and Tatiana Pouschine, 1992, Junk equity, Forbes 149, March 2, 40–42.

Teitelman, Robert, 1990, Gene dreams: Wall Street, academia and the rise of biotechnology (Basic Books, New York, NY).

U.S. Department of Commerce, Patent and Trademark Office, Office of Patent Depository Library Programs (USPTO/OPDLP), 1989, ASSIST disk notes, Mimeo. (USPTO/OPDLP, Washington, DC).

U.S. Department of Commerce, Patent and Trademark Office, Office of Patent Depository Library Programs (USPTO/OPDLP), 1990, CASSIS/BIB user's guide (USPTO/OPDLP, Washington, DC).

U.S. General Accounting Office (USGAO), 1989, Assessment of small business innovation research programs (USGAO, Washington, DC).

Venture Economics, 1988a, Exiting venture capital investments (Venture Economics, Needham, MA).

Venture Economics, 1988b and earlier years, Guide to European venture capital sources (Venture Economics, London).

Venture Economics, 1991, Untitled documentation of databases, Mimeo. (Venture Economics, New York, NY).

Venture Economics, 1992 and earlier years, Pratt's guide to venture capital sources (Venture Economics, New York, NY).

Welch, Ivo, 1989, Seasoned offerings, imitation costs, and the underpricing of initial public offerings, Journal of Finance 44, 421–449.

[8]

The Pricing of Initial Public Offerings: Tests of Adverse-Selection and Signaling Theories

Roni Michaely
Cornell University

Wayne H. Shaw
University of Colorado at Boulder

We test the empirical implications of several models of IPO underpricing. Consistent with the winner's-curse hypothesis, we show that in markets where investors know a priori that they do not have to compete with informed investors, IPOs are not underpriced. We also show that IPOs underwritten by reputable investment banks experience significantly less underpricing and perform significantly better in the long run. We do not find empirical support for the signaling models that try to explain why firms underprice. In fact, we find that (1) firms that underprice more return to the reissue market less frequently, and for lesser amounts, than firms that underprice less, and (2) firms that underprice less experience higher earnings and pay higher dividends, contrary to the models' predictions.

We would like to thank Franklin Allen, Michael Barclay, Randolph Beatty, Pradeep Chintagunta, Bob Gibbons, Maureen O'Hara, Tim Opler, Jay Ritter, Ivo Welch, William Wilhelm, Kent Womack, and seminar participants at the University of Colorado at Boulder, the Cornell–Rochester Symposium, MIT, New York University, Rice University, the Stockholm School of Economics, the University of Texas–Austin, the University of Waterloo, the Wharton School, the Workshop in International Corporate Finance at the HEC Group, Tel-Aviv University, and the University of Utah for many helpful comments, and Barbara Lougee and Heather Wier for their research assistance. Special thanks are due to an anonymous referee and Rick Green (the editor) for extensive comments and suggestions that improved the article markedly. An earlier version entitled, "Asymmetric Information, Adverse Selection, and the Pricing of Initial Public Offerings," was presented at the 1992 Western Finance Association meetings. Address correspondence to Roni Michaely, Johnson Graduate School of Management, Cornell University, Ithaca, NY 14853-4201.

The Review of Financial Studies Summer 1994 Vol. 7, No. 2, pp. 279–319
© 1994 The Review of Financial Studies 0893-9454/94/$1.50

The Review of Financial Studies / v 7 n 2 1994

The underpricing of initial public offerings (IPOs) is a well-documented phenomenon.[1] For example, Ibbotson, Sindelar, and Ritter (1988) find that the average first-day IPO return is 16.3 percent in the years 1960–1987. Several reasons why a firm would willingly underprice its securities at the cost of limiting the funds received have been proposed. This article tests the implications of several such theoretical explanations of IPO underpricing. We derive empirical implications for the winner's curse [Rock (1986), Beatty and Ritter (1986), Carter and Manaster (1990)] and signaling-based models [Allen and Faulhaber (1989), Grinblatt and Hwang (1989), Welch (1989)] and test them using a sample of IPOs from the years 1984–1988.[2]

Rock (1986) constructs a model for the IPO market with two types of investors. The first consists of outside investors who have better knowledge about the prospective cash flow than does the entrepreneur. The second type, uninformed outside investors, lack special knowledge about the firm's future cash flow. This information asymmetry may lead to a "lemons problem," where the uninformed investors end up primarily with the less successful IPOs. Keeping them in the market, therefore, requires an additional premium—the average underpricing of all IPOs. Ibbotson (1975) conjectures that new issues may be underpriced to "leave a good taste in investors' mouths." In a formalization of this statement, Allen and Faulhaber (1989), Grinblatt and Hwang (1989), and Welch (1989) hypothesize that the owner's incentive to leave a good taste is due to the possibility of coming back to the market to sell securities on more favorable terms.

The basic idea behind the tests of the adverse-selection models is quite simple. First, underpricing should decrease as information becomes less heterogeneous across investor groups. At the extreme, when all outside investors possess the same information about the firm, there should not be any underpricing, according to Rock's model. Second, through the choice of the underwriter, the firm can reduce some of the uncertainty about its prospects and therefore reduce the need for underpricing [Carter and Manaster (1990)].

To test these propositions, we compare the underpricing in two markets in which the degree of information heterogeneity differs substantially. Our sample consists of two data sets: (1) a sample of IPO master limited partnerships (MLPs) and (2) a sample of "regular"

---

[1] Logue (1973) and Ibbotson (1975) were among the first to document the apparent underpricing. Ritter (1984) shows that the underpricing in the oil and gas industry in 1980 was much larger than the average underpricing; Ibbotson and Jaffe (1975) conclude that the level of underpricing is cyclical. See Smith (1986) for a review of empirical evidence on this issue.

[2] Both classes of models rely on asymmetric information. However, in the adverse-selection models the uninformed investor moves first, and in the signaling model the informed participant moves first. See Kreps (1990, pp. 630, 638).

IPOs. The special feature of the MLP IPOs that enables us to test Rock's model is that institutional investors largely avoid them and the market knows that. The main reason for institutional investors' lack of interest is that the income received from the MLPs is classified as unrelated business income. Hence, even non-tax-paying entities such as pension funds would have to pay tax on earnings from MLPs they own. In addition, corporations do not get the dividend exclusion from taxes on income from MLPs.

Investment bankers tend to favor their large and established customers in allocating shares of initial public offerings [see Rock (1986), Benveniste and Spindt (1989), Benveniste and Wilhelm (1990), among others]. These customers are also more likely to be the better informed investors. We associate these investors with institutions.[3] The retail (or uninformed) investors will face an allocation bias whether the institutional investors receive larger allocations in the better IPOs because they bid more for them (as a result of their superior information) or because they are favored by the investment bankers.[4] Prior knowledge of the absence of the informed investors reduces the winner's curse problem and consequently the need for underpricing. We find that although the regular IPO group shows a mean initial-day return of 8.5 percent, statistically significantly different from zero, the MLP IPO group has a mean initial-day return of -0.04 percent, insignificantly different from zero. Even when controlling for the ex ante level of uncertainty (approximated by the dollar value of the IPO and the line of business in which the firm operates), we find that non-MLP IPOs experience significantly greater underpricing than MLP IPOs. Our findings support the explanation that the ex ante difference in market structure between MLP IPOs and non-MLP IPOs (i.e., investors in the MLP IPOs know a priori that they are competing to a much smaller extent with other investors who possess superior information) is the reason for the lack of MLP IPO underpricing. These results are consistent with Rock's (1986) winner's curse explanation of why firms underprice.

---

[3] The claim that institutional investors have access to better information than retail investors because of their size and continuing relationship with the investment bankers also appeared in the April 26, 1992, *New York Times* (page 1):

> Privileged information given to institutional investors puts less sophisticated investors at a disadvantage. Mainly because of the potential liability of an unfulfilled forecast, few new issuers publish earnings-per-share projections in their offering prospectuses, which brokers are confined to using to sell a new issue to the public. But our research shows that the vast majority of the 358 issuers that raised $15.8 billion through IPOs last year provided earnings projections during the "road shows" held for institutional investors weeks in advance of the offering. (In IPOs, the more data the better.)

[4] It is likely that other, noninstitutional investors are informed as well, but as long as the fraction of informed investors is higher among the institutional investors our analysis holds.

The Review of Financial Studies / v 7 n 2 1994

Using Rock's framework, Carter and Manaster (1990) model the role of the investment banker's reputation. They show that more prestigious investment bankers are associated with less risky IPOs. To preserve its reputation, the prestigious underwriter screens the firms that go public and selects the less risky ones, using information unavailable to the general public. This, in turn, reduces the uncertainty and information asymmetry between informed and uninformed investors. Investors know that by subscribing to issues of reputable investment banks they face less risk, and, consequently, the initial-day return is lower for these issues. Using investment bankers' capital as a proxy for their reputation (investment bankers with greater capital have more to lose from a loss of reputation), we find that reputation plays an important role in explaining the initial-day return. Although our findings indicate that the investment banker's reputation and the issue size are highly correlated (the correlation coefficient is .75), controlling for reputation we find that larger issues experience greater underpricing. We also show that IPOs issued by more reputable investment banks perform significantly better in the long run.

In Section 2.3 we test several empirical implications of the signaling-based models of IPOs underpricing. Empirically, these models imply a positive association between underpricing and the probability and amount of a seasoned equity (or debt) issue. The decisions on how much to underprice and whether to reissue equity, however, are not separate. In considering whether to underprice, an issuer takes into account the possibility of reentering the market for a seasoned issue some time in the future. Hence, the decision on the amount offered to the public in the seasoned issue is endogenous and made simultaneously with the decision of what signal to send to the market during the IPO through underpricing. We test this proposition using a simultaneous equations model. Contrary to the signaling models' predictions, we find that firms that underprice more enter the reissue market less frequently, and for smaller amounts, than firms that underprice less.

Allen and Faulhaber (1989) argue that earnings performance and dividend policy after the IPO help the market revise its views about the firm's quality. They suggest the market views firms that underprice and pay high dividends (high earnings) more favorably than firms that follow the same dividend policy (earnings) but do not underprice. Consequently, their model implies that (1) firms that underprice more are more likely to have higher dividends (earnings), and (2) the market reacts more favorably to dividend announcements by firms that underprice more. We examine the relationship between underpricing, dividend policy, earnings, and firm value. We find that firms that pay dividends or experience higher earnings during the first two years of trading show significantly lower underpricing, contrary to the model's prediction. Not surprisingly, a dividend increase results in a significant price reaction in the three days around the announcement. There is no relationship, however, between the market reaction to the dividend announcement and the degree of underpricing. In Grinblatt and Hwang (1989), insider holdings as well as underpricing signal the firm's value. Their model's predictions of positive relationships between insider holdings and underpricing (for a given level of variance), and between the firm's value and the degree of underpricing, are not supported by the data.

In summary, our results support the winner's curse argument proposed by Rock (1986) that the purpose of underpricing is to entice less informed investors into the IPO market. We also show that larger IPOs and those issued by more reputable investment bankers experience less underpricing. For a given level of underwriter prestige, however, larger, more diffuse issues require greater underpricing to ensure successful placement. In contrast, we find little evidence that high-quality IPOs "leave money on the table" to signal their quality. Finally, we provide evidence that IPOs issued by more prestigious investment banks significantly outperform those issued by less prestigious underwriters.

The article is organized as follows. We describe the data and sample selection in Section 1. The empirical implications of the IPOs models are developed and tested in Section 2 and Section 3 concludes the study.

1. Sample Description

Our sample firms are obtained from the 1984–1988 editions of the *Directory of Corporate Financing.* Firms are selected from the list of corporate security offerings if (1) they make a firm commitment offering of at least $1 per unit, (2) the unit contains only a single share of stock (no warrants attached), (3) the issue is an initial public offering, and (4) the firm is subsequently listed on COMPUSTAT. A total of 947 firm offerings meet all four requirements.[5]

The return data are extracted from the 1990 Center for Research in Security Prices (CRSP) daily tapes. Initial return is calculated using the offer price and the first-day closing price. The offer price is taken

---

[5] A total of 1180 firm-commitment IPOs with a unit price above $1 were found. A total of 187 IPOs were eliminated from the sample because they included other rights such as warrants. Twenty-five offerings of ADRs on foreign stocks and 24 IPOs that did not appear on COMPUSTAT were excluded. Out of the 24 non-COMPUSTAT firms, 22 still traded in 1991, one merged into another firm, and one stopped trading after one year. No closed-end funds or REITs are included in the sample.

The Review of Financial Studies / v 7 n 2 1994

from the *Directory of Corporate Financing,* and the first-day closing price is taken from the 1990 CRSP tapes when available; otherwise, it is collected from the *Wall Street Journal* (*WSJ*). The long-run performance, defined as the two-year excess return, is calculated as the stock's geometric return, starting with the day after the firm goes public, minus the value-weighted geometric market return for the same period.[6] If a firm goes bankrupt during the period (21 firms out of 889 non-MLP IPOs), it is assumed that its return is equal to zero for the remaining days in the period. If a firm is acquired (six firms in our sample), the cash purchase price is used as the final market price.

Table 1 provides a distribution of the sample firms by year. As Ibbotson, Sindelar, and Ritter (1988) document for an earlier period, the number of offerings varies greatly by year, from a low of 106 in 1984 to a high of 314 in 1986. As indicated in the last column of Table 1, the initial return is significantly different from zero for each year in the sample period. The level of underpricing is positively correlated with the number of offerings in that year. For example, the average underpricing in 1984, the year with the lowest number of IPOs, is 4.51 percent, compared with average underpricing of 8.13 percent in 1986, the year with the most IPOs. The firms in the sample come from a variety of industries (Table 1, Panel B). At the one-digit Standard Industrial Classification (SIC) level, all industry groups are represented, with the largest number of firms in technical manufacturing (255), service (142), and financial services (130). At the four-digit SIC level, 284 industries are represented, with a maximum of 31 firms from an industry. Seventeen industries contain 10 or more firms. Included in the sample are 58 master limited partnership IPOs. The majority of the MLP IPOs are in 1986 and 1987. The initial return on the MLPs is insignificantly different from zero in four of the five years in the sample period. Because MLPs are treated differently by the federal income tax laws (for example, they do not pay an entity-level tax), they will be analyzed separately to gain further insights into the return behavior of IPOs.

Table 2 provides descriptive statistics for the 947 sample firms. The average return for the first trading day is 7.27 percent, significant at the .001 level.[7] The range, however, is dramatic, with a minimum first-day return of -29.87 percent and a maximum of 136.81 percent.

---

[6] Calculating the performance over a three-year period instead of a two-year period yields similar results.

[7] We also calculate the first-day return using the average high–low prices. The mean initial return is 7.43 percent.

Table 1
Initial return and the distribution of IPOs across years (1984–1988) and industry

A: The distribution of initial public offerings, in our sample period, across years

| | Number of firms | | Initial-day return | |
Year	MLPs	Total	MLPs	Total
1984	2	106	−0.0206 (−0.435)	0.0451 (4.008)
1985	8	152	0.0002 (0.085)	0.0705 (7.154)
1986	18	314	−0.0009 (−0.347)	0.0813 (7.957)
1987	25	257	0.0033 (0.728)	0.0791 (8.168)
1988	5	118	0.0093 (2.04)	0.0634 (5.618)
	58	947		

B: The distribution of IPOs across industry groups using the one-digit Standard Industrial Classification code

| | | Number of firms | |
SIC code	Industry type	MLPs	Total
0	Agriculture production	2	10
1	Mineral production	8	32
2	Heavy industry	3	117
3	Technical manufacturing	1	255
4	Regulated industries	9	70
5	Service	6	142
6	Financial services	19	130
7	Commercial services	9	117
8	Miscellaneous services	1	74
		58	947

All IPOs are firm-commitment single-unit offers with an offer price of at least $1 per share. The initial return is calculated using the offer price and the closing price on the first trading day (taken from the CRSP tapes). *t*-Statistics appear in parentheses.

Nearly two-thirds (65.4 percent) of the firms experienced positive first-day returns, and 21.4 percent incur negative returns. No price movement is experienced by 13.2 percent of the firms. The size of the IPO varies greatly across the sample. The mean dollar value of the transaction is $32.158 million, with a range from $675,000 to $1.456 billion. The price per share ranges from $1 to $56.50.

The percentage of common stock owned by insiders and institutions is obtained from *Spectrum* and 10K reports.[8] Data are available on insider holdings for 621 firms and on institutional holdings for 844 firms. Both groups have significant average holdings: 38 percent

---

[8] Insider and institutional holdings are defined by *Spectrum* as beneficial holdings as reported under SEC requirements in the proxies.

The Review of Financial Studies / v 7 n 2 1994

Table 2
Univariate descriptive statistics on selected variables for 947 initial public offerings between 1984 and 1988

A: 947 Initial public offerings between 1984–1988

	Initial return	IPO size[1]	Percentage of shares held by insiders	Percentage of shares held by institutions	Long-term debt to total assets	Net income to total assets	Earnings-to-price ratio[2]
Mean	0.0727	32.158	0.3895	0.2618	0.2230	0.0126	0.0378
Minimum	−0.2987	0.675	0.0000	0.0000	0.0000	−3.6413	−0.8540
Maximum	1.3681	1456.000	1.0000	1.0000	1.7858	1.4231	5.6700
Number of observations	(947)	(947)	(621)	(844)	(944)	(944)	(944)

B: Comparison of financial and nonfinancial IPOs (means)

	Initial return	IPO size	Percentage of shares held by insiders	Percentage of shares held by institutions	Number of shareholders relative to IPO size	Long-term debt to total assets	Net income to total assets	Earnings-to-price ratio
Financial	0.0236	55.978	0.2851	0.2835	0.0496	0.2119	0.0157	0.0457
	(111)	(111)	(69)	(72)	(110)	(110)	(110)	(110)
Nonfinancial	0.0850	23.594	0.3972	0.2740	0.0682	0.2190	0.0113	0.0396
	(778)	(778)	(495)	(717)	(776)	(776)	(776)	(776)
t-Test of the difference[3]	6.863	3.146	2.925	0.276	1.290	0.306	0.274	0.387

Descriptive statistics on selected variables for 947 initial public offerings between 1984 and 1988 (Panel A). The initial-day return is calculated using the offer price and the price at the end of the first trading day. The IPO size is calculated as the offer price multiplied by the number of shares offered. The percentage held by insiders and institutions and the number of shareholders (relative to the IPO size) are taken from the *Spectrum* books published within a quarter of the IPO date. The accounting variables are taken from the first annual reports after the IPO. In Panel B, the sample is separated into financial and nonfinancial IPOs (excluding MLPs). The number of observations appears in parentheses.

[1] In millions of dollars.

[2] First annual earnings reported after the IPO relative to the offer price.

[3] When the assumption of equal variance between the two groups is rejected, test statistics are calculated under the assumption of an unequal variance.

by insiders and 26 percent by institutions. The range for both groups extends from 0 to 100 percent.

Table 2 also includes some selected accounting data and ratios for the first year-end after the IPO for 944 of the 947 sample firms. One of the three missing firms was acquired before filing an annual report, and two firms filed for bankruptcy shortly after the IPO. The data shown were collected from COMPUSTAT, with missing values obtained from copies of firms' annual reports. Long-term debt averages only 22 percent of total assets. Extreme observations are obvious on both ends, however, since 118 firms have no long-term debt, and six firms have long-term debt exceeding their total assets. Table 2 also provides information on the firms' earnings performance in the year after they go public. Although they earn a median 5.5 percent return on total assets, approximately 22.4 percent of the firms lose money in the first year of operations. The mean earnings-to-price ratio statistic, reported in the last column of the table, is 3.78 percent.

Following Ritter's (1984) findings, we separate the non-MLP IPOs sample into financial and nonfinancial firms. Indeed, as Table 2, Panel B reveals, there are substantial differences between the two groups of IPOs. The majority of the IPOs are nonfinancial (778 versus 111), and their initial return is significantly higher than that of the financial IPOs, 8.50 percent compared with 2.36 percent. The mean issue size of the financial IPOs is more than double the nonfinancial size, $55.9 million versus $23.6 million. The average debt-to-total-assets ratios are almost identical, at about 21 percent. Among the ownership variables, only the average portion held by insiders differs: 39.7 percent in the nonfinancial firms, compared with 28.5 percent in the financial firms.

Finally, we record the lead underwriter in each public offering, as disclosed in the *Directory of Corporate Financing*. For this sample, 179 different underwriters are employed. Only 22 underwriters lead in more than 10 transactions, but six underwriters lead in approximately one-third of the transactions. To compute the underwriter reputation variable, we collect information about their capital position from the 1986 *Securities Industry Yearbook*. Underwriters are ranked from high to low according to their capital.

2. Hypotheses and Empirical Results

2.1 The winner's curse hypothesis
Rock (1986) develops a model that relies on information asymmetry between investors, some of whom are informed and others of whom are not. The outside informed investors possess better knowledge about the future prospects of the firm than uninformed investors. Consequently, they will bid for more shares of the more successful firms, which will leave the uninformed investors with a disproportionate amount of the less successful issues. In addition, since the allocation is not on a pro rata basis, the bias against uninformed investors can be even larger if the investment bankers favor the informed investors. Because market participants are rational, the uninformed investors require a higher average return to compensate them for their allocation disadvantage—hence the underpricing in the IPO market. If, however, there are issues in which the uninformed traders

The Review of Financial Studies / v 7 n 2 1994

have a priori knowledge that the informed traders will not participate, they do not face an allocation disadvantage, and underpricing is not required to induce them to participate in the market.

Implication 1. *In issues with an a priori knowledge of information homogeneity, the "lemons problem" does not exist and there is no need for underpricing.*

In most instances, however, there is no such a priori knowledge, and the trading population differs in its information. Then underpricing is necessary to attract the disadvantaged uninformed investors, who will not consider the new issue unless its price is low enough to compensate them for the winner's curse problem.

We associate the informed investors in the IPO market with the institutional investors. Institutional investors hold and trade large quantities of shares, and are most likely to be the better informed shareholders.[9] As large traders, they are also the most likely to be favored by the investment bankers when an issue is oversubscribed, and since there are no restrictions on how the shares of the newly formed firm should be distributed, their advantage is magnified.[10]

2.1.1 An analysis of master limited partnerships IPOs. The unique feature of MLP IPOs is that institutions are minor participants in them.[11] There are several reasons why institutions and corporations find MLPs unattractive. First, MLPs are taxed as partnerships, with the only tax applied at the unitholders' level on income earned. Because of this taxation difference, all equity holders, including tax-free institutions, must pay taxes on earnings from MLPs they own. Second, corporations do not qualify for the tax exemption on dividends received from MLPs. Third, owners of MLPs cede control to the MLP general partner. For example, investors do not have any voting power or power to remove management from office. Institutions and other large investors may find it unattractive to invest in entities in which they have to cede so much control to management. Fourth, there are significant administrative costs associated with institutional holdings of MLPs. For example, the general partner has the sole authority to agree to changes made upon audit by the IRS even though the limited partners must pay tax on their pro rata share of the income. Finally, even the

---

[9] See, for example, Grossman and Hart (1980) and Shleifer and Vishny (1986) for a discussion of why large shareholders are more likely to possess more information. Also see note 3.

[10] It is reasonable to expect some noninstitutional traders to be informed or some institutional investors to be uninformed. We merely assume that the concentration of informed traders is higher among the institutional investors.

[11] For a more detailed description of the distinctive characteristics of MLPs, see the Appendix.

filing deadlines can cause administrative inconveniences for the limited partners. While corporate partners must file tax returns, or at least pay the tax due to avoid an underpayment penalty, by March 15, the partnership return is not due until April 15. This filing difference may cause a corporation to file for an extension even if it is ready to file on time. In addition, given that institutional investors are not the natural holders of MLPs, Benveniste and Spindt (1989) show that investment bankers are unlikely to be willing to award them MLP IPOs, since they know they will try to resell them immediately.

The minor role of institutional investors as buyers of MLP IPOs and the market's a priori knowledge of this role reduce the potential bias against individual investors that exists in other IPOs.[12] This characteristic of the MLP IPO sample enables us to test Rock's assertion that the degree of underpricing is positively related to the degree of information heterogeneity among market participants. To make the analysis of the MLP IPOs more informative, we compare the MLP IPO sample results with those for the non-MLP IPOs.

Table 3 compares the samples of nonfinancial MLP and corporate IPOs.[13] The table contains summary statistics on the initial performance of the two samples and some fundamental characteristics of the firms. The mean initial-day return is insignificantly different from zero (−0.04 percent) for the MLP group but positive and significant for the corporate sample (8.50 percent).[14] The difference between the two returns is significant ($t = 13.62$). The 8.5 percent return for the corporate sample is similar to the figure reported by Ibbotson, Sindelar, and Ritter (1988) for IPOs with an initial price exceeding $3 per share for the years 1975–1984. In the second column of the table, we compare offer size for the two samples. The mean MLP offer is more than four times the size of the mean offer of the corporate sample ($115.68 million compared with $23.6 million). This differ-

---

[12] There is also evidence in the popular press that MLPs are designed for individual investors. For example, an article from the June 11, 1987, *WSJ* states: "Limited partnership sales are surging as sponsors cast their products for middle-class investors." Finally, our test of Implication 1 goes through even if some institutions participate in the MLP market. As long as the informed participation in this market is significantly lower than in the "regular" IPO market, and this fact is known a priori to market participants, Rock's model predicts less underpricing in this market.

[13] The comparison of the financial MLP IPOs with the financial corporate IPOs yields similar results and is omitted from this table for the sake of brevity. Muscarella (1988) reports an initial-day return of 0.24 percent, insignificantly different for zero, for a sample of 50 MLPs, but stops short of providing an explanation for the lack of underpricing.

[14] If the average initial return for the MLP sample is zero, but the dispersion of initial return is high, institutional investors could capture a positive initial return by purchasing the appropriate issues at the offering. However, this is not the case: the maximum initial return is 6.1 percent and the minimum is −3.5 percent. Fifty-three out of 58 MLPs exhibit initial returns lower than 2.1 percent. We examined whether the very small price movement on the first day of trading in the MLP IPOs sample is due to lack of trading activity. The mean (median) first-day turnover in the MLP sample is 9.28 percent (8.90 percent), with an average of 619,970 shares traded.

The Review of Financial Studies / v 7 n 2 1994

Table 3
A comparison of the characteristics of MLP IPOs and non-MLP IPOs

	Initial return	IPO size	Percent held by insiders	Percent held by institutions	Number of shareholders relative to IPO size
MLP	−0.0004	115.682	0.5247	0.0765	0.0843
(nonfinancial IPOs)	(39)	(39)	(38)	(37)	(39)
Corporate	0.0850	23.594	0.3972	0.2740	0.0624
(nonfinancial IPOs)	(778)	(778)	(495)	(717)	(773)
t-Statistics of the difference[1]	13.620	8.469	1.824	6.478	0.774

A comparison of initial-day return, IPO size, insiders and institutional holdings, and the number of shareholders relative to the IPO size, between nonfinancial MLP IPOs and nonfinancial IPOs, in the years 1984–1988. The initial-day return is calculated using the offer price and the price at the end of the first trading day. The IPO size is calculated as the offer price multiplied by the number of shares offered. The percentage held by insiders and institutions and the number of shareholders are taken from the *Spectrum* books published within a quarter of the IPO date. The number of observations appears in parentheses.

[1] When the assumption of equal variance between the two groups is rejected, test statistics are calculated under the assumption of an unequal variance.

ence is significant at the 1 percent level. As subsequent analyses will reveal, the size of the IPO plays a significant role in determining the degree of underpricing.[15] In columns 3, 4, and 5, we report the mean value of three ownership variables for the two samples, insider and institutional holdings, and number of shareholders relative to dollar value of the IPO. The mean insider holding is higher for the MLP sample than for the corporate sample: 52.5 percent compared with 39.7 percent (the *t*-statistic of the difference is 1.824). In contrast, the holdings of institutional investors are almost four times larger in the corporate group than in the MLP group: 27.4 percent versus 7.5 percent, with a *t*-statistic of the difference of 6.48.[16] The dispersion of shares (measured as the postoffering total number of shareholders divided by the dollar value of the IPO) is not significantly different across the two groups, with a mean value of 0.0843 for the MLP sample and 0.0624 for the corporate sample.

[15] Beatty and Ritter (1986) find that the level of uncertainty affects the degree of underpricing, consistent with a cross-sectional implication of Rock's (1986) model that they develop. They estimate uncertainty as the inverse of issue size. Indeed, Ritter (1987) finds that more speculative firms tend to raise smaller amounts of money than less risky firms; that is, uncertainty and size are correlated. Our results show that issue size has a significant role in explaining the degree of underpricing, but that it is not the only factor that accounts for the cross-sectional differences in underpricing across IPOs.

[16] In all MLP IPOs where institutions hold more than 10 percent of equity after the IPO, we further investigate the institutions' identities. In seven of the eight cases, the institutions holding the MLP are affiliated with the corporate sponsor of the MLP, even before the MLP IPO. For example, Fine Homes International, a real estate limited partnership, was created in May 1987 by Merrill Lynch. Merrill Lynch manages several mutual funds. The institutional investors for Fine Homes were the mutual funds managed by Merrill Lynch.

The results thus far reveal significant differences between the MLP IPOs and the corporate IPOs, both in their initial-day return and in some of their fundamental characteristics. Most notable are the differences in the issue size and the institutional holdings. The fact that the market recognizes a priori that institutional investors are not major participants in the MLP IPOs is of crucial importance to our experiment, since it gives us an opportunity to test Implication 1. This implication states that the winner's curse will be less pronounced in a market in which agents have prior knowledge of the absence of informed investors.

Given the results of Table 3, we construct three corporate IPO control samples and compare their initial return with the MLP IPOs' initial return. First, we control for industry effect. Ritter (1984) has shown that underpricing varies dramatically across industries. Since MLPs tend to concentrate in the oil and gas and real estate industries (see Table 1, Panel B), a comparison with a sample of IPOs from diverse industries may not be appropriate. For each MLP IPO, we matched a corporate IPO with the same four-digit SIC code and with the closest IPO size.[17] The results are reported in Table 4, Panel A. The initial return for the MLP IPOs (both financial and nonfinancial) is 0.12 percent, insignificantly different from zero. The matched sample shows a mean initial return of 4.5 percent, significantly different from zero. The *t*-statistic of the difference between the mean initial return of the two samples is 4.821.[18] Second, we control for the size of the IPO. It has been shown that larger IPOs show less underpricing [see, for example, Beatty and Ritter (1986)], presumably because larger IPOs have lower uncertainty. Table 4, Panel B indicates that even when we control for ex ante uncertainty, the corporate IPOs show significant underpricing while the MLP IPOs do not. The initial day return is 2.9 percent for the non-MLP group and -0.04 percent for the MLP group. On the other hand, the institutional holdings are significantly higher for the corporate group, 38 percent versus 7.6 percent, with a *t*-statistic of the difference of 4.572. That is, IPO size in and of itself cannot be used as an ex ante proxy for whether informed (institutional) investors participate in an IPO in a significant way. As shown in Table 4, Panel C, however, it is not the ex post fraction held by institutions that causes the difference in the initial return between

---

[17] In instances where a matched IPO cannot be found using the four-digit SIC code, we use the two-digit SIC code instead. We are able to find a match for 80 percent of the MLPs at the four-digit SIC code level. We repeat the experiment with this subsample. The results do not change in a significant way.

[18] The *t*-statistic of the difference is based on a pairwise comparison. In the last column of Table 4 we report the results of the rank statistics. They are practically identical to the results achieved using the parametric test.

The Review of Financial Studies / v 7 n 2 1994

the two groups. Even when the fraction held by institutions is held constant, the non-MLP group shows a significantly higher initial return.[19] This result is consistent with our assertion that the ex ante knowledge of lack of participation by informed investors in the MLP IPO market is important in explaining why MLPs are not underpriced. It seems that even when we control for asset structure (Panel A) and ex ante risk (Panel B), MLP IPOs show significantly lower initial returns than equivalent corporate IPOs.

2.1.2. Discussion. There are several possible objections to our explanation of why MLP IPOs are not underpriced, in that the experiment reported in Table 4 does not control for additional fundamental differences between MLP IPOs and corporate IPOs. First, the lack of underpricing in the MLP sample may be consistent with the higher fraction of equity held by insiders [Leland and Pyle (1977)]. Second, MLP IPOs are generally issued by the most prestigious underwriters, which might suggest less underpricing.[20] Third, since the parent corporation of the MLP IPO is publicly traded, it may be easier to obtain information about MLPs than about other IPOs, thus lowering the uncertainty and underpricing. Fourth, the organizational form per se may create an equity security that is less risky than an otherwise identical security.

We try to address the first two points using regression analysis. The log of the gross proceeds, insider holdings, a set of dummy variables for industry affiliation and the year in which the IPO was issued, a dummy variable that takes the value of 1 if the firm is non-MLP and 0 otherwise, and a proxy for the prestige of the underwriter are the independent variables; the initial return is the dependent variable. The MLP dummy coefficient is 0.061, which implies that corporate IPOs experience an initial-day return of 6.1 percent above MLP firms (significant at the 1 percent level). This result is similar to that reported in Table 4, Panel B. The insider holdings variable is negative and insignificantly different from zero. The prestige and gross proceeds coefficients are positive and significant at the 5 percent level.[21]

The third objection can be analyzed by comparing our results with those of Schipper and Smith (1986), Muscarella and Vetsuypens

---

[19] Given a corporate IPO sample of 889, we were able to match the MLP sample quite accurately. When matching by size (Panel B), the mean size is 121.357 and 115.68 for the corporate and MLP samples respectively, with a *t*-statistic of the difference of −0.26. When matching by institutions (Panel C), the mean institutional holdings are 7.59 percent and 7.65 percent, respectively, with a *t*-statistic of the difference of 0.0134.

[20] The role of the underwriter's reputation in determining the degree of underpricing is discussed in much more detail in the next section.

[21] Robust *t*-statistics [White (1980)] yield identical results.

Pricing Initial Public Offerings

Table 4
Differences in initial-day returns for MLP IPOs and non-MLP IPOs matched by industry, size, and institutional holdings

		MLP	Non-MLP	*t*-Statistics of the difference[1]	Rank statistics[2]
	A: Matched by SIC code				
n = 58	Initial return	0.0012	0.0451	4.821	4.447
		(0.558)	(5.126)		
	B: Matched by size				
n = 39	Initial return	−0.0004	0.0291	3.386	3.884
		(0.198)	(3.479)		
	Fraction held by institutions	0.0765	0.3801	4.572	3.373
	C: Matched by percentage held by institutions				
n = 39	Initial return	−0.0004	0.0679	2.818	3.113
		(0.198)	(2.809)		

A comparison of the initial-day return for MLP IPOs and a sample of corporate IPOs issued between 1984–1988, matched by industry classification (Panel A), size (Panel B), and the fraction of institutional holdings (Panel C). In Panel A, each MLP IPO is matched with a non-MLP IPO with the same four-digit SIC code, closest in size. If no match is found using the four-digit SIC code, the MLP IPO is matched using the two-digit SIC code. In Panels B and C, only nonfinancial IPOs are included. *t*-Statistics are in parentheses.

[1] *t*-Statistics of the difference are calculated on the basis of pairwise comparison.
[2] Wilcoxon rank statistics.

(1989), and Wang, Chan, and Gau (1992). Schipper and Smith (1986) find a mean initial return of 4.9 percent for 41 equity carve-outs during the period 1963–1983, and Muscarella and Vetsuypens (1989) report an initial return of 2.1 percent for 76 reverse LBOs during the period 1986–1987. The feature common to their samples and ours is that the firms involved are larger than the average corporate IPOs and that prior knowledge about their quality is more readily available. In the case of MLP IPOs and equity carve-outs, the parent company is publicly traded, which enables investors to gather more information about the newly traded firm, and in the case of reverse LBOs, the firm itself has been traded publicly. Indeed, all three samples show lower average returns than the "regular" IPO sample. Both the equity carve-out sample and the reverse LBO sample have an initial return significantly different than zero, whereas the MLP IPOs sample does not. This difference is consistent with the assertion of a positive association between information heterogeneity and the underpricing of IPOs (Implication 1).

As with MLP IPOs, institutional investors do not generally invest in IPOs of real estate investment trusts (REITs). Indeed, Wang, Chan, and Gau (1992) find that for a sample of 87 REIT IPOs the average initial day return is −2.82 percent, even though there is considerable uncertainty about their value. This result is consistent with the expla-

The Review of Financial Studies / v 7 n 2 1994

nation that when the winner's-curse problem does not exist, there is no incentive for the issuer to underprice.

The fourth point is related to the uniqueness of the MLP organizational form. To analyze this question, we examine the differences in profitability and expenditures for corporations and MLPs in the oil and gas industry. We find MLPs have acquisition and development costs commensurate with those of corporations. MLP IPOs underperform similar corporate IPOs in several ways, however. The MLPs are less profitable primarily because of higher operating costs for a given level of sales. The MLPs also underperform the corporations in terms of stock returns for the two years after going public. For example, matching MLPs and corporations by SIC code (as in Table 4, Panel A), we find that, whereas MLPs experience a two-year excess return of -21 percent, the SIC matched set of non-MLP IPOs experiences only a -2 percent excess return. In addition, the business failure rate of oil and gas industry MLPs is approximately 50 percent during the period we examine, significantly higher than the rate for corporations. That is, we find no evidence that MLPs' equity is in any way less risky than that of otherwise identical corporations.[22]

Finally, if MLPs have no intention of reissuing equity after the IPO, the results presented here may also be consistent with the signaling models. That is, if there is no reissue, there is no incentive to send the costly signal of underpricing. This is not the case, however: 9 out of 58 MLPs reissue equity in the first two years of operation.

In summary, we find support for the notion that there is a link between the heterogeneity of investors' information and IPO underpricing. For MLP IPOs, in which institutional (informed) investors scarcely participate, we find no underpricing. We attribute this result to the more homogeneous individual investor clientele of the MLP IPOs. We also provide evidence that the lack of underpricing is not due to size differences, industry affiliation, or lesser uncertainty about the future value of the MLPs.

2.2 Investment banker's reputation hypothesis
In Carter and Manaster (1990), the reputable investment banks take the less risky IPOs and less reputable investment banks underwrite the more risky IPOs. Consequently, their model predicts that the initial return on the IPO is negatively correlated with the investment banker's reputation.

---

[22] Since the general partner in MLPs has full control over the operation, cannot be voted out by the unitholders, and has only a small equity stake in the entity, the agency problem may be more severe in this organizational form than in corporations, consistent with our findings of poorer long-run performance and a higher failure rate for the MLPs.

Implication 2. *The more prestigious the investment bank, the lower the expected initial return on the IPO.*

2.2.1 Empirical analysis. The value of the underwriter's reputation depends not only on its activity in the IPO market, but on the entire array of activities with which it is involved. With each new issue the investment bank undertakes, it risks the present value of its distribution channels: the bigger the investment bank, the more severe the consequences of lost reputation. Therefore, we use the investment bank's capital as a proxy for its prestige.[23] The investment bank with the largest capital is ranked first, and the one with the smallest amount of capital is ranked last. For the 889 IPOs in the sample (MLP IPOs are excluded), there are 179 lead underwriters.[24]

Table 5 reports several tests of the hypothesis that there are significant differences in the characteristics of IPOs led by prestigious and less prestigious underwriters. Twenty-three out of 179 underwriters, who handled 50.05 percent of the transactions, are classified as prestigious. Indeed, the IPOs associated with more prestigious underwriters (449 out of 889 issues) exhibit significantly lower initial returns than the IPOs associated with the less prestigious group: 4.5 percent versus 10.9 percent. This is not the only significant difference, however. Issues are more than five times as large for the prestigious underwriters group as for the less prestigious group, $46.24 versus $8.65 million. Insiders hold 34.6 percent and 42.7 percent in the prestigious and less prestigious groups, respectively. There is no significant difference between the two groups in the percentage of equity held by institutions, although the absolute amount held by institutions is naturally larger for the prestigious underwriters group.[25]

---

[23] Using capital as a proxy for reputation is also consistent with the implication of the certification hypotheses [Booth and Smith (1986)].

[24] Using multivariate regression analysis, and using rank on the tombstone announcement as a proxy for underwriters' prestige, Carter and Manaster (1990) find the reputation variable to be significant, whereas James and Wier (1990) find it to be insignificant. We also compare our ranking with the one used by Carter and Manaster (1990). Seventy-six underwriters are in both groups. We divide our sample into nine equal groups. All underwriters in the first group are assigned a rank of 9, and those in the last group are assigned a rank of 1. The Spearman rank correlation coefficient between the Carter and Manaster ranking and ours is .86.

[25] Carter and Manaster (1990) argue that ". . . since informed investor capital migrates to the highly uncertain IPOs [issued by the less prestigious underwriter], the underpricing and subsequent run-up for these firms are greater" (p. 1046). The results in Table 5 indeed show that underpricing for the IPOs in the less prestigious group is greater. However, the fraction held by informed investors (the institutions) is the same, which seems to invalidate either Carter and Manaster's conjecture or our proxy for informed traders. Since, as Carter and Manaster argue, informed traders maximize the value of their information acquisition, they will take into account not only the degree of uncertainty in a given issue, but also its size: the bigger the IPO, the greater the potential gains from acquiring information about the issue. Since the prestigious underwriters offer larger issues, our finding of similar fractional holdings by institutions in the two groups is not surprising.

The Review of Financial Studies / v 7 n 2 1994

Table 5
A comparison of the characteristics of IPOs issued by prestigious and less prestigious underwriters

Variable	Less prestigious underwriter	Prestigious underwriter	t-Statistics of the difference[1]
Return	0.1097 (440)	0.0452 (449)	6.221
IPO size	8.65 (440)	46.24 (449)	8.056
INSID	0.4276 (259)	0.3460 (346)	3.2395
INSTIT	0.2856 (389)	0.2694 (400)	1.063
SHHOLD	0.0821 (433)	0.0422 (448)	4.583
Two-year excess return	−0.2682 (440)	−0.0152 (449)	3.760

A comparison of initial-day return, IPO price, IPO size, and insider and institutional holdings between IPOs handled by reputable underwriters and IPOs handled by less reputable underwriters. Underwriters are ranked according to the size of their capital. Twenty-three underwriters out of 179 are classified as prestigious. The initial-day return is calculated using the offer price and the price at the end of the first trading day. IPO size is calculated as the offer price multiplied by the number of shares offered. The percentage held by insiders (INSID) and institutions (INSTIT) and the number of shareholders relative to the IPO size (SHHOLD) are taken from the *Spectrum* books published within a quarter of the IPO date. The number of transactions is in parentheses.
[1] When the assumption of equal variance between the two groups is rejected, test statistics are calculated under the assumption of an unequal variance.

The difference in long-run performance between the IPOs issued by the prestigious and the less prestigious underwriters is striking. The latter group shows a two-year negative excess return of 26.8 percent, whereas the former group shows a 1.5 percent negative excess return. The difference is statistically significant at the 1 percent level. It seems that prestigious underwriters indeed issue "better" IPOs (significantly better long-run performance), and the initial return of these IPOs is lower because of lower uncertainty. Because of the substantial difference in the size of the IPOs (a mean issue size of 8.65 and 46.24 million for the less prestigious and the prestigious groups respectively), however, it is hard to discern thus far whether the difference in performance is due to the size of the IPO or issuer's prestige. This distinction is important for evaluating the validity of the reputation-based models. If by observing the issue size alone, potential investors can infer the same information about the uncertainty level they can gain by observing the underwriter's reputation, issuers will not have an incentive to pay the additional costs associated with dealing with the more reputable investment bankers.

To examine this issue, we first rank all IPOs by issue size, beginning with the largest. Then for each firm, we assign the prestige rank of

Table 6
The distribution of IPOs and their initial-day return categorized by size and underwriters' prestige

Issue size (v) →	All	1 v < 4.91	2 4.91 < v < 8.90	3 8.90 < v < 15.19	4 15.19 < v < 28.9	5 v > 28.9
All		0.1472 (8.462) [176]	0.0681 (8.294) [179]	0.0611 (7.550) [178]	0.0590 (5.710) [178]	0.0521 (4.854) [178]
Underwriter						
1 Most capital	0.0366 (4.462) [193]	0.0100 (—) [1]	0.0483 (2.609) [6]	0.0191 (2.363) [32]	0.0258 (3.349) [61]	0.0470 (3.095) [93]
2	0.0487 (6.470) [179]	−0.0388 (−8.052) [2]	0.0078 (0.667) [16]	0.0592 (3.819) [58]	0.0628 (4.377) [53]	0.0408 (3.259) [58]
3	0.0583 (6.900) [161]	0.0538 (2.225) [11]	0.0596 (4.108) [41]	0.0596 (4.795) [50]	0.0422 (4.066) [38]	0.0883 (1.900) [21]
4	0.0816 (7.010) [176]	0.0759 (3.464) [37]	0.0570 (5.460) [73]	0.0820 (3.862) [42]	0.1838 (2.597) [20]	0.0701 (1.375) [4]
5 Least capital	0.1618 (8.415) [180]	0.1806 (7.897) [125]	0.1204 (5.119) [43]	0.1306 (2.220) [9]	0.0000 (—) [1]	0.0983 (22.953) [2]

The sample of IPOs from 1984 to 1988 is divided into 25 groups according to issue size (in millions of dollars) and the reputation of the issuing underwriter. *t*-Statistics of the null hypothesis that the initial return equals zero appears in parentheses. The number of IPOs appears in brackets.

the underwriter and calculate the Spearman rank correlation between the two. The Spearman correlation is positive (.752) and significant at the .0001 level. Next, we partition the sample into quintiles by issue size and brokerage prestige, resulting in a 5 × 5 matrix of initial-day returns. The results are reported in Table 6 and in Figure 1. The results reveal three interesting phenomena. First, reputable investment banks issue large IPOs, while less reputable investment banks issue small IPOs. For example, the underwriters with the most capital (first quintile) issue 93 IPOs from the largest issue quintile and only one from the smallest issue quintile. The underwriters with the least capital issue only three IPOs from the two largest-size IPO quintiles. Second, initial-day return increases monotonically as the reputation of the investment bank decreases (first column), from 3.7 to 16.2 percent. A similar pattern is maintained within each size-based group (columns 2 through 6). Third, initial IPO return decreases as the issue size increases (first row), from 5.21 percent for the largest size group to 14.72 percent for the smallest size group. This relationship between size and initial return is not always maintained, however, when we control for the reputation of the underwriter. For example, for the second most prestigious group of underwriters, the mean

The Review of Financial Studies / v 7 n 2 1994

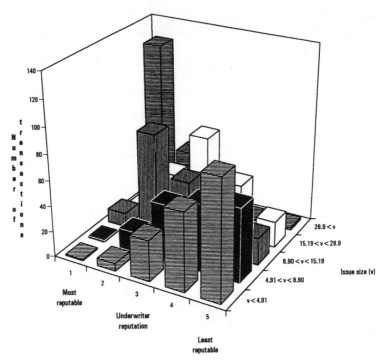

Figure 1
Number of IPOs by value and underwriter size quintiles
The reputation of underwriters is based on the equity capital. The issue size of the IPO offerings is in millions.

initial returns are −3.8, 0.78, 5.9, 6.3, and 4.1 percent from the smallest to the largest IPO issues group. Only for the IPO group issued by the least reputable investment bankers does the initial return decrease with size. These conclusions also emerge from a regression analysis for each size and prestige quintile: for all but the largest size quintile, the prestige coefficient is positive and significantly different from zero. The size coefficient is positive for the first four prestige groups (and significantly different from zero for groups 3 and 4), and negative but insignificant for the least reputable quintile.

These results can be interpreted as follows. The reputation of the investment banker resolves some of the uncertainty about the quality of the IPO. The better the investment banker's reputation, the less risky the issue is, and the lower the required initial-day return. Larger issues, however, require greater distribution efforts by the investment banker [Baron (1982)] and the dispersion of the issue to a larger group of investors; hence, there is larger underpricing.[26] (We estimate the dispersion by the total number of shareholders in relation to the dollar value of the IPO.)

Indeed, the regression results reported below indicate that the marginal effect of the number of shareholders (in relation to the dollar value of IPO) has a positive effect on the initial-day return.

$$\text{Initial return} = -0.0312 + 0.0012\text{BROK} + 0.021\text{SIZE}$$
$$\phantom{\text{Initial return} = }(0.533)\quad(6.566)(3.019)$$

$$+\ 0.0219\,\text{SHHOLD} + \text{industry and year}\qquad(1)$$
$$(4.622)\text{dummy variables,}$$

$$\bar{R}^2 = 0.111\quad(\text{number of observations is }881),$$

where SIZE = log of the gross proceeds (millions of dollars)

BROK = prestige variable based on the investment banker's capital; the first-ranked investment banker has the highest prestige and the last-ranked has the lowest prestige

SHHOLD = number of shareholders in relation to the IPO size

$\bar{R}^2$ = adjusted R^2; t-statistics are reported in parentheses

The brokerage prestige coefficient is positive and highly significant, indicating that IPOs issued by less reputable bankers experience higher initial-day returns.[27] The positive size coefficient is consistent with the assertion that, for a given brokerage prestige-level, larger issues show more underpricing.[28,29] Finally, the number-of-shareholders variable shows that the larger the dispersion of the stockholdings, the greater the underpricing. That is, given the investment

---

[26] One may argue that the IPO size can be used as an indicator of the degree of information heterogeneity. For example, it may be that the fraction held by informed (institutional) investors in large IPOs is trivial, which may affect equilibrium underpricing, according to Rock. However, we do not find support for such a relationship. The fraction held by institutions is almost uniformly distributed across size deciles.

[27] We rerun Equation (1) with the fraction of shares held by insiders as an additional independent variable. The prestige, size, and shareholders coefficients are almost identical to what has been reported above. The insider-holdings coefficient is negative ($-.013$) but insignificantly different from zero ($t = -0.856$). Because of data limitations, the number of observations in this regression is 621 instead of 889. We also added the Carter and Manaster reputation variable to Equation (1). Its coefficient is found to be insignificantly different from zero, while the capital-based reputation coefficient is highly significant.

[28] We also checked whether size affects initial return in a nonlinear way by adding size squared as an additional independent variable in Equation (1). Its coefficient is found to be insignificant.

[29] The positive and significant size coefficient may also be a manifestation of the "partial adjustment" phenomenon [Ibbotson, Sindelar, and Ritter (1988)]. After the investment banker is chosen and the preliminary prospectus is issued, if demand is strong, there is a higher initial return and the offering price and number of shares are sometimes adjusted upward.

The Review of Financial Studies / v 7 n 2 1994

banker's prestige, larger IPOs require more effort to distribute; hence, the underpricing is greater and the investor base is wider.[30]

Finally, we examine the relationship between the reputation variable and the long-run performance of the IPOs, measured by their two-year excess returns over the market portfolio. We divide the sample into two groups based on brokerage prestige and calculate the two-year excess return for each group. As reported in the last row of Table 5, long-run performance is significantly better for the more prestigious group than for the less prestigious group, -1.52 and -26.8 percent respectively.[31] Controlling for time and industry variation, the regression analysis reported below indicates that IPOs issued by more reputable brokerages perform better in the long run:

$$2 \text{ yr. EXR} = \begin{array}{cc} 0.0668 & - \ 0.0028\text{BROK} \\ (0.406) & (-2.32) \end{array}$$

$$\begin{array}{cc} + \ 0.0665\text{SIZE} & + \text{ industry and year} \\ (1.514) & \text{dummy variables,} \end{array} \qquad (2)$$

$$\bar{R}^2 = 0.034 \quad \begin{array}{l} \text{[number of observations} \\ \text{is 889 and variables} \\ \text{definitions are as in} \\ \text{Equation (1)].}^{32} \end{array}$$

In summary, using investment banks' capital as a measure of prestige, we find that IPOs underwritten by more prestigious investment banks experience less underpricing than IPOs underwritten by less prestigious banks. Consistent with prior literature, we show that larger IPOs experience less underpricing. However, we show that for a given

---

[30] We also run two univariate regressions when the dependent variable is the initial return. In the first, the independent variable is the brokerage prestige, resulting in a positive and highly significant coefficient. In the second regression, the independent variable is the issue size. Its coefficient is $-.0252$ with a t-statistic of -5.39, illustrating that size alone is negatively associated with initial return. However, its marginal effect is positive when controlling for issuer's reputation, as has been demonstrated in the text. Given a correlation of .75 between the issue size and the prestige variable, it is likely that the regressors are collinear. Belsley, Kuh, and Welsch (1980) describe a procedure for detecting collinearity. The procedure calculates a condition number that provides a measure of the potential sensitivity of the solution vector, b, to small changes in the elements of X and Y. Using this procedure, we find that a principal component associated with a high condition index contributes strongly to the variance of both the issue size and the broker variable, indicative of some linear dependencies between the two variables.

[31] Ritter (1991) finds that issuing firms underperform the value-weighted index by about 12 percent in the first three years of operation.

[32] We rerun Equation (2) with the fraction held by insiders and the fraction held by institutions (at the time of the IPO) as additional independent variables. The insider's coefficient is positive but insignificant ($t = 0.82$), and the institutions' coefficient is insignificantly negative ($t = 0.275$). The prestige coefficient remains significant. Because of data limitations the sample size is reduced by more than one-third. t-Statistics for the variables in Equations (1) and (2) are also calculated using the White (1980) procedure. The results are virtually identical to what has been reported in the text.

level of underwritter prestige, the larger IPOs experience greater underpricing. This may be a result of the greater distribution efforts by the investment banker for these issues. Finally, we show that in the long run, IPOs issued by prestigious investment bankers perform significantly better than those issued by less prestigious investment bankers.

2.3 The signaling hypothesis
2.3.1 Allen and Faulhauber (1989). In Allen and Faulhaber (1989), Grinblatt and Hwang (1989), and Welch (1989), "good" firms try to distinguish themselves from "bad" firms by incurring a cost that the less successful firms cannot profitably sustain. This cost is the underpricing of the initial issue. In Allen and Faulhaber's model, investors update their prior beliefs about the value of the firm through its earnings or dividend policy. High dividends (earnings) tend to upgrade their valuation of the firm, and low dividends (earnings) tend to downgrade it. High dividends (or earnings) after the IPO will be more effective in revising the market's prior beliefs for firms that underprice more. The model implies that the better firms will underprice more, will have higher earnings, will initiate dividends earlier, will have a higher payout ratio, and will experience a more favorable market reaction to the dividend announcement.

Implication 3A. There is a positive relation between the degree of underpricing and the subsequent earnings performance and dividend policy of the firm.

We define dividend policy in this context in terms of the interval between the IPO and the dividend initiation, and by the dividend yield, calculated at the first dividend payment.

Implication 3B. The effect of the dividend announcement should be positively related to the IPO underpricing. That is, firms that are less underpriced should experience a less favorable price reaction when the dividend is announced.[33]

Our test of Allen and Faulhaber's model consists of three experi-

---

[33] Allen and Faulhaber's (1989) model suggests that underpricing is a consequence of a separating equilibrium. When a pooling equilibrium occurs, firms will not underprice. Since in each year of our sample period we observe significant underpricing, our test of Allen and Faulhaber concentrates on their separating equilibrium implications. Among other things, a separating equilibrium is more likely to occur when the probability of successful implementation is low. In such a case investors will be surprised to see high dividends after the implementation, and they will revise their prior beliefs dramatically. Good firms that do not underprice will not experience the same change in beliefs when they pay a high dividend.

The Review of Financial Studies / v 7 n 2 1994

ments. First, we test whether greater underpricing is associated with higher earnings or with higher dividend yield. Second, we examine whether greater underpricing is associated with distributing dividends sooner rather than later. Finally, we test whether the market reaction to changes in dividend policy is related to the degree of underpricing. According to the theory, in equilibrium, firms that underprice more will experience a more positive market reaction to a dividend increase than firms that do not underprice.[34] The other major implications of the model concern the timing and the size of the seasoned equity issue. The reward for being perceived as a good firm rather than a bad firm is a more favorable environment for an issue of seasoned equity. This feature is common to all the signaling models discussed here and will be dealt with when we test the Welch (1989) model in the next section.

In Table 7, Panel A, we divide the sample of IPOs into two groups. The first group (685 firms) has positive earnings in the first year of public operation, and the second group (196 firms) has negative earnings. The initial return is 6.8 percent for the positive earnings group and 10.87 percent for the negative-earnings group, both significantly different from zero. Contrary to the model prediction, the initial return of the group with negative earnings is significantly higher than the initial return of the positive-earnings group. The results using regression analysis, where the dependent variable is the first-year net income normalized by the IPO size, leads to the same conclusion. The first-day return coefficient is negative ($-.0492$) and significant ($t = 2.84$). That is, greater underpricing is associated with lower earnings.[35]

In Table 7, Panel B, we again divide the IPO sample into two groups. The first group (704 firms) does not pay any cash dividend in the first three years of public operation; the 185 companies in the second group pay cash dividends in this period. Both initial returns are positive and significantly different from zero. Contrary to the implications of the Allen and Faulhaber model, however, the zero-yield group has an initial-day return significantly higher than that of the positive-yield group, with a t-statistic of the difference of 4.2. In Panel C, we divide the dividend-paying stocks into high- and low-yield groups. The initial return decreases as the yield increases, from 6.0 percent for the low-yield group to 2.31 percent for the high-yield group.

---

[34] In the Allen and Faulhaber model, investors condition their beliefs on the degree of underpricing. Firms that underprice more are considered better firms. However, good firms face a positive probability of unsuccessful implementation, and of then becoming bad firms. High earnings (dividends) help investors revise their prior beliefs about whether the implementation was successful.

[35] Inclusion of year and industry dummy variables does not affect this result.

Table 7
Initial return measured for 889 IPOs between 1984 and 1988 categorized by earnings (panel A) and dividend yield (panels B and C)

	Panel A		
	Earnings > 0	Earnings < 0	*t*-Statistic of the difference[1]
Initial-day return	6.804 (12.287) [685]	10.870 (8.140) [196]	2.770

	Panel B		
	Yield = 0	Yield < 0	*t*-Statistic of the difference[1]
Initial-day return	8.676 (14.131) [704]	4.150 (4.689) [185]	4.201

	Panel C		
	Yield = 0	Yield < 0.0246	Yield > 0.0246
Initial-day return	8.676 (14.131) [704]	6.007 (4.234) [92]	2.313 (2.232) [93]

A comparison of the mean initial-day return when the sample is divided according to whether the firm has positive or negative earnings in the first year of operation (Panel A). In Panel B, we compare the mean initial-day return when the sample is divided according to whether the firm does or does not pay dividends in the first three years of public operation. In Panel C, we divide the IPOs that pay dividends in the first three years of operation into high- and low-yield groups. The dividend yield is calculated using the first dividend over the price on the day prior to the announcement. All dividends are annualized. *t*-Statistics are in parentheses and number of observations is in brackets.

[1] When the assumption of equal variance between the two groups is rejected, test statistics are calculated under the assumption of an unequal variance.

Next, we use a linear regression analysis to test the hypothesis that firms that underprice more pay a higher divided. The dependent variable is the initial-day return. The explanatory variables are the dividend yield (measured at the first dividend announcement day) and a dummy variable that takes the value of 1 if the firm pays dividends and zero otherwise. The relationship between underpricing and subsequent dividend policy may manifest itself not only through the amount of dividends paid but also through how soon after the IPO a dividend is paid. A more successful implementation will allow the firm to pay dividends sooner. Therefore, we add time as an explanatory variable to the regression. The time variable is measured as the reciprocal of the interval between the initial public offering and the first dividend announcement. If no dividend is paid, the time variable takes the value of zero. The results are reported in Table 8. Contrary to Implication 3A, both the dividend yield and the dividend dummy coefficients have negative signs, implying a lower initial return for

The Review of Financial Studies / v 7 n 2 1994

Table 8
The relationship between dividend payout and initial-day return of IPOs

	Constant	Dividend yield	Yield dummy	Time[1]	$\overline{R}^2$	N
(1)	0.0868	−0.5546	−0.0242		.0151	889
	(14.144)	(−4.349)	(−1.755)			
(2)	0.0806			−0.7025	.0059	889
	(14.639)			(−3.589)		
(3)	0.0868	−0.5801	−0.0156	−0.3395	.0173	889
	(14.142)	(−4.381)	(−0.964)	(−2.188)		

The dependent variable is the degree of underpricing. The explanatory variables are the dividend yield, a dummy variable that takes the value of 1 if the firm pays dividends in the first two years of operation and 0 otherwise, and a time variable that measures the time between the IPO and the dividend yield. Standard errors are adjusted for heteroskedasticity using White's (1980) procedure. *t*-Statistics are reported in parentheses. The degree of underpricing is measured using the closing price on the first trading day and the price at which the IPO is offered. The dividend yield is calculated using the first dividend over the price on the day prior to the dividend announcement. The time variable is measured in days.

[1] The time variable is measured as the reciprocal of the interval between the initial public offering and the first dividend announcement. If no dividend is paid, the time variable takes the value of zero.

dividend-paying stocks.[36] The coefficient of the interval between the IPO and the first dividend is negative and significant. It seems that firms that underprice less tend to pay higher dividends and to pay them sooner rather than later. There is no indication that greater underpricing is positively related to subsequent dividend policy.[37]

Allen and Faulhaber's (1989) model also implies that dividend payment causes investors to revise their expectations about the firm's prospects—the greater the underpricing, the greater the effect of the dividend announcement in revising the market's expectations (Implication 3B). To test this hypothesis, we calculate the excess return on the three days surrounding the announcement of the first dividend for each dividend-paying stock in the sample.[38] The return behavior around the dividend announcement day cannot be analyzed with a linear regression since its estimators may be inconsistent as a result

[36] The finding that firms with high dividends or high earnings also underprice less is consistent with the legal liability hypothesis as well [Tinic (1988), Hughes and Thakor (1992)].

[37] Examining only the dividend-paying stocks, we divide the sample into two groups according to initial return. The first group contains all stocks with a nonpositive initial-day return (82 securities), and the second group contains all stocks with a positive initial-day return (103 securities). The mean dividend yields are 7.25 percent for the nonpositive return group and 4.37 percent for the positive return group, insignificantly different from each other ($t = 1.58$).

[38] Announcements of dividend initiation cause a significant stock-price reaction [see, for example, Michaely et al. (1994)]. The excess return in the three days around the dividend initiation announcement is 0.85 percent, significant at the 5 percent level (see Table 10, Panel B). We exclude companies that pay the first dividend within 60 days of the IPO, since most of those companies had paid dividends prior to the IPO. Inclusion of those announcements, however, does not change the results.

of the truncation bias.[39] The decision to pay dividends is endogenous, which is not reflected in the cross-sectional estimator. Eckbo, Maksimovic, and Williams (1990) derive consistent estimators using a latent variables model. These estimators account for the presence of the potential truncation bias. Let D be a dummy variable that has a value of 1 if a dividend is paid and a value of 0 otherwise. Suppose that D^*, the latent counterpart of D, is generated by the model

$$D^* = Z\gamma - \epsilon_D, \tag{3}$$

where Z is a vector of instruments (initial return, brokerage prestige, and percentage held by institutions) that are related to the likelihood that a dividend will be paid and ϵ_D is an error term. The estimator for γ is a probit. Consistent estimates of the parameters are obtained from

$$ER_i = \beta_0 + \beta_1 \cdot Yield_i + \beta_2 \cdot Init\ Ret_i + \beta_3 \cdot time_i + \beta_4 E[\epsilon_D \mid \epsilon_D < Z\gamma] + \epsilon_R. \tag{4}$$

The specification (4) indicates that the cross-sectional structure of announcement returns comprises information associated with the decision to announce any dividend as well as the information transmitted by the dividend yield and the degree of underpricing.

The explanatory variables in (4) are the stock dividend yield, the IPO initial return, the length of time between the IPO and the dividend initiation, and Mill's ratio $\phi(Zr)/\Phi(Zr)$, where ϕ is the normal density function and Φ is the normal cdf. As reported in Table 9, the initial-return coefficient is negative (insignificant), implying that a higher initial return is associated with a smaller dividend announcement effect. Mill's ratio coefficient is positive but insignificant, suggesting that the insider's superior knowledge does not play an important role in this context. These variables do not seem to have any power in explaining the market reaction around the dividend announcement. These results are inconsistent with Implication 3B.

Overall, we find no support for a hypothesis that initial underpricing is used to signal underlying IPO quality or that it can be translated into better understanding of future dividends and earnings announcements. Whereas Allen and Faulhaber (1989) predict a positive relation between underpricing and future earnings performance and dividend levels, we find the opposite result holds. Firms with higher earnings and those that initiate dividends experience less initial underpricing. Also, the market does not apparently react differently to the announcements of dividend initiation by firms that underprice and those that do not.

---

[39] We would like to thank the referee for pointing this out to us.

The Review of Financial Studies / v 7 n 2 1994

Table 9
The effect of initial underpricing and dividend yield on stock prices at announcement of the first dividend after the IPO

	Constant	Dividend yield	Time	Initial return	Mill's ratio	$\bar{R}^2$	N
(1)	−0.0759 (−1.247)			−0.0949 (−1.03)	0.056 (1.42)	.0015	118
(2)	0.0459 (−0.847)	−0.0354 (−0.167)			0.035 (1.04)	−.0094	118
(3)	−0.0525 (−0.974)	−0.057 (−0.267)	0.00005 (1.560)		0.032 (0.015)	.0059	118
(4)	−0.0795 (−1.308)	−0.1015 (−0.475)	0.00004 (1.478)	−0.0919 (−0.968)	0.053 (1.22)	.0052	118

The dependent variable is the excess return on the three days surrounding the announcement of the first dividend. The explanatory variables are the dividend yield, the degree of underpricing, the time between the IPO and the announcement of the first dividend, and Mill's ratio, estimated from the Probit model [Equation (3)]. (Implication 3B states that the higher the underpricing, the more positive should be the market reaction to the dividend initiation announcement.)

2.3.2 Welch (1989). Welch's model, as well as Grinblatt and Hwang's (1989) and Allen and Faulhaber's (1989), formalizes the notion that good firms underprice to "leave a good taste in investors' mouths." The hypothesis is that the owner's incentive to leave a good taste is the possibility of coming back to the market for the sale of additional securities on more favorable terms.[40] Welch's model explicitly accounts for the possibility of subsequent issuance of equity or debt in the secondary market. The entrepreneur of a high-quality firm will underprice to distinguish his firm from the low-quality firm. He will be rewarded at the time of the seasoned issue by a higher price for the shares. The underpricing is a credible signal if the imitation costs for the low-quality firm are high enough. In fact, the entrepreneur faces a joint decision of how much to underprice and whether to reenter the market at a later time for the subsequent issue of equity or debt.[41]

Implication 4A. *There is a positive relationship between the degree of initial underpricing and the amount of the subsequent seasoned issue.*

In addition, Welch's model implies that good firms, which underprice

---

[40] This justification for underpricing appears in the popular press as well. For example, the March 4, 1992, "Heard on the Street" column in the *Wall Street Journal* states ". . . companies may be receptive to a low price because they will be back to sell stock in a year or so" (p. C1).

[41] Indeed, Welch (1989) presents evidence that about one-fourth of the IPO firms came back to the market to raise capital through seasoned equity offerings in the 10 years following the IPO. From January 1977 to December 1987, 395 seasoned offerings were found. Of these, 288 were for firms that went public between 1977 and 1982.

more, experience a less unfavorable price response at the time of the seasoned issue.

Implication 4B. *The price reaction at the time of a seasoned issue announcement will be less unfavorable for firms that underprice more.*

Empirically, the model implies a positive association between underpricing and the success of the seasoned equity issue (or a debt issue). We measure success in terms of the size of the seasoned issue in relation to the initial public offering and the market reaction to the seasoned issue. Of the 889 non-MLP IPOs, 84 firms issue debt and 216 firms issue seasoned equity in the first three years of operation. As reported in Table 10, neither type of issue is clustered in any particular year, with 78, 63, and 75 seasoned equity offerings, and 30, 20, and 34 debt offerings in the first, second, and third years of operation. Consistent with the existing evidence, both seasoned equity offerings and debt offerings are perceived as bad news about the firm, and consequently the stock price drops at their announcement.[42] In our sample, the three-day excess return is -0.79 percent with a t-statistic of -1.805 around the seasoned equity offerings, and -0.88 percent with a t-statistic of -1.363 for the debt offerings (Table 10, Panel B).

To test the relationship between underpricing and subsequent issuance decisions, we first divide the sample into two groups. The first group comprises all firms that issue additional equity in the first three years of operation. All firms that do not have an equity offering are included in the second group. A comparison of the two groups' initial-return and long-run performance is shown in Table 11, Panel A. The results are striking. Although there is no significant difference in initial underpricing between the two groups (8.84 percent for the firms that issue and 7.38 percent for the firms that do not), the two-year excess return is 38.3 percent for the firms that issue, compared with -39.4 percent for the firms that do not. The t-statistic of the difference is 11.55. Likewise, in Table 11, Panel B, the IPO firms are divided according to whether they issue public debt in the three years after the IPO. As with the seasoned equity issue, there is no significant difference in the initial return between the two groups (7.94 percent for the firms that issue debt and 7.71 percent for the firms that do not), but the two-year excess return is 16.7 percent for the firms that

---

[42] See, for example, Asquith and Mullins (1986), Eckbo (1986), Masulis and Korwar (1986), and Mikkelson and Partch (1986).

The Review of Financial Studies / v 7 n 2 1994

Table 10
Frequency and timing of future dividend payments and equity or debt offerings

	A			
	1st year	2nd year	3rd year	Total
Dividends	142	20	23	185
Seasoned equity	78	63	75	216
Debt issue	30	20	34	84

	B		
	Excess return (%)	t-Statistics	No. of observations
Dividend initiations[1]	0.8455	2.15	118
Seasoned equity offerings[2]	−0.79	−1.805	197
Debt issue[3]	−0.88	−1.363	72

In Panel A we report the number of firms that initiated dividends or issued additional securities (equity or debt) in the three years following their IPOs. Panel B presents the cumulative excess return in the three days around each of these events and its significance.

[1] Excess return is calculated for all dividend initiations in the first two years of public operations, excluding dividends that were announced in the first 60 days after the IPO.

[2] Nine seasoned offerings by MLPs and 10 offerings without identifiable announcement days are excluded.

[3] Debt offerings by MLPs and offerings without identifiable announcement days are excluded.

issue, compared with −24.23 percent for the firms that do not. The difference is significant with a t-statistic of 8.3. These results seem to indicate that while there is no relationship between initial underpricing and subsequent debt or equity issues, only firms that perform well reissue equity. The former finding is inconsistent with Implication 4A of a positive association between underpricing and seasoned equity issue policy.[43]

The decisions on how much to underprice and whether to reissue equity are not independent. Whether the issuer desires to "leave a good taste in investors' mouths" by underpricing depends on whether he thinks he will subsequently go back to the market to raise more capital. That is, the issuer faces two simultaneous decisions: how much to underprice, and whether and how much he would like to reissue. The decision about the amount offered in the seasoned issue is endogenous and is made simultaneously with the decision about what signal to send to the market during the IPO through underpricing. This is the major implication of all the IPO signaling models.

Using a simultaneous equations model, we test the proposition of

---

[43] A priori, one may expect the opposite relationship between issuance decisions and performance (or earnings). Firms with high earnings have less need for cash flow and therefore will go to the market less often. Our findings are consistent with the assertion that "better" firms also face more positive NPV projects and hence need outside financing above and beyond their internally generated cash flow.

Table 11
**Initial underpricing conditional on the later issuance of a seasoned equity offering: A
comparison of mean initial returns and two-year excess returns for firms that issue and
do not issue seasoned equity (Panel A) or debt (Panel B) in the first three years of operation**

	A: Seasoned equity issues		
	Firms that issued seasoned equity	Firms that did not issue seasoned equity	t-Statistics of the difference[1]
Initial return	0.0884 (7.913) [216]	0.0738 (12.5) [673]	−1.1954
Two-year excess return	0.383 (4.54)	−0.394 (14.7)	−11.548

	B: Debt issues		
	Firms that issued debt	Firms that did not issue debt	t-Statistics of the difference[1]
Initial return	0.0794 (4.1) [84]	0.0771 (14.22) [805]	−0.1221
Two-year excess return	0.162 (1.934)	−0.2423 (−7.615)	−8.304

t-Statistics are reported in parentheses, and numbers of observations are in brackets.
[1] When the assumption of equal variance between the two groups is rejected, test statistics are calculated under the assumption of an unequal variance.

a positive association between the degree of underpricing and the seasoned equity issuance decision. In the first equation, the dependent variable is the initial underpricing (InitR), and the independent variables are the size of the seasoned issue in relation to the IPO size (Rel Size), the log of the dollar value of the IPO (SIZE), the brokerage prestige variable (BROK), and a set of industry and year dummy variables. In the second equation (Tobit), the dependent variable is the relative size of the seasoned equity issue (Rel Size), and the independent variables are the initial underpricing (InitR), the IPO size (SIZE), the excess return in the 60 days after the IPO (Ret 60) and the two years after the IPO (Ret 2), and a set of industry and year dummy variables. The 60-day excess return and the two-year excess return variables try to capture the effect of the after-market performance on the seasoned issuance decision. Given that one variable is observed (underpricing) and the other is censored (relative size of the seasoned equity offering), we estimate the regression coefficients and their asymptotic covariance matrix following Amemiya (1979).

$$\text{InitR} = -0.06744 + 0.00221(\text{Rel Size}) + 0.009(\text{SIZE})$$
$$\quad (-1.15) \qquad\quad (1.18) \qquad\qquad (1.56)$$
$$+ 0.0013(\text{BROK}) + \text{industry and year} \qquad (5a)$$
$$\quad (6.95) \qquad\qquad \text{dummy variables}$$

The Review of Financial Studies / v 7 n 2 1994

$$\text{Rel Size} = \begin{array}{cc} -4.556 & - 7.686(\text{InitR}) + 0.059(\text{SIZE}) \\ (-1.455) & (-1.92) \qquad\qquad (0.29) \end{array}$$

$$+ 2.321(\text{Ret } 60) + 0.971(\text{Ret } 2) \\ (4.06) \qquad\qquad (6.22)$$

$$+ \text{ industry and year} \qquad\qquad\qquad (5b) \\ \text{dummy variables}$$

The statistically insignificant coefficient of the relative issue size in Equation (5a) indicates that the decision on whether to reissue has no significant effect on the decision about how much to underprice ($t = 1.18$). Consistent with prior analysis, the brokerage prestige coefficient is positive and highly significant, indicating that firms going public with less reputable brokers show higher initial returns. Contrary to the implications of the signaling models, the coefficient of the initial return in Equation (5b) is negative and significant, indicating that the likelihood of seasoned equity offerings is inversely related to initial return. That is, IPO firms that are less underpriced are more likely to reissue equity and for larger amounts. The 60-day return and the two-year return coefficients are positive and significant, indicating that firms that perform well after the IPO tend to reissue more equity.[44]

The analysis reveals that the decision to reissue (or to pay dividends) is closely related to the firm's success in the market in its first years of public operation. Successful firms reissue (and pay dividends), and unsuccessful firms do not. On the other hand, our findings do not support the proposition that greater underpricing is associated with a higher likelihood of further reissuance of debt or equity.

Finally, we test the model's prediction that stocks with greater initial underpricing will experience a less unfavorable price reaction at the time of the seasoned equity issue. We account for management's superior information about the seasoned issue in the way described for Equations (3) and (4). The only difference is that the decision

---

[44] Unlike in the linear regression model, heteroskedasticity results in biased estimators in the Tobit regression. The system of Equations (5a) and (5b) is reestimated when the standard error of the Tobit model is assumed to be a function of the issue size and initial return [see, for example, Maddala (1983)] $\sigma_i^2 = \exp(\gamma + X\beta)^2$. The results of the heteroskedastic Tobit are quite similar to those of the homoskedastic model. The only difference is that the asymptotic t-ratio of the initial return in Equation (5b) has changed from -1.92 to -1.66. We repeat the entire analysis when the IPO proceeds and the amount of seasoned equity issues are adjusted for inflation. None of the results change. Jegadeesh, Weinstein, and Welch (1991) test the relationship between underpricing and subsequent equity issue using a Tobit model. Contrary to our findings, their analysis indicates that firms that underprice more are more likely to return to the market for subsequent seasoned equity offerings. However, they do not take into account the inherent simultaneity in the seasoned equity issuance decision as described in Equations (5a) and (5b) and in the text. When we run Equation (5b) by itself, we still find the initial return to be negative, but it is insignificantly different from zero ($t = -1.54$). Hence, the null hypothesis of no relationship between underpricing and subsequent issuance decisions cannot be rejected.

variable is whether to reissue equity (debt) instead of the dividend decision analyzed in Equation (3). We try to explain the three-day excess return around seasoned equity and debt offerings (Table 12, first and second rows) by the relative size of the seasoned offering, the log size of the seasoned issue, the initial underpricing, the interval between the IPO and the announcement of the seasoned issue, and Mill's ratio. Contrary to the model's prediction, when the dependent variable is the excess return around the seasoned equity announcement, the initial-return coefficient is negative and significant, implying that stocks with more underpricing experience a less favorable price reaction at the time of the seasoned equity issue. The seasoned issue size coefficient is negative, indicating that the market reacts more severely to larger issues. Both the relative size of the seasoned issue and the time coefficients are insignificant. The excess return around debt issue announcements (second regression in Table 12) is lower for larger seasoned issues ($t = -2.918$). The initial underpricing has no significant effect on the excess return around the debt announcement, and the time coefficient is positive but insignificant.

In summary, according to the signaling models, the decisions about the extent of the initial underpricing and the subsequent reissuance are made simultaneously, so we test for the relationship between these two variables using a set of simultaneous equations. Contrary to the model's prediction, we find that firms that underprice more tend to go to the reissue market less often and for lesser amounts. These results hold even after we control for several variables that are important in the underpricing decision, such as firm size, underwriter prestige, the year of the IPO, and industry affiliation. Finally we find no support for the models' assertion that firms that underprice more will experience less unfavorable price reactions when they issue seasoned equity.

2.3.3 Grinblatt and Hwang (1989). In this model, a firm employs two signals to convey the mean and variance of its future cash flow: the degree of underpricing and the fraction of shares held by insiders. We test three empirical implications of the model that are related to the interaction between insider holdings, the degree of underpricing, and the value of the firm.[45]

Implication 5A. The initial return on the IPO is positively related to the fraction held by insiders for a given variance level.

Implication 5B. Firm value is positively related to the degree of underpricing for a given fraction held by insiders.

---

[45] See Grinblatt and Hwang (1989, p. 415).

The Review of Financial Studies / v 7 n 2 1994

Table 12
The relationship of excess returns around the seasoned equity offering and selected variables

		Constant	Relative size of seasoned offering	Log SO	Initial return	Log time	Mill's ratio	$\bar{R}^2$	N
(1)	Equity	0.1582	0.0013	−0.0105	−0.0869	−0.0089	−0.064	.0218	197
		(2.240)	(0.707)	(−1.687)	(−2.563)	(−1.297)	(−1.526)		
(2)	Debt	−0.032	−0.0006	−0.0163	−0.032	0.0078	0.0281	.1638	70
		(−0.751)	(−1.596)	(−2.918)	(−0.499)	(1.384)	(1.695)		

The dependent variable is the excess return for the three days around the announcement of the first seasoned equity offering (first row), or debt issue (second row) within the first three years after the IPO. The explanatory variables are the size of the offering relative to the IPO, the log size of the seasonal issue (SO), the initial day return on the IPO, the time between the IPO and the seasoned equity offering announcement, and Mill's ratio estimated from the Probit model.

Table 13
Comparison of the percent held by insiders for nonfinancial IPOs in the years 1984–1988

	1 Initial return		2 Two-year excess return		3 IPO size		4 Brokerage prestige	
	Negative (or zero)	Positive	Negative	Positive	Small	Large	Low	High
Percent held by insiders	0.3873	0.3819	0.3869	0.3768	0.4367	0.3349	0.427	0.346
Number of observations	278	611	601	288	445	444	440	449
t-Statistics of the difference[1]		0.1924		0.377		4.077		3.22

In the first part of the table, we divide the IPO sample according to whether the first-day return is positive or negative. In the second part we divide the sample according to whether the two-year excess return is positive or negative. In the third part we partition the sample according to the IPO size, and in the fourth according to whether the issuing underwriter is in the high- or low-prestige group.
[1] When the assumption of equal variance between the two groups is rejected, test statistics are calculated under the assumption of an unequal variance.

Implication 5C. *Firm value is positively related to the degree of underpricing for a given variance level.*

Given our prior findings about the effect of brokerage prestige and size, we compare the amount held by insiders when the sample is partitioned into two groups according to (1) positive or negative initial return, (2) positive or negative two-year excess return, (3) IPO size (small/large), and (4) brokerage prestige (high/low). The statistics are reported in Table 13. There is no significant difference in the amount held by insiders between the positive and the negative initial-return groups: 38.2 percent and 38.7 percent. The amount held by insiders does not vary significantly with long-run performance: 38.7 percent and 37.7 for the negative and positive two-year excess return. However, there are significantly more insiders in the small IPO group: 43.7 percent compared with 33.5 percent in the large group, as well as in the low-prestige group, 42.7 percent compared with 34.6 percent in the high-prestige group.

Direct tests of Implications 5A, 5B, and 5C of the Grinblatt and Hwang model consist of three regressions, reported in Table 14. Implication 5A states that the initial return is positively related to the fraction held by insiders, given a variance level. Using the variance of the securities in the 60 days after the initial offering, we regress the initial return on the estimated variance and the fraction held by insiders. The coefficients for both the variance and insider holdings are insignificant, and there is no indication that the percentage of shares held by insiders has any significant power to explain the initial-day return, even when the variance is held constant. James and Wier

The Review of Financial Studies / v 7 n 2 1994

Table 14
Test of the Grinblatt and Hwang (1989) model

	(1) Dependent variable	(2) Intercept	(3) Variance	(4) Insiders	(5) Initial return	(6) Ad. R^2	(7) N
1	Initial return	0.0579 (8.338)	3.9770 (0.428)	−0.0061 (−0.423)		−.0005	545
2	2-year return	−0.1368 (−2.051)		0.0869 (0.598)	0.0431 (0.084)	−.0031	545
3	2-year return	−0.1308 (−2.829)	−22.3790 (−1.096)		0.2429 (0.725)	−.0004	850
4	2-year return	−0.1001 (−2.258)	−31.6530 (−1.623)	0.1168 (0.760)	0.0548 (0.112)	.0016	545

Regressions of initial-day return and two-year excess return on the firm's variance, fraction held by insiders, and initial return. Initial return is calculated using the offering price and the closing price on the first trading day. The firm's variance is calculated as the variance of returns for the 60 days immediately following the IPO. The fraction held by insiders is taken from the *Spectrum* books in the month following the IPO date. The variance matrix is estimated using White's (1980) procedure. *t*-Statistics are reported in parentheses.

(1990), using a sample of firms with close borrowing relationships with banks, find similar results. One might argue that in their sample insider holdings are less useful as an instrument to reveal information, because more information is already known to the outsiders (banks and their customers) through their prior dealings. This objection does not apply to our sample and we find the same result.

Implication 5B states that the value of the firm is positively related to the degree of underpricing for a given fraction held by insiders. We estimate the firm's value as the percentage change in its equity value from its second day of trading to the two-year trading date, calculated as the two-year excess return including dividends. The results in Table 14, row 2 show that neither the initial-day return nor the percentage held by insiders has significant power to explain the two-year return. Finally, Implication 5C states that given a variance level, the firm's value is related to the degree of underpricing. Regressing the initial-day underpricing and the 60-day variance on the two-year return indicates that the initial-day return does not have significant marginal power ($t = 0.112$) to explain the two-year return when variance is held constant.[46]

In summary, our results do not support the Grinblatt and Hwang (1989) model. The insider holdings variable has no significant power to explain the initial-day return even when variance is held constant. There is no evidence that insider holdings provide a credible signal of firm quality that reduces uncertainty and, therefore, initial under-

---

[46] When the variance of the firm is calculated over two years instead of 60 days, or when its value is measured over three years instead of two, the results are essentially the same.

pricing. Neither the initial-day return nor the fraction held by insiders seems to explain the value of the firm two years after it goes public.

3. Concluding Remarks

The basic question addressed in these tests is whether firms going public underprice to compensate uninformed investors who end up with a disproportionate share of the weaker IPOs, or to send a signal, albeit a costly one, of their underlying strength.

Our findings support the adverse-selection models that attribute underpricing to the presence of information asymmetries between outside informed and uninformed investors. When investors are relatively homogeneous, as for MLP IPOs, we do not find any underpricing. Even when we control for size, the line of business in which the firm operates, the prestige of its investment banker, and the fraction of equity held by insiders, we find that the underpricing is significantly less in the MLP IPO market, where the uninformed investors do not face a winner's-curse problem. Second, we demonstrate that underwriter quality lessens the need to underprice, apparently by reducing the information asymmetries. The link between underwriter quality and IPO quality is also demonstrated by the fact that IPOs issued by more prestigious underwriters perform better over the two years after the IPO. Finally, we show that the most prestigious underwriters generally avoid taking smaller IPOs to market. We show, however, that for a given level of prestige, larger IPOs with more diverse shareholders require a greater underpricing. This suggests that larger IPOs may be more difficult to market.

We find little support for the models suggesting that firms underprice to signal their quality or because they intend to return to the market with secondary security issues. Instead, we find that firms that underprice more have weaker future earnings performance, fewer dividend initiations and smaller dividends, and less frequent trips to the market with secondary equity and debt issues.

These results suggest several guidelines that may be of interest to financial managers and investors at large. First, firms that go public should not underprice their offering because they may be considering subsequent securities issues. There is no need to underprice to "go back to the well." Second, firms issued by more reputable investment banks are required to leave less money on the table than firms issued by less reputable investment banks (excluding fees). All else being equal, therefore, issuing firms should have an incentive to use prestigious investment banks. This incentive is reinforced by our finding that shares issued by more reputable investment banks perform significantly better in the long run.

The Review of Financial Studies / v 7 n 2 1994

Appendix: Master Limited Partnerships

The first master limited partnership (MLP) was created in 1981 when Apache Oil rolled up 33 oil and gas partnerships into a publicly traded company, Apache Petroleum. By June 30, 1987, 99 MLPs were traded on the NYSE and AMEX. MLPs have generally been created in two ways. In the first, an entire corporation is converted into a partnership. In this case, the shareholders swap the stock they own in the corporation for limited ownership units in the MLP. The second and more popular method is for a corporation to spin off one line of business into an MLP. It then pays units in the new MLP as a dividend on its own stock or alternatively sells the units directly to the public.

In most instances, the sponsoring corporation maintains an interest in the MLP as the general partner. As general partner, the corporation receives a fee for operating the MLP. Virtually all of the remaining income (usually 99 percent) is credited to the partnership accounts of the limited partners. Most MLPs operate in two industries, oil and gas and real estate. One unique characteristic of the MLPs is that they are aggressively marketed on the basis of a high dividend yield, usually around 12 percent per annum, compared with an average 2 percent for corporations in the same industries.

From a corporate control standpoint, MLPs offer certain advantages to the general partner. All of the operating control is vested with the general partner. MLP unitholders have no vote on decisions made or on the makeup of the board of directors. Even if one person owned all the units of the MLP, he could not remove the general partner. In other words, a hostile takeover of an MLP is not feasible.

The advantages of the partnership structure are primarily tax motivated. First, the MLP does not pay a tax at the entity level. Instead, each limited partner pays tax at his own personal income tax rate on his share of the MLP's taxable income, computed on the basis of his ownership percentage. Second, since the unitholder pays tax on the income earned, any dividend received is not taxed. Therefore, the partnership escapes the double taxation of income incurred by corporations. Also, the tax incurred is at the personal rate, which since 1986 has been lower than the corporate rate.

There are some potential tax-related pitfalls in having a business classified as an MLP. First, the unitholder must pay tax on his share of the MLPs income even if no dividends are paid. Second, since 1988, if the MLP generates a loss, the loss cannot offset income from other ventures the unitholder is involved in. The losses can only be carried forward to offset future income from that MLP. Finally, since the income from MLPs is classified as unrelated business income for tax-exempt entities, normally non-tax-paying entities such as pension funds must pay tax on earnings from MLPs they own. Corporations also do not get a dividends-received exclusion on income from MLPs. In contrast, 70 percent or more of dividends from corporations are excluded from income.

The units of MLPs have primarily been owned by individual investors, in part because of this unfavorable tax treatment of corporate and tax-exempt unitholders. MLPs are generally structured with only one line of business, usually with a passive income source such as royalties or rents. The Revenue Act of 1987 guarantees this type of structure will remain in the future. Any MLPs created after December 17, 1987, will be taxed as corporations unless that have only one passive line of business. Any existing MLPs that add a new line of business will lose their partnership designation. Also, in 1997 all MLPs except those with a passive line of business will lose their partnership taxation status.

References

Allen, F., and G. Faulhaber, 1989, "Signaling by Underpricing in the IPO Market," *Journal of Financial Economics*, 23, 303–323.

Amemiya, Takeshi, 1979, "The Estimation of a Simultaneous Equation Tobit Model," *International Economic Review*, 20, 169–181.

Asquith, P., and D. W. Mullins, Jr., 1986, "Equity Issues and Offering Dilution," *Journal of Financial Economics*, 15, 61–89.

Baron, D., 1982, "A Model of the Demand for Investment Banking Advising and Distribution Services for New Issues," *Journal of Finance*, 37, 955–976.

Beatty, R., and J. Ritter, 1986, "Investment Banking, Reputation and the Underpricing of Initial Public Offerings," *Journal of Financial Economics*, 15, 213–232.

Belsley, D., E. Kuh, and R. E. Welsch, *Regression Diagnostics*, Wiley, New York, 1980.

Benveniste, L., and P. Spindt, 1989, "How Investment Bankers Determine the Offer Price and Allocation of New Issues," *Journal of Financial Economics*, 24, 343–362.

Benveniste, L., and W. Wilhelm, 1990, "A Comparative Analysis of IPO Proceeds under Alternative Regulatory Environments," *Journal of Financial Economics*, 28, 173–208.

Booth, J., and R. Smith, 1986, "Capital Raising, Underwriting and the Certification Hypothesis," *Journal of Financial Economics*, 15, 261–281.

Carter, R., and S. Manaster, 1990, "Initial Public Offering and Underwriter Reputation," *Journal of Finance*, 45, 1045–1067.

Eckbo, B. E., 1986, "Valuation Effects of Corporate Debt Offerings," *Journal of Financial Economics*, 15, 119–151.

Eckbo, B. E., V. Maksimovic, and J. Williams, 1990, "Consistent Estimation of Cross-Sectional Models in Event Studies," *Review of Financial Studies*, 3, 343–365.

Grinblatt, M., and C. Hwang, 1989, "Signaling and the Pricing of New Issues," *Journal of Finance*, 44, 393–420.

The Review of Financial Studies / v 7 n 2 1994

Grossman, S., and O. Hart, 1980, "Takeover Bids, The Free Rider Problem and the Theory of the Corporation," *Bell Journal of Economics,* Spring, 42–64.

Hughes, P., and A. Thakor, 1992, "Litigation Risk, Intermediation, and the Underpricing of Initial Public Offerings," *The Review of Financial Studies,* 5, 709–742.

Ibbotson, R., 1975, "Price Performance of Common Stock New Issues," *Journal of Financial Economics,* 2, 235–272.

Ibbotson, R., and J. Jaffe, 1975, "Hot Issue Markets," *Journal of Finance,* 30, 1027–1042.

Ibbotson, R., J. Sindelar, and J. Ritter, 1988, "Initial Public Offerings," *Journal of Applied Corporate Finance,* V1, 37–45.

James, C., and P. Wier, 1990, "Borrowing Relationships, Intermediation, and the Cost of Issuing Public Securities," *Journal of Financial Economics,* 28, 149–173.

Jegadeesh, N., M. Weinstein, and I. Welch, 1993, "An Empirical Investigation of IPO Underpricing and Subsequent Equity Offerings," *Journal of Financial Economics,* 34, 153–175.

Koh, F., and T. Walter, 1989, "A Direct Test of Rock's Model of the Pricing of Unseasoned Issues," *Journal of Financial Economics,* 23, 251–272.

Kreps, D., 1990, *A Course in Microeconomic Theory,* Princeton University Press, Princeton, NJ.

Leland, H., and D. Pyle, 1977, "Information Asymmetries, Financial Structure and Financial Inter-mediation," *Journal of Finance,* 32, 371–387.

Logue, D., 1973, "On the Pricing of Unseasoned Equity Issues, 1965–69," *Journal of Financial and Quantitative Analysis,* 8, 91–103.

Maddala, G., 1983, *Limited Dependent and Qualitative Variables in Econometrics,* Cambridge University Press, London and New York.

Masulis, R. W., and A. N. Korwar, 1986, "Seasoned Equity Offerings: An Empirical Investigation," *Journal of Financial Economics,* 15, 91–118.

Michaely, R., R. Thaler, and J. K. Womack, 1994, "Price Reactions to Dividend Initiation and Omissions, Overreaction or Drift?" working paper, Cornell University.

Mikkelson, W. H., and M. M. Partch, 1986, "Valuation Effects of Security Offerings: An Empirical Investigation," *Journal of Financial Economics,* 15, 31–60.

Muscarella, C., 1988, "Price Performance of Master Limited Partnership Units," *The Financial Review,* 23, 513–521.

Muscarella, C., and M. Vetsuypens, 1989, "The Underpricing of 'Second' Initial Public Offerings," *Journal of Financial Research,* 12, 183–192.

Ritter, J., 1984, "The 'Hot Issue' Market of 1980," *Journal of Business,* 57, 215–241.

Ritter, J., 1987, "The Costs of Going Public," *Journal of Financial Economics,* 19, 269–282.

Ritter, J., 1991, "The Long-Run Performance of Initial Public Offerings," *Journal of Finance,* 46, 3–27.

Rock, K., 1986, "Why New Issues are Underpriced," *Journal of Financial Economics,* 15, 187–212.

Schipper, K., and A. Smith, 1986, "A Comparison of Equity Carve-outs and Seasoned Equity Offerings: Share Price Effect and Corporate Restructuring," *Journal of Financial Economics,* 15, 153–186.

Shleifer, A., and R. Vishny, 1986, "Large Shareholders and Corporate Control," *Journal of Political Economy,* 94, 461–488.

Smith, C., Jr., 1986, "Investment Banking and the Capital Acquisition Process," *Journal of Financial Economics,* 15, 3–29.

Pricing Initial Public Offerings

Tinic, S., 1988, "Anatomy of Initial Public Offerings of Common Stock," *Journal of Finance*, 43, 789–822.

Wang, K., S. H. Chan, and G. Gau, 1992, "Initial Public Offerings of Equity Securities: Anomalous Evidence Using REITs," *Journal of Financial Economics*, 31, 381–410.

Welch, I., 1989, "Seasoned Offerings, Imitation Costs and the Underpricing of Initial Public Offerings," *Journal of Finance*, 44, 421–449.

White, H., 1980, "A Heteroscedasticity Consistent Covaraince Matrix Estimator and a Direct Test of Heteroscedasticity," *Econometrica* 48, 817–838.

[9]

Journal of Financial Economics 23 (1989) 251-272. North-Holland

G12

A DIRECT TEST OF ROCK'S MODEL OF THE PRICING OF UNSEASONED ISSUES*

Francis KOH

National University of Singapore

Terry WALTER

University of Sydney, Sydney, NSW, 2006 Australia

Received December 1987, final version received October 1988

Unique data availability and institutional arrangements for new issues in Singapore allow a direct test of the empirical implications of Rock's model of pricing unseasoned new issues. Our empirical results are consistent with the model. Specifically we find that the unseasoned new issues' anomaly disappears when the rationing associated with new issues is incorporated into the analysis. The winner's curse is evident in allocation patterns used in Singapore.

1. Introduction

That unseasoned new issues are underpriced is well documented in the empirical finance literature.[1] This paper directly tests Rock's (1986) model, which explains why, in equilibrium, new issues are underpriced. The crucial empirical test of Rock's model involves observing the extent to which shares are rationed on the offer date. If the model is correct, weighting the returns by the probabilities of obtaining an allocation should leave the uninformed investor earning the riskless rate [Rock (1986, p. 205)]. Such a test has not been conducted previously because the necessary data are generally not available. The unique institutional arrangements governing the new issues market in Singapore, however, which make evidence on rationing publicly available, permit a direct test.

In Rock's model rationing per se is insufficient to explain underpricing; it is also necessary to show that rationing occurs more often for 'good' than for 'bad' shares. This winner's curse causes an uninformed investor to lower his

---

*This paper has benefited from comments of participants at a research workshop at the Australian Graduate School of Management. The comments and suggestions of Alan Farley, Kevin Rock (the referee), and Clifford Smith (the editor) were especially helpful.

[1]See, for example, Ibbotson (1975), Ibbotson and Jaffe (1975), Ritter (1984), and Finn and Higham (1986). See Smith (1986) for a review of this literature.

valuation of new issues because informed demand makes the probability of receiving an allocation lower for underpriced (i.e., positive initial-listing-day excess returns) than for overpriced (i.e., negative initial-listing-day excess returns) new issues. Accordingly, uninformed investors withdraw from the market until the issue price falls sufficiently to compensate them for the bias in allocation. The model predicts an equilibrium offer price that includes a finite discount to attract uninformed investors to the issue.[2]

Beatty and Ritter (1986) extend Rock's analysis and show that equilibrium for informed investors occurs when the cost of information search equals the expected gain from applications for underpriced new issues. Uninformed investors' equilibrium exists when the expected losses associated with applications for overpriced issues equal the expected gains from applications for underpriced issues.

An appendix describes in detail the institutional arrangements for new issues in Singapore. A key feature of this market is that the basis used for rationing when issues are oversubscribed is disclosed publicly. The balloting of issues (i.e., a random selection from all applications) takes place in public and is evenhanded in the sense that all applications of a particular size have an equal probability of being accepted. These procedures ensure that applicants for a particular number of shares face a fair game.

Singapore operates under the general principles of British company law. New shares can be issued to the public when accompanied by a prospectus registered with the relevant statutory authority. The prospectus details the number of shares to be issued and the issue price, neither of which can be changed during the course of the issue. A prospectus in Singapore is typically issued three to four weeks before the applications closing date and there are further three to four weeks before initial stock-exchange listing. Thus the issuer is committed to a price decided on in advance over a lengthy period. In addition, the prospectus sets out information to enable an investor to evaluate the offer, including the purposes of the issue, historical accounting and other information related to the issuing company, a one-year-ahead earnings forecast by directors (with auditor comments), other statutory information (for example, details of material contracts), and prescribed reports (i.e., the directors', accountants', valuers', and auditors').

Our empirical tests confirm the major empirical implications of Rock's theory. First, uninformed investors' returns on the difference between subscription and first-day listing prices are not statistically different from the riskless rate. Rationing of new issues explains the unseasoned new issues' anomaly. Second, the winner's curse is strongly evident. Third, our results

---

[2]For a discussion of why an issuer would want to attract uninformed investor participation see Rock (1986, p. 195). Issues in Singapore may require uninformed participation to meet stock-exchange listing requirements. These are described in the appendix.

show that there is a significant positive correlation between oversubscription
levels and first-day returns. Further, if the size of an application is a reasonable proxy for the distinction between informed and uninformed investors,
additional results consistent with the model are obtained. Informed investors
are found to respond to greater expected underpricing by expanding demand.
This demand expansion is consistent with rationality in the new-issues market,
and is contrary to the frequently expressed view that this market is driven by
fads. Fourth, the results hold when the new issues are categorized by underwriter and size.

2. Data and methods

2.1. Data

Details of all new issues since the incorporation of the Singapore Stock
Exchange (SSE) in 1973 listed on the SSE before June 1987 are extracted from
monthly SSE journals. Seventy new issues result. We search the files for these
70 companies at the SSE library to extract the details of the allocation basis
adopted and find data for 48 issues. Before 1980 few firms routinely filed these
details with the exchange. A comprehensive search is made of the daily
business newspapers (the *Business Times* and the *Straits Time*) for the period
between the application-closing date stated in the prospectus and the listing
date. This produces data on the allocation basis for a further ten issues. We
call the remaining companies and their underwriters for the data (with
subsequent written confirmation of the request), and establish a further eight
data points. Thus, for 66 of the 70 firms we are able to establish information
on the allocation system adopted. This allows us to calculate the probability of
an allocation, conditional on the size of an application, for each issue.

Other data are relevant to our experiment. First-day sales prices (high, low,
and last sale) are extracted from the daily trading summaries of the SSE. The
issue price per share, the number of shares offered, the underwriter and the
applications-close date are collected from the prospectus. The risk-free rate of .
interest and the prime rate prevailing during this listing lag (i.e., applications-
close date to listing) are extracted from publications of the Monetary Authority of Singapore (MAS).

2.2. Method

Our approach is to simulate the returns produced by applying for various
lots in each new issue. A lot is 1,000 shares and our results model the returns
for application strategies in the range of 1 to 1,000 lots.

Our aim is to test Rock's implication that the uninformed investor should
earn the risk-free rate, conditional on the rationing process associated with

various issues and ranges of application. We assume that a mechanical strategy of applying for n lots in each new issue is consistent with being uninformed.

When an application is made for shares in a new issue in Singapore a real payment must be made. After the company has determined the successful applicants, application monies are refunded to unsuccessful applicants. This may involve a complete refund if the applicant is balloted out or a partial refund when pro-rata allocations are made. The period for which funds are tied up depends on the size of the application (large refunds are processed earlier), the pattern and level of subscriptions received (the clerical effort), the speed of the postal service, and the efficiency of the underwriter. Discussions with underwriters suggest that this period averages between four days (for large investors) and ten days (for small investors), though there are cross-sectional differences due to the factors mentioned above. We assume that funds are tied up in accord with the following:

$$T_s = 10 - (n_s \cdot 6/1{,}000)$$

where T_s is the time in days and n_s the number of lots applied for, where $s = 1, \ldots, 1{,}000$.

As we show in the next section, our analysis can bear this assumption. We assume each application involves an opportunity interest cost of 2% above prime, calculated for the period funds are tied up as defined above. Fixed costs of the application are assumed to be S\$5, and represent the cost of obtaining a banker's draft, postage costs, and other application processing costs. Brokerage is ignored.

These cost assumptions are based on average conditions prevailing in the market. They are obviously arbitrary for individual issues. The results are driven, however, not by the way we model the cost of the application, but by the probability of receiving an allocation.

3. Results

Fig. 1 presents the normal unseasoned-new-issues experiment results. Returns (X) for the 66 issues (i) and 1,000 strategies (s) are defined as follows:

$$X_{i,s} = \ln\left[\frac{P_i \cdot N_s - I_{i,s} - FC}{S_i \cdot N_s}\right] - R_i,$$

where

$X_{i,s}$ = return for issue i and strategy s measured from the applications-close date to the initial-listing date,
P_i = last sale price for issue i on the first day of trading,
N_s = number of shares applied for in strategy s,
$I_{i,s}$ = interest cost associated with the application for issue i and strategy s,
FC = fixed cost of an application,
S_i = subscription price for issue i stated in the prospectus,

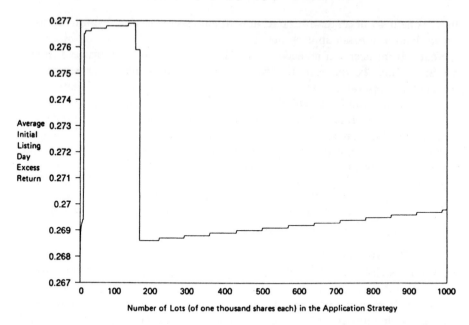

Fig. 1. Average initial-listing-day excess return for 66 new issues made between January 1973 and June 1987 on the Singapore Stock Exchange for investment strategies in the range of one to 1,000 lots (of 1,000 shares each) on the assumption that no rationing occurs. The estimated *t*-statistics that these excess returns are greater than zero are in the range of 4.01 to 4.24.

R_i = continuously compounded risk-free return over the period from application to listing for issue i.

These returns are then averaged for the sample of 66 issues for which we have data.

The assumption in fig. 1 is that a full allocation of the requested shares is granted, though we incorporate the cost of an application (i.e., interest costs and fixed costs) as described in the previous section.

Irrespective of the investment strategy adopted, the unseasoned new issues' anomaly is present in fig. 1. Returns of approximately 27% above the risk-free rate (with associated *t*-statistics of greater than 4.0) are obtained.[3, 4] There is a

---

[3] The *t*-statistics on the excess returns differing from zero must be interpreted cautiously because the distribution of excess returns is generally skewed toward positive returns. We calculated skewness and kurtosis coefficients for our excess-return distributions, and although these suggest departures from a normal distribution, the extent of the departure is insufficient to reject the use of a *t*-statistic.

[4] Skewness coefficients for fig. 1 returns are in the range of 0.86 to 0.92 and suggest the distribution is skewed to positive returns. At this stage we are assuming that rationing does not operate in allocations of new issues and accordingly induce positive skewness.

slight benefit associated with larger-investment strategies because of the assumed fixed cost of an application.[5]

What returns accrue if no account is taken of cost? The short answer is that they are essentially identical to those in fig. 1, so a full figure is not presented. In summary these are:

1–10	lots returns of 0.274,	with t-statistics of 4.19,
11–154	lots returns of 0.281,	with t-statistics of 4.29,
155–162	lots returns of 0.280,	with t-statistics of 4.22,
163–1,000	lots returns of 0.273,	with t-statistics of 4.07.

The cost of application explains a difference in returns of less than $\frac{1}{2}$ of 1 percent. As we show below, incorporating rationing has a far more dramatic effect.

Fig. 2 presents probabilities of receiving an allocation conditional on an application size of 1,000 to 1 million shares, for new issues on the SSE. Three proportions are plotted. The first relate to all new issues for which data are available, the second covers the underpriced issues (ex post identification), and the third covers the overpriced issues (again identified ex post). Three points emerge. First the data reveal a systematic preference in the allocation system for small investors.[6] Across all issues the probability of an allocation when 1,000 shares are applied for is 0.35, which is more than twice the probability of success (0.16) when 1 million shares are sought. Second, the winner's curse is evident in that the chance of an allocation in overpriced issues is more than three times the chance of an allocation in underpriced issues. Third, underpriced issues ($n = 57$) are far more common than overpriced issues ($n = 9$). However, an investor's ability to exploit this underpricing to secure the returns apparent in fig. 1 is reduced because, as fig. 2 clearly shows, investors, on average, are allocated higher proportions of the losers.[7] In addition, the costs of an application are ignored. Applications for new issues on the SSE must be accompanied by payment of a cash equivalent (i.e., a banker's draft, cashier's order, etc.) and thus there is an opportunity loss associated with placing these funds with the issuer.

---

[5] The discontinuities in these results at 11, 155, and 163 lots are caused by three issues in which the maximum allowable application size was 10, 154, and 162 lots, respectively. These limits were imposed to comply with regulations that limit the maximum individual shareholding in newspaper companies (two cases) and in a chemical company.

[6] The subscription price for the issues in this study is in the range of S$1 to S$5, with a mean of S$1.76. S$2.1 equals approximately US$1, so an application for one lot involves an amount of approximately US$840.

[7] It is interesting to note that only three of these issues were undersubscribed, while six were oversubscribed. The average oversubscription for these six was, however, only 3.1 times, compared to 29.4 times for the total sample.

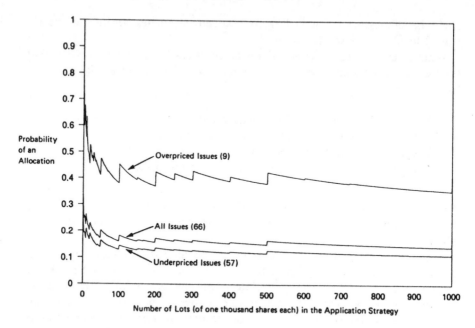

Fig. 2. Probability of receiving an allocation of shares in 66 new issues made between January 1973 and June 1987 on the Singapore Stock Exchange for investment strategies in the range of one to 1,000 lots (of 1,000 shares each) and subdivisions according to whether the issue was underpriced (57 issues) or overpriced (9 issues).

The allocation bias also depends on the extent of underpricing, although these results are not reported in fig. 2. The probability of receiving an allocation in new issues where the excess return is positive but less than 30 percent is in the range of 0.48 (for an application for one lot) to 0.23 (for 1,000 lots). The corresponding probabilities for issues with initial returns greater than 30 percent are 0.16 and 0.06, respectively, less than one third the size.

Fig. 3 results plot average returns (after incorporating rationing and application costs) against the number of lots in the application strategy. Returns ($X_{i,s}$) are calculated as follows,[8] and these are then summed and averaged for

---

[8] Rock argues that the overall return should be formed by weighting the individual return, given an allocation, by the probability of receiving an allocation. For example. if there is only one issue, which rises 40 percent on the first day, and there is a 50 percent chance of a successful application, the return is defined as 0.5 ln(1.4). Our definition is slightly different and calculates the return as ln[1 + (0.5 × 0.4)]. We use this definition to more easily keep track of the costs associated with various application strategies. In any event the results are essentially the same. The alternative return metric suggested by Rock produces average returns in the range of 1.1 percent (one lot) to −1.4 percent (99 lots). None of these are estimated to be significant.

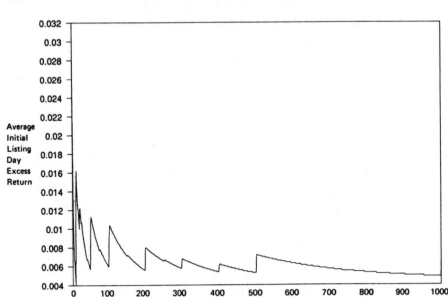

Fig. 3. Average initial-listing-day excess return for 66 new issues made between January 1973 and June 1987 on the Singapore Stock Exchange for investment strategies in the range of one to 1,000 lots (of 1,000 shares each) after incorporating the actual rationing process adopted in each new issue. The estimated *t*-statistics that these excess returns are greater than zero are all less than 1.0 with the exception of that for an investment strategy of one lot, where the estimated *t*-statistic is 1.51

the sample for each strategy,

$$X_{i,s} = \ln\left[\frac{P_i \cdot a_{i,s} + S_i(N_s - a_{i,s}) - I_{i,s} - FC}{S_i \cdot N_s}\right] - R_i$$

where $a_{i,s}$ is the allocation received in issue i for strategy s, and other terms are as previously defined.

These results are in marked contrast to fig. 1. Average returns are in the range of 3.12 percent (one lot) to 0.49 percent (999 lots). The jumps in the average returns in fig. 2 are caused by changes in the probability of allocation at certain round lot sizes that issuing companies frequently use to ration shares in oversubscribed issues. No application strategy produces returns significantly different from zero. Only one *t*-statistic exceeds one: the *t*-statistic on the return associated with the strategy of applying for 1,000 shares in each new

Table 1

Correlations between initial-listing-day excess returns and the application and allocation patterns in 38 new issues made between January 1973 and June 1987 on the Singapore Stock Exchange for which sufficient data exist to split total applications and allocations into subcategories based on application size.

Correlations between proportions applied for or allocated to investors and initial-listing-day excess returns	Demand by investors applying for			
	1,000 shares (i.e., small investors)	2,000 to 99,000 shares (i.e., medium/ small investors)	100,000 to 249,000 shares (i.e., medium investors)	250,000 shares or more (i.e., large investors)
Proportions applied for	−0.888	−0.363[a]	−0.030	0.275[a]
Proportions allocated to	−0.064	−0.415[a]	0.173	0.357[a]

[a] Significant at 5 percent level, one-tailed test.

issue is 1.51.[9] Adopting this strategy would have produced 54 positive returns and only 12 negative returns. Recall however from fig. 2 that the probability of receiving an allocation of overpriced securities is approximately three times that of receiving an allocation in underpriced securities, and thus statistical significance would be overstated by using a binomial test on the sign of the initial return.

Table 1 provides additional evidence on the bias in the allocation system faced by the uninformed investor. Thirty-eight of the 66 new issues provide sufficient data for this test. We are concerned with the question of whether large- or small-investor applications and allotment patterns differ for issues that are over- and underpriced. If the size of an investor's application is a reasonable proxy for his information, Rock's analysis suggests there should be a negative correlation between underpricing and the proportion of an issue subscribed for and allocated to small (uninformed) investors. This association is caused where informed investors withdraw from overpriced issues (negative initial-listing-day excess returns) and thus cause a high proportion of the issue to go to the uninformed, but swamp the underpriced issues with applications (positive initial-listing-day excess returns) and thus cause a low proportion of the issue to go to the uninformed. Conversely, the large (informed) investors should dominate the underpriced hot issues, leading to a positive correlation between underpricing and the proportion of the issue they apply for and receive. Finally, general market response to underpricing should be evidenced by a strong correlation between oversubscription levels and underpricing.

[9] Skewness coefficients for fig. 3 are in the range of −0.11 to 0.72 and suggest returns are generally positively skewed.

The average underpricing for the 38 issues for which sufficient data exist to determine both application and allotment patterns is 34.7 percent. These issues are on average oversubscribed 40 times, with a range of 2.2 to 248.1. The Spearman rank correlation between oversubscription levels and initial-day returns is 0.951, which is significant at 1 percent.

In general the correlations in table 1 are significant and in the expected direction. There is a negative correlation of -0.088 between the proportion of an issue applied for by small investors and initial-day returns. This negative correlation is much more pronounced and is statistically significant (the correlation of -0.363 is significant at 5 percent) for medium/small investors. Small investors' application strategies tend to be inversely related to the success of the issue. Recall however that there is a systematic preference in the allocation system for small investors and that on average new issues are underpriced. These factors produce a lower negative correlation (-0.064) for small investors between allocated proportions and returns than between application proportions and returns. Small (naive) investors' application strategies are cushioned by the allocation process.[10] The applications of large investors are positively and significantly correlated (0.275) with the issues outcome, as expected. Large investors follow wealth-increasing application strategies at the small investors' expense.[11]

These correlations do not perfectly capture the responsiveness of investors in the various size categories to expected underpricing. The highly significant correlation between oversubscription levels and initial-listing-day excess returns is not driven solely by demand from a particular class or category of investor; rather, it is a phenomenon that pervades the applications of all investor classes. It is less pronounced, however, for small investors and more pervasive for large investors.

Table 2 explores the issue of investor responsiveness in more detail. Using the same size-of-application definitions for small and large investors employed in table 1, we calculate the proportion that total shares applied for by investors in each category bears to the total shares offered. This proportion is used as the dependent variable in four regressions (i.e., four size-of-application investor categories) in which initial-day returns are the independent variable. The dependent variable, which is a subscription rate by category, is a measure of the extent to which investors in a particular size-of-application class are

---

[10] There is always the possibility that informed investors might attempt to take advantage of the preferential allocations afforded small applicants by breaking up their purchases into smaller lot sizes. Indeed this practice occurred in the early years of the SSE. It is now illegal, however, to submit multiple applications. Further, the prospectus states that all applications by an investor are declared void when an investor submits multiple applications. The evidence in table 1 is consistent with relatively little 'gaming' of the allocation mechanism by informed investors.

[11] The results in fig. 1 are insensitive to different definitions of boundaries for application strategy size.

Table 2

Regression results for four regressions that employ the initial-listing-day return as the independent variable and subscription level achieved within various subcategories of the total application pool as the dependent variable for 38 new issues made between January 1973 and June 1987 on the Singapore Stock Exchange for which sufficient data exist to split total applications into various subcategories based on application size.

Regression results and related statistics	Demand by investors applying for			
	1,000 shares (i.e., small investors)	2,000 to 99,000 shares (i.e., medium/ small investors)	100,000 to 249,000 shares (i.e., medium investors)	250,000 shares or more (i.e., large investors)
Estimated coefficient	10.102	13.234	23.112	93.408
T-ratio	4.582	5.355	5.071	5.195
R-square	0.368	0.443	0.417	0.428
T-ratio on difference between the coefficient for large investors and other categories	4.599	4.418	3.790	—

able to respond to actual levels of underpricing. Small-investor class definitions serve as a proxy for uninformed demand. The theory predicts that the estimated coefficient on small-investor subscription levels, which is a measure of how responsive these investors are to actual underpricing, should be smaller than the estimated coefficient on larger-investor categories. We also calculate and report a t-statistic on the difference between the estimated coefficient for the large-investor definition and smaller-investor definitions.

The evidence in table 2 is striking. Although small investors are responsive to greater underpricing (the estimated coefficient, 10.102, is positive and significant, $t = 4.582$), they are far less responsive than larger investors (coefficient of 93.408, $t = 5.195$). Returns in these regressions are defined as the natural log of first-day price over subscription price; thus a coefficient of 10.102 implies that small investors will increase their applications by 10.102 percent for each 1 percent underpricing.[12] By contrast large investors are approximately nine times as responsive. The t-statistic on the differences in the estimated small- and large-investor-group coefficient is 4.599. The sensitivity with which large investors respond to underpricing is evidence consistent with rational behavior in the initial-public-offer (IPO) market. This contrasts with

---

[12] Rock (1986, p. 185) argues that it is essential to establish that uninformed demand expands as issue price is reduced because unless an issuer can increase the chance of a full subscription in any state of the world by attracting uninformed investors to the offering, there is no point whatsoever in pricing the shares at a discount. This evidence is consistent with demand expansion by uninformed investors.

the position of many commentators who view the IPO market as being dominated by fads.

These regression results can be used to estimate a subscription price which is sufficiently low to ensure that uninformed demand alone will fully subscribe the issue.[13] In the Rock model a rational issuer would not price an issue below the price at which uninformed demand alone will fully subscribe the issue, so the analysis below can be seen as an additional test of the descriptive validity of Rock's model in Singapore.

Our data allow us to calculate total investor demand for these 38 issues, and to split this into informed and uninformed demand by assuming that the size of an application is a reasonable proxy for an investor's access to information about an issue. We initially take the strictest definition of an uninformed investor our data allow us to make, that is, we define uninformed investors to be only those who apply for 1,000 shares. If observed uninformed demand is less than the total issue, the price at which uninformed investors alone will fully subscribe the issue must be below the actual subscription price, i.e., the underpricing was insufficient to attract uninformed demand to subscribe the issue fully. There are six cases in this category. For the 32 other cases we estimate the price at which uninformed demand alone will fully subscribe the issue by employing the following methods.

Across all issues, uninformed demand by investors in the smallest application category for a new issue expands by 10.102 percent for each 1 percent of underpricing. We work back from the first-day (observed) market price to an estimate of the full-subscription price by reducing the market price by e^x percent, where x equals

$$\frac{(\text{Uninformed Demand} - \text{Issue Size})}{\text{Issue Size}} \bigg/ 10.102.$$

For example, Sing Investments and Finance Limited offered 5 million shares at \$S2.50 per share. Sing's last sale on the first day of trading was \$S3.20. Applications for 1,000 shares were received from 18,740 investors; thus uninformed demand was 18.74 million, 3.748 times the issue size. Using the above formula we calculate

$$x = [(18,740 - 5,000)/5,000]/10.102 = [2.748]/10.102 = 0.272.$$

Thus a 27.2 percent level of underpricing would produce uninformed demand equal to the total issue. We estimate the price at which uninformed demand alone will fully subscribe the issue to be \$S3.20$/e^{0.272}$ = \$S3.20/1.313 = \$S2.43. This is below the actual issue price and thus consistent with rational issuer behavior. Adopting this definition of uninformed demand produces 20 out of

---

[13] This price is called the 'full-subscription' price by Rock.

Table 3

Number of issues where the uninformed demand alone fully subscribes the issue for alternative levels of uninformed demand (in lots of 1,000 shares) for 38 issues made between January 1973 and June 1987 on the Singapore Stock Exchange.

Critical level of uninformed demand in lots of 1,000 shares	Number of issues where uninformed demand alone fully subscribes the issue
1	20[a]
10	29
11	30
12	31
15	32
21	34
50	38[b]

[a] Using the strictest definition of uninformed demand allowed by our data produces 20 (out of 38) cases which are consistent with rational issuer behavior.

[b] All 38 issues are characterized by rational issuer behavior if uninformed demand includes applications up to 50,000 shares.

38 estimates of the price at which uninformed demand alone fully subscribes the issue that are less than the actual issue price, that is, consistent with rational issue behavior. By loosening the definition of uninformed demand to include larger applications for the 18 inconsistent issues, we calculate the cut-off size of an application that would need to be included as a component of uninformed demand to produce an estimated price at which uninformed demand alone fully subscribes the issue which is below the issue price. These larger applications are divided by 13.234, which is the estimate of increase in demand by investors in the range of 2,000 to 99,000 shares per 1 percent of underpricing (see table 2). Table 3 contains these critical levels of uninformed demand.

It can be seen that all 38 issues are rationally priced providing uninformed demand is defined to include investors applying for up to 50,000 shares.[14] Such a definition is necessary in four cases. These four issues represent U.S. dollar applications ranging between approximately $25,000 and $80,000. Twenty-nine issues are consistent with the Rock model when uninformed demand is defined as applications for up to 10,000 shares (US$5,000–US$16,000).

Figs. 4 and 5 are subdivisions of the results in fig. 3. Fig. 4 breaks the sample up by underwriter, and fig. 5 looks at the question of an association between initial returns and issue size.

[14] A potential way to discriminate between informed and uninformed investors is to rely on the correlation data in table 1. These suggest that investors who submit orders for less than 50,000 shares are (comparatively) uninformed because the adverse selection effect is most severe for this group.

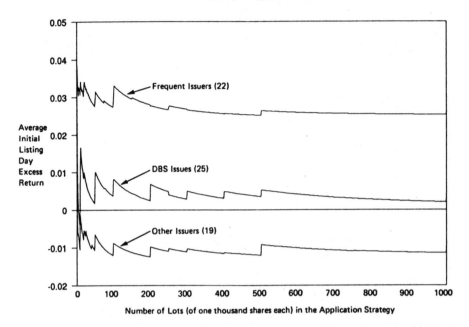

Fig. 4. Average initial-listing-day excess return for 66 new issues made between January 1973 and June 1987 on the Singapore Stock Exchange split by underwriter identity into 25 issues underwritten by the Development Bank of Singapore, Ltd. (DBS), 22 issues underwritten by Wardley Limited, United Chase Merchant Bankers Limited, and Singapore International Merchant Bank Limited (frequent issuers), and 19 issues underwritten by others (other issuers) for investment strategies in the range of one to 1,000 lots (of 1,000 shares each) after incorporating the actual rationing process adopted in each new issue. The estimated t-statistics that these excess returns are greater than zero are (i) all less than 1.2 for the DBS issues, (ii) in the range of 1.01 to 1.54 for the frequent issuers, and (iii) all less than 0.13 and generally negative for the other issuers.

The Development Bank of Singapore Ltd. (DBS) underwrote or jointly underwrote 25 new issues during the period studied. As revealed in fig. 4, a strategy of investing in DBS issues would not have produced statistically significant excess returns. The 22 issues underwritten by the 'Frequent Issuers' (United Chase Merchant Bankers Limited, Singapore International Merchant Bank Limited, and Wardley Limited) generally produce positive returns of 2.5 to 3 percent, but again these are insignificant at conventional levels.[15] 'Other Issuers' ($n = 19$) returns are generally insignificantly negative. Taken together, fig. 4 results reveal some underwriter effect [consistent with Beatty and Ritter (1986)], but this effect is not substantial.

Fig. 5 splits the sample by size of issue into the 22 largest, the next 22, and the smallest 22 issues. Although this subdivision again does not reveal signifi-

---

[15] These return distributions are highly positively skewed and cast doubt on the appropriateness of t-statistics.

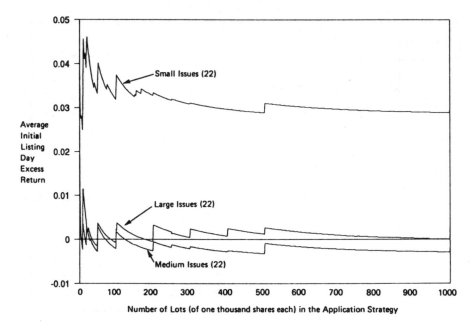

Fig. 5. Average initial-listing-day excess return for 66 new issues made between January 1973 and June 1987 on the Singapore Stock Exchange split by size of the issue into the 22 largest issues, the medium issues, and the smallest issues for investment strategies in the range of one to 1,000 lots (of 1,000 shares each) after incorporating the actual rationing process adopted in each new issue. The estimated t-statistics that these excess returns are greater than zero are (i) all less than 0.95 for the large issues, (ii) less than 0.61 and generally negative for the medium issues, and (iii) in the range of 0.63 to 1.33 for the small issues.

cant returns[16] after rationing is incorporated, there is some slight size effect. The smaller issues are generally most underpriced and the medium-sized group is most overpriced, given the actual rationing processes adopted. Except for lots of 1,000 and 2,000 shares, the average listing-day returns for the larger issues are less than 1 percent. The subdivision depicted in fig. 5 can be achieved only after the size of all issues is known. Thus fig. 5 results violate fair-game requirements in that an ex ante investment strategy of this nature is not feasible.

4. Conclusions

Rock's (1986) model of the pricing of new issues predicts that the difference between subscription price and first-day listing price should yield uninformed investors the risk-free rate of return. Empirical test of this model in the United

---

[16] The returns for the smaller issues are highly positively skewed, whereas those for the medium-size issue group are negatively skewed.

States and elsewhere is impossible because information on the rationing process adopted by underwriters and issuers is not observable. (Presumably underwriters are reluctant to release these data because they may show bias in the allocation process.)

The new-issues market in Singapore is unbiased in the sense that all investors applying for the same number of shares have an equal chance of success. Further, the method of allocation adopted on an issue-by-issue basis is publicly disclosed. Singapore thus provides the opportunity to test the predictions of Rock's model.

Our tests confirm Rock's major empirical implications. Uninformed investors' returns are not statistically different from the risk-free rate of return. Rationing is the major reason for the apparent excess returns on unseasoned new issues. Rationing is shown to be applied far more stringently in underpriced (i.e., positive initial-listing-day excess returns) than in overpriced (i.e., negative initial-listing-day excess returns) issues. Rock argues that this bias in rationing produces an equilibrium offer price with a finite discount sufficient to attract uninformed investors to the issue. Our results are consistent with this proposition for both the total sample and for subdivisions based on underwriter identity and issue size. Additional analysis suggests that issuing companies price new issues rationally in the sense that the actual issue price is set above an estimate of the price at which uninformed demand alone would subscribe an issue.

Appendix

The new-issues market in Singapore

Between the incorporation of the Singapore Stock Exchange (SSE) in 1973 and June 1987 there were 70 new public issues. Sixty-one of these were underpriced, in the sense that if application costs and rationing are ignored the initial-day price (measured by the last sale price) exceeds the subscription price.

Rationing is, however, pervasive in Singapore. For 66 of the 70 new issues for which we have data, oversubscription levels average 29.4 times (standard deviation 44.6). Only seven issues were undersubscribed (three of these were overpriced), while the maximum oversubscription level was 248.1 times. With such substantial levels of oversubscription the question arises whether an incentive exists for the company or underwriter to underprice so as to benefit from interest on the excess-application float. In general the answer is no. First, applications that are rejected by the balloting process are not banked by the underwriter but are returned directly to the applicant. Second, application money on partial allotments is trust money and generally does not earn interest. Some underwriting agreements, however, specifically mention the treatment of interest on partially successful applications. If the issuer is to receive interest it is generally seen as an offset to the negotiated underwriting fee. Third, most application forms state that refunds to partially successful applicants will be made without interest.

As described below, the allocation system used in Singapore is a fair game (within applications for the same number of shares) and accordingly oversubscription levels should, in equilibrium, be driven by expected gains (a function of rationing, subscription price, expected listing price, and time) and costs (interest and application costs). Participants in the new-issue market will not be deterred from entry because of perceived bias by underwriters or issuers in the allocation process.

Another important characteristic of the new-issues market in Singapore is that an application for shares in a new issue must be accompanied by payment in the form of a banker's draft, a bank check, a cashier's order, or a postal order. (In one case personal checks were permitted.) All payments of these types involve funds being actually withdrawn from an applicant's bank account and accordingly incur the opportunity cost of foregone interest revenue. An application constitutes an offer by the applicant to acquire shares in the company. As such it can be withdrawn at any stage prior to acceptance by the issuing company. Although the law allows an applicant to withdraw an offer, this is very rarely done in Singapore initial public offerings.

New issues in Singapore proceed in accord with the general principles of British company law and are of the firm-commitment type, in which the issuer and its investment bank (usually the underwriter) agree on the price and quantity of securities to be issued.

These amounts are detailed in a prospectus and cannot be changed by the issuing company during the issue. The prospectus contains the application form and discloses relevant investment information for the issue, including accounting and other information on past performance, a one-year-ahead earnings forecast by directors (with auditor comments), the objectives of the issue, valuers', directors', and accountants' reports, and other general and statutory information. Under British company law an issue of shares to the public cannot be made unless it is accompanied by a prospectus registered with the appropriate regulatory body or bodies. (In Singapore the body is the Registrar of Companies and Businesses.) A prospectus is typically open for applications for 3–4 weeks and another 3–4 weeks elapse between the closing date for applications and the initial stock-exchange listing. Printing lags add further to the period between the decision on an issue price and a market assessment of worth.

Typically 10 percent of the shares offered are reserved for priority allocation to employees of the issuing company. The other 90 percent are allocated to the public in such a way as to ensure that all applicants for a certain number of shares have an equal chance of obtaining shares. This process can sometimes involve balloting (i.e., a random selection from all applications). When a ballot is required it is conducted in public and is overseen by representatives of the SSE, the Monetary Authority of Singapore (MAS), and the issuing company auditor.

Where oversubscription occurs the investment bank or underwriter, having determined actual subscription patterns, recommends various feasible allocation systems to the issuer. These can involve combinations of full allocation, pro-rata allocation, and balloting. Following the selection of an allocation basis by the issuing firm, a public announcement describes the method adopted. (An example of a complete-disclosure and of a partial-disclosure announcement are given below.) A complete disclosure differs from a partial disclosure in that the former allows both the application and allotment patterns to be reconstructed. With a partial disclosure only the probability of an allocation, conditional on an application of a particular size, can be determined. Although the allocation basis adopted systematically gives proportionally more shares to small investors (see fig. 2), applicants for the same number of shares are treated equally. Different firms and underwriters adopt different schemes in deriving allocation categories, which depend in part on actual subscription patterns received. Apart from the general bias toward small investors, it seems unlikely that the basis of allocation for any particular issue can be predicted [see Koh and Walter (1987)], though some application strategies seem (at this stage) undesirable. For instance, it seems better to apply for 1 million shares than for 999,000 (see fig. 2).

Some interesting anecdotes have emerged. First, in the issue by Singapore Bus Services (1978) Limited, all applications by investors who owned a car (data were obtained by the underwriter from the Registry of Vehicles) or for more than 5,000 shares were rejected, even though no mention of this was made in the prospectus. Second, on two occasions a preference was given to applications from investors using Central Provident Fund Investment Account deposits. Third, the largest public issue, by the flagship of Singapore, Singapore International Airlines Limited (SIA), while oversubscribed, was overpriced. The SIA float followed closely on the heels of the announcement that Pan Electric Industries Limited, one of the largest listed firms in Singapore, was to be liquidated. Fourth, the recent issue by Sembawang Maritime Limited attracted total subscriptions of $S6.8 billion, compared with $S81 million offered. The applications received represented 15 percent of the total market capitalization of all companies listed on the SSE and 20 percent of Singapore's GDP.

The listing requirements of the SSE impose some restrictions on issuers in deciding on allocation and rationing systems that partly explain the preference afforded small investors. Section 102 of the SSE listing requirements states: 'Companies applying for quotation of ordinary shares are, as a general rule, expected to meet the following criteria:

(1) It has a paid-up capital of at least $4,000,000.

(2) At least $1,500,000 or 25% of the issued and paid-up capital (whichever is the greater) is in the hands of not less than 500 shareholders.

(3) A minimum percentage of the issued and paid-up capital is in the hands of shareholders each holding not less than 500 shares and not more than 10,000 shares:

Nominal value of issued and paid-up capital	Minimum percentage
less than $50 million	20%
$50 million and above and less than $100 million	15% or $10 million whichever is the greater
$100 million and above	10% or $15 million whichever is the greater

In complying with this distribution, the following are to be excluded:

(a) Holdings by parent, or companies deemed to be related by virtue of Section 6 of the Companies Act.

(b) Holdings by directors (including those of persons designated directors under the Companies Act).'

If there is a correspondence between small investors and uninformed investors in the Rock (1986) sense, this SSE institutional arrangement might partly explain why firms in a Singapore context seek uninformed participation in the new-issue process. Alternatively, firms might seek uninformed investor participation as a way of expanding their customer base, by appealing to shareholder loyalty to buy the company product. [In the Singapore Bus Services (1978) Limited float all successful applicants received 500 shares. A holding of 500 shares entitles the shareholder to a bus concession pass and presumably directly creates incentives for shareholder loyalty, as do shareholder discounts, which are common in retailing. If this explanation is valid, there should be an empirical relationship between small-investor participation and the extent to which the firm's products are sold directly to the public.

270   *F. Koh and T. Walter, The pricing of unseasoned issues*

Retailers, for example, should have larger small-investor participation than, say, property developers.]

Sample Announcement, Complete Disclosure

ANNOUNCEMENT

AVIMO SINGAPORE LIMITED

OFFER FOR SALE OF 18,750,000 SHARES OF $0.20 EACH
AT $1.75 PER SHARE

The Directors of Avimo Singapore Limited are pleased to announce that at the close of the Application List at 12 noon, 21 April, 1987, there were 108,787 applicants applying for 1,754,990,000 shares, totalling $3,071,232,500. The offer for sale is approximately 104 times subscribed compared with the 16,875,000 shares available to the public for subscription at $1.75 per share.

The following table sets out the details on the applications received and the basis of allotment:

Denominations of shares applied for ('000)	No. of applicants	Total no. of shares applied for ('000)	Percent of total applications (%)	Balloting ratio	No. of shares allotted per successful applicant ('000)	No. of shares ('000)	Percent of the offer for sale (%)
1–4	93,207	103,719	5.9	1 : 27	1	3,391	20.1
5–9	2,022	10,784	0.6	1 : 12	1	168	1.0
10–49	7,464	88,404	5.0	2 : 15	1	995	5.9
50–99	1,099	56,385	3.2	5 : 9	1	610	3.6
100–199	3,629	367,300	20.9	—	1	3,629	21.5
200–299	134	29,418	1.7	—	2	268	1.6
300–399	19	5,737	0.3	—	3	57	0.4
400–499	10	4,004	0.2	—	4	40	0.2
500–749	633	317,611	18.1	—	5	3,165	18.8
750–999	9	7,850	0.5	—	6	54	0.3
1,000–1,999	482	486,133	27.7	—	7	3,374	20.0
2,000–2,999	44	91,530	5.2	—	11	484	2.9
3,000–3,999	5	15,100	0.9	—	14	70	0.4
4,000–4,999	3	12,000	0.7	—	16	48	0.3
5,000–5,999	21	105,013	6.0	—	18	378	2.2
6,000–7,999	1	6,000	0.3	—	20	20	0.1
8,000–9,999	1	8,000	0.5	—	24	24	0.1
10,000–10,001	4	40,002	2.3	—	25	100	0.6
	108,787	1,754,990	100.0			16,875	100.0

The 1,875,000 shares reserved for the management and staff of the Company and those who have contributed to the success of the Company have been fully subscribed.

The Directors of Avimo Singapore Limited wish to thank all applicants for their confidence in the Company. Unsuccessful applications and refund cheques for (partially) successful applications will be sent to applicants as soon as possible.

Issued for and on behalf of Avimo Singapore Limited

N.M. Rothschild & Sons (Singapore) Limited
22 April 1987

Sample Announcement, Partial Disclosure

PRESS RELEASE

HOTEL TAI-PAN LIMITED
(Incorporated in the Republic of Singapore)

NEW ISSUE OF 22,500,000 SHARES OF $1.00 EACH AT $1.30 PER SHARE

The Directors of Hotel Tai-Pan Limited ('The Company') are pleased to announce that at the time of the closing of the Application List at 2:00 p.m. on 23rd July 1981, a total of 74,148 applications in respect of 288,463,000 shares in the company had been received. The application monies amounted in aggregate to $375,001,900. The issue was therefore subscribed approximately 13 times.

No. of shares applied for	Balloting ratio	No. of shares allotted per successful application
1,000	1 : 10	1,000
2,000 to 5,000	1 : 5	1,000
6,000 to 10,000	1 : 2	1,000
11,000 to 20,000	no balloting	1,000
21,000 to 50,000	"	2,000
51,000 to 100,000	"	4,000
101,000 to 150,000	"	5,000
151,000 to 200,000	"	9,000
201,000 to 300,000	"	14,000
301,000 to 400,000	"	16,000
401,000 to 500,000	"	24,000
501,000 to 500,000	"	30,000
1,000,00 and above	"	55,000

Every effort will be made to ensure the expeditious processing of successful applications and the return of the application monies to unsuccessful and partially successful applicants.

Issued for and on behalf of Hotel Tai-Pan Limited

By Wardley Limited

24 July 1981

References

Beatty, R.P. and J.R. Ritter, 1986, Investment banking, reputation, and the underpricing of initial public offerings, Journal of Financial Economics 15, 213–232.

Finn, F. and R. Higham, 1986, The performance of unseasoned new equity issues-cum-stock exchange listings in Australia, Working paper (University of Queensland, Brisbane).

Ibbotson, R.G., 1975, Price performance of common stock new issues, Journal of Financial Economics 2, 235–272.

Ibbotson, R.G. and J. Jaffe, 1975, 'Hot issue' markets, Journal of Finance 30, 1027–1042.

Koh, F. and T. Walter, 1987, Allocation patterns for new issues in Singapore, Working paper (National University of Singapore).

Ritter, J., 1984, The 'hot issues' market of 1980, Journal of Business 57, 215–240.

Rock, K., 1986, Why new issues are underpriced, Journal of Financial Economics 15, 187–212.

Smith, C.W., 1986, Investment banking and the capital acquisition process, Journal of Financial Economics 15, 3–29.

[10]

Journal of Financial Economics 37 (1995) 239–257

Evidence on the strategic allocation of initial public offerings

Kathleen Weiss Hanley[a], William J. Wilhelm, Jr.[*, b]

[a]University of Maryland, College Park, MD 20742, USA
[b]Boston College, Chestnut Hill, MA 02167, USA

(Received August 1993; final version received May 1994)

Abstract

The evidence reported in this paper suggests that institutional investors capture a large fraction of the short-run profits associated with IPOs. The favored status enjoyed by institutional investors in underpriced offerings appears, however, to carry a *quid pro quo* expectation that they will participate in less-attractive issues as well. This finding conforms with the Benveniste and Spindt (1989) and Benveniste and Wilhelm (1990) prediction that U.S. underwriters behave strategically in the allocation of IPOs.

Key words: Initial public offerings; Share allocation; Institutional investors
JEL classification: G24

1. Introduction

Initial public offerings of equity (IPOs) are commonly oversubscribed (Ibbotson, 1975; Koh and Walter, 1989). In many countries, underwriters are legally bound to evenhandedly allocate shares among subscribers when oversubscription occurs (Loughran, Ritter, and Rydqvist, 1994). By contrast, underwriters bringing issues to market in the U.S. follow a 'book-building' approach in which offer prices are conditioned on nonbinding pre-offer indications of

*Corresponding author.

The authors thank Larry Benveniste, Cliff Holderness, Albert Kyle, Robyn McLaughlin, Wayne Mikkelson, Vikram Nanda, Jay Ritter (the referee), Paul Seguin, Clifford Smith (the editor), Bob Taggart, and seminar participants at Boston College, Duke University, the University of Michigan, the Securities and Exchange Commission, and the 1993 meeting of the Western Finance Association for comments on earlier drafts of the paper.

interest and IPO shares are allocated in a discriminatory fashion. Although the initial distribution of IPOs is private information, underwriters are criticized for favoring institutional investors with large shares of underpriced offerings. Popular accounts leave the impression that this favoritism occurs at the expense of retail investors or, more colorfully, that the status of retail investors has been reduced to that of 'peasant(s) among a cartel of aristocrats' (*Forbes*, May 25, 1992).

In this paper we present the first direct evidence of institutional domination of the short-run profits associated with IPOs. Drawing on distribution data for a sample of 38 IPOs managed (or co-managed) by a single underwriter during the period 1983–1988, we find that approximately 70% of the shares in under-priced offerings are allocated to institutional investors. Balancing their apparent preferential treatment in underpriced offerings, however, is the fact that institutional investors take similarly large positions in overpriced offerings. Moreover, we find that institutional investors are allocated large proportions of issues for which pre-offer interest is weak and also of issues for which it is strong. Thus the data support the conclusion that institutional investors capture the lion's share of profits associated with underpriced offerings, but only at the cost of active participation in less attractive offerings. Interestingly, *Business Week* estimates (April 4, 1994) that institutional investors purchase 80% of the shares in 'hot' deals but only 60% of the shares in 'normal' deals. Although it is not clear how these estimates were obtained or how deals are classified, our findings suggest that their estimates overstate the variation in institutional participation across offers. Moreover, our interpretation of the evidence stands in sharp contrast to their characterization of the market.

We also document a statistically significant positive correlation between initial institutional holdings and post-offer domestic institutional holdings reported in 13(f) filings with the SEC. This observation serves as the basis for an investigation of the population of IPOs brought to market during the 1983–1987 period for which post-offer institutional holding data are available. Using public reports of post-offer institutional holdings as a proxy for (unobservable) initial holdings, we report evidence consistent with our findings for the sample of IPOs for which initial institutional holding data are available.

It is often claimed that institutional investors are well-informed relative to retail investors. Even if this claim is true, our findings suggest that institutional investors are unable to use their information advantage to avoid investing in overpriced offerings. This interpretation of the evidence apparently casts doubt on the explanatory power of Rock's (1986) argument that informed investors impose a winner's curse on uninformed investors by demanding larger allocations of (rationed) offerings identified as underpriced and smaller allocations of those identified as overpriced. Moreover, the evidence is difficult to reconcile with Rock's prediction that uninformed investors earn the riskless rate when profits are weighted by the probability of receiving an allocation.

Of course, Rock (1986) assumes that it is costless for informed investors to abstain from participating in less-attractive offerings. In the U.S., however, failure to participate in such offerings can cost an investor the opportunity to participate in future offerings. The information-gathering theory proposed by Benveniste and Spindt (1989) predicts that the threat of exclusion from under-priced offerings (made credible by the underwriter's discriminatory power) can induce institutional investors to participate in (overpriced) offerings in which they would otherwise have little interest. Thus the favored status enjoyed by institutional investors in underpriced offerings carries a *quid pro quo* expectation consistent with the pattern observed in the data.

The following section describes the unique dataset on which the study is based. We show that although the sample is small and confined to IPOs brought to market by a single underwriter, it is in most respects representative of the population of firm-commitment offerings during the sample period. In Section 3 we investigate the sample for which initial institutional holdings are available, as well as the population of firm-commitment offerings brought to market during the sample period, for evidence on the degree to which institutional investors capture the benefits associated with IPOs. Section 4 offers a discussion of the theoretical and policy implications of our findings, and Section 5 concludes.

2. Data

2.1. Sample description

Our sample includes all 38 firm commitment IPOs managed (or co-managed) by a single (anonymous) underwriter during the 1983–1988 period. The data are derived from internal reports produced to market the firm's underwriting services. Although these reports are not available to the general public, they are shared freely with prospective issuing clients. In addition to the size and price of the offerings, the reports document the firm's distributional efforts and aftermarket support for its issues.

The firm reports allocation statistics for both institutional (domestic and foreign) and retail investors. Institutional investors are similar to one another in that they participate repeatedly in the firm's IPOs, although the institutional investor pool for each IPO is not necessarily the same. Representatives of the firm suggest viewing the institutional investor pool as including several distinct clienteles of investors. Some institutional investors participate only in IPOs of firms in particular industries. Others express interest only in 'growth' or 'value' stocks. Only a small fraction of the firm's institutional investor pool participates in most of the firm's offerings. Common to each clientele, however, is the expression of repeated interest in IPOs within their area of interest and the

242   *K.W. Hanley, W.J. Wilhelm, Jr./Journal of Financial Economics 37 (1995) 239–257*

Table 1
Fraction of shares allocated to each of four investor classes for the 38 sample issues brought to market during the 1983–1988 period

	Mean	Median	Std. dev.	Maximium	Minimum
Institutional (domestic)	50.3%	53.7%	15.5%	77.6%	5.0%
Institutional (foreign)	16.6%	14.3%	9.8%	40.4%	0.0%
Total institutional	66.8%	71.7%	15.8%	88.6%	6.6%
Retail	28.0%	24.3%	15.3%	93.4%	11.4%
External retail	5.1%	3.0%	5.7%	22.3%	0.0%
Total retail	33.2%	28.3%	15.8%	93.4%	11.4%

expectation of such interest by the firm. Finally, although representatives of the firm claim that institutional investors are not coerced to participate in IPOs, it is understood by both parties that allocation decisions are contingent on an investor's history with the firm. Thus an investor's ability to skim the cream from the pool of IPOs within an expressed area of interest is limited by the threat of being excluded from future offerings.

Retail investors are drawn mainly from the firm's existing retail brokerage accounts. Once allocated to an individual broker, distribution of IPO shares among retail investors is at the discretion of the broker, although the firm claims that IPO shares are never allocated to new accounts. A small fraction of retail allocations are the result of shares allocated to and distributed by firm employees who are registered brokers but who operate in some other capacity within the firm. For example, bond traders within the firm may also be registered brokers providing brokerage services to small clienteles of investors in addition to carrying out their trading responsibilities to the firm. Shares in this category are not allocated to retail accounts of the firm and are therefore referred to as *external* retail allocations.

Table 1 reports summary statistics for the distribution of IPOs across the four investor classes (domestic institutional, foreign institutional, retail, and external retail). Percentage allocations reflect the actual number of shares issued (including those issued through the exercise of the overallotment option). The firm claims to maintain a target institutional (domestic and foreign) allocation of 60%. The statistics reported in Table 1 indicate that the average institutional allocation (66.8%) is somewhat larger than this target during the sample period. In no case is an entire issue allocated to either institutional or retail investors.

Since initial distribution data are not generally available to researchers, we also investigate the degree to which publicly available reports of post-offer institutional holdings are correlated with initial institutional holdings. The SEC requires that domestic institutions controlling more than $100 million in equity

K.W. Hanley, W.J. Wilhelm, Jr./Journal of Financial Economics 37 (1995) 239–257   243

report their holdings on a quarterly basis. We collect the number of shares held by institutions as of the end of the calendar quarter in which the IPO took place from *Spectrum3: 13(f) Institutional Stock Holdings Survey* (e.g., March 31 holdings for IPOs between January 1 and March 31). We divide the number of shares owned by institutions by the number of shares outstanding to obtain a measure of post-offer institutional holdings. Assuming that other syndicate members follow an allocation strategy identical to that of the sample underwriter, the Pearson correlation between this measure of post-offer holdings and initial (domestic) institutional holdings is 0.91 ($p = 0.0001$). Similarly, the Spearman rank correlation coefficient is 0.76 ($p = 0.0001$). Of course, this comparison of initial and post-offer institutional holdings is indirect. Only large domestic institutions are required to report. Moreover, the sample underwriter distributes on average only 48.2% (median: 46.1%) of each issue, and there is surely variation across the allocation strategies followed by the remainder of the syndicate. Thus a direct comparison of initial and post-offer holdings is impossible. On the other hand, if our sample is representative of the population of firm-commitment offerings brought to market during the sample period, reported post-offer institutional holdings are a potentially useful proxy for initial institutional holdings.

2.2. Comparison of sample and population characteristics

We investigate the degree to which our sample is representative of the population by comparing the sample IPOs and underwriter to the 'population' of 1,477 firm-commitment IPOs brought to market during the 1983–1987 period as compiled by the *Investment Dealers' Digest Corporate Database* and *Securities Data Corporation* and screened by Hanley (1993). The population contains only IPOs subsequently traded in the over-the-counter market (as reported in the Standard and Poors Stock Price Record); we exclude unit offers and issues of financial institutions. The exclusion of IPOs listed on either the NYSE or Amex has the effect of eliminating closed-end funds and many of the reverse LBOs. Table 2 indicates that both the sample of 38 IPOs and the population of firm-commitment offerings (including an additional 156 issues brought to market in 1988) are distributed similarly across the sample period. Approximately one-half of both the sample and population IPOs were brought to market during the high-volume years of 1983 and 1986.

Table 3 provides a comparison of various characteristics of the IPO population and the 38-issue sample. Taken as a whole, the evidence suggests that the sample is representative of the population of IPOs during the sample period. For example, the difference between the 8.63% mean initial return for the sample and the population mean of 8.64% is not statistically significant at conventional significance levels, nor is the difference between the sample and population mean dollar value of shares offered. Further, the average size of the

244   *K.W. Hanley, W.J. Wilhelm, Jr./Journal of Financial Economics 37 (1995) 239–257*

Table 2
Distribution of IPOs across the sample period for both the sample of 38 IPOs and the population of
IPOs brought to market during the sample period

The population of IPOs is comprised of all IPOs brought to market and subsequently traded in the
over-the-counter market as compiled by the *Investment Dealers' Digest Corporate Database* and
Securities Data Corporation, excluding financial institutions and unit offers. (Percent of total is
reported in parentheses.)

Year	Sample	Population
1983	10 (26.3%)	468 (28.7%)
1984	4 (10.5%)	196 (12.0%)
1985	6 (15.8%)	203 (12.4%)
1986	9 (23.9%)	376 (23.0%)
1987	7 (18.4%)	234 (14.3%)
1988	2 (5.3%)	156 (9.6%)
Total	38	1,633

sample firms, measured by assets or revenue, is not statistically different from
that of the average firm in the population. On the other hand, a Wilcoxon
rank-sum test rejects ($p = 0.01$) the null hypothesis of equality for each of these
characteristics of the sample and population IPOs, with the exception of the
initial return.

Megginson and Weiss (1991) show that market share, defined as the total
dollar amount underwritten by a given underwriter divided by total IPO capital
raised during the sample period ($70.3 billion), yields underwriter rankings
similar to those produced by Carter and Manaster (1990). Using market share to
measure reputation, Table 3 indicates that the sample underwriter's reputation
is similar to that of the mean for the population. (If the issue has more than one
lead underwriter, market share is defined to be the average market share of the
lead underwriters, so that average market share varies within the sample as
a consequence of co-management.) In contrast, the cost of engaging the sample
underwriter is significantly lower than the mean cost for the population. Finally,
both the sample mean gross spread as a proportion of the offering amount and
the mean value of relative offering expenses are statistically different from the
corresponding population values.

3. Share allocation and institutional profits

Table 4 begins our investigation of the conjecture that underwriters favor
institutional investors with large proportions of underpriced offerings; it cat-
egorizes sample IPOs according to whether the initial return from the offer price

K.W. Hanley, W.J. Wilhelm, Jr./Journal of Financial Economics 37 (1995) 239–257   245

Table 3
Comparison of the 38-issue sample with the population of 1,477 firm-commitment IPOs brought to market during the period 1983–1987.

Sample and population characteristics are drawn from the *Investment Dealers' Digest Corporate Database* and the Center for Research in Securities Prices daily return file. (Median values are reported in parentheses.)

	Sample	Population	t-statistic for difference in means
Initial return	8.6%	8.6%	− 0.01
	(3.2%)	(2.0%)	
Offering price	$14.0	$9.9	6.22
	(12.9)	(9.5)	
Amount offered	$24.9	$15.7	1.59
(in millions)	(14.6)	(9.3)	
Pre-issue assets	$97.3	$67.1	0.90
(in millions)	(47.9)	(11.5)	
Preceding year's revenue	$79.6	$65.8	0.93
(in millions)	(57.8)	(18.6)	
Gross spread as a percent	7.1%	7.9%	− 8.69
of offering amount	(7.1%)	(7.5%)	
Offering expenses as a percent	3.0%	5.0%	− 5.43
of offering amount	(2.7%)	(4.0%)	
Average market share	3.0%	3.5%	− 0.99
of lead underwriters[a]	(1.3%)	(1.5%)	

[a]Market share is the total dollar amount underwritten by an underwriter divided by the total capital raised by all issues classified as IPOs by the *Investment Dealers' Digest Corporate Database* ($70.3 billion during the 1983–1987 period). If the issue has more than one lead underwriter, then market share is the average market share of the lead underwriters. Therefore, issues underwritten by the sample underwriter may differ in the average market share of the lead underwriters as a result of co-management.

to the close of the first day of trading is negative (overpriced), zero, or positive (underpriced). Among the 38 sample offerings for which initial institutional holdings (domestic and foreign) are observable, 24 are underpriced. The mean return from a strategy of purchasing underpriced issues at the offer price and liquidating at the close of the first day of trading is 14.7%. Institutions purchased 70.4% of the shares in underpriced offerings distributed by the sample underwriter thereby capturing $20,809,992 (73%) of the $28,681,776 total first-day profits generated by underpriced offers. (Recall that the sample underwriter distributes on average only 48.2% of the shares offered.) Assuming that the remainder of the syndicate follows an identical distribution pattern, institutions capture $41,514,336 of the $56,804,160 first-day profits generated by underpriced offers. Of course, since lower-ranked members of the syndicate tend to be regional retail firms, it is likely that this assumption leads to overstatement

Table 4
Initial returns and distribution characteristics for the sample of 38 IPOs

Sample IPOs are classified by the size of their initial return. Dollar profit (loss) is calculated assuming that shares distributed by the sample underwriter are purchased at the offer price and liquidated at the close of the first day of trading. [Median values are reported in brackets.]

	Initial returns less than zero	Initial returns equal to zero	Initial returns greater than zero
Number of issues	9	5	24
Initial return	− 1.7%	0.0%	14.7%
	[− 1.4%]	[0.0%]	[12.7%]
Percent of issue sold to institutional investors	64.8%	53.4%	70.4%
	[71.6%]	[63.4%]	[73.3%]
Mean $ profit (loss) earned by institutional investors	($133,351)	$0.00	$867,083
	[($117,500)]	[$0.00]	[$554,600]
Total $ profit (loss) earned by institutional investors	($1,200,159)		$20,809,992
Total $ profits (losses)	($1,718,568)		$28,681,776

of the fraction of first-day profits captured by institutional investors. Simply assuming that the remainder of the issue is allocated to retail investors yields a lower bound of 37% on first-day profits captured by institutional investors. Thus the 38-issue sample for which initial institutional holdings are observable supports the conjecture that institutions capture the majority of the profits generated by underpriced IPOs.

On the other hand, institutional investors also purchase a relatively large fraction of the nine overpriced offerings. In fact, the median percentage of overpriced shares purchased by institutional investors differs little from the median for underpriced offerings. Although an institutional trading strategy of purchasing at the offer and liquidating at the close of the first day of trading results in losses of $1,200,159, or 70% of the $1,718,568 total losses, these losses are less than 10% of the $20,809,992 in profits generated by following the same strategy with underpriced issues. The difference in magnitude between profits and losses is related to both the relatively small number (nine) of overpriced issues and the relatively small absolute initial return (− 1.7%).[1] It is also worth

---

[1] We observe a similar pattern within the population of firm-commitment offerings for which reports of post-offer institutional holdings are available. In contrast to the 671 underpriced issues, only 242 (21%) of the population issues are overpriced. Similarly, the mean initial return for overpriced issues is − 4.22%, whereas the mean initial return for underpriced issues is 14.05%. A partial explanation for the relatively small losses on overpriced issues in both the sample and the population is that underwriters make efforts to support weak issues for a limited period of time following the offering (Miller and Reilly, 1987; Ruud, 1993; Hanley, Kumar, and Seguin, 1993).

Table 5
Ordinary least-squares estimates of coefficients from cross-sectional regressions of initial returns on the fraction of the issue purchased by institutional investors

Panel A contains regression results for the 38-issue sample for which initial institutional holdings are observable. Panel B contains regression results for the 1,168 firm-commitment offerings brought to market during the 1983–1987 period using post-offer reports of domestic institutional holdings as a proxy for initial institutional holdings. Market share is included to proxy for underwriter reputation and is defined as the total dollar amount underwritten by an underwriter divided by the total capital raised through IPOs during the 1983–1987 period. (*t*-statistics are reported in parentheses.)

Initial return$_i$ = a_0 + a_1 Institutional$_i$ + a_2 Market share$_i$ + e_i

Intercept	% of issue sold to institutional investors	Average market share of lead underwriters	F-value	Adjusted R^2
Panel A: 38-issue sample				
− 0.061	0.22		2.55	0.04
(− 0.64)	(1.60)			
Panel B: Population				
0.075	− 0.008		0.45	0.00
(12.15)	(− 0.67)			
0.089	0.007	− 0.472	12.15	0.019
(13.18)	(0.58)	(− 4.88)		

noting that although the sample underwriter distributes 50% of the shares in underpriced offers, it distributes only 40% of the shares in overpriced offerings.

The mean percentage of institutional holdings for both overpriced issues and issues with an initial return of zero is sensitive to the exclusion of outliers. In only four cases is the fraction of the issue allocated to institutional investors less than 50%. In only one instance does this occur for an underpriced issue. Among those issues with zero initial returns, one issue exhibits an institutional allocation of only 6.6%. (Interest in this issue was so weak that the initial offer of 1.3 million shares was reduced to 900,000 shares; the firm ultimately sold 575,000 primary shares and held the remainder from the market.) The next-smallest institutional allocation of 27.6% occurs among the overpriced issues. All other issues exhibit institutional allocations in excess of 42%. Excluding these two outliers from the sample we find mean percentage institutional holdings of 69.5% among overpriced issues and 65% among issues with zero initial returns. Thus, initial institutional holdings appear to be largely independent of the degree to which an issue is underpriced.

Further evidence in support of this conclusion is provided by regressing an issue's initial return on the fraction of the issue purchased by institutional investors. The regression results for the 38-issue sample, reported in panel A of Table 5, support the conclusion that variation in the fraction of an issue allocated to institutional investors does not explain a statistically significant proportion of the cross-sectional variation in initial returns. This conclusion is insensitive to the exclusion of outliers and alternative specifications of the regression model.[2]

In panel B of Table 5 we corroborate these results with similar evidence from the population of 1,168 issues brought to market during the 1983–1987 period for which post-offer institutional holdings are available. (When no institutional holdings are reported, the issue is excluded from the sample, because it is impossible to distinguish issues held entirely by retail investors from those with unreported institutional holdings.) The first regression simply uses post-offer institutional holdings as a proxy for initial institutional holdings. The second regression also controls for the fact that, in contrast to the 38-issue sample, underwriter reputation varies considerably across the population. We use the market-share variable described earlier as a proxy for underwriter reputation. Similar to the findings of Carter and Manaster (1990), issues with smaller initial returns are associated with more reputable underwriters. In neither case, however, does variation in reported post-offer holdings explain a statistically significant proportion of the cross-sectional variation in initial returns.

Thus far the evidence is consistent with the hypothesis that institutional investors are favored in the distribution of underpriced issues but that such treatment comes in exchange for participation in overpriced issues. Of course it is possible that institutional investors are simply unable to distinguish between (ex ante) underpriced and overpriced issues. It is perhaps more relevant, then, to ask whether retail investors are systematically excluded from issues drawing strong institutional interest prior to the offering. Since underwriters condition the final offer price (as well as the number of shares offered) on pre-offer institutional indications of interest, we follow Hanley (1993) and assume that issues with offer prices greater than the upper bound of the price (file) range disclosed in the issuing firm's preliminary prospectus drew relatively strong institutional interest prior to the offering. Similarly, we assume that issues priced within the offer range drew moderate interest and those offered at prices below the lower bound of the offer range drew relatively weak interest prior to the offering.

---

[2]Hanley (1993) finds a statistically significant direct relation between initial returns and the percentage deviation of the offer price from the mean of the offer range. Including this variable in the regression model produces similar results, but has no qualitative effect on the institutional-holding coefficient. Defining the institutional-holding variable to be the natural log of the fraction of the issue purchased by institutional investors yields similar results. Finally, when the sample is divided into underpriced offerings and all others, both parametric and nonparametric tests fail to reject the hypothesis that initial institutional holdings are the same for both groups. Again, the conclusion is insensitive to exclusion of outliers.

K.W. Hanley, W.J. Wilhelm, Jr./Journal of Financial Economics 37 (1995) 239–257   249

Table 6
Initial returns and distribution characteristics for the sample of 38 IPOs

Sample IPOs are classified by the relation of their final offer price to the file range in the preliminary prospectus. Mean dollar profit (loss) earned by institutional investors is calculated per issue assuming that all shares distributed by the sample underwriter to institutional investors are purchased at the offer price and liquidated at the close of the first day of trading. [Median values are reported in brackets.]

	Final offer price less than the file range	Final offer price within the file range	Final offer price greater than the file range
Number of issues	8	20	10
Initial return	− 2.1%	8.2%	18.0%
	[− 1.9%]	[4.4%]	[12.0%]
Percent of issue sold to institutional investors	59.2%	67.7%	71.1%
	[64.5%]	[70.1%]	[73.0%]
Mean $ profit (loss) earned by institutional investors	($118,598)	$550,588	$917,951
	[($80,563)]	[$229,800]	[$435,568]

For two of the sample IPOs, the preliminary prospectus provides a single price rather than a range of prices. In both of these cases the offer price exceeds the preliminary price, and the issues were therefore designated as having sold above the offer range. In one case we were unable to obtain information about the suggested offer range and therefore assumed that the issue sold within the offer range. Under these assumptions Table 6 indicates that 18 of the IPOs in the current sample are offered at prices outside of the offer range. Of these, 10 are offered at prices greater than the upper bound of the offer range.

Consistent with Hanley's (1993) findings, we observe a direct relation between the initial return and the level of the offer price relative to the offer range. The mean initial return for IPOs offered at prices less than the lower bound of the offer range is − 2.1%. In contrast, the mean initial returns for IPOs offered at prices within the offer range or above the upper bound of the offer range are 8.2% and 18.0%, respectively. Mean first-day dollar returns on shares distributed by the sample underwriter range from a loss of $118,598 for issues offered at prices less than the lower bound of the offer range to a profit of $917,951 for issues offered at prices greater than the upper bound of the offer range.

The relation between the fraction of the issue allocated to institutional investors and the level of the offer price relative to the offer range is less pronounced. Institutional investors purchase approximately 71% of the shares distributed by the sample underwriter in issues with offer prices in excess of the upper bound of the offer range, 68% of the shares in issues with offer prices

250   *K.W. Hanley, W.J. Wilhelm, Jr./Journal of Financial Economics 37 (1995) 239–257*

Table 7
Ordinary least-squares estimates of coefficients from cross-sectional regressions of the percentage
deviation of the offer price from the mean of the file range on the fraction of the issue purchased by
institutional investors

Panel A contains regression results for the 38-issue sample for which initial institutional holdings are
observable. Panel B contains regression results for the 1,168 firm-commitment offerings brought to
market during the 1983–1987 period using post-offer reports of domestic institutional holdings as
a proxy for initial institutional holdings. Market share is included as a proxy for underwriter
reputation and is defined as the total dollar amount underwritten by an underwriter divided by the
total capital raised through IPOs during the 1983–1987 period. (*t*-statistics are reported in parentheses.)

Initial return$_i = a_0 + a_1$ Institutional$_i + a_2$ Market share$_i + e_i$

Intercept	% of issue sold to institutional investors	Average market share of lead underwriters	*F*-value	Adjusted R^2
Panel A: 38-issue sample				
− 0.155	0.250		3.34	0.061
(− 1.67)	(1.83)			
Panel B: Population				
− 0.053	0.024		3.26	0.002
(− 8.28)	(1.80)			
− 0.042	0.037	− 0.395	9.27	0.014
(− 5.90)	(2.74)	(− 3.91)		

within the offer range, and 59% of the shares in issues with offer prices less than
the lower bound of the offer range.[3] However, the class of issues with offer prices
less than the lower bound of the offer range contains the issue for which only
6.6% of the shares were allocated to institutional investors. Excluding this issue
from the sample, we observe a mean institutional allocation of 67% for the class
of issues.

We investigate the statistical significance of the relation between pre-offer
institutional interest and the fraction of the issue purchased by institutional
investors by regressing the percentage deviation of the offer price from the mean
of the offer range on the fraction of the issue allocated to institutional investors
for the 37 issues for which the offer range was known. The results reported in
panel A of Table 7 indicate that the relation between institutional allocations

---

[3]In contrast to the distribution pattern among over- and underpriced offers, the sample underwriter
distributed approximately the same fraction of issues with offer prices less than the lower bound of
the offer range (47.3%) and issues with offer prices greater than the upper bound of the offer range
(46.6%). For issues with offer prices within the offer range, the sample underwriter distributed 49.4%
of the shares sold.

K.W. Hanley, W.J. Wilhelm, Jr./Journal of Financial Economics 37 (1995) 239–257   251

and pre-offer interest is statistically significant at the 10% level. Excluding the two outliers from the sample, however, we cannot reject the null hypothesis of no relation between institutional allocations and pre-offer interest at conventional levels of significance. On the other hand, both parametric and nonparametric difference tests reject at conventional significance levels ($p = 0.05$) the hypothesis that institutional allocations for issues priced above the mean of the offer range equal the allocations for those priced at or below the mean.

Similar results for the population of 1,168 issues brought to market during the 1983–1987 period are reported in panel B of Table 7. Regressing the percentage deviation of the offer price from the mean of the offer range on post-offer institutional holdings alone yields results similar to those obtained for the 37-issue sample. On the other hand, after controlling for differences in underwriter reputation, variation in post-offer institutional holdings explains a statistically significant proportion of the cross-sectional variation in the proxy for pre-offer interest. We obtain similar results using the absolute percentage deviation of the offer price from the mean of the offer range. We also control for market-wide movements by including the holding-period return from the filing date to the offer date for the NASDAQ equally-weighted index contained in the Center for Research in Securities Prices (CRSP) data file. Similar to the findings of Hanley (1993), this variable accounts for a statistically significant fraction of the variation in the independent variable. The remainder of our conclusions are robust to this addition to the model, however.

In summary, the evidence suggests that institutional investors do receive larger allocations of underpriced offerings. However, because institutions also take large positions in overpriced offerings there is no evidence of a statistically significant relation between institutional holdings and initial returns for either the sample of 38 issues for which initial holdings are observable or the population of firm-commitment offerings brought to market during the sample period. Although there is some evidence that institutional allocations are directly related to pre-offer interest, again we find that institutions are allocated large proportions of issues for which pre-offer interest is weak as well as of issues for which it is strong.[4]

4. Discussion

A number of theories have been advanced to explain the apparent short-run average underpricing of IPOs. Among these theories, several predict a relation

---

[4] Ritter (1991) suggests that evidence of long-run underperformance of IPOs reflects overly optimistic expectations among investors. If institutional investors are relatively sophisticated and therefore less likely to fall prey to fads in IPOs, we should observe a direct relation between an IPO's long-run performance and the fraction of the issue purchased by institutional investors. Although the 38-issue sample yields evidence consistent with this prediction, the population does not.

252 *K.W. Hanley, W.J. Wilhelm, Jr./Journal of Financial Economics 37 (1995) 239-257*

between the degree of underpricing and the distribution of shares among various investor clienteles. Rock (1986), for example, predicts that well-informed investors will dominate underpriced issues and systematically avoid overpriced issues. Assuming that the successful placement of IPOs rests on the continued participation of uninformed investors, a passive underwriter will find it necessary to underprice IPOs on average such that uninformed investors earn the riskless rate of return when profits are weighted by the probability of receiving an allocation.

This stylized model appears to capture the essence of primary markets in countries where underwriters play a relatively passive role in bringing new issues to market. In Singapore, for example, underwriters generally set prices independently of the market response to the issuing firm's prospectus. Moreover, rationing of oversubscribed shares is generally '... evenhanded in the sense that all applications of a particular size have an equal probability of being accepted' (Koh and Walter, 1989). When underwriters do discriminate in the allocation of shares, it is generally because of public policy concerns such as the desire to allocate a fraction of the approximately $2 billion privatization of Singapore Telecom to the domestic retail market. Thus underwriters act primarily as passive agents for the issuing firm. Under these circumstances Koh and Walter (1989) confirm the presence of a winner's curse in Singapore. Keloharju (1993) finds evidence of a winner's curse in Finland, where underwriters behave in a similarly passive manner.

In contrast, if institutional investors are well-informed relative to retail investors, the evidence reported in Section 3 suggests that the simple model analyzed by Rock (1986) cannot capture the full range of price and distribution outcomes observed in the U.S. Although institutional investors receive a large fraction of the shares in underpriced offerings, they also purchase a similarly large fraction of overpriced shares. In other words, if institutional investors are well-informed relative to retail investors, they are unable to use their information advantage over time to avoid investing in overpriced offerings.

Moreover, retail investors earn substantial average first-day profits from participation in the 38 sample issues: $193,510 per issue, or about 1.5% of the average dollar value of shares issued (based on the total market value at the offer price for the 38 sample issues, including shares sold through the overallotment option, of $1028.22 million and the total first-day profit of $56.8 million from purchasing at the offer price and liquidating at the first-day closing price). In fact, even if 100% of the shares in overpriced issues were purchased by retail investors during this period, their average first-day profit would remain positive unless institutional investors purchased in excess of 94% of the shares in underpriced offerings. (If we assume an identical distribution pattern among other members of the underwriting syndicate, retail investors earn an average first-day profit on the entire issue of $362,088, and average first-day retail profits remain positive unless institutional investors purchase in excess of 91.2% of the shares in underpriced offerings.) Of course, this analysis ignores the effect of rationing on *expected* returns. On the

K.W. Hanley, W.J. Wilhelm, Jr./Journal of Financial Economics 37 (1995) 239–257 253

other hand, the relative stability of the total retail allocation suggests that rationing alone will not diminish the attractiveness of IPOs to retail investors unless the degree of adverse selection within the retail pool dominates that which occurs across the pools of retail and institutional investors.

Of course, Rock (1986) assumes that underwriters respond passively in the presence of adverse selection, an apt characterization of the traditional underwriting practices in Finland and Singapore. In contrast, the information-gathering theory suggests that the practice of book-building followed by U.S. underwriters reflects an effort to mitigate the consequences of asymmetric information. The underwriter's leverage derives from the opportunity under U.S. securities regulation to condition both offer prices and share allocations on nonbinding indications of interest solicited from a pool of regular institutional investors. The power to discriminate in the allocation of shares introduces the threat of exclusion from underpriced offerings. This threat can be sufficient to make understating interest in an issue or declining to participate in less-attractive issues quite costly from the perspective of institutional investors. Although underpricing is still necessary to provide an incentive for institutional investors to give accurate indications of interest, a strategy favoring institutional investors with underpriced issues can lead to greater expected net proceeds than would be possible if no information were gathered and the full burden of adverse selection were borne.

For our purposes the key predictions of the information-gathering theory are that underpriced shares will be concentrated among institutional investors and that institutional investors can occasionally be called upon to invest in (overpriced) issues in which they would otherwise have little interest. The first prediction derives from the use of underpricing as an incentive to surrender private information and the observation that institutional investors are the focus of the underwriter's pre-offer information-gathering effort. Efficient use of the incentive requires concentration of underpricing among the segment of the investor population surrendering private information. Since retail investors have no voice in the pre-offer marketing effort, they should receive underpriced shares only if institutional demand falls short of the total shares issued or when the underwriter's information-gathering effort yields no information (and for incentive reasons it is necessary to allocate the issue to retail investors). In the latter case, underpricing is necessary because the underwriter's efforts have failed, and the market is characterized by the presence of adverse selection.[5]

---

[5] Benveniste and Wilhelm (1990) predict that investors providing negative indications of interest will be excluded from the offer. This feature of the models the result of both the discrete information structure (Benveniste and Wilhelm, 1990, footnote 5), and the absence of repeated trade between the underwriter and investors. Relaxing either or both of these restrictions reduces the importance of excluding investors providing negative indications for incentive purposes. For the remainder of the discussion we use a hybrid of the Benveniste and Wilhelm (1990) model in which repeat trade occurs to guide our interpretation of the evidence.

The sample underwriter's allocation of 70% of the shares in underpriced offerings to institutional investors is consistent with the efficient use of underpricing as an incentive. Of course, this finding is also consistent with Rock's prediction that informed investors will dominate underpriced offerings. Thus the prediction that institutional investors can be induced to purchase shares in less-attractive issues is crucial to any attempt to distinguish between the two theories. Benveniste and Spindt (1989) demonstrate that this prediction arises in a repeated-trade setting where underwriters can force investors to purchase shares of issues from which they expect to incur losses as long as these losses are offset by expected profits from their inclusion in future underpriced offerings. By trading repeatedly with a stable pool of investors, the underwriter effectively gains additional leverage over investors with private information. The underwriter is thus able to reduce expected underpricing while preserving the incentive-compatibility of providing accurate indications of interest. The finding that institutional investors also purchase a large fraction of shares in overpriced offerings is consistent with this element of the information-gathering theory. Finding active institutional participation in issues drawing relatively weak interest prior to the offering lends further weight to the argument.

If participation in less-attractive issues is the price of inclusion in underpriced offerings, we should observe several related patterns in the data. For example, the underwriter investigated in this study, perhaps in an effort to avoid alienating both the investing public and its regulators, claims to earmark 40% of the shares in each issue for distribution among retail investors. If this claim is true, then issues with initial institutional holdings well in excess of 60% might represent cases in which pre-offer demand was weak and institutional investors were compelled to purchase a larger fraction of the issue. In such cases we might expect the underwriter to be less aggressive in its use of the overallotment option and institutional investors to be more aggressive in flipping their initial holdings. Dividing the 38-issue sample into quartiles according to initial institutional holdings, we find evidence consistent with both conjectures. In the presence of post-offer price support, the burden associated with participation in less-attractive issues is therefore diminished.

Alternatively, Welch (1992) interprets the underwriter as an institution aimed at inhibiting communication among potential investors. In Welch's (1992) model, asymmetric information creates the potential for a *cascade* in which investors deciding whether to purchase shares in an IPO ignore their private information in favor of information inferred from previous sales. Issuers benefit from cascades, and cascades are more likely to occur when communication among investors is limited. Welch (1992, footnote 31) conjectures that '... the relationship between an investor and a selling investment bank is far more adversarial than the relationships among investors'. Assuming that investors do communicate with one another, one might also conjecture that given the atomistic nature of retail investors, communication occurs to a greater degree

K.W. Hanley, W.J. Wilhelm, Jr./Journal of Financial Economics 37 (1995) 239–257   255

among institutional investors. Marketing an issue to retail investors would then appear to be the more attractive alternative. In this regard, our evidence is inconsistent with the cascade theory. Of course, it is possible that retail distribution channels are operationally inefficient relative to institutional channels. Benveniste and Bu-Saba (1993) compare cascade and information-gathering strategies and demonstrate that information gathering generates higher expected proceeds for the issuing firm. On the other hand, cascades reduce uncertainty about the level of proceeds.

Obviously, the data are insufficient to reach a definitive conclusion regarding the relative explanatory power of these theories, in part because the theories are not mutually exclusive, positing that asymmetric information among potential investors lies at the root of IPO underpricing. Rock (1986), however, does not consider mechanisms for resolving the information problem, and consequently underpricing is a reflection of the winner's curse faced by uninformed investors. In contrast, Benveniste and Wilhelm (1990) demonstrate that under some conditions underwriters have the incentive and leverage necessary to resolve informational asymmetries among investors. Under these circumstances, underpricing is the cost of eliciting private information. Although much of the evidence is consistent with the hypothesis that underwriters allocate IPO shares strategically in an attempt to mitigate the adverse selection described by Rock (1986), a stronger conclusion would require data not incorporated in this study. For example, we cannot observe the degree to which sample IPOs are rationed, nor can we observe variation in allocation patterns within the institutional and retail investor pools. More importantly, we cannot be certain that institutional investors are indeed well-informed relative to retail investors. If the distribution of information is more heterogeneous within rather than across the two investor classes, our evidence provides little insight into the relative merit of the two theories in the absence of rationing and within-class allocation data.

Of course, it is difficult to explain the favored status enjoyed by institutional investors if institutional investors are not well-informed relative to retail investors. One possible explanation is that investment banks bundle IPOs with other services in a manner described by Smith (1977) and Chalk and Peavy (1987), although this explanation does not account for the similarly large institutional allocations in overpriced issues. Alternatively, institutional distribution channels may simply be more efficient. If so, however, it is not clear why retail investors would receive even a small allocation of IPO shares unless investment banks are concerned that exclusion of retail investors from IPOs will limit the breadth of share distribution, harm relations with retail investors, or, perhaps worse, draw the attention of the regulatory community.

It should also be noted that recent evidence on the role of post-offer price supports by underwriters (Hanley, Kumar, and Seguin, 1993; Ruud, 1993) suggests that even if the information-gathering theory is an accurate description of the underwriting process for firm-commitment offerings in the U.S., the equilibrium is likely to be considerably more complicated than previously understood. In its current form, the information-gathering theory assumes that underwriters use a combination of underpricing, discriminatory allocation, and repeat transactions to elicit information from institutional investors. Although both post-offer price supports and rapid liquidation of shares (or flipping) impose a burden on underwriters, it is likely that such post-offer efforts complement pre-offer information gathering. It has been suggested that underwriters exercise control over the level of flipping among at least some of their investors by threatening exclusion from future IPOs (see the *Wall Street Journal*, December 29, 1993). Underwriters can then discriminate in the magnitude of expected profits allocated to individual investors by providing price support but limiting investor access to their artificially high bid price. In other words, although U.S. underwriters must sell IPO shares at a fixed price, their post-offer activities may permit them to replicate the effect of discriminatory pricing. Benveniste and Wilhelm (1990) demonstrate that the ability to set prices in a discriminatory manner leads to higher expected proceeds.

5. Conclusion

The evidence reported in this paper suggests that institutional investors are indeed the recipients of a large fraction of the short-run profits associated with IPOs. Although quite profitable, the favored status enjoyed by institutional investors in underpriced offerings appears to carry a *quid pro quo* expectation that they will participate in less-attractive issues as well. This pattern in the data suggests that U.S. underwriters behave strategically in their use of the freedom to discriminate in the allocation of IPOs. If this interpretation is accurate, our findings contradict the conventional wisdom that the apparent discriminatory practices of U.S. underwriters warrant criticism. Rather, the ability to engage in such practices may promote efficiency in U.S. capital markets by diminishing the consequences of an otherwise substantial market imperfection, and may in turn, shed light on the increasing popularity of the book-building approach to marketing IPOs (*The Economist*, January 9, 1993).

References

Benveniste, Lawrence M. and Walid Bu-Saba, 1993, Bookbuilding versus fixed price: An analysis of competing strategies for marketing IPOs, Working paper (Boston College, Chestnut Hill, MA).

Benveniste, Lawrence M. and Paul A. Spindt, 1989, How investment bankers determine the offer price and allocation of initial public offerings, Journal of Financial Economics 24, 343–362.

Benveniste, Lawrence M. and William J. Wilhelm, 1990, A comparative analysis of IPO proceeds under alternative regulatory environments, Journal of Financial Economics 28, 173–207.

K.W. Hanley, W.J. Wilhelm, Jr./Journal of Financial Economics 37 (1995) 239–257 257

Carter, Richard and Steven Manaster, 1990, Initial public offerings and underwriter reputation, Journal of Finance 45, 1045–1068.

Chalk, Andrew J. and John W. Peavy, 1987, Why you'll never get a 'hot' new issue, AAII Journal 9, 16–20.

Hanley, Kathleen Weiss, 1993, Underpricing of initial public offerings and the partial adjustment phenomenon, Journal of Financial Economics 34, 231–250 .

Hanley, Kathleen Weiss, A. Arun Kumar, and Paul J. Seguin, 1993, Price stabilization in the market for new issues, Journal of Financial Economics 34, 177–198.

Ibbotson, Roger G., 1975, Price performance of common stock new issues, Journal of Financial Economics 2, 235–272.

Keloharju, Matti, 1993, The winner's curse, legal liability, and the long-run performance of initial public offerings in Finland, Journal of Financial Economics 34, 251–277.

Koh, Francis and Terry Walter, 1989, A direct test of Rock's model of the pricing of unseasoned issues, Journal of Financial Economics 23, 251–272.

Loughran, Tim, Jay R. Ritter, and Kristian Rydqvist, 1994, Initial public offerings: International insights, Pacific-Basin Finance Journal, forthcoming.

Megginson, William L. and Kathleen A. Weiss, 1991, Venture capitalist certification in initial public offerings, Journal of Finance 46, 879–903.

Miller, Robert E. and Frank K. Reilly, 1987, An examination of mispricing, returns, and uncertainty for initial public offerings, Financial Management 16, 33–38.

Ritter, Jay R., 1991, The long-run performance of initial public offerings, Journal of Finance 46, 3–28.

Rock, Kevin, 1986, Why new issues are underpriced, Journal of Financial Economics 15, 187–212.

Ruud, Judith F., 1993, Underwriter price support and the IPO underpricing puzzle, Journal of Financial Economics 34, 135–152.

Smith, Clifford W., 1977, Alternative methods for raising capital: Rights versus underwritten offerings, Journal of Financial Economics 5, 273–307.

Welch, Ivo, 1992, Sequential sales, learning, and cascades, Journal of Finance 47, 695–732.

THE JOURNAL OF FINANCE • VOL. LII, NO. 2 • JUNE 1997

Analyst Following of Initial Public Offerings

RAGHURAM RAJAN and HENRI SERVAES*

ABSTRACT

We examine data on analyst following for a sample of initial public offerings completed between 1975 and 1987 to see how they relate to three well-documented IPO anomalies. We find that higher underpricing leads to increased analyst following. Analysts are overoptimistic about the earnings potential and long term growth prospects of recent IPOs. More firms complete IPOs when analysts are particularly optimistic about the growth prospects of recent IPOs. In the long run, IPOs have better stock performance when analysts ascribe low growth potential rather than high growth potential. These results suggest that the anomalies may be partially driven by overoptimism.

THREE WELL-DOCUMENTED "ANOMALIES" associated with initial public offerings (IPO) are underpricing, hot issue markets, and long-run underperformance. Can data on analyst following or analyst forecast accuracy help us understand these phenomena better? There is an ongoing debate about whether these anomalies are examples of market inefficiency, and if so, whether they are caused by the behavior of irrational investors or whether they reflect institutional constraints. Consider the long run underperformance of initial public offerings documented by Ritter (1991). The immediate question is whether the underperformance persists after precise adjustment for priced risk. If indeed IPOs underperform on a risk adjusted basis, the next question is whether the underperformance is because of institutional constraints—such as short sales restrictions—in the IPO market, or whether it is because of systematic overoptimism on the part of investors. The problem with investigating these issues using data on returns and prices only is that the researcher cannot tell if ex post realized returns for a security are low because the ex ante estimated cash flows were too high (either because of overoptimism on the part of all investors or because short sales constraints prevented the beliefs of pessimistic investors

* Rajan is from the University of Chicago and Servaes is from the University of North Carolina at Chapel Hill. Part of this research was completed when Servaes was visiting London Business School. Some of the results reported in this article were contained in a previous version of a related working paper: "The Effect of Market Conditions on Initial Public Offerings" (March 1994). We thank Mike Cooper, David Denis, Jennifer Francis, Joshua Lerner, Ernst Maug, Peter Pope, René Stulz, Sunil Wahal, Marc Zenner, an anonymous referee, and seminar participants at INSEAD, Katholieke Universiteit Leuven, London Business School, North Carolina State University, Norwegian School of Management, Stockholm School of Economics, University of Lausanne, and the University of North Carolina at Chapel Hill for helpful comments and suggestions and Jay Ritter and Michel Vetsuypens for allowing us to use their databases. IBES kindly allowed the use of their data on analyst following. This research was partially supported by the McColl Faculty Fellowship (Servaes), and NSF grant SBR 9423645 (Rajan).

from being reflected in the price) or because the expected returns were low. One possible way to disentangle the two is to look at investor expectations. To the extent that brokerage house analysts reflect or drive investor expectations, data on analyst following and forecast accuracy may throw more light on the debate.

With this in mind, we explore whether the behavior of analysts is related to the IPO anomalies. In particular, we address four questions: (i) Is analyst following related to the extent an initial public offering is underpriced? (ii) Do analysts make systematic errors in forecasting the performance of the firm undertaking the IPO? (iii) Is the number of IPOs coming to the market related to analyst (over)optimism? (iv) Is the long run performance of IPOs related to analyst (over)optimism?

We have to correct for a number of factors before we attempt to interpret the results. A growing literature has shown that analysts do not pick the firms they follow at random, nor are they unbiased in their forecasts. O'Brien and Bhushan (1990) find that analyst following increases with institutional ownership and industry growth. Pearson (1992) documents a positive relation between analyst following and beta, firm value, and the number of firms operating in an industry, and a negative relation between analyst following and the market model residual standard deviation. Several papers have documented that analysts tend to be overoptimistic (see, for example, Abarbanell (1991) and Brown, Foster, and Noreen (1985)). Dugar and Nathan (1995) and Lin and McNichols (1995) argue that part of the overoptimism may be because some analysts work for investment banks that have a relationship with the firm being analyzed, and issue optimistic forecasts for fear of jeopardizing the relationship. McNichols and O'Brien (1996) argue that the documented overoptimism may also stem from a selection bias; analysts typically start following stocks they are optimistic about. Finally, while many of these studies show that investors adjust for potential biases in analyst recommendations, investor behavior does appear to be affected by analysts. Irvine (1994) finds that trading volume and brokerage market share increase after a brokerage firm releases an investment report.

Even after correcting for previously documented influences, we obtain some interesting results. First, we find that more underpriced issues attract larger analyst following. Analysts then systematically overestimate the earnings of these companies, with forecast errors averaging 5 percent of the firm's stock price. As the forecast window (the length of time between making the forecast and the period for which the forecast is made) increases, so does the forecast error. Thus, analysts are not only overoptimistic, they are more overoptimistic about a firm's long term prospects than a firm's short term prospects. These forecast errors are lower after we make size and industry adjustments, but they remain highly significant. This indicates that the overoptimism of analysts for IPOs is only partly a reflection of their overoptimism in general. In addition, since their forecasts worsen with the forecast horizon, investors who rely on analyst forecasts to make investment decisions, are likely to purchase these shares at inflated prices.[1] We also study long-run (five years) earnings growth forecasts and find that within six months of the IPO, analysts predict that these firms will grow approximately six percentage points faster than their industry peers. These long run growth predictions decline substantially over the following months, which suggests that analysts eventually realize that the predicted growth cannot be attained.

Second, we document a positive relation between the number of IPOs coming to market in a given industry in a given quarter and several measures of analyst long-term earnings growth projections for recent IPOs in these industries. This finding is, perhaps, not surprising, since firms in industries with higher growth projections are likely to need more funds to finance this growth and an IPO may be the best method of obtaining these funds. However, we know that these growth projections are overly optimistic. Hence, these results suggest that firms take advantage of this optimism by raising funds from the public. What lends credence to this interpretation is that the number of firms coming to market is also positively correlated with the magnitude of the (matched firm adjusted) earnings forecast errors made by analysts for recent IPOs.

Finally, we relate analyst long-term growth projections to the aftermarket stock price performance of IPOs and find dramatic results. When firms are subdivided into quartiles according to their long-term growth projections, firms with the highest projected growth substantially underperform three benchmarks, whereas firms with the lowest growth projections outperform these benchmarks. The difference in returns between the two extreme quartiles is more than 100 percent. This indicates that investors appear to believe the inflated long-term growth.

A number of other articles also attempt to document and explain IPO anomalies. Loughran and Ritter (1995) report that IPOs completed in the 1970 to 1990 period have generated average annual returns of only five percent over the five year period subsequent to the offering. They argue that firms take advantage of windows of opportunity to issue stock publicly; these are periods when investors are willing to pay high prices, relative to some historical benchmarks, for corporate assets in certain industries. Rajan and Servaes (1995) present evidence consistent with this notion: more firms conduct IPOs when seasoned firms in their industries are trading at high multiples relative to the stock market and relative to historical levels. They also find that firms coming to market during these periods have poor aftermarket stock price performance. Lerner (1994) studies a sample of 350 privately held venture-backed biotechnology firms and finds that these firms go public when equity valuations are high. Jain and Kini (1994) and Mikkelson and Shah (1994) analyze the earnings performance of firms that conduct IPOs; these firms

---

[1] As indicated in the introductory paragraph, we cannot tell whether our results are because the investing public believes analyst forecasts or because analyst forecasts reflect the beliefs of the investing public. In other words, we establish correlation but not causality. However, we speculate about the likely source in the conclusion.

perform very well prior to the IPO, but very poorly afterwards. For a sample of 284 firms that went public in the 1980 to 1983 period, Mikkelson and Shah find that the median pretax operating cash flow per dollar of assets is only four cents during the first three years after the IPO. Our article differs from these in its focus on analyst data, and in its attempt to find a common link between underpricing and the other two IPO anomalies.

Finally, Teoh, Wong, and Rao (1995), find that firms with extensive discretionary accounting accruals perform poorly in the aftermarket. They argue that firms adopt these accrual adjustments to manipulate reported earnings before and soon after the IPO. Investors may not fully understand the implications of this manipulation for future earnings growth, which leads to a revaluation of share prices in the aftermarket. Our article suggests that one reason investors do not understand these implications is that they receive poor information from analysts.

The remainder of this article is organized as follows. Section I describes the data collection process and presents some descriptive statistics. Section II contains our results and Section III concludes.

I. Data Collection and Description

We gather a sample of firm commitment IPOs completed between 1975 and the second quarter of 1987 from databases compiled by Ritter (1984, 1991), Loughran and Ritter (1995), and Barry, Muscarella, and Vetsuypens (1991). Stock price data are obtained from the Center for Research in Security Prices (CRSP) and analyst following information from Institutional Brokers Estimate System (IBES). Table I describes the sample over time and contains data on underpricing. Underpricing is computed as the difference between the first aftermarket price and the offer price, divided by the offer price. As documented previously, there is substantial variation in the number of issues coming to market over time (see Ibbotson and Jaffe (1975) and Ritter (1984)) and IPOs are underpriced, on average (see Ibbotson (1975)). Average underpricing is 10.03 percent over the sample period, and, except for 1975, IPOs are underpriced each year. There is also substantial time-series variation in underpricing, with a low of -0.88 percent in 1975 and a high of 28.99 percent in 1980.

More than half of the firms in our sample (56.3 percent) are covered on the IBES database at some point in time after the offering. However, because we are interested in the behavior of analysts shortly after the IPO, much of the ensuing analyses focus on those firms covered by IBES within one year or three years of the offering. The one-year sample consists of 935 firms, or approximately one third of the original sample. The three-year sample consists of 1410 firms, which is more than 52 percent of the original sample. Also note that IBES coverage improves over time. Except for 1975, IBES coverage within one year of going public was rather sporadic over the 1975 to 1981 period. Coverage improved substantially in 1982, and by 1986 more than half of the IPOs were covered by at least one analyst within 12 months of going public. Interestingly, there is no relation between the number of IPOs and analyst following. With

Analyst Following of Initial Public Offerings   511

Table I

Distribution of Sample Over Time and Underpricing Information

Underpricing is computed as: (First Aftermarket Price − Offer Price)/Offer Price. Only firm commitment offers are included in the sample. Number on Institutional Brokers Estimate System (IBES) refers to the number of initial public offering (IPO) firms who are listed on the IBES database. Number on IBES < 1 (3) year(s) refers to the number of firms who are listed on the IBES database within 1 (3) years of their IPO. Fraction refers to the fraction of IPOs listed on IBES within the specified period.

Year	Number of IPOs	Average Underpricing	Number on IBES (Fraction)	Number on IBES < 1 year (Fraction)	Number on IBES < 3 years (Fraction)
75	11	−0.0088	8 (0.73)	3 (0.27)	7 (0.64)
76	28	0.0030	15 (0.54)	0 (0.00)	11 (0.39)
77	20	0.0660	6 (0.30)	0 (0.00)	3 (0.15)
78	24	0.1413	15 (0.63)	1 (0.04)	12 (0.50)
79	49	0.1351	25 (0.51)	0 (0.00)	20 (0.41)
80	125	0.2899	48 (0.38)	5 (0.04)	44 (0.35)
81	320	0.1186	131 (0.41)	24 (0.08)	107 (0.33)
82	107	0.1032	58 (0.54)	28 (0.26)	50 (0.47)
83	651	0.1100	355 (0.55)	260 (0.40)	327 (0.50)
84	336	0.0662	157 (0.47)	86 (0.26)	138 (0.41)
85	276	0.0877	177 (0.64)	110 (0.40)	171 (0.62)
86	551	0.0785	376 (0.68)	286 (0.52)	360 (0.65)
87 (6 months)	227	0.0677	164 (0.72)	132 (0.58)	160 (0.70)
Total	2725	0.1003	1535 (0.56)	935 (0.34)	1410 (0.52)

limited analyst resources (and time needed to increase trained capacity), one might expect that fewer IPOs are followed during hot issue periods, but this is not consistent with the evidence presented in Table I. Thus capacity constraints (number of available analysts) do not seem to be a problem for the period under study.

II. Results

A. Analyst Following and Underpricing

We first explore the determinants of analyst interest in a firm and, in particular, we investigate whether analyst following is related to the extent of underpricing. IBES collects all forecasts from a group of analysts who agree to provide them in return for free use of IBES products or data. Consequently, if IBES's choice of analysts is random, the data are unbiased. However, it is possible that some biases creep into IBES's choice of analysts. For instance, it may be easier for IBES to obtain forecasts from analysts of the major brokerage houses. These analysts may be more likely to ignore small firms trading on regional exchanges. If this is the case, there are two reasons why firms may not be followed: either analysts do not deem the firm worthy of following or IBES does not get forecasts from the analysts most likely to follow the firm.

To correct for a potential selection bias in the IPOs for which we have no evidence of analyst following, we employ Heckman's (1979) two stage process. In the first stage, we attempt to correct for potential selection biases in IBES's choice of analysts. In the second stage, we investigate the determinants of analyst following (including underpricing).

In the second stage, the dependent variable is the average number of analysts making earnings forecasts per forecast period during the year after the IPO. This is a measure of analyst interest in the firm. The explanatory variables are firm size (the log of market value of equity computed at the first after market price), which should be positively correlated with analyst interest. Since analysts typically specialize in particular industries, there are likely to be more analysts with the potential to follow IPOs in industries with more seasoned firms. So, we also include the number of seasoned firms (firms on COMPUSTAT for more than three years at the time of the IPO) in the two-digit Standard Industrial Classification (SIC) code of the IPO firm. Finally, we include the degree of underpricing.

The first stage explains why the dependent variable is not missing. We could report the regression only for the observations that are not missing, but we would then be losing some potential information in the data.[2] As argued above, the data could be missing because of a selection bias in IBES coverage or it could be missing because of a lack of analyst interest.

In the first stage regression, we include variables that ought to proxy for the potential selection bias. As Table I indicates, IBES's coverage improves over time. So clearly, the inclusion of year dummies is warranted in the first stage regression. Furthermore, IBES is more likely to have relationships with analysts in large brokerages headquartered in the financial centers than with analysts from small brokerages in remote areas. Since the clients of the latter are likely to be smaller, and not listed on a major exchange, we include firm size, and an indicator if the firm is not listed on a major exchange (i.e., not on New York Stock Exchange (NYSE), American Stock Exchange (AMEX), or National Association of Securities Dealers Automated Quotation (Nasdaq). We also include the number of firms in the industry at the time of the IPO. Finally, since IBES's choice of analysts may be biased toward those following certain industries, we include dummies for the 13 most important two-digit SIC industries in our database.

The results are reported in the first regression model presented in Panels A and B of Table II. The average number of analysts making forecasts is strongly positively related to firm size ($\beta = 0.59$, $t = 17.8$). It is also strongly positively related to the degree of underpricing ($\beta = 0.99$, $t = 6.51$). A one standard deviation increase in underpricing (an increase by 0.26) increases the number of analysts following the firm in the first year by 0.25.[3] Since there are 0.7 analysts following a firm on average in the first year, the coefficient is also

---

[2] All the results we report hold qualitatively when we confine the regression only to firms for whom we have analyst following data in the first three years.

[3] The marginal effect reported is for the latent variable.

Table II

Determinants of Analyst Following

Panel A presents the second stage estimates (using Heckman's (1979) two step procedure) of the determinants of analyst following. Panel B contains coefficient estimates for the first stage model, which is a maximum likelihood probit model that determines when the dependent variable in the second stage is not missing. Underpricing is computed as: (First aftermarket price–Offer price)/ Offer price. AV1 is the average number of analyst forecasts per reporting period during the first year after the initial public offering (IPO). Other explanatory variables are: (i) the logarithm of the market value of equity, computed on the first trading day; (ii) the number of firms listed on COMPUSTAT for more than three years at the time of the IPO who are also in the same two-digit industry; (iii) the number of lead managers to the IPO. The first regression is estimated using all firms with available data. The second regression is estimated for IPOs from 1985 onwards. Underpricing is subdivided into four categories in the second regression model, depending on the level of underpricing. p values are in parentheses.

	Full sample	1985 to 1987
Panel A: Second Stage Estimates: Dependent Variable is AV1.		
Underpricing	0.99 (0.00)	
Underpricing * Indicator if negative		2.03 (0.34)
Indicator if underpricing is zero		0.03 (0.75)
Underpricing * Indicator if positive but less than the median of positive observations		0.66 (0.64)
Underpricing * Indicator if positive but more than the median of positive observations		0.80 (0.00)
Log equity size	0.59 (0.00)	0.41 (0.00)
Number of firms in industry	0.002 (0.00)	0.002 (0.00)
Number of lead managers to the issue		0.13 (0.00)
Prob > Chi^2	0.000	0.000
Number of observations	2274	803

Panel B: First Stage Estimates (Explaining When the Dependent Variable in the Second Stage is not Missing)

Estimated model: Analyst following is not missing if:

$c + c_1 \cdots c_n$ (Year indicators) $+ c_{n+1}$ (Log size equity) $+ c_{n+2}$ (number of firms in 2-digit industry) $+ c_{n+3} \cdots c_{n+15}$ (*industry dummies*) $+ c_{n+16}$ (Equity not traded on a major exchange) $+ f > 0$

The constant and the coefficients on industry and year indicators are not reported.

Log equity size	0.64 (0.02)	0.67 (0.00)
Not traded on a major exchange	−0.37 (0.00)	−0.50 (0.00)
Number of firms in industry	0.002 (0.09)	0.005 (0.00)
Prob > Chi^2	0.000	0.000
Number of observations	2274	803

economically meaningful. The correlation between underpricing and following is robust to a variety of different specifications and to the inclusion of additional variables such as trading volume in the first 100 days (a proxy for the demand for analyst services), turnover (which may be a proxy for the stability of shareholdings), stock price volatility (a proxy for the risk of the stock), and past and future growth of the industry. It is also robust to changes in the dependent variable to (i) the average number of analysts making earnings forecasts per forecast period during the three years after the IPO, (ii) the total number of forecasts in the first year, or (iii) the total number of forecasts in the first three years after the IPO. These results are available on request from the authors.

IBES's coverage, as we have seen, was much better during the latter half of the sample period. Hence, the dependent variable should be less noisy if we only consider IPOs from 1985 onwards. Also, lead managers to an issue would like to sustain interest in IPOs they bring to market, and are more likely to encourage their analysts to follow them. So, we include the number of lead managers to the issue that we collected from the Investment Dealers Digest for all IPOs after 1984. Finally, we want to see if it is the absolute price movement at the open (i.e., both underpricing and overpricing) that attracts analyst interest, or whether it is significant underpricing only. We therefore partition the underpricing variable into overpricing (negative "underpricing"), underpricing if zero, underpricing if positive and less than the median of positive observations, and underpricing if positive and greater than the median of positive observations.

The coefficient estimates in the second model show that the number of lead managers is significantly positively related with analyst following, even after controlling for firm size. But underpricing is still important. However, only the coefficient for extreme underpricing is statistically different from zero ($\beta = 0.8$, $t = 3.19$). Also, it appears that analysts lose interest if an issue is overpriced, although the coefficient, while economically large, is measured very imprecisely.[4]

Overall, these results suggest that firms that underprice attract analyst interest. Clearly, there could be a common omitted variable that drives both underpricing and analyst following, but it is not obvious what it is. On the other hand, there are theories that suggest that underpricing may, in fact, drive the extent of analyst interest. Chemmanur (1993) argues (p. 286) that "insiders of high value firms are motivated to maximize outsider information production so that this information will be reflected in the secondary market price of their firm's equity, increasing its expected value. However, since information production is costly, only a lower IPO share price will induce more outsiders to produce information. The equilibrium offer price may involve some underpricing. . . ." To the extent that analysts are agents of outsiders, our finding supports Chemmanur's hypothesis. A number of articles take a less rational view of investors (see Ibbotson and Ritter (1995) for a more detailed

---

[4] We also verify that these results are not caused by outliers.

review). Shiller's (1990) "impresario" hypothesis is that the market for IPOs is subject to fads and IPOs are underpriced by investment bankers (the impresarios) to create the appearance of excess demand, just as the promoter of a rock concert attempts to make it an "event." Rajan and Servaes (1995) argue that to ensure the success of an issue, investment bankers have to underprice to deal with potential "feedback" trader risk.[5] Finally, we will shortly present evidence that analysts tend to be systematically overoptimistic. It is possible that firms underprice with the direct aim of attracting analysts, who will then keep the firm stock price high until such time as the promoters have unloaded further shares. We now turn to tests of the accuracy of analyst forecasts.

B. Earnings Forecast Errors

We focus on firms listed on IBES within one year of their IPO and examine the accuracy of analyst forecasts made over the two years after going public. Including firms listed on IBES after one year would obscure some of the results, because forecast errors would be influenced both by the addition of new firms as well as revisions in forecasts of firms already listed. Moreover, we are interested in how analysts make earnings forecasts for recent IPOs. Firms that went public more than one year before the first forecast is made are less useful for this purpose. Forecast errors are computed as: (Actual earnings − Earnings forecast)/Stock price at the time of the earnings forecast. Thus we gather data on the firm's stock price at the time the forecast is made and employ this as a deflator of the forecast error.

Forecasts are available on a monthly basis and made for periods up to two fiscal years in the future. Obviously, forecast accuracy improves over time. We therefore report forecast accuracy for different forecast windows, defined as the number of months between the time the forecast is made and the fiscal year end for which the forecast is made. To gauge whether forecasts become more accurate over time, we separately report forecasts made within one year of the IPO, and forecasts made between one and two years after the IPO. We also report matching firm adjusted forecast errors. A matching firm is selected by ranking, according to market value of equity, all seasoned firms in the same industry (two-digit level) for which forecasts with the same window are available. The firm closest in size to the IPO firm is selected.

Forecast errors are reported in Table III. Panel A contains the forecasts made within one year of the IPO. The results indicate that analysts are systematically overoptimistic with regard to the earnings of firms that recently went public (see also Ali (1996)). The forecast error as a percentage of the stock price is −3.36 percent for forecasts made for a three-month window; the error

---

[5] Feedback traders are investors whose demand is based on prior returns. If they observe that the first trading price is below the offer price, they may sell the offer short, which will further depress the stock price. Rational investors, who anticipate the behavior of feedback traders, will ensure that this behavior is already reflected in the first trading price. Investment banks who stabilize the issue in the aftermarket protect themselves from this feedback trader risk by underpricing.

Table III

Analyst Earnings Forecast Errors for Initial Public Offerings (IPOs)

The sample consists of all forecasts made by analysts for earnings in the two year period following the IPO. Only forecasts made for firms listed on Institutional Brokers Estimate System (IBES) within one year of the IPO are included. The forecast error is computed as: (Actual earnings − Earnings forecast)/Stock price at the time of the earnings forecast. We report forecast errors for forecast windows of three through 21 months in three-month intervals. Window is the number of months between the time the forecast is made and the fiscal year end for which the forecast is made. Matched firm adjusted forecast errors are computed by subtracting the forecast error of the firm with the same two-digit Standard Industrial Classification (SIC) code closest in size to the IPO firm, if this firm has been listed on COMPUSTAT for at least three years. The number of observations in the matched firm adjusted sample is smaller because no matched firms can be found for certain forecast windows. p-values are in parentheses.

Window	Forecast Error	Number	Matched Firm Adjusted Forecast Error	Number
Panel A: Forecasts Made Within One Year of the IPO				
3 months	−0.0336 (0.00)	412	−0.0165 (0.06)	340
6 months	−0.0445 (0.00)	400	−0.0147 (0.07)	324
9 months	−0.0449 (0.00)	442	−0.0167 (0.00)	329
12 months	−0.0577 (0.00)	327	−0.0321 (0.01)	263
15 months	−0.0456 (0.00)	310	−0.0112 (0.20)	255
18 months	−0.0430 (0.00)	268	−0.0122 (0.10)	212
21 months	−0.0486 (0.00)	175	0.0033 (0.71)	118
Panel B: Forecasts Made Between One and Two Years After the IPO				
3 months	−0.0321 (0.00)	685	−0.0182 (0.01)	436
6 months	−0.0345 (0.00)	660	−0.0130 (0.03)	426
9 months	−0.0414 (0.00)	629	−0.0192 (0.00)	364
12 months	−0.0534 (0.00)	610	−0.0205 (0.00)	421
15 months	−0.0586 (0.00)	548	−0.0244 (0.00)	358
18 months	−0.0603 (0.00)	469	−0.0103 (0.20)	294
21 months	−0.0509 (0.00)	246	−0.0108 (0.41)	130

increases with the window up to 12 months when the forecast error is −5.77 percent. Note that the number of observations is smaller than the 935 firms for which IBES data are available (see Table I) because not all firms have forecasts available for all forecast windows. Matched firm adjusted forecast errors remain negative and significant for the three to 12 month period, but they are generally less than half of the raw forecast error. For example, for the 12 month window, raw forecast errors average −5.77 percent, whereas matched firm adjusted errors are −3.21 percent. These results indicate that the previously documented overoptimism on the part of analysts is about twice as severe for IPOs.

Panel B contains the errors for forecasts made between one and two years after the IPO. A comparison of Panels A and B illustrates that forecast accuracy does not improve as the firm becomes more seasoned. The errors presented in both panels are very similar. For example, the average forecast error is −0.0449 for the nine month window in the first year after the IPO and −0.0414 in the second year after the IPO. Similarly, there is little variation over the two years in matched firm adjusted forecast errors. For instance, the average matched firm adjusted forecast error is −0.0147 for the six month window in the first year after the IPO and −0.0130 in the second year after the IPO. The *t*-tests indicate that none of the differences in forecast errors between Panels A and B are significant at conventional significance levels (10 percent or better).

We also estimate cross-sectional regression models of forecast errors on firm size, the number of analysts following the firm, industry dummies, and an indicator variable, set equal to one if the firm went public in the previous two years, and zero otherwise. The coefficient on the IPO dummy is significant for all windows, and close to the matched firm adjusted forecast error reported in Table III.

Clearly, one does not have to rely on irrationality to explain this finding. It could stem, for instance, from selection bias: IPOs are underwritten by investment banks who are optimistic about the underwritten firm's prospects. It is natural for analysts from these investment banks also to be optimistic. Alternatively, conflicts of interest may prevent analysts from investment banks that are associated with the firm making the offering from being objective about the firm (see Dugar and Nathan (1995), Lin and McNichols (1995), Michaely and Womack (1996)). By definition, all IPOs have recently been underwritten, so we cannot fully separate selection bias or agency explanations of the forecast errors from explanations based on irrational investors. We can, however, test whether factors correlated with agency or selection bias problems also correlate with the size of the forecast errors.

We know the number of lead underwriters to an issue. Typically, there is a quality threshold below which firms are not underwritten. If an investment bank has a positive signal about a firm that pushes it above the threshold, it agrees to be a lead underwriter. Hence, there is a selection bias in firms that are underwritten. If investment banks independently agree to be lead underwriter, then the number of lead underwriters is a measure of the number of independent positive signals on the firm. The more the positive signals, the more likely is the firm to be truly above the underwriting threshold and the less the selection bias. If forecast errors stem from selection bias, then the more lead underwriters the lower should be the forecast error.

By contrast, if forecast errors are because of agency problems, then the more lead underwriters there are to an issue, the more likely it is that forecasts of independent analysts will be swamped by forecasts of analysts who have vested interests in the success of the issue, and the greater should be the bias in forecasts. Finally, if forecast errors are due to universal overoptimism about IPOs, there should be no consistent relation between the magnitude of the forecast errors and the number of lead underwriters to the IPO. The last is indeed the case. For instance, for the three month window forecasts, overoptimism clearly increases with the number of underwriters (from −0.004 for IPOs with one underwriter to −0.063 for IPOs with more than three) while for the 21 month window, it clearly decreases (forecast errors go from −0.012 for IPOs with one underwriter to +0.069 for IPOs with more than three). For other windows, there is no clear relation. The correlation between the number of lead underwriters and the forecast error is significantly negative only for the three month window, and only at the 10 percent level, suggesting that any relationship is very weak. Finally, the number of lead underwriters may proxy for size. Including size in regression models of forecast errors on the number of lead underwriters does not affect our results. Larger firms have smaller forecast errors, but the effect of the number of lead managers is only significant (and negative) for the three month window (*p*-value = 0.07).[6]

Overall, the results of Table III suggest that analyst earnings forecasts for firms that have recently gone public have an upward bias, and this bias is larger than the previously documented bias for seasoned firms. The bias increases with the forecast window and persists after controlling for size, industry, and the number of analysts following the firm. While we cannot rule out agency or selection bias related explanations of the forecast errors, systematic overoptimism on the part of analysts seems part of the explanation. Of course, we will obtain more support for this interpretation if we find that these errors are related to the number of IPOs coming to market (suggesting that firms time their issues to take advantage of mispricing). Before testing this conjecture, we analyze analyst predictions of firm growth.

C. Long-Term Earnings Growth Projections

In addition to earnings forecasts, analysts also make long term earnings growth projections. While there is no formal definition of what constitutes long term, discussions with IBES suggest that a five-year horizon is representative for what analysts have in mind when these forecasts are made. The fuzziness of the horizon and the existence of firms with currently negative earnings implies that we cannot, with great confidence, adjust this measure by the actual realizations to get firm-by-firm measures of analyst overoptimism (although averages are likely to be more meaningful). Thus, a priori, the long term earnings growth forecasts should be thought of as a measure of the *relative* optimism of analysts. We will, however, provide some evidence from an analysis of ex post returns that it may also be a proxy for the degree of overoptimism by the analysts.

---

[6] Another potential explanation for our results stems from the selection bias inherent in an analyst's decision to follow a firm. As McNichols and O'Brien (1996) argue, only optimistic analysts start following firms. So recommendations by analysts (e.g., buy, hold, or sell) who have just started following firms are typically positive. But they also argue that analysts have a greater incentive to collect information about newly added stocks. This explains their somewhat surprising finding that earnings forecasts made by these analysts tend to be less upward biased. Our finding that forecasts for IPOs (which are, by definition, newly followed) are more optimistic than for seasoned firms suggests, at the very least, that there is a different underlying explanation than the one proposed by McNichols and O'Brien.

Analyst Following of Initial Public Offerings 519

Table IV
Forecasts of Long Term Earnings Growth for Initial Public Offerings (IPOs)

Time refers to the time period after the IPO that the forecast is made. Industry-adjusted long term growth rates are computed by subtracting the average of all firms with the same two-digit industry code, for all firms listed on COMPUSTAT for at least three years. Only forecasts made the last month of each quarter after the IPO are listed. The table contains forecasts for all firms listed on Institutional Brokers Estimate System (IBES) within one year of the IPO.

Time	Long Term Growth Forecast (in %)	Number	Industry-Adjusted Long Term Growth Forecast (in %) (p-Value)	Number
3 months	23.19	28	5.42 (0.07)	27
6 months	23.73	252	5.43 (0.00)	238
9 months	22.45	433	4.22 (0.00)	400
12 months	22.03	526	3.22 (0.03)	480
15 months	21.13	568	3.08 (0.00)	520
18 months	20.26	585	3.27 (0.00)	530
21 months	19.63	582	3.02 (0.00)	530
24 months	19.77	566	3.04 (0.00)	516
27 months	19.02	568	2.40 (0.00)	515
30 months	18.14	571	1.81 (0.00)	516
33 months	17.84	547	1.64 (0.00)	490
36 months	17.61	537	1.39 (0.01)	484

Table IV contains a detailed analysis of long-term growth forecasts generated over the three-year period following the IPO. We only focus on corporations listed on IBES within 12 months of their IPO and report the average of the growth forecasts for the last month of each quarter. The initial long term earnings growth forecasts are high (23–24 percent), and they fall considerably by the third year after the IPO. IPOs are expected to grow five percentage points faster than their industry in the three to six month period after the IPO. By the end of the first year, these expectations fall to approximately three percent faster than the industry and by the end of the third year, IPOs are expected to grow only 1.4 percent faster than the industry rate.[7]

One explanation for this downward drift in industry-adjusted growth rates is that analysts (and investors) are overoptimistic about the prospects of IPOs, but they adjust their expectations over time. This could account for the long run underperformance of IPOs. A more mundane explanation is that much of the growth of IPO earnings is concentrated within the first few years after the IPO. But, to account for the revision over the first year in five-year industry adjusted growth rates in Table IV, a crude calculation shows that earnings

---

[7] One problem with these numbers is that more firms are added to the IBES database as we increase the time period after going public (up to one year). However, if we restrict ourselves to firms listed on the IBES database within three months of the IPO, the results are similar to those reported in Table IV.

from the average IPO should increase at a nine percent faster rate than the
industry over the first three years.[8] This seems rather high. In addition, it is
inconsistent with Jain and Kini (1994) and Mikkelson and Shah (1994) who
find that firms have poor earnings growth in the year following the IPO.

These results suggest that analysts are also overoptimistic about the long-
term growth opportunities of IPOs (and we support this later with evidence
that the higher the long term earnings growth forecasts, the lower, on average,
are returns).

Which measure—earnings forecast errors or long term earnings growth
projections—should be used in our analysis? While the former is a more direct
proxy for overoptimism, it has the disadvantage of being based on ex post data,
and therefore it is mechanically correlated with long term returns. Furthermore, earnings forecasts do not seem to be adjusted downwards rapidly and, as
illustrated in Table III, for a given forecast window, they do not improve in
accuracy over time.[9] There may also be greater selection problems associated
with earnings forecasts.[10] In what follows we will investigate the relationship
between both measures and the number of firms coming to market. Finally, we
will examine the correlation between long term earnings growth forecasts and
ex post returns. We will not use forecast errors in this case because it contains
ex post data.

---

[8] If we assume that the expected growth is uniform over the next five years, the growth rate for
the first three years should have been approximately 27 percent, which is nine percent above
expected industry growth at the start of the first year and the second year, and 10 percent above
expected industry growth at the start of the third year.

[9] We check whether earnings forecasts (as compared to forecast errors) decline over time. We
analyze earnings forecasts for the end of the next fiscal year (window between 13 and 24 months)
and track this number over the three years following the IPO. Expected earnings per share are
$1.16 one year after the IPO (adjusted for splits), $1.18 after two years, and $1.16 after three
years. As a fraction of the stock price, this is 0.108 one year after the IPO, 0.096 after two years,
and 0.089 after three years. Thus, while analysts project high growth rates, the projected earnings
are actually flat. Given the slight increase in the stock price over time, there is a decline in the
forecast to price ratio.

[10] McNichols and O'Brien (1996) provide evidence that analysts disproportionately tend to
follow successful firms and stop following unsuccessful firms. It is possible that this bias is
concentrated more in earnings forecasts than in growth forecasts. This may explain why earnings
forecasts in the second year persist in being high even though growth forecasts are revised
downward—earnings forecasts in the second year contain a disproportionate number of winners.
We find evidence consistent with this. At the end of one year after the IPO, we have 734 firms
being followed, with an average of 2.99 analysts reporting earnings forecasts per firm. The average
number of analysts reporting earnings forecasts for these firms goes up to 3.75 at the end of the
second year, an increase of about 25 percent. The comparable figures for the 526 firms reporting
growth forecasts at the end of the first year is 1.73 and 2.06, implying growth of about 20 percent.
But the distribution of analysts among good and poorly performing firms at the end of the second
year is more skewed for earnings forecasts. Firms in the lowest quartile of return performance
have only 72 percent of the mean number of analysts (=3.75) reporting earnings forecasts,
whereas firms in the highest quartile have 123 percent of the mean number of analysts reporting
earnings forecasts. The corresponding figures for growth forecasts of 77 percent and 114 percent
suggests less bias.

D. Analyst Optimism and Windows of Opportunity

In this section we examine whether the long term earnings growth projections and earnings forecasts are related to the frequency with which firms engage in IPOs. If analysts are systematically overoptimistic about the prospects of IPOs and if there is substantial time series variation in this overoptimism, more firms should come to the market when this overoptimism is particularly severe. This is consistent with the "window of opportunity" arguments discussed by Ritter (1991), Lerner (1994), Loughran and Ritter (1995), and Rajan and Servaes (1995), and the "investor sentiment" evidence presented by Lee, Shleifer, and Thaler (1991). Lee *et al.* find that more IPOs come to market when closed-end funds trade at a low discount compared to net asset values; they interpret the closed-end fund discount as a measure of investor sentiment. Growth forecasts are, perhaps, a more direct measure of sentiment and a finding of positive correlation will add validity to the interpretation of Lee *et al.*

The focus in this analysis is on those industries (defined at the two-digit SIC code level) with at least 50 IPOs over our sample period. Approximately 62 percent of the firms in our sample are from industries that meet this selection criterion. The reason for limiting our analysis to industries with many IPOs is that we construct measures of analyst forecasts for recent IPOs in each industry. Obviously, such measures cannot be computed for industries with only sporadic IPO activity.

Specifically, we count the number of IPOs in each quarter in each industry and relate this frequency to measures of analyst forecasts computed on a quarterly basis. Four measures of analyst forecasts are employed: (a) long term earnings growth projections for all recent (<1 year) IPOs; (b) long term earnings growth projections for all recent IPOs, computed separately for each industry; (c) industry long term earnings growth projections for all industries with recent IPOs; (d) industry-adjusted long term earnings growth projections for all recent IPOs. Firms in the industry sample have to be listed on COMPUSTAT for at least three years. We employ forecasts made during the last month of each quarter. If no forecasts are available for the last month of the quarter, we use the second month, and if no forecasts are available for the second month, we use the first month.

Table V presents the results for the four measures of analyst forecasts. Tobit models are estimated because the dependent variable is truncated at zero. Panel A includes our earnings growth forecast measure as an explanatory variable, together with 12 industry dummies defined at the two-digit level (coefficients not reported). The column heading describes the growth measure employed in the model presented in that column. Our measures of long term earnings growth forecasts are positive in all models and significant in three of the four models. Interestingly, the model in column (i) has the largest explanatory power. In that model all long term earnings growth forecasts for IPOs completed over the last year are averaged by quarter. Thus, this explanatory variable is the same for each industry. The result is also economically signif-

Table V

Tobit Regressions of the Number of Initial Public Offerings (IPOs) Coming to Market During a Quarter on Long Term Earnings Growth Forecasts and Control Variables

The dependent variable is the number of IPOs coming to market in a quarter in a (two-digit) industry. Only 13 industries with at least 50 IPOs over the sample period are included in the analysis. Four long term earnings growth measures are employed as explanatory variables: (i) LT IPO earnings growth is the average long term earnings growth forecast for all firms that went public in the previous 12 month period; (ii) LT IPO earnings growth by industry is the average long term earnings growth forecast for all firms in the same two-digit Standard Industrial Classification (SIC) code industry that went public in the previous 12 month period; (iii) LT industry earnings growth is the average long term earnings growth forecast for all seasoned firms (>3 years on COMPUSTAT) in the same two-digit SIC code industry; (iv) LT IPO industry-adjusted earnings growth is the long term earnings growth forecast for all firms in the same two-digit SIC code industry that went public in the previous 12 months period, minus the same forecast for all seasoned firms in that industry. Only forecasts made during the last month of each quarter are employed. Historical MB is the average equity market to book ratio for seasoned firms in the industry (listed at least three years) at the end of the previous quarter, divided by the same measure averaged over all quarters in the five surrounding years. Relative MB is the average equity market to book ratio for seasoned firms in the industry (listed at least three years) at the end of the previous quarter, divided by the market to book ratio for all seasoned firms in the market at the end of that quarter. MARKET MB is the equally weighted equity market to book ratio for all seasoned firms in the market in the previous quarter, divided by the same measure averaged over all quarters in the five years surrounding that quarter. *p*-values are in parentheses.

	Explanatory Variable			
	LT IPO Earnings Growth	LT IPO Earnings Growth by Industry	LT Industry Earnings Growth	LT IPO Industry-Adjusted Earnings Growth
Panel A: Excluding Control Variables				
Intercept	−3.845	0.564	3.402	3.479
	(0.010)	(0.68)	(0.02)	(0.01)
Growth measure	0.323	0.125	0.010	0.062
	(0.00)	(0.00)	(0.75)	(0.00)
Pseudo R^2	0.117	0.058	0.037	0.047
Number	299	165	165	165
Panel B: Including Control Variables				
Intercept	−32.120	−49.086	−50.607	−50.696
	(0.00)	(0.00)	(0.00)	(0.00)
Growth measure	0.186	0.079	0.000	0.040
	(0.00)	(0.00)	(0.99)	(0.02)
Historical MB	−2.827	−14.097	−11.238	−14.423
	(0.47)	(0.04)	(0.11)	(0.04)
Relative MB	8.275	15.603	16.882	17.627
	(0.00)	(0.00)	(0.00)	(0.00)
Market MB	21.456	41.972	40.756	42.844
	(0.00)	(0.00)	(0.00)	(0.00)
Pseudo R^2	0.162	0.128	0.116	0.122
Number	299	165	165	165

icant. An increase in the long term earnings growth projections of seven percentage points (= one standard deviation) increases the number of IPOs per industry per quarter by 2.4 (= one half of its standard deviation).[11] This result suggests that analyst optimism may not be industry specific but applies to all IPOs during a particular period. When analysts project high earnings growth for recent IPOs, regardless of their industry, the number of new IPOs increases, consistent with the conjecture that firms exploit these "windows of opportunity" to go public.

Two other long-term growth forecast measures also yield significant results: (i) long-term earnings growth forecasts for recent IPOs, computed by industry; and (ii) industry-adjusted long-term earnings growth forecasts for recent IPOs. Note that the number of observations in these models is smaller because we lack forecasts for recent IPOs in some industries in some quarters.[12]

Arguably, finding a relation between long term earnings growth forecasts and the number of firms engaging in an IPO is not that surprising. Firms with high future growth projections need funds to finance this growth, and selling shares to the public is one method of obtaining new financing. There are at least two reasons, however, why this argument is not entirely convincing. First, evidence presented in the previous section suggests that analyst growth projections are biased upwards; hence, the forecasts employed in the regression models presented in Table V are poor predictors of actual firm growth, and the resulting need for funds. Second, the third model presented in Table V indicates that the frequency of new IPOs is not related to industry growth projections. The coefficient on industry growth is small, and not significantly different from zero. Firms engage in an IPO when recent IPOs in that industry (and IPOs in general) are expected to grow quickly, but not when the seasoned firms in their industry are expected to grow quickly. These results are more consistent with the argument that firms go public when analysts (and, coincidentally or consequently, the public) are optimistic than with the argument that firms go public because they need to finance future growth.

In Panel B of Table V, we add a number of control variables to the estimated regression models to verify the robustness of our results. Historical MB is the average ratio of the market value of equity and the book value of equity for all seasoned firms in the industry (listed at least three years) at the end of the quarter prior to the IPO, divided by the same measure averaged over all quarters in the five years surrounding that quarter. Relative MB is the average equity market-to-book ratio for seasoned firms in the industry at the end of the previous quarter, divided by the market-to-book ratio for all seasoned firms in the market at the end of that quarter. These measures capture whether firms in the industry are trading at high multiples relative to their

---

[11] Note that this interpretation is based on an uncensored model, while the estimated model is actually censored.

[12] There are two reasons for the lack of forecasts: (i) in some years there are no IPOs in some industries, which implies that no forecasts are made; and (ii) as noted previously, IBES coverage is sporadic during the early years of the sample period.

historical levels (historical MB) or relative to the other firms in the market (relative MB). Both measures can be interpreted as proxies for growth opportunities in the industry or as proxies for investor sentiment (Rajan and Servaes (1995)). In the regression models, the coefficient on relative MB is always positive and significant; but, contrary to expectations, historical MB is always negative and it is significant in some specifications. This negative coefficient is caused by multicollinearity, however. When relative MB is not included in the regression models, the coefficient on historical MB is always positive and significant at the 10 percent level or better in three of the four models.

We also include market MB, which is the market-to-book ratio of all seasoned firms in the market, divided by the same measure averaged over all quarters in the five surrounding years. This variable measures whether the stock market is peaking and is included in the model to capture Loughran and Ritter's (1995) argument that IPOs come to market near market peaks. Its coefficient is always positive and significant. More importantly, for our purpose, however, is that the coefficients on the long term earnings growth forecast measures remain significant in the relevant three specifications.

In unreported models, we also find no qualitative differences in the significance or the magnitude of the reported coefficients when we include the following control variables: (i) the feedback risk measure proposed by Rajan and Servaes (1995), computed as the abnormal trading volume on the second trading day following the IPO;[13] (ii) a measure of future investment growth for each industry, computed as the average ratio of investment to sales for the three following years, divided by this ratio for the past year; (iii) three measures of general business conditions, proposed by Fama and French (1989) and Choe, Masulis, and Nanda (1993): the dividend yield for the S&P 500, the default spread, and the term spread.[14]

Finally, instead of growth forecasts, we use earnings forecast errors and adjust them as in (a), (b), (c), and (d) above, except that we use matched firm data when adjustments are made, and not industry data. (i.e., for all recent IPOs, we employ (a) raw forecast errors, (b) raw forecast errors, computed by industry, (c) matched firm forecast errors, (d) matched firm adjusted forecast errors). This analysis examines whether analyst overoptimism leads to more IPOs. We generally find a positive relation between forecast errors and IPO frequency (not reported). The relation is only significant for one measure, however, and that is the average matched firm adjusted earnings forecast error. Arguably, this measure best reflects IPO optimism, because it adjusts for both the general bias in earnings forecasts and any industry-specific idiosyncracies in earnings. This measure remains significant when the control variables are included in the regressions.

---

[13] Feedback trading leads to increased trading volume on the second day following the IPO, after one price change has been observed.

[14] The default spread is computed as the difference between the yield on Baa and Aaa bonds, and the term spread is computed as the difference between the yield on ten year treasury bonds and treasury bills. Both measures, together with the dividend yield on the S&P 500, are obtained from Citibase.

In sum, the results are consistent with a scenario where firms take advantage of windows of opportunity, as suggested by Ritter (1991) and others. The evidence indicates that these windows are at least partially related to analyst overoptimism about recent IPOs.

E. Analyst Optimism and Long-Run Stock Price Performance

The previous findings indicate that firms come to market when analysts are optimistic, and that analysts overestimate the earnings and growth potential of these firms once they complete their IPO. If analyst expectations influence, or represent, market expectations, we expect firms to perform poorly in the long run as earnings materialize below analyst predictions. Furthermore, the poor performance should be correlated with analyst optimism. We provide a detailed examination of this conjecture in this subsection.

To determine the long run performance of IPOs, we compare the five year returns of the firms in our sample to three benchmarks: (i) the NYSE/AMEX value weighted index; (ii) the smallest decile of the NYSE/AMEX firms; (iii) a matching sample. The matched firm meets the following criteria: (i) it has been listed on COMPUSTAT for at least three years; (ii) it operates in the same two-digit SIC code industry as the IPO firm; (iii) it is closest in size (market value of equity) to the IPO firm. The market value of the IPO firm's equity is computed on the first day of trading, thereby taking into account the stock price change on that day.[15]

Table VI verifies that the IPOs in our sample perform poorly in the long run. Over the five year period following their IPO, companies have raw returns of only 23.8 percent. Adjusting for either of the three benchmarks yields negative returns, ranging from -17.0 percent (smallest NYSE/AMEX decile) to -47.1 percent (NYSE/AMEX adjusted). Also note that there is substantial variation in the long run performance of IPOs over time. This is what would be expected if there is substantial time series variation in analyst overoptimism.

For our tests, we divide firms into quartiles according to their industry-adjusted long term growth forecasts and compare the benchmark adjusted stock returns for the IPOs in the different quartiles. We employ the first long term earnings growth forecast made in the year after the IPO. We exclude returns computed over the first 252 trading days (approximately one year) from our analysis, because not all growth forecasts are available during this period. The results presented in Table VII are striking. The firms with the lowest industry-adjusted growth forecasts (less than -0.0478) outperform the NYSE/AMEX index by 35.6 percent, the smallest NYSE/AMEX decile by 78.1 percent, and the matched sample by 74.1 percent. The firms with the highest industry-adjusted growth forecasts underperform the NYSE/AMEX index by

---

[15] Our matching procedure is similar to the procedure followed by Ritter (1991) with the following differences: (i) Ritter matches at the three-digit level, if possible; we match at the two-digit level; (ii) if a two-digit match cannot be found, Ritter employs a firm from a similar industry, whereas we do not assign a matching firm in that case; (iii) Ritter's matching firms can only be used once every three years, while we do not impose that restriction.

Table VI
Average Five Year Performance According to Several Benchmarks by Year of Going Public

Returns are computed for 1260 trading days starting from the second trading day. The adjusted returns are computed by subtracting the five-year return on New York Stock Exchange/American Stock Exchange (NYSE/AMEX) (value weighted), the smallest decile of NYSE/AMEX, and a matched firm from the five-year raw return. The firm closest in size (traded on NYSE, AMEX, or Nasdaq) to the Initial Public Offering (IPO) firm from the same two-digit Standard Industrial Classification (SIC) industry is used as a matching firm if it has been listed for at least three years. If firms are delisted, returns are only computed until the delisting.

Year	Raw Return	NYSE/AMEX Adjusted Return	NYSE/AMEX Smallest Decile Adjusted Return	Matched Firm Adjusted Return
75	1.1123	0.3868	−1.0964	−0.2260
76	2.1569	1.6706	0.6405	0.0036
77	2.2194	1.6968	0.7113	0.9836
78	2.0037	1.2153	0.3611	−0.1752
79	0.7239	−0.0253	−1.0217	−0.6812
80	−0.0416	−0.6859	−1.2514	−1.7097
81	0.1900	−0.6977	−1.1047	−1.7027
82	0.8568	−0.4530	−0.6384	−0.6583
83	0.0564	−0.6210	−0.1373	−0.2859
84	0.4361	−0.4895	0.1761	−0.0806
85	0.1577	−0.5781	−0.0284	−0.1008
86	0.0956	−0.4751	0.1040	0.0207
87 (6 months)	0.2017	−0.2552	0.1764	−0.1804
	0.2383	−0.4714	−0.1703	−0.4064

62.8 percent, the smallest 10 percent of the NYSE/AMEX stocks by 19.5 percent, and the matched firm sample by 35.9 percent. Thus, the difference in performance between the high and low growth forecast quartiles is close to 100 percent. Note that the return differences between the high and low growth quartiles are significant at the one percent level for all three benchmarks. In addition, many of the differences between the other quartiles are also highly significant. These results support our conjecture that analyst optimism is also reflected in the stock price performance of these firms.

We also verify whether the size effects and market to book effects reported by Fama and French (1992) can explain some of the patterns reported in Table VII. However, we do not find systematic differences in market-to-book ratios and sizes for the firms in the four quartiles.

The results presented in Table VII indicate an economically significant inverse relation between the long run performance of IPOs and analyst forecasts of their long term growth potential. This suggests that investors bid up the prices of firms above their fundamentals when analysts predict high growth rates and drive down the prices of firms below their fundamentals

Table VII
Long Term Returns on Initial Public Offerings (IPOs) by Forecasted Industry Adjusted Growth Quartiles

The first long term growth forecast reported for a firm after the IPO is employed in this analysis. Industry-adjusted long term growth forecasts are computed by subtracting the average long term growth forecast for all seasoned firms in the industry. Industry is defined at the two-digit Standard Industrial Classification (SIC) code level. Seasoned firms have to be listed on COMPUS-TAT for at least three years. Returns are computed over the 1008 trading day (approximately four years) period starting 252 days after the IPO. New York Stock Exchange/American Stock Exchange (NYSE/AMEX) adjusted returns are computed as: raw return for IPO firm − return on Center for Research in Security Prices (CRSP) NYSE/AMEX index over the same period. NYSE/AMEX smallest decile adjusted returns are computed as: raw return for the IPO firm − return on smallest decile of NYSE/AMEX firms over the same period. Matching firm adjusted returns are computed as: raw return for the IPO firm − return on the seasoned firm in the industry which is closest in size.

Industry-Adjusted Long Term Growth Forecast Quartiles	NYSE/AMEX Adjusted 4-Year Return[a]	NYSE/AMEX Smallest Decile Adjusted 4-Year Return[b]	Matched Firm Adjusted 4-Year Return[c]
Less than −0.0478	0.3561 (123)	0.7813 (123)	0.7413 (122)
−0.0478 to 0.0152	−0.2305 (125)	0.1656 (125)	0.0333 (125)
0.0152 to 0.0960	−0.5665 (122)	−0.1404 (122)	−0.3228 (119)
Greater than 0.0960	−0.6282 (126)	−0.1948 (126)	−0.3586 (122)

[a] All the returns in this column are significantly different from each other at the one percent level, based on pairwise t-tests.

[b] All the returns in this column are significantly different from each other at the one percent level, based on pairwise t-tests, except for the returns in the second and third quartiles, which are significantly different from each other at the five percent level.

[c] The return in the first quartile is significantly different from the return in all other quartiles at the one percent level; the return in the second quartile is significantly different from the return in the fourth quartile at the 10 percent level; the returns in the third and fourth quartiles are not significantly different from each other; the returns in the second and third quartiles are not significantly different from each other.

when analysts predict low growth rate. LaPorta (1996) provides related evidence. He examines all stocks listed on CRSP, COMPUSTAT, and IBES over the 1982 to 1991 period and finds a significant negative relation between these predicted growth rates and future returns. He also finds that analysts subsequently reduce earnings forecasts and earnings growth forecasts for those firms that were previously predicted to grow quickly. Our results indicate, however, that the growth forecasts remain above the industry average for at least three years. In addition, returns continue to be negative for high growth stocks for several years after the initial forecast is made.[16]

---

[16] For example, the NYSE adjusted returns for firms in the highest industry-adjusted growth forecast quartile are −20 percent in the two-year period starting three years after the IPO.

III. Conclusion

This article presents four major results. First, analyst following is positively related to IPO underpricing. Second, analysts are overoptimistic about the earnings and growth performance of IPOs, and this overoptimism is not a reflection of their overoptimism in general: the upward bias in earnings forecasts is more substantial for IPOs than for matched firms in their industries. Third, analyst growth forecasts and the magnitude of earnings forecast errors for recent IPOs are positively related to the number of IPOs coming to market. Fourth, firms perform poorly in the long run when analysts are more optimistic about their long run growth projections.

While there is a substantial literature on both initial public offerings and analyst forecasts, this article, we believe, is the first to study both. Underpricing seems, at least in part, an effort to attract interest. The windows of opportunity that open up for IPOs in the "hot-issue" periods appear to be driven by inflated expectations that eventually lead to poor long run returns. The most important question raised by this article is whether analysts reflect, or influence, the market's expectations. Most of the work on analysts thus far (see Dugar and Nathan (1995), for example), and information producers in general (see Kroszner and Rajan (1997)), suggests that the market is typically aware of any agency or selection biases influencing their behavior and adjusts for it. If this is so, our finding that analyst misperceptions are correlated over time with the frequency of new issues while they are cross-sectionally correlated with excess returns suggests that these misperceptions are not solely driven by agency or selection bias, but also partially reflect beliefs already widely held by the market. If this conjecture can be better established, it would suggest that analyst forecasts provide information about investor expectations for cash flows, and can be used in tests of market efficiency.

REFERENCES

Abarbanell, Jeffery, 1991, Do analysts' earnings forecasts incorporate information in prior stock price changes?, *Journal of Accounting and Economics* 14, 147–165.

Ali, Ashiq, 1996, Bias in analysts' earnings forecasts as an explanation for the long-run underperformance of stocks following equity offerings, Working paper, University of Arizona.

Barry Christopher B., Chris J. Muscarella, and Michael R. Vetsuypens, 1991, Underwriter warrants, underwriter compensation, and the costs of going public, *Journal of Financial Economics* 29, 113–135.

Brown, Phillip, George Foster, and Eric Noreen, 1985, Security analysts multi-year earnings forecasts and the capital market, *Studies in Accounting Research* No. 21.

Chemmanur, Thomas, 1993, The pricing of initial public offerings: A dynamic model with information production, *Journal of Finance* 48, 285–304.

Choe, Hyuk, Ronald W. Masulis, and Vikram Nanda, 1993, Common stock offerings across the business cycle: Theory and evidence, *Journal of Empirical Finance* 1, 3–31.

Dugar, A., and S. Nathan, 1995, The effect of investment banking relationships on financial analysts' earnings forecasts and investment recommendations, Working paper, Michigan State University.

Fama, Eugene F., and Kenneth R. French, 1989, Business conditions and expected returns on stocks and bonds, *Journal of Financial Economics* 25, 23–49.

Heckman, James, 1979, Sample selection bias as a specification error, *Econometrica* 47, 153–161.

Analyst Following of Initial Public Offerings   529

Ibbotson, Roger G, 1975, Price performance of common stock new issues, *Journal of Financial Economics* 2, 235–272.

Ibbotson, Roger G., and Jeffrey F. Jaffe, 1975, "Hot issue" markets, *Journal of Finance* 30, 1027–1042.

Ibbotson, Roger G., and Jay R. Ritter, 1995, Initial public offerings, in Jarrow, R. A., V. Maksimovic, and W. T. Ziemba, Eds.: *North Holland Handbooks of Operations Research and Management Science: Finance* (North Holland, The Netherlands).

Irvine, Paul J. A., 1994, Do analysts' reports generate trade for their firms? Evidence from the Toronto Stock Exchange, Working paper, University of Rochester.

Jain, Bharat A., and Omesh Kini, 1994, The post-issue operating performance of IPO firms, *Journal of Finance* 49, 1699–1726.

Kroszner, Randall, and Raghuram Rajan, 1997, Organization structure and credibility: Evidence from the underwriting activities of commercial banks before Glass Steagall, *Journal of Monetary Economics*, Forthcoming.

La Porta, Rafael, 1996, Expectations and the cross-section of stock returns, *Journal of Finance* 51, 1715–1742.

Lee, Charles M. C., Andrei Shleifer, and Richard H. Thaler, 1991, Investor sentiment and the closed-end fund puzzle, *Journal of Finance* 46, 75–109.

Lerner, Joshua, 1994, Venture capitalists and the decision to go public, *Journal of Financial Economics* 35, 293–316.

Lin, H., and M. McNichols, 1995, Underwriter relationships and analysts' research reports, Working paper, Stanford University.

Loughran, Tim, and Jay R. Ritter, 1995, The new issues puzzle, *Journal of Finance* 50, 23–51.

McNichols, M., and P. O'Brien, 1996, Self selection and analyst coverage, Working paper, University of Michigan.

Michaely, Roni and Kent L. Womack, 1996, Conflict of interest and the credibility of underwriter analyst recommendations, Working paper, Cornell University.

Mikkelson, Wayne H., and Ken Shah, 1994, Performance of companies around initial public offerings, Working paper, University of Oregon and University of Auckland.

O'Brien, Patricia C., and Ravi Bhushan, 1990, Analyst following and institutional ownership, *Journal of Accounting Research* 28 Supplement, 55–76.

Pearson, Neil D, 1992, Determinants of the production of information, Working paper, University of Rochester.

Rajan, Raghuram, and Henri Servaes, 1995, The effect of market conditions on initial public offerings, Working paper, University of Chicago and University of North Carolina at Chapel Hill.

Ritter, Jay R., 1984, The "hot issue" market of 1980, *Journal of Business* 32, 215–240.

Ritter, Jay R., 1991, The long-run performance of initial public offerings, *Journal of Finance* 46, 3–27.

Shiller, Robert, 1990, Speculative prices and popular models, *Journal of Economic Perspectives* 4, 55–65.

Teoh, Siew, T. J. Wong, and Gita Rao, 1995, Earnings management and the subsequent performance of initial public offerings, Working paper, UCLA.

[12]

THE JOURNAL OF FINANCE • VOL. LII, NO. 5 • DECEMBER 1997

Myth or Reality? The Long-Run Underperformance of Initial Public Offerings: Evidence from Venture and Nonventure Capital-Backed Companies

ALON BRAV and PAUL A. GOMPERS*

ABSTRACT

We investigate the long-run underperformance of recent initial public offering (IPO) firms in a sample of 934 venture-backed IPOs from 1972–1992 and 3,407 nonventure-backed IPOs from 1975–1992. We find that venture-backed IPOs outperform non-venture-backed IPOs using equal weighted returns. Value weighting significantly reduces performance differences and substantially reduces underperformance for nonventure-backed IPOs. In tests using several comparable benchmarks and the Fama-French (1993) three factor asset pricing model, venture-backed companies do not significantly underperform, while the smallest nonventure-backed firms do. Underperformance, however, is not an IPO effect. Similar size and book-to-market firms that have not issued equity perform as poorly as IPOs.

RITTER (1991) AND LOUGHRAN and Ritter (1995) document severe underperformance of initial public offerings (IPOs) during the past twenty years suggesting that investors may systematically be too optimistic about the prospects of firms that are issuing equity for the first time. Recent work has shown that underperformance extends to other countries as well as to seasoned equity offerings. We address three primary issues related to the underperformance of new issues. First, we examine whether venture capitalists, who specialize in financing promising startup companies and bringing them public, affect the long-run performance of newly public firms. We find that venture-backed firms do indeed outperform nonventure-backed IPOs over a five-year period, but only when returns are weighted equally.

The second set of tests examines the effects of using different benchmarks and different methods of measuring performance to gauge the robustness of IPO underperformance. We find that underperformance in the nonventure-

* Duke University and Harvard University and NBER. Jay Ritter and Charles Lee provided access to data. Victor Hollender and Laura Miller provided research assistance. We thank Chris Géczy, J.B. Heaton, Steve Kaplan, Shmuel Kandel, Marc Lipson, Andrew Metrick, Mark Mitchell, Steve Orpurt, Jay Ritter, Raghu Rajan, Stephen Schurman, Andrei Shleifer, René Stulz, Richard Thaler, Rob Vishny, Luigi Zingales, an anonymous referee, and seminar participants at Boston University, Tel Aviv University, the University of Chicago, the University of Georgia, the University of Rochester, Virginia Tech, the NBER Corporate Finance Summer Institute, and the Financial Decision and Control Workshop at Harvard Business School for helpful comments and suggestions. Financial support was provided by the Center for Research in Security Prices, University of Chicago. Any errors or omissions are our own.

backed sample is driven primarily by small issuers, i.e., those with market capitalizations less than $50 million. Value weighting returns significantly reduces underperformance relative to the benchmarks we examine. In Fama-French (1993) three factor time series regressions, portfolios of venture-backed IPOs do not underperform. Partitioning the nonventure-backed sample on the basis of size demonstrates that underperformance primarily resides in small nonventure-backed issuers. Fama-French's three factor model cannot explain the underperformance of these small, nonventure-backed firms.

Finally, this article provides initial evidence on the sources of underperformance. We find that returns of IPO firms are highly correlated in calendar time even if the firms go public in different years. Because small nonventure-backed IPOs are more likely to be held by individuals, bouts of investor sentiment are a possible explanation for their severe underperformance. Individuals are arguably more likely to be influenced by fads or lack complete information. We also provide initial evidence that the returns of small, non-venture-backed companies covary with the change in the discount on closed-end funds. Lee, Shleifer, and Thaler (1991) argue that this discount is a useful benchmark for investor sentiment. Alternatively, unexpected real shocks may have affected small growth firms during this time period. We find, however, that underperformance is not exclusively an IPO effect. When issuing firms are matched to size and book-to-market portfolios that exclude all recent firms that have issued equity, IPOs do not underperform. Underperformance is a characteristic of small, low book-to-market firms regardless of whether they are IPO firms or not.

The rest of the article is organized as follows: Section I presents relevant aspects of the venture capital market that are important in public firm formation. A discussion of behavioral finance and rational asset pricing explanations for long-run pricing anomalies is presented in Section II. The data are presented in Section III. Underperformance is examined in Section IV. Section V concludes the article and discusses some possible explanations for the underperformance of small, nonventure-backed IPOs.

I. Venture Capitalists and the Creation of Public Firms

Gompers (1995) shows that venture capital firms specialize in collecting and evaluating information on startup and growth companies. These types of companies are the most prone to asymmetric information and potential capital constraints discussed in Fazzari, Hubbard, and Petersen (1988) and Hoshi, Kashyap, and Scharfstein (1991). Because venture capitalists provide access to top-tier national investment and commercial bankers and may partly overcome informational asymmetries that are associated with startup companies, we expect that the investment behavior of venture-backed firms would be less dependent upon internally generated cash flows. Venture capitalists stay on the board of directors long after the IPO and may continue to provide access to capital that nonventure-backed firms lack. Additionally, the venture capitalist may put management structures in place that help the firm perform better in the long run.

If venture-backed companies are better on average than nonventure-backed companies, the market should incorporate these expectations into the price of the offering and long-run stock price performance should be similar for the two groups. Barry, Muscarella, Peavy, and Vetsuypens (1990) and Megginson and Weiss (1991) find evidence that markets react favorably to the presence of venture capital financing at the time of an IPO.

If the market underestimates the importance of a venture capitalist in the pricing of new issues, long-run stock price performance may differ. (Conversely, the market may not discount the shares of nonventure-backed companies enough.) Such underestimation may result because individuals (who are potentially more susceptible to fads and sentiment) hold a larger fraction of shares after the IPO for nonventure-backed firms (Megginson and Weiss (1991)).

Venture capitalists may affect who holds the firm's shares after an IPO. Venture capitalists have contacts with top-tier, national investment banks and may be able to entice more and higher quality analysts to follow their firms, thus lowering potential asymmetric information between the firm and investors. Similarly, because institutional investors are the primary source of capital for venture funds, institutions may be more willing to hold equity in firms that have been taken public by venture capitalists with whom they have invested. The greater availability of information and the higher institutional shareholding may make venture-backed companies' prices less susceptible to investor sentiment.

Another possible explanation for better long-run performance by venture-backed IPOs is venture capitalists' reputational concerns. Gompers (1996) demonstrates that reputational concerns affect the decisions venture capitalists make when they take firms public. Because venture capitalists repeatedly bring firms public, if they become associated with failures in the public market, they may tarnish their reputation and ability to bring firms public in the future. Venture capitalists may consequently be less willing to hype a stock or overprice it.

II. Initial Public Offerings and Underperformance

A. Behavioral Finance

Behavioral economics demonstrates that individuals often violate Bayes' Rule and rational choice theories when making decisions under uncertainty in experimental settings (Kahneman and Tversky (1982)). Financial economists have also discovered long-run pricing anomalies that have been attributed to investor sentiment. Behavioral theories posit that investors weight recent results too heavily or extrapolate recent trends too much. Eventually, overly optimistic investors are disappointed and subsequent returns decline.

DeBondt and Thaler (1985, 1987) demonstrate that buying past losers and selling past winners is a profitable trading strategy. Risk, as measured by beta or the standard deviation of stock returns, does not seem to explain the results. Lakonishok, Shleifer, and Vishny (LSV) (1994) show that many "value" strategies also seem to exhibit abnormally high returns. LSV form portfolios based on earnings-to-price ratios, sales growth, earnings growth, or cash flow-to-price and find that "value" stocks outperform "glamour" stocks without appreciably affecting risk. In addition, La Porta (1996) shows that selling stocks with high forecasted earnings growth and buying low projected earnings growth stocks produces excess returns. These articles imply that investors are too optimistic about stocks that have had good performance in the recent past and too pessimistic about stocks that have performed poorly.

In addition to accounting or stock market-based trading strategies, researchers have examined financing events as sources of potential trading strategies. Ross (1977) and Myers and Majluf (1984) show that the choice of financing strategy can send a signal to the market about firm valuation. Event studies around equity or debt issues (e.g., Mikkelson and Partch (1986), Asquith and Mullins (1986)) assume that all information implied by the financing choice is fully and immediately incorporated into the company's stock price. The literature on long-run abnormal performance assumes that managers have superior information about future returns and use that information to benefit current shareholders, and the market underreacts to the informational content of the financing event.

Ritter (1991) and Loughran and Ritter (1995) show that nominal five-year buy-and-hold returns are 50 percent lower for recent IPOs (which earned 16 percent) than they are for comparable size-matched firms (which earned 66 percent). Teoh, Welch, and Wong (1997) show that IPO underperformance is positively related to the size of discretionary accruals in the fiscal year of the IPO. Larger accruals in the IPO year are associated with more negative performance. Teoh *et al.* believe that the level of discretionary accruals is a proxy for earnings management and that investors are systematically fooled by the boosted earnings.

If investor sentiment is an important factor in the underperformance of IPOs, small IPOs may be more affected. Individuals are more likely to hold the shares of small IPO firms. Many institutions like pension funds and insurance companies refrain from holding shares of very small companies. Taking a meaningful position in a small firm may make an institution a large blockholder in the company. Because the Securities and Exchange Commission (SEC) restricts trading by 5 percent shareholders, institutions may want to avoid this level of ownership. Individual investors may also be more subject to fads (Lee, Shleifer, and Thaler (1991)) or may be more likely to suffer from asymmetric information. Lee, Shleifer, and Thaler use the discount on closed-end funds as a measure of investor sentiment. If investor sentiment affects returns and if closed-end fund discounts measure investor sentiment, then the returns on small IPOs would be correlated with the change in the average closed-end fund discount. Decreases in the average discount imply that investors are more optimistic and should be correlated with higher returns for small issuers.

B. Rational Asset Pricing Explanations

Recent work claims that multifactor asset pricing models can potentially explain many pricing anomalies in the financial economics literature. In particular, Fama and French (1996) argue that the "value" strategies in Lakonishok, Shleifer, and Vishny (1994) and the buying losers-selling winners strategy of DeBondt and Thaler (1985, 1987) are consistent with their three-factor asset pricing model.

Fama (1994) and Fama and French (1996) argue that their three factor pricing model is consistent with Merton's (1973) I-CAPM. While the choice of factor mimicking portfolios is not unique, sensitivities to Fama and French's three factors (related to the market return, size, and book-to-market ratio) have economic interpretations. Fama and French claim that anomalous performance is explained by not completely controlling for risk factors.

Tests of underperformance, however, suffer from the joint hypothesis problem discussed by Fama (1976). The assumption of a particular asset pricing model means that tests of performance are conditional on that model's correctly predicting stock price behavior. If we reject the null hypothesis, then either the pricing model is incorrect or investors may be irrational. Similarly, if factors like book-to-market explain underperformance, it does not necessarily verify the model. The results may just reflect that investor sentiment is correlated with measures like book-to-market. We do not wish to argue whether factors like book-to-market reflect rational market risk measures or investor sentiment. The tests we perform are consistent with either interpretation. Another problem with long-run performance tests, however, is the nonstandard distribution of long-run returns. Both Barber and Lyon (1996) and Kothari and Warner (1996) show that typical tests performed in the literature suffer from potential biases. While Barber and Lyon show that size and book-to-market adjusted returns give unbiased test estimates of underperformance for random portfolios (which we report in Figs. 5 and 6), neither article addresses the cross-sectional or time series correlation in returns when tests are predicated on an event.

III. Data

Our sample of initial public offerings is collected from various sources. The venture-backed companies are taken from three primary sources. First, firms are identified as venture-backed IPOs in the *Venture Capital Journal* for issues from 1972 through 1992. Second, firms that are in the sample of distributions in Gompers and Lerner (1996b) but are not listed in the *Venture Capital Journal* are added to the venture-backed sample. Finally, if offering memoranda for venture capital limited partnerships used in Gompers and Lerner (1996a, 1996c) list a company as being venture financed but it is not listed in either of the previous two sources, it is added to the venture-backed sample. Jay Ritter provides data on initial public offerings for the period 1975–1984. IPOs are identified in various issues of the *Investment Dealers'*

Digest of Corporate Financing for the period 1975–1992. Any firm not listed in the sample of venture-backed IPOs is classified as nonventure-backed. The data include name of the offering company, date of the offering, size of the issue, issue price, number of secondary shares, and the underwriter.

Our sample differs from that of Loughran and Ritter in two respects. First, our sample period is not completely overlapping. Loughran and Ritter look at IPOs from 1970 to 1990 and measure performance using stock returns through December 31, 1992. We look at IPOs conducted over the period 1975 to 1992 using stock returns through December 31, 1994. The different sample period does not change the qualitative results because we replicate Loughran and Ritter's underperformance in our sample period as well. Second, we eliminate all unit offerings from our sample. Unit offerings, which contain a share of equity and a warrant, tend to be made by very small, risky companies. Calculating the return to an investor in the IPO is difficult because only the share trades publicly. Value weighted results would change very little because unit offering companies are usually small.

For inclusion in our sample, a firm performing an initial public offering must be followed by the Center for Research in Security Prices (CRSP) at some point after the offering date. Our final sample includes 934 venture-backed IPOs and 3,407 nonventure-backed IPOs; 81.3 percent of the venture-backed sample are still CRSP-listed five years after their IPO. A slightly smaller fraction of nonventure-backed IPOs, 76.7 percent, are CRSP-listed after five years. The frequency of mergers appears low. Only 11.2 percent of the venture-backed IPOs and 9.7 percent of the nonventure sample merge within the first five years. The number of liquidations, bankruptcies, and other delisting events is small for both groups as well. Only 7.5 percent of the venture-backed IPOs are delisted for these reasons in the first five years while 13.3 percent of nonventure IPOs are.

We also examine the size and book-to-market characteristics of our sample. Each quarter we divide all NYSE stocks into ten size groups. An equal number of NYSE firms is allocated to each of the ten groups and quarterly size breakpoints are recorded. Similarly, we divide all NYSE stocks into five book-to-market groups each quarter with an equal number of NYSE firms in each group. The intersection of the ten size and five book-to-market groups leads to 50 possible quarterly classifications for an IPO firm. We calculate the market value of equity at the first CRSP-listed closing price. For book value of equity, we use COMPUSTAT and record the first book value after the IPO as long as it is within one year of the offering date.[1] The bias in book value should not be too great because the increment in book value due to retained earnings in the first year is likely to be very small. Our sample of venture-backed IPOs is heavily weighted in the smallest and lowest book-to-market firms: 38.5

---

[1] When we match firms on the basis of book-to-market values, we lose 778 firms because they lack COMPUSTAT data within one year of the offering. For most results, this is unimportant because tests do not rely on book values. Where book-to-market ratios are used either to sort firms or match firms, the 778 firms are excluded.

percent are in the lowest size decile with another 27.2 percent in the second decile, while 84.0 percent of the venture-backed IPOs are in the lowest book-to-market quintile. Most venture-backed firms are young, growth companies. These firms may have many good investment opportunities for which they need to raise cash. On the other hand, their low book-to-market ratios may just be indicators of relative overpricing. Loughran and Ritter (1995) and Lerner (1994) claim that issuers time the market for new shares when their firms are relatively overvalued.

Most nonventure-backed firms are also small and low book-to-market, but a substantial number of firms fall in larger size deciles or higher book-to-market quintiles: 58.6 percent of firms are in the lowest size decile, 20 percent more than are in the lowest decile for the venture-backed sample, and 73.2 percent of the nonventure-backed firms fall in the lowest book-to-market quintile. However, 7.3 percent are in the two highest book-to-market quintiles. The differences between venture and nonventure-backed IPOs may result from greater heterogeneity in nonventure-backed IPOs.

IV. Underperformance of Initial Public Offerings

A. Full Sample Results

Ritter (1991) and Loughran and Ritter (1995) document underperformance of IPO firms using several benchmarks. Our approach is an attempt to replicate their work and extend it along several dimensions. Several benchmarks are utilized throughout this article. First, as in Loughran and Ritter, the performance of IPO firms is matched to four broad market indexes: the S&P 500, Nasdaq value weighted composite index, NYSE/AMEX value weighted index, and NYSE/AMEX equal weighted index (all of which include dividends). Performance of IPOs is also compared to Fama-French (1994) industry portfolios and size and book-to-market matched portfolios that have been purged of recent IPO and seasoned equity offering (SEO) firms.[2]

Matching firms to industry portfolios avoids the noise of selecting individual firms and can control for unexpected events that affect the returns of entire industries. We use the 49 industry portfolios created in Fama and French (1994). While the Standard Industrial Classification (SIC) codes may be non-adjacent, industry groupings sort firms into the similar lines of business.

Comparing performance to size and book-to-market portfolios seems reasonable given the effects documented by Fama and French (1992, 1993) showing that size and book-to-market are important determinants of the cross section of stock returns. We form 25 (5 × 5) value-weighted portfolios of all NYSE/AMEX and Nasdaq stocks on the basis of size and the ratio of book equity to market equity. We match each IPO on those two dimensions to the corresponding portfolio for comparison.

---

[2] We purge SEO firms from our benchmark portfolios as well, since it has been argued (Loughran and Ritter (1995)) that these firms underperform after they make a seasoned offering.

We form the size and book-to-market portfolios as described in Brav, Géczy, and Gompers (1995). Starting in January 1964, we use all NYSE stocks to create size quintile breakpoints with an equal number of NYSE firms in each size quintile.[3] Size is measured as the number of shares outstanding times the stock price at the end of the preceding month. We obtain our accounting measures from the COMPUSTAT quarterly and annual files and define book value as book common equity plus balance sheet deferred taxes and investment tax credits for the fiscal quarter ending two quarters before the sorting date. This is the same definition as in Fama and French (1992). If the book value is missing from the quarterly statements, we search for it in the annual files.[4] Within each size quintile we form five book-to-market portfolios with an equal number of NYSE firms in each book-to-market quintile to form 25 (5 × 5) size and book-to-market portfolios.[5] Value weighted returns are calculated for each portfolio for the next three months. We repeat the above procedure for April, July, and October of each year. In order to avoid comparing IPO firms to themselves, we eliminate IPO and SEO firms from the various portfolios for five years after their equity issue. Each issue is matched to its corresponding benchmark portfolio. Each quarter the matching is repeated, creating a separate benchmark for each issue. We then proceed to equal (value) weight IPO firm returns and the individual benchmark returns resulting in equal (value) weighted portfolios adjusted for book-to-market and size. We thus allow for time-varying firm risk characteristics of each IPO and each matching firm portfolio.

We do not, however, replicate Loughran and Ritter's size-matched firm adjustment for several reasons. Matching on the basis of size alone ignores evidence that book-to-market is related to returns. Book-to-market seems particularly important for small firms (Fama and French (1992)). Matching to small nonissuers makes it likely that firms in the matching sample are disproportionately long-term losers, i.e., high book-to-market firms. IPO firms tend to be small and low book-to-market. The delisting frequency is low for the IPO sample and their risk of financial distress in the first five years may be small. A similar sized small firm that has not issued equity in the previous five years is probably a poorly performing firm with few growth prospects and is probably not an appropriate risk match for the IPO firm if book-to-market is important. These firms may have higher returns because their risk of financial distress is higher. They are likely to be the DeBondt and Thaler (1985) underperformers that we know have high returns. This bias is especially strong prior to 1978 because Nasdaq returns only start in December 1972. Therefore, all size-matched firms would come from the NYSE and AMEX, potentially biasing the matched firms even more towards long-term losers, i.e., very high book-to-market firms.

---

[3] Fama and French (1992) use only NYSE stocks in order to ensure dispersion of the number of firms across portfolios.

[4] For firms that are missing altogether from the quarterly files, we use the annual files.

[5] We do not include stocks with negative book values.

Table I

Five-Year Post-Initial Public Offering (IPO) Returns and Wealth Relatives Versus Various Benchmarks

The sample is all venture-backed IPOs from 1972 through 1992 and all nonventure-backed IPOs from 1975 through 1992. Five-year equal weighted returns on IPOs are compared with alternative benchmarks. For each IPO, the returns are calculated by compounding daily returns up to the end of the month of the IPO and from then on compounding monthly returns for 59 months. If the IPO is delisted before the 59th month we compound the return until the delisting date. Wealth relatives are calculated as $\Sigma(1 + R_{i,T})/\Sigma(1 + R_{bench,T})$, where $R_{i,T}$ is the buy and hold return on IPO i for period T and $R_{bench,T}$ is the buy and hold return on the benchmark portfolio over the same period. Size and book-to-market benchmark portfolios are formed by intersecting five size quintiles and five book-to-market quintiles (5 × 5) and removing all firms which have issued equity in the previous five years in either an IPO or a seasoned equity offering. All IPO and benchmark returns are taken from the Center for Research in Security Prices files.

Benchmarks	Venture-Backed IPOs			Nonventure-Backed IPOs		
	IPO Return	Benchmark Return	Wealth Relative	IPO Return	Benchmark Return	Wealth Relative
Panel A: Five Year Equal Weighted Buy-and-Hold Returns						
S&P 500 index	44.6	65.3	0.88	22.5	71.8	0.71
Nasdaq composite	44.6	53.7	0.94	22.5	52.4	0.80
NYSE/AMEX value-weighted	44.6	61.4	0.90	22.5	66.4	0.75
NYSE/AMEX equal-weighted	44.6	60.8	0.90	22.5	55.7	0.79
Size and book-to-market (5×5)	46.4	29.9	1.13	21.7	20.8	1.01
Fama-French industry portfolio	46.8	51.2	0.97	26.2	60.0	0.79
Panel B: Five Year Value Weighted Buy-and-Hold Returns						
S&P 500 index	43.4	64.5	0.87	39.3	62.4	0.86
Nasdaq Composite	43.4	50.4	0.95	39.3	51.1	0.92
NYSE/AMEX value-weighted	43.4	60.0	0.90	39.3	57.6	0.88
NYSE/AMEX equal-weighted	43.4	56.4	0.92	39.3	47.7	0.94
Size and book-to-market (5×5)	41.9	37.6	1.03	33.0	38.7	0.96
Fama-French industry portfolio	46.0	45.0	1.01	45.2	53.2	0.95

Tests in this article calculate returns two ways, although we only report buy-and-hold results. First, as in Ritter (1991) and Loughran and Ritter (1995), we calculate buy-and-hold returns. No portfolio rebalancing is assumed in these calculations. We also calculate full five-year returns assuming monthly portfolio rebalancing. While the absolute level of returns changes, qualitative results are unchanged if returns are calculated using monthly rebalancing.

Table I presents the long-run buy-and-hold performance for our sample. We follow each offering event using both the CRSP daily and monthly tapes. Compound daily returns are calculated from the offering date until the end of the offering month. We then compound their returns using the monthly tapes for the earlier of 59 months or the delisting date. Firms that drop out will have IPO returns and benchmark returns that are calculated over a shorter time period. Where available, we include the firm's delisting return. Our interval is set to match Loughran and Ritter's results (1995). In Panel A we weight equally the returns for each IPO and their benchmark. As in Loughran and Ritter (1995), we calculate wealth relatives for the five-year period after IPO by taking the ratio of one plus the IPO portfolio return over one plus the return on the chosen benchmark. Wealth relatives less than one mean that the IPO portfolio has underperformed relative to its benchmark.

The results weighting returns equally show that venture-backed IPOs outperform nonventure-backed IPOs by a wide margin. Over five years, venture-backed IPOs earn 44.6 percent on average, while nonventure-backed IPOs earn 22.5 percent.[6] The five year equally weighted wealth relatives show large differences in performance as well. Wealth relatives for the venture capital sample are all close to 0.9. Wealth relatives for the nonventure capital sample are substantially lower and range as low as 0.71 against the S&P 500 index.

Controlling for industry returns leaves performance differences as well. Using Fama-French (1994) industry portfolios, the venture capital sample shows little underperformance. The five-year wealth relative is 0.97. Nonventure-backed IPOs show substantial underperformance relative to their industry benchmarks, 0.79 for the five year wealth relative.

Two interpretations of the industry results are possible. First, the benchmark industry returns for the venture-backed sample are lower than the industry returns for the nonventure-backed sample. Thus, venture-backed IPOs may be concentrated in industries that have lower risk and therefore expected returns should be lower. Second, the relatively lower industry returns may reflect the venture capitalist's ability to time industry overpricing.

Wealth relatives versus size and book-to-market portfolios demonstrate that underperformance is not an IPO effect. When IPOs and SEOs are excluded from size and book-to-market portfolios, we find that venture-backed IPOs significantly outperform their relative portfolio returns (average wealth relative of 1.13) while nonventure-backed IPOs perform as well as the benchmark portfolios. The poor performance documented by Loughran and Ritter (1995) is not due to sample firms being initial public offering firms, but rather results from the types of firms they are, i.e., primarily small and low book-to-market firms.

Although the time frame of our sample is slightly different from Loughran and Ritter, our wealth relatives for NYSE/AMEX value and equal weighted indexes, the Nasdaq value weighted composite, and the S&P 500 are virtually identical to theirs. For example, five-year performance versus the NYSE/AMEX equally weighted and S&P 500 indexes produces wealth relatives of 0.78 and 0.84 in Loughran and Ritter's sample while (in unreported results), our entire sample (venture and nonventure-backed IPOs) produces wealth

---

[6] The five-year buy-and-hold returns are not true five-year returns because the average holding period is less than 60 months. Firms may take several months to be listed on the CRSP data tapes and so the first several return observations may be missing. Similarly, firms are delisted and so are only traded for some shorter period of time than the sample period. Finally, IPOs in the last two years have truncated returns because observations on returns only run through December 1994. The average holding period is approximately 47 months.

relatives of 0.78 and 0.82. Nonventure-backed IPOs perform worse than Loughran and Ritter's results.

Panel B of Table I presents results in which returns of IPOs and their reference benchmarks are weighted by the issuing firm's first available market value. If we are concerned about how important IPO underperformance affects investors' wealth, then value weighted results may be more meaningful. Five-year value weighted nominal returns on nonventure-backed IPOs are higher than when returns are weighted equally. Value weighted returns on the benchmark portfolios are similar to the equally weighted benchmark returns. This increases wealth relatives at five years for the nonventure capital sample and leaves venture capital wealth relatives relatively unchanged. Value weighted performance looks similar for the two groups with little overall underperformance. Five-year wealth relatives are closer to one. Large nonventure-backed IPOs perform substantially better than smaller nonventure-backed firms.

B. Yearly Cohort Results

Ritter (1991) and Loughran and Ritter (1995) document clear patterns in the underperformance of IPOs. In particular, years of greatest IPO activity are associated with the most severe underperformance. Results in Panel A of Table II present equal weighted, buy-and-hold cohort results versus the NYSE/AMEX equal weighted index.[7] Nominal returns and wealth relatives are high in the late 1970s but fall sharply in the early and middle 1980s. While five-year returns increase in the late 1980s and early 1990s, they increase more in the venture-backed sample. Our five-year return patterns closely follow Loughran and Ritter's results. For the venture-backed IPOs, underperformance is concentrated in the 1979 to 1985 cohorts while for the nonventure-backed sample, five-year underperformance is prevalent from 1978 forward. These results are largely consistent with the results of Ritter (1991) and Loughran and Ritter (1995), who find similar time series patterns of underperformance.

We also investigate how value weighting affects yearly cohort buy-and-hold patterns in Panel B. Each IPO is given a weight proportional to its market value of equity using the first available CRSP-listed closing price. Value weighting has different effects on the venture capital and nonventure capital samples. Value weighting the venture capital IPOs has little impact on the pattern of performance. Value weighting returns of the nonventure capital sample improves their nominal performance and wealth relatives in most cohorts. There is still some evidence of underperformance in the early 1980s, but it is much smaller. Most five-year nonventure capital wealth relatives are closer to one.

---

[7] We use the NYSE/AMEX equal weighted index because it produces wealth relatives that are somewhere in the middle of all benchmarks utilized. Replacing the NYSE/AMEX equal weighted index with the S&P 500, Nasdaq composite index, or industry portfolios does not affect the time series pattern of underperformance in any significant manner. Similarly, monthly portfolio rebalancing yields qualitatively similar results.

Table II

Long-Run Performance of Initial Public Offerings (IPOs) by Cohort Year Versus NYSE/AMEX Equal-Weighted Index

The sample is all venture-backed IPOs and all nonventure-backed IPOs from 1976 through 1992. For each IPO, the returns are calculated by compounding daily returns up to the end of the month of the IPO and from then on compounding monthly returns for 59 months. If the IPO is delisted before the 59th month, we compound the return until the delisting date. Wealth relatives are calculated as $\Sigma(1 + R_{i,T})/\Sigma(1 + R_{\text{bench},T})$, where $R_{i,T}$ is the buy and hold return on the IPO i for period T and $R_{\text{bench},T}$ is the buy and hold return on the benchmark portfolio over the same period. All IPO and benchmark returns are taken from the Center for Research in Security Prices files.

	Venture-backed IPOs				Nonventure-backed IPOs			
Year	Number	IPO Return	NYSE/AMEX	Wealth Relative	Number	IPO Return	NYSE/AMEX	Wealth Relative
	Panel A: Equal Weighted Five-Year Buy-and-Hold Returns							
1976	16	310.2	193.2	1.40	14	192.8	189.8	1.01
1977	13	253.1	128.9	1.54	9	103.0	119.0	0.93
1978	8	525.0	226.9	1.91	24	99.6	160.8	0.77
1979	8	71.1	164.4	0.65	44	51.0	141.8	0.62
1980	27	48.8	115.1	0.69	107	−23.4	107.0	0.37
1981	63	24.4	121.0	0.56	241	5.9	114.0	0.49
1982	25	32.8	142.8	0.55	75	110.8	128.9	0.92
1983	117	−14.7	51.1	0.56	507	3.6	50.7	0.69
1984	52	2.1	71.0	0.60	258	46.7	66.1	0.88
1985	46	12.6	40.4	0.80	253	5.3	41.5	0.74
1986	94	79.0	30.1	1.38	505	4.0	30.3	0.80
1987	78	25.3	27.1	0.99	379	12.3	26.0	0.89
1988	35	120.6	59.4	1.38	183	95.4	63.3	1.20
1989	33	141.1	58.3	1.52	129	48.9	58.2	0.94
1990	40	−14.3	67.8	0.51	116	30.7	66.5	0.79
1991	111	38.2	49.3	0.93	208	26.3	49.6	0.84
1992	147	17.7	28.3	0.92	343	15.0	27.7	0.90
	Panel B: Value Weighted Five Year Buy-and-Hold Returns							
1976	16	166.8	208.0	0.87	14	228.7	183.0	1.16
1977	13	438.1	152.1	2.14	9	200.4	118.6	1.37
1978	8	529.4	218.1	1.98	24	141.8	181.7	0.86
1979	8	7.1	156.7	0.42	44	87.9	150.7	0.75
1980	27	1.3	115.6	0.47	107	−32.4	108.6	0.32
1981	63	37.6	127.1	0.61	241	22.6	122.6	0.55
1982	25	−25.7	125.3	0.33	75	81.1	108.2	0.87
1983	117	−26.0	53.3	0.48	507	21.8	54.7	0.79
1984	52	0.0	75.2	0.57	258	67.6	71.4	0.98
1985	46	26.5	43.3	0.88	253	13.9	39.4	0.82
1986	94	201.6	32.5	2.28	505	25.3	32.0	0.95
1987	77	20.1	29.8	0.93	379	39.2	25.4	1.11
1988	35	120.5	58.9	1.39	183	72.0	68.5	1.03
1989	33	130.6	59.0	1.45	129	65.4	61.5	1.02
1990	40	7.9	66.1	0.65	116	45.8	65.9	0.88
1991	111	46.9	48.3	0.99	208	49.8	50.7	0.99
1992	145	25.4	28.2	0.98	343	29.2	27.5	1.01

The Long-Run Underperformance of Initial Public Offerings 1803

The yearly cohort results suggest several patterns that we examine more deeply. The level and pattern of underperformance previously documented seem to be sensitive to the method of calculating returns. When returns are value weighted, underperformance of nonventure-backed IPOs is reduced in most years.

C. Calendar Time Results

Event time results that are presented above may be misleading about the pervasiveness of underperformance. Cohort returns in Table II may overstate the actual number of years in which IPOs underperform because the returns of recent IPO firms may be correlated. If firms that have recently gone public are similar in terms of size, industry, or other characteristics, then their returns will be highly correlated in calendar time. For example, if a shock to the economy in 1983 substantially decreased the value of firms that issued equity, then it makes the cohort years from 1979 through 1983 underperform, even though all the underperformance is concentrated in one year. Similarly, as discussed in De Long, Shleifer, Summers, and Waldmann (1990), investor sentiment is likely to be market-wide rather than specific to a particular firm and may cause returns to be correlated in calendar time.

To address this correlation we calculate the annual return on a strategy that invests in recent IPO firms. In Panel A of Table III we calculate the monthly return on portfolios that buy equal amounts of all IPO firms that went public within the previous five years. We calculate the annual return by compounding monthly returns on the IPO portfolios starting in January and ending in December of each year. These calendar time returns are presented and compared to calendar time returns on the NYSE/AMEX equal weighted index and the Nasdaq composite index. The wealth relatives on the venture capital IPO portfolio are above one in nine of nineteen years and are higher than the nonventure capital portfolio wealth relative in eleven of nineteen years. Underperformance for the venture capital sample is primarily concentrated from 1983 through 1986 and is concentrated from 1981 through 1987 for the nonventure capital portfolio.

In Panel B, the calendar time portfolio is formed by investing an amount that is proportional to the market value of the IPO firm's equity in a given month. Value weighting the calendar time portfolio does not have a major impact on the pattern of underperformance for venture-backed IPOs, but reduces underperformance in the nonventure-backed sample.

The cross-sectional correlation between cohort years can be seen graphically in Figures 1 and 2. The cumulative wealth relative is calculated for each IPO cohort year from 1979 through 1982 by taking the ratio of one plus the compound return on the portfolio that invests in each IPO that went public in a given year divided by the compound return on the Nasdaq composite index. Figure 1 plots the cumulative wealth relative for venture-backed IPOs and Figure 2 plots the cumulative wealth relative for nonventure-backed IPOs. All

Table III

Calendar Time Initial Public Offering (IPO) Performance

Annual performance of initial public offerings from 1976 through 1992 relative to the New York Stock Exchange/American Stock Exchange (NYSE/AMEX) value weighted index and the Nasdaq value weighted composite index. The sample is all venture capital (VC) IPOs from 1972 through 1992 and all nonventure-backed (nonVC) IPOs from 1975 through 1992. Each month, the return on all IPOs that went public within the past five years is calculated. The annual return in each year is the compound return from January through December of these average monthly returns. The annual benchmark returns are the compounded monthly returns on either the NYSE/AMEX value weighted or Nasdaq composite index. IPO and benchmark returns are taken from the Center for Research in Security Prices files.

Year	VC-IPOs	nonVC-IPOs	NYSE/ AMEX	VC Wealth Relative	nonVC Wealth Relative	Nasdaq	VC Wealth Relative	nonVC Wealth Relative
Panel A: Equal Weighted IPO Calendar-time Portfolio Returns								
1976	48.9	14.6	26.5	1.18	0.91	29.3	1.15	0.89
1977	32.3	22.2	−4.2	1.38	1.28	10.5	1.20	1.11
1978	44.7	10.5	7.8	1.34	1.03	16.1	1.25	0.95
1979	43.8	53.9	23.6	1.16	1.25	32.3	1.09	1.16
1980	78.0	89.7	32.7	1.34	1.43	37.7	1.29	1.38
1981	−7.1	−20.9	−4.3	0.97	0.83	−0.7	0.94	0.80
1982	34.6	5.8	20.2	1.12	0.88	22.4	1.10	0.87
1983	10.5	28.5	23.1	0.90	1.04	21.3	0.91	1.06'
1984	−34.4	−21.1	5.1	0.62	0.75	−9.1	0.72	0.87
1985	30.1	23.5	31.2	0.99	0.94	33.8	0.97	0.92
1986	−8.9	3.4	16.9	0.78	0.88	8.0	0.84	0.96
1987	−11.4	−19.9	2.8	0.86	0.78	−4.6	0.93	0.84
1988	23.9	20.1	17.5	1.05	1.02	18.4	1.05	1.01
1989	7.9	11.4	29.4	0.83	0.86	21.1	0.89	0.92
1990	−15.0	−27.3	−4.8	0.89	0.76	−15.3	1.00	0.86
1991	97.4	50.5	30.6	1.51	1.15	60.0	1.23	0.94
1992	8.1	19.1	8.0	1.00	1.10	16.3	0.93	1.02
1993[1]	5.3	16.1	11.0	0.95	1.05	14.5	0.92	1.01
1994[1]	−3.1	−10.5	−0.3	0.97	0.90	−2.3	0.99	0.92
Panel B: Value Weighted IPO Calendar-time Portfolio Returns								
1976	1.1	2.7	26.5	0.80	0.81	29.3	0.78	0.79
1977	13.3	−5.9	−4.2	1.18	0.98	10.5	1.03	0.85
1978	44.9	12.7	7.8	1.34	1.05	16.1	1.25	0.97
1979	27.8	49.6	23.6	1.03	1.21	32.3	0.97	1.13
1980	67.3	99.3	32.7	1.26	1.50	37.7	1.22	1.45
1981	−7.6	−21.7	−4.3	0.97	0.82	−0.7	0.93	0.79
1982	29.6	14.6	20.2	1.08	0.95	22.4	1.06	0.94
1983	2.2	16.9	23.1	0.83	0.95	21.3	0.84	0.96
1984	−30.2	−19.4	5.1	0.66	0.77	−9.1	0.77	0.89
1985	21.4	30.5	31.2	0.93	0.99	33.8	0.91	0.97
1986	−7.0	8.9	16.9	0.80	0.93	8.0	0.86	1.01
1987	5.5	−11.3	2.8	1.03	0.86	−4.6	1.11	0.93
1988	14.0	15.4	17.5	0.97	0.98	18.4	0.96	0.97
1989	32.4	20.8	29.4	1.02	0.93	21.1	1.10	1.00
1990	0.1	−12.6	−4.8	1.05	0.92	−15.3	1.18	1.03
1991	78.6	38.3	30.6	1.37	1.06	60.0	1.12	0.86
1992	7.5	10.9	8.0	1.00	1.03	16.3	0.92	0.95
1993[1]	10.48	38.3	11.0	1.00	1.25	14.5	0.97	1.21
1994[1]	−4.7	10.9	−0.3	0.96	1.11	−2.3	0.98	1.14

[1] Returns for 1993 and 1994 only include IPOs that went public prior to December 31, 1992.

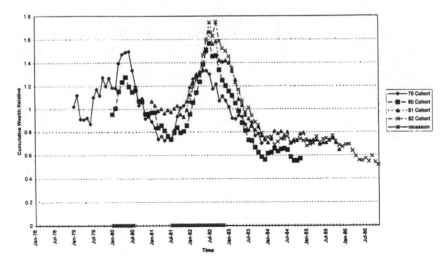

Figure 1. Time series of wealth relatives for selected venture-backed initial public offering (IPO) yearly cohorts. The sample is all venture-backed IPOs from 1979 through 1982. Performance of the portfolio of IPO firms is compared to the Nasdaq composite benchmark. The cumulative wealth relative from issue date through the calendar month is plotted by taking the ratio of one plus the equal weighted buy-and-hold return for the portfolio of issuing firms in a cohort year starting from the beginning of the cohort year up to the given month divided by one plus the compounded Nasdaq return over the same time period.

cohort years move in almost identical time series patterns. Relative returns decline sharply for all cohorts in mid-1980, rise in parallel from January 1982 through the end of 1982 and then decline in 1983. The time series correlation of the yearly cohorts illustrates the need to be concerned about interpretation of test statistics. Viewing each IPO as an independent event probably overstates the significance of estimated underperformance. Knowing that underperformance is concentrated in time may also help determine its causes.

D. Pricing the IPOs

If IPOs underperform on a risk-adjusted basis, portfolios of IPOs should consistently underperform relative to an explicit asset pricing model. Recent work by Fama and French (1993) indicates that a three factor model may explain the cross section of stock returns. Their three factors are: RMRF, which is the excess return on the value weighted market portfolio; SMB, the return on a zero investment portfolio formed by subtracting the return on a large firm portfolio from the return on a small firm portfolio;[8] and HML, the return on a zero investment portfolio calculated as the return on a portfolio of

---

[8] The breakpoints for small and large firms are determined by NYSE firms alone, but the portfolios contain all firms traded on NYSE, AMEX, and Nasdaq exchanges.

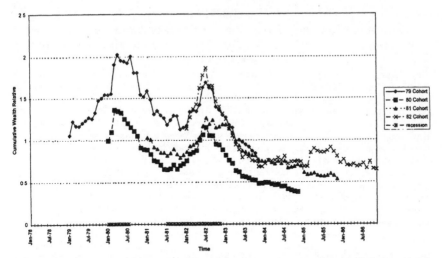

Figure 2. Time series of wealth relatives for selected nonventure-backed initial public offering (IPO) yearly cohorts. The sample is all nonventure-backed IPOs from 1979 through 1982. Performance of the portfolio of IPO firms is compared to the Nasdaq composite benchmark. The cumulative wealth relative from issue date through the calendar month is plotted by taking the ratio of one plus the equal weighted buy-and-hold return for the portfolio of issuing firms in a cohort year starting from the beginning of the cohort year up to the given month divided by one plus the compounded Nasdaq return over the same time period.

high book-to-market stocks minus the return on a portfolio of low book-to-market stocks.[9] We use the intercept from time series regressions as an indicator of risk-adjusted performance to determine whether the results documented by Ritter (1991) and Loughran and Ritter (1995) are consistent with the Fama-French model. The intercepts in these regressions have an interpretation analogous to Jensen's alpha in the Capital Asset Pricing Model (CAPM) framework. This approach has the added benefit that we can make statistical inferences given the assumption of multivariate normality of the residuals. This was not possible in our previous analysis due to the right skewness of long horizon returns. The disadvantage of this approach is that it weights each month equally in minimizing the sum of squares. This point can be appreciated by noting that a monthly observation in mid-1976 (the average of a few IPOs) gets the same weight as a monthly observation in mid-1986 (the average of a large number of IPOs). If underperformance is correlated with the number of IPOs in our portfolios, the Fama-French results will reduce the measured underperformance.

---

[9] The high book-to-market portfolio represents the top 30 percent of all firms on COMPUSTAT while the low book-to-market portfolio contains firms in the lowest 30 percent of the COMPUSTAT universe of firms.

Table IV

Fama-French (1993) Three Factor Regression on Initial Public Offering (IPO) Portfolios for the Whole Sample and Sorted on the Basis of Size

The sample is all venture capital IPOs from 1972 through 1992 and all nonventure-backed IPOs from 1975 through 1992. Portfolios of IPOs are formed by including all issues that were done within the previous five years. RMRF is the value weighted market return on all NYSE/AMEX/ Nasdaq firms (RM) minus the risk free rate (RF) which is the one-month Treasury bill rate. SMB (small minus big) is the difference each month between the return on small firms and big firms. HML (high minus low) is the difference each month between the return on a portfolio of high book-to-market stocks and the return on a portfolio of low book-to-market stocks. The first two columns present results for the entire sample. The next three columns show portfolios sorted by size. Every six months an equal number of stocks are allocated to one of three size portfolios. Size breakpoints are the same for both the venture and nonventure-backed samples. Portfolio returns are the equal weighted returns for IPOs within that tercile. IPOs are allowed to switch allocation every six months. All regressions are for January 1977 through December 1994 for a total of 216 observations (t-statistics are in parentheses).

	Full Sample Equal Weighted	Full Sample Value Weighted	Equal Weighted Size Terciles		
			Small	2	Large
Panel A: Venture Capital IPOs					
Intercepts	0.0007	0.0015	0.0001	−0.0004	0.0023
	(0.35)	(0.55)	(0.02)	(−0.20)	(0.93)
RMRF	1.0978	1.2127	0.9481	1.1096	1.2333
	(22.97)	(17.64)	(11.28)	(19.41)	(19.46)
SMB	1.2745	1.1131	1.6841	1.3237	1.1373
	(18.57)	(10.37)	(12.91)	(14.83)	(11.49)
HML	−0.6807	−1.0659	−0.2765	−0.6734	−1.1373
	(−8.24)	(−8.96)	(−1.90)	(−6.81)	(−9.95)
Adjusted R^2	0.889	0.821	0.687	0.846	0.849
Panel B: Nonventure Capital IPOs					
Intercepts	−0.0052	−0.0029	−0.0056	−0.0056	−0.0004
	(−2.80)	(−1.84)	(−1.63)	(−2.72)	(−0.27)
RMRF	0.9422	1.0486	0.8073	0.9900	1.0312
	(19.94)	(26.12)	(9.24)	(18.74)	(26.40)
SMB	1.1450	0.6612	1.3870	1.2245	0.8322
	(15.52)	(10.55)	(10.17)	(14.85)	(13.65)
HML	−0.1069	−0.3405	0.1909	−0.1906	−0.3229
	(−1.31)	(−4.90)	(1.26)	(−2.08)	(−4.77)
Adjusted R^2	0.825	0.868	0.544	0.813	0.879

Table IV presents the three-factor time series regression results. IPO portfolio returns are regressed on RMRF, SMB, and HML. For the equal and value weighted venture-backed IPO portfolios presented in Panel A, results cannot reject the three-factor model. The intercepts are 0.0007 and 0.0015. Panel B presents results for nonventure-backed IPOs. When the nonventure-backed returns are weighted equally, the intercept is −0.0052 (52 basis points per month) with a t-statistic of −2.80 indicating severe underperformance. Value weighting nonventure capital returns produces a smaller intercept, -0.0029 with a t-statistic of -1.84.[10]

The coefficients on HML for venture-backed IPOs (-0.6807 and -1.0659) indicate that their returns covary with low book-to-market (growth) firms. When returns are value weighted, loadings on SMB decline but the loadings on HML become more negative for both IPO groups. The returns on larger IPO firms (in market value) tend to covary more with the returns of growth companies.

Every six months we divide the sample into three size portfolios based on the previous month's IPO size distribution using all IPOs to determine the breakpoints. The portfolios are rebalanced monthly and IPOs are allowed to switch portfolios every half year. We estimate equal weighted regressions within each size group. The venture capital terciles never underperform. No intercept is below -0.0004 and none is significant. The pattern for nonventure-backed IPOs verifies our earlier results. Underperformance is concentrated in the two smallest terciles. Intercepts for the smallest two size terciles in the nonventure-backed sample are large, -0.0056, with t-statistics of -1.63 and -2.72. Coefficients on SMB decline monotonically from the portfolio of smallest issuers to largest issuers. Returns of the smallest IPOs covary more with returns on small stocks.

Coefficients on HML show two interesting patterns. Coefficients for venture-backed IPO portfolios decline monotonically. The larger the firm, the more it covaries with low book-to-market firms. Venture-backed firms are similar in age and amount of capital invested (book value of assets). Venture-backed firms become large by having high market values. Large firms (in market value) will have low book-to-market ratios and hence covary with growth companies.

This pattern is not as clear in the nonventure-backed sample. First, the smallest tercile has a positive coefficient on HML and the largest two portfolios have negative coefficients. Similarly, venture-backed IPOs load more negatively on HML than nonventure-backed firms, indicating that venture-backed returns covary more with the returns of growth companies.

The results indicate that IPO underperformance is driven by nonventure-backed IPOs in the smallest decile of firms based on NYSE breakpoints. Over 50 percent of nonventure-backed firms are in the smallest size decile when breakpoints are determined by NYSE-listed firms. Therefore, all firms in the nonventure capital smallest portfolio of Table IV are from the smallest size decile.

---

[10] Loughran and Ritter (1995) also run Fama-French three-factor regressions and find negative intercepts for all issuer portfolios. Loughran and Ritter's regressions, however, combine IPO and SEO firms. Their regressions are therefore not directly comparable to our results. Loughran and Ritter also sort issuing firms into large and small issuers, but use the median firm on NYSE/AMEX to determine the size breakpoint. This cutoff would leave very few IPO firms in the large issuing firm portfolio.

Table V presents the results sorting firms on the basis of book-to-market ratios.[11] Panel A shows that for the equal weighted venture-backed IPO portfolio, no book-to-market portfolio underperforms. Nonventure-backed firms, however, show substantial underperformance in all terciles. Underperformance ranges from −0.0042 to −0.0055.

Panels C and D show that value weighting again reduces the influence of small firm underperformance. The lowest book-to-market portfolio for the venture-backed IPOs now has a positive intercept of 0.0036 (36 basis points per month). No other venture or nonventure-backed IPO tercile has significant underperformance relative to the Fama-French three-factor model. The Fama-French results provide evidence that underperformance remains even after controlling for size and book-to-market in time series regressions. Venture-backed IPOs do not underperform whether the results are run on the entire sample or sortings based on size or book-to-market. Nonventure-backed IPOs exhibit severe underperformance (primarily concentrated in the smaller issuers) even relative to the Fama-French model.

In order to address the source of the underperformance, we rerun the Fama-French three factor regressions including an index that measures the change in the average discount on closed-end funds. We construct the index as in Lee, Shleifer, and Thaler (1991). The discount on a closed-end fund is the difference between the fund's net asset value and its price divided by the net asset value. We value weight the discount across funds in a particular month and then calculate the change in the level of the index from the previous month. Lee, Shleifer, and Thaler argue that the average discount reflects the relative level of investor sentiment. If this is the case, we expect the change in the discount to be related to returns of firms that underperform relative to the Fama-French three-factor model. When the change in discount is positive, i.e., the average discount increases, individual investors may be more pessimistic and returns on firms affected by investor sentiment should fall. Conversely, when the change in average discount is negative, individual investors are becoming more optimistic and returns should rise.

Table VI confirms our predictions. The change in discount is negatively related to returns of the smallest group of firms, the smallest venture-backed companies and the smallest two terciles of nonventure-backed firms. These firms are potentially most affected by investor sentiment. The negative relation between changes in the closed-end fund discount and returns of small IPO firms indicates that investor sentiment might be an important source of underperformance. Sophisticated investors may not enter this market because the cost of gathering information about these firms may outweigh the potential returns from correcting the mispricing. Informed investors may also not want to bet against noise traders if prices can move further out of line in the

---

[11] Results for the whole sample are not the same as in Table IV because sorting by book-to-market is predicated on having book equity data from COMPUSTAT. Some firms are on CRSP but not on COMPUSTAT, so the number of firms in Table IV is larger than the number of firms in Table V by 778 observations.

Table V

Fama-French (1993) Three Factor Regression on Initial Public Offering (IPO) Portfolios for the Whole Sample and Sorted on the Basis of Book-to-Market Ratio

The sample is all venture capital IPOs from 1972 through 1992 and all nonventure-backed IPOs from 1975 through 1992. Portfolios of IPOs are formed by including all issues that were done within the previous five years. RMRF is the value weighted market return on all NYSE/AMEX/Nasdaq firms (RM) minus the risk free rate (RF) which is the one-month Treasury bill rate. SMB (small minus big) is the difference each month between the return on small firms and big firms. HML (high minus low) is the difference each month between the return on a portfolio of high book-to-market stocks and the return on a portfolio of low book-to-market stocks. The first column presents results for the entire sample. The next three columns show portfolios sorted by book-to-market ratio. Every six months an equal number of stocks are allocated to one of the three book-to-market portfolios. Book-to-market breakpoints are the same for venture and nonventure-backed samples. Portfolio returns are either equal weighted or value weighted returns for IPOs within that tercile. IPOs are allowed to switch allocation every six months. All regressions are for January 1977 through December 1994 for a total of 216 observations (t-statistics are in parentheses).

		Book-to-Market Terciles		
	Full Sample	Low	2	High
Panel A: Venture Capital IPOs–Equal Weighted Portfolios				
Intercepts	0.0029	−0.0009	0.0026	−0.0007
	(0.15)	(−0.36)	(0.89)	(−0.23)
RMRF	1.0893	1.1128	1.1154	1.0400
	(20.94)	(16.51)	(14.75)	(13.70)
SMB	1.3416	1.2160	1.2801	1.5242
	(16.52)	(11.56)	(10.83)	(12.86)
HML	−0.6864	−0.9806	−0.8044	−0.2760
	(−7.63)	(−8.41)	(−6.15)	(−2.10)
Adjusted R^2	0.868	0.812	0.766	0.730
Panel B: Nonventure Capital IPOs–Equal Weighted Portfolios				
Intercepts	−0.0051	−0.0042	−0.0055	−0.0054
	(−2.90)	(−1.61)	(−2.60)	(−2.33)
RMRF	0.9762	1.0394	0.9881	0.9017
	(21.71)	(15.47)	(18.16)	(15.08)
SMB	1.1946	1.2839	1.1803	1.1264
	(17.02)	(12.24)	(13.90)	(12.07)
HML	−0.1667	−0.4977	−0.2641	0.2575
	(−2.14)	(−4.28)	(−2.81)	(2.49)
Adjusted R^2	0.852	0.770	0.805	0.703
Panel C: Venture Capital IPOs–Value Weighted Portfolios				
Intercepts	0.0012	0.0036	0.0029	−0.0030
	(0.42)	(1.09)	(0.86)	(−1.01)
RMRF	1.1991	1.1814	1.1772	1.1664
	(16.89)	(13.82)	(13.58)	(15.38)
SMB	1.0283	0.9384	1.2043	1.3184
	(9.28)	(7.03)	(8.90)	(11.13)
HML	−1.0470	−1.2152	−0.9706	−0.5252
	(−8.52)	(−8.22)	(−6.47)	(−4.00)
Adjusted R^2	0.804	0.744	0.734	0.756

Table V.—*Continued*

	Full Sample	Book-to-Market Terciles		
		Low	2	High
Panel D: Nonventure Capital IPOs–Value Weighted Portfolios				
Intercepts	−0.0012	0.0021	−0.0015	−0.0039
	(−0.59)	(0.66)	(−0.71)	(−1.81)
RMRF	1.0438	1.0771	1.0631	1.0269
	(20.59)	(13.55)	(20.03)	(18.86)
SMB	0.6870	0.8899	0.7483	0.5189
	(8.68)	(7.17)	(9.03)	(6.10)
HML	−0.4282	−0.7053	−0.3632	−0.0090
	(−4.88)	(−5.12)	(−3.96)	(−0.10)
Adjusted R^2	0.813	0.698	0.802	0.732

short-run. Finally, short selling may be constrained because shares cannot be borrowed.

E. Cross-Sectional Results

Given the results from the Fama-French (1993) three factor regressions, we explore how raw returns and wealth relatives vary with size and book-to-market. In Table VII we present summary statistics for size and book-to-market quintiles of the full sample and the subsets of venture-backed and nonventure-backed IPOs. In Panel A, we sort the entire sample of IPOs by their real (constant 1992 dollars) market value at the first available CRSP listed closing price. Equal numbers of IPOs are allocated to each size quintile. We impose the same cutoffs for venture-backed and nonventure-backed IPOs. Size increases from an average of $11.5 million in the first quintile to $445.2 million in the biggest. Comparing average book-to-market ratios for the two subgroups demonstrates that venture-backed IPOs have substantially lower average book-to-market ratios within any given size quintile. The smallest two size quintiles have disproportionately more nonventure-backed IPOs. This reflects the larger average size of venture-backed IPO firms.[12] Differences in book-to-market ratios might reflect different industry compositions between the two groups. Venture capitalists back more firms in high growth, low book-to-market industries.

In Panel B IPOs are sorted into book-to-market quintiles. Average book-to-market ratios increase from 0.053 in the lowest quintile to 3.142 in the highest. Once again, significant differences are apparent across the two samples. Average size of the venture-backed IPOs is higher in the first through third

[12] No time series bias is imparted by sorting the entire sample by the total sample breakpoints. No trend or pattern in real size (in 1992 dollars) or book-to-market ratios is evident that would lead to dramatic differences in the yearly representation in size or book-to-market quintiles.

Table VI

Fama-French (1993) Three Factor Regression on Initial Public Offering (IPO) Portfolios Including the Change in the Average Closed-End Fund Discount

The sample is all venture capital IPOs from 1972 through 1992 and all nonventure-backed IPOs from 1975 through 1992. Portfolios of IPOs are formed by including all issues that were done within the previous five years. RMRF is the value weighted market return on all NYSE/AMEX/ Nasdaq firms (RM) minus the risk free rate (RF) which is the one-month Treasury bill rate. SMB (small minus big) is the difference each month between the return on small firms and big firms. HML (high minus low) is the difference each month between the return on a portfolio of high book-to-market stocks and the return on a portfolio of low book-to-market stocks. ΔDiscount represents the change in the average discount on closed end-funds from the end of last month to the end of this month. The first two columns present results for the entire sample. The next three columns show portfolios sorted by size. Every six months an equal number of stocks are allocated to one of the three size portfolios. Size breakpoints are the same for both venture and nonventure-backed samples. Portfolio returns are the equal weighted returns for IPOs within that tercile. IPOs are allowed to switch allocation every six months. All regressions are for January 1977 through May 1992 for a total of 185 observations (*t*-statistics are in parentheses).

	Full Sample Equal Weighted	Full Sample Value Weighted	Equal Weighted Size Terciles		
			Small	2	Large
Panel A: Venture-backed IPOs					
Intercepts	0.0009	0.0018	0.0011	−0.0008	0.0024
	(0.44)	(0.59)	(0.31)	(−0.34)	(0.89)
RMRF	1.0934	1.2043	0.9145	1.1258	1.2377
	(21.10)	(15.85)	(10.08)	(18.34)	(18.06)
SMB	1.3855	1.1071	1.7154	1.2986	1.1406
	(17.28)	(9.41)	(12.22)	(13.67)	(10.75)
HML	−0.7104	−1.0881	−0.4078	−0.6400	−1.0818
	(−7.51)	(−7.85)	(−2.47)	(−5.71)	(−8.65)
ΔDiscount	−0.0002	0.0018	−0.0038	0.0001	0.0031
	(−0.22)	(1.24)	(−2.18)	(0.06)	(2.34)
Adjusted R^2	0.891	0.819	0.701	0.850	0.853
Panel B: Nonventure Capital IPOs					
Intercepts	−0.0049	−0.0032	−0.0050	−0.0053	−0.0004
	(−2.38)	(−1.80)	(−1.28)	(−2.32)	(−0.52)
RMRF	0.9121	1.0271	0.7801	0.9480	1.0096
	(17.61)	(23.28)	(8.03)	(16.66)	(23.50)
SMB	1.1650	0.6853	1.3910	1.2554	0.8581
	(14.53)	(10.04)	(9.25)	(14.26)	(12.91)
HML	−0.2155	−0.4172	0.0862	−0.3313	−0.4045
	(−2.28)	(−5.18)	(0.48)	(−3.19)	(−5.16)
ΔDiscount	−0.0022	−0.0000	−0.0030	−0.0031	−0.0005
	(−2.23)	(−0.06)	(−2.62)	(−2.87)	(−0.64)
Adjusted R^2	0.829	0.871	0.543	0.824	0.882

The Long-Run Underperformance of Initial Public Offerings 1813

Table VII

Summary Statistics for Size and Book-to-Market Quintiles

The sample is all venture capital initial public offerings (IPOs) from 1972 through 1992 and all nonventure-backed IPOs from 1975 through 1992. IPOs are divided into quintiles based on size (market value of equity at the first Center for Research in Security Prices (CRSP) listed closing price in constant 1992 dollars) or book-to-market at the time of IPO. The first book value of equity after the IPO is taken from COMPUSTAT as long as it is within one year of the offering date. An equal number of IPOs from the entire sample are allocated to each quintile. Breakpoints are the same for venture and nonventure-backed samples. Size is in millions of 1992 dollars. (Medians are in parentheses.)

Panel A: Summary Data for Size Quintiles					
		Venture-backed IPOs		Nonventure-backed IPOs	
Size Quintile	Average Size	Average Book-to-Market	Number of Firms	Average Book-to-Market	Number of Firms
Small	$ 11.5	0.465 (0.323)	58	1.901 (0.295)	806
2	$ 26.1	0.360 (0.326)	132	0.531 (0.286)	732
3	$ 52.3	0.326 (0.286)	220	0.892 (0.305)	648
4	$101.3	0.248 (0.097)	285	0.907 (0.310)	579
Large	$445.2	0.187 (0.235)	237	0.709 (0.280)	622

Panel B: Summary Data for Book-to-Market Quintiles					
		Venture-backed IPOs		Nonventure-backed IPOs	
Book-to-Market Quintile	Average Book-to-Market	Average Size	Number of Firms	Average Size	Number of Firms
Low	0.053	$201.4 ($125.8)	198	$115.6 ($43.8)	404
2	0.167	$147.1 ($103.8)	182	$149.8 ($51.8)	420
3	0.277	$117.2 ($81.1)	181	$101.9 ($45.7)	422
4	0.400	$ 90.2 ($68.6)	157	$103.4 ($39.2)	447
High	3.142	$ 72.4 ($48.8)	92	$200.5 ($57.8)	510

quintiles, but lower in the fourth and fifth quintiles. Venture-backed growth (low book-to-market) firms tend to be larger and venture capital value (high book-to-market) firms tend to be smaller than comparable nonventure-backed IPOs. Except for the highest book-to-market quintile, the quintiles have roughly constant proportions of venture and nonventure-backed IPOs. The highest book-to-market quintile has substantially more nonventure-backed IPOs than venture-backed IPOs. This may indicate that venture capitalists avoid investment in industries that have high book-to-market ratios (value industries) or that the nonventure-backed firms simply have lower growth expectations.

Figure 3 plots the average equal weighted nominal five year buy-and-hold return for each size quintile classifying IPOs as venture or nonventure-backed. Venture-backed IPOs show no size effect. Performance of the smallest quintile of venture-backed IPOs looks very similar to performance of the largest. A

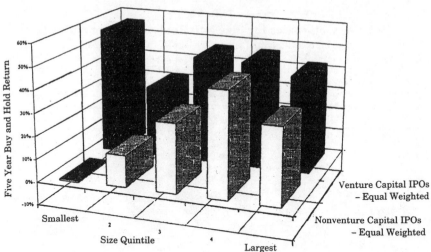

Figure 3. Five year equal weighted buy-and-hold returns for venture and nonventure-backed initial public offerings (IPOs) by size quintile. The sample is 3,407 nonventure-backed IPOs from 1975 through 1992 and 934 venture-backed IPOs from 1972 through 1992. Each sample of IPOs is sorted into size quintiles based on the real (1992 dollars) size at the first closing price listed by the Center for Research in Security Prices. Size breakpoints are the same for the venture and nonventure-backed samples. Quintile returns are the average buy-and-hold return for IPOs in that quintile.

pronounced size effect is apparent in the nonventure-backed firms, however. Average nominal returns on nonventure-backed IPOs in size quintile 1 are *negative*.

Equal weighted nominal five-year buy-and-hold returns for book-to-market quintiles are shown in Figure 4. Returns show an increase from lowest to highest quintile. The increase across book-to-market quintiles is substantially larger for nonventure-backed firms. On an equal weighted basis, all nonventure-backed book-to-market quintiles underperform the venture-backed quintiles.

Figures 5 and 6 show that underperformance of small, low book-to-market IPO firms is not due to their status as equity issuers. We sort the IPO firms into their appropriate 25 (5 × 5) size and book-to-market portfolio based on the NYSE breakpoints that are discussed above. The five year buy-and-hold return on the IPO firms is compared to the five year buy-and-hold return on the size and book-to-market portfolio that excludes IPO and SEO firms for five years after issue. Figure 5 plots the average excess returns of the venture capital-backed IPO sample by portfolio. Adjusting for size and book-to-market returns, no strong pattern of performance is seen. Small, low book-to-market venture-backed IPOs (380 of 934 firms) outperform the small, low book-to-market benchmark by 42 percent.

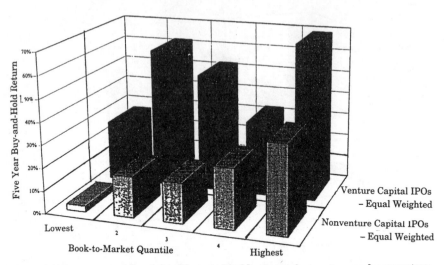

Figure 4. Five year equal weighted buy-and-hold returns for venture and nonventure-backed initial public offerings (IPOs) by book-to-market quintile. The sample is 3,407 nonventure-backed IPOs from 1975 through 1992 and 934 venture-backed IPOs from 1972 through 1992. Each sample of IPOs is sorted into book-to-market quintiles based on the real (1992 dollars) market value at the first closing price listed by the Center for Research in Security Prices and first available book value of equity. Book-to-market breakpoints are the same for both samples. Quintile returns are the average buy-and-hold return for IPOs in that quintile.

Figure 6 plots size and book-to-market excess returns for nonventure capi-tal-backed IPO firms. The small, low book-to-market nonventure-backed IPO firms (which make up 1,465 of the 3,407 firms) outperform similar nonissuing firms by 12 percent. This positive relative performance is not the result of large returns by the IPO firms; they only earn an average of 5 percent over five years. Small, low book-to-market nonissuing firms, however, earn an average of −7 percent over the same time period. Portfolios further from the small, low book-to-market portfolio have far fewer issuing firms. Standard errors for the estimates of mean excess returns would be much larger and hence little emphasis should be placed on their significance. For the majority of the sample, i.e., the corner of the figure near the small, low book-to-market portfolio, relative performance is close to 0.

These results indicate that IPO underperformance is not an issuing firm effect. It is a small, low book-to-market effect. Similar size and book-to-market nonissuing firms perform just as poorly as IPO firms do. This does not imply that returns are normal on a risk-adjusted basis. In fact, small, low book-to-market firms appear to earn almost zero nominal returns over a five-year period that starts with IPO issuance. It may be difficult to explain this low return with a risk-based model.

In Table VIII we present cross-sectional estimates of the determinants of five year buy-and-hold wealth relatives using the Nasdaq composite index as

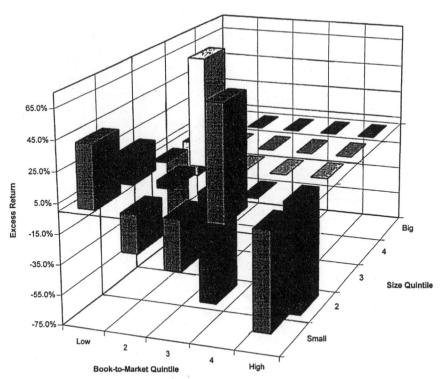

Figure 5. Five year excess returns for venture capital-backed initial public offerings (IPOs) by size and book to market portfolio. The sample is 934 venture-backed IPOs from 1972–1992. Twenty-five (5 × 5) size and book-to-market portfolios are formed based on the New York Stock Exchange (NYSE) breakpoints. IPO firms are assigned to their appropriate size and book-to-market portfolio at issue. The five-year excess return is calculated by subtracting the five-year buy-and-hold return on the size and book-to-market portfolio that excludes all IPO and SEO firms for five years after issue from the five-year buy-and-hold return on the IPO firm. The average excess return is plotted for each size and book-to-market portfolio.

the benchmark.[13] The dependent variable is the logarithm of the five-year wealth relative. The independent variables are the natural logarithm of the firm's market value of equity (in 1992 dollars) at the first available CRSP listed closing price, a dummy variable indicating if the firm was venture-backed, the natural logarithm of the firm's book value of equity to market value, and the lagged dividend price ratio for the entire market. We include the dividend price ratio to determine whether overall market pricing affects long-run returns.

The results demonstrate that size is an important determinant of relative returns. Across all specifications, the coefficient on logarithm of IPO firm size is positive and highly significant. This result captures the essence of value

[13] Because of the large cross-section that we employ, the standard 5 percent significance level should be reduced.

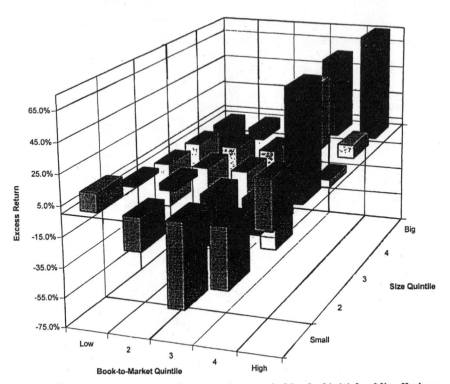

Figure 6. Five year excess returns for nonventure capital-backed initial public offerings (IPOs) by size and book to market portfolio. The sample is 3,407 venture-backed IPOs from 1975–1992. Twenty-five (5 × 5) size and book-to-market portfolios are formed based on the New York Stock Exchange (NYSE) breakpoints. IPO firms are assigned to their appropriate size and book-to-market portfolio at issue. The five-year excess return is calculated by subtracting the five-year buy-and-hold return on the size and book-to-market portfolio that excludes all IPO and SEO firms for five years after issue from the five-year buy-and-hold return on the IPO firm. The average excess return is plotted for each size and book-to-market portfolio.

weighting returns. The presence of a venture capitalist is positively related to a firm's wealth relative, although the coefficient is only marginally significant.[14] The coefficients on lagged dividend price ratio are negative and significant. If the dividend price ratio captures the general level of market prices, IPOs that go public during periods of higher market valuation perform worse over the subsequent five years relative to the market as a whole. Finally, book-to-market has an important impact on returns at five-year horizons. The coefficient on the book-to-market ratio is positive and highly significant. The positive relationship between book-to-market ratio and relative performance is

---

[14] If the regressions are run on firms below the median size, the coefficient on the venture capital dummy variable is positive and significant indicating that returns are significantly different for small venture and nonventure-backed companies.

Table VIII

Cross-Sectional Regressions on Buy-and-Hold Returns and Wealth Relatives

The sample of initial public offerings (IPOs) is all venture-backed IPOs that went public between 1972 and 1992 and all nonventure-capital-backed IPOs that went public between 1975 and 1992. The dependent variable is the logarithm of the five year wealth relatives using the Nasdaq composite index as the benchmark. The independent variables are the natural logarithm of the market value of the firm's equity in billions of 1992 dollars valued at the closing price on the first day for which a price from the Center for Research in Security Prices database is available, a dummy variable that equals one if the firm was venture-backed, the natural logarithm of the book-to-market ratio when the firm goes public, and the lagged dividend price ratio for the market. (t-statistics are in parentheses.)

Independent Variables	Dependent Variable: Logarithm of Five-Year Wealth Relative				
Logarithm of firm size	0.2063				0.1944
	(12.68)				(10.44)
Venture-backed dummy variable		0.0953			0.0992
		(1.94)			(1.93)
Logarithm of book-to-market ratio			0.1414		0.1321
			(7.44)		(7.03)
Lagged dividend price ratio				−0.2445	−0.1386
				(−9.81)	(−5.03)
Constant	−1.6919	−0.8923	−0.7190	0.0768	−0.9904
	(−25.01)	(−39.11)	(−20.54)	(0.77)	(−6.91)
Adjusted-R^2	0.035	0.001	0.015	0.021	0.062
Number	4332	4341	3563	4341	3563

consistent with both Fama-French's interpretation of book-to-market as a priced risk factor and Loughran and Ritter's belief that it proxies for relative overpricing.

V. Conclusions

The underperformance documented in Ritter (1991) and Loughran and Ritter (1995) comes primarily from small, nonventure-backed IPOs. We replicate Loughran and Ritter's results and show that returns on nonventure-backed IPOs are significantly below those of venture-backed IPOs and below relevant benchmarks when returns are weighted equally. We test performance against several broad market indexes, Fama-French (1994) industry portfolios, and matched size and book-to-market portfolios to test the robustness of our results. Differences in performance between the groups and the level of underperformance are reduced once returns are value weighted.

We also show that underperformance documented by Loughran and Ritter is not unique to firms issuing equity. Eliminating IPOs and SEOs from size and book-to-market portfolios demonstrates that IPOs perform no worse than similar nonissuing firms. This argues that we should look more broadly at types of firms that underperform and not treat IPO firms as a different group.

While small, low book-to-market IPOs perform no differently from similar small, low book-to-market nonissuing firms, the pattern of relative performance in other portfolios needs to be examined in greater detail. Some of the IPO size and book-to-market portfolios appear to exhibit either under or overperformance. Examination of the time series and cross sectional properties of these patterns may be important in determining the source of performance anomalies.

The underperformance of small, low book-to-market firms may have various explanations. First, unexpected shocks may have hit small growth companies in the early and middle 1980s. The correlation of returns in calendar time may argue in favor of this explanation. Fama and French (1995) show that the earnings of small firms declined in the early 1980s but did not recover when those of large firms did. This experience was different from previous recessions. It is possible that small growth firms were constrained either in the capital or product markets after the recession. These constraints may have been unanticipated. This explanation argues that we should not view each IPO (or firm) as an event, i.e., they are not all independent observations. Correcting for the cross-sectional correlation is critical.

A second explanation for the underperformance of small, low book-to-market firms is investor sentiment. The evidence from Fama-French three factor regressions with and without the change in closed-end fund discount supports this alternative. If the IPO is small, "you can fool some of the people all of the time." If any type of firm is likely to be subject to fads and investor sentiment, it is these firms. Their equity is held primarily by individuals. Megginson and Weiss (1991) show that institutional holdings of equity after an IPO are substantially higher for venture-backed IPOs than they are for nonventure-backed IPOs. The relatively higher institutional holdings may occur because institutions have greater information on small, venture-backed firms through their investment in venture capital funds. Furthermore, because institutions invest such large amounts of money, holding an investment in a small firm may mean that the institutional investor becomes a 5 percent shareholder, something that many institutions want to avoid for regulatory reasons. The ability to short sell small firms is extremely limited because it may be difficult to borrow their stock certificates. Fields (1996) has shown that long-run IPO performance is positively related to institutional holdings. Fields' effects may similarly extend to nonissuing small growth companies.

Asymmetric information is also likely to be more prevalent for small firms because individuals spend considerably less time tracking returns than institutional investors do. Small nonventure-backed firms go public with lower tier underwriters than similar venture-backed firms (Barry, Muscarella, Peavy, and Vetsuypens (1990)) and may have fewer and lower quality analysts following the company after the offering.[15] Carter, Dark, and Singh (1998) and Nanda, Yi, and Yun (1995) have shown that the quality of the underwriter is related to long-run performance of IPOs, consistent with greater asymmetric information being associated with lower returns. It might not pay for a sophis-

---

[15] Michaely and Shaw (1991) provide evidence that underwriter reputation is positively related to the long-run performance of IPOs.

ticated investor to research a small firm because they cannot recoup costs of information gathering and trading. The absolute return that an investor can make is small because the dollar size of the stake they can take is limited by firm size.

Finally, individuals might derive utility from buying the shares of small, low book-to-market firms because they value them like a lottery ticket. Black (1986) argues that many finance anomalies may only be explained by this type of utility-based theory. Returns on small nonventure-backed IPOs are more highly skewed than returns on either large IPO firms or similar sized venture-backed IPO firms.

Ritter (1991) and Loughran and Ritter (1995) have discovered an area that may allow us to test the foundations of investor sentiment and rational pricing. Future tests that identify elements of investor sentiment may show that individual investors are less than perfectly rational. Alternatively, real factors may be responsible for the measured underperformance.

What are the implications of our results? First, most institutional investors will not be significantly hurt by investing in IPOs. They usually do not buy the small issues that perform the worst. Underperformance of small growth companies may be important for capital allocation, however. If the cost of capital for small growth companies is periodically distorted, their investment behavior may be adversely affected. If any of these small firms are future industry leaders, then we should be concerned about this mispricing. Further research is clearly warranted.

REFERENCES

Asquith, Paul, and David Mullins, 1986, Equity issues and offering dilution, *Journal of Financial Economics* 15, 61–89.

Barber, Brad, and John Lyon, 1996, Detecting long-run abnormal stock returns: The empirical power and specification of test statistics, Working paper, University of California, Davis.

Barry, Christopher, Chris Muscarella, John Peavy, III, and Michael Vetsuypens, 1990, The role of venture capital in the creation of public companies: Evidence from the going-public process, *Journal of Financial Economics* 27, 447–476.

Black, Fischer, 1986, Noise, *Journal of Finance* 41, 529–543.

Brav, Alon, Chris Géczy, and Paul Gompers, 1995, Underperformance of seasoned equity offerings revisited, Working paper, University of Chicago and Harvard University.

Carter, Richard, Frederick Dark, and Ajai Singh, 1998, Underwriter reputation, initial returns, and the long-run performance of IPO stocks, *Journal of Finance* forthcoming.

De Bondt, Werner, and Richard Thaler, 1985, Does the stock market overreact?, *Journal of Finance* 40, 793–808.

De Bondt, Werner, and Richard Thaler, 1987, Further evidence on investor overreaction and stock market seasonality, *Journal of Finance* 42, 557–581.

De Long, J. Bradford, Andrei Shleifer, Lawrence H. Summers, and Robert Waldmann, 1990, Noise trader risk in financial markets, *Journal of Political Economy* 98, 703–738.

Fama, Eugene, 1976, *The Foundations of Finance* (New York, Basic Books.)

Fama, Eugene, 1994, Multifactor portfolio efficiency and multifactor asset pricing, Working paper, University of Chicago.

Fama, Eugene, and Kenneth French, 1992, The cross-section of expected stock returns, *Journal of Finance* 47, 427–466.

Fama, Eugene, and Kenneth French, 1993, Common risk factors in the returns of stocks and bonds, *Journal of Financial Economics* 33, 3–55.

Fama, Eugene, and Kenneth French, 1994, Industry cost-of-equity capital, Working paper, University of Chicago and Yale University.

Fama, Eugene, and Kenneth French, 1996, Multifactor explanations of asset pricing anomalies, *Journal of Finance* 51, 55–84.

Fazzari, Steve, R. Glen Hubbard, and Bruce Petersen, 1988, Investment and finance reconsidered, *Brookings Papers on Economic Activity* 19, 141–195.

Fields, Laura, 1996, Is institutional investment in initial public offerings related to the long-run performance of these firms?, Working paper, Penn State University.

Gompers, Paul, 1995, Optimal investment, monitoring, and the staging of venture capital, *Journal of Finance* 50, 1461–1490.

Gompers, Paul, 1996, Grandstanding in the venture capital industry, *Journal of Financial Economics* 42, 133–156.

Gompers, Paul, and Josh Lerner, 1996a, The use of covenants: An empirical analysis of venture capital partnership agreements, *Journal of Law and Economics* 39, forthcoming.

Gompers, Paul, and Josh Lerner, 1996b, Venture capital distributions: Inside information, downward sloping demand curves, or corporate control, Working paper, Harvard University.

Gompers, Paul, and Josh Lerner, 1996c, An analysis of compensation in the US venture capital partnership, Working paper, Harvard University.

Hoshi, Takeo, Anil Kashyap, and David Scharfstein, 1991, Corporate structure, liquidity, and investment, *Quarterly Journal of Economics* 106, 33–60.

Kahneman, Daniel, and Amos Tversky, 1982, Intuitive prediction: Biases and corrective procedures, In Daniel Kahneman, Paul Slovic, and Amos Tversky, Eds: *Judgement under Uncertainty: Heuristics and Biases* (Cambridge University Press, London).

Kothari, S. P., and Jerry Warner, 1996, Measuring long-horizon security price performance, Working paper, University of Rochester.

Lakonishok, Josef, Andrei Shleifer, and Robert Vishny, 1994, Contrarian investment, extrapolation, and risk, *Journal of Finance* 49, 1541–1578.

La Porta, Rafael, 1996, Expectations and the cross-section of stock returns, *Journal of Finance* 51, 1715–1742.

Lee, Charles, Andrei Shleifer, and Richard Thaler, 1991, Investor sentiment and the closed-end fund puzzle, *Journal of Finance* 46, 29–48.

Lerner, Josh, 1994, Venture capital and the oversight of privately-held firms, *Journal of Financial Economics* 35, 293–316.

Loughran, Tim, and Jay Ritter, 1995, The new issues puzzle, *Journal of Finance* 50, 23–52.

Megginson, William, and Kathleen Weiss, 1991, Venture capitalist certification in initial public offerings, *Journal of Finance* 46, 879–903.

Merton, Robert, 1973, An intertemporal capital asset pricing model, *Econometrica* 41, 867–887.

Michaely, Roni, and Wayne H. Shaw, 1991, The pricing of initial public offerings: Tests of adverse selection and signaling theories, *The Review of Financial Studies* 7, 279–319.

Mikkelson, Wayne, and M. Megan Partch, 1986, Stock price effects and costs of secondary distributions, *Journal of Financial Economics* 15, 31–60.

Myers, Stewart, and N. S. Majluf, 1984, Corporate financing and investment decisions when firms have information that investors do not have, *Journal of Financial Economics* 13, 187–221.

Nanda, Vikram, Jong-Hwan Yi, and Youngkeol Yun, 1995, IPO long-run performance and underwriter reputation, Working paper, University of Michigan.

Ritter, Jay, 1991, The long-run performance of initial public offerings, *Journal of Finance* 42, 365–394.

Ross, Stephen, 1977, The determination of financial structure: The incentive signaling approach, *Bell Journal of Economics* 8, 23–40.

Teoh, Siew, Ivo Welch, and T. J. Wong, 1997, Earnings management and the long-run market performance of initial public offerings, Working paper, UCLA.

Part III
Dividend Policy and Equity Management: Secondary Offerings, Splits and Share Repurchases

[13]

THE JOURNAL OF FINANCE • VOL. L, NO. 2 • JUNE 1995

Price Reactions to Dividend Initiations and Omissions: Overreaction or Drift?

RONI MICHAELY, RICHARD H. THALER, and
KENT L. WOMACK*

ABSTRACT

This article investigates market reactions to initiations and omissions of cash dividend payments. Consistent with prior literature we find that the magnitude of short-run price reactions to omissions are greater than for initiations. In the year following the announcements, prices continue to drift in the same direction, though the drift following omissions is stronger and more robust. This post-dividend initiation/omission price drift is distinct from and more pronounced than that following earnings surprises. A trading rule employing both samples earns positive returns in 22 out of 25 years. We find little evidence for clientele shifts in either sample.

WHEN A FIRM INITIATES the payment of a cash dividend, or omits such a payment, the firm is making an extremely visible and qualitative change in corporate policy. What effect do such abrupt changes have on returns? We investigate both the immediate (three-day) reaction to initiation or omission announcements and the long-term post-announcement price performance.

Consistent with prior studies of dividend omissions (Healy and Palepu (1988)), and initiations ((Asquith and Mullins (1983) and Healy and Palepu (1988)), we find that omission announcements are associated with a mean price drop of about 7 percent, and initiations are associated with a price increase of over 3 percent. The center of our investigation, however, focuses on whether there are subsequent excess returns after the market has had an initial chance to react to the announcement of a change in dividend policy. There are three reasons why one might expect significant excess returns in years following the announcement.

First, many authors (e.g., Ball and Brown (1968), Foster, Olsen, and Shevlin (1984), and Bernard and Thomas (1989, 1990)) find evidence for what has come to be called "post-earnings-announcement drift." This research

* Michaely and Thaler are from the Johnson Graduate School of Management, Cornell University. Thaler is also with the National Bureau of Economic Research. Kent Womack is from Amos Tuck School of Business Administration, Dartmouth College. The authors thank the seminar participants at Chicago, Cornell, Illinois, MIT, and Wisconsin and especially Vic Bernard, Laurie Bagwell, Eugene Fama, Steven Kaplan, Charles Lee, Jay Ritter, and David Scharfstein for helpful comments. We also benefited greatly from the comments of the referee and René Stulz, the editor. Errors are ours alone.

shows that when firms make surprising quarterly earnings announcements, prices continue to move in the same direction for the next three quarters, especially on the days surrounding the next two quarterly earnings announcements. Since dividend omissions and initiations are similar to earnings surprises, one might expect a similar drift in prices following the change in policy. That is, prices of firms that omit a dividend would drift down, after the immediate reaction to the omission, and prices of firms that initiate would drift up. Post-earnings-announcement drift can be interpreted as a type of underreaction. The initial price move is insufficient, leaving room for a subsequent drift.

A second literature provides some reason to expect exactly the opposite pattern of prices. Numerous studies find evidence for overreaction or mean reversion in prices. For example, De Bondt and Thaler (1985, 1987) document that those firms that exhibit the most extreme price performance over long time periods (such as 3 to 5 years) tend to display mean reverting excess returns in the subsequent time period. (This tendency is stronger for losers than for winners.) Similar results are obtained by many other researchers in other markets and for different time periods.[1] One study is directly applicable. Bremer and Sweeny (1991) study all the one day price changes of greater than 10 percent for a sample of large New York Stock Exchange companies. They find that over the next six days, the prices of the losers rebounded by about 30 percent of the original loss. Once again there is no rebound for the winners. De Bondt and Thaler characterize these results as evidence of overreaction to the accumulation of bad news during the formation period. One might expect a similar reaction to the omission of a dividend, especially since firms that take this action are likely to be long-term losers. The overreaction literature also suggests that the price patterns might be different for omissions and initiations, with a rebound only for the omissions.

A third reason why one might expect excess returns following a dividend initiation or omission is the likelihood that such actions could cause a change in the type of stockholders owning the company. This is known as a clientele effect. Changes in a firm's stockholder clientele may occur because some individual stockholders dislike cash dividends for tax reasons, while others may prefer the cash payments (Black and Scholes (1974), and Shefrin and Statman (1984)). Similarly, some institutions may either have a preference for dividends or be required by charter to own stock only in dividend paying companies, i.e., various "prudent man" rules. For all these reasons, it is plausible to suppose that dividend initiations and omissions may create a change in ownership. Of course, this does not necessarily imply that there will also be predictable excess returns. In an efficient market, prices will quickly adapt to a new equilibrium, even if the change in clientele is not

---

[1] See De Bondt and Thaler (1989) for a review as well as the more recent contributions of Chopra, Lakonishok, and Ritter (1992) and Lakonishok, Shleifer, and Vishny (1994).

instantaneous. That is, the new equilibrium price will reflect the eventual supply and demand after adjustments in ownership are complete. Nevertheless, if changes in ownership are gradual, price changes might be gradual too, with prices drifting as a result of "price pressure."[2] The existence of clientele effects does not make a crisp prediction about long-term price movements, but offers another reason to investigate this question.

Two earlier papers offer some hints as to how our investigation will turn out. First, Charest (1978) studies the price reactions to announced changes in dividend policies. His events include all changes in dividend payout of 10 cents per share or more, not just initiations and omissions. Although there are some limitations to his study because of the time at which it was written (for example, he does most of his analysis with monthly data for the time period 1947 to 1968), Charest finds small but significant drift after dividend changes. That is, excess returns are positive in the months following the announcement of a dividend increase, and excess returns are negative in the months following the announcement of dividend cuts. More recently, Christie (1990) studies the returns of dividend and nondividend paying stocks. He finds that nondividend paying firms earn negative size-adjusted returns. Although most of his article combines firms that have omitted a dividend with those that have never paid a dividend, he does report one analysis for omitting firms that shows negative returns relative to a size-matched dividend-paying sample. The results we present are consistent with and extend both of these earlier efforts.

The specific events investigated here (initiations and omissions) also provide us with a unique opportunity to analyze the question of whether the market responses to good news (initiations) and bad news (omissions) are symmetric. A quick glance at the data reveals that the absolute magnitude of the price change is larger for omissions than for initiations. However, other questions require some analysis: Are the reactions (both in the short- and long-run) proportional to the change in dividend yield, or does the announcement have a fixed effect? Does the market treat initiation and omission announcements symmetrically? Are omissions more serious events? Are those omissions when the cash dividend is replaced by a stock dividend treated differently by the market? We provide evidence on all of these issues.

The outline of the article is as follows. Section I begins with a summary of our data and some descriptive statistics about the sample of initiations and omissions. In Section II we then examine the short-run market reactions to both types of events in the three days surrounding the announcement. Section III contains the long-term return results, Section IV examines the asymmetry between the initiations (good news) and omissions (bad news) events, and Section V offers tests of the robustness of the long-term excess returns. Section VI investigates clientele effects, and Section VII concludes the article.

---

[2] For similar arguments, see Shleifer (1986) and Harris and Gurel (1986).

I. Sample Selection and Methodology

A. Initiation Sample Selection

Using the Center for Research in Security Prices (CRSP) tapes, we collect all New York Stock Exchange (NYSE)/American Stock Exchange (AMEX) companies that initiated dividends during 1964 to 1988. We define a dividend initiation as the first cash dividend payment reported on the CRSP Master File. (Reinstitution of a cash dividend is not considered a dividend initiation for our purposes.) The following criteria are used for inclusion in our initiation sample:

1. The company must have been traded on the NYSE or AMEX for two years prior to the initiation of the first cash dividend. This criterion was chosen for two reasons. It helps us to select an adequate preevent period for comparison of returns and it eliminates new listings on the NYSE or AMEX that had been paying dividends while on National Association of Securities Dealers Automated Quotation System (NASDAQ) or on another exchange before being listed.[3] While this criterion excludes a number of potential initiation candidates, we feel that it protects the cleanness of the remaining initiation events by eliminating candidates that had listed or had gone public on the NYSE or AMEX with some preannounced intention to pay dividends in the near future.
2. All closed-end funds and all companies paying monthly dividends were excluded from the sample.
3. All foreign companies (usually traded in American Depositary Receipts (ADRs)) were excluded from the sample, since payment conventions in other countries sometimes make checking the periodicity or regularity of payments difficult.

The resulting sample contains 561 cash dividend initiation events. The initiation declarations are widely spread over 25 years, as shown in Table I, Panel A. The number of firms initiating each year shows a positive correlation ($\rho = +0.44$) with percentage changes in aggregate U.S. corporate profits (as reported by the Federal Reserve Board). Also shown in Table I are the market-capitalization distribution (Panel B), price range (Panel C), and industry representation (Panel D) of the initiation sample. For Panel B, we divide the entire sample into deciles according to market capitalization of NYSE/AMEX stocks at the beginning of the year. The first row in Panel B of Table I shows the frequency distribution across deciles of our initiation sample. Firms that initiate dividends are somewhat smaller than the average firm in the NYSE/AMEX universe. Although 21.5 percent of these firms are in the smallest two deciles, only 5 percent are in the largest two deciles. The median is in the 4th decile. The median price per share of initiating firms is

---

[3] It is still possible that a few firms that had previously paid a dividend enter our sample. For example, a firm that had paid a dividend on NASDAQ but was not paying one when listed on NYSE or AMEX would meet our criteria when it resumed paying a dividend.

approximately $10, as reported in the first row of Panel C. We also tabulate the industry representation of both samples in Panel D of Table I. One hundred and seventy-five industries are represented in the initiation sample (defined by the 3-digit SIC code). No industry is represented by more than 25 observations, and the average number of observations in any one industry is 3.2. There is no discernible concentration in any one industry in a given time period. As shown in Panel D, the maximum number of initiations from one industry in any given sample year is 5, which is 20 percent of the sample in that year (1972).

B. Omission Sample Selection

Unlike initiations, declarations of dividend omissions are not recorded on the CRSP tapes. The CRSP files contain announcement dates for dividend declarations, but no dates for the subsequent omissions of regular or irregular payouts. Hence, our sample construction strategy is to select from the CRSP Master File those companies that had existed on the NYSE or AMEX for more than one year and had paid regular, periodic cash dividends and then omitted such payments during 1964 to 1988. Specifically, for a company's dividend record to be considered as a *potential* omission event in our sample, one of the following must have occurred:

1. The company declared at least six consecutive quarterly cash payments and then paid no cash payment in a calendar quarter.
2. The company declared at least three consecutive semi-annual cash payments and then paid no cash payments in the next six months.
3. The company declared at least two consecutive annual cash payments and then paid no cash payments in the next year.

The above search identified more than 1,500 potential omission events in the 1964 to 1988 period. Then, searching the *Wall Street Journal (WSJ) Index* and *Moody's Dividend Record*, we were able to positively identify 887 exact dates of omissions for our sample.[4] Typical reasons for excluding *potential* omission events from our sample are listed below.

1. Timing differences between fiscal quarterly payments and the calendar quarter search algorithm described above. It is quite common for quarterly dividend payments to be unequally spaced throughout the year. For example, payments are usually declared and paid at a regular interval after earnings reporting times. However, fiscal fourth quarter and, hence, annual earnings reports are regularly reported longer after the close of the fiscal fourth quarter than announcements and payments

---

[4] To demonstrate the comprehensive nature of our sample of omissions, our final sample (after exclusions for data availability described below) for the years 1969 to 1980 is 476 omission events (887 in the entire 25 year sample) versus 172 in the same period by Healy and Palepu (1988). Their criteria are indeed more strict, requiring ten continuous years of dividend payments before a chosen omission event.

Table I
Descriptive Statistics of Dividend Initiations and Omissions, 1964 to 1988

Included in the initiation sample are all New York Stock Exchange (NYSE)/American Stock Exchange (AMEX) companies that traded for at least two years before the first dividend announcement, as recorded on the CRSP tapes. Foreign companies, American Depositary Receipts (ADRs) closed-end funds, and companies that pay monthly dividends are excluded. Firms are included in the omission sample if they are traded on the NYSE/AMEX for at least two years, skipped at least one dividend and had an identifiable omission announcement in the *WSJ* Index. The annual aggregate percentage change in U.S. corporate profits is gathered from the Federal Reserve publications, and the percentage change in the NYSE Index is taken from the *NYSE Fact Book*.

Panel A: Distribution of Dividend Initiations and Omissions by Year, 1964–1988

Year	Omissions	Omissions Percentage of Sample	Initiations	Initiations Percentage of Sample	Change in U.S. Corp. Profits (%)	Change in NYSE Index (%) (Excluding Dividends)
1964	12	1.4	39	6.9	12.5	14.4
1965	15	1.7	26	4.8	16.5	9.5
1966	18	2.0	17	3.0	8.2	-12.6
1967	29	3.3	11	2.0	-5.2	23.1
1968	22	2.5	10	1.8	9.8	9.4
1969	41	4.6	10	1.8	-3.1	-12.5
1970	98	11.0	8	1.4	-11.2	-2.5
1971	47	5.3	15	2.7	14.9	12.3
1972	28	3.2	31	5.5	15.8	14.3
1973	21	2.4	57	10.1	25.2	-19.6
1974	58	6.5	35	6.2	8.8	-30.3
1975	47	5.3	53	9.4	-3.4	31.9
1976	24	2.7	77	13.7	25.9	21.5
1977	20	2.3	51	9.1	20.5	-9.3
1978	18	2.0	21	3.7	16.5	2.1
1979	30	3.4	17	3.0	10.1	15.5
1980	44	5.0	14	2.5	-7.8	25.7
1981	47	5.3	10	1.8	-4.5	-8.7
1982	74	8.3	9	1.6	-25.1	14.0
1983	19	2.1	7	1.2	22.4	17.5

Table I—Continued

Panel A: Distribution of Dividend Initiations and Omissions by Year, 1964–1988

Year	Omissions	Omissions Percentage of Sample	Initiations	Initiations Percentage of Sample	Change in U.S. Corp. Profits (%)	Change in NYSE Index (%) (Excluding Dividends)
1984	27	3.0	6	1.1	15.6	1.3
1985	50	5.6	6	1.1	−6.5	26.1
1986	52	5.9	10	1.8	−1.2	14.0
1987	27	3.0	9	1.6	24.2	−0.3
1988	19	2.1	12	2.1	15.0	13.0
Totals	887	100.0	561	100.0		

Panel B: Market Capitalization Deciles (1st Decile Firms are the Smallest Size Firms)

Decile	1st	2nd	3rd	4th	5th	6th	7th	8th	9th	10th
Initiations (%)	8.0	13.5	18.5	14.1	14.6	11.4	8.6	6.1	3.9	1.2
Omissions (%)	14.5	18.0	15.3	12.1	12.5	8.7	9.6	5.2	2.9	1.1

Panel C: Stock Price Per Share of Initiating and Omitting Firms (Day Before the Event).

Price ($)	< 5	5–10	10–15	15–20	20–30	30–40	40–50	> 50
Initiations (%)	20.1	30.1	17.8	11.9	11.2	4.5	1.6	2.3
Omissions (%)	17.9	39.7	20.4	10.1	7.2	2.5	0.6	1.1

Panel D: Industry Representation of Dividend Initiations and Omissions by Year, 1964–1988

Year	Omissions	Omissions Industries Represented (3-Digit SIC)	Omissions Maximum in Any One Industry	Initiations	Initiations Industries Represented (3-Digit SIC)	Initiations Maximum in Any One Industry
1964	12	11	2	39	33	2
1965	15	14	2	26	24	2
1966	18	14	3	17	16	2
1967	29	25	2	11	11	1
1968	22	19	2	10	10	1
1969	41	33	5	10	10	1
1970	98	65	5	8	8	1
1971	47	39	3	15	14	2

Table I—*Continued*

Panel D: Industry Representation of Dividend Initiations and Omissions by Year, 1964–1988

Year	Omissions	Industries Represented (3-Digit SIC)	Maximum in Any One Industry	Initiations	Industries Represented (3-Digit SIC)	Maximum in Any One Industry
1972	28	24	4	31	25	5
1973	21	21	1	57	45	4
1974	58	33	13	35	29	3
1975	47	40	3	53	43	3
1976	24	21	2	77	46	4
1977	20	17	2	51	41	3
1978	18	17	2	21	15	3
1979	30	29	5	17	14	2
1980	44	33	5	14	13	2
1981	47	37	4	10	9	2
1982	74	54	3	9	9	1
1983	19	17	2	7	7	1
1984	27	25	4	6	6	1
1985	50	35	6	6	6	1
1986	52	36	2	10	9	2
1987	27	25	1	9	8	2
1988	19	19	1	12	12	1
Totals, all years	887	210	28	561	175	25

after the close of the previous three fiscal quarters. In the case of these timing differences, multiple payments in a contiguous calendar quarter were ascertained (approximately 450 exclusions).

2. Companies declaring monthly dividends, and closed-end funds were excluded (100 exclusions).

3. No record of an omission announcement could be found in the *WSJ Index* or *Moody's Dividend Record*, or the *WSJ Index* made it clear that no dividend omission had occurred during the suspicious time period (40 exclusions).

4. Payment of a cash dividend was not actually omitted but changed to another type of cash payout such as a return-of-capital payment (20 exclusions).

5. The company preannounced the likelihood of an omission within one month of the official announcement data (10 exclusions).

This procedure results in a sample of 887 cash dividend omission events widely spaced over the 25-year period (Table I, Panel A). Although the number of omissions shows a negative correlation with the value of yearly changes in corporate profits ($\rho = -0.74$) and the one-year-lagged NYSE Index ($\rho = -0.43$), the size and length of our sample prevent any year or economic cycle from dominating our inquiry. The market capitalization, price distribution, and industry representation of the omission sample is quite similar to the initiation sample: over 65 percent of the omitting firms are in the top eight size deciles (second row, Panel B), and over 82 percent traded in a price range greater than five dollars (second row, Panel C). Two hundred and ten industries are represented (second row, Panel D). Out of the 887 omissions, the largest number of omissions from one industry is 28, and the average number in any industry is 4.2. The maximum number of observations from one industry in any given sample year is 13, which is 22 percent of the sample in that year (1974).

In order to compare the results we obtain for initiations and omissions with the post-earnings-announcement drift literature, and to check for contemporaneous earnings announcements, we also require earnings data for as many of the firms in the initiation and omission samples as possible. To obtain this data, we search the COMPUSTAT tapes for the period 1972 to 1988 for all the firms in our samples. We then select those firms where we can identify at least five consecutive recorded earnings announcement dates around the initiation or omission date. In most cases, 12 consecutive earnings dates are available. A total of 235 initiation and 290 omission firms can be matched, or 36 percent of our sample.[5] If the selection requirement is only the positive identification of the earnings date at or immediately prior to the omission event, we can identify 379 omitting firms. The latter subsample is used to

[5] There are several reasons for our failure to find COMPUSTAT data for our entire sample. The two most important are: (1) earnings report dates are not available of the COMPUSTAT tapes before 1972 (our samples includes observations starting in 1964); and (2) COMPUSTAT data are sparse for smaller companies.

ensure that the reaction to the omission announcement is not due to an announcement of contemporaneous negative earnings.

C. Methodology: Excess Return Calculations

To evaluate the performance of the firms in our initiation and omission samples before, during, and after the events (initiation or omission), we calculate the returns from a buy-and-hold strategy.[6] We compare those returns to four benchmark portfolio returns. More precisely, for each stock, the excess return is defined as the geometrically compounded (buy-and-hold) return on the stock minus the geometrically compounded return on either (1) the equally-weighted CRSP index including dividends, (2) the appropriate CRSP market-capitalization decile, (3) the equally-weighted market index adjusted for the beta of each stock, or (4) a matching firm in the same industry (two-digit SIC code) that is closest in market capitalization:

$$ER_{j(a \text{ to } b)} = \prod_{t=a}^{b} (1 + R_{jt}) - \prod_{t=a}^{b} (1 + MR_t) \tag{1}$$

where $ER_{j(a \text{ to } b)}$ = Excess return for firm j from time period a to b. For the three-day event period, the time period (a to b) is trading days $t = -1, 0, +1$. For the monthly periods before or after the event, the returns are calculated assuming 21 trading days for each month. That is, the 12-month return is actually a 252-trading-day (12×21 days) return.[7] R_{jt} = raw return for observation firm j on day t. MR_t = return on the equally-weighted or beta-adjusted market index, the market capitalization decile, or the industry-and-size matched firm on day t.

The average excess returns for each period are then:

$$\overline{ER} = \frac{1}{N} \sum_{j=1}^{N} ER_j \tag{2}$$

For clarity and ease of exposition, the article initially reports the CRSP equally-weighted excess returns as the benchmark. We focus on this benchmark because it is the least noisy and most easily replicable for other researchers. However, we also report results with beta-adjusted, size-adjusted, and industry-and-size-matched portfolio returns in Section V, when we examine the robustness of our long-run findings.

II. Short-Run Reactions to Omissions and Initiations

We compute excess returns for the firms in both samples, for the time period before the event, and for the three-day window around the event (from

---

[6] Our methodology has been strongly influenced by Ritter (1991) and Loughran and Ritter (1995).

[7] Whenever we calculate excess returns for a time period greater than one month, we use the equal-weighted monthly returns or the capitalization-decile price index from the CRSP indices tapes to minimize the bias from compounding daily returns (see Blume and Stambaugh (1983), Roll (1983), and Canina *et al.* (1994)).

the day before the announcement to the day after). These excess returns are presented in Table II. Not surprisingly, the average performance of the stocks that initiate dividends is significantly better than the benchmark portfolios in the year prior to initiation. The initiation portfolio excess return in the prior year is +15.1 percent. During the three-day announcement (event) period, the initiation portfolios experience a significant additional excess return of +3.4 percent ($t = 11.08$). These returns are observed even though the average magnitude of the annual dividend yield is a relatively modest 0.9 percent. (The initial yield is annualized by extrapolating from the first payment and is calculated using the price on the day before the dividend initiation announcement).

Firms omitting dividends perform quite poorly in the year before the omission declaration, consistent with the evidence presented in DeAngelo, DeAngelo, and Skinner (1992). The average excess return is −31.8 percent. As with the initiation sample, the reaction to the omission announcement is in the same direction as the price movement in the period before the announcement: omitting firms experience an additional excess return of −7.0 percent in the three days around the announcement. This highly significant drop in price is a response to a major change in dividend policy. The average yield prior to the omission announcement is an annualized 6.7 percent, much larger than the average yield for firms initiating dividends.

A. Contemporaneous Events and Omission Announcements

The pronounced market reaction to dividend omissions might be attributable to other concurrent events. To investigate this possibility, we search the COMPUSTAT file for earnings announcements in the three-day window around the omission announcement date, and the *WSJ* Index for other concurrent events. The only events occurring in more than 5 percent of the omission sample are announcements of a stock dividend in lieu of the (omitted) cash dividend, and earnings announcements.[8] We therefore investigate these two subsamples separately.

About 10 percent of the omitting firms (92 of the 887) replace the cash dividend with a stock dividend. Table II shows how these firms do, relative to those eliminating all payments. These firms have somewhat better performance in the year before the omission, with excess returns of −21.9 percent (compared to −33.0 percent for those eliminating all payouts), and the price reaction to the switch from a cash to a stock dividend at the announcement is only −3.1 percent, (versus −7.4 percent, a significant difference). This latter result is consistent with the view that the market perceives stock dividends as a positive signal of firm quality (e.g., Brennan and Copeland (1988)). However, as we discuss below, the long-term performance for these firms is worse than that for firms that eliminated all dividends.

---

[8] Other typical news events reported are corporate restructurings, takeover announcements, liquidations, and bankruptcies. The number of these concurring events is very small (less than 5 percent of total observations).

Table II
Market-Adjusted Returns for Periods Before and At Announcement Date for Corporations Initiating and Omitting Cash Dividends

Market-adjusted buy-and-hold returns for the initiation and omission samples (1964 to 1988) are calculated for the one year and three months prior to the three-day event period and for the event period centered around the event day. Buy-and-hold (market-adjusted) returns are calculated as follows:

$$ER_{j(a \text{ to } b)} = \prod_{t=a}^{b}(1 + R_{jt}) - \prod_{t=a}^{b}(1 + MR_t)$$

where $ER_{j(a \text{ to } b)}$ = Excess return for firm j from time period a to b, R_{jt} = raw return for firm j in day or month t, MR_t = return on the CRSP NYSE/AMEX equally-weighted market index for day or month t. The EW market geometrically compounded return is calculated from the monthly and daily CRSP return tapes. t-Statistics are calculated based on the cross-sectional variance in the mean excess return in the relevant period. Dividend yield is defined as the annualized dividend over the price the day before the event. In Panel A excess returns are calculated for the entire samples of initiations and omissions. In Panel B those firms in the omission sample that paid a stock dividend in lieu of the cash dividend are shown separately from the rest. In Panel C the mean excess returns of a subsample of firms that had contemporaneous earnings announcements are compared to the firms that did not have contemporaneous announcements. t-Statistics are reported in parentheses.

		From Day −254 to Day −2	From Day −65 to Day −2	From Day −1 to Day +1	Dividend Yield (%)
			Market-Adjusted Excess Returns for Holding Period Relative to Event Day (%)		
Panel A: Entire Samples					
Initiations	$n = 561$	15.1 (6.4)	4.7 (5.2)	3.4 (11.08)	0.9
Omissions	$n = 887$	−31.8 (−31.6)	−11.2 (−18.9)	−7.0 (−24.75)	6.7
Panel B: Separating the Omission Sample into Stocks that Paid and Substituted and Did Not Substitute a Stock for Cash Dividend					
Stock dividend in lieu	$n = 92$	−21.9	−7.5	−3.1	5.5
No stock dividend	$n = 795$	−33.0	−11.6	−7.4	6.9
t-Statistic of difference		(3.62)	(2.32)	(5.45)	
Panel C: Separating the Omission Sample into Firms that Had and Did Not Have Concurrent Earnings and Omission Announcements (in the Three-Day Event Window)					
Contemporaneous earnings announcement	$n = 93$	−34.1	−13.2	−8.0	
Omission announcement only	$n = 286$	−34.6	−11.7	−5.5	
t-Statistic of difference		(0.14)	(0.79)	(2.63)	

To investigate the influence of concurrent earnings announcements, we use our subsample of 379 stocks that were successfully matched with COMPUSTAT. Ninety-three of the 379 companies made an earnings announcement in one of the three days around the dividend omission announcement. For these 93 companies, the mean excess return in the three-day event window (omission announcement and earnings announcement) is -8.0 percent, whereas the mean for companies without an earnings announcement is -5.5 percent (See Table II, Panel C). Each of these excess returns is significantly different from zero, and the t-test comparing these two means indicates that the means are statistically different. Clearly, there is some incremental (negative) information content in the earnings release, although, as we discuss in Section III, the longer-run performance of the two groups is practically identical.

III. Long-Run Price Responses

Table III and Figure 1 display the return performance for up to three years after initiations and omissions events. As before, the benchmark portfolio is the equally-weighted market index. For initiating firms, the stock prices continue to rise even after the initiation announcement: the first year excess return is 7.5 percent, significantly different from zero ($t = 3.37$) and the three-year excess return is $+24.8$ percent ($t = 3.81$). (T-statistics are calculated using the cross-sectional variance of excess returns as in Korajczyk, Lucas, and McDonald (1991) and Michaely and Shaw (1994).[9] For the omit-

---

[9] Since the time periods of our events partially overlap, the excess returns we calculate are not strictly independent. For several reasons, however, this does not create a serious problem regarding our statistical tests. First, the extent to which our samples (initiations and omissions) overlap is small. As shown in Table I, our firms are well spread over the 25-year sample period. When we calculate one-year returns, about 5 percent of the observations (partially) overlap, while there is partial overlap for 15 percent of the observations for three year returns. Second, even when samples fully overlap in time, the correlation in excess returns depends on the mix of industries. Bernard (1987), for example, shows that within industries the average correlation of one-year excess returns is about 30 percent, but across industries it is only 6 percent. Once again a look at Table I shows that our observations come from many industries, reducing the potential severity of the problem.

Nevertheless, we explicitly test the magnitude of the correlation in the excess returns in our sample as follows. For each event in each sample (the initiations and the omissions) we compute one-year excess returns and then sort the observations chronologically. Call the excess return for the first observation in our sample XR_1 and so forth. We then compute the correlations between XR_i and XR_{i+1}, then the correlations between XR_i and XR_{i+2}, and so forth, up to a "lag" of 60 observations. The average correlation over the first 25 "lags" is less than 5 percent and is essentially white noise thereafter (both for one-year and three-year excess returns). This level of correlation is small, as was to be expected.

The next step is to investigate whether this correlation, however small, affects our inference procedure. Sefcik and Thompson (1986, Table 2, and page 327) show how the t-statistics should be adjusted in the presence of such correlation. The basic idea is that the t-statistics can be adjusted by the average correlation of the residuals. In our case, the average correlation is 0.14 percent. We then proceed to calculate the adjusted t-statistics for the one- and three-year returns as described in Sefcik and Thompson (1986). Not surprisingly (given the low correlation), none of our conclusions change.

Table III
Market-Adjusted Returns for Periods At and After Announcement Date for Corporations Initiating and Omitting Cash Dividends

Market-adjusted buy-and-hold returns for the initiation and omission samples (1964 to 1988) are calculated for the three-day event period and for the three-month, one-year, two-year, and three-year periods beginning two trading days after the event day. In Panel A excess returns are calculated for the entire samples of initiations and omissions. In Panel B the omission sample is divided into firms that paid a stock dividend in lieu of the cash dividend and those that did not. In Panel C the mean excess return of subsample firms that had contemporaneous earnings announcements are compared to the ones that did not have a contemporaneous announcement. *t*-Statistics are reported in parentheses.

		Market-Adjusted Excess Returns for Holding Period Relative to Event Day (%)				
		From Day −1 to Day +1	From Day +2 to Day +65	From Day +2 to Day +254	From Day +2 to Day +506	From Day +2 to Day +758
Panel A: Entire Sample						
Initiations	n = 887	3.4 (11.08)	1.8 (1.97)	7.5 (3.37)	15.6 (3.47)	24.8 (3.81)
Omissions	n = 561	−7.0 (−24.75)	−4.6 (−6.34)	−11.0 (−6.33)	−15.0 (−5.88)	−15.3 (−4.15)
Panel B: Separating the Omission Sample into Stocks that Paid and Substituted and Did Not Substitute a Stock for Cash Dividend						
Stock dividend in lieu	n = 92	−3.1	−7.6	−15.2	−21.9	−31.3
No stock dividend	n = 795	−7.4	−4.3	−10.5	−14.1	−13.5
t-Statistic of difference		(5.45)	(1.74)	(0.85)	(0.94)	(1.77)
Panel C: Separating the Omission Sample into Firms that Had and Did Not Have Concurrent Earnings and Omission Announcements (in the Three-Day Event Window)						
Contemporaneous earnings announcement	n = 93	−8.0	−6.0	−11.9	−12.0	−18.2
Omission announcement only	n = 286	−5.5	−5.3	−12.9	−19.5	−19.7
t-Statistic of difference		(2.63)	(0.34)	(0.14)	(0.74)	(0.12)

Price Reactions to Dividend Initiations and Omissions   587

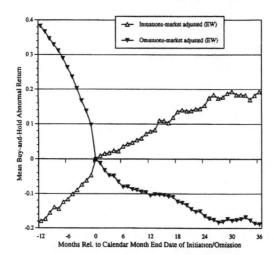

Figure 1. Buy-and-hold adjusted returns for corporations initiating and omitting cash dividends in the period 1964 to 1988. Buy-and-hold market-adjusted returns for the initiation and omission samples are calculated from the one year before to three years after the event. The market-adjusted benchmark compares the security return to the equally-weighted index return. Buy-and-hold returns are calculated as follows:

$$ER_{j(a \text{ to } b)} = \prod_{t=a}^{b}(1 + R_{jt}) - \prod_{t=a}^{b}(1 + MR_{t})$$

where $ER_{j(a \text{ to } b)}$ = Excess return for firm j from time period a to b, R_{jt} = raw return for firm j for month t, MR_{t} = return on the equally-weighted market index for month t.

ting firms, we observe a drift in the opposite direction: the first year excess return is -11.0 percent, measured from the second day after the announcement, and is -15.3 percent after three years. Both excess returns are significant with t-statistics of 6.33 and 4.15, respectively. It should be noted, however, that the long-term results of the omission sample are more robust than those of the initiation sample. That is, the omission sample excess return shows a significant drift for one and three years after the event regardless of the benchmark portfolio used. The drift after initiations, however, is significant only for some benchmarks and time intervals.

We also examine the long-run performance of firms with and without concurrent earnings announcements at the time of the omission announcement (reported in Table III, Panel C). The price behavior of the two subsamples is quite similar to the entire sample: a price drop of 11.9 percent and 12.9 percent after one year, and 18.2 and 19.7 percent after three years. We cannot reject the hypotheses that the return behavior of the two groups is identical in each of those time intervals.

The drift, however, is even more pronounced for the subsample of firms that replace the cash dividend with a stock dividend. Recall that the three-day return for these firms is smaller than for the firms that omit all payouts (−3.1 versus −7.4 percent). This difference is more than offset over the following three years. As Table III, Panel B shows, the three-year buy-and-hold excess returns are −31.3 percent for stock-dividend payers versus −13.5 percent for the rest of the sample. (A test of these returns being different produces a t-statistic of 1.77.) This combination of a smaller initial reaction followed by a much larger drift is indeed curious.

The difference between the stock-dividend-paying firms and the others, interesting as it may be, is not the major story here. Of greater interest are the excess returns following initiations and omissions, excess returns that are both economically and statistically significant, and persist for a year or more. The negative excess returns following omissions are particularly surprising since we began our investigation believing that subsequent positive excess returns (consistent with overreaction) were as likely as drift.[10] This raises questions regarding the comparability of our omission sample with those of De Bondt and Thaler (1985, 1987, 1989 (who find price reversals)) as well as Bernard and Thomas (1989, 1990 (who find drift)).

Are the negative excess returns experienced by the omission firms comparable to those of De Bondt and Thaler's "losers"? To examine this we compute the excess returns for the four-year period prior to the announcement. We find that the excess returns over this period were −45.6 percent. For the sake of comparison, consider the excess returns of the first and second quintile of stocks (ranked on the basis of four year monthly cumulative average market-adjusted returns) reported in De Bondt and Thaler (1987). They find that the first quintile (the big losers) have four year excess returns of −81 percent, while the second quintile have excess returns of −32 percent. Our sample of omission firms falls between these two levels, but this negative performance is severe enough to expect mean reversion based on De Bondt and Thaler's results of positive excess returns over the next four years for both quintiles (25 percent for the first quintile and 12 percent for the second quintile). Thus, while the omission firms are not the most extreme losers, their stock prices have lost enough to make one think that a price reversal is likely.

There is another interesting comparison that can be made between our omission sample and De Bondt and Thaler's losers. De Bondt and Thaler find that the excess returns to their losers occurred primarily in January. In light of this, we compute monthly excess returns for the omission sample in the twelve calendar months following the month of the omission event. We find that the omission portfolio actually does very well in January. The mean return for this month is +4.6 percent. (Part of this excess return is attributable to the small firm sizes in the omission sample, but compared to the size-matched portfolio the omission portfolio still earns a 3.1 percent excess

---

[10] There is less contrast between the positive drift for our initiation sample and the negative returns to De Bondt and Thaler's winners, since the latter were small and not significant.

return in January.) The negative excess returns occur in the other months, particularly in the fourth quarter.[11]

While our results are inconsistent with overreaction, are they consistent with post-earnings-announcement drift. Have we simply rediscovered this phenomenon? We have already shown that (for the subsample of omitting firms for which we have earnings data) only one quarter of the firms omitting a dividend actually made concurrent earnings announcements, and that the concurrence of the two announcements seems to have little effect on the long-term drift. However, even if firms do not announce earnings at the same time as the dividend omission, they might still have negative earnings surprises in surrounding quarters. To investigate this, we calculate earnings surprises in the year before and after the event for all the firms where we have sufficient data. The earnings surprise is defined as the difference between this quarter's earnings (E_t) and the earnings four quarters earlier, (E_{t-4}) scaled by price at the end of quarter $t - 4$, which is prior to the (E_{t-4}) announcement (Bernard and Thomas (1990)). The earnings numbers we use are "earnings before extraordinary items" as reported by COMPUSTAT. We also calculate excess returns for the three days surrounding each earnings announcement.

The results are shown in Table IV. As expected, initiating firms experience positive earnings surprises and excess returns for the earnings announcements preceding the dividend initiation, and omitting firms have negative earnings surprises and excess returns before the omission announcement. What about the subsequent earnings announcements? After an earnings surprise, Bernard and Thomas find significant excess returns (in the same direction) for three quarters, and then a significant excess return in the opposite direction one year after the event. Do our firms show the same pattern? Unfortunately, with our small sample size (compared to the thousands of events studied by Bernard and Thomas) it is not possible to say anything definitive. We do see excess returns of 1.3 and 0.9 percent in the two quarters after an initiation (the first of which is significant) and a significant -1.1 percent excess return in the quarter following an omission. However, no other excess returns are significantly different from zero.

Another comparison with Bernard and Thomas is possible. They find that the magnitude of the drift is highly correlated with the size of the initial earnings surprise. To see whether our drift displays a similar pattern we have divided both our samples into thirds based on the change in dividend yield (the dividend surprise) at the time of the announcement. We then calculate the excess returns for the year before and three years after the event. These results are shown in Table V. Unlike Bernard and Thomas, we find no clear relationship between the size of the "dividend surprise" and the subsequent drift. The excess returns in the year following the event are

---

[11] There is no strong seasonal pattern in the excess returns in the initiation sample. The January excess return is 0.6 percent using the equally-weighted index as a benchmark and -1.5 percent on a size-adjusted basis. Neither are significantly different from zero.

Table IV

Price Reactions to Earnings Announcements from One Year Before and to One Year After the Dividend Announcements

We collect available (beginning in 1972) quarterly earnings announcement dates and earnings before extraordinary items for dividend-initiating and omitting firms. Earnings surprises (*ES*) are calculated using the seasonal random walk model as in Bernard and Thomas (1990). That is:

$$ES_{qtr\,t} = \frac{EBEI_t - EBEI_{t-4}}{PRICE_{end\,of\,qtr\,t-4}}$$ where *EBEI* is the earnings before extraordinary items and *PRICE*

is the stock price at the end of the prior measurement period. Excess returns are calculated as market-adjusted buy-and-hold returns for the three-day periods centered around the earnings announcement day for each quarterly report.

Panel A: Initiations				
Quarter Relative to Initiation Day	No. of Observations	Mean Earnings Surprise (%)	Mean Excess Return (%)	*t*-Statistic of *ER* = 0
− 4	174	+2.6	1.6	2.45
− 3	203	+2.9	1.0	1.85
− 2	212	+2.7	0.9	1.82
− 1	181	+2.4	1.0	1.94
0*	42	+2.5	6.0	4.84
1	227	+2.6	1.3	2.53
2	235	+1.7	0.9	1.22
3	231	+1.2	−0.2	0.58
4	227	−0.1	0.0	0.09

Panel B: Omissions				
Quarter Relative to Omission Day	No. of Observations	Mean Earnings Surprise (%)	Mean Excess Return (%)	*t*-Statistic
− 4	248	−1.4	−1.6	4.86
− 3	277	−2.2	−2.2	0.30
− 2	278	−3.5	−1.5	4.04
− 1	204	−4.0	−2.1	4.89
0*	86	−5.4	−8.8	9.77
1	281	−6.6	−1.1	2.92
2	290	−4.1	0.4	0.93
3	297	−1.1	0.4	0.96
4	278	2.2	0.1	0.37

* Quarter 0 represents quarterly earnings announcements that were coincident with the initiation and omission three-day event period windows.

Price Reactions to Dividend Initiations and Omissions   591

Table V

Market-Adjusted Returns for Firms Initiating and Omitting Dividends, Separated into Thirds by Change in Yield

Post-event market-adjusted returns are shown for three equal-number-of-observation groups based on the magnitude of the yield change. Returns are market-adjusted (equally-weighted index) buy-and-hold returns.

		Market-Adjusted Return (%) for Holding Periods Relative to Event Day		
	From Day −254 to Day −2	From Day −1 to Day +1	From Day +2 to Day +254	From Day +2 to Day +758
Panel A: Initiations				
Yield change 0.0–0.5%	22.3	1.6	4.5	15.1
Yield change 0.5–0.93%	13.6	2.8	10.5	39.9
Yield change 0.93–8.0%	9.5	5.7	7.6	19.9
Panel B: Omissions				
Yield change 0.0–3.9%	−23.7	−4.2	−10.0	−17.2
Yield change 3.9–6.9%	−33.4	−6.6	−12.9	−16.3
Yield change 7.0–77%	−38.4	−10.3	−9.8	−12.2

actually greatest (in absolute value) in the middle group for both omissions and initiations. For the omissions, the three-year drift is, if anything, inversely related to the size of the yield change.

IV. Symmetry in Market Reactions to Initiations and Omissions

A. Short-Run Reactions

The more pronounced initial price reaction to omissions than to initiations is not unique to our sample. Healy and Palepu (1988) for example, find a 3.9 percent increase for a sample of 131 initiations and a 9.5 percent decrease for a sample of 172 omissions. In fact, this differential holds for simple dividend increases and decreases as well. Aharony and Swary (1980), for instance, find that dividend decreases are associated with a price drop of about 3.5 percent while dividend increases are associated with a price increase of about 1 percent.

If dividend changes convey information about the future prospects of the firm (as postulated by Bhattacharya (1979) and Miller and Rock (1985)), then the differential response to omissions and initiations might suggest that negative changes have more information content (perhaps because they are more unusual). Bhattacharya's (1979) and Myers and Majluf's (1984) results also suggest that for an equivalent dividend change, the price impact of a dividend decrease should be greater than the impact of a dividend increase (since the cost of making up a deficit in cash flow is greater than the cost of having a surplus). However, if dividend changes have information content, then presumably the information transmitted is related to the size of the change in the dividend. Initiating or omitting a 5 percent dividend should be more informative than initiating or omitting a dividend paying a 1 percent yield. If we assume that information content is proportional to the magnitude of the change, then the conclusion that omissions are more informative than initiations is reversed. The average change in yield at initiation is only 0.9 percent while the change in yield at omission is 6.7 percent. Thus, while the price change upon the announcement of an omission is twice the change for an omission, this change is in response to an event 7 times larger. Perhaps it is initiations that are more informative!

To investigate this issue more rigorously, we use a series of regressions of the excess returns on the change in yield.[12] We do so using two measures of the change in yield: in the first, the last dividend paid is annualized and divided by the stock price on the day before the announcement, and, in the second, the annualized dividend on the day before the announcement is divided by the price one year before the announcement. The use of the current price needs no justification. The argument for the older price is that

---

[12] Asquith and Mullins (1983) examine whether the larger price reaction to dividend initiations relative to regular dividend increases is because of larger change in yield. They conclude that even after accounting for the yield differences, initiations convey more information.

Price Reactions to Dividend Initiations and Omissions 593

prices have changed over the year since the level of the dividend was set (an average drop of 31 percent below the market for the omission sample), and so the current yield somewhat overstates the "intended" yield. We also add dummy variables to test whether the effect is symmetric between initiations and omissions:

$$ER_i \cdot M_i = \alpha_0 + \alpha_1 Q_i + \alpha_2 \left(\frac{D}{P}\right)_i \cdot M_i + \alpha_3 Q_i \left(\frac{D}{P}\right)_i \cdot M_i + \varepsilon_i \text{ for } i = 1 \text{ to } N$$

(3)

where

ER_i is the three-day excess return for security i,

$M_i = -1$ if the observation is an omission or 1 if the observation is an initiation,

$Q_i = 1$ if omission and 0 if initiation,

$\left(\dfrac{D}{P}\right)_i$ is the ratio of the annualized dividend to the price.

The results are reported in Table VI. When we use the previous day's price to scale the change in dividend yield (first row) we find that both the slope and intercepts differ between the initiation and omission samples. The intercept dummy is positive and the slope dummy is negative, both significant at the 1 percent level. This result suggests that the omission announcement per se is a more dramatic event than an initiation, but that the effect of a unit change in yield has a larger effect on prices for initiations than for omissions. Using an F-test, we can reject the hypothesis that the slope and intercept are equal for omissions and initiations at the 0.01 percent level. However, if the year-old price is used to define the change in yield (second row of Table VI), the differences between the slopes and intercepts for initiations and omissions are statistically insignificant. Likewise, we cannot reject the joint hypothesis that the intercept and slopes are equal for omissions and initiations using an F-test.

To see whether either of these results might be due to outliers in the sample, we have also run the same regressions using grouped data. To do so, we divided both samples into ten groups ranked by change in yield and reexamined the relationship between excess return and yield using the means for these deciles. The results are shown in the third and fourth rows of Table VI. Regardless of whether we divide the annualized dividend by previous day price (third row) or prior year price (fourth row), neither the intercept dummy nor the slope dummy is significantly different from zero. Similarly, the F-statistics also indicate that the intercept and the slope are equal for omissions and initiations (p-values of 0.34 and 0.62 using the two yield definitions respectively). Overall, the results show that the market reaction to the dividend change is significantly related to the magnitude of the change. When the "stale" price is used in the definition of yield, there is no asymmetry between the market reactions to initiation and omission announcements.

Table VI

Dividend Yield Changes as A Determinant of the Price Reaction around Initiation and Omission Announcements

Using multivariate linear regression, we investigate the relationship between the market reaction to the initiation/omission announcement and the change in yield:

$$ER_i \cdot M_i = \alpha_0 + \alpha_1 Q_i + \alpha_2 \left(\frac{D}{P}\right)_i \cdot M_i + \alpha_3 Q_i \left(\frac{D}{P}\right)_i \cdot M_i + \varepsilon_i, \quad i = 1 \ldots N$$

where ER_i is the three-day excess return for security i, $M_i = -1$ if the observation is an omission or $= 1$ if the observation is an initiation, $Q_i = 1$ if omission and 0 if initiation, $(\frac{D}{P})_i$ is the ratio of the annualized dividend to the price on the day before (first and third regressions) or the year before the announcement (second and fourth regressions). To reduce the outliers effects in the last two regressions, observations are grouped according to their yield into 10 omissions and 10 initiations deciles. The F-statistics tests the joint hypotheses that both the intercept and the slope dummies are insignificantly different from zero. t-Statistics are in parentheses.

Intercept α_0	Intercept Dummy $\alpha_1^* Q_i$	Yield Coefficient α_2	Slope Dummy Coefficient α_3	F-Test (probability)	R^2	N
		Panel A: When Yield = D/P_{t-1}				
0.011 (2.43)	0.029 (4.91)	2.117 (5.59)	-1.67 (-4.40)	13.47 (0.00)	0.16	1448
		Panel B: When Yield = D/P_{t-250}				
0.019 (4.52)	0.004 (0.53)	0.997 (3.88)	0.10 (0.36)	0.70 (0.50)	0.14	1448
		Panel C: When Yield = D/P_{t-1}, Grouped Data				
0.0097 (1.75)	0.009 (1.05)	1.62 (3.04)	-0.81 (-0.54)	1.13 (0.35)	0.90	20
		Panel D: When Yield = D/P_{t-250}, Grouped Data				
0.010 (2.06)	-0.003 (-0.34)	1.16 (3.51)	0.32 (0.90)	2.01 (0.62)	0.92	20

B. Long-Run Response

We have documented price drifts associated with both omission and initiation announcements. These deviations from the market efficiency paradigm are not unique to our study. However, the specific events investigated here (initiations and omissions) provide us with a unique opportunity to analyze the question of whether the long-run market response to good news (initiations) and to bad news (omission) is symmetric. Similar to the immediate response to these events, it appears that the absolute magnitude and the duration of the drift are more pronounced for omissions than for initiations. The magnitude of the drift may depend on the intensity of the news (i.e., the magnitude of the change in yield). It is also possible that the drift will be more pronounced for stocks that are thinly traded, i.e., low turnover. These stocks may experience slower price responses to informational events, including initiations and omissions.

To investigate these issues, we estimate a set of regressions (not reported) similar to the ones we used in the analysis of the short-term reactions (equation (3)). The independent variables are the stock's dividend yield, its average daily turnover in the year after the event, and a dummy variable, Q_i, that takes the value of one if the event is an omission and zero if an initiation. The dependent variables are the one-year and the three-year excess returns. No discernible pattern is found for either the one or the three-year excess returns: neither the yield nor the liquidity coefficients are significant. The long-term drift, and the asymmetry in the drifts between initiations and omissions, cannot be explained by the magnitude of the change in the yield, nor by the stock's subsequent liquidity.

V. Robustness

There are several possible concerns one might have about the results presented so far. First, are the long-run excess returns sensitive to the particular benchmark selected? Second, could the excess returns be attributable to changes in risk? Third, are the excess returns concentrated in particular industries or years? Finally, do the excess returns imply a viable trading rule?

A. The Benchmark Portfolio

We have argued that the equally-weighted index is an appropriate benchmark to use in computing excess returns for our samples. However, both samples have somewhat higher concentrations of small firms that the NYSE/AMEX population (as shown in Table I, the median firm in both samples lies in the 4th decile) so it is possible that our results could be influenced by the size effect. To test for this possibility we recalculate excess returns using size-adjusted portfolios. To do this, we calculate excess returns by subtracting the CRSP NYSE/AMEX market capitalization decile return appropriate to each firm from that firm's return. (Firm size is measured as the market value of equity at the beginning of the event year).

Another possibility is that our samples may be concentrated in particular industries, and a few select industries are producing the excess returns. To check out this possibility, we also construct industry-and-size-matched portfolios. For each firm in our samples we select the (nonevent) firm from the same two-digit SIC code that is closest in size at the beginning of the year. It should be noted however, that controlling for industry may not be appropriate in our case. That is, if the initiation or omission events coincide with industry-wide misvaluation, controlling for industry effects will reduce our ability to identify abnormal performance.

The results are described in Table VII. For the most part, the results are qualitatively the same as those obtained using the equally-weighted index. In both samples, the returns prior to the event, and those in the event window, are very close to those shown before in Table II. Since both of our samples overweight small capitalization firms, and since small stocks generally outperformed large stocks during our sample period, using size-adjusted returns as a benchmark reduces the reported excess returns on average. For the omission sample, the postevent (negative) excess returns are thus more pronounced: the one-year excess returns are -12.7 percent for the size-adjusted portfolio, -14.7 percent for the industry-and-size-matched portfolio, and -11.3 percent for the beta-adjusted portfolio, compared to -11.0 percent using the equally-weighted index. The three-year cumulative returns are -19.6, -16.0, -19.7, and -15.3 percent, respectively. All are significant.

For the same reasons, the positive excess returns for initiations also become smaller when using the size-adjusted benchmarks, especially the three-year returns. The one-year and the three-year mean excess returns are significant for both the beta-adjusted and size-adjusted benchmarks. The long-run excess returns are positive but insignificant when the industry-and-size-matched benchmark is used. Of course, the industry-and-size-matched portfolio procedure introduces considerable additional noise into the excess return calculations because of the higher variance of the firm-by-firm matching comparisons relative to portfolio comparisons, so we put the most weight on the market-adjusted (with or without beta) and size-adjusted returns.

In Table VII we also report median excess returns using the equally-weighted index. Although medians are not very interesting from an investment perspective, they can tell us to what extent the portfolio returns are produced by outliers or asymmetries in returns. Since individual firm returns are typically right skewed (negative returns are bounded at -100 percent), median returns are usually lower than mean returns (especially for long-term returns), and our results are no exception. Thus, the median excess returns for the omissions are more negative, whereas the median excess returns for the initiations are closer to zero.

Table VII

Beta-Adjusted, Size-Adjusted, and Industry-Matched Returns for Corporations Initiating and Omitting Dividends

Table VII compares market-adjusted, beta-adjusted, size-adjusted, and industry-matched buy-and-hold returns for the initiation and omission samples. We calculate the buy-and-hold return for the initiating and omitting firms as:

$$ER_{j(a\ to\ b)} = \prod_{t=a}^{b}(1 + R_{jt}) - \prod_{t=a}^{b}(1 + MR_t)$$

where $ER_{j(a\ to\ b)}$ = Excess return for firm j from time period a to b, R_{jt} = raw return for firm j in day or month t, MR_t is either the return on (1) the equally-weighted market, (2) the equally-weighted market times the appropriate firm beta, (3) the appropriate market capitalization decile for New York Stock Exchange/American Stock Exchange firms on the CRSP tape, or (4) a matching firm (closest by size with the appropriate SIC code), in day or month t. If the matching firm was delisted before the sample firm, the equally-weighted market index was substituted for the matching-firm return. t-Statistics are calculated based on the cross-sectional variance of the excess returns in the relevant period and are reported in parentheses.

	Excess Returns (%) for Holding Periods Relative to Event Day			
	From Day −254 to Day −2 (1 Yr. Preevent)	From Day −1 to Day +1 (Event Return)	From Day +2 to Day +254 (1 Yr. Postevent)	From Day +2 to Day +758 (3 Yr. Postevent)
Panel A: Initiations				
Mean, market-adjusted (EW)	15.1 (6.4)	3.4 (11.08)	7.5 (3.37)	24.8 (3.81)
Mean, beta-adjusted	13.2 (5.4)	3.4 (10.82)	6.2 (2.65)	13.9 (2.05)
Mean, size-decile adjusted	13.8 (5.96)	3.4 (11.19)	6.0 (2.69)	12.1 (1.89)
Mean, industry-and-size-matched portfolio	13.5 (4.6)	3.0 (7.40)	0.76 (0.25)	8.6 (1.07)
Median, market-adjusted (EW)	0.6	2.3	1.7	−1.4
Panel B: Omissions				
Mean, market-adjusted (EW)	−31.8 (−31.6)	−7.0 (−24.75)	−11.0 (−6.33)	−15.3 (−4.15)
Mean, beta-adjusted	−31.4 (−26.5)	−7.0 (−24.61)	−11.3 (−6.08)	−16.0 (−4.12)
Mean, size-decile-adjusted	−32.9 (−32.02)	−7.0 (−24.92)	−12.7 (−7.39)	−19.6 (−5.41)
Mean, industry-and-size-matched portfolio	−28.1 (−16.1)	−7.1 (−21.10)	−14.7 (−6.00)	−19.7 (−4.13)
Median, market-adjusted (EW)	−32.5	−6.3	−18.1	−32.0

B. Beta Risk Changes

Can the excess returns after initiation and omission announcements be explained by changes in systematic risk as measured by beta? While such an explanation is always possible, a change in beta-risk seems unlikely to explain our results because of the direction of the drifts that we observe. After initiations, prices drift up while after omissions, they drift down, so a risk change hypothesis must argue that firms become riskier after initiations and less risky after omissions. It is worth noting that such a risk shift is precisely the opposite pattern of the risk changes that some authors (e.g., Chan (1988) and Ball and Kothari (1989)) have proposed as an explanation of De Bondt and Thaler's findings. Nevertheless, for completeness we have investigated this issue by taking the CRSP estimated beta of each stock in our samples for the calendar year of the event and the years before and after. These betas are calculated using the daily returns in that year. For the omissions, the three betas are, in order, 1.06, 0.95, and 1.08. For the initiations the three betas are: 1.34, 1.35, and 1.24. If we simply compare the preannouncement year betas with the postannouncement year betas, we find that both samples show movement in the wrong direction to support a risk explanation.

Of course, beta may not be the best measure of risk. Fama and French (1993) have argued that returns are best explained by size and the ratio of market value to book value. We have reported size-adjusted returns but not returns correcting for price to book. However, it is clear what direction this correction would take. The initiation sample will tend to be high price-to-book (i.e., growth stocks) and the omission sample will tend to be low price-to-book (i.e., value stocks). Therefore, the drifts we observe will become more pronounced if we compare the returns to other stocks with these characteristics.

C. Event Clustering

While Table I (Panel A) indicates that neither the initiations nor the omissions events are clustered in one particular time period, it is still possible that the excess returns are dominated by a shorter subperiod. Perhaps the drift existed in the 60s, was recognized, and has since disappeared. We investigate this possibility by splitting our samples into two time periods so that there are equal numbers of observation in each subperiod. (The split occurs in 1975 for the initiation sample and 1976 for the omissions.) We then evaluate the portfolio performance (relative to the equally-weighted index) before, during, and after the events for each subperiod. The results are reported in Table VIII.

In general, we find that excess returns, before and after the announcements, are more pronounced in the second subperiod than in the first. For the initiation sample, the average excess returns in the year before the event is +8.6 percent for the 1966 to 75 period compared with +21.6 percent for the 1975 to 88 period. The excess return in the three years after the event is +11.1 percent in the first subperiod and is +38.4 percent in the second.

Table VIII
Market-Adjusted Returns for Firms Initiating and Omitting Dividends When the Sample is Divided Into Two Time Periods

Market-adjusted buy-and-hold returns for the initiation and omission samples (1964 to 1988) are calculated for the year before, the three days of, and for the one-, two-, and three-year periods after the events. Each sample is divided into two time periods so that the number of events in each time period is equal.

		Market-Adjusted Returns (%) for Holding Period Relative to Event Day			
	From Day −254 to Day −2	From Day −1 to Day +1	From Day +2 to Day +254	From Day +2 to Day +506	From Day +2 to Day +758
Panel A: Initiations					
1966–1975 $n = 280$	8.6	3.1	1.7	2.7	11.1
1975–1988 $n = 281$	21.6	3.7	13.3	28.3	38.4
Panel B: Omissions					
1966–1976 $n = 443$	−27.6	−8.0	−7.5	−8.9	−6.8
1976–1988 $n = 444$	−36.0	−6.0	−14.6	−21.1	−23.9

Similarly, the three-year post-omission-announcement drift is −6.8 percent and −23.9 percent for the first and second subperiods respectively. A comparable picture emerges when we compare the performance in each time period to the size-adjusted portfolios. We have no explanation for why the magnitude of the post-event drift increases in the second sub-periods.

D. Returns to a Trading Rule

As a final test of the robustness of the results, we calculate the returns to a simple trading rule. For each initiation event in our sample we buy a given long position (say $1,000) in the stock at the closing price on the day after the initiation announcement, and offset this position by selling short the market (as measured by the CRSP equally-weighted index). Similarly, for every omission event we sell the stock short at the closing price the day after the announcement, and take an offsetting long position in the equally-weighted index. We hold the positions for one year (actually 252 trading days). Then, although these are theoretically zero investment portfolios, we compute returns as a percentage of the long positions.[13]

In order to see how this strategy performs on a year-by-year basis, we have assigned the profits of any given event to the year in which the event occurred, i.e., the year in which the trades were initiated. The results are shown in Figure 2. The average return across all the years is +9.7 percent. The returns are positive in 22 out of the 25 years, and there is only one bad year for the strategy, 1966. We conclude from this exercise that the excess returns from this anomaly are not produced by any one time period, and appear to be economically significant.

VI. Clientele Effects

Common Wall Street wisdom has it that stocks differ in their clienteles. For example, it is well known that institutions primarily hold stocks in large firms, and small firms are held primarily by individuals. Firms with different dividend policies are also thought to have different clienteles for two distinct reasons, one economic and one psychological. First, if dividends are taxed at a higher rate than capital gains, then high-yield stocks should be relatively more attractive to stockholders with low (or zero) marginal tax rates. Second, as Shefrin and Statman (1984) have argued, some individuals may prefer to own stock in dividend paying companies because they employ the rule "spend the dividends, don't touch the principal" as a self-control device. Utilities, for example, are held primarily by individuals, though they pay high dividends (see Lee, Shleifer, and Thaler (1991)). Of course, if stockholders do sort themselves according to their preferences for dividend income versus capital

---

[13] We make no claims that this exercise represents a real investment opportunity. The purpose of the calculation is to see whether the excess returns are concentrated in specific time periods. We therefore make no calculations regarding transactions costs.

Price Reactions to Dividend Initiations and Omissions 601

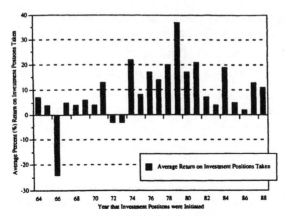

Figure 2. A naive trading strategy capturing abnormal returns to dividend initiations and omissions. For each initiation event in our sample we buy an equal-dollar long position in the stock at the closing price on the day after the initiation announcement, and offset this investment with a short position in the CRSP equally-weighted index. Similarly, for every omission event we sell the stock short at the closing price the day after the announcement, and buy an offsetting long position in the equally-weighted index. Both positions are held for one year (252 trading days). Returns are calculated as a percentage of the long position. The figure displays the average return in each year to the trading strategy: the returns displayed are for positions initiated in the year shown, but closed out in the following year. The average return across all years is +9.7 percent.

gains, then the announcement of a dividend omission or initiation should produce a significant shift in clientele. At the time of the omission, the average firm in our sample was paying out an annual yield of 6.7 percent, so the change in yield is substantial. For this reason, omissions are a particularly interesting case to look at for evidence of clientele shifts. (Initiations, with their much smaller 0.9 percent average yield, would presumably create a smaller clientele shift.) The fact that we also find long-term price drifts after dividend initiations and omissions suggests another reason to check for clientele shifts, since price pressure effects might be a plausible explanation for the drifts. With this motivation, we examine clientele effects in two ways, first by monitoring volume, and second by checking for shifts in institutional ownership.

One way of looking for evidence of a clientele shift is to see whether the turnover rate for firms that initiate or omit dividends shows a marked change following the announcement. To examine this we measure the trading volume for each firm in our sample for the 125 trading days (6 months) before the event day and for the 250 days after the event. Normal volume is defined as the portfolio's average turnover in days -125 to -5 where day zero is the event day. We then compute the portfolio's abnormal volume, AV_t, (defined as the ratio of daily turnover to normal turnover) and its standard deviation as follows:

For each stock we calculate the daily turnover TO_{it}, defined as the number of shares traded over the number of shares outstanding.

$$TO_{it} = \frac{\text{Number of shares traded}_{it}}{\text{Number shares outstanding}_{it}} \quad \begin{array}{l} i = 1 \ldots N \\ t = -125 \ldots 250 \end{array} \quad (4)$$

where N is the number of firms in the sample.

Next the average daily turnover for each event is calculated using the daily turnover in days -125 to -6:

$$\overline{TO_i} = \sum_{t=-125}^{-6} TO_{it}/120 \quad (5)$$

Then, the portfolio daily turnover for day t is defined as the simple average turnover for all securities in the sample (either initiations or omissions).

$$TO_t = \frac{1}{N} \sum_{i=1}^{N} \frac{TO_{it}}{\overline{TO_i}} \quad t = -125 \ldots 250 \quad (6)$$

Finally, the abnormal volume (in percentage terms) for day t is defined as

$$AV_t = TO_t - 1 \quad t = -125 \ldots 250 \quad (7)$$

and its standard deviation is:

$$S.D.(AV_t) = \frac{1}{(119)} \sum_{t=-125}^{-6} \left(AV_t - \overline{AV} \right)^2 \quad (8)$$

where

$$\overline{AV} = \frac{\sum_{t=-125}^{-6} AV_t}{120} \quad (9)$$

The results are displayed in Table IX and Figures 3 (initiations) and 4 (omissions). The average daily turnover for the omission and initiation portfolios is 0.223 and 0.233 percent, respectively, implying an annual turnover of 56 percent, somewhat lower than the average NYSE daily turnover. The results for the initiation sample show that in the eleven days around the initiation announcement, abnormal volume is positive, and significantly positive in days -3 to $+3$. However, the increase in turnover is not very large. The average cumulative turnover in those eleven days is only 3.23 percent compared with the normal eleven day turnover of 2.56 percent. Also, as Figure 3 shows, there is no appreciable increase in turnover in the subsequent year.

Firms that omit dividends show a similar pattern shown in the second column of Table IX. Significantly positive abnormal volume is detected up to nine days after the omission date, but the cumulative average turnover in the eleven days around the announcement is 3.62 percent, compared with a normal eleven day turnover of 2.45 percent. Once again, there is no discernible change in volume in the year following the omission announcement.

Table IX

Abnormal Trading Volume Around Dividend Initiation and Omission Announcements

Abnormal volume is calculated for the 21 days centered around the initiation/omission announcement. Normal volume is defined as the average daily turnover in day -125 to -5 relative to the event, and abnormal volume is the daily turnover in the event day minus the average daily turnover, relative to the daily average turnover. The standard deviation of turnover is calculated in the estimation period (day -125 to day -5) from the average daily turnover.

	(1) Dividend Initiations		(2) Dividend Omissions	
Day Relative to Announcement Date	Abnormal Volume (%)	t-Statistic	Abnormal Volume (%)	t-Statistic
-10	10.6	1.68	-0.4	-0.07
-9	-0.6	-0.09	-0.4	-0.07
-8	17.0	2.67	3.8	0.61
-7	0.8	0.13	-4.1	-0.65
-6	4.0	0.63	-5.8	-0.94
-5	9.0	1.42	-6.6	-1.06
-4	7.0	1.10	1.7	0.28
-3	15.9	2.51	8.6	1.39
-2	20.5	3.22	4.6	0.74
-1	18.8	2.95	126.1	20.31
0	81.9	12.89	191.0	30.77
1	82.5	12.99	98.8	15.92
2	40.3	6.35	55.2	8.90
3	32.5	5.12	42.8	6.89
4	10.2	1.61	26.6	4.28
5	6.2	0.97	30.0	4.84
6	7.1	1.11	38.8	6.25
7	2.5	0.40	12.9	2.07
8	-1.8	-0.29	11.2	1.80
9	3.3	0.52	15.9	2.56
10	0.9	0.14	0.0	-0.01

The relatively minor increase in volume during the event window, and the absence of an increase thereafter, strongly suggests that if there are changes in clientele, they are not very dramatic.[14] Of course, changes in clientele could occur (albeit gradually) without an increase in volume. We have, therefore, also undertaken a direct investigation of whether the share of institutional ownership changes after a dividend omission.[15] To do this we used the *Standard and Poor's Stock Guide* to obtain an estimate of the

[14] In investigating volume and price changes of 192 firms that initiated dividends, Richardson, Sefcik, and Thompson (1986) conclude that the volume increase is primarily in response to the news contained in the initiation announcement.

[15] We also tried to collect data on institutional ownership for initiating firms but could not obtain a large enough sample size to make an analysis possible. The problem is that many initiating firms are too small to be included in the *Standard and Poor's Stock Guide*, the source of our ownership data.

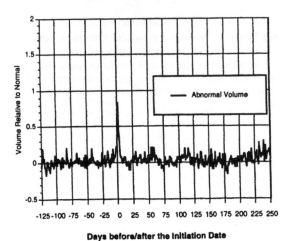

Days before/after the Initiation Date

Figure 3. Abnormal trading volume around dividend initiation announcements.
Abnormal volume from the six months before the initiation announcements to one year after the announcements is calculated. Normal volume is defined as the average daily turnover in day -125 to -5 relative to the event, and abnormal volume is the daily turnover minus the average daily turnover in the estimation period, relative to the daily average turnover.

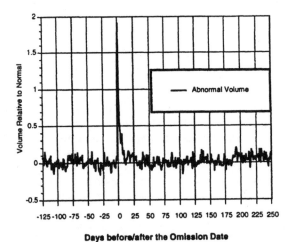

Days before/after the Omission Date

Figure 4. Abnormal trading volume around dividend omission announcements. Abnormal volume from the six months before the omission announcements to one year after the announcements is calculated. Normal volume is defined as the average daily turnover in day -125 to -5 relative to the event, and abnormal volume is the daily turnover minus the average daily turnover in the estimation period, relative to the daily average turnover.

percentage of shares held by institutions for the three years before and three years after the omission announcement. The data on institutional holdings began to appear in the *Stock Guide* in 1979, so we are able to obtain three years of data prior to omissions only for events occurring in 1982 and later. For this reason, and because not every firm is listed in the *Stock Guide*, our sample of omitting firms falls from 887 to 168.[16] For these 168 firms, we then computed the average institutional ownership share for the three years preceding the event and the three years after the event. Averaging across all firms, we find that the mean institutional holdings before the omission announcement are 30.0 percent (18.1 percent standard deviation) while the mean postevent share is 30.9 percent (17.6 percent). This adds further support to the impression that dividend omissions do not produce dramatic changes in ownership.

VII. Summary and Conclusion

We investigate the immediate and long-term effects of dividend initiation and omission announcements. Consistent with prior studies, we find that the short-run price impact of dividend omissions is negative and that of initiations is positive. Initiation reactions are about one-half the magnitude of the market reaction to omission announcements. The change in yield, however, is about seven times larger for the omission announcements. We show that the market reaction to a dividend omission announcement is no greater than to an initiation for a given change in yield.

The most surprising of our findings concerns the significant long-term drifts following announcements of initiations and especially omissions. These drifts are surprising on several counts. First, from an efficient market perspective, predictable excess returns are always surprising. In the case of the omissions, where the drift is large and robust, our attempts to correct for risk or size only make the excess returns larger. It also seems that these drift patterns are quite consistent through time: we show that in 22 out of 25 years examined in the study, the combined initiating and omitting firms' drifts result in abnormal profits. Second, firms that omit a dividend are prior losers, not unlike those studied by De Bondt and Thaler who find significantly positive excess returns. Third, while the negative drift resembles that found by Bernard and Thomas and others who have investigated post earnings announcement drift, this is not the same phenomenon. The drift here is more pronounced, lasts longer, and does not appear to occur primarily around subsequent earnings announcements. Fourth, we can find no evidence of important changes in volume or clientele, which mitigates price pressure as a potential explanation for the anomalous drift.

---

[16] We also deleted firms when the year to year changes were so wild as to suggest that one of the observations was an error. For example, if the institutional holdings for three consecutive years were recorded as 20, 2, 23 percent, we suspected that the middle year was an error and dropped the observation.

It is apparent that both the immediate and the long-term reaction to omission announcements is greater (in absolute value) than to initiation announcements. We are able to explain (at least partially) the asymmetry in the short-term reaction by the difference in the magnitude of the yield change between these two types of events. We cannot find any explanation for the long-term differences in price behavior between initiations and omissions. Neither the intensity of the news (i.e., the change in yield) nor the stock's liquidity can explain the larger drift observed for omissions. Finally, we show that those firms substituting stock dividends for cash dividends experience a smaller price drop at the announcement, but that these stocks perform even worse than nonstock-dividend-paying firms in the long run.

Although our long-term drift results are surprising, they are consistent with several other recent articles. Ikenberry, Lakonishok, and Vermaelen (1995) find positive long-term excess returns following the open-market share repurchases while Loughran and Ritter (1995) find negative long-term excess returns following seasoned equity issues. In both of these cases, firms are making announcements that the market might perceive to be signals regarding the intrinsic value of the stock. Share repurchases indicate that the stock price is too low, while equity issues suggest the opposite. The long-term returns imply that these signals are accurate, but the fact that the price adjustment seems to take months instead of minutes suggests that the market is, in some sense, underreacting to the announcements. The findings of Jegadeesh and Titman (1993) can also be interpreted as underreaction in the three-months to one-year time horizon. In another relevant article Womack (1995) finds similar drift after changes in brokerage recommendations. When brokerage firms add a stock to their "buy" list or "sell" list, there are both immediate and delayed excess returns. We hope future research will help us understand why the market appears to overreact in some circumstances and to underreact in others.

REFERENCES

Aharony, Joseph, and Itzhak Swary, 1980, Quarterly dividend and earnings announcements and stockholders' returns: An empirical analysis, *Journal of Finance* 35, 1–12.

Asquith, Paul, and David W. Mullins, 1983, The impact of initiating dividend payments on shareholder wealth, *Journal of Business* 56, 77–96.

Ball, Ray, and Philip Brown, 1968, An empirical evaluation of accounting income numbers, *Journal of Accounting Research*, 159–178.

Ball, Ray, and S. P. Kothari, 1989, Nonstationary expected returns: Implications for tests of market efficiency and serial correlation in returns, *Journal of Financial Economics* 25, 51–74.

Bernard, Victor L., 1987, Cross-sectional dependence and problems in inference in market-based accounting research, *Journal of Accounting Research* 25, 1–47.

Bernard, Victor L., and Jacob K. Thomas, 1989, Post-earnings-announcement drift: Delayed price response or risk premium?, *Journal of Accounting Research* 27, 1–36.

———, 1990, Evidence that stock prices do not fully reflect the implications of current earnings for future earnings, *Journal of Accounting and Economics* 13, 305–340.

Bhattacharya, Sudipto, 1979, Imperfect information, dividend policy, and "the bird in the hand" fallacy, *Bell Journal of Economics* 10, 259–270.

Black, Fisher, and Myron Scholes, 1974, The effects of dividend yield and dividend policy on common stock prices and returns, *Journal of Financial Economics* 1, 1–22.

Blume, Marshall E., and Robert F. Stambaugh, 1983, Biases in computed returns: An application to the size effect, *Journal of Financial Economics* 12, 387–404.

Brennan, Michael, and Thomas Copeland, 1988, Stock splits, stock prices, and transaction costs, *Journal of Financial Economics* 22, 83–101.

Bremer, Marc, and Richard J. Sweeny, 1991, The reversal of large stock-price decreases, *Journal of Finance* 46, 747–754.

Canina, Linda, Roni Michaely, Richard H. Thaler, and Kent L. Womack, 1995, A warning about using the daily equal-weighted index to compute long-run returns, Working paper, Cornell University.

Chan, K. C., 1988, On the contrarian investment strategy, *Journal of Business* 61, 147–164.

Charest, Guy, 1978, Dividend information, stock returns and market efficiency—II, *Journal of Financial Economics* 6, 297–330.

Chopra, Navin, Josef Lakonishok, and Jay R. Ritter, 1992, Measuring abnormal performance: Do stocks overreact?, *Journal of Financial Economics* 31, 235–268.

Christie, William G., 1990, Dividend yield and expected returns: The zero-dividend puzzle, *Journal of Financial Economics* 28, 1990.

DeAngelo, Harry, Linda DeAngelo, and Douglas Skinner, 1992, Dividends and losses, *Journal of Finance* 47, 1837–1864.

De Bondt, Werner, and Richard Thaler, 1985, Does the stock market overreact?, *Journal of Finance* 40, 793–808.

———, 1987, Further evidence on investor overreaction and stock market seasonality, *Journal of Finance* 42, 557–581.

———, 1989, Anomalies: A mean-reverting walk down Wall Street, *Journal of Economic Perspectives* Winter, 189–202.

Fama, Eugene, and Kenneth French, 1993, Common risk factors in the returns of stocks and bonds, *Journal of Financial Economics* 33, 3–56.

Foster, George, Chris Olsen, and Terry Shevlin, 1984, Earnings releases, anomalies, and the behavior of security returns, *The Accounting Review* 59, 574–603.

Harris, Lawrence, and Eitan Gurel, 1986, Price and volume effects associated with changes in the S&P 500: New evidence for the existence of price pressures, *Journal of Finance* 41, 815–830.

Healy, Paul, and Krishna Palepu, 1988, Earnings information conveyed by dividend initiations and omissions, *Journal of Financial Economics* 21, 149–175.

Ikenberry, David, Josef Lakonishok, and Theo Vermaelen, 1995, Market underreaction to open market share repurchases, *Journal of Financial Economics*, Forthcoming.

Jegadeesh, Narasimhan, and Sheridan Titman, 1993, Returns to buying winners and selling losers: Implications for stock market efficiency, *Journal of Finance* 48, 65–91.

Korajczyk, Robert A., Deborah J. Lucas, and Robert L. McDonald, 1991, The effect of information releases on the pricing and timing of equity issues, *Review of Financial Studies* 4, 685–708.

Lakonishok, Josef, Andrei Shleifer, and Robert Vishny, 1994, Contrarian investment, extrapolation and risk, *Journal of Finance* 49, 1541–1578.

Lee, Charles, Andrei Shleifer, and Richard Thaler, 1991, Investor sentiment and the closed-end fund puzzle, *Journal of Finance* 46, 75–109.

Loughran, Tim, and Jay R. Ritter, 1995, The new issues puzzle, *Journal of Finance* 50, 23–51.

Michaely, Roni, and Wayne Shaw, 1994, The pricing of initial public offerings: Tests of adverse selection and signaling theories, *Review of Financial Studies* 7, 279–319.

Miller, Merton H., and Kevin Rock, 1985, Dividend policy under asymmetric information, *Journal of Finance* 40, 1031–1051.

Myers, Stewart C., and Nicholas Majluf, 1984, Corporate financing and investment decisions when firms have information that investors do not have, *Journal of Financial Economics* 13, 187–221.

Richardson, Gordon, Stephan Sefcik, and Rex Thompson, 1986, A test of dividend irrelevance using volume reactions to a change in dividend policy, *Journal of Financial Economics* 17, 313–333.

Ritter, Jay R., 1991, The long-run performance of initial public offerings, *Journal of Finance* 46, 3–28.

Roll, Richard, 1983, On computing mean returns and the small firm premium, *Journal of Financial Economics* 12, 371–386.

Sefcik, Stephan, and Rex Thompson, 1986, An approach to statistical inference in cross-sectional models with security abnormal returns as dependent variable, *Journal of Accounting Research* 24, 316–334.

Shefrin, Hersh M., and Meir Statman, 1984, Explaining investor preference for cash dividends, *Journal of Financial Economics* 13, 253–282.

Shleifer, Andrei, 1986, Do demand curves for stocks slope down?, *Journal of Finance* 41, 579–590.

Womack, Kent L., 1995, Do brokerage analysts' recommendations have investment value?, Working paper, Dartmouth College.

[14]

Signaling, Investment Opportunities, and Dividend Announcements

Pyung Sig Yoon
Laura T. Starks
University of Texas at Austin

This article examines potential explanations for the wealth effects surrounding dividend change announcements. We find that new information concerning managers' investment policies is not revealed at the time of the dividend announcement. We also find that dividend increases (decreases) are associated with subsequent significant increases (decreases) in capital expenditures over the three years following the dividend change, and that dividend change announcements are associated with revisions in analysts' forecasts of current earnings. These results are consistent with the cash flow signaling hypothesis rather than the free cash flow hypothesis as an explanation for the observed stock price reactions to dividend change announcements.

It is widely accepted that announcements of changes in dividend payouts affect firm value.[1] There is an ongoing debate, however, concerning why dividend

---

Previous drafts of this work were titled "Cash Flow Signaling Hypothesis vs. Free Cash Flow Hypothesis: The Case of Dividend Announcements." A previous version was presented at the annual meeting of the Western Finance Association, Vancouver, Canada, June 1993. The authors would like to thank Robert Bliss, David Chapman, Richard Green (the editor), David Ikenberry, Meeta Kothare, Ken Lehn, John Martin, Roni Michaely, Robert Parrino, A. J. Senchack, Tom Shively, two anonymous referees, and especially Chris James and Paul Laux for helpful comments. Address correspondence to Laura T. Starks, Department of Finance, University of Texas at Austin, Austin, TX 78712-1179.

[1] Studies that document the wealth effects of dividend change announcements include Aharony and Swary (1980), Asquith and Mullins (1983), Bajaj and Vijh (1990), Eades, Hess, and Kim (1985), Kalay and Loewenstein (1985, 1986), and Pettit (1972).

The Review of Financial Studies / v 8 n 4 1995

changes affect firm value. At the heart of this debate is the question of exactly what information is being conveyed to the market by the dividend change. The primary explanation has been the cash flow signaling hypothesis as developed in theoretical models by Bhattacharya (1979), John and Williams (1985), Kalay (1980), and Miller and Rock (1985). These authors argue that since managers possess more information about the firm's cash flows than do individuals outside the firm, the managers have incentives to unambiguously "signal" that information to investors. According to these models then, dividend changes convey managers' information about future and/or current cash flows.

An alternate, although not mutually exclusive, explanation is that changes in dividends reflect changes in managers' investment policies given their opportunity set [John and Lang (1991) and Lang and Litzenberger (1989)]. This explanation is based on the free cash flow hypothesis suggested by Jensen (1986). The free cash flow hypothesis asserts that managers with substantial free cash flow will invest it at below the cost of capital or waste it on organizational inefficiencies rather than distribute it to shareholders. On the other hand, these managers could change their investment policies and increase dividends, thus paying out current cash that would otherwise be invested in low-return projects or wasted [Jensen (1986), p. 324]. While Jensen (1986) does not explicitly state that changes in dividends reflect changes in the managers' investment policies, his free cash flow hypothesis predicts that changes in wasteful investments for firms with poor investment opportunities should have significant valuation effects.

Lang and Litzenberger (1989) focus on this implication of the free cash flow hypothesis. They argue that the free cash flow hypothesis does a better job of explaining stock price reaction to dividend change announcements than does the cash flow signaling hypothesis. According to their argument, a significant stock price reaction would be observed for dividend changes when the dividends affect the level of cash flows available for wasteful investments. The rationale is that for firms that are overinvesting, a dividend increase implies a reduction in management's policy of overinvesting, while a dividend decrease implies further overinvestment. Thus, the information content of a dividend change announcement depends on the severity of the firm's agency problems, that is, how much the firm is overinvesting.

According to Lang and Litzenberger (1989) a significant stock price response should be observed _only_ when dividend changes affect investors' expectations about the size of the firm's future investment in negative net present-value projects. Note then that this interpretation of the free cash flow hypothesis requires that dividend change announcements provide information concerning changes in managers' actions.

The difference between the cash flow signaling hypothesis and the Lang-Litzenberger (1989) interpretation of the free cash flow hypothesis can be summarized as follows: Under the cash flow signaling hypothesis, the dividend change provides information about current and/or future cash flows, while under the free cash flow hypothesis, the dividend change provides information about changes in the managers' misuse of cash flows.

Using Tobin's q ratio as a proxy for the overinvestment problem, Lang and Litzenberger (1989) conclude that their empirical results are more consistent with the free cash flow hypothesis than the cash flow signaling hypothesis. They find a differential market reaction between firms that are overinvesting and firms that are not. Based on analysts' earnings forecasts, they also conclude that the dividend change does not provide information about the firm's current cash flows.

A number of other studies have tested the free cash flow and cash flow signaling hypotheses by examining whether the effects of the firm's investment opportunities or the signaling of current and future cash flow is the primary explanation for stock price reaction to firm announcements. Evidence has been mixed. While some empirical studies have presented evidence supporting the free cash flow hypothesis,[2] others have found evidence counter to its implications.[3] Our interest is in determining which hypothesis is more appropriate for explaining the information conveyed in dividend change announcements. Accordingly, we analyze the extent to which the dividend changes themselves are related to the firms' investment opportunities and the extent to which the wealth effects from the dividend change announcement are related to the investment opportunities or cash flow signaling.

The results indicate that cross-sectional differences in observed dividend policy are related to investment opportunities. In a sample of firms with large dividend changes we find that firms with poor investment opportunities have higher dividend yields. Such a relationship is consistent with Jensen's (1986) free cash flow hypothesis in which

---

[2] For example, evidence in favor of the free cash flow hypothesis is presented by Pilotte (1992) for security offering announcements, Keown, Laux, and Martin (1992) for joint venture announcements, Lang, Stulz, and Walkling (1991) for tender offers, Perfect, Peterson, and Peterson (1994) for self-tender offers, and Lehn and Poulsen (1989) for going-private transactions.

[3] Servaes (1994) finds no evidence of overinvestment on the part of takeover targets. Howe, He, and Kao (1992) find no difference between high-q and low-q firms in the market's reaction to one-time cash flow events such as share repurchase and specially designated dividends. Denis, Denis, and Sarin (1992) report that firms with Tobin's q less than one have significantly greater stock price reactions to dividend change announcements largely because they pay higher dividends and their dividend changes are of greater magnitude.

The Review of Financial Studies / v 8 n 4 1995

firms with fewer growth opportunities should have higher dividend yields. It is also consistent with Smith and Watts' (1992) empirical finding that firms with more assets in place and fewer growth options have higher payout ratios.

The focus in Jensen (1986) and Smith and Watts (1992) is on the *level* of dividend payments, whereas our focus is on the *change* in dividends. We find that the information revealed at the time of the dividend change announcement is more consistent with the prediction of the cash flow signaling hypothesis. After controlling for the size of the dividend change, the anticipated dividend yield, and the market value of the firm, there is no difference in the magnitude of stock price reactions to dividend announcements across firms with different investment opportunities (measured by Tobin's q ratio or an alternate proxy, the direction of insider trading). This result is counter to the prediction of Lang and Litzenberger's (1989) version of the free cash flow hypothesis in which they contend that the absolute value of the announcement abnormal return should be larger for firms with poor investment opportunities than for firms with good investment opportunities.

However, a regression analysis of the observed wealth effects segmented by investment opportunity sets cannot be considered definitive evidence against the free cash flow hypothesis because the control variables (the magnitude of the change, the dividend yield, and the market value of the firm) are also related to the firm's investment opportunities. A more appropriate approach to testing the free cash flow and cash flow signaling hypotheses is to analyze the sources of the wealth effects suggested by those two hypotheses. Consequently we investigate (1) the extent to which dividend changes are related to subsequent changes in wasteful investment (as predicted by the free cash flow hypothesis) and (2) the extent to which dividend changes are associated with changes in cash flow expectations (as predicted by the cash flow signaling hypothesis).

If dividend changes reflect modifications in management's policy toward overinvesting, then we should observe a change in capital expenditures following the dividend increase or decrease. Specifically we should observe overinvesting firms reducing their capital expenditures after dividend increases. However, our results are not consistent with this prediction of the free cash flow hypothesis. We find that, in general, there are significant increases (decreases) in capital expenditures after dividend increases (decreases) for firms regardless of their investment opportunities.

We also conduct a thorough investigation of whether changes in investors' expectations associated with dividend change announcements are related to current and/or future cash flow expectations. Using revisions of analysts' forecasts for current earnings, we provide evidence that announcements of dividend increases and decreases cause analysts to revise their *current* earnings forecasts in a manner generally consistent with the cash flow signaling hypothesis. In contrast, when we examine revisions of analysts' forecasts for *future* earnings, we document significant changes only for dividend decreasing firms. Analysts do not significantly revise their expectations of future earnings for dividend increasing firms. This finding is particularly important because previous researchers have not examined changes in long-run earnings expectations around dividend change announcements, although it has been frequently stated that dividend changes release managers' information about both current and future cash flows. This finding is also consistent with the empirical evidence that a dividend decrease results in a larger stock market reaction than would an equivalent dividend increase.

In the next section we describe the data and explain our proxies for the quality of the investment opportunity set. We then analyze firm characteristics between firms with good investment opportunities versus firms with poor investment opportunities in Section 2. After we examine the wealth effects of dividend change announcements in Section 3, we investigate the sources of these wealth effects by analyzing changes in capital expenditures in Section 4 and changes in cash flow expectations in Section 5. Concluding comments are presented in Section 6.

1. Data and Proxies for Investment Opportunity Set

1.1 Data

The sample of 3748 dividend increase and 431 dividend decrease announcements over the period 1969 to 1988 consists of all NYSE stocks from the Center for Research in Security Prices (CRSP) monthly master file that satisfy the following criteria:

1. We restrict our attention to regular quarterly U.S. cash dividends per share. Based on the naive expectations model, the unexpected dividend change is defined to be the proportional change in dividends from the previous quarter. Warther (1994) argues that due to the coarseness of the signaling equilibrium, not all dividend changes contain information. In order to ensure that any potential information signal is significant, we impose the restriction that the dividend change must be at least 10 percent.

2. The announcement does not represent a dividend initiation or omission.

The Review of Financial Studies / v 8 n 4 1995

3. A stock split or stock dividend does not occur during the month before or the month in which the dividend change announcement is made.

4. Daily return data for the 200 trading days surrounding the announcement are available from the CRSP daily return master file.

5. Empirical estimates of Tobin's q ratios are available from the National Bureau of Economic Research (NBER) manufacturing sector master file.[4]

1.2 Proxy for the investment opportunity set

A central issue in any test of the free cash flow hypothesis is the question of a measure for firms' investment opportunities. We employ two proxies, the often-used Tobin's q ratio and the direction of insider trading. As suggested by Lang and Litzenberger (1989) and Lang, Stulz, and Walkling (1991) our first proxy for the investment opportunities available is Tobin's q ratio, defined as the ratio of the market value of the firm's assets to their replacement costs. Although most empirical estimates of Tobin's q ratios are built on Lindenberg and Ross (1981),[5] the classification of q ratios into high-q and low-q firms varies by author. For example, Lang and Litzenberger define a value-maximizing firm as one with a one year q greater than unity, while Lang, Stulz, and Walkling (1991) define a high-q firm as one with a three year average q greater than one. Since a cutoff of one has some theoretical appeal, we take a one-year q greater than one as a basic cutoff point for high- and low-q firms. We also use two other cutoff points: a three year average q greater than unity and a one year q greater than the median within a calendar year.[6]

Although the estimated Tobin's q ratio is commonly employed as a proxy for the investment opportunity set, it has several potential problems. First, the estimate is of the average q ratio, but as pointed

---

[4] Since the NBER file contains only industrial firms, the problems associated with dividend announcements for regulated firms are avoided.

[5] The empirical estimates of Tobin's q ratios are computed slightly differently by authors, but most of them are built on Lindenberg and Ross (1981). Perfect and Wiles (1994) construct four procedures to estimate q ratios (primarily based on the methodology developed by Lindenberg and Ross). Their results indicate that the methods tend to produce equivalent empirical results with one exception: a q ratio computed using book values of long-term debt and total assets.

[6] Servaes (1991) provides reasons why a cutoff of one may not be appropriate. For example, the median Tobin's q may differ from one. Specifically, examining the median Tobin's q across all firms in the NBER file each year over the period 1968 to 1987, we find that the median ranges from 0.61 (in 1975) to 1.93 (in 1969). The median Tobin's q by year for our sample is consistent with these population parameters. Since we find that the equality of the medians across years can be rejected at any reasonable significance level, we checked the robustness of our results by using the median Tobin's q ratio by year as an alternative cutoff point to separate high-q firms from low-q firms. We also test the results with an industry median q ratio as a cutoff point. Our results are not sensitive to the q classification process.

out by Lang and Litzenberger (1989), the differences in investment opportunities would be found in the *marginal q* ratio. Second, measurement errors induce noise in estimated q ratios. Third, estimated q ratios may be based on outdated information. In calculating Tobin's q ratio, the market value of the firm's assets and their replacement cost are evaluated at the year end before the announcement. For example, if one assumed that dividend announcements are made evenly across the following year, the estimated q ratios would be six months old, on average, and consequently would not contain any private information developed just prior to the dividend change announcements.

Because of these problems, we also employ a second proxy for the investment opportunities available. John and Lang (1991) suggest that the direction of insider trading activity combined with the dividend announcements may be a better proxy for the investment opportunity set than the average q ratio. Following John and Lang, we construct an insider trading index based on insider open market sale and purchase transactions for the period of two quarters prior to the dividend change announcements. Since our results using this alternate proxy are consistent with the Tobin's q results, we do not report them here.

2. Differences in Firm Characteristics Between High-q and Low-q Firms

We begin our empirical analysis by comparing firm characteristics of high-q firms with those of low-q firms in order to identify any significant differences between the two groups. Previous studies have identified three factors as influential on the stock market reaction to dividend change announcements: the firm's dividend yield, the firm's size, and the magnitude of the dividend change. The first variable, dividend yield, has been suggested as a proxy for clientele effects. Bajaj and Vijh (1990) posit that if investors with preferences for dividends are the marginal investors in high-yield stocks, the price reaction to a dividend change should be larger, the higher the anticipated yield of the stock. They find that for high-yield stocks, price reactions to dividend increases are significantly more positive and to dividend decreases significantly more negative. Fehrs, Benesh, and Peterson (1988) report similar results. The second variable reflects omitted market pricing factors such as the information asymmetry between large versus small firms. Eddy and Seifert (1988) document that abnormal returns from the announcements of large dividend increases are greater for small firms than for large firms. Finally, the third variable is suggested by dividend signaling models which predict that large dividend changes are used to signal large changes in cash flows.

The Review of Financial Studies / v 8 n 4 1995

The free cash flow hypothesis predicts that these firm characteristics should systematically differ between high-q versus low-q firms. In particular, Jensen (1986) argues that firms with more growth opportunities should have lower dividend yields. Consistent with this prediction, Smith and Watts (1992) document that firms with more assets-in-place and fewer growth options have higher dividend payout ratios. [This finding is also consistent with Easterbrook (1984) and Rozeff (1982).] In addition, a firm's size is related to its q. As pointed out by Smith and Watts, size is a function of the firm's investment opportunity set. That is, those firms with more growth opportunities are more likely to become larger. Thus, the free cash flow hypothesis based on contracting arguments predicts a negative relationship between dividend yields and Tobin's q ratios, and a positive relationship between size and Tobin's q.

On the other hand, cash flow signaling models generally do not have direct predictions for differences across high-q and low-q firms in terms of dividend yield, firm size, and the magnitude of dividend changes.

Panel A in Table 1 reports the averages of dividend change, dividend yield, and firm size by the sign of the dividend changes and the level of the Tobin's q ratios.[7] In our sample there are 3748 dividend increases and 431 dividend decreases announced from 1969 through 1988. While there is not a large difference in the proportion of dividend increase announcements for high-q and low-q firms, for dividend decreases, 87 announcements (20 percent) are classified to a group of high-q firms and 344 (80 percent) to a group of low-q firms. This result is consistent with the view that firms in general cut their dividend payments when their performance is poor [DeAngelo, DeAngelo, and Skinner (1992)].

We find that the characteristics of dividend change announcements for high-q firms tend to be systematically different from those of low-q firms. For both dividend increases and decreases, the means of the anticipated dividend yield and the dividend change for high-q firms are significantly smaller than those for low-q firms. In addition, for dividend increases there is a significant positive relationship between firm size and Tobin's q ratios: the equality of mean firm size between the two groups can be rejected at any reasonable significance level.

---

[7] The anticipated dividend yield in this article is measured by dividing the sum of all dividend payments for the year preceding the announcement by the end-of-year stock price. The firm's size is measured as the market value of the firm's assets at the end of the year preceding the announcement. The dividend change is computed by dividing the dividend change in dollars by the end-of-month stock price before the announcement.

Signaling, Investment Opportunities, and Dividend Announcements

Table 1
Dividend change, yield, and firm size by sign of dividend change and Tobin's q[1]

Panel A: Characteristics of dividend change announcements

	No. of observations	Average change	Average size	Average yield
A.1. Dividend increases				
$q < 1$	2062 (55%)	0.0021	1215	0.042
$q > 1$	1686 (45%)	0.0012	2054	0.022
Mean difference		0.0009	−839	0.020
$(q < 1) - (q > 1)$		(25.96)	$(-16.32)^2$	(41.68)
A.2. Dividend decreases				
$q < 1$	344 (80%)	−0.0082	1,015	0.072
$q > 1$	87 (20%)	−0.0061	1,194	0.040
Mean difference		−0.0021	−179	0.032
$(q < 1) - (q > 1)$		(−3.20)	$(-0.24)^2$	(12.52)

Panel B: Spearman correlation matrix for all sample[3]

	Change	Log(size)	Yield	Tobin's q
Change	1.00			
Log(size)	−0.18	1.00		
Yield	0.24	−0.17	1.00	
Tobin's q	−0.37	0.29	−0.65	1.00

[1] Our sample consists of 3748 dividend increases and 431 dividend decreases announced over the period 1969 to 1988 that meet the following criteria: (1) The announcement date is available from the CRSP monthly master file. (2) Daily return data for the 200 trading days surrounding the announcements are available. (3) The announcement does not represent a dividend initiation or omission. (4) A stock split or stock dividend does not fall a month before or during the month in which the announcement is made. (5) The dividend change is at least 10 percent compared with the previous quarter. (6) Empirical estimates of Tobin's q ratios are available from the NBER manufacturing sector master file. Tobin's q ratios are estimated as the market value of the firm's assets divided by replacement costs, both are evaluated at the year end before the announcement from the NBER tape. The change is computed by dividing dividend change in dollars by the end-of-month stock price before the announcement. The size is the year-end market value of the firm (in million $) obtained from the NBER tape. The yield is measured by dividing all dividend payments for a year before the announcement by the end-of-year stock price. T-statistics are in parentheses.

[2] T-statistics are based on the logarithm of firm size.

[3] All correlations are significant at the 0.01% level.

However, for dividend decreases, the mean differences in firm size between the two groups are not significant.

The evidence to this point indicates that there are cross-sectional differences in dividend changes that are related to a firm's investment opportunities: low-q firms have higher dividend yields and larger dividend changes, and are smaller in size. These relationships indicate a potential problem in testing the free cash flow hypothesis directly against the cash flow signaling hypothesis. For example, while dividend yield reflects dividend clientele effects, it could also be regarded as another proxy for investment opportunities. In the extreme case, firms with many good investment opportunities would pay no dividends at all. This point is further reflected in the Spearman rank

The Review of Financial Studies / v 8 n 4 1995

correlations between the Tobin's q ratios and the three control variables presented in Panel B of Table 1. The correlations between the q ratio and dividend yield, dividend change, and firm size are all statistically significant, being -0.65, -0.37, and 0.29, respectively, suggesting that the control variables may also be proxying for investment opportunities.

In this section we have pointed out that the dividend change itself depends on a firm's investment opportunities. In the next section we measure the stock market reaction to the dividend change announcement, conditional on the market's prior information concerning the firm's investment opportunities.

3. Investment Opportunities and Abnormal Returns

The free cash flow hypothesis implies that dividend changes by low-q firms will lessen or aggravate the overinvestment and accordingly affect the market value of the firm. On the other hand, dividend changes by high-q firms would not be expected to have a particular effect on stock prices. There is no reason that a change in the dividend should affect the level of the optimal investment because the firms are not assumed to be overinvesting [see Lang and Litzenberger (1989)]. Thus, according to their hypothesis, dividend change announcements for high-q firms should not have information content, not because they are fully anticipated, but because dividend changes do not affect the market's assessment of managers' investment policies. (Under some plausible assumptions, Lang and Litzenberger derive these predictions in their model.) Thus, for either dividend increases or decreases, the prediction is that announcements of dividend changes by high-q firms should have no significant impact on the firms' stock prices, whereas announcements of dividend changes by low-q firms should have a substantial effect on stock prices, implying that the absolute value of the abnormal return is larger for low-q firms than for high-q firms. In contrast, the cash flow signaling hypothesis predicts significant price reactions regardless of the level of q ratios, implying a symmetrical impact between high-q and low-q firms for either dividend increases or decreases.

Table 2 reports three day cumulative average abnormal returns (CAAR), summed over days -1 to $+1$ relative to the announcement date, and average abnormal returns on the announcement day by the sign of the dividend changes and by the level of the Tobin's q ratios. Abnormal returns are estimated from the market model using the CRSP equally weighted index and Scholes-Williams betas.[8] We find

---

[8] The estimation period covers days -100 to -8 and days $+8$ to $+100$ (a total of 186 days).

significant cumulative average abnormal returns for all four groups, ranging in absolute value from 0.67 percent for dividend increases of high-q firms to 5.30 percent for dividend decreases of low-q firms. Note that the free cash flow hypothesis implies that for high-q firms, dividend changes should have no impact on the managers' investment policies, and therefore no impact on firms' stock prices. The significance of abnormal returns for all four groups is consistent with the predictions of the cash flow signaling hypothesis.[9] The results for the average abnormal returns on the announcement day are consistent with those for the cumulative average abnormal returns.

We find a larger share price reaction for dividend decreases than for increases. This result is consistent with the cash flow signaling models of Bhattacharya (1979) and Kalay (1980). Bhattacharya assumes that the cost of making up a cash flow deficit is more than the benefit of a cash flow surplus of the same size. Kalay argues that managers' reluctance to cut dividends is a necessary condition for dividends to convey information. Thus, both papers suggest that dividend decreases are more costly. On the other hand, as posited by Lang and Litzenberger (1989), the free cash flow hypothesis implies that for high-q firms, neither dividend increase nor decrease announcements should have any impact on stock prices.

For dividend decreases, the cumulative average abnormal return for high-q firms is not significantly different from that of low-q firms; a result counter to the free cash flow hypothesis. In contrast, for dividend increases, the cumulative average abnormal return for low-q firms is significantly larger than that of high-q firms. This result is not

---

The announcement period abnormal returns are summed over days -1 to $+1$ due to possible information leakage and announcements being made after trading hours on the announcement day. Our results remain qualitatively the same with the CRSP value-weighted index rather than the CRSP equal-weighted index as our market proxy. Similar results are also obtained when we calculate the two day cumulative abnormal returns.

[9] While, on average, our results indicate that stock prices react favorably to dividend increases and unfavorably to dividend decreases, these results are not uniform across the sample. The stock price reactions to dividend increase announcements for 43 percent of the high-q firms and 34 percent of the low-q firms are negative. Similarly, 24 percent of the high-q firms and 18 percent of the low- firms have positive stock price reactions to dividend decrease announcements. While these results could be interpreted as evidence counter to the cash flow signaling hypothesis, they may be due to the problem of determining the market's *conditional* expected dividend, especially for dividend increases. In our empirical analysis, we have adopted the naive dividend expectation model, which implies that the expected dividend change is zero on average. However, this model may not be realistic, not only because many firms tend to increase dividends in the same quarter every year, but also because the model does not incorporate the market's most recent expectation since the last dividend payment. The lower percentage of stock price reactions in the opposite direction for dividend decreases than dividend increases supports the view that the problem of determining the market's conditional expected dividend is more serious for dividend increases. Regardless, the fact that there are a number of reactions in the opposite direction to the dividend change does not present a serious problem in testing which hypothesis is more consistent with the observed market reactions because the competing free cash flow hypothesis also does not predict negative reactions to dividend increases and positive reactions to dividend decreases.

The Review of Financial Studies / v 8 n 4 1995

Table 2
Cumulative average abnormal returns by sign of dividend changes and level of q ratios[1]

	Dividend increases	Dividend decreases	Differences in absolute values of means (decreases − increases)
$q < 1$			
No. of obs.	2062	344	
CAAR	1.537 (17.41)	−5.299 (−14.67)	3.762 (10.11)
Percent positive	66%	18%	
AAR	0.969 (16.70)	−3.197 (−12.24)	2.228 (8.33)
$q > 1$			
No. of obs.	1686	87	
CAAR	0.670 (7.18)	−4.599 (−6.14)	3.929 (5.21)
Percentage positive	57%	24%	
AAR	0.350 (6.13)	−2.689 (−5.13)	2.339 (4.44)
$(q < 1) - (q > 1)$			
Mean difference on CAAR	0.867 (6.75)	−0.700 (−0.86)	
Mean difference on AAR	0.619 (7.61)	−0.508 (−0.87)	

[1] Our sample consists of 3748 dividend increases and 431 dividend decreases announced over the period 1969 to 1988 that meet the following criteria: (1) The announcement date is available from the CRSP monthly master file. (2) Daily return data for the 200 trading days surrounding the announcements are available. (3) The announcement does not represent a dividend initiation or omission. (4) A stock split or stock dividend does not fall a month before or during the month in which the announcement is made. (5) The dividend change is at least 10 percent compared with the previous quarter. (6) Empirical estimates of Tobin's q ratios are available from the NBER manufacturing sector master file. Tobin's q are estimated as the market value of the firm's assets divided by replacement costs, both are evaluated year end before the announcement from the NBER tapes. Abnormal returns are estimated from the market model using the CRSP equally weighted index and Scholes-Williams betas. The estimation period is over days −100 to −8 and days 8 to 100. CAAR refers to the three day (day −1, day 0, and day 1) cumulative average abnormal returns. AAR refers to the average abnormal returns on the announcement day. Percent positive refers to the percentage of positive cumulative abnormal returns. T-statistics are reported in parentheses.

predicted by the cash flow signaling hypothesis, but is predicted by the free cash flow hypothesis.

Previous articles document that the abnormal returns to dividend increase announcements are positively related to dividend change and dividend yield, but negatively related to the firm size. We have shown in Table 1 that for dividend increases, low-q firms have higher dividend change, higher dividend yield, and smaller firm size than high-q firms. Accordingly, we include these three control variables along with a dummy for high-q firms, $D_{high\ q}$, in a regression of the cumulative abnormal returns of the dividend increase announcements.

$$CAR = \underset{(t=1.51)}{0.50} + \underset{(t=8.73)}{481\,CHANGE} + \underset{(t=4.50)}{19.08\,YIELD}$$

$$- \underset{(t=-3.28)}{0.14\,LOG(SIZE)} + \underset{(t=0.57)}{0.09\,D_{high\ q}.}$$

$$F\text{-statistic} = 4.75, \quad R^2 = 0.05.$$

The regression indicates that the relationships between the abnormal returns and each of the three control variables are consistent with the findings of previous studies, and that Tobin's q ratios are not significantly related to abnormal returns once the three control variables are considered.

These results indicate that a differential price reaction between high-q and low-q firms for dividend increases may be caused by a difference in firm characteristics rather than differences in investment opportunities. Our regression results are not definitive evidence against the free cash flow hypothesis because dividend change, dividend yield, and firm size are all related to a firm's investment opportunity. Accordingly, in the next section we directly examine the sources of the wealth effects suggested by the two hypotheses.

4. The Effect of Dividend Change Announcements on Capital Expenditures

We have presented evidence that the information revealed in the dividend change announcement appears to be more of a reflection of cash flows than a reaction to managers' actions in the context of the free cash flow hypothesis. A further test of this conjecture can be obtained by examining whether changes in the firm's investment policies after the announcements are consistent with the free cash flow hypothesis predictions. Under the free cash flow hypothesis, an announcement of a dividend change will have an effect on the firm's stock price if the size of the firm's future investment in negative net present value projects is expected to change. Thus, since low-q firms invest in negative net present value projects, there should be a decrease in wasteful capital expenditures after dividend increases and an increase in wasteful investment after dividend decreases. The implication is that a change in capital expenditures would cause significant stock price reactions for low-q firms. It also predicts no significant change in capital expenditures for high-q firms, implying no effect on stock prices.

We use capital expenditures (COMPUSTAT data item 128) to measure new investment by the dividend change firms. The analysis measures the percentage changes in capital expenditures in the first three full fiscal years after a dividend change (years $+1$, $+2$, and $+3$) compared to the last fiscal year before a dividend change (year -1). We measure capital expenditures in levels and as a fraction of the end-of-period total assets. To control for industry effects, we also present an industry-adjusted percentage change in capital expendi-

The Review of Financial Studies / v 8 n 4 1995

Table 3
Relations between dividend change announcements and subsequent capital expenditures[1]

Panel A: Dividend increases and $q < 1$

	From year i to year j		
	−1 to +1	−1 to +2	−1 to +3
A.1. Capital expenditures	$n = 1626$	$n = 1626$	$n = 1517$
Percentage change	39.68%***	52.10%***	65.87%***
Industry adjusted percentage change	8.31%***	1.13%***	1.11%***
A.2. Capital expenditures/Assets	$n = 1626$	$n = 1626$	$n = 1517$
Percentage change	12.22%***	11.54%***	11.13%***
Industry adjusted percentage change	4.59%***	0.30%***	0.70%***

Panel B: Dividend increases and $q > 1$

	From year i to year j		
	−1 to +1	−1 to +2	−1 to +3
B.1. Capital expenditures	$n = 1168$	$n = 1175$	$n = 1083$
Percentage change	41.63%***	51.05%***	69.80%***
Industry adjusted percentage change	9.82%***	0.76%***	1.37%***
B.2. Capital expenditures/Assets	$n = 1168$	$n = 1175$	$n = 1083$
Percentage change	6.38%***	0.70%	−0.57%
Industry adjusted percentage change	5.25%***	0.00%	0.00%

** Significance at the 5 percent level.
*** Significance at the 1 percent level.
[1]Median percentage change and industry adjusted change in capital expenditures and in capital expenditures as a percentage of assets by sign of dividend changes and q ratios. Year-1 is the fiscal year ending prior to dividend change announcements. Year +1 is the first full fiscal year after dividend change announcements. Significance levels are based on two-tailed Wilcoxon signed rank tests. Industry adjusted change for a given period equals the difference between the change for dividend change company and the median change for a sample of companies in the same industry during that period. The firms in the same industry are those that have the same four-digit SIC code. The observation was excluded if there are less than three firms in the same industry.

tures. The industry-adjusted percentage change is defined as the percentage change in capital expenditures minus the median percentage change over the same period for all firms in the same four-digit SIC code as the dividend change firm.[10] The results by sign of dividend changes and level of q ratio are reported in Table 3.

Table 3 shows that there are significant increases (decreases) in the level of capital expenditures after dividend increases (decreases). This result holds regardless of the industry adjustment. The change in capital expenditures is more pronounced for low-q firms than high-

---

[10] When there were fewer than three firms in the same industry, that observation was excluded. The results remain the same under the "same industry" definition with the two-digit SIC code.

Signaling, Investment Opportunities, and Dividend Announcements

Table 3
(Continued)

Panel C: Dividend decreases and $q < 1$

	From year i to year j		
	-1 to $+1$	-1 to $+2$	-1 to $+3$
C.1. Capital expenditures	$n = 269$	$n = 266$	$n = 245$
Percentage change	$-37.76\%^{***}$	$-18.49\%^{***}$	-3.70%
Industry adjusted percentage change	$-24.92\%^{***}$	$-19.71\%^{***}$	$-15.51\%^{***}$
C.2. Capital expenditures/Assets	$n = 269$	$n = 266$	$n = 245$
Percentage change	$-33.39\%^{***}$	$-20.38\%^{***}$	$-10.50\%^{***}$
Industry adjusted percentage change	$-16.30\%^{***}$	$-8.16\%^{***}$	$-2.76\%^{***}$

Panel D: Dividend decreases and $q > 1$

	From year i to year j		
	-1 to $+1$	-1 to $+2$	-1 to $+3$
D.1. Capital expenditures	$n = 67$	$n = 72$	$n = 68$
Percentage change	1.29%	-4.53%	$16.26\%^{**}$
Industry adjusted percentage rate	$-14.53\%^{***}$	$-17.32\%^{***}$	-13.19%
D.2. Capital expenditures/Assets	$n = 67$	$n = 72$	$n = 68$
Percentage change	-13.47%	$-21.00\%^{**}$	$-9.63\%^{**}$
Industry adjusted percentage change	-3.19%	$-5.35\%^{***}$	0.00%

** Significant at the 5 percent level.
*** Significant at the 1 percent level.

q firms for both dividend increases and decreases. This is in sharp contrast to the implication of the free cash flow hypothesis that dividend increases would reduce overinvestment and dividend decreases would increase wasteful investment.[11] For low-q firms with dividend increases (shown in Panel A), the level of investment significantly increases in years $+1$, $+2$, and $+3$ relative to year -1. The industry-adjusted changes are also significant for all periods, although they are small in years $+2$ and $+3$. For completeness, Panel B contains the changes in capital expenditures for high-q firms with dividend increases. These results are similar to those for the low-q firms. Panels C and D indicate that for both high- and low-q firms that decrease their dividends, there are reductions in capital expenditures over the next three years. In particular, for the low-q firms, the industry-adjusted changes are all negative and significant, equal to -24.92 percent, -19.71 percent, and -15.51 percent.

---

[11] If the firm issues debt or equity to finance a dividend increase, a change in dividends will not induce a corresponding change in investment. The conclusions are not affected by the exclusion of those cases from our sample.

The Review of Financial Studies / v 8 n 4 1995

The analysis provided in this section directly examines the source of the valuation effects suggested by the free cash flow hypothesis. We find no evidence that dividend increase (decrease) firms reduce (increase) their level of investment.[12] On the other hand, our finding is not inconsistent with the cash flow signaling hypothesis; if dividend changes signal management's belief about the firm's future prospects, dividend increase firms are able to invest more and dividend decrease firms could be expected to cut capital expenditures.

5. Dividend Change Announcements and Current versus Future Earnings Expectations

Theories and empirical tests of the cash flow signaling model as an explanation for stock market reaction to dividend announcements typically state that dividend announcements provide information about current and/or future cash flows. According to Miller and Rock (1985, p. 1037), dividend announcements act as "the missing piece of the sources/uses constraint which the market needs to establish the firm's *current* earnings." According to their model, although dividend announcements may provide information about future expected earnings, it is only indirectly. In this section we investigate the extent to which the dividend announcement provides information about current and future earnings expectations. To do so, rather than inferring these changes from observed stock price reactions which are also affected by other factors, we use a direct measure of changes in investors' expectations: changes in analysts' earnings forecasts.

5.1 Analysts' earnings forecasts as a proxy for cash flow expectations

There is mixed evidence concerning whether analysts change their forecasts of current earnings after dividend announcements. Ofer and Siegel (1987) report that analysts revise their earnings forecasts fol-

---

[12] The relationship between the previously observed wealth effects and the investment opportunity set depends to some extent on how we define high- and low-q firms. For example, if we happen to assign low-q firms to the high-q firm category by mistake, we could erroneously observe a significant stock price reaction to dividend change announcements of high-q firms. In contrast, our results employing capital expenditure changes are not diminished by a poor proxy. The free cash flow hypothesis predicts a significant change in wasteful capital expenditures in the direction opposite to that of dividend changes for low-q firms. It also predicts no particular change in capital expenditures for high-q firms. In this case, if we assign low-q firms into the high-q firm category, we may observe a significant decrease in capital expenditures after dividend increases and a significant increase after dividend decreases for both high- and low-q firms. Conversely, if we assign high-q firms into the low-q firm category, we may observe an insignificant change in capital expenditures for both high- and low-q firms. Our evidence that dividend increase (decrease) firms increase (reduce) their level of investment significantly for both high- and low-q firms is not related to how we determine high- and low-q firms. This is strong evidence against the free cash flow hypothesis as an explanation for the wealth effects of dividend change announcements.

lowing the announcement of an unexpected dividend change. They find that the revision is positively related to the size of the unexpected dividend change. Similarly, Healy and Palepu (1987) show that dividend initiations and omissions are leading indicators of superior and inferior earnings performance, respectively. On the other hand, Lang and Litzenberger (1989) report that announcements of sizable dividend changes are not significantly related to changes in analysts' forecasts. In this section we analyze the extent to which the announcement of an unexpected dividend change has a significant effect on the revision of current and future cash flow expectations. The proxies for investors' cash flow expectations are analysts' forecasts for the current year earnings and their five year growth forecasts. These forecasts are obtained from the Institutional Broker Estimate System (IBES) database developed by IBES Inc. The IBES database used here contains summary statistics of analysts' earnings forecasts made by major brokerage firms for about 2000 firms listed on the NYSE and AMEX over the period 1976 to 1989. Since the IBES database short-term analysts' earnings forecasts covers the period 1976 to 1989, our sample is reduced to 2505 dividend increases and 205 dividend decreases. Similarly, the forecasts of the five year earnings growth rates are available from 1981 to 1989, so that the sample is further reduced to 883 increases and 131 decreases.

5.2 Revisions of short-term analysts' earnings forecasts

The cash flow signaling hypothesis predicts that dividend change announcements will cause investors to revise their cash flow expectations in the same direction as the dividend surprise. To test this implication we measure the elasticity of the change in the median of analysts' current earnings forecasts with respect to dividend changes, computed by dividing the percentage change of the postannouncement median earnings forecast (compared to the preannouncement median earnings forecast) by the percentage dividend change. The use of the median provides more conservative statistics than the mean because the median is less sensitive to extreme earnings revisions.

Table 4 reports the mean elasticity of the change in the median of analysts' forecasts with respect to dividend changes. Similar to the Healy and Palepu (1987) and Ofer and Siegel (1987) results, and in contrast to the Lang and Litzenberger (1989) results, we find that both dividend increases and decreases are associated with positive mean elasticity. In addition, consistent with the observed larger stock price reaction to dividend decreases, the magnitude of forecast revisions is greater for the dividend decreases than the increases. We also divide the dividend increases and decreases into two groups according to their investment opportunities (i.e., Tobin's q ratio). Three of the

The Review of Financial Studies / v 8 n 4 1995

Table 4
The impact of dividend change announcements on current cash flow expectations[1]

	$q < 1$	$q > 1$	$(q < 1) - (q > 1)$
Panel A: Dividend increases			
No. of observations	1284	1221	
Average elasticity	0.08	0.01	0.07
(*t*-stat *p*-value)	(0.00)	(0.06)	(0.00)
Positive/0/negative	636/313/335	468/400/353	
Panel B: Dividend decreases			
No. of observations	171	34	
Average elasticity	0.56	0.27	0.29
(*t*-stat *p*-value)	(0.00)	(0.00)	(0.00)
Positive/0/negative	145/14/12	22/7/5	

[1] Our sample consists of 2505 dividend increases and 205 dividend decreases announced over the period 1976 to 1988 that meet the following criteria: (1) The announcement date is available from the CRSP monthly master file. (2) Daily return data for the 200 trading days surrounding the announcements are available. (3) The announcement does not represent a dividend initiation or omission. (4) A stock split or stock dividend does not fall a month before or during the month in which the announcement is made. (5) The dividend change is at least 10 percent compared with the previous quarter. (6) Empirical estimates of Tobin's q ratios are available from the NBER manufacturing sector master file. (7) Firms should be included in the Investment Broker Estimation System (*IBES*) database. The elasticity is measured by dividing percentage change of postannouncement median earnings forecast compared to preannouncement median earnings forecast by the percentage dividend change. The elasticity is set to 1 (−1) if it is greater (less) than 1 (−1).

four groups have significantly positive mean elasticities. The one exception is the group of high-q firms that increased dividends. Note that positive elasticity implies that the medians of analysts' earnings forecasts change in the same direction as the dividend changes. The most significant effect on cash flow expectations occurs for low-q firms with dividend decreases. The mean elasticity is 0.56. Further, out of 171 announcements, 145 have positive elasticity. For high-q firms that decrease their dividend, the mean elasticity is 0.27. Out of the 34 announcements, there were only 5 in which analysts revised their forecasts in the direction opposite to the dividend change. Low-q and high-q firms that increase their dividends have mean elasticities of 0.08 and 0.01, respectively.[13]

According to the cash flow signaling hypothesis, the magnitudes of signaling will be differentiated by the level of asymmetry in information between managers and shareholders. As shown in Table 1, low-q firms tend to be smaller in size and have a larger dividend change.

[13] Brous (1992) and O'Brien (1988) have found that analysts tend to be overly optimistic in their initial annual earnings forecasts. Consequently, analysts' earnings forecasts are systematically lowered each month up to the fiscal year end. The results reported in Table 4 do not control for this optimism bias. To check for the extent to which an optimism bias may affect our results, we follow the procedure discussed in Brous and Kini (1993) and find qualitatively similar results.

Since asymmetry in information is greater for smaller firms and larger dividend changes, the results that the magnitude of forecast revisions is greater for low-q than high-q firms should be expected.

5.3 Revisions of long-term growth rate of earnings

In this section our goal is to determine the extent to which cash flow signaling from dividends reflects future earnings as opposed to current earnings. Analysts' forecasts of current earnings are dominated by the forecasts of earnings from assets in place rather than from growth options. To measure changes in the market's perceptions of growth options we use analysts' forecasts of the long-term growth rate of earnings.

Specifically, for each dividend announcement, we measure forecast revisions from the previous month as the proportional change in the analysts' forecasts of five year earnings growth. The abnormal forecast revision of analysts' five year growth of future earnings is computed by subtracting the average forecast revision estimated over the estimation period (months -24 to -7 and months 7 to 24) from the forecast revision for each month in the event period (months -6 to 6 relative to the dividend month). The results are shown in Table 5 for months -4 to 4 relative to the dividend month. The results are divided by the sign of the dividend change and by the level of investment opportunities.

For both low- and high-q firms, we find that analysts' forecasts of five year earnings growth do not significantly change when firms have a large increase in their dividends. Although this result could be due to firms financing increased dividend payments through the issuance of debt or equity, Long, Malitz, and Sefcik (1994) find that firms do not issue debt to increase dividends. Thus, the results suggest that, consistent with Miller and Rock's (1985) signaling model, dividend increases release managers' information about current cash flows rather than future cash flows. This is also consistent with Lintner's (1956) finding that for healthy firms, the current earnings are the major determinant of the dividend change.

We find a somewhat different result for dividend decreases. As shown in Panel B, while the average abnormal forecast revisions are also not significantly different from zero as measured by z-statistics, the proportion of firms with positive abnormal forecast revisions for the announcement month and for the following three months are all significantly less than 50 percent. This result is basically driven by low-q firms. (The results for high-q firms with dividend decreases should be interpreted carefully as there are only 19 observations.) Thus, unlike dividend increases, dividend decreases appear to signal managers' views on both current and long-term cash flows.

Our finding that analysts lower their long-term earnings growth

The Review of Financial Studies / v 8 n 4 1995

Table 5
Monthly average abnormal forecast revisions of the five-year growth of earnings per share[1]

Forecast month	All			$q < 1$			$q > 1$		
	n	Average abnormal forecast revisions	Proportion positive	n	Average abnormal forecast revisions	Proportion positive	n	Average abnormal forecast revisions	Proportion positive
Panel A: Dividend increases									
-4	815	-0.0047	0.52	242	-0.0106	0.50	573	-0.0022	0.52
-3	827	-0.0002	0.54	246	0.0028	0.47	581	-0.0015	0.57***
-2	831	-0.0048	0.51	248	-0.0149	0.45*	583	-0.0006	0.53
-1	853	-0.0024	0.51	258	-0.0107	0.46	595	0.0012	0.53
0	883	0.0035	0.49	270	0.0142	0.47	613	-0.0012	0.50
1	880	-0.0030	0.51	269	-0.0083	0.48	611	-0.0007	0.53
2	877	0.0001	0.50	268	-0.0086	0.46	609	0.0040	0.51
3	879	0.0058	0.52	269	0.0222	0.49	610	-0.0014	0.53
4	876	-0.0036	0.48***[2]	267	0.0001	0.48	609	-0.0052	0.48*
Panel B: Dividend decreases									
-4	116	-0.0196	0.40**	98	-0.0192	0.41**	18	-0.0213	0.33
-3	122	0.0172	0.47	104	0.0194	0.49	18	0.0042	0.33
-2	124	-0.0047	0.33***	105	-0.0108	0.32***	19	0.0286	0.37
-1	127	-0.0087	0.32***	108	-0.0072	0.35***	19	-0.0172	0.16*
0	131	-0.0038	0.36***	112	-0.0147	0.35***	19	0.0603	0.42
1	131	-0.0237	0.40***	112	-0.0244	0.39***	19	-0.0195	0.42
2	130	-0.0349	0.38**	111	-0.0413	0.36***	19	0.0029	0.47
3	129	0.0314	0.39**	110	0.0390	0.40*	19	-0.0123	0.32
4	130	0.0389	0.43	111	0.0463	0.31***	19	-0.0040	0.42

[1] The abnormal forecast revisions are computed by subtracting average forecast revisions estimated from the estimation period (months -24 to -7 and 7 to 24) from the forecast revisions for months -4 to 4. The forecast revision is defined to be the proportional change in analysts' forecast of five-year growth rate of future earnings from the previous month. Test statistics on the proportion positive are Wilcoxon signed rank test.

[2] *, (**, ***) denotes significance at the 10, 5 and 1 percent level, respectively.

forecasts following dividend decrease announcements contributes to the existing literature concerning the type of information contained in dividend announcements. DeAngelo, DeAngelo, and Skinner (1992) analyze the dividend reduction decision of firms with current losses. They conclude that dividend changes have some incremental information about future earnings over that conveyed by current earnings in the sense of improving the ability of current earnings to predict future earnings. Our result is complimentary to theirs and provides direct evidence that dividend decrease announcements contain information on future earnings. This result is also consistent with Warther's (1994) coarse dividend signaling model in which he predicts that dividends are more likely to have information when they are decreased than when they are increased. In his model, only the "worst" firms cut dividends, so that firms that do not cut their dividends reveal only that they are not among the worst firms. This implies that dividend reductions are more informative about future earnings prospects than are dividend increases.

Our finding that only dividend decreases release information on long-term earnings growth also provides an empirical explanation as to why dividend decreases are associated with a larger absolute magnitude of stock price reaction than are dividend increases. For our sample, the CAAR of −5.16 percent for the dividend decrease announcements is over four times as large (in absolute value) as the CAAR of 1.15 percent for the dividend increase announcements. This differential stock price reaction between dividend increase and decrease announcements could be due to the problem of determining the market's conditional expected dividend, since dividend decrease firms have greater dividend yields and larger absolute values of dividend changes, and are smaller in size (see Table 1). However, the differential still holds after controlling for these variables. We conclude that the analyst forecast revision result suggests that the differential reaction can be explained in part by information relevant to the long-term earnings growth rate.

6. Concluding Comments

In this article we have provided tests of whether the information revealed by dividend change announcements is more consistent with the cash flow signaling hypothesis or the Lang and Litzenberger (1989) version of the free cash flow hypothesis. We find that the stock price reaction to large (at least 10 percent) dividend change announcements is generally consistent with the predictions of the cash flow signaling hypothesis. Although we find that for dividend increases, the abnormal return for low-q firms is significantly larger than that of high-q

The Review of Financial Studies / v 8 n 4 1995

firms, this differential reaction does not persist after controlling for dividend change, dividend yield, and firm size.

Due to the relationships between the three control variables and the investment opportunity set, we take an alternate approach to discriminate between the cash flow signaling and free cash flow hypotheses as explanations of the wealth effects surrounding dividend change announcements. We directly examine the sources of the wealth effects suggested by the two hypotheses. We find that dividend increase (decrease) firms experience significant increases (decreases) in capital expenditures over the three years following the dividend change, a result that is inconsistent with the implications of the free cash flow hypothesis for dividend change announcements. We also provide significant evidence that announcements of dividend increases and decreases cause analysts to revise their current earnings forecasts in a manner generally consistent with the cash flow signaling hypothesis. In addition, we find that analysts tend to lower their long-term earnings growth forecasts following dividend decrease announcements, but not following dividend increase announcements. This result potentially explains why dividend decreases cause a larger stock price reaction than do dividend increases.

A central issue in any test of the free cash flow hypothesis is the question of a measure for a firm's investment opportunities. Our choices for proxies for the investment opportunity set were Tobin's q ratio and the direction of insider trading. If our choices were poor proxies for the investment opportunity set, our results on the market reaction by the investment opportunity set are biased against the free cash flow hypothesis. The examination of the sources of the valuation effects provides clearer evidence than the analysis of the wealth effects, not only because the observed stock price reactions are affected by confounding factors, but also because our conclusion from the examination of capital expenditure changes does not particularly depend on how good a proxy Tobin's q ratio is. That is, we find significant changes in capital expenditures in the direction opposite to the prediction by the free cash flow hypothesis for both high-q and low-q firms, although the magnitude of the changes for high-q firms are smaller than that of low-q firms.

Although our results indicate that the free cash flow hypothesis does not explain the information effects of dividend change announcements, we cannot rule out the possibility that the free cash flow hypothesis explains the observed cross-sectional differences in dividend policy. In particular, the fact that low-q firms have higher dividend yield and larger dividend change than high-q firms is consistent with the implications of the free cash flow hypothesis [Smith and Watts (1992)].

1016

Signaling, Investment Opportunities, and Dividend Announcements

References

Aharony, J., and I. Swary, 1980, "Quarterly Dividend and Earnings Announcements and Stockholder's Returns: An Empirical Analysis," *Journal of Finance*, 35, 1–12.

Asquith, P., and D. Mullins, 1983, "The Impact of Initiating Dividend Payments on Shareholders' Wealth," *Journal of Business*, 56, 77–96.

Bajaj, M., and A. Vijh, 1990, "Dividend Clienteles and the Information Content of Dividend Changes," *Journal of Financial Economics*, 26, 193–219.

Bhattacharya, S., 1979, "Imperfect Information, Dividend Policy, and the 'Bird in the Hand' Fallacy," *Bell Journal of Economics*, 10, 259–270.

Brous, P., 1992, "Common Stock Offerings and Earnings Expectations: A Test of the Release of Unfavorable Information," *Journal of Finance*, 47, 1517–1536.

Brous, P., and O. Kini, 1993, "A Rexamination of Analysts' Earnings Forecasts for Takeover Targets," *Journal of Financial Economics*, 33, 201–226.

DeAngelo, H., L. DeAngelo, and D. Skinner, 1992, "Dividends and Losses," *Journal of Finance*, 47, 1837–1863.

Denis, D., D. Denis, and A. Sarin, 1992, "The Information Content of Dividend Changes: Cash Flow Signaling, Overinvestment, and Dividend Clienteles," working paper, Virginia Polytechnic Institute and State University.

Eades, K., P. Hess, and E. Kim, 1985, "Market Rationality and Dividend Announcements," *Journal of Financial Economics*, 15, 3–34.

Easterbrook, F. H., 1984, "Two Agency-Cost Explanations of Dividends," *American Economic Review*, 74, 650–659.

Eddy, A., and B. Seifert, 1988, "Firm Size and Dividend Announcements," *Journal of Financial Research*, 11, 295–302.

Fehrs, D., G. Benesh, and D. Peterson, 1988, "Evidence of a Relation between Stock Price Reactions around Cash Dividend Changes and Yields," *Journal of Financial Research*, 11, 111–123.

Healy, P., and K. Palepu, 1988, "Earnings Information Conveyed by Dividend Initiations and Omissions," *Journal of Financial Economics*, 21, 149–176.

Howe, K., J. He, and W. Kao, 1992, "One-time Cash Flow Announcements and Free Cash-Flow Theory: Share Repurchase and Special Dividends," *Journal of Finance*, 47, 1963–1975.

Jensen, M., 1986, "Agency Costs of Free Cash Flow, Corporate Finance, and the Market for Takeovers," *American Economic Review*, 76, 323–329.

John, K., and L. Lang, 1991, "Insider Trading around Dividend Announcements: Theory and Evidence," *Journal of Finance*, 46, 1361–1389.

John, K., and J. Williams, 1985, "Dividends, Dilution and Taxes: A Signaling Equilibrium," *Journal of Finance*, 40, 1053–1070.

Kalay, A., 1980, "Signaling, Information Content, and the Reluctance to Cut Dividends," *Journal of Financial and Quantitative Analysis*, 15, 855–869.

Kalay, A., and U. Loewenstein, 1985, "Predictable Events and Excess Returns: The Case of Dividend Announcements," *Journal of Financial Economics*, 14, 423–449.

Kalay, A., and U. Loewenstein, 1986, "The Information Content of the Timing of Dividend Announcements," *Journal of Financial Economics*, 16, 373–388.

The Review of Financial Studies / v 8 n 4 1995

Keown, A., P. Laux, and J. Martin, 1992, "Joint Ventures, Latent Assets and the Information Content of Corporate Announcements," working paper, Virginia Polytechnic Institute and State University and University of Texas at Austin.

Lang, L., and R. Litzenberger, 1989, "Dividend Announcements: Cash Flow Signaling vs. Free Cash Flow Hypothesis?," *Journal of Financial Economics*, 24, 181–191.

Lang, L., R. Stulz, and R. Walkling, 1991, "A Test of the Free Cash Flow Hypothesis: The Case of Bidder Returns," *Journal of Financial Economics*, 29, 315–335.

Lehn, K., and A. Poulsen, 1989, "Free Cash Flow and Stockholder Gains in Going Private Transactions," *Journal of Finance*, 44, 771–789.

Lindenberg, E., and S. Ross, 1981, "Tobin's Q Ratio and Industrial Organization," *Journal of Business*, 54, 1–32.

Lintner, J., 1956, "Distribution of Incomes of Corporations among Dividends, Retained Earnings and Taxes," *American Economic Review*, 46, 97–113.

Long, M., I. Malitz, and S. Sefcik, 1994, "An Empirical Examination of Dividend Policy Following Debt Issues," *Journal of Financial and Quantitative Analysis*, 29, 131–144.

Miller, M. H., and K. Rock, 1985, "Dividend Policy under Asymmetric Information," *Journal of Finance*, 40, 1031–1051.

O'Brien, P. C., 1988, "Analysts' Forecasts as Earnings Expectations," *Journal of Accounting and Economics*, 10,187–221.

Ofer, A., and D. Siegel, 1987, "Corporate Financial Policy, Information, and Market Expectations: An Empirical Investigation of Dividends," *Journal of Finance*, 42, 889–911.

Perfect, S., D. Peterson, and P. Peterson, 1994, "Self-Tender Offers: Differentiating the Effects of Free Cash Flow and Cash Flow Signaling," forthcoming in *Journal of Banking and Finance*.

Perfect, S., and K. Wiles, 1994, "Alternative Constructions of Tobin's Q: An Empirical Comparison," *Journal of Empirical Finance*, 1, 313–341.

Pettit, R., 1972, "Dividend Announcements, Security Performance, and Capital Market Efficiency," *Journal of Finance*, 28, 993–1007.

Pilotte, E., 1992, "Growth Opportunities and the Stock Price Response to New Financing," *Journal of Business*, 65, 371–394.

Rozeff, M. S., 1982, "Growth, Beta, and Agency Costs as Determinants of Dividend Payout Ratios," *Journal of Financial Research*, 5, 249–259.

Servaes, H., 1991, "Tobin's Q and the Gains from Takeovers," *Journal of Finance*, 46, 409–419.

Servaes, H., 1994, "Do Takeover Targets Overinvest?," *Review of Financial Studies*, 7, 253–277.

Smith, C., and R. Watts, 1992, "The Investment Opportunity Set and Corporate Financing, Dividend, and Compensation Policies," *Journal of Financial Economics*, 32, 263–292.

Warther, V., 1994, "Dividend Smoothing: A Sleeping Dogs Explanation," working paper, University of Southern California.

[15]

JOURNAL OF FINANCIAL AND QUANTITATIVE ANALYSIS VOL. 19, NO. 2, JUNE 1984

Repurchase Tender Offers, Signaling, and Managerial Incentives

Theo Vermaelen*

I. Introduction

One of the main principles of corporate finan
maximize the market value of the outstanding securi
managers and security holders may have divergent (
sumed that various market forces keep managerial and shareholders goals in
line. Out of the extensive literature on this issue, three such market forces
emerge. First, non-value-maximizing firms are prime targets for take-over bids
(e.g., see [14]): bidding firms could acquire control over the shares of the target
firm, replace the management, follow a value-maximizing strategy, and realize a
profit from the resulting appeciation of the target shares. Second, outside shareholders may charge managers-owners *ex ante* by discounting stock prices for
expected managerial expropriation, which may induce managers to accept various restrictions on their behavior (e.g., see [11]). Third, shareholders may
charge managers *ex post*, indirectly via the discipline imposed by a competitive
managerial labor market (e.g., [8]). Note the difference from the previous
mechanism: Jensen and Meckling [11] assume that managerial wages are fixed so
that all the adjustment for expected expropriation is reflected in stock prices (and,
ultimately, in costly monitoring and bonding devices). In Fama's [8] model, all
the adjustment occurs in the managerial labor market, so that the value of the
firm remains unaffected by expected managerial expropriation.

To what extent each of these forces is relevant is an empirical issue. Past
empirical research has mainly focused on managerial incentives to implement
various accounting techniques (e.g., [9], [10], [2], and [12]). In this paper, we
investigate managerial incentives in a different setting, i.e., signaling inside information via repurchase tender offers. The justification for treating stock repurchase as an information signal stems from results reported by previous research.

* Catholic University of Leuven and European Institute for Advanced Studies in Management,
Brussels. The author has benefited from comments by Michael Brennan, George Constantinides,
Nelson De Pril, Doug Diamond, Merton Miller, Eli Talmor (especially), and the participants of the
finance workshops at the University of British Columbia, the University of North Carolina at Chapel
Hill, and the University of Chicago. This paper was presented at the 1983 European Finance Associa-
tion meetings.

Dann [5], Masulis [15], Rosenfeld [19], and Vermaelen [23] report significant abnormal returns of approximately 15 percent (on the average) after repurchase tender offer announcements. After testing for various hypotheses, Dann and Vermaelen conclude that disclosure of new information is the principal explanation of this value increase. Vermaelen goes on to put the event in a framework consistent with the signaling literature, but in contrast to past theoretical studies on signaling (e.g., [21], [20], [13], and [17]), his analysis does not provide an explicit solution to an equilibrium signaling function. As will become clear below, identifying such an exact specification is necessary (or at least very helpful) in testing for some of the above-mentioned incentive issues.

The purpose of this paper is threefold. First, the stock repurchase decision is formulated within a managerial incentive framework and a corresponding (partial) signaling function is derived. Second, because this signaling function is defined conditional upon implicit managerial benefits, it becomes possible to obtain a market estimate of these benefits by using a sample of 131 announcements of tender offers. Third, using a nonlinear least squares estimation procedure, we test whether the market sets security prices as if managerial benefits are related to specific incentive "candidates," by using data on executive compensation and take-over bids. Hence, this paper addresses the signaling and managerial incentive issues both theoretically and empirically. Moreover, different from previous empirical tests of signaling hypotheses ([7], [23]), an *explicit* test of a financial signaling model is provided.

The results support the joint hypothesis that (i) repurchase tender offers convey inside information, (ii) perceived managerial benefits are positive and significant, and (iii) managerial incentives related to preventing take-over bids and executive stock options are taken into account by the market when it prices securities after the repurchase announcement. So the results provide some tentative support for the hypothesis that stock prices reflect adverse managerial incentives, which is the underlying assumption in most of the agency literature (e.g., see [11]).

This paper is organized as follows. In Section II, a closed-form solution to an equilibrium signaling function is developed and its theoretical properties are discussed. The predictions of the model are contrasted with the predictions of two alternative models that involve *ex post* setting up (see [8]). The data base discussed in Section III is used in Section IV to test for various hypotheses and implications of the model(s). Section V summarizes our findings.

II. Repurchase Tender Offers as a Signal: Theory

In a repurchase tender offer, the company offers to buy a specified amount of stock at a given price, (the tender price, which is typically above the market price) until a given expiration date (usually three weeks to one month after the offer). The company generally reserves the right to buy more than the amount specified, to extend the offer, or to purchase the shares *pro rata*. The firm can set maximum or minimum limits on the amount sought. Minimum constraints imply that the firm may withdraw the offer if fewer shares are tendered than desired. The vast majority of tender offers are "maximum limit" offers: management agrees to buy all the shares tendered if fewer than the amount specified are tendered. In the theoretical analysis below (and also in the empirical tests), the offers are maximum limit offers.

In the following discussion, we assume that insiders have some information, $\bar{I}$, which represents the difference between the "true" market value of the outstanding shares (known to insiders) and the market value before the announcement of the repurchase tender offer. As in most signaling models (see [22] for an extensive discussion of the general procedure), we proceed in two steps. First, we look at the problem from the point of view of the manager (insiders, agents) who determine the parameters of the tender offer (i.e., the fraction of shares repurchased and the tender price) to maximize the value of a compensation or incentive "package." Second, we invoke a "rationality" condition that, in equilibrium, the signal is determined by the market such that the *perceived* value of the information, I, equals the true value, $\bar{I}$. Combining this condition with the managers' optimal decision produces an exact functional relationship between the perceived (or signaled) value change and the various signals considered.

A. The Model

Assume managers-signalers must determine how many shares to repurchase at a specific tender price, P_T. The repurchase decision is assumed to affect the present value of their total compensation, C, in two ways.

First, part of their compensation, $W(I)$, depends on the perceived value of information signaled to the market, I. I is the total dollar-value increase of the shares as a result of the repurchase, and $W'(I) > 0$. These benefits represent the *gross* signaling benefits. One of the main purposes of this paper is to determine what and how large these benefits are, or better, whether $W(I)$ is perceived by the market as being related to gains from increases in the value of executive stock options or managerial benefits arising from a reduction in take-over threats. For the time being, no generality is lost by not defining a more specific format of this compensation package.

To determine the *net* signaling benefits, consider the following scenario. Assume that, whether the firm signals or not, the true value of information will be revealed to outsiders (e.g., via annual reports) at some time in the future, say T periods (days) from now. Also, redefine $\bar{I}$ as the *present value* of this information. Insiders-managers hold M_O shares before the repurchase; further, assume that they will not tender their shares and that they plan to hold on to their shares until day T. Define $\bar{P}$ as the value of the "true" stock price today; this is the prevailing price if all market participants could costlessly observe $\bar{I}$. Per definition, $\bar{P} = P_O + \bar{I}/N_O$, where P_O is the price per share before the repurchase announcement and N_O is the number of shares outstanding. If the firm repurchases N_p shares at $P_T > \bar{P}$, the total cost to the insiders equals $(P_T - \bar{P})F_P M_O/ (1 - F_P)$, where $F_P = N_P/N_O$. Indeed, when $P_T > \bar{P}$, the nontendering shareholders are buying N_P shares from the tendering shareholders at a price above their true value. This does not imply that all non-insider shareholders will tender their shares: the existence of capital gains taxes may induce shareholders to hold on to their shares. Thus, the net signaling benefits to insiders are equal to

(1) $C = W(I) - \left(P_T - P_O - \bar{I}/N_O\right)F_P M_O / \left(1 - F_P\right) .$

The managerial decision problem then reduces to determining the fraction of shares repurchased and the tender price to maximize C. Although the management controls two variables (P_T and F_P), we will assume that P_T is a *parameter*, not a decision variable. This assumption does not imply that P_T is set randomly; in the Appendix it is shown that a rational management will always set $P_T > \bar{P}$. Since the main purpose is to obtain a model that is both empirically testable and that captures the essence of the informational theory of stock repurchases, we will assume for simplicity the following sequential decision process: (i) the insiders set P_T above $\bar{P}$; and (ii) given P_T and the other parameters of the model, they determine F_P to maximize C.[1]

Differentiating (1) with respect to F_P, we find the first-order condition:[2]

(2) $\dfrac{\partial W(I)}{\partial F_P} = -M_O\left(P_O - P_T + \bar{I}/N_O\right)/\left(1 - F_P\right)^2 .$

To arrive at an equilibrium value for the perceived value of information, $I(F_P)$, we will proceed along the lines of previous research (e.g., see [22] and [20]). First we invoke the rationality condition that the signaling equilibrium will be fully revealing, such that

(3) $I\left(F_P\right) = \bar{I} .$

This condition mainly states that no informational equilibrium can be reached unless the perceived value of the value change equals the true value, given the signals and given the managerial decision process described above. If condition (3) does not hold, the market will change its perception about I, in the same way as in regular equilibrium models prices will change if demand does not equal supply. Totally differentiating (3) and realizing that in equilibrium F_P is a function of I,

(4) $\dfrac{\partial I}{\partial F_P} \dfrac{\partial F_P}{\partial I} = 1 .$

Also, in (2) we can write $\partial W/\partial F_P$ as $w(\partial I/\partial F_P)$ where w is assumed to be a

---

[1] Applying the multiple signaling model in [22], we obtain a differential equation similar to (5), except for an additional term $F_P(\partial P_T/\partial I)$, added to the left-hand side of equation (5). This new equation has no closed-form solution. It also is assumed that the information content of P_T is only an indirect one: i.e., via the behavior of the decision variable F_P. The signaling function $I(F_P)$ is defined, therefore, conditional upon a given observed value of P_T.

[2] The second-order condition will be derived later (footnote 3).

constant. Combining (2), (3), and (4) we obtain a first-order partial differential equation in F_P as a function of I

$$(5) \quad -\frac{\left(P_O - P_T + I\left(F_P\right)/N_O\right)}{\left(1 - F_P\right)} \frac{\partial F_P}{\partial I} = w\left(1 - F_P\right)/M_O .$$

If we impose the boundary condition that $I = 0$ when $F_P = 0$, the solution to (5) is straightforward and equal to

$$(6) \quad I = \left(P_T - P_O\right)N_O\left[1 - \exp\left(-M_O F_P/N_O w\left(1 - F_P\right)\right)\right]$$

Dividing both sides of (6) by $P_O N_O$ and defining M_0/N_0 as the fraction of insider holdings m_0, we obtain

$$(7) \quad \alpha \equiv I/N_O P_O = \frac{\left(P_T - P_O\right)}{P_O}\left[1 - \exp\left(-m_O F_P/w\left(1 - F_P\right)\right)\right] ,$$

where α represents the value of information (if the market sets prices according to our signaling model) expressed as an "abnormal" return per share. Recall that, per definition, $\bar{I}/N_O P_O = (\bar{P} - P_O)/P_O$, which is the abnormal return one would observe if the stock price moves to its true value and this is exactly what should happen if the signals are fully revealing.[3]

In the analysis above, the assumption that insiders-managers hold on to their M_O shares until the true value of information becomes publicly available may seem questionable. However, empirically, insiders generally do not tender their shares and they make this commitment known in the offering circular. Moreover, even if they wished to unload their shares afterwards (i.e., after the expiration of the offer), the larger m_O, the more difficult it becomes to do this quietly, i.e., without adversely affecting the market price of the stock. So indirectly, m_O will be perceived as a positive signal by the market, although the observed value of α may be less than predicted on the basis of expression (7). It should be emphasized that the fact that managers hold on to their shares until the true information becomes known to all market participants (at some future time) does not imply that managers have no incentive to signal. As will be discussed below in detail, *early* release of information may be important to insiders (e.g., to prevent outside take-over bids at a price below the true stock price).

B. Properties of the Value of Information

First, redefining $(P_T - P_O)/P_O$ as *PREMIUM*, it follows that the premium,

---

[3] Using (7), we can derive the second-order condition for a local maximum as $[\exp(-x)]$ $[-m_0/w - (2F_P - 2)](P_T - P_O) + (\bar{P} - P_T)(2 - 2F_P) \leqslant 0$ where $x = m_0 F_P/(w(1 - F_P))$. As $P_T > \bar{P}$, $P_T > P_O$ and $F_P < 1$, it follows that $m_0/w > 2 - 2F_P$ is a sufficient condition for a maximum. To check the reasonableness of this condition, note that $F_P > 0$ so that the right-hand side is always smaller than 2. So as long as the fraction of insider holdings is at least twice the marginal signaling benefit, a local maximum will always exist.

the fraction repurchased, and the fraction of insider holdings are positively related to α (denoted as ''positive signals''),[4] while the marginal signaling benefits are negatively related to α. Specifically,

$$(8) \qquad \frac{\partial \alpha}{\partial PREMIUM} \geq 0 \quad \text{and} \quad \frac{\partial^2 \alpha}{\partial (PREMIUM)^2} = 0,$$

$$(9) \qquad \frac{\partial \alpha}{\partial F_P} \geq 0 \quad \text{and} \quad \frac{\partial^2 \alpha}{\partial F_P^2} \gtreqqless 0 \text{ if } 2 - 2F_P \gtreqqless m_O/w$$

$$(10) \qquad \frac{\partial \alpha}{\partial m_O} \geq 0 \quad \text{and} \quad \frac{\partial^2 \alpha}{\partial m_O^2} \leq 0$$

$$(11) \qquad \frac{\partial \alpha}{\partial w} \leq 0 \quad \text{and} \quad \frac{\partial^2 \alpha}{\partial w^2} \gtreqqless 0 \text{ if } 2 \gtreqqless m_O F_P / w \left(1 - F_P \right).$$

Note from the expressions and conditions above that the direction of the *marginal* impact can be established unambiguously only for the premium and the fraction of insider holdings.

Further insight is provided by Figure 1. The curve OBA represents α as a function of F_P (which can range between 0 and 1) for given values of the premium (shown on the vertical axis), the fraction of insider holdings, and the marginal signaling benefit (w). The specific curvature arises from condition (9): at small values of F_P, the curve is convex; at larger values of F_P, the second-order condition (9) will reverse so that the curvature becomes concave. Note that for all values of F_P, the value of information is never larger than the premium. Only when $F_P = 1$ is α equal to the premium. This point will never be reached, however; because insiders are assumed not to tender their shares, F_P can never be larger than $1 - m_O$. So the effective signaling function is not OA, but the kinked curve OBC.

When the premium is doubled, from *PREMIUM'* to *PREMIUM''*, the signaling function shifts out to OFE. Note that, because of (7), doubling the premium will double α at any given level of F_P (so that, e.g., FB = BS). Note also that $\alpha = 0$ when *either* F_P, m_O or the premium are zero. When $w = 0$, $\alpha = PREMIUM$, and the signaling function reduces to OXA.

C.   Signaling and *Ex Post* Settling Up

Fama [8] argues that agency problems resulting from moral hazard are of no consequence to the value of the firm if the manager can be charged *ex post* for

---

[4] We deviate here from the classification proposed by Spence [21], who makes a distinction between *indices* and *signals*. Indices are observable firm characteristics that are largely outside the control of the firm at the time of the repurchase (such as, e.g., the fraction of insider holdings). Signals are directly observable variables that are directly controllable by the firm (the fraction purchased). In this paper, we always use the term ''signal'' for so-called ''indices.''

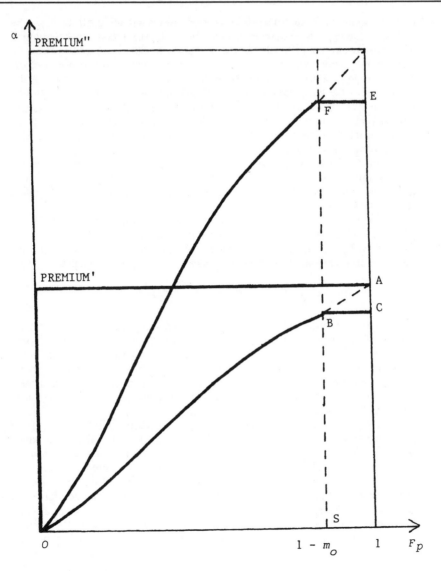

FIGURE 1

Value of Information as a Function of F_P, for Different Values of the Premium

169

past expropriation. In such a world, managers always will tell the truth,[5] e.g., by making a simple public statement that the true stock price is equal to $\overline{P}$. Failing to do so will result in penalties to the extent that the outside shareholders (who are assumed to control managerial compensation *ex post*) are hurt because of incorrect signaling. We try to answer the following question in this section. If the insiders have the *alternative* to reveal the information *costlessly and truthfully* via a public statement and full *ex post* settling up is possible, (i) will insiders still have an incentive to signal information via a repurchase tender offer, and, if so, (ii) how is the decision variable F_P affected? In answering this question, we consider two alternative cases.

Case 1. The gross signaling benefits $W(\bar{I}) = W(I)$ are independent of the way the information is revealed to the market: for a given I, gross benefits obtained via repurchase, $W_r(I(F_P))$, are equal to gross benefits via a simple public statement, $W_P(I)$.

It should be obvious from (1) that in the above circumstances (with $W_r = W_P$), rational insiders will never engage in a repurchase tender offer unless $P_T = \overline{P} \equiv P_O + \bar{I}/N_O$, i.e., unless the marginal signaling cost is zero.[6] Or, in a fully revealing signaling equilibrium the market will set prices such that

(12) $$\alpha' \equiv I/N_O P_O = \left(P_T - P_O \right)/P_O .$$

Thus, if *ex post* settling up is possible and the gross signaling benefits are independent of the way the true information is revealed, the market will set prices such that the abnormal return after the repurchase announcement is equal to the premium. In this case, repurchases will take place all along with public statements by insiders, but a rational market always will expect that rational managers never will engage in actions that are costly to the management themselves or to the other shareholders.

Case 2. $W_r(I(F_P)) > W_P(I)$, or the gross signaling benefits are higher if the information is revealed through a repurchase tender offer than via a public statement. (For example, thwarting an outside take-over bid may be more effective (for the same value increase I) via repurchase than via a public statement.)[7]

First, recall how the repurchase decision imposes a cost on non-tendering shareholders (equation (1)). The repurchase is costly because the non-tendering shareholders are buying N_P shares at a price $P_T > \overline{P}$. In our signaling model, we have assumed that part of these costs (i.e., $(P_T - \overline{P})N_P(1 - M_O/(N_O - N_P))$) are borne by the non-insider, shareholders who do not tender, possibly because of capital gains taxes. If these shareholders are able to charge the insiders *ex post* so that insiders bear *all* the signaling costs (i.e., $(P_T - \overline{P})N_P$), then the revised net signaling benefits are equal to $C' = W_r(F_P) - N_P(P_T - \overline{P})$.

---

[5] See [1], footnote 3.

[6] Equation (12) cannot be considered as a "special case" of (7): equation (7) is derived under the assumption that no alternative cheaper signaling mechanism exists.

[7] Because part of the shares are retired, the insiders end up with a larger fraction of the remaining shares than before the repurchase. This strengthening of control may enhance their power to prevent a successful take-over bid.

In this case (with $W_r > W_P$), it is possible that C' is larger than W_P for $P_T > \overline{P}$. The revised first-order condition (2) now becomes

(13)
$$w\frac{\partial I}{\partial F_P} = -N_0\left(\overline{P} - P_T\right) .$$

Using condition (13) with the rationality condition (3), it can be shown (using the same procedure as above) that the signaling equilibrium function reduces to

(14)
$$\alpha'' = \frac{\left(P_T - P_O\right)}{P_O}\left[1 - \exp\left(-F_P/w\right)\right] .$$

Again, it can be verified easily that the premium and the fraction purchased will be perceived as positive signals. The main difference between (14) and (7) is that the insider-holdings variable no longer enters the equilibrium valuation: with *ex post* settling up, insiders carry the total burden of the expropriation, not just the expropriation of their personal holdings.

It is important to emphasize that, contrary to [8], even with *ex post* settling up, the solution in the case of information asymmetry differs from the one under perfect information. Thus, the moral hazard problem of false signaling *cannot* be resolved just because the market is aware of it and penalizes the manager.

To summarize, the analysis in this section allows us to test the joint hypothesis that (i) repurchases reveal information, (ii) they can exist next to alternative, costless fully revealing signaling mechanisms, and (iii) full *ex post* settling up is possible. Depending on the assumptions about W_r/W_P, we are able to formulate two predictions (different from α in (7)) about abnormal returns observed after a repurchase tender offer. The purpose of the remainder of this paper is to test the predictions of (7) against the competing predictions (12) and (14).

III. Empirical Evidence: Preliminaries

A. Repurchase Tender Offer Data Base

The data base is the same as the one used in [23]. Data on tender offers for the years 1962-1977 were compiled from the *Financial Daily Card Service* (Financial Information, Inc., N.J.), *Corporations in Conflict: The Tender Offer* (Ann Arbor, MI: Masterco Press, Inc. 1966), and the *Standard and Poors Corporation Called Bond Record*. These publications give the effective date (generally a few days after the announcement date), the expiration date, and the terms of the offer. The announcement date was found in the *Wall Street Journal* and the *Wall Street Journal Index*. In selecting the sample, the following rules were observed: (i) no other event was reported in the three days surrounding the announcement day; (ii) tender offers that were not stated in maximum limit form or were not directed to all shareholders were deleted; and (iii) offers announced with the intention to become a private company or which resulted in a delisting from the exchange in the month after the expiration date were not included. The number of shares outstanding was obtained from the *Standard and Poors Corporation Security Owners Stock Guide*.

B.　Predictions of the Model and Estimation of the Model Inputs

As pointed out before, $\alpha = I/P_O N_O$ (as described in (7)) is equal to $(\overline{P} - P_O)/P_O$, the abnormal return per share resulting from the tender offer. So, equation (7), together with conditions (8) through (11), makes *explicit* predictions about the relationship between abnormal announcement returns and w, F_P, m_O, and the tender premium. To test the validity of these predictions, we need estimates of the value of information $\hat{\alpha}$, and the value of the signals F_P, $(P_T - P_O)/P_O$, m_O, and w.

An *estimate of the value of information* is obtained as follows. In a semi-strong efficient capital market, the price after the expiration of the offer but before the true value of information is revealed, P_E, multiplied by the remaining number of shares outstanding, N_E, must equal the value of the shares before the announcement minus the value of the repurchased shares, $P_T N_P$, plus the market estimate of the dollar change in the value of the shares, $\hat{I}$ or

(15) $$P_E N_E = P_O N_O - P_T N_P + \hat{I} .$$

Using this envelope condition, the abnormal announcement return is estimated as $\hat{I}/P_O N_O = \hat{\alpha}$. P_O is estimated by the price per share 5 days before the announcement of the offer and P_E is estimated by the price per share 10 days after the expiration of the offer (adjusted for market movements; see [23], p. 156).[8]

Data on the *premium*, the *fraction purchased*, and the target fraction (i.e., the fraction of shares the firm was *willing* to repurchase) were obtained from the sources mentioned above. When the offer was undersubscribed, we replaced the fraction purchased by the target fraction, F_T. This adjustment was made to incorporate the fact that, unlike the assumption in our signaling model, management does not have complete control over the repurchase decision. Firms *offer* to repurchase a target fraction F_T, so the actual amount repurchased depends on the response of the shareholders. The firm always commits itself to repurchase all shares tendered below the target amount, so the target fraction represents management's willingness to bear the specific signaling costs. The unforseen fact that (because of capital gains taxes) fewer shares than sought are tendered should not in itself be a determinant of the information content of the offer. Indeed, when the offer is *undersubscribed*, management has not determined F_P on the basis of $\overline{I}$ (as we have assumed all along), but has set F_T on the basis of that information. So, in this case, we expect a closer relationship between $\overline{I}$ and F_T than between $\overline{I}$ and F_P. At the same time, when the offer is *oversubscribed*, management has the power to repurchase the target fraction (and allocate *pro rata*) or buy all the

---

[8] We do not use announcement returns for two reasons: (1) announcement returns are biased estimates of α (see [23], pp. 145-146); and (2) around the announcement (before the expiration of the offer), the fraction purchased is not known (yet). Of course, our alternative estimation method is not free of criticism: estimates of the value of information may be too high or too low if, during the ± one-month offer period, other company-specific good or bad news becomes available (e.g., dividend announcements). However, this will only increase the variability of our estimate and will not induce a systematic bias if good and bad news are more or less randomly distributed.

shares tendered. Thus, only for the oversubscribed offers, F_P can be considered as an actual managerial decision variable.[9]

For our 131-firm sample, data on *insider holdings* were obtained from 3 sources: (1) the annual proxy statement lists the amount of insider holdings in the firm; the missing data were obtained either (2) via a questionnaire; or (3) by going through the *S.E.C. Official Summary of Insider Transactions* for the three years preceding the announcement. The last method is likely to understate the total amount of insider holdings because only the holdings of individuals who engage in a transaction are reported.

The final input in our model are the *marginal signaling incentives, w*. Initially, as a first pass, we will estimate w via a cross-sectional regression based on equation (7). Thus, we obtain a market estimate of w, conditional upon (7) being the correct pricing mechanism *and w being constant across firms*. This allows us to test the joint hypothesis that (7) represents the relevant pricing mechanism and managerial (marginal) signaling benefits are positive (or better, the market believes that they are positive). In a second approach, we will specify *w as a function of specific incentive candidates, $w(a_i, \ldots, a_n)$* where the a_i denote the incentive candidates. This allows us to test the joint hypothesis that (7) represents the relevant pricing mechanism and the market perceives the a_i as being related to signaling incentives. In this paper, the following managerial signaling incentives are considered: prevention of take-over bids and executive stock options.

1. Prevention of Outside Take-Over Bids

Insiders-managers may want to prevent outsiders from gaining control of the firm. Specifically, if insiders know the firm is undervalued, they might want to prevent successful take-over bids at "low" offer premiums. Note that, in relating this incentive to $W(I)$ (and w), these managerial benefits depend on the increase in the value of the shares, I, as a result of the repurchase. Or, equivalently, we assume that the threat of an outside take-over bid is smaller at higher firm values, *ceteris paribus*. Note that in this case $W(I)$ does not necessarily refer to "selfish" managerial incentives (e.g., preserving their jobs), but it also could represent the managerial incentive to promote the interests of the non-insider shareholders: non-insiders may be better off without a take-over bid than with a take-over bid at a low offer premium. Admittedly, it is not clear how to quantify these managerial incentives, but their expected value should be positively correlated with the probability of take-over. Two measures of this probability can be considered. First, an aggregate level of take-over activity is used, i.e., the number of take-over bids in the year of the repurchase announcement as reported by Bradley [3] in a study of interfirm cash tender offers. Table 1 shows the distribution of our 131 repurchases and Bradley's 212 take-over bids from January 1962 until December 1977. Spearman rank correlations and simple correlations between the number of repurchases and take-over bid announcements

---

[9] Buying more than required (in the case of oversubscribed offers) can be rationalized in our model as a way to change the terms of the tender offer *ex post*; i.e., management increases F_P, perhaps because it has revised (upwards) its own estimate of the true value of the shares. Note that, empirically, the decision to buy more than required generally increases the price of the shares (and, therefore, benefits the management via a higher $W(I)$).

are equal to .74 and .80, respectively. For both events, 1973 and 1974 are the most active years, while 1971 is the least active year in the seventies. So there exists at least some suggestive evidence that take-over threats increase repurchase incentives. To test directly whether the *market* relates adverse signaling incentives to take-over bids, an individual level of take-over activity is employed (i.e., the number of announcements relating to potential take-over bids for the companies shares, as announced in the *Wall Street Journal* during the six months before the repurchase). In the tables that follow, we will denote this number as *BIDS*. Using our notation from above, *BIDS* is one of the incentive variables a_i specified in the incentive function $w(a_i, \ldots, a_n)$. The prediction of our model is that, if the threat of take-over bids is perceived by the market as an incentive to signal, w will be a positive function of *BIDS*.

TABLE 1

Relationship between Repurchase Tender Offers and Take-Over Bids

Year	Number of Take-Over[a] Bid Announcements	Number of Repurchase Announcements
1962	3	4
1963	12	4
1964	7	4
1965	11	4
1966	21	6
1967	10	2
1968	9	1
1969	10	4
1970	5	3
1971	2	2
1972	3	7
1973	28	32
1974	31	18
1975	17	8
1976	21	17
1977	22	15

a) Data are taken from [3].

2. Executive Stock Options

One obvious way to benefit from releasing positive information is to buy the shares before the announcement and sell them afterwards. SEC regulations forbid trading on the basis of inside information so that, considering the relative rarity of a repurchase tender offer, considerable legal risk may be involved in trying to benefit from short-term insider trading. Indirectly, managerial stock options allow circumvention of the legal impediments: managers can benefit via an increase in the value of the stock options after the repurchase announcement. Implicitly, we assume that the *marginal* signaling benefits, w, are proportional[10] to $n(\partial p/\partial I)$ where n is the number of unexercised options and p is the option price. The Black-Scholes option pricing model predicts that $\partial p/\partial I$ is propor-

---

[10] $N(d_1)$ is the value of the cumulative standard normal distribution function at d_1.

tional to $N(d_1)$ where $d_1 = [\ln(P_0/E) + (r + s^2/2)t]/s\sqrt{t}$, and where E is the exercise price, r is the instantaneous interest rate, s is the instantaneous standard deviation of the rate of return on the stock, P_0 is the stock price, and t is the time to maturity of the option.[11] That is, the marginal benefit from increasing the stock price should be a positive function of the number of stock options and the log of the ratio of the stock price relative to the exercise price of the options. Or, using the notation from above, these two variables are two of the incentive variables a_i specified in our incentive function. If the market perceives these variables as additional managerial incentives to signal, w will be positively related to these variables.

Of course, we do not claim that this list of incentives is exhaustive. Insiders may benefit in many other ways, e.g., by compensation tied to *earnings per share* numbers: if the firm repurchases shares as an alternative to paying a dividend, earnings per share will increase. Managers also may be compensated on the basis of *performance units,* (i.e., phantom stock) or may receive side payments from tendering shareholders. Another plausible incentive may be the fact that if managers are concerned about the wealth of the *current* shareholders, they should not issue new equity or acquire other firms in exchange for shares when the stock is undervalued. The repurchase is then a prelude to facilitate future equity financing or future acquisitions. The problem with these incentives is that it is difficult (or in the case of side payments, impossible) to use them in an empirical analysis. Except for insider holdings and stock options, firms have a lot of discretion in reporting the exact nature of their compensation packages. This creates an error in the variables problem and makes the (scarce) data on these items unsuitable for empirical investigation.

IV. Empirical Results

A. Data Description

Table 2 summarizes the characteristics of the distribution of the estimated value of information (computed via (15)) and the various signals. The value of $\hat{\alpha}$ ranges between -16.3 percent and 69.4 percent and has a mean value of 15.7 percent.[12] The mean premium equals 22.7 percent and on the average 14.7 percent of the shares are repurchased (F_P). The fraction of insider holdings, m_0, has a mean of 17 percent and ranges from .1 percent to 87 percent.

Proxy statements were available for only 91 firms. In 76 of these, managers were found to be compensated by (unexercised) stock options, with the fraction

---

[11] Approximately, because, technically speaking, executive stock options are warrants. Thus, the formula ignores any dilution effects created by an increase in the number of shares outstanding. Also because of the standard assumptions of the Black-Scholes option pricing model: no dividends are paid, etc.

[12] In 14 cases (or 10.7 percent), the observed returns were negative. This does not necessarily mean that the tender offer *per se* revealed negative information; indeed, other (negative) company-specific news may have been revealed during the offer period. In the same way, because of release of other ''good'' company-specific news, the observed abnormal returns may overstate the information content of the offer. This implies that we can make meaningful statements about only the average value of information (see also footnote 8).

of options (as a percentage of shares outstanding) ranging from 0.1 to 21.8 percent. The final column in Table 2 refers to the value of P_O/E for the 76 firms in which executives receive stock options. With regard to other characteristics of the compensation scheme, we found evidence in four offers of compensation on the basis of earnings per share and in six offers managers were compensated on the basis of stock performance units. Finally, with respect to the probability of take-over threat, only in four cases was a *Wall Street Journal* announcement found that indicated other firms were planning a take-over bid. The fact that so few announcements were found may well have something to do with the legal problems caused by frustrating an outsider take-over bid. As Nathan and Sobel [18] note, courts frequently look at the "compelling reason" or the "sole or primary purpose" for a transaction. If the sole or primary reason is to perpetuate the control of the present management, there is a violation of fiduciary duty.

TABLE 2

Distribution Characteristics of Various Variables in Our Signaling Model [a]

Decile	α	Premium	F_P	m_O	f_O	P_O/E
Min.	−.163	−.188	.01	.001	0	.096
0.1	−.02	.059	.05	.005	0	.344
0.2	+.023	.101	.06	.020	0.002	.447
0.3	.06	.127	.08	036	0.004	.522
0.4	.095	.159	.10	.058	0.006	.705
0.5	.153	196	.12	.088	0.009	.759
0.6	.173	.241	.14	.137	0.014	.961
0.7	.220	.273	.18	.215	0.018	1.16
0.8	.280	.333	.22	.330	0.026	1.26
0.9	.350	.429	.29	.481	0.039	1.70
Max.	.694	.846	.60	.87	0.218	13.93
Mean	.157	.227	.147	.175	0.017	1.14
Std Dev.	.155	.175	.108	.199	0.027	1.72

a) Notes: α is the value of information per share.
  Premium is the abnormal return to the tendering shareholders.
  F_P is the fraction purchased.
  m_O is the fraction of insider holdings.
  f_O is the fraction of executive stock options; this distribution is based on 91 available proxy statements.
  P_O/E is the price per share 5 days before the announcement divided by the weighted average exercise price of the executive stock options; this distribution is based on 76 firms that reported positive amounts of executive stock options.

B. Consistency with the Theoretical Predictions

One more-or-less straightforward method of testing the predictions of the signaling model (and its derivatives) is to regress[13] the value of information, $\hat{\alpha}$ (as estimated by the market) on the variables-signals that are readily observable, i.e., the premium, the fraction purchased, and the fraction of insider holdings.

---

[13] All cases, also the ones for which *a* was not found positive, are used in the regressions. Otherwise we would introduce an upward bias in our regression coefficients (see also footnotes 8 and 12).

Note that this approach is only a "first pass" in the sense that it ignores the interaction between different variables, as predicted by the signaling function (7). Except for the adjustment of F_P (see above), this approach is essentially a replication of Vermaelen's [23] analysis.

The regression in Table 3 shows the regression coefficients (with *t*-values in parentheses) obtained by regressing the perceived value of information against the variables-signals. From the second derivatives in equations (8) through (11), we expect that the effect of the premium on $\hat{\alpha}$ should be proportional, the effect of F_P is unclear, and the effect of the fraction of insider holdings should be marginally declining. Hence, the log-specification of m_O and the linear specification of F_P.

TABLE 3

OLS Estimation of $\alpha = \hat{\beta}_0 + \hat{\beta}_1 \, PREMIUM + \hat{\beta}_2 F_P + \hat{\beta}_3 \ln(m_O) + e$

$\hat{\beta}_0$	$t(\hat{\beta}_0)$	$\hat{\beta}_1$	$t(\hat{\beta}_1)$	$\hat{\beta}_2$	$t(\hat{\beta}_2)$	$\hat{\beta}_3$	$t(\hat{\beta}_3)$
0.074	(0.61)	0.589	(11.00)	0.242	(3.09)	0.012	(2.31)
	$\overline{R}^2 = 0.614$				$\sigma(\hat{e}) = 0.096$		

Explanation: *PREMIUM* = tender price relative to the price 5 days before the announcement minus 1.
Dependent variable is the abnormal return per share around the announcement.
F_P is the target fraction for undersubscribed offers and the fraction purchased for oversubscribed offers.
m_O is the fraction of insider holdings before the announcement.

The resulting regression shows that the impact of all signals is positive and statistically significant at the 5 percent significance level and the model explains approximately 61 percent of the cross-sectional variance of the perceived value of information.

Although, strictly speaking, the model is misspecified according to our analysis in equation (7), the fact that the premium is by far the most significant signal is very much consistent with the predictions of our theoretical analysis. Indeed, from Figure 1, it follows that the premium puts an upper boundary on the value of information: whatever the value of F_P, w, or m_O, α always will be smaller than the premium. Moreover, equation (7) shows that α is homogeneous of degree 1 in the premium.[14] Thus, the expected regression coefficient on the premium is equal to 1. Using the same equation (7) it can be verified easily that the theoretically expected regression coefficients on the fraction of insider holdings and the fraction purchased are much smaller.[15] This illustrates that the theoretically crucial importance of the insider holdings variable (note that $\alpha = 0$ if $m_O = 0$) will not necessarily show up via a large regression coefficient.

---

[14] The coefficient in Table 3 is less than 1 (.59). Of course, this should not be surprising; the linear regression is only a "first pass" test of the model.

[15] For example, to test for homogeneity in F_P, multiply F_P in (7) with a constant factor x. Call this function $b(xF_P)$. It is easy to verify that $x\,a$ is always greater than $b(xF_P)$. Indeed, the term in parentheses in (7) can never become greater than 1.

The observation that, on the average, the premium is significantly higher than the value of information[16] is consistent with (7) (and also with (14)), but inconsistent with the first *ex post* settling up version (equation 12)). The finding that the insider-holdings variable is statistically significant is inconsistent with (14). Therefore, for the remaining part of the empirical tests, we confine ourselves to testing the implications of α in (7).

The next step involves obtaining an estimate of the implicit perceived managerial benefits, $W(I)$. We estimated the marginal benefit, w, as a regression coefficient in the following cross-sectional regression

$$\hat{\alpha}_i = PREMIUM_i \left[1 - \exp\left(-\gamma_i / w\right) \right] + \tilde{\epsilon}_i$$

where $\gamma_i = m_{oi} F_{Pi} / (1 - F_{Pi})$ and i refers to offer i.

Thus, we test the joint hypothesis that our model is correctly specified and that w is constant across firms and positive. The regression was estimated using a nonlinear least squares estimation procedure, which is equivalent to maximum likelihood estimation under the assumption that the errors are normally distributed. The resulting estimate for w is shown in the first row of Table 4 and indicates that w is approximately equal to 2.01 percent and highly significant ($t = 6.50$). Under our assumption, $W(I) = wI$. The average I in the sample is $17.985 million so that, on the average, $W(I)$ is equal to approximately $361,000. The *net* average (perceived by the market) managerial benefit then can be computed via equation (1): with an average signaling cost of $99,000, the net average signaling benefit, C, equals $262,000.

Finally, in order to test whether w is perceived (by the market) as related to the managerial incentives above, we estimated w as a function of (i) the fraction of executive stock options (f_O), (ii) the number of previous take-over bid announcements ($BIDS$), and (iii) the ln (P_O/E) multiplied by the fraction of stock options.[17] Estimates were obtained using the same nonlinear least squares estimation procedure, using the 76 cases in which managers were found to be compensated by stock options. The results are shown in Table 4. All coefficients on the incentive variables are positive and statistically significant at the 5 percent significance level. For comparison, we also show the regression that assumes that w is a constant for the same 76 observations. The specification that estimates w as a function of the incentive candidates explains approximately 68 percent or 4 percent more of the cross-sectional variation of $\hat{\alpha}$ and the standard error of the residuals is smaller. The fact that the total variation is not entirely explained by the model is, of course, not surprising. It generally takes at least a month before a

---

[16] Some of the results mentioned in [23] also are consistent with the model; e.g., as predicted by the model, stock prices fall significantly after the expiration of the offer. Also, in large firms, where m_O is very small, the value of information is much smaller than average.

[17] Ln p_O/E was not included as a separate independent variable because it would cause underflow/overflow problems in the estimation of the exponential function. This procedure creates a multicollinearity problem: f_O tends to be larger when ln (P_O/E) is small (i.e., stock options are unexercised when they are not in the money), so that f_O and ln (P_O/E) are negatively correlated. The positive regression coefficients on both variables do indicate, however, that executive stock option compensation matters, although collinearity makes it difficult to separate the impact of the number of options and the extent to which they are in the money.

tender offer expires. Because we computed the perceived value of information on the basis of post-expiration returns, $\hat{\alpha}$ will be influenced by other company-specific news that becomes available during the offer period.

TABLE 4

Maximum Likelihood Estimation of

$$\alpha = PREMIUM \left(1 - \exp\left[\frac{-F_P m_O}{1 - F_P} \frac{1}{\hat{w}}\right]\right) + \epsilon$$

---

1) $\hat{w}$ constant—all 131 observations

| $\hat{w} = 0.0201$ | $t(\hat{w}) = 6.50$ | $\bar{R}^2 = 0.57$ | $\sigma(\hat{\epsilon}) = 0.1169$ |

2) $\hat{w}$ constant—76 observations

| $\hat{w} = 0.0086$ | $t(\hat{w}) = 3.94$ | $\bar{R}^2 = 0.64$ | $\sigma(\hat{\epsilon}) = 0.1174$ |

3) $\hat{w} = \hat{\gamma}_0 + \hat{\gamma}_1 BIDS + \hat{\gamma}_2 f_0 + \hat{\gamma}_3(f_0 \ln(P_0/E))$.

| $\hat{\gamma}_0 = 0.0076$ | $\hat{\gamma}_1 = 0.029$ | $\hat{\gamma}_2 = 0.327$ | $\hat{\gamma}_3 = 0.249$ |
| $t(\hat{\gamma}_0) = 2.69$ | $t(\hat{\gamma}_1) = 2.07$ | $t(\hat{\gamma}_2) = 2.11$ | $t(\hat{\gamma}_3) = 2.71$ |

$\bar{R}^2 = 0.681$

$\sigma(\hat{\epsilon}) = 0.106$

Explanation: *PREMIUM* = tender price relative to the price 5 days before the announcement minus 1; F_P is the target fraction for undersubscribed offers and the fraction purchased for oversubscribed offers.
f_0 is the fraction of executive stock options.
P_0 is the price per share 5 days before the announcement.
E is the weighted average exercise price of the stock options.
BIDS = number of take-over bid announcements preceding the repurchase offer.

V. Conclusions

This paper provides theoretical and empirical support for the hypothesis that repurchase tender offers can be analysed in a signaling framework consistent with the existing signaling literature. The premiums offered, the target fraction, and the fraction of insider holdings are perceived as positive signals. In this setting, the market apparently sets prices as if managers-insiders are obtaining significant net signaling benefits, partially related to preventing take-over bids and increasing the value of executive stock options. The analysis in this paper could possibly be extended to other company-specific events that involve buying back shares at a premium, such as leverage-increasing exchange offers (see [16]) and targeted share repurchases (see [4] and [6]).[18]

---

[18] Possibly with an alternative managerial incentive specification that does not uniquely depend on the value increase of the shares but also on other factors (see, e.g., the "managerial entrenchment hypothesis" in [6]).

179

References

[1] Barnea, Amir; Robert Haugen; and Lemma Senbet. "A Rationale for Debt Maturity Structure and Call Provisions in the Agency Theoretic Framework." *Journal of Finance*, Vol. 35 (December 1980), pp. 1223-1234.

[2] Bowen, Robert; Eric Noreen; and John Lacey. "Determinants of the Corporate Decision to Capitalize Interest." *Journal of Accounting and Economics*, Vol. 3 (August 1981), pp. 151-179.

[3] Bradley, Michael. "An Analysis of Interfirm Cash Tender Offers." Unpublished Ph.D. dissertation. University of Chicago (1978).

[4] Bradley, Michael, and Lee Wakeman. "The Wealth Effects of Targeted Share Repurchases." *Journal of Financial Economics*, Vol. 11 (April 1983), pp. 301-328.

[5] Dann, Larry. "Common Stock Repurchases: An Analysis of Returns to Bondholders and Stockholders." *Journal of Financial Economics*, Vol. 9 (June 1981), pp. 115-138.

[6] Dann, Larry, and Harry De Angelo. "Standstill Arguments, Privately Negotiated Stock Repurchases and the Market for Corporate Control." *Journal of Financial Economics*, Vol. 11 (April 1983), pp. 275-300.

[7] Downes, David, and Robert Heinkel. "Signalling and the Value of Unseasoned New Issues." *Journal of Finance*, Vol. 37 (March 1982), pp. 1-10.

[8] Fama, Eugene. "Agency Problems and the Theory of the Firm." *Journal of Political Economy*, Vol. 88 (April 1980), pp. 288-307.

[9] Hagerman, R., and M. Zmijewski. "Some Economic Determinants of Accounting Policy Choice." *Journal of Accounting and Economics*, Vol. 1 (August 1979), pp. 141-161.

[10] Holthausen, Robert. "Evidence of the Effect of Bond Covenants and Management Compensation Contracts on the Choice of Accounting Techniques: the Case of Depreciation Switchback." *Journal of Accounting and Economics*, Vol. 3 (March 1981), pp. 73-109.

[11] Jensen, Michael, and William Meckling. "The Theory of the Firm: Managerial Behavior, Agency Cost and Ownership Structure." *Journal of Financial Economics*, Vol. 3 (October 1976), pp. 305-360.

[12] Larcker, David. "The Association between Performance Plan Adoption and Corporate Capital Investment." *Journal of Accounting and Economics*, Vol. 2 (April 1983), pp. 1-30.

[13] Leland, Hayne, and David Pyle. "Informational Asymmetries, Financial Structure and Financial Intermediation." *Journal of Finance*, Vol. 32 (May 1977), pp. 371-388.

[14] Manne, Henry. "Mergers and the Market for Corporate Control." *Journal of Political Economy*, Vol. 73 (April 1965), pp. 110-120.

[15] Masulis, Ronald. "Stock Repurchase by Tender Offer: An Analysis of Common Stock Price Changes." *Journal of Finance*, Vol. 35 (May 1980), pp. 305-318.

[16] —————————. "The Effects of Capital Structure Change on Security Prices: a Study of Exchange Offers." *Journal of Financial Economics*, Vol. 8 (June 1980), pp. 139-178.

[17] Miller, Merton, and Kevin Rock. "Dividend Policy under Asymmetric Information." Unpublished manuscript, University of Chicago (1982).

[18] Nathan, Charles, and Marilyn Sobel. "Corporate Stock Repurchase in the Context of Unsolicited Take-over Bids." *Business Lawyer*, Vol. 35 (July 1980), pp. 172-192.

[19] Rosenfeld, A. "Repurchase Offers: Information Adjusted Premiums and Shareholders' Response." Working paper. Krannert Graduate School of Management, Purdue University (1982).

[20] Ross, Stephen. "The Determination of Financial Structure: the Incentive Signalling Approach." *Bell Journal of Economics*, Vol. 8 (Spring 1977), pp. 23-40.

[21] Spence, Michael. "Job Market Signalling." *Quarterly Journal of Economics*, Vol. 87 (August 1973), pp. 355-374.

[22] Talmor, Eli. "Asymmetric Information, Signalling and Optimal Corporate Financial Decisions." *Journal of Financial and Quantitative Analysis*, Vol. 16 (November 1981), pp. 413-436.

[23] Vermaelen, Theo. "Common Stock Repurchases and Market Signalling: An Empirical Study." *Journal of Financial Economics*, Vol. 9 (June 1981), pp. 139-184.

Appendix

Proof that rational managers will always set $P_T > \overline{P}$:

Substituting (6) in the manager's objective function (1), we obtain

(A1)
$$C = W\left[(P_T - P_O)N_O(1 - \exp(-x))\right]$$
$$- \frac{M_O F_P}{1 - F_P}\left[P_T - P_O - \overline{I}/N_O\right]$$

where $x = M_O F_P / N_O w (1 - F_P)$.

Taking first derivatives with respect to F_P, we obtain the first-order condition:

(A2)
$$w(P_T - P_O)N_O \exp(-x)\frac{M_O}{N_O w\left(1 - F_P\right)^2} = \frac{M_O}{\left(1 - F_P\right)^2}(P_T - \overline{P}).$$

(A3)
$$\text{or},\quad (P_T - P_O)\exp(-x) = (P_T - \overline{P}).$$

Since $\exp(-x) > 0$ and $P_T > P_O$, it must be that $P_T > \overline{P}$.

This completes the proof.

181

[16]

Journal of Financial Economics 39 (1995) 181–208

Market underreaction to open market share repurchases

David Ikenberry[a], Josef Lakonishok[*,b], Theo Vermaelen[c,d]

[a]*Jesse H. Jones Graduate School of Business Administration, Rice University, Houston, TX 77005, USA*
[b]*University of Illinois at Urbana–Champaign, Champaign, IL 61820, USA*
[c]*INSEAD, 77305 Fontainebleau Cedex, France*
[d]*University of Limburg, 6200 MD Maastricht, The Netherlands*

(Received January 1994; final version received February 1995)

Abstract

We examine long-run firm performance following open market share repurchase announcements, 1980–1990. We find that the average abnormal four-year buy-and-hold return measured after the initial announcement is 12.1%. For 'value' stocks, companies more likely to be repurchasing shares because of undervaluation, the average abnormal return is 45.3%. For repurchases announced by 'glamour' stocks, where undervaluation is less likely to be an important motive, no positive drift in abnormal returns is observed. Thus, at least with respect to value stocks, the market errs in its initial response and appears to ignore much of the information conveyed through repurchase announcements.

Key words: Stock repurchase
JEL classification: G14; G32

---

*Corresponding author.

We appreciate the comments of Amir Barnea, Louis Chan, Kent Daniel, Bala Dharan, Narashimhan Jegadeesh, George Kanatas, Steve Kaplan, Tim Loughran, Matt Maher, Robert McDonald, Bill Nelson, Tim Opler, Graeme Rankine, Jay Ritter, Andrei Shleifer, Richard Shockley, David Smith, Kay Stice, Robert Vishny, and *JFE* editor Jerold Warner. We extend thanks to Eugene Fama (the referee), who also provided us with monthly factor returns. This paper has been presented at the 1994 NBER Behavioral Finance meeting, the 1994 NBER Corporate Finance meeting, the Spring 1994 CRSP Seminar on the Analysis of Security Prices, the 1994 Western Finance Association meetings, the 1994 European Q-group meetings in Lausanne, the 1994 European Finance Association meetings in Brussels, the 1995 American Finance Association meetings, the University of Chicago, the University of Houston, Texas A&M University, and Rice University.

1. Introduction

Corporations distribute substantial sums of wealth to shareholders by repurchasing their own stock. From 1980 to 1990, the aggregate value of stock repurchased on the New York Stock Exchange (NYSE), the American Stock Exchange (ASE), and the National Association of Securities Dealers Automated Quotations (NASDAQ) was about one-third of the value distributed as cash dividends. Toward the end of the 1980s, the dollars involved in repurchases increased substantially, becoming nearly half the amount paid as cash dividends. Framed differently, the dollar value of stock repurchases announced between 1985 and 1993 was nearly three times larger than that raised through initial public offerings (IPOs).[1] In 1994, stock buybacks continued at a record pace, more than $65 billion were announced. Firms can reacquire shares either through tender offers or through open market transactions. Historically, managers have chosen the latter approach by wide margins. For example, 90% of the dollar value of all share repurchases announced between 1985 and 1993 were to be completed through open market transactions. In this paper, we examine the long-run performance of firms that chose this approach for repurchasing shares.

The literature provides a lengthy list of motivations for why corporations might repurchase their own shares: capital structure adjustment, takeover defense, signaling, excess cash distribution, substitution for cash dividends, and wealth expropriation from bondholders. While all of these reasons are plausible, signaling has emerged as one of the most prevalent explanations (Vermaelen, 1981; Dann, 1981; Asquith and Mullins, 1986; Ofer and Thakor, 1987; Constantinides and Grundy, 1989). The Traditional Signaling Hypothesis, or TSH, is motivated by asymmetric information between the marketplace and a firm's managers. If, in management's assessment, the firm is undervalued, they might choose to buy back stock. Making such an announcement is thus argued as serving a valuable signal to a less informed marketplace. If markets respond efficiently, prices should adjust immediately in an unbiased manner. The new equilibrium price should fully reflect the 'true' value of the new information, and no wealth transfer should occur between long-term shareholders and those selling shares to the firm.

When managers are asked why they repurchase shares on the open market, the most commonly cited reason is 'undervaluation' and that their shares represent a 'good investment', two reasons seemingly consistent with the TSH (Baker, Gallagher, and Morgan, 1981; Dann, 1983; Wansley, Lane, and Sarkar,

---

[1] From 1985 to 1993, the total value of all announced share repurchases recorded by Securities Data Company was $334 billion (excluding REITs and closed-end funds). The comparable dollar value of initial public offerings over the same period was $114 billion.

D. Ikenberry et al./Journal of Financial Economics 39 (1995) 181–208   183

1989). Yet, paradoxically, if prices adjust instantaneously, how can the stock be a good investment for long-term shareholders? In an efficient market, the stock should no longer be undervalued after the announcement, thus eliminating the motivation to undertake the repurchase.

However, managers typically do not announce that they are canceling a repurchase program. This would suggest that the initial market reaction is too low. Given that the average market reaction is only on the order of 3%, this would indeed seem to be the case. It hardly seems plausible that managers would, first, have the ability to recognize such small valuation errors, and second, choose to react to such minor discrepancies. Placed in perspective, 3% is not that much greater than the daily standard deviation of returns for many stocks. If managers are reacquiring shares because of mispricing, it is likely that they perceive substantially greater valuation errors. For example, in October 1993, Midland Resources Inc., a U.S.-based oil and gas concern, announced an open market share repurchase for 5% of its shares. At the announcement, the chairman was quoted as saying: 'If you look at the amount of our reserves, we think (our stock) should be trading for about twice its current value. What it boils down to is, if you can buy a dollar for 50 cents, why not buy it?'

We hypothesize that the market treats repurchase announcements with skepticism, leading prices to adjust slowly over time. We refer to this as the Underreaction Hypothesis, or UH. Evidence consistent with this hypothesis has been documented in a study on fixed-price tender offer stock repurchases. Lakonishok and Vermaelen (1990) find that on average, prices remain at bargain levels for at least two years. Other examples of delayed market reactions include IPOs (Ritter, 1991), mergers (Agrawal, Jaffe, and Mandelker, 1992), proxy contests (Ikenberry and Lakonishok, 1993), and spinoffs (Cusatis, Miles, and Woolridge, 1993). In what is essentially the mirror image of a stock repurchase, Loughran and Ritter (1995) observe a sluggish response by the market to seasoned equity offerings.

Is it possible that the market fully incorporates the information conveyed through an open market repurchase? If so, we should observe that stock prices following the announcement are unbiased, and that long-run performance is not above average. Or, alternatively, do managers in fact really know what they are doing and are correct in their assessment that their stock is a good investment, even after the repurchase announcement? These fundamental questions motivate the remainder of this paper.

We examine a sample of 1,239 open market share repurchases announced between January 1980 and December 1990 by firms whose shares traded on the NYSE, ASE, or NASDAQ. Similar to the findings reported in earlier research, the average market response to the announcement of an open market share repurchase is 3.5%. Furthermore, this initial reaction is consistent with several predictions of the TSH. For example, the market reacts more favorably to announcements made by low market capitalization firms and by firms announcing large repurchase programs.

The most striking finding of this paper is that the information conveyed by open market share repurchases is largely ignored. Managers of firms that repurchase their own shares appear to have been correct, on average, in assuming that they can buy shares at bargain prices to the benefit of their long-term shareholders. Beginning in the month following the repurchase announcement, the average buy-and-hold return over the next four years is more than 12% above that of a control portfolio.

If undervaluation is an important motive overall, it should be particularly important for out-of-favor stocks, which tend to have high book-to-market ratios. Yet, surprisingly, the market reaction to repurchase announcements is similar across all book-to-market groups. Over the long run, however, the largest abnormal returns following buyback announcements are observed in high book-to-market firms. The average return over the next four years for a buy-and-hold portfolio of these stocks is 45.3% above that of a control portfolio of similar size and book-to-market firms. For low book-to-market firms, no abnormal performance is observed in long-run returns.

The remainder of the paper is organized as follows: In Section 2, we describe the data and our sample. Issues regarding performance measurement and significance tests are discussed in Section 3. In Section 4, we examine daily returns surrounding the announcement of open market share repurchases. In Section 5, we examine long-run performance. In Section 6, we explore the determinants of long-run performance. In Section 7, we check the robustness of our findings. Conclusions are provided in Section 8.

2. Data

Our sample was formed by identifying all announcements reported in the *Wall Street Journal* from January 1980 through December 1990 that stated that a firm intended to repurchase its own common stock through open market transactions. We examine all open market share repurchase announcements without regard to whether the programs were actually completed. We further require that these firms be included on the daily Center for Research in Security Prices (CRSP) NYSE and ASE tapes or daily CRSP NASDAQ tapes, as well as the annual industrial Compustat file at the time of the announcement. For most of our analysis, we exclude all announcements made in the fourth quarter of 1987. Following the 1987 crash, 777 NYSE, ASE, and NASDAQ firms announced either new or increased share repurchase programs totalling over $45 billion, largely in response to their low post-crash share prices. Although we also examined announcements made during this period, these cases are not included in the results we report in order to avoid having this unusual period dominate our study.

D. Ikenberry et al./Journal of Financial Economics 39 (1995) 181–208   185

Table 1 shows the distribution of the repurchase announcements by year, the average percentage of shares repurchased, and the dollar value of the repurchase announcements. These repurchases, if fully completed, would have totalled $142 billion. Over the entire 11-year period, sample companies announced repurchases for, on average, 6.6% of their outstanding shares. This percentage generally rose over our sample period. Table 1 also shows the distribution of announcements according to firm size. Size deciles were determined in the month prior to the announcement, and were based on market equity value relative to the universe of all NYSE and ASE stocks covered by both CRSP and Compustat. Our sample has a bias favoring larger firms. Nearly one-third of our sample is ranked in the two largest size deciles.

3. Methodology

3.1. Performance measurement

We examine both short-term returns surrounding the announcement and long-term performance following the announcement. Short-term performance is calculated over various windows from 20 days before to 10 days following the announcement. When abnormal returns are calculated over such short intervals, the results are not overly sensitive to the benchmark used. Thus, we report results using a straightforward approach, calculating abnormal returns in relation to the CRSP equal-weighted index of NYSE and ASE firms. We also calculated short-term performance relative to other benchmarks, including the CRSP value-weighted index as well as a size-based approach, but the results were essentially the same.

Care must be taken when calculating long-run performance, because the findings can be sensitive to the procedures used (see Chopra, Lakonishok, and Ritter, 1992). In this paper, we pursue two different approaches. The first is the more common technique based on cumulative abnormal returns (CARs) relative to some benchmark. The second approach calculates long-run abnormal performance assuming a buy-and-hold strategy. For both of these methods, abnormal returns are calculated relative to four benchmarks: the CRSP equal- and value-weighted indices of NYSE and ASE firms, a size-based benchmark, and a size- and book-to-market-based benchmark. This last benchmark is motivated by the recent work of Fama and French (1992, 1993) and Lakonishok, Shleifer, and Vishny (1994).[2]

---

[2]To distinguish 'value' stocks from 'glamour' stocks, a variety of ratios exist aside from book-to-market. From example, Lakonishok, Shleifer, and Vishny (1994) find that classifying stocks by cash-flow-to-price produces an even larger spread in returns than does sorting by book-to-market. However, sorting on the basis of cash-flow-to-price poses some difficulties when cash flow becomes negative. Hence, we classify firms using book-to-market ratios.

Table 1
Descriptive statistics for open market share repurchase announcements between January 1980 and December 1990

This table reports the number of open market share repurchases announced in the *Wall Street Journal* by year for ASE, NYSE, and NASDAQ firms, the dollar value of these announcements, the percent of shares announced for repurchase, and the size decile rank of the firms when the announcement was made. In some cases, firms did not state the number of shares they intended to repurchase. Size decile rankings are determined relative to all ASE and NYSE firms on the annual industrial Compustat tape in the month prior to the repurchase announcement, where the smallest firms are ranked in decile 1.

Year	n	$ (billion)	Mean % of share announced	Percent of shares announced for repurchase					Size decile rank at announcement				
				0 to 2.5%	2.5 to 5%	5 to 10%	Above 10%	Not stated	Small 1-2	3-4	5-6	7-8	Large 9-10
1980	86	1.429	4.73	31	20	27	6	2	9	15	16	18	28
1981	95	3.013	5.24	29	26	23	13	4	13	12	16	21	33
1982	128	3.106	5.74	25	38	42	18	5	22	14	35	21	33
1983	43	1.645	5.05	11	18	9	3	2	5	4	6	10	18
1984	203	10.105	5.57	34	78	53	24	14	35	39	50	28	51
1985	113	14.380	7.45	22	30	34	24	3	16	23	17	18	39
1986	145	17.189	7.12	30	36	37	33	9	17	27	26	29	46
1987	92	27.380	7.92	14	20	31	26	1	10	15	14	18	35
1988	121	14.967	7.15	20	30	38	26	7	17	15	23	24	42
1989	117	31.971	8.53	18	28	35	33	3	14	15	17	24	47
1990	96	17.403	7.84	10	28	37	21	0	14	18	15	18	31
All years	1239	142.587	6.64	244	352	366	227	50	172	197	235	229	406

For 1987 all announcements made in the fourth quarter are excluded.

D. Ikenberry et al. /Journal of Financial Economics 39 (1995) 181–208   187

3.1.1. The CAR approach

Under the CAR approach, abnormal returns are calculated each month relative to a benchmark, and then aggregated over time. This procedure assumes monthly rebalancing, with sample firms receiving equal portfolio weights each month. Furthermore, abnormal performance is not based on compounded returns. Although takeovers and bankruptcies reduce the number of firms in the sample as event-time progresses, these cases are not excluded from our analysis. Abnormal performance is measured using the returns to all companies existing in a given event month, even those that eventually depart the sample.

Calculating performance relative to the CRSP equal- and value-weighted indices is straightforward and requires no further discussion. To calculate abnormal returns adjusted for size, we form ten size-based portfolios at the end of April each year, using all NYSE and ASE firms on both CRSP and Compustat. Monthly returns are calculated for these ten portfolios over the next year, assuming equal weighting. These returns are then used as benchmarks to measure abnormal performance. Each month, abnormal returns are calculated for each repurchase firm relative to its respective size benchmark. CARs are then calculated by averaging across all repurchase firms each month, and summing over time.

To calculate abnormal returns controlling for both size and book-to-market, each of the ten size deciles discussed above is further sorted by book-to-market ratio into quintiles. Quintile 1 contains the 20% of all stocks in a given size decile with the lowest book-to-market ratios. At the other extreme are the 20% of firms within a given size decile with the highest ratios. This sorting results in 50 benchmark portfolios for each month (10 size deciles times 5 book-to-market quintiles). As is done when we adjust only for size, all firms are ranked at the end of each April for the following 12 months. We assume a four-month lag in reporting financial results to avoid any look-ahead bias. Thus, for companies whose fiscal year ends in December, the book equity value will be recent. For firms with fiscal year-ends following December but preceding April, we calculate book-to-market ratios using book equity values from the prior year. Abnormal performance for each of the repurchase firms is then calculated using the appropriate size and book-to-market benchmark.[3]

---

[3]As a check on the validity of this approach, we examined whether a randomly drawn sample with the same size and book-to-market characteristics would also produce abnormal performance. We did this by pooling the announcement dates of all repurchases firms along with their corresponding size and book-to-market rankings. We then formed a random sample by arbitrarily drawing from this pool 2,500 times and assigning the announcement date to a randomly chosen NYSE or ASE firm that had the same size and book-to-market ranking at that point in time. In each of the 48 months following the 'event' month, the cumulative abnormal return for this random sample was less than $\pm 1.5\%$, using the size and book-to-market approach, and was always within one standard error. When performance was measured using the CRSP equal- or value-weighted index of NYSE and ASE stocks, CARs were in excess of two standard errors in many cases.

3.1.2. The buy-and-hold approach

The results obtained using the CAR approach should be regarded as descriptive in nature, since they do not represent a realistic investment strategy. However, our second approach presents a more feasible strategy. We assume an equal-weighted buy-and-hold investment in all repurchase firms beginning in the month following the announcement and continuing for 12 months. After one year, the portfolio is rebalanced, thus reducing the possibility that a small set of firms will dominate the return calculations. The multi-year total return to this investment strategy is calculated by compounding average annual returns over time.

If a firms departs the sample prematurely, we assume the investment is sold at the last available price on CRSP, and that the proceeds from this sale are reinvested for the remainder of the year in that firm's benchmark portfolio. At the end of the year, the portfolio is rebalanced, using only the surviving firms. Firms used to calculate benchmark returns were treated similarly.

To calculate abnormal performance, we form four benchmarks. These are similar in spirit to the four benchmarks created for the CAR approach, but calculated in a manner consistent with the buy-and-hold investment strategy. To save space, we report results only for the size and book-to-market benchmark approach. To form the reference portfolio, all firms listed on the NYSE and ASE and also carried on Compustat are sorted each month into one of 50 size and book-to-market portfolios, as described earlier. Beginning in the next month, the one-year buy-and-hold return is calculated for each firm in a given portfolio. The equal-weighted average of all annual returns in a given portfolio is then used as a benchmark return for firms ranked in that particular size and book-to-market rank at that point in time. Thus, this procedure leads us to compute annual buy-and-hold returns for each of the 50 benchmark portfolios each calendar month.

In addition to annual returns, we also measure compounded abnormal performance for two, three, and four years following the repurchase announcement. To calculate a two-year abnormal return, we take the difference between the compounded two-year return to repurchase firms, assuming rebalancing after the first year, and that of the reference portfolio.[4] Abnormal performance in years three and four is treated similarly.

3.2. Significance testing

Significance levels are calculated for daily, monthly, and annual returns. For daily cumulative abnormal returns, we use the event-time methodology outlined

---

[4]The size and book-to-market ranking of a particular firm may change from year to year. To accommodate this, we also allow the benchmark used to compute abnormal performance to change over time.

D. Ikenberry et al./Journal of Financial Economics 39 (1995) 181–208   189

by Brown and Warner (1985). Here, standard errors are estimated from the time series of daily portfolio abnormal returns calculated over days -250 to -21 relative to the repurchase announcement. Autocorrelation in daily abnormal returns in this study is low. Corrections we made for autocorrelation had essentially no impact on the results. Thus, we present t-tests that assume zero autocorrelation. To estimate significance levels for monthly CARs, we also use the event-time methodology described by Brown and Warner (1980). Standard errors are calculated in a similar fashion, using months -36 to $+48$ relative to the repurchase announcements. As before, we calculate t-tests assuming time independence, since corrections for autocorrelation had essentially no impact on the analysis.

For a variety of reasons, the approach described above is not appropriate when examining annual buy-and-hold or compounded multi-year returns. For example, estimating standard errors using an event-time approach requires a reasonable number of annual observations. Many firms simply do not have a long history of returns. Moreover, for those firms where the availability of returns is not an issue, it is questionable whether the return distribution is stable over such a long period of time. Further, since buy-and-hold returns are compounded rather than cumulated over time, multi-year standard errors cannot be simply inferred from annual standard errors. And finally, the skewness of long-run returns and the clustering of observations in time also pose problems for traditional significance tests.

Therefore, statistical inference of annual buy-and-hold and compounded multi-year returns is done via bootstrapping, as applied by Brock, Lakonishok, and LeBaron (1992) in their examination of technical trading strategies. Under this approach, we generate the empirical distribution of annual buy-and-hold and multi-year compounded abnormal returns under the null hypothesis. Specifically, for each repurchase announcement in our sample, we randomly select with replacement a firm listed on the NYSE or ASE that has the same size and book-to-market ranking at that point in time. We treat this randomly chosen company as if it had announced a repurchase on the same day as the corresponding repurchase firm. This matching process continues until each firm in our repurchase sample is represented in this pseudo-portfolio. This portfolio will have one randomly drawn firm for each actual repurchase firm, matched in time with similar size and book-to-market characteristics. After forming a single pseudo-portfolio, we estimate long-run performance in the same manner as we did for the repurchase sample. This yields one observation of the abnormal performance obtained from randomly forming a portfolio with the same characteristics as our repurchase sample. This entire process is repeated until we have 1,000 pseudo-portfolios, and thus 1,000 abnormal return observations. This provides us with an empirical approximation of the distribution of abnormal returns drawn under the null model specific to our sample. The null hypothesis is rejected at the α percent level if the abnormal return obtained from the repurchase sample is greater than the $(1 - \alpha)$ percentile abnormal return observed in the empirical distribution. The appeal of the bootstrap approach is that it avoids many of the problems that plague *t*-tests regarding assumptions over normality, stationarity, and time independence of observations. Departures from these basic assumptions are especially worrisome for returns calculated over long intervals, such as a year or more. To the extent that these problems exist in long-run returns, they are also present in our pseudo-portfolios, and thus are controlled for in our tests.

We also examine long-run firm performance by time period as well as by book-to-market ranking at the time of the repurchase announcement. The associated *p*-values are estimated by repeating the entire bootstrap procedure for each subsample. For example, when we report long-run performance for high book-to-market stocks announcing buybacks, the associated *p*-values are derived from the distribution of abnormal returns obtained from 1,000 pseudo-portfolios specifically matched to this particular subsample.

4. The market reaction to open market share repurchase announcements

Table 2 provides a comprehensive analysis of short-term abnormal returns surrounding repurchase announcements in our sample. Looking at repurchase announcements overall, there are negative abnormal returns prior to the announcement, measured from days -20 to -3, totalling -3.07%. The average market reaction, measured from two days before through two days following publication of the announcement in the *Wall Street Journal*, is 3.54%. Following the announcement, returns appear on average to be quite similar to those of the market. This evidence is similar to the findings reported by other researchers examining repurchase announcements (for example, Vermaelen, 1981; Comment and Jarrell, 1991).

The initial market reaction changes only slightly across subperiods, decreasing from 4.25% between 1980 and 1983 to 2.33% in the period 1987 to 1990. Consistent with the TSH, larger share repurchase programs are received more favorably by the market. For example, the mean announcement period abnormal return is 4.51% for programs which are for more than 10% of outstanding shares. For those programs which are for less than 2.5% of outstanding shares, the average market reaction is 2.58%.

Table 2 also reports short-term announcement returns according to the reason provided in the abstract of the *Wall Street Journal Index*. Some caution should be exercised here, since it is difficult to assess management's true motivation for the repurchase by reading such abbreviated press statements. Furthermore, no reason was mentioned in nearly 85% of the cases. But for the few cases in which a reason was mentioned, undervaluation was a prominent theme. For the 38 cases in which undervaluation was specifically mentioned,

D. Ikenberry et al. / Journal of Financial Economics 39 (1995) 181–208   191

both the negative drift prior to the announcement (− 5.52%) and the market reaction at the announcement (5.31%) were comparatively large.

The size decile panel in Table 2 shows short-term performance by firm size. The market reaction shows clear differences across size groups. Firms ranked in the two smallest size deciles show the highest abnormal returns on average, 8.19%, more than double that observed overall. Those in the two largest size deciles exhibit an abnormal return of only 2.09%. If firm size is viewed as a proxy for information asymmetries, the observed relationship between size and abnormal returns is consistent with the TSH.

Separating the various motivations for undertaking an open market stock repurchase is difficult. One approach is to examine announcement returns in relation to book-to-market ratios. Firms with low book-to-market ratios are likely to repurchase shares for reasons other than undervaluation. At the other extreme, repurchases announced by firms with high book-to-market ratios, or value stocks, are more likely to have undervaluation as their primary motivation. However, we see in Table 2 that the market reaction to the repurchase announcement is similar across the five book-to-market quintiles. The average market reaction for firms in quintile 1 (glamour stocks) is 3.36%, while it is 3.56% for firms in quintile 5 (value stocks).

To further clarify the nature of announcement returns, we regressed announcement returns on various firm characteristics. To control for the possibility that positive announcement returns reflect mean reversion arising from negative returns observed prior to the announcement, we also included in the regression the CAR from days − 20 to − 3. Although not reported here, the results are consistent with the evidence reported in Table 2, even after controlling for the impact of return reversals. As the percentage of shares announced for repurchase increases, the market reaction increases, and as firm size increases, announcement returns decline substantially. Yet, as before, the regression results provide no indication that the book-to-market ratio has any impact on the market reaction to repurchase announcements.

5. The long-term performance of firms repurchasing their own shares

Fig. 1 plots CARs up to 48 months following a repurchase announcement, using four different benchmarks. These CARs are calculated beginning in month 1, and thus exclude the initial market reaction to the announcement. The picture that emerges is that firms that announce an open market stock repurchase tend to perform abnormally well in the long run. Focusing on size-adjusted returns, the CAR from month 1 to 36 is 8.69% ($t = 2.50$). Following month 36, abnormal returns are close to zero. This positive drift cannot be explained by the book-to-market effect. When returns are adjusted for both size and book-to-market, the CAR from month 1 to 36 is nearly the same, 8.17% ($t = 2.37$). Focusing only on

192 D. Ikenberry et al./Journal of Financial Economics 39 (1995) 181–208

Table 2

Abnormal returns on and around the announcement of open market share repurchases, 1980 to 1990

The table reports abnormal returns (in percent) measured with respect to the CRSP equal-weighted index over days −20 to −3, −2 to +2, and +3 to +10 relative to the announcement of an open market share repurchase made during the period January 1980 through December 1990 (t-statistics reported in parentheses). Abnormal returns are reported for all sample firms and by time period, the percentage of shares announced for repurchase, the reason stated by the company for the repurchase (if any), the size decile rank, and the book-to-market quintile rank in the month prior to announcement.

	n	Days relative to repurchase announcement		
		−20 to −3	−2 to +2	+3 to +10
All firms	1239	−3.07 (−9.91)	3.54 (21.72)	0.21 (1.00)
Time period				
1980 to 1983	352	−3.59 (−6.40)	4.25 (14.37)	0.91 (2.42)
1984 to 1986	461	−2.86 (−6.47)	4.12 (17.71)	−0.03 (−0.09)
1987 to 1990	426	−2.86 (−5.79)	2.33 (8.94)	−0.12 (−0.36)
Percent intended to repurchase				
0 to 2.5%	241	−4.68 (−8.11)	2.58 (8.50)	0.77 (2.00)
2.5 to 5%	335	−4.01 (−7.78)	2.87 (10.54)	0.12 (0.34)
5 to 10%	367	−2.80 (−5.22)	3.86 (13.64)	0.11 (0.30)
At or above 10%	246	−0.59 (−0.83)	4.51 (12.02)	−0.24 (−0.52)
Not disclosed	50	−3.09 (−2.01)	5.57 (6.88)	1.03 (1.01)

D. Ikenberry et al. / Journal of Financial Economics 39 (1995) 181–208   193

Stated reason			
Undervalued	38	−5.52 (−3.38)	5.31 (6.17)	−1.29 (−1.18)
Anti-takeover	7	6.79 (2.09)	5.50 (3.21)	3.76 (1.74)
ESOP or stock option	82	−1.69 (−1.70)	3.00 (5.71)	0.24 (0.36)
Acquisition	9	−3.87 (−1.39)	2.56 (1.75)	1.49 (0.80)
General corp. purposes	16	−1.32 (−0.67)	1.83 (1.77)	2.27 (1.73)
Other	27	−2.79 (−1.73)	2.52 (2.98)	−1.19 (−1.11)
Not disclosed	1060	−3.18 (−9.57)	3.57 (20.40)	0.23 (1.03)
Size decile			
1–2 (small firms)	172	−3.91 (−3.12)	8.19 (12.41)	0.70 (0.83)
3–4	197	−5.71 (−6.62)	4.67 (10.27)	−0.76 (−1.32)
5–6	235	−2.99 (−4.50)	3.08 (8.79)	0.20 (0.46)
7–8	229	−3.53 (−6.08)	2.13 (6.96)	0.70 (1.80)
9–10 (large firms)	406	−1.21 (−3.61)	2.09 (11.84)	0.19 (0.86)
Book-to-market quintile			
1 (glamour stocks)	201	−3.53 (−3.78)	3.36 (6.84)	0.11 (0.18)
2	260	−4.30 (−6.72)	3.14 (9.32)	0.48 (1.12)
3	276	−2.72 (−4.50)	4.07 (12.80)	0.15 (0.37)
4	230	−2.54 (−4.06)	3.46 (10.51)	0.21 (0.49)
5 (value stocks)	241	−2.17 (−3.76)	3.56 (11.71)	0.07 (0.18)

194   *D. Ikenberry et al./Journal of Financial Economics 39 (1995) 181–208*

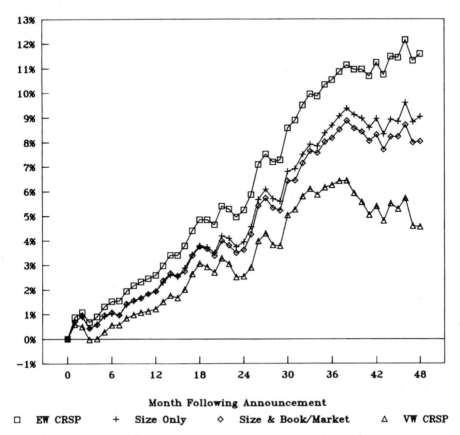

Month Following Announcement

□ **EW CRSP**   + **Size Only**   ◇ **Size & Book/Market**   △ **VW CRSP**

Fig. 1. Comparative monthly cumulative abnormal returns following open market share repurchase announcements, 1980–1990.

This figure plots the cumulative abnormal return (CAR) up to 48 months following the announcement of an open market share repurchase. Abnormal returns are calculated using four different methods; market-adjusted returns using the CRSP equal-weighted index of ASE and NYSE firms (EW CRSP), size-adjusted returns using equal-weighted portfolio returns of NYSE and ASE firms from the same size decile (Size Only), size and book-to-market adjusted returns using equal-weighted portfolio returns of NYSE and ASE firms from the same size decile and book-to-market quintile (Size & Book/Market), and market-adjusted returns using the CRSP value-weighted index of NYSE and ASE firms (VW CRSP).

the initial market reaction (3.5%), about 70% of the total valuation impact is ignored.

The picture is slightly different when the CRSP value-weighted index is used as a benchmark. Although post-announcement abnormal returns are positive, they are lower than when either the size-only or size and book-to-market

D. Ikenberry et al. / Journal of Financial Economics 39 (1995) 181–208 195

benchmarks are used, and are about half that observed using the CRSP equal-weighted index. This occurs because large firms substantially outperformed smaller firms during the latter portion of our sample period.

Although the CAR approach is straightforward, the analysis is best regarded as descriptive in nature. A more appealing approach is the buy-and-hold procedure described earlier. The results using such an approach are reported in Table 3.[5] The left-hand side of Table 3 shows mean annual returns from buying an equal-weighted portfolio of repurchasing firms, beginning in the month following the announcement and for the subsequent four years. To the right of this column are returns to the reference portfolio, calculated using the size and book-to-market benchmarks corresponding to the repurchase sample. The right side of Table 3 reports total compounded buy-and-hold returns up to four years, allowing for annual rebalancing. Results are also presented for two subperiods; announcements made in years 1980 to 1985 and those made in years 1986 to 1990.

The average return in the first year following the repurchase announcement is 20.80%, 2.04% more than the reference portfolio. This difference in annual returns increases to 2.31% and 4.59% in years 2 and 3, respectively. As we observed in Fig. 1, the phenomenon appears to dissipate by year 4, when the difference is close to zero. Although not reported in the tables, we also examined performance in year 5 and again found abnormal returns close to zero (− 0.13%).

Turning to compounded returns, the difference in performance after four years is substantial, 12.14%. The *p*-value associated with this abnormal return is 0.012. In Fig. 2, we plot the empirical distribution of four-year compounded abnormal returns under the null hypothesis based on our bootstrapping procedure, using 1,000 replications. From this figure, we see that the probability that a random portfolio will exhibit abnormal performance as high as our repurchase sample is remote. In our case, only 12 of the 1,000 pseudo-portfolios demonstrated compounded abnormal returns higher than 12.14% after four years. Focusing on year 3, the difference in compounded returns between the repurchase and the reference portfolio is 12.60% with a corresponding *p*-value of 0.000, meaning that none of the 1,000 pseudo-portfolios performed as well. Apparently, investing in companies that announce buybacks is a profitable long-run strategy, at least over the decade of the 1980s.

When we turn our attention to the two subperiods, we observe some differences in long-run performance. In the early subperiod, 1980–1985, the compounded abnormal return is 16.02% in year 3. This value decreases slightly to

---

[5]Because book-equity values were not available for some firms, the number of firms in this table differs slightly from that reported in Table 2.

Table 3
Annual buy-and-hold returns following open market share repurchase announcements, 1980 to 1990

This table reports annual and compounded buy-and-hold returns (in percent) following open market share repurchase announcements for up to four years. Equal-weighted portfolios are formed for all announcements between 1980 and 1990, and for two subperiods, 1980 through 1985 and 1986 through 1990. The reference portfolio is formed using benchmark returns corresponding to the repurchase sample, matched on the basis of size and book-to-market ranking. Compounded holding-period returns assume annual rebalancing. Significance levels are determined via bootstrapping.

	n	Annual buy-and-hold returns				Compounded holding-period returns			
		Repurchase firms	Reference portfolio	Diff.	p-value	Repurchase firms	Reference portfolio	Diff.	p-value
All firms									
Year 1	1208	20.80	18.76	2.04	0.064	20.80	18.76	2.04	0.064
Year 2	1188	18.12	15.81	2.31	0.098	42.69	37.53	5.16	0.011
Year 3	1047	21.77	17.18	4.59	0.002	73.75	61.15	12.60	0.000
Year 4	893	8.56	9.51	−0.96	0.892	88.62	76.48	12.14	0.012
1980 to 1985									
Year 1	646	32.36	28.89	3.47	0.029	32.36	28.89	3.47	0.029
Year 2	637	25.23	21.76	3.47	0.017	65.75	56.93	8.82	0.002
Year 3	615	21.79	18.43	3.36	0.035	101.87	85.85	16.02	0.000
Year 4	583	10.38	12.07	−1.68	0.938	122.83	108.28	14.55	0.024
1986 to 1990									
Year 1	562	7.52	7.11	0.41	0.444	7.52	7.11	0.41	0.444
Year 2	551	9.91	8.93	0.97	0.338	18.17	16.68	1.49	0.349
Year 3	432	21.73	15.39	6.34	0.008	43.85	34.64	9.21	0.032
Year 4	310	5.12	4.71	0.41	0.531	51.22	40.98	10.24	0.092

D. Ikenberry et al. / Journal of Financial Economics 39 (1995) 181–208   197

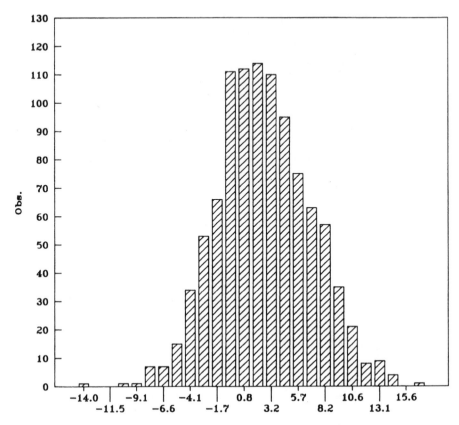

Fig. 2. Compounded four-year abnormal performance (in percent) adjusted for size and book-to-market under the null hypothesis for open market share repurchase announcements between January 1980 and December 1990.

This histogram plots the empirical distribution of four-year compounded abnormal returns for 1000 bootstrap portfolios specific to our sample of repurchase announcements. Each portfolio is formed by taking the post-announcement returns for a given sample firm and replacing them with the returns to a firm randomly chosen from the NYSE or ASE with the same size and book-to-market classification at that point in time. This is done for each firm in the sample, thus forming a single portfolio. This entire process is then repeated until 1000 such portfolios are formed. The compounded abnormal performance from these randomly formed portfolios provides us with an empirical estimate of the distribution relevant to the entire sample of repurchase announcements in our study. The empirical distributions for subsamples are unique and are therefore estimated separately.

14.55% in year 4. In both years, abnormal performance is statistically significant at traditional confidence levels. In the later subperiod, 1986–1990, compounded abnormal performance after year 3 is 9.21% and is highly significant. In year 4, compounded abnormal performance increases slightly to 10.24%, but is only marginally significant. Of course, some variation from one subperiod to another is to be expected. Yet the impact of year 3 in the later subperiod and the focus of our study on the 1980s may give some cause for concern regarding robustness. Nevertheless, the results overall are significant. Moreover, we can look to other related papers which report evidence consistent with our findings. For example, Nelson (1994) uses CRSP data from 1926 to 1985 to examine firms that made substantial changes in the number of shares outstanding. He reports superior long-run performance for companies that decrease shares outstanding, most of which occurs prior to year 4. He also finds inferior long-run performance for firms that increase shares. In the context of tender offer repurchases, Lakonishok and Vermaelen (1990) also report evidence of a prolonged positive drift for announcements made between 1962 and 1986.

6. Undervaluation as a motive for open market share repurchases

6.1. Long-term performance by book-to-market quintile

Undervaluation appears to be an important factor motivating companies to repurchase shares. However, a variety of other motives also exist. An interesting question is whether the excess long-run performance we observe overall is more pronounced in those cases that are more clearly motivated by undervaluation. Identifying such firms *ex ante* is, of course, a challenge. One possibility, though, is to examine long-run performance conditional on book-to-market ratios.

Several recent studies report that firms with high book-to-market ratios have substantially higher returns than those with low book-to-market ratios. Lakonishok, Shleifer, and Vishny (1994) find that this difference cannot be explained by risk, but is instead due to behavioral and institutional considerations. Many underpriced stocks have high book-to-market ratios. If the propensity to repurchase shares is related to the degree of underpricing, one would expect the most undervalued firms among those with high book-to-market ratios to be active in buybacks. If the market underreacts to buyback announcements, high book-to-market firms announcing buybacks should not only outperform the overall market, but also outperform a benchmark that adjusts for book-to-market. To some degree, this argument parallels that of Lakonishok, Shleifer, and Vishny (1994). They observe that not all high book-to-market stocks are truly out-of-favor. Using a variety of two-way classifications, they find differences in the stock returns of high book-to-market firms. For example, high book-to-market stocks that performed well in the past substantially underperform high book-to-market stocks with poor past performance, or firms that might be considered truly out-of-favor.

On the other hand, if managers in low book-to-market firms have the same ability to recognize undervaluation, they too will tend to announce buybacks when their stock is undervalued. However, Lakonishok, Shleifer, and Vishny (1994) suggest that few of these stocks are truly underpriced. If underpricing were the only motive for repurchasing shares, one would expect few low book-to-market companies to be involved in buybacks. Yet the evidence in Table 2 shows that the propensity for low book-to-market firms to announce buybacks is nearly the same as for high book-to-market firms. Thus, for these firms, the motivation for repurchasing shares would not seem to be dominated by undervaluation. For example, managers in low book-to-market firms may view buybacks as a way to artificially support prices that have typically risen dramatically in the recent past. In addition, executives in low book-to-market firms are more likely than executives in high book-to-market firms to take advantage of prior stock performance by exercising options. As these options are exercised, many firms choose to repurchase shares to avoid dilution in ownership. And finally, given the relatively superior past performance of low book-to-market companies, managers in these firms may be more prone to hubris, and thus repurchase shares that are not underpriced. Thus, for firms with low book-to-market ratios, true undervaluation would not appear to be as important a motive for repurchasing shares as it would be for firms at the other end of the spectrum.

In Table 4, we report long-run performance by book-to-market ranking at the time of the repurchase announcement. Focusing on high book-to-market (or value) stocks in quintile 5, the results are striking. Here, the compounded four-year buy-and-hold return is 135.91%, 45.29% above the reference portfolio return of similar size and book-to-market companies. The associated *p*-value here is 0.000, meaning that none of the 1,000 pseudo-portfolios specifically formed for this subsample performed as well.[6] This extraordinary performance is not limited to a small number of cases. Value stocks comprise 26.2% of the sample measured on a dollar-weighted basis. To check the robustness of our findings for value stocks, we also calculated long-run performance for this group on a year-by-year basis. In each case, four-year compounded abnormal returns were positive.[7]

---

[6]As we observed overall, the positive drift observed in value stocks repurchasing shares is generally confined to the first three years. By year 4, the difference between this portfolio and its respective benchmark, though positive (3.23%), is not significant using traditional confidence levels. As a check, we also examined performance in year 5, and found that the difference narrows further to 2.06%.

[7]Four-year compounded abnormal returns can be computed for those announcements made prior to 1989. The aveage four-year compounded abnormal return on a year-by-year basis is as follows: 1980, 57.1%; 1981, 23.5%; 1982, 213.1%; 1983, 25.5%; 1984, 13.0%; 1985, 72.6%; 1986, 15.0%; 1987, 15.4%; 1988, 32.4%.

Table 4
Annual and compounded buy-and-hold returns by book-to-market quintile following open market share repurchase announcements, 1980 to 1990

This table reports annual and compounded buy-and-hold returns (in percent) for equal-weighted portfolios of firms announcing open market share repurchases, for up to four years following an open market share repurchase announcement by book-to-market quintile ranking. Ranks are determined by sorting into size deciles all NYSE and ASE firms on the annual industrial Compustat tape. Each decile is further sorted into quintiles on the basis of book-to-market, with the lowest ratios assigned to quintile 1. Firms that could not be ranked at the time of the announcement are excluded. The reference portfolio comprises benchmark returns matched to the repurchase sample on the basis of size and book-to-market. Compounded holding-period returns assume annual rebalancing. Significance levels are determined via bootstrapping.

		Annual buy-and-hold returns				Compounded holding-period returns			
	n	Repurchase firms	Reference portfolio	Diff.	p-value	Repurchase firms	Reference portfolio	Diff.	p-value
Book-to-market quintile 1 (glamour stocks)									
Year 1	201	15.72	16.83	−1.11	0.687	15.72	16.83	−1.11	0.687
Year 2	195	17.86	16.60	1.26	0.136	36.40	36.22	0.18	0.526
Year 3	184	12.00	13.61	−1.61	0.568	52.77	54.75	−1.98	0.397
Year 4	158	4.98	6.42	−1.44	0.330	60.38	64.69	−4.31	0.358

D. Ikenberry et al./Journal of Financial Economics 39 (1995) 181–208

Book-to-market quintile 2

Year 1	260	20.59	18.43	2.16	0.206	20.59	18.43	2.16	0.206
Year 2	250	12.34	15.07	−2.73	0.487	35.47	36.28	−0.81	0.625
Year 3	223	22.39	17.29	5.10	0.070	65.80	59.84	5.96	0.220
Year 4	191	3.20	6.99	−3.79	0.668	71.10	71.02	0.08	0.498

Book-to-market quintile 3

Year 1	276	19.49	16.46	3.03	0.087	19.49	16.46	3.03	0.087
Year 2	268	18.23	17.33	0.90	0.487	41.27	36.64	4.63	0.174
Year 3	225	20.77	16.57	4.20	0.070	70.61	59.29	11.32	0.058
Year 4	184	7.45	10.35	−2.90	0.635	83.32	75.78	7.54	0.308

Book-to-market quintile 4

Year 1	230	23.43	22.84	0.59	0.374	23.43	22.84	0.59	0.374
Year 2	228	15.16	12.73	2.43	0.178	42.14	38.48	3.66	0.197
Year 3	198	24.05	18.32	5.73	0.067	76.32	63.85	12.47	0.058
Year 4	172	12.44	11.06	1.38	0.567	98.24	81.97	16.27	0.144

Book-to-market quintile 5 (value stocks)

Year 1	241	24.15	19.49	4.66	0.054	24.15	19.49	4.66	0.054
Year 2	234	26.01	17.23	8.78	0.003	56.44	40.08	6.36	0.003
Year 3	199	29.81	20.49	9.32	0.013	103.07	68.78	34.29	0.000
Year 4	169	16.17	12.94	3.23	0.389	135.91	90.62	45.29	0.000

Although we might expect the quintile 5 stocks in our sample to be the most undervalued at the time of the announcement, long-run abnormal performance is not exclusive to this subset. For example, firms in quintile 4, which constitute 21.3% of our sample when measured on a dollar-weighted basis, show average abnormal performance of 12.47% after year 3 with an associated *p*-value of 0.058. As we move from value stocks toward glamour stocks, long-run performance declines. For example, the mean four-year compounded abnormal return for glamour stocks in quintile 1 is slightly negative, -4.31%.

To investigate further the impact of the book-to-market variable, we examine the determinants of long-run performance following announcements. We do this by estimating a cross-sectional regression where the four-year compounded abnormal return is the dependent variable. If a firm leaves the sample midway through the four-year period, we assume that the stock is sold and that the proceeds are reinvested in the reference portfolio so that four-year performance is available for all companies in our sample. The independent variables are the book-to-market quintile ranking, the size decile ranking, the fraction of shares they intend to repurchase, and the three-year abnormal return prior to the repurchase to control for mean reversion in returns. Although we do not report these results here, book-to-market is by far the strongest variable related to long-run performance.

7. Robustness

In this section, we examine the robustness of our findings, especially with respect to repurchases announced by value stocks where abnormal returns are particularly high. Specifically, we explore three issues: the impact of takeovers, performance measurement, and multiple announcements.

7.1. The impact of takeovers

It is possible that the abnormal performance observed for firms repurchasing shares is caused by an unusually high incidence of takeovers. To the extent that this is not anticipated by the market, the upward drift may be a consequence of takeover premiums. This might be a particularly relevant issue for value stocks, whose relatively low prices may have been attractive to bidding firms. To investigate this possibility, we compared long-run performance overall with that observed for only those firms that survived at least four years following the announcement. Three-year compounded abnormal performance for announcements made between 1980 and 1988 is 13.0%. Of this group, 84.4% survived. Focusing only on survivors, the three-year compounded abnormal return diminishes to 6.7%, though still significant.

D. Ikenberry et al. / Journal of Financial Economics 39 (1995) 181–208   203

For repurchase firms ranked in the highest book-to-market quintile, returns also diminish when we focus on survivors, yet abnormal performance is still extremely positive. Here, compounded three-year abnormal performance falls from 39.7% using all eligible firms to 31.6% when only survivors are examined. The survival rate in this group (86.2%) differs little from that observed overall. Thus, the presence of takeovers in our sample does not appear to explain the abnormal returns of firms that repurchase shares, particularly in those cases in which book-to-market ratios are high and long-run performance is so positive.

7.2. Performance measurement

Fama and French (1993) suggest a three-factor model to measure abnormal performance. The first factor is the excess return to a value-weighted portfolio of NYSE, ASE, and NASDAQ stocks. The second and third factors represent size and book-to-market factors. These two factors are formed by sorting NYSE, ASE, and NASDAQ stocks on the basis of market equity into either a small-cap or large-cap portfolio measured relative to the median NYSE stock at the end of each June. These same stocks are also independently sorted on the basis of book-to-market into one of three portfolios. Those whose low book-to-market ratios rank them in the bottom 30% of all NYSE stocks are sorted into the first portfolio. Those with ratio values among the middle 40% of all NYSE stocks are included in the second portfolio, while the third portfolio contains those stocks with high book-to-market ratios that rank them among the top 30% of NYSE stocks. Value-weighted returns are calculated on a monthly basis for six portfolios defined from the intersection of the two size portfolios and three book-to-market portfolios. The size factor in the Fama–French three-factor model is then calculated monthly by taking the difference in the average return between the three small-cap portfolios and the three large-cap portfolios. The book-to-market factor is calculated similarly, taking the difference in the average return between the two high book-to-market portfolios and the two low book-to-market portfolios.

To use this procedure, we form a time series of monthly returns in calendar time. Specifically, we buy companies at the end of the month in which a repurchase announcement is made and keep them for 36 months. The composition of the portfolio changes over time. Each month, the portfolio is rebalanced, new firms are added as they make announcements, and old firms are removed. This results in a time series of monthly returns for announcements between 1980 and 1990. The main puzzle is the extraordinary performance obtained for value stocks. Thus, we again form portfolios based on book-to-market rankings at the time of the repurchase announcement. Excess monthly returns are then regressed on the three Fama–French factors. We exclude from our analysis returns during the first six months of 1980. In these initial months, the number of firms in each portfolio is small. The alpha from each regression is a monthly estimate of abnormal performance similar in spirit to Jensen's alpha, but controls for size and book-to-market factors in addition to the overall market.

This approach differs from the buy-and-hold procedure in several respects. First, returns are rebalanced monthly, thus the abnormal performance measured under this approach is less representative of a realistic investment strategy. Second, this procedure assumes that the coefficients are stable over time, which implies that the characteristics of the portfolios are not changing.

The results are reported in Table 5. The alpha obtained in the first regression using book-to-market quintile 1 stocks (glamour stocks) is − 0.30% per month, though not significant from zero at traditional confidence levels. The alpha obtained using book-to-market quintile 5 stocks (value stocks) is 0.43% per month and is highly significant. The spread in performance between high and low book-to-market firms repurchasing their shares is 0.73% per month, or 8.76% per year, and is consistent with our earlier findings. Gibbons, Ross, and Shanken (1989) suggest an F-statistic to test more formally whether the alphas produced in these regressions are jointly equal to zero. The F-statistic associated with our analysis is 2.624, with an associated probability level of 0.973, thus rejecting the hypothesis that the alphas are jointly equal to zero.[8]

Although not reported here, we also applied the Fama–French three-factor model in a Returns Across Time and Securities (RATS) framework, which aligns returns in event time. This approach relaxes assumptions regarding parameter stability. Thus, alphas are calculated monthly for 36 months following the repurchase announcement. The difference in alphas between high and low book-to-market stocks averages 0.69% per month, a result similar to the calendar-time approach.

7.3. Multiple announcements

Nearly one-fourth of our cases are firms that had a repurchase announcement in the prior three years. We examined whether these cases were somehow affecting our results. Firms making repeat repurchase announcements do show strong performance. Compounded abnormal performance after three years for these firms is 15.0%. Yet, repeat announcements cannot explain the abnormal performance we observe overall. Focusing on those firms that announced buybacks for the first time, or those that have not made an announcement in

---

[8] Based on our early approach, we have interpreted the long run to be either three or four years. Here, we report analysis for a 36-month holding period. However, our results are not overly sensitive to the holding period assumed. When we extend the holding period to 48 months, the difference in alpha between quintile 1 and quantile 5 is essentially the same as before (0.74% per month). The associated F-statistics is 2.308 with a probability level of 0.952, which again rejects the hypothesis that the alphas from the five regressions are jointly equal to zero.

D. Ikenberry et al. / Journal of Financial Economics 39 (1995) 181–208

Table 5

Fama–French three-factor model regression coefficients

Below are coefficients obtained from regressing excess monthly portfolio returns on the following three-factor model, as suggested by Fama and French (1993):

$$r_{p,t} - r_{f,t} = \alpha + \beta_m(r_{m,t} - r_{f,t}) + \beta_s(r_{small,t} - r_{large,t}) + \beta_{bm}(r_{high,t} - r_{low,t}) + \varepsilon_t,$$

where $r_p - r_{f,t}$ is the excess portfolio return in month t, $(r_{m,t} - r_{f,t})$ is an overall market factor formed by calculating the excess portfolio return to a value- weighted portfolio of NYSE, ASE, and NASDAQ firms. $r_{small,t} - r_{large,t}$ is a size factor and $r_{high,t} - r_{low,t}$ is a book-to-market factor. These two factors are calculated by first identifying NYSE, ASE, and NASDAQ stocks as either 'small' or 'large' relative to the median market equity value of NYSE stocks at the end of each June. These same stocks are independently sorted into one of three portfolios on the basis of their book-to-market ratio. These three portfolios are defined as those with low book-to-market ratios among the bottom 30% of all NYSE stocks, those with ratio values among the middle 40% of NYSE stocks and, finally, those with high book-to-market ratio values among the top 30% of NYSE stocks. Value-weighted returns are calculated on a monthly basis for six portfolios defined from the intersection of the two size portfolios and three book-to-market portfolios. The size factor is then calculated monthly by taking the difference in the average return between the three small-cap portfolios and three large-cap portfolios. The book-to-market factor is calculated by taking the difference in the average monthly return between the two high book-to-market portfolios and the two low book-to-market portfolios. Portfolio returns for the repurchase sample are formed in calendar time. We assume that sample firms are bought at the end of the month in which an open market repurchase announcement is made. New firms are added each month as announcements occur and are removed 36 months following the announcement. Portfolios are formed by book-to-market rank at the time of the announcement for repurchase announcements between 1980 and 1990. Because of small samples during the initial months, portfolio returns obtained for the first six months of 1980 are ignored.

Book-to-market rank	α	β_m	β_s	β_{bm}	R^2
1 (glamour stocks)	− 0.30 ($t = -1.23$)	1.04	0.86	0.02	80.3
2	0.07 ($t = 0.45$)	1.06	0.59	0.00	90.3
3	0.12 ($t = 0.93$)	1.03	0.67	0.28	92.3
4	0.13 ($t = 0.97$)	1.00	0.62	0.34	90.3
5 (value stocks)	0.43 ($t = 3.30$)	1.08	0.62	0.42	92.1

three years, compounded three-year abnormal performance is still impressive, 11.3%.

This finding is also true of high book-to-market stocks. Here, firms making their first repurchase announcement in three years show compounded abnormal performance three years after the announcement of 26.3%. High book-to-

206   *D. Ikenberry et al./Journal of Financial Economics 39 (1995) 181–208*

market stocks making a repeat announcement have compounded abnormal performance after three years of 56.4%. If managers seek to acquire shares from the market at bargain prices, rather than announce one large share repurchase, they might instead opt for a series of smaller announcements stretching over several years. Furthermore, if the market underreacts to the first announcement, managers with strong conviction that their shares remain undervalued may choose to make additional announcements.

8. Conclusions

The literature is rich with reasons for why companies repurchase their own stock, ranging from signaling to being a substitute for cash dividends. Yet managers rarely mention these reasons. Instead, they frequently claim that they are repurchasing shares because prevailing market prices 'undervalue' the stock and that it is a 'good investment'. Despite this public endorsement, the average market response to the news of an open market share repurchase is only 3.5%. Such a small reaction seems inconsistent with the undervaluation theme voiced by managers. Either the market ignores a substantial portion of this undervaluation signal, or managers are overly optimistic about their firm's value.

We find that on average, the market underreacts to open market share repurchase announcements. Using a buy-and-hold strategy, four-year abnormal performance following the announcement is more than 12%. When the announcement and long-run returns are combined, the magnitude of the total undervaluation is about 15%, a level more consistent with manager's claims of mispricing.

Undervaluation is an important reason motivating share repurchases, but other reasons also exist. To distinguish undervaluation from these other motivations, we sort firms on the basis of book-to-market ratios. Undervaluation is more likely to drive repurchases by high book-to-market companies, while other reasons may motivate repurchases announced by companies with low ratios. For those cases in which undervaluation is the dominant reason, a more substantial post-announcement drift might be expected, even after controlling for overall book-to-market effects in stock returns. For example, Lakonishok, Shleifer, and Vishny (1994) show that not all high book-to-market stocks are true out-of-favor stocks. True out-of-favor stocks will show higher returns in the future compared with high book-to-market stocks in general. High book-to-market firms that announce stock buybacks seem more likely to be truly out-of-favor. This indeed appears to be the case. Firms ranked in the top book-to-market quintile have four-year abnormal performance of 45.3% following the repurchase announcement. This occurs using a benchmark that explicitly controls for size and book-to-market effects in stock returns. This impressive performance cannot be explained by an abnormally high incidence of takeovers.

Firms in the bottom two book-to-market quintiles exhibit abnormal returns close to zero or slightly negative, suggesting that true undervaluation was not a primary motive in these cases. Although book-to-market is closely associated with long-run performance, the initial market reaction to repurchase announcements is surprisingly similar across all book-to-market groups.

This evidence is consistent with other studies that find that managers have market-timing ability. A recent paper by Loughran and Ritter (1994) examines the long-run performance of seasoned equity offerings, a corporate action that is the antithesis of a share repurchase. They find evidence of timing ability by observing that managers tend to issue shares when stock prices are high, and that the worst long-run performance occurs following periods of heavy offering activity. Seyhun (1990) finds that managers successfully timed trades of shares in their own firms following the 1987 crash. We find further evidence that managers possess timing abilities. For some reason, the initial market reaction to management's decision to either issue or remove shares is largely ignored by investors in the short run.

This paper adds to a growing body of literature that finds that the market reaction to news is not always completed over short time periods, an assumption made in many event studies. The full impact of corporate announcements can extend over several years. Other examples of such protracted adjustments include initial as well as seasoned equity offerings, mergers, spinoffs, proxy contests, and, in a related context, fixed-price repurchase tender offers. Given the diverse settings of this research, serious concerns should be raised as to the appropriateness of measuring abnormal performance over short windows to assess the economic impact of corporate decisions. Why the market reaction extends over such long periods of time is an intriguing issue that requires further work. Some answers to this puzzle are provided by Shleifer and Vishny (1990), who discuss how market inefficiencies can occur in investments with long horizons.

References

Agrawal, Anup, Jeffrey F. Jaffe, and Gershon N. Mandelker, 1992, The post-merger performance of acquiring firms in acquisitions: A re-examination of an anomaly, Journal of Finance 47, 1605–1621.

Asquith, Paul and David W. Mullins, Jr., 1986, Signalling with dividends, stock repurchases and equity issues, Financial Management 15, 27–44.

Baker, H. Kent, Patricia L. Gallagher, and Karen E. Morgan, 1981, Management's view of stock repurchase, Journal of Financial Research 4, 233–247.

Brock, William, Josef Lakonishok, and Blake LeBaron, 1992, Simple technical trading rules and the stochastic properties of stock returns, Journal of Finance 47, 1731–1764.

Brown, Stephen J. and Jerold B. Warner, 1980, Measuring security price performance, Journal of Financial Economics 8, 205–258.

Brown, Stephen J. and Jerold B. Warner, 1985, Using daily stock returns: The case of event studies, Journal of Financial Economics 14, 3–31.

Chopra, Navin, Josef Lakonishok, and Jay R. Ritter, 1992, Measuring abnormal performance: Do stocks overreact?, Journal of Financial Economics 31, 235–268.

Comment, Robert and Gregg A. Jarrell, 1991, The relative signalling power of Dutch auction and fixed price tender offers and open market share repurchases, Journal of Finance 46, 1243–1271.

Constantinides, George M. and Bruce D. Grundy, 1989, Optimal investment with stock repurchase and financing as signals, Review of Financial Studies 2, 445–465.

Cusatis, Patrick J., John A. Miles, and J. Randall Woolridge, 1993, Restructuring through spinoffs: The stock market evidence, Journal of Financial Economics 33, 293–311.

Dann, Larry Y., 1981, Common stock repurchases: An analysis of returns to bondholders and stockholders, Journal of Financial Economics 9, 113–138.

Dann, Larry Y., 1983, Is your common stock really worth buying back?, Directors & Boards 7, no. 4, 23–29.

Fama, Eugene F. and Kenneth R. French, 1992, The cross-section of expected returns, Journal of Finance 47, 427–466.

Fama, Eugene F. and Kenneth R. French, 1993, Common risk factors in the returns on stocks and bonds, Journal of Financial Economics 33, 3–56.

Gibbons, Michael R., Stephen A. Ross, and Jay Shanken, 1989, A test of the efficiency of a given portfolio, Econometrica 57, 1121–1152.

Ikenberry, David and Josef Lakonishok, 1993, Corporate governance through the proxy contest: Evidence and implications, Journal of Business 66, 405–435.

Lakonishok, Josef and Theo Vermaelen, 1990, Anomalous price behavior around repurchase tender offers, Journal of Finance 45, 455–477.

Lakonishok, Josef, Andrei Shleifer, and Robert W. Vishny, 1994, Contrarian investing, extrapolation and risk, Journal of Finance 49, 1541–1578.

Loughran, Tim and Jay R. Ritter, 1995, The new issues puzzle, Journal of Finance 50, 23–51.

Nelson, William R., 1994, Do firms buy low and sell high? Evidence of excess returns on firms that issue or repurchase equity, Working paper (Federal Reserve System, Washington, DC).

Ofer, Aharon R. and Anjan V. Thakor, 1987, A theory of stock price response to alternative corporate disbursement methods: Stock repurchases and dividends, Journal of Finance 42, 365–394.

Ritter, Jay R., 1991, The long-run performance of initial public offerings, Journal of Finance 46, 1–27.

Seyhun, H. Nejat, 1990, Overreaction or fundamentals: Some lessons from insiders' response to the market crash of 1987, Journal of Finance 45, 1363–1388.

Shleifer, Andrei and Robert W. Vishny, 1990, Equilibrium short horizon of investors and firms, American Economic Review 80, 148–153.

Vermaelen, Theo, 1981, Common stock repurchases and market signalling, Journal of Financial Economics 9, 139–183.

Wansley, James W., William R. Lane, and Salil Sarkar, 1989, Management's view of share repurchase and tender premiums, Financial Management 18, 97–110.

[17]

THE JOURNAL OF FINANCE • VOL. XLVII, NO. 1 • MARCH 1992

Dutch Auction Repurchases: An Analysis of Shareholder Heterogeneity

LAURIE SIMON BAGWELL*

ABSTRACT

This paper documents that firms face upward-sloping supply curves when they repurchase shares in a Dutch auction, and it analyzes the market reaction to these offers. The announcement price increase is highly correlated with the ultimate repurchase premium. Prices decline at expiration only for pro-rated offers. The cumulative return is positive and highly correlated with the repurchase premium, excepting pro-rated offers. Much of this price increase is consistent with movement along an upward-sloping supply curve. Trading volume around the Dutch auction parallels fixed-price repurchases. Supply elasticity is larger for firms with large trading volume, firms included in the S&P 500 Index, and takeover targets.

THIS PAPER DOCUMENTS THAT firms face upward-sloping supply curves when they repurchase shares in a Dutch auction. Until now, there has been little direct empirical assessment of the elasticity of the supply curve for corporate equity. At issue is whether or not the hypothesis of shareholder homogeneity of valuations, and therefore perfect supply elasticity, is a good approximation to actual markets. Both the advantages and limitations of assuming homogeneous valuations are highlighted in *The Theory of Finance* by Fama and Miller (1972), who in discussing the perfect capital market observed that

> no such market exists in the real world, nor could it. Rather, what we have here is an idealization . . . permit(ing) us to focus more sharply on a limited number of aspects of the problem and usually greatly facilitat(ing) both the derivation and statement of the sought-for empirical generalizations. In the nature of the case, however, the generalizations so obtained can never be anything more than approximations to the real phenomena that they are supposed to represent. The question is whether, considered as approximations, they are close enough; and this, of course, is a question that can only be answered empirically and in light of the specific uses to which the approximations are put. (pp 21–22)

* From the Department of Finance, Northwestern University. I would like to thank Kyle Bagwell, Doug Bernheim, Dave Brown, Harry DeAngelo, Mike Fishman, Kathleen Hagerty, Bob Hodrick, Ken Judd, Narayana Kocherlakota, two anonymous referees and René Stulz (the editor) for their comments. I also thank the seminar participants at Duke, Indiana, Northwestern, Ohio State, Princeton and Stanford Universities, the Universities of Chicago and Michigan, the 1991 NBER Summer Institute on Corporate Finance and Banking and the Sixth World Congress of the Econometric Society. I am grateful to Donald Jacobs for his assistance in obtaining the data and to Latha Ramchand for her research assistance. Financial support from National Science Foundation Grant SES-8821666 is gratefully acknowledged.

This paper's provocative empirical findings imply that the hypothesis of homogeneous valuations is not a good approximation for understanding Dutch auction stock repurchases.

I examine 32 Dutch auction stock repurchases which took place between 1981 and 1988. In a Dutch auction, the company states the number of shares it will buy during a stipulated period, and it sets a price range between which shareholder bids will be accepted. The repurchase price is the lowest price necessary to acquire the number of shares sought. Though not publicly available, I have obtained the individual shareholder bids in these auctions directly from the companies. Shareholder valuations are not homogeneous; rather, in each repurchase, the bids differ markedly across shareholders. This indicates that the repurchasing firms encounter upward-sloping supply curves for their shares.

I then analyze the share price reaction to the repurchase. Prices increase 7.7% on average at the announcement of a Dutch auction. The correlation between the announcement day return and the ultimate repurchase premium is over 80%. Prices decline 1.9% on average at expiration. This decline is, however, limited to repurchases with pro-rated offers, where firms buy back fewer shares than were tendered at or below the purchase price. Firms with pro-rated offers have a −6.9% expiration return on average and a negative correlation between their expiration return and the repurchase premium of 63%. Firms with non-pro-rated offers have zero expiration return on average and little correlation between their expiration return and the repurchase premium. The sample average cumulative return during the period beginning the day before the announcement through the expiration of the offer is 6.7%. For non-pro-rated offers, the sample cumulative return is 9.8%, with a correlation between the cumulative return and the repurchase premium of 87%. For pro-rated offers, the sample cumulative return is zero, with a correlation between the cumulative return and the repurchase premium of only 35%.

The average elasticity measure implies that to purchase 15% of the outstanding stock, a firm must offer a 9.1% premium above its pre-announcement market price. Much of the observed 7.7% price increase therefore may be movement along an upward-sloping supply curve. This is confirmed by the high correlation between the announcement return and the ultimate repurchase premium. In light of the evidence in this paper, all homogeneous valuation explanations of the market reaction to the announcement of these offers, including signaling models wherein homogeneous shareholder valuations are revised in response to the repurchase, are suspect. Hybrid models which allow signaling in the presence of heterogeneous valuations, however, seem consistent with the evidence.

The difference between the expiration day price reaction for pro-rated and non-pro-rated offers can be explained with movement along an upward-sloping supply curve. The firm buys back all shares tendered at or below the purchase price in a non-pro-rated offer. The documented facts that there is typically no price decline at expiration, that the offer results in a large cumulative return, and that there is a high correlation between the cumulative return and the repurchase premium are all consistent with an alteration of the marginal holder of stock to one with a higher reservation price, the repurchase price. By contrast, the firm buys back fewer shares than were tendered at or below the purchase price in a pro-rated offer. For these cases the expiration day return is typically negative even when most of the shares submitted for sale are bought back, the cumulative return is zero, and there is little correlation between the cumulative return and the repurchase premium. These facts are consistent with there being no change in the marginal shareholder. Since the marginal valuation is below the purchase price, the price falls at expiration.

In addition, this paper documents that changes in trading volume around Dutch auction repurchases are comparable to the findings for fixed-price repurchases. On average, volume increases dramatically during the repurchase, and it appears to fall below pre-announcement levels after the expiration of the offer. Cross-sectional analysis indicates that the share price elasticity calculated from the individual bids is larger for firms with large trading volume, firms included in the S&P 500 Index, and firms that have been takeover targets.

The organization of the paper is as follows. Section I describes the Dutch auction stock repurchase and the data. Section II documents the upward-sloping supply curves. Section III evaluates the market reaction to these offers. Section IV argues that an explanation emphasizing shareholder heterogeneity is consistent with the evidence. Section V measures trading volume around the Dutch auction repurchases. Section VI examines the cross-sectional variability in supply elasticity. Section VII concludes that the presence of heterogeneous shareholder valuations may be an important determinant of the market reaction to any event which alters the marginal shareholder.

I. Dutch Auction Repurchases

The first firm to utilize the Dutch auction was Todd Shipyards in 1981. Planning a tender offer at $28 for between 200,000 and 550,000 of its 5,500,000 shares, Todd instead was convinced by Bear Stearns to offer a Dutch auction at a price not to exceed $28 (although shareholders could tender for less). The fee paid to Bear Stearns would be 30% of the savings if the ultimate purchase price was less than $28. Todd chose the Dutch auction, and the purchase price was $26.50.[1]

Including the Todd Shipyards offer, 52 Dutch auction repurchases commenced prior to December 31, 1988. Thirty-nine of these firms were traded on the NYSE, seven on the AMEX, and six OTC (NASDAQ). The firms are listed in Appendix A. The sample was created from a search of *The Wall*

---

[1] *Wall Street Journal*, September 23, 1981.

Street Journal (hereafter WSJ), *The Business Periodicals Index*, and correspondence with Morgan Stanley and Bear Stearns. Since firms publicly
disclose only the final terms of the offer (and not the individual shareholder
tenders), I wrote the Chief Executive Officer at each of the 52 companies and
requested the shareholder tendering responses. I was ultimately provided
with the data for 32 of these firms (approximately 60%).[2] Fourteen of the
firms requested confidentiality.

The fundamental difference between the fixed-price tender offer and the
Dutch auction repurchase is that the tender offer is made for one price,
whereas the Dutch auction offer specifies a range from which shares will
ultimately be purchased.[3] Shareholders are invited to tender their stock, if
they desire, at any price within the stated range. The firm compiles these
responses, creating the supply curve for the stock, and pays as the purchase
price the lowest price that allows it to buy the number of shares sought in the
offer. Under the nondiscrimination or "best-price provision" required by the
SEC, the purchase price is paid to all investors who tendered at or below that
price. Item 1 of Schedule 13E-4 requires the firm to specify exactly at the
time of the offer the number of shares to be repurchased. Nevertheless, prior
to two SEC no-action letters in 1987, this was not always enforced, due to
questions of interpretation, and therefore sometimes firms instead specified a
range of shares that were sought.[4]

If the number of shares tendered exceeds the number sought, the company
purchases less than all shares tendered at or below the purchase price on a
pro-rata basis to all who tendered at or below the purchase price. That is, the
firm repurchases shares in proportion to the total number of shares tendered.
If too few shares are tendered, the firm either cancels the offer (provided it
had been made conditional on a minimum acceptance), or buys back all
tendered shares at the maximum price.

The announcement day of the offer is defined as the earliest trading day at
which the principal terms of the offer were publicly available.[5] The expiration day of the offer is defined as the earliest trading day to end after the
offer expired. Most of the offers expired at midnight, in which case the next
trading day is designated the expiration day. These dates were determined

---

[2] The data are analyzed for 31 firms. Hospital Corporation is excluded due to confounding
circumstances during its offer. After the October 1987 market crash, the minimum specified
price for the offer was over 50% above the market price at expiration of the offer. Eighty-six
percent of the outstanding shares were tendered at this price. Interestingly, an additional 6% of
the outstanding shares were tendered at higher prices in the offer's range.

[3] Dutch auctions are permitted under Rule 13e-4 governing tender offers, if conducted pur-
suant to certain procedures (as described in SEC Release No. 23421, fn. 64, July 11, 1986).

[4] Moreover, Rule 13e-4(f)(1)(ii) provides that, in the event of an increase in the percentage of
securities sought by more than 2%, the offer must be extended at least 10 business days from the
date that notice of the increase is given. I am grateful to the staff attorneys at the SEC for
providing me with this information.

[5] In the one case where the price terms of the offer were changed, the announcement date of
the final offer terms is used.

by examining WSJ announcements, SEC 8-K reports, news releases provided by the firms, and the offering statements. These sources were consulted to find also (1) the date the offer commenced, (2) the number of outstanding shares of the repurchasing firm, (3) the number of shares sought, and (4) the tender price range. The number of shares tendered and repurchased were obtained from the firms and confirmed with SEC 13E-4 filings.

Most bids are submitted at the very end of the offer's duration.[6] This is not surprising, given the shareholders' option to submit or revoke their bids until the expiration of the offer. At the time shareholders tender, they cannot observe the tendering responses of others. Moreover, tendering borrowed shares (short tendering) is prohibited by the SEC.

The range of premia offered, percentage of equity sought and acquired, and other terms of the offers for the sample are given in Table I.[7] The purchase price is 13.4% higher on average than the closing market price on the day preceding the announcement of the offer. The price range specified by the firm is on average from 2.64% to 17.17% above the pre-announcement price. On average, these firms have sought to acquire between 18.03% and 20.07% of their outstanding shares. The mean duration of the offer is 22 business days. The mean fraction of outstanding shares reacquired was 15.28%, where 17.84% of the outstanding shares were tendered at or below the purchase price, and 23.87% were tendered within the price range of the offer. None of these firms made more than one Dutch auction offer in the 1981–1988 time period.

II. The Evidence

For each firm in the sample, the tendering responses are ordered from lowest to highest prices. This schedule of offers is the supply curve for shares that the company faced in the repurchase. Documenting significant upward slope to the supply curves contradicts the perfect supply elasticity hypothesis.

Appendix B provides the Dutch auction supply curves for the 17 firms which did not require confidentiality. The supply curves display an upward slope. The bid prices are normalized so that the pre-announcement market price is 100. The normalized quantities measure the cumulative percentage of outstanding shares tendered at or below a given price.

Consider as an example the 1986 Dutch auction in which J. P. Stevens offered to buy back up to 13% of its outstanding stock. The highest normalized bid in the specified range was 114, or a 14% premium above the pre-announcement market price, while the lowest bid was 102, or 2% above the pre-announcement market price. Twenty-nine percent of the outstanding shares were tendered at various prices within this range.

---

[6] This observation arose repeatedly during discourse with executives of the firms who conducted the Dutch auctions.

[7] The terms and outcomes of this sample of Dutch auction repurchases are comparable to the sample in Comment and Jarrell (1991), which includes all Dutch auctions between 1984–1989.

Table I

Descriptive Statistics of the Sample

This table reports the mean and median values of the terms and the outcomes for 31 firms conducting Dutch auction stock repurchases, 1981–1988.

Statistic	Mean	Median
1. Purchase price premium percentage relative to market price one day prior to announcement	13.43	11.46
2. Purchase price premium percentage relative to market price one month prior to announcement	11.60	8.91
3. Lower bound price premium percentage relative to market price one day prior to announcement	2.64	4.19
4. Upper bound price premium percentage relative to market price one day prior to announcement	17.17	16.06
5. Lower bound percentage of outstanding shares sought	18.03	12.18
6. Upper bound percentage of outstanding shares sought	20.07	15.86
7. Percentage of outstanding shares tendered in price range	23.87	17.87
8. Percentage of outstanding shares tendered at or below purchase price	17.84	12.07
9. Percentage of outstanding shares acquired	15.28	12.07
10. Duration of offer (number of trading days from open to close)	22.13	21.00

A. Upward-Sloping Supply Curves: Alternative Measures

Because fourteen firms required confidential use of the shareholder tendering responses, this section provides various measures of the average slope of the supply curves in the sample. Table II provides the difference between the bid corresponding to the 6th percentile tender and the bid corresponding to the 1st percentile tender, scaled by the pre-announcement market price.[8] Similar calculations are made to determine the difference between the 11th percentile and the 6th percentile tendering bids, and between the 16th percentile and the 11th percentile tendering bids for each of the 31 firms.[9]

In Row 1, the difference between the 6th percentile bid and the 1st percentile bid is 4.5%. The reported average understates the true average premium, since five of the firms were excluded, because less than 6% of the outstanding shares tendered in the price range offered. That is, the observations in which the smallest percentage of stockholders were willing to sell their shares are omitted.

The average difference between the 11th percentile bid and the 6th percentile bid is 2.6%. Again, the reported average underestimates the true average. Nine firms are omitted because they have less than 11% of their outstanding shares tendering. The difference between the 16th percentile bid and the 11th percentile bid is 2.0%. This is based on 19 firms, because an additional three have less than 16% tendering within the range.

Therefore, the average difference between the 16th percentile bid and the 1st percentile bid is 9.1%.[10] This 9.1% price premium to obtain 15% of the outstanding stocks implies an average elasticity measure of 1.65.

I next measure the extent of the upward slope by computing 31 separate least squares best fits of the firms' supply curves. Again, price is normalized so that the pre-announcement price is equal to 100 for each firm, and quantity is normalized to measure the cumulative percentage of outstanding shares tendered at or below each price. Points on the supply curves are denoted $P_{ji} - Q_{ji}$, where subscript j represents different price-quantity points on firm i's supply curve. The results from the individual firm regressions:

$$P_{ji} = \alpha_i + \beta_i Q_{ji} + \varepsilon_{ji}$$

are reported in Table III. The average slope is 1.46, with a median of .95. These least squares best fit results suggest that for the typical firm in this sample, to acquire an additional 10% of the outstanding stock, one must offer an average (median) additional premium of 14.6% (9.5%) of the

---

[8] On average the lower range price is 2.64% above the pre-announcement market price. Any shareholders willing to sell between the market price and the lower bound price would bid the lower bound price. Therefore, elasticity measurements begin at 1% of the outstanding shares.

[9] Five percent quantity intervals are small enough to allow the elasticity to vary within the supply curve, yet large enough to avoid some of the effects of tendering lumpiness. They allow useful stylized facts about the nature of the supply curve, while never assuming that this piece-wise linear curve is the best functional description of a supply curve.

[10] For the 19 firms where at least 16% of the outstanding shares tendered, the difference between the 16th percentile price and the 1st percentile price varies from 0% to 23.3%.

Table II

Arc Elasticity Measures of the Dutch Auction Supply Curves

This table reports the difference between the bid corresponding to the 6th percentile tender and the bid corresponding to the 1st percentile tender, scaled by the pre-announcement market price, for firms conducting Dutch auction stock repurchases, 1981–1988. Similar calculations are made to determine the differences between the 11th percentile and the 6th percentile tendering bids, and between the 16th percentile and 11th percentile tendering bids for each of the firms. The implied elasticities are also calculated.

5% Quantity Change Intervals (%)	Mean % Price Change	Median % Price Change	Mean Arc $\eta = \%Q/\%P$	No. of Firms
1–6	4.54	3.66	1.10	26
6–11	2.55	2.01	1.96	22
11–16	1.99	1.69	2.51	19
Sum: 1–16	9.08		1.65*	

*This figure is computed using the mean sum price change over the 15% quantity interval.

Table III

Best Fit Line Measures of the Dutch Auction Supply Curves

This table reports the slope of the normalized supply curve for each of 31 firms conducting Dutch auction stock repurchases, 1981–1988. For each firm, the pre-announcement price is set at 100 and quantity is normalized as the cumulative percentage of outstanding shares tendered at or below each price. Points on the supply curves are denoted $P_{ji} - Q_{ji}$, where subscript j represents different price-quantity pairs for firm i. The regressions are $P_{ji} = \alpha_i + \beta_i Q_{ji} + \varepsilon_{ji}$. The slopes are then sorted from highest to lowest, with the average slope equal to 1.46.

β_i	t-Statistic	p Value	Firm Name
7.37	1.94	.084	Farwest
4.96	3.33	.045	Sage
4.79	5.08	.000	Standard
2.43	7.28	.000	Axia
2.31	52.44	.000	Pennwalt
1.98	3.63	.001	Confidential
1.86	4.88	.000	Todd
1.73	3.48	.007	Confidential
1.57	8.81	.000	Knogo
1.47	7.39	.000	Confidential
1.39	8.44	.000	Ralston
1.31	8.83	.000	Confidential
1.18	12.57	.011	Confidential
1.02	6.75	.000	Confidential
0.96	6.39	.000	Barnes
0.95	29.73	.000	RJR Nabisco
0.87	8.83	.000	Confidential
0.78	8.42	.000	NL Ind.
0.67	11.67	.000	Jostens
0.67	11.92	.000	Carl Karcher
0.66	11.51	.000	Confidential
0.60	11.05	.000	Gen. Sig.
0.53	26.23	.000	Confidential
0.50	4.16	.009	Confidential
0.44	27.24	.000	Confidential
0.40	8.34	.000	J P Stevens
0.38	9.91	.000	Whittaker
0.36	4.99	.000	Confidential
0.36	9.77	.000	Confidential
0.35	7.48	.001	FMC
0.31	18.12	.000	Confidential

preannouncement market price. This implies an average (median) elasticity of .68 (1.05).

B. *Other Evidence of Upward-Sloping Supply Curves*

The results in this section provide direct evidence that firms face upward-sloping supply curves when they repurchase shares in a Dutch auction. Evidence consistent with upward-sloping supply curves has been detected in similar transactions. For example, Bradley, Desai, and Kim (1988) find that the premium paid in interfirm tender offers is increasing in the fraction of target shares purchased by the acquirer, while Brown and Ryngaert (1990) find a positive relation between the premium and the fraction of outstanding shares tendered in fixed-price repurchase tender offers.

Holthausen, Leftwich, and Mayers (1990) consider buyer-initiated block transactions, finding that buyers of large blocks of stock pay a premium above the price before the block transaction, with the premium representing a permanent price effect. This premium increases with the size of the block traded, evidence consistent with upward-sloping supply curves.[11] Shleifer (1986) finds that the share price increase at the announcement of the inclusion of firms to the S&P 500 Index is positively related to the increased buying of the shares by Index funds. Since being included in the Index does not necessarily signal any information about stock value, the findings suggest that the price increase is being driven by increased demand in the presence of upward-sloping supply curves. The innovation of the Dutch auction evidence is that it is direct evidence of the upward-sloping supply curves faced by the repurchasing firms.

C. Sources of Upward-Sloping Supply Curves

Heterogeneous tendering responses could result from various sources, the first being heterogeneous (private) valuations due to objective characteristics like capital gains tax lock-in as in Bagwell (1991a) or Stulz (1988), or transaction costs as in Mayshar (1981) or Bagwell and Judd (1989). In this case, the different bids across shareholders reflect buyers' distinct valuations. In a Technical Appendix (available from the author), I demonstrate natural conditions under which shareholders optimally bid their true (private) reservation values. Similar to standard findings for second-price auctions (for example, Vickrey (1961)), atomistic shareholders truthfully reveal their reservation prices in Dutch auction stock repurchases. That is, a price-taking shareholder who does not expect to alter the outcome of the repurchase by his behavior offers to sell his shares at their true valuation. Second, differential reservation prices may arise from asymmetric information about a common valuation as in Milgrom and Weber (1982). Third, they may result from differences of opinion as in Miller (1977) or Varian (1985).[12]

---

[11] Scholes (1972) finds a permanent negative price reaction to the sale of large blocks. Greater price changes occur if the seller is presumed to have adverse information motivating the sale. Mikkelson and Partch (1985) reconsider block sales in light of a downward-sloping demand curve, documenting a significant negative price reaction to seller-initiated secondary distributions regardless of the type of seller, with the magnitude of the price response positively related to the size of the offering. Loderer, Cooney, and Van Drunen (1991) find that stock offerings by regulated firms depress stock prices, even after controlling for information releases.

[12] If these differences of opinion are generated by the repurchase, then the observed tendering differences might overestimate the heterogeneity of valuations that would be present absent the repurchase.

III. Price Reaction: Announcement, Expiration, and Cumulative Excess Returns

The next two sections evaluate the share price reaction to Dutch auction stock repurchases. The market response to announcements is measured with daily stock excess returns, obtained from the CRSP Daily Returns File. A firm's daily excess return is its daily return less a CRSP equally weighted market return. Table IV presents the cross-sectional mean excess return on the equally weighted portfolio of the sample securities, in event time. The announcement day excess return for the sample is 7.7%, with 27 of the 31 (87%) individual security returns positive.[13] This is significantly different from zero at the 1% level, with a t-statistic of 5.7. In contrast, the mean portfolio daily excess return for the 50-day period beginning 60 days prior to the announcement day is not significantly different from zero.

I also compute the daily stock excess returns at the Dutch auction expiration.[14] The expiration day portfolio excess return is -1.9%. This is significantly different from zero at the 5% level, with a t-statistic of -2.2. Unlike the announcement day effect which is positive for 27 of 31 firms, 9 of the 30 (30%) individual security excess returns are positive on the expiration day.[15] In contrast, the mean portfolio daily excess return for the 50-day period beginning 10 days after the expiration day is not significantly different from zero.

The average cumulative excess return for the period beginning the day before the announcement through the expiration day is 6.7%, with 24 of the 30 (80%) individual security cumulative returns positive. This is significantly different from zero at the 1% level, with a t-statistic of 3.3.

A. Price Reaction: The Importance of Pro Rata

I next examine whether the pro-ration of an offer is an important determinant of the magnitudes of the excess returns reported above. Panel A of Table V shows that firms with non-pro-rated offers experience no significant price reduction at expiration, while firms with offers that are pro-rated experience a negative price reaction at expiration.[16] For the 22 firms whose repurchase offers were not pro-rated, the average expiration day excess return is -0.1%, which is not significantly different from zero. Only 13 out of 22 (59%) individual security excess returns are negative on the expiration

---

[13] Comment and Jarrell (1991) find a three-day return of 7.5%. Kamma, Kanatas, and Raymar (1990) find a 6.6% return, with 86% positive on the announcement day.

[14] Expiration statistics are computed for 30 firms, excluding Excello Corporation. Five days after the expiration, Textron bid for Excello, successfully acquiring it within two weeks. The takeover bid generated significant price reaction and trading volume.

[15] Kamma, Kanatas, and Raymar (1990) find a -1.3% average abnormal residual at the expiration, with 30% of the expiration abnormal returns positive.

[16] This analysis excludes two firms whose offers were canceled.

Table IV

Excess Returns Around the Dutch Auction Stock Repurchase

This table reports one-day and cumulative common stock rates of return net of market around the Dutch auction repurchase for 31 firms conducting Dutch auction stock repurchases, 1981–1988.

Panel A: Daily excess returns are daily returns less a CRSP equally weighted market return.

Time Period	Mean Rate of Return, %	Standard Deviation, %	t-Statistic (H0: Mean Return = 0)	p Value (H0: Mean Return = 0)	No. Pos.: No. Neg.
Announcement day	7.668	7.431	5.745	.000	27:4
Expiration day	−1.939	4.836	−2.196	.036	9:21
60 days before to 10 days before announcement (31 firms)	0.001	0.480	0.021	.983	
10 days after to 60 days after expiration (30 firms)	−0.050	0.280	−1.261	.213	

Panel B: Cumulative returns are daily excess returns cumulated around the Dutch auction repurchase.

Time Period	Cumulative Rate of Return, %	Standard Deviation, %	t-Statistic (H0: Mean Return = 0)	p Value (H0: Mean Return = 0)	No. Pos.: No. Neg.
Day before announcement through expiration	6.728	11.021	3.344	.002	24:6

day.[17] In contrast, for the six firms where the repurchase offer was pro-rated, the average expiration day excess return is −6.9%, significantly different from zero at the 5% level, with a *t*-statistic of −2.8. All six individual security excess returns are negative on the expiration day, ranging from −1.7% to −18.4%.[18] The null hypothesis that the expiration excess returns of the two subsamples are the same is rejected at the 1% level, with a *t*-statistic of 4.4. These findings are consistent with the expiration day price reaction found in Dann (1981) and Masulis (1980) for fixed-price tender offers.

Panel B presents the cumulative excess returns during the repurchase. For non-pro-rata firms, the cumulative excess return from the day before the announcement through expiration is 9.8%. This is significant at the 1% level, with a *t*-statistic of 5.9. 20 of the 22 (91%) individual security cumulative excess returns are positive. Since firms with offers that are not pro-rated experience no significant price decline at expiration, the positive announcement effect remains. By contrast, the cumulative excess return for the pro-rata firms is .1%, which is not significantly different from zero. 4 of the 6 (67%) individual security cumulative excess returns are positive. Since firms with offers that are pro-rated suffer a price decline at expiration, the announcement effect is offset. The null hypothesis that the cumulative excess returns of the two subsamples are the same is rejected at the 5% level, with a *t*-statistic of 2.1.

Potentially, there is a fundamental difference between the interpretation of oversubscription in fixed-price repurchases and Dutch auction repurchases. In fixed-price tender offers, oversubscribed offers are associated with larger post-expiration price declines because high tendering rates occur when the offer price is high relative to the expected post-expiration price (Brown and Ryngaert (1990)). In Dutch auctions the purchase price is determined by shareholder tendering responses rather than being set by the firm. Therefore, an offer is not always pro-rated because the offer price was set in excess of that necessary to obtain the shares sought. While oversubscription in Dutch auctions can occur because even the lower range price terms were generous, oversubscription can also occur because there is a mass of tenders at the purchase price, due to the lumpiness of bidding schedules.

To examine this distinction, I compare those pro-rated offers where the purchase price was the lowest price of the specified range, suggesting that even the lowest price was generous, to those offers where the purchase price was above the minimum price, suggesting that the pro-ration reflects tendering lumpiness. Panel C reports the expiration day excess returns for the

---

[17] Of these 22, none closed at the lowest price in the range, nine closed at some price within the range, and the remaining 13 closed at the highest price in the range. Of these 13, 10 were undersubscribed; the number of shares tendered in the range was below the lower bound of shares sought.

[18] For these six offers, three closed at the lowest price in the range, two at some price within the range, and the remaining one closed at the highest price in the range.

Table V

Expiration and Cumulative Returns: The Importance of Pro-Ration

This table reports the relationship between pro-ration and expiration and cumulative excess returns, for 31 firms conducting Dutch auction stock repurchases, 1981–1988.

Panel A: Firms with non-pro-rated offers experience no significance price reduction on the expiration day, while offers that are pro-rated experience a significant negative price reaction at expiration.

Sample	No. of Firms	Expiration Day Excess Return, %	t-Statistic (H0: Mean Return = 0)	p Value (H0: Mean Return = 0)	No. Pos.: No. Neg.
Non-pro-rata firms	22	−0.107	−0.214	.833	9:13
Pro-rata firms	6	−6.900	−2.798	.038	0:6
Difference across samples (H0: same mean)			−4.359	.000	

Panel B: Firms with non-pro-rated offers experience significant cumulative excess returns from the day before the announcement through expiration, while firms with offers that are pro-rated experience no cumulative return.

Sample	Cumulative Excess Rate of Return, %	Standard Deviation, %	t-Statistic (H0: Mean Return = 0)	p Value (H0: Mean Return = 0)	No. Pos.: No. Neg
Non-pro-rata firms	9.788	7.768	5.910	.000	20:2
Pro-rata firms	0.133	16.404	0.020	.985	4:2
Difference across samples (H0: same mean)			2.091	.046	

Table V-*Continued*

Panel C: Pro-rated firms closing at the minimum price are compared to those closing above the minimum price.

Subsample of Pro-rata Firms	No. of Firms	Expiration Day Excess Return, %	t-Statistic (H0: Mean Return = 0)	p Value (H0: Mean Return = 0)	Range of Excess Returns	Range of Pro-rata Fractions
Offers closing at minimum price	3	-8.567	-1.698	.232	-1.7, -5.6, -18.4	.52 .60 .98
Offers closing above minimum price	3	-5.233	-3.544	.071	-2.8, -5.0, -7.9	.88 .92 .97
Difference across samples (H0: same mean)			0.634	.561		

subsamples. The offers closing at the lowest price of the specified range have a larger price decline on average (although the difference across samples is not significant), as might be expected given the nature of their oversubscription. The offers closing above the minimum price, however, also experience significant price decline at expiration, even though they repurchase between 88% and 97% of the shares tendered at or below the purchase price.

B. Price Reaction: Comparison to the Purchase Price Premium Ultimately Paid

It is interesting to compare the stock price reaction to the Dutch auction repurchases to the purchase price premium ultimately paid by each firm. The purchase price premium is computed as the premium of the purchase price above the pre-announcement price, scaled by the pre-announcement price.

Panel A of Table VI reports that the sample correlation between the announcement day excess return and the purchase price premium is 86%. In contrast, there is little correlation between the expiration day excess return and the purchase price premium. The correlation between the cumulative return from the period beginning the day before the announcement through expiration and the purchase price premium is 64%.

Panel B reports the correlation between firm excess returns and the purchase premium, based on whether the firm's offer was pro-rated. Both non-pro-rata and pro-rata firms experience high correlation between the announcement excess return and the purchase price premium, with correlations of 89% and 80%, respectively. One notable difference between the subsamples is the correlation between the expiration excess return and the purchase price premium. Firms with non-pro-rated offers have a small positive correlation of 14%, while firms with pro-rated offers have a significant negative correlation of 63%. This difference is also captured in the correlation between the cumulative excess return and the purchase price premium. Firms with non-pro-rated offers have a significant positive correlation of 87%, while firms with pro-rated offers have a much smaller correlation of 35%.

IV. Interpreting the Price Reaction Evidence

In this section I examine an explanation of the market price reaction documented in section III: one effect of a repurchase on price is due to an upward-sloping supply curve. If the supply curve is less than perfectly elastic, movement along the supply curve in a non-pro-rata repurchase changes the marginal shareholder to one having a higher reservation price, while a pro-rata repurchase does not.

Common explanations of the price reaction generally assume that homogeneous shareholder valuations are revised in response to the repurchase. Vermaelen (1984), for example, suggests that the willingness of a firm to pay a premium for its shares "signals" favorable information about the firm.

Table VI

The Correlation Between Stock Excess Returns and Purchase Premium

This table reports the correlation between firm excess returns and the purchase premium paid, for 31 firms conducting Dutch auction stock repurchases, 1981–1988. The purchase premium is calculated as the purchase price of the repurchase less the pre-announcement market price, scaled by the pre-announcement market price.

Panel A: This panel reports the correlation between firm excess returns and the purchase premium.

Time Period Return	Correlation Between Return and Purchase Premium	No. of Firms*
Announcement day excess return	.862	29
Expiration day excess return	.028	28
Day before announcement through expiration cumulative excess return	.638	28

Panel B: This panel reports the correlation between firm excess returns and the purchase premium, based on whether the firm's offer was pro-rated.

	Excess Return Correlation		Day before Announcement Through Expiration	
Subsample	Announcement	Expiration	Cumulative	No. of Firms
Non-pro-rata firms	.893	.136	.869	22
Pro-rata firms	.800	−.625	.350	6

*This correlation can be computed only for firms with completed (not canceled) repurchases.

Jensen (1986) argues that firm value is enhanced by disgorging free cash that otherwise would be used inefficiently. The alternative explanation developed here in no way precludes signaling nor free cash considerations; on the contrary, if asymmetric information underlies the heterogeneity of shareholder valuations, then the change to a new marginal shareholder may be tantamount to a change in the information impounded in the market price. The fundamental distinction, therefore, is that the explanation developed in this section incorporates heterogeneous valuations explicitly into any explanation of the stock price reaction to the repurchase.

To introduce the heterogeneous valuations hypothesis, I begin by abstracting from many of the potentially salient components of the market reaction to the repurchase. When the cumulative excess return from the day before the announcement through expiration is positive for non-pro-rated offers, there are numerous explanations. The price increase could reflect only revised information in the presence of homogeneous valuations, as measured by the movement from point a to point b in Figure 1. The evidence presented in section II, however, does not favor this interpretation. By contrast, the price increase could reflect only changes in the marginal shareholder, as measured by the movement from point a to point b in Figure 2. Recall that this explanation, which does not include revisions in shareholder valuations, nevertheless does not rule out a signaling hypothesis based on heterogeneous valuations. As well, the price reaction could incorporate interactions of revised valuations and changes in the marginal shareholder, for example from point a to point c in Figure 2. The lack of a definitive model of the sources of shareholder heterogeneity, and therefore how shareholder valuations change due to the repurchase, limits our ability to distinguish between the second and third hypotheses. Therefore, I refer to such hypotheses, relying on movement along an upward-sloping supply curve, collectively as the heterogeneous valuations hypothesis.

The heterogeneous valuations hypothesis is consistent with all of the price reaction evidence presented above. The typical Dutch auction repurchase buys 15% of the outstanding shares and increases the market price at its announcement by 7.7%. If we assume that the repurchase caused only movement along the supply curve, recall that the average elasticity measure implies that to purchase 15% of the outstanding stock, a firm must offer a 9.1% premium above its pre-announcement price. Since the average announcement price increase is less than that, one consistent explanation of the price increase is that it results from shareholder heterogeneity.[19] This is confirmed by the high correlation between the announcement return and the ultimate repurchase premium.

The expiration price decline only for pro-rated offers is also consistent with shareholder heterogeneity. An important distinction between pro-rated and

---

[19] Bagwell (1991b) reconsiders the price reaction at the announcement of other corporate events in light of an upward-sloping supply curve.

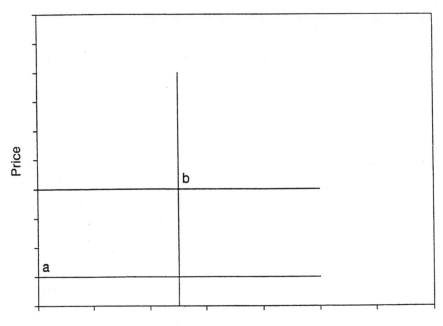

Quantity Repurchased

Figure 1. Explanations of the price reaction to non-pro-rated Dutch auction repur-chases. The positive cumulative excess return from the day before the announcement through expiration could reflect only revised information in the presence of homogeneous valuations, as measured by the movement from point a to point b. The evidence presented in section II, however, does not favor this interpretation.

non-pro-rated offers in the Dutch auction is the effect on the marginal shareholder. In a non-pro-rated offer the reservation price of the post-offer marginal shareholder is at least the purchase price. Movement along the supply curve causes a persistent price increase, and hence there is no price decline at expiration. In a pro-rated repurchase each selling shareholder retains a positive number of shares. Thus, in the pro-rated repurchase the marginal shareholder is not changed by the offer. The reservation price of the marginal shareholder after the offer is less than the purchase price and therefore the price declines at expiration.

This hypothesis is confirmed by the cumulative excess returns from the day before the announcement through expiration. While for the sample the cumulative return is 6.7%, this is driven by non-pro-rated offers, with a 9.8% cumulative return. There is zero cumulative return for pro-rated offers. While the cumulative return is highly correlated with the purchase premium for non-pro-rated firms, it is not highly correlated for pro-rata firms.

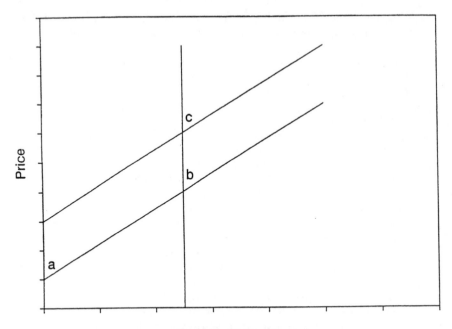

Quantity Repurchased

Figure 2. Explanations of the price reaction to non-pro-rated Dutch auction repur-chases. By contrast to Figure 1, the positive cumulative excess return from the day before the announcement through expiration could reflect only changes in the marginal shareholder, as measured by the movement from point a to point b. Recall that this explanation, which does not include revisions in shareholder valuations, nevertheless does not rule out a signaling hypothesis based on heterogeneous valuations. As well, the price reaction could incorporate interactions of revised valuations and changes in the marginal shareholder, for example from point a to point c.

V. Abnormal Trading Volume

This section documents the pattern of trading volume during the period surrounding the Dutch auction repurchase. In the presence of an upward-sloping supply curve, a non-pro-rata (pro-rata) repurchase removes all (some) of the shareholders with valuations at or below the purchase price. After repurchases one might expect a decline in trading volume, with few trades being made at the post-repurchase price, as well as increases in bid-ask spreads. Models based on asymmetric information about common valuations seem not to predict a reduction in trading volume. Therefore, examination of trading volume patterns may produce corroborative evidence of shareholder heterogeneity.

Trading data were obtained from the CRSP tapes and the S&P Daily Stock

Price Record. The ratio of daily trading volume relative to estimated "normal" pre-repurchase volume is computed analogously to Lakonishok and Vermaelen (1990). For each firm, the trading volume around the announcement and expiration are compared to the average number of shares traded per day in the period from 50 days to 25 days prior to the announcement of the Dutch auction. The average ratio of trading volume relative to the estimates of average volume for the sample are reported in Table VII.

Panel A shows that the pattern of trading volume around the repurchase announcement is similar to the volume pattern found in fixed-price tender offers. In the ten days prior to the announcement, trading volume almost never exceeds 200% of the normal trading volume. Also comparable to fixed-price repurchases, substantial increases in trading activity follow the announcement of the Dutch auction. Average trading volume is very high on the announcement day, over 800% of normal volume. The median volume level is four times the usual volume, with 87% of the firms experiencing above-normal volume. On each of the first ten days after the announcement, volume on average is over 250% of normal volume. The magnitude of the post-announcement increase appears slightly smaller than found in fixed-price tender offers where 300% increases occur on average.

Panel B shows that on average the trading volume is at least twice as large as normal in each of the ten days prior to the expiration day. On the day before expiration, there is over three times the normal trading volume. The median level is 230% of normal, with 77% of the firms experiencing above-normal volume. This finding is comparable to that found for the expiration day for fixed-price repurchases. The expiration day here, in contrast, does not demonstrate significant increase in trading volume, with an average of 132% of normal levels, a normal median level, and exactly half of the firms above normal levels. This result may stem from the timing convention used here to define the expiration day. In particular, since 25 of the 30 (83%) offers expired at midnight, the next trading day is denoted the expiration day, and not the calendar day of the expiration.

It appears that by the second day past expiration unusual trading volume disappears, and daily volume may even be lower than preceding the announcement of the repurchase. Most of the firms have below-normal volume levels, and the median levels are lower than the lowest figure from the pre-announcement period. By the tenth day after expiration the trading volume appears similar to that found in the period preceding the announcement of the repurchase. While these results are inconclusive, lacking statistical significance at traditional levels, trading volume does appear temporarily lower following the expiration of the offer.[20] Similar findings emerged for fixed-price repurchases in Lakonishok and Vermaelen (1990). Further

---

[20] I was unable to conclude whether the trading volume following the expiration is a function of whether the offer was pro-rated.

Table VII

Abnormal Trading Volume Around Dutch Auction Repurchases

This table reports the number of shares traded around the announcement and expiration of the offer relative to normal, which is the average daily trading volume computed from days −50 to −25 relative to the announcement. Under the null hypothesis, the mean ratio is one. Note that the median ratio for normal periods is less than one, and the percentage of positive cases is less than 50%.

Panel A: Trading volume around the announcement of the offer (31 firms).

Day	−20	−19	−10	−9	−8	−7	−6	−5	−4	−3	−2	−1
Mean	1.20	1.03	1.21	1.76	0.79[c]	0.91	1.54	1.27	1.11	1.23	1.05	1.17
Med.	0.66	0.79	0.72	0.70	0.68	0.76	0.68	0.74	0.81	0.78	0.89	0.97
% > 1	32	42	32	42	32	29	39	42	35	42	39	45

Day	0	1	2	3	4	5	6	7	8	9	10	20
Mean	8.83[a]	4.30[a]	2.75[a]	2.04[a]	2.47[a]	2.45[b]	2.59[b]	2.85[c]	2.58[b]	2.28[b]	1.53	1.53[b]
Med.	4.13	2.31	2.48	1.85	1.34	1.20	1.40	1.31	1.31	1.05	1.09	.87
% > 1	87	84	68	65	61	58	61	68	61	52	55	45

Panel B: Trading volume around the expiration of the offer (30 firms).

Day	−10	−9	−8	−7	−6	−5	−4	−3	−2	−1
Mean	1.90[c]	2.74	2.43[b]	2.35[c]	2.48[b]	2.29[b]	3.58	2.98[a]	2.12[a]	3.61[b]
Med.	1.12	1.15	1.32	1.15	1.17	1.17	1.48	1.56	1.69	2.30
% > 1	53	57	67	57	70	60	60	60	63	77

Day	0	1	2	3	4	5	6	7	8	9	10
Mean	1.32	1.24	1.40	1.10	0.88	0.86	1.36	0.95	0.94	1.58	1.00
Med.	1.00	0.95	0.54	0.51	0.64	0.64	0.66	0.91	0.80	0.94	0.62
% > 1	52	47	23	13	27	27	40	40	33	43	33

[a]Significantly different from one at the 1% level (two-tailed test).
[b]Significantly different from one at the 5% level (two-tailed test).
[c]Significantly different from one at the 10% level (two-tailed test).

empirical work, therefore, should explore possible reductions in trading volume resulting from similar corporate events.

VI. Cross-Sectional Variations in Supply Elasticity

This section examines the characteristics of firms that face less elastic supply curves when they repurchase stock using the Dutch auction. Although the robustness of the results is limited by the smallness of this sample, the findings suggest that firms with low trading volume, firms not included in the S&P 500 Index, and firms that are not takeover targets face supply curves with greater upward slope. There is no difference based on whether a firm required confidential use of the shareholder tendering responses.

I examine first the relation between a stock's trading volume and its Dutch auction supply curve elasticity. Firms with large daily trading volume prior to the offer are more likely to have many shareholders with valuations close to the market price, since many shares are transactable at or near the market price, and hence may possess more elastic supply curves. Daily trading volume, obtained from the CRSP tapes and the S&P Daily Stock Price Record, is averaged over the period from 50 days to 25 days prior to the announcement of the Dutch auction. This window is the same as used to calculate "normal" volume in section V. Firms with no more than the sample median of 54,508 shares traded per day on average are classified as "Thin" stocks, while those with daily trading volume above the median are considered "Thick" stocks.[21]

A second (although less precise) proxy for liquidity is inclusion in the S&P 500 Index. Index funds as well as non-index institutions generate significant volume for these stocks.[22] Fourteen of the 31 firms were included in the S&P 500 Index at the time of the repurchase.

Second, I document whether firms initiating Dutch auction repurchases in the presence of rumored or actual takeover activity have different elasticities than firms without takeover activity. Takeover activity might increase the valuation dispersion by generating uncertainty about the takeover's outcome. Alternatively, if takeover activity has encouraged shareholders to sell to arbitrageurs, then more agreement in tendering prices could be observed after these transactions were completed. Also, if the target of a takeover is an endogenous choice, firms with relatively elastic supply curves are easier to take over. Based on WSJ accounts, takeover activity was considered to exist if at any time from one year before the announcement of the repurchase until expiration of the repurchase either (1) there were takeover rumors published, (2) an outsider acquired a significant holding, (3) antitakeover amendments were implemented, or (4) an actual takeover bid was made. Twelve firms satisfied at least one of the conditions for takeover activity.

---

[21] The mean daily trading volume for the 31 firms is 118,375 shares per day.

[22] For discussion, see Shleifer (1986), Harris and Gurel (1986), and Pruitt and Wei (1989).

Third, I investigate whether the 14 firms that demanded confidentiality in my use of the tendering data have significantly different elasticities than the firms which allowed free disclosure of the data. I am interested in whether the sample collected here is representative of all Dutch auction repurchases or is biased because the firms were willing to reveal the shareholder tendering responses. If confidential firms are not different than nonconfidential ones within Dutch auction firms that provided shareholder tendering data, it is less likely that the ones that provided data are different from those that refused to provide data.

The results are reported in Panels A through D of Table VIII. Firms with large daily trading volume have an average elasticity of 2.4, significantly greater than the elasticity of 1.3 for those with lighter volume. Firms included in the S&P 500 Index have an average elasticity of 1.9, somewhat greater than the elasticity of 1.4 for those that are not, although the differences are not statistically significant. Firms with takeover activity have an average elasticity of 2.2, greater than the elasticity of 1.4 for those that are not targets, especially above the bottom decile of the supply curve. There are no discernible differences across the elasticities of firms depending on whether the firm allowed free disclosure of the shareholder tendering responses.

I also consider these factors collectively in a multiple regression, allowing for correlation and interaction between these factors, using the regressions:

$$NP_i = \alpha + \beta_1 D_{1i} + \beta_2 D_{2i} + \beta_3 D_{3i} + \beta_4 D_{4i} + \varepsilon_i$$

where NP_i measures for firm i the difference between bids, for example, corresponding to the 6th percentile tender and the bid corresponding to the 1st percentile tender, scaled by the pre-announcement market price, and $D1$, $D2$, $D3$, and $D4$ are dummy variables whose sample values are:

$D1 = 1$ if the firm has "Thick" volume, else 0
$D2 = 1$ if the firm is included in the S&P 500 Index, else 0
$D3 = 1$ if the firm is a takeover target, else 0
$D4 = 1$ if the firm required confidentiality, else 0.

The results of the multiple regression analysis (table not reported) confirm the bivariate cross-sectional variations in supply curve elasticities documented in Panels A through D. Firms with large trading volume, firms included in the S&P 500 Index, and takeover targets have more elastic supply curves. Whether a firm required confidentiality never significantly influences the elasticities, and including a dummy for confidentiality in the multiple regressions consistently lessens the statistical significance against the hypothesis of no cross-sectional differences. Moreover, there appear to be interactions between trading volume, takeover activity, and inclusion in the S&P 500 Index, warranting further examination with larger samples.

It is also interesting that even the subsamples of more elastic firms, including firms with heavy trading volume, firms that are included in the

Table VIII
Arc Elasticity Measures: Cross-Sectional Variation

This table reports the percentage price change necessary to acquire additional shares, scaled by the pre-announcement price, going from 1% to 6% of outstanding shares, 6% to 11%, and 11% to 16%. The cross-sectional variations in the price change (and implied elasticity) are reported for subsamples of firms based on the size of their trading volume, whether they are included in the S&P 500 Index, whether they have been the target of takeover activity, and whether they required confidential use of the data, for 31 firms conducting Dutch auction stock repurchases, 1981–1988.

Panel A: Sixteen firms had no more than the sample median of 54,508 shares traded per day and are considered "Thin" stocks, while 15 firms had daily trading volume above the median and are considered "Thick" stocks.

% Price Change for 5% Quantity Changes: Intervals	Thick Firms	Thin Firms	Price Diff. of Means t-Statistic	p Value	Mean Thick Arc η = %Q/%P	Mean Thin Arc η = %Q/%P	No. Thick: No. Thin
1-6	2.83	5.92	-2.05	.051	1.77	0.85	14:12
6-11	1.80	3.36	-1.56	.133	2.78	1.49	12:10
11-16	1.52	2.53	-1.12	.280	3.29	1.98	12:7
Sum: 1-16	6.15	11.81			2.44*	1.27*	

Panel B: Fourteen firms were included in the S&P 500 Index at the time of repurchase, while 17 were not.

% Price Change for 5% Quantity Changes: Intervals	S&P 500 Firms	Non-S&P 500 Firms	Price Diff. of Means t-Statistic	p Value	Mean S&P Arc η = %Q/%P	Mean Non-S&P Arc η = %Q/%P	No. S&P: No. Non-S&P
1-6	3.49	5.59	-1.35	.191	1.43	0.89	13:13
6-11	2.61	2.48	0.13	.900	1.92	2.02	11:11
11-16	1.62	2.50	-1.01	.328	3.09	2.00	11:8
Sum: 1-16	7.72	10.57			1.94*	1.42*	

Table VIII-Continued

Panel C: Twelve firms were takeover targets in the year preceding or during the repurchase, while 19 were not.

% Price Change for 5% Quantity Changes: Intervals	Takeover Firms	Non-takeover Firms	Price Diff. of Means t-Statistic	p Value	Mean Takeover Arc $\eta = \%Q/\%P$	Mean Non-takeover Arc $\eta = \%Q/\%P$	No. Takeover: No. Non-takeover
1–6	3.71	5.15	−0.90	.379	1.35	0.97	11:15
6–11	1.64	3.31	−1.69	.106	3.05	1.51	10:12
11–16	1.43	2.49	−1.25	.229	3.50	2.01	9:10
Sum: 1–16	6.78	10.95			2.21*	1.37*	

Panel D: Fourteen firms required confidential use of the tendering bids, while 17 did not.

% Price Change for 5% Quantity Changes: Intervals	Confident Firms	Non-confident Firms	Price Diff. of Means t-Statistic	p Value	Mean Confident Arc $\eta = \%Q/\%P$	Mean Non confident Arc $\eta = \%Q/\%P$	No. Confident: No. Non-confident
1–6	4.95	4.24	0.43	.670	1.01	1.18	11:15
6–11	2.03	2.90	−0.83	.418	2.46	1.72	9:13
11–16	1.87	2.10	−0.26	.798	2.67	2.38	9:10
Sum: 1–16	8.85	9.24			1.70*	1.62*	

*This figure is computed using the mean sum price change over the 15% quantity interval.

S&P 500 Index, or takeover targets, have an average elasticity of approximately two. This suggests that the model of perfect supply elasticity is not appropriate even for these firms.

VII. Conclusion

Finance theory often assumes that the supply curve for shares is perfectly elastic. Nevertheless, this paper provides direct evidence that repurchasing firms face significantly upward-sloping supply curves for their shares. Shareholders' valuations differ dramatically, as revealed by their bids in Dutch auction repurchases of stock.

The average elasticity measure implies that to purchase 15% of the outstanding stock, a firm must offer a 9.1% premium above its pre-announcement market price. Much of the observed 7.7% announcement day price increase therefore is consistent with movement along an upward-sloping supply curve. This is confirmed by the high correlation between the announcement return and the ultimate repurchase premium. The expiration price decline only for pro-rated offers is also consistent with shareholder heterogeneity. In a non-pro-rated offer, movement along the supply curve causes a persistent price increase, and hence there is no price decline at expiration. By contrast, in a pro-rated repurchase the marginal shareholder is not changed by the offer, and hence there is a price decline at expiration. This is confirmed by the cumulative excess returns from the day before the announcement through expiration.

The findings force a reconsideration of all hypotheses which rely on homogeneity of valuations, and underscore the need to explicitly incorporate upward-sloping supply curves into explanations of the market reaction to the repurchase. Shareholder heterogeneity and signaling need not be in conflict; yet, for a true understanding of the price reaction, an explicit model of the sources of shareholder heterogeneity, and therefore how shareholder valuations change due to the repurchase, is imperative. This evidence herein also leaves unanswered the question of whether some of the price changes observed during other repurchases, takeovers, or large block transactions may also be due to upward-sloping supply curves.

Changes in trading volume around Dutch auction repurchases are comparable to the findings for fixed-price repurchases. On average, volume increases dramatically during the repurchase, and it appears to fall below pre-announcement levels after the expiration of the offer. Future research should examine post-expiration trading activity for similar corporate events.

The share price elasticity calculated from the individual bids is larger for firms with large trading volume, firms included in the S&P 500 Index, and firms that have been the targets of takeover activity. In future research, I will differentiate between various potential sources of the observed cross-sectional variation in Dutch auction supply curve elasticity. These sources include taxation, transaction costs, and the divergence of information and opinion.

Appendix A
Firms Conducting Dutch Auction Stock Repurchases:
1981–1988

Alco Standard Corp.
American Presidents Co.
Axia Inc.
Barnes Group Inc.
Brown-Forman Corp.
Cabot Corp.
Caesars World Inc.
Chelsea Industries Inc.
CSX Corp.
Equitable Bancorp.
Excello Corp.
Far West Financial Corp.
FHP International Corp.
FMC Corp.
Geico Corp.
Gelco Corp.
General Signal Corp.
Graco Inc.
Holiday Corp.
Hospital Corp. of America
Household International Inc.
Jewelcor Inc.
Jostens Inc.
Carl Karcher Enterprises Inc.
Knogo Corp.
Masco Industries Inc.
May Department Stores Co.
MEM Company
NL Industries Inc.
Pennwalt Corp.
Progressive Corp.
Quadrex Corp.
Quantum Chemical Corp.
Quantum Corp.
Ralston Purina Co.
Resorts International Inc.
Rex-Noreco Inc.
RJR Nabisco Inc.
Sage Energy Company
Schlumberger LTD
SmithKline Beckman Corp.
Standard Brands Paint Co.
Sterling Software Inc.
J. P. Stevens and Company
Superior Surgical
Tektronix Inc.
Tenneco Inc.
Todd Shipyards
Torchmark Corp.
TRW Inc.
Vulcan Materials
Whittaker Corp.

Appendix B
Dutch Auction Supply Curves

For each firm, the shareholder tendering responses from the Dutch auction are ordered from lowest to highest prices within the price range of the offer. This schedule of offers is the supply curve for the shares that the company faces in the repurchase. This table documents the supply curves for the 17 firms not requesting confidentiality. The prices at which shares were tendered are normalized with the pre-announcement price set to 100. Quantity is normalized to measure the cumulative percentage of outstanding shares tendered at or below each price. The percent sought is the upper bound of outstanding shares sought.

Axia		Far West		FMC		Jostens	
Price Range: 15,21		Price Range: 8,10.5		Price Range: 51,54		Price Range: 33.5,37	
Pre-ann. Price: 17.75		Pre-ann. Price: 9.375		Pre-ann. Price: 48.625		Pre-ann. Price: 32.5	
Percent Sought: 7.5		Percent Sought: 8.5		Percent Sought: 18.2		Percent Sought: 16.9	
Price	Quantity	Price	Quantity	Price	Quantity	Price	Quantity
84.51	0.100	85.33	0.037	104.88	7.576	103.08	0.896
85.92	0.100	88.00	0.038	105.91	7.818	103.85	0.896
87.32	0.100	90.67	0.038	106.94	11.181	104.62	0.982
88.73	0.100	93.33	0.039	107.97	12.572	105.39	0.982
90.14	0.100	96.00	0.040	108.98	15.282	106.15	0.983
91.55	0.100	98.67	0.041	110.03	17.636	106.92	1.089
92.96	0.100	101.33	0.042	111.05	24.903	107.69	2.705
94.37	0.100	104.00	0.043			108.46	4.030
95.78	0.117	106.67	0.071			109.23	5.956
97.18	0.119	109.33	0.224			110.00	6.638
98.59	0.121	112.00	2.216			110.77	9.869
100.00	0.198					111.54	10.160
101.41	0.396					112.31	11.482
102.82	0.594					113.08	12.237
104.23	1.488					113.85	14.195
105.63	1.709						
107.04	2.156						
108.45	2.208						
109.86	3.896						
111.27	4.893						
112.68	5.987						
114.08	6.236						
115.49	8.586						
116.90	9.206						
118.31	12.989						

General Signal

Price Range: 44,51
Pre-ann. Price: 43.75
Percent Sought: 31.5

Price	Quantity	Price	Quantity
100.57	7.422	108.86	10.854
100.86	7.597	109.14	10.855
101.14	7.597	109.43	11.921
101.43	7.597	109.71	12.210
101.71	7.597	110.00	12.350
102.00	7.597	110.29	12.358
102.29	7.597	110.57	12.360
102.57	7.597	110.86	12.364
102.86	8.799	111.14	12.364
103.14	8.799	111.43	12.366
103.43	8.974	111.71	12.368
103.71	8.974	112.00	13.222
104.00	9.092	112.29	13.222
104.29	9.092	112.57	13.311
104.57	9.092	112.86	13.320
104.86	9.092	113.14	14.149
105.14	9.868	113.43	14.709
105.43	9.868	113.71	16.130
105.71	10.030	114.00	19.278
106.00	10.030	114.29	21.618
106.29	10.031	114.57	22.768
106.57	10.031	114.86	22.881
106.86	10.032	115.14	22.883
107.14	10.032	115.43	27.029
107.43	10.847	115.71	27.036
107.71	10.847	116.00	28.270
108.00	10.849	116.29	28.465
108.29	10.850	116.57	38.210
108.57	10.854		

Pennwalt

Price Range: 85,97
Pre-ann. Price: 90
Percent Sought: 37.6

Price	Quantity	Price	Quantity
94.44	72.519	102.50	76.118
94.72	72.779	102.78	76.158
95.00	72.792	103.06	76.168
95.28	72.795	103.33	76.456
95.56	72.902	103.61	76.462
95.83	72.903	103.89	76.465
96.11	72.922	104.17	76.516
96.39	72.928	104.44	76.629
96.67	73.191	104.72	76.631
96.94	73.196	105.00	76.633
97.22	73.450	105.28	76.641
97.50	73.478	105.56	77.426
97.78	73.828	105.83	77.428
98.06	73.829	106.11	77.436
98.33	73.923	106.39	77.441
98.61	73.929	106.67	77.474
98.89	74.150	106.94	77.474
99.17	74.150	107.22	77.592
99.44	74.158	107.50	77.623
99.72	74.202	107.78	77.916
100.00	74.987		
100.28	75.006		
100.56	75.014		
100.83	75.037		
101.11	75.651		
101.39	75.659		
101.67	75.670		
101.94	75.817		
102.22	76.105		

Ralston Purina
Price Range: 76,85
Pre-ann. Price: 79.125
Percent Sought: 7.4

Standard Brands
Price Range: 25,28
Pre-ann. Price: 21.5
Percent Sought: 53.1

Carl Karcher
Price Range: 21,24
Pre-ann. Price: 19.125
Percent Sought: 17.1

Ralston Purina				Standard Brands		Carl Karcher	
Price	Quantity	Price	Quantity	Price	Quantity	Price	Quantity
96.05	1.074	101.26	1.111	116.28	84.165	109.80	3.056
96.21	1.074	101.42	1.112	116.86	84.169	110.46	3.056
96.37	1.074	101.58	1.112	117.44	84.188	111.11	3.069
96.52	1.074	101.74	1.116	118.02	84.249	111.76	3.069
96.68	1.074	101.89	1.117	118.60	84.249	112.42	3.428
96.84	1.074	102.05	1.117	119.19	84.277	113.07	3.829
96.99	1.074	102.21	1.118	119.77	84.283	113.73	3.832
97.16	1.074	102.37	1.637	120.35	84.524	114.38	3.834
97.31	1.075	102.53	1.637	120.93	84.524	115.03	4.402
97.47	1.075	102.69	1.637	121.51	84.543	115.69	4.408
97.63	1.075	102.84	1.723	122.09	84.546	116.34	4.409
97.79	1.075	103.00	1.723	122.67	84.647	116.99	4.420
97.95	1.075	103.16	1.738	123.26	84.651	117.65	6.605
98.10	1.075	103.32	1.738	123.84	84.661	118.30	6.680
98.26	1.075	103.48	1.938	124.42	84.666	118.95	7.805
98.42	1.075	103.63	1.939	125.00	84.929	119.61	7.967
98.58	1.076	103.79	1.939	125.58	84.930	120.26	15.315
98.74	1.076	103.95	1.939	126.16	84.930	120.92	15.320
98.89	1.076	104.11	2.676	126.74	84.932	121.57	16.019
99.05	1.076	104.27	2.676	127.33	84.964	122.22	16.072
99.21	1.076	104.42	2.773	127.91	84.964	122.88	17.657
99.37	1.076	104.58	2.774	128.49	84.975	123.53	17.693
99.53	1.076	104.74	3.689	129.07	84.976	124.18	18.127
99.68	1.076	104.89	3.690	129.65	87.463	124.84	18.166
99.84	1.078	105.06	4.362	130.23		125.49	23.685
100.00	1.078	105.21	4.513				
100.16	1.078	105.37	5.675				
100.32	1.078	105.53	5.729				
100.47	1.080	105.69	6.299				
100.63	1.080	105.85	6.302				
100.79	1.080	106.00	8.178				
100.95	1.081	106.16					
101.11	1.111						

Barnes Group		J.P. Stevens		Whittaker		Todd Shipyards	
Price Range: 24.5,28		Price Range: 34,38		Price Range: 30,34		Price Range: 21,28	
Pre-ann. Price: 23.5		Pre-ann. Price: 33.375		Pre-ann. Price: 27.25		Pre-ann. Price: 24.25	
Percent Sought: 15		Percent Sought: 13		Percent Sought: 46.5		Percent Sought: 10	
Price	Quantity	Price	Quantity	Price	Quantity	Price	Quantity
104.26	0.428	101.87	2.685	110.09	3.864	86.60	0.000
105.32	0.428	102.62	2.687	111.01	3.864	98.97	0.007
106.38	0.436	103.37	2.689	111.93	3.869	100.00	0.043
107.45	0.436	104.12	2.803	112.84	3.870	102.06	0.063
108.51	0.437	104.87	3.178	113.76	4.609	103.09	0.166
109.57	0.438	105.62	3.179	114.68	4.611	105.15	1.496
110.64	0.799	106.37	3.191	115.59	4.618	106.19	2.043
111.70	0.809	107.12	3.636	116.51	4.780	107.22	3.621
112.77	1.463	107.87	5.363	117.43	7.712	108.25	3.639
113.83	1.564	108.61	6.641	118.35	12.514	109.28	7.149
114.89	5.652	109.36	10.063	119.27	13.943	110.31	7.150
115.96	8.385	110.11	11.159	120.18	21.575	111.34	7.152
117.02	8.991	110.86	15.554	121.10	25.317	113.40	7.225
118.09	10.734	111.61	16.966	122.02	27.534	115.46	7.234
119.15	12.070	112.36	21.748	122.94	28.813		
		113.11	23.429	123.85	29.753		
		113.86	29.420	124.77	35.689		

Knogo		NL Industries		RJR Nabisco		Sage Energy	
Price Range:	15,18	Price Range:	15.125,16	Price Range:	52,58	Price Range:	6.5,8.5
Pre-ann. Price:	12.875	Pre-ann. Price:	14.125	Pre-ann. Price:	48	Pre-ann. Price:	6.875
Percent Sought:	47.6	Percent Sought:	16.7	Percent Sought:	8.1	Percent Sought:	8.3
Price	Quantity	Price	Quantity	Price	Quantity	Price	Quantity
116.50	4.625	107.08	48.064	108.33	6.715	94.55	0.019
118.45	4.625	107.96	50.695	109.38	6.964	101.82	0.019
120.39	4.641	108.85	51.324	110.42	7.710	109.09	0.393
122.33	4.641	109.73	53.444	111.46	8.396	116.36	1.915
124.27	5.373	110.62	53.776	112.50	10.169	123.64	4.842
126.21	5.728	111.50	54.267	113.54	10.865		
128.16	6.484	112.39	54.495	114.58	12.873		
130.09	8.547	113.27	56.518	115.63	13.350		
132.04	10.105			116.67	15.087		
133.98	11.067			117.71	16.057		
135.92	13.497			118.75	17.252		
137.86	14.284			119.79	17.489		
139.81	18.178			120.83	18.646		

104   *The Journal of Finance*

REFERENCES

Bagwell, Laurie Simon, 1991a, Share repurchase and takeover deterrence, *Rand Journal of Economics* 22, 72–88.

——, 1991b, Shareholder heterogeneity: Evidence and implications, *American Economic Review* 81, 218–221.

—— and Kenneth L. Judd, 1989, Transaction costs and corporate control, Unpublished manuscript, Northwestern University.

Bradley, M., A. Desai, and E. H. Kim, 1988, Synergistic gains from corporate acquisitions and their division between the stockholders of target and acquiring firms, *Journal of Financial Economics* 21, 4–40.

Brown, David T. and Michael Ryngaert, 1990, Heterogeneous shareholders: Evidence from buybacks and control contests, Unpublished manuscript, University of Florida.

Comment, Robert and Greg A. Jarrell, 1991, The relative signalling power of Dutch auction and fixed-price self-tender offers and open-market share repurchases, *Journal of Finance* 46, 1243–1271.

Dann, Larry Y., 1981, Common stock repurchases: An analysis of returns to bondholders and stockholders, *Journal of Financial Economics* 9, 113–138.

Fama, Eugene F. and Merton H. Miller, 1972, *The Theory of Finance* (Dryden Press, Hinsdale, IL).

Harris, Lawrence and Eitan Gurel, 1986, Price and volume effects associated with changes in the S&P 500: New evidence for the existence of price pressures, *Journal of Finance* 41, 815–829.

Holthausen, Robert, Richard Leftwich, and David Mayers, 1990, Large-block transactions: The speed of response, and temporary and permanent stock-price effects, *Journal of Financial Economics* 26, 71–95.

Jensen, Michael, 1986, Agency costs of free cash flow, corporate finance and takeovers, *American Economic Review* 76, 323–329.

Kamma, Sreenivas, George Kanatas, and Steven Raymar, 1990, Dutch auction vs. fixed-price self-tender offers for common stock: An empirical examination, Unpublished manuscript, Indiana University.

Lakonishok, Josef and Theo Vermaelen, 1990, Anomalous price behavior around repurchase tender offers, *Journal of Finance* 45, 455–477.

Loderer, Claudio, John Cooney, and Leonard Van Drunen, 1991, The price elasticity of demand for common stock, *Journal of Finance* 46, 621–651.

Masulis, Ronald W., 1980, Stock repurchase by tender offer: An analysis of the causes of common stock price changes, *Journal of Finance* 35, 305–321.

Mayshar, Joram, 1981, Transaction costs and the pricing of assets, *Journal of Finance* 36, 583–597.

Mikkelson, Wayne and Megan Partch, 1985, Stock price effects and costs of secondary distributions, *Journal of Financial Economics* 14, 165–194.

Milgrom, Paul and Robert Weber, 1982, A theory of auctions and competitive bidding, *Econometrica* 50, 1089–1122.

Miller, Edward, 1977, Risk, uncertainty, and divergence of opinion, *Journal of Finance* 32, 1151–1168.

Pruitt, Stephen and K. C. John Wei, 1989, Institutional ownership and changes in the S&P 500, *Journal of Finance* 44, 509–513.

Scholes, Myron, 1972, The market for securities: Substitution versus price pressure and the effects of information on share prices, *Journal of Business* 45, 179–211.

Shleifer, Andrei, 1986, Do demand curves for stock slope down? *Journal of Finance* 41, 579–590.

Stulz, René M., 1988, Managerial control of voting rights: Financial policies and the market for corporate control, *Journal of Financial Economics* 20, 25–54.

Varian, Hal R., 1985, Divergence of opinion in complete markets, *Journal of Finance* 40, 309–317.

Vermaelen, Theo, 1981, Common stock repurchases and market signalling: An empirical study, *Journal of Financial Economics* 9, 139–183.

———, 1984, Repurchase tender offers, signalling and managerial incentives, *Journal of Financial and Quantitative Analysis* 19, 163–181.

Vickrey, William, 1961, Counterspeculation, auctions, and competitive sealed tenders, *Journal of Finance* 16, 8–37.

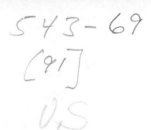

[18]

THE JOURNAL OF FINANCE • VOL. XLVI, NO. 5 • DECEMBER 1991

Stock Prices and the Supply of Information

MICHAEL J. BRENNAN and PATRICIA J. HUGHES*

ABSTRACT

We develop a model in which the dependence of the brokerage commission rate on share price provides an incentive for brokers to produce research reports on firms with low share prices. Stock splits therefore affect the attention paid to a firm by investment analysts. Managers with favorable private information about their firms have an incentive to split their firm's shares in order to reveal the information to investors. We find empirical evidence that is consistent with the major new prediction of the model, that the number of analysts following a firm is inversely related to its share price.

THE CLASSICAL THEORY OF finance assigns great importance to the aggregate market value of the equity of a firm, but has no role for the number of shares in a firm's capital stock, or for the price of a single share. Consequently, the attention paid to this seemingly irrelevant variable by firms, investors, and brokers, as well as by legal and regulatory authorities, has so far defied plausible explanation. It is clear that firms attempt to manage the unit price of their shares by stock splits and occasional reverse splits, and there is a strong relation between the price per share and the size of the firm.[1] Moreover, investors pay attention to stock splits, the abnormal return consequent on a split announcement being strongly related to the projected post-split share price. This reaction has been explained by Brennan and Copeland (1988a) as the rational response to a costly signal by the firm. The basis of their argument is that it is costly for a firm to reduce its share price by splitting because the structure of brokerage commissions makes it more costly to trade in low priced shares. The relation between splits and trading

---

* Irwin and Goldyne Hearsh Professor of Banking and Finance at University of California, Los Angeles, and University of Southern California, respectively. We are grateful to Craig Holden and Jim Brandon for research assistance. We also thank Yuk-Shee Chan, Linda DeAngelo, John Hand, Prem Jain, Pat O'Brien, Brett Trueman, Ivo Welch, Fred Weston, workshop participants at Cornell, London Business School, London School of Economics, Stanford, UC Berkeley, UCLA, UC Riverside, USC, and University of Texas (Austin), and the referees and Rene Stulz for helpful comments. A previous version of this paper was presented at the 1990 meetings of the American Accounting Association, the French Finance Association, the IMI in Rome, and the Western Finance Association.

[1] Stoll and Whaley (1983) show that, based upon portfolios formed on firm size, average price per share is monotonically increasing in size, and both the mean portfolio return and beta are monotonically decreasing in size.

costs has been acknowledged in the business press,[2] and the signaling argument finds support in the work of McNichols and Dravid (1990) and others who show that stock splits are followed by unexpected increases in earnings. Less easy to explain is the change in stock price behavior following the date the split becomes effective. Ohlson and Penman (1985) observe an increase in the variance of returns following the split ex-date, and Brennan and Copeland (1988b) find that the systematic risk of firms also increases following the split.

The Brennan and Copeland signaling model is at best a partial explanation of the stock price reaction to split announcements, for it relies on the observed structure of brokerage commissions which is taken as exogenous. Yet why should brokerage commissions depend on such a seemingly irrelevant variable as the share price? And why should legal and regulatory authorities also be concerned about the level of the price per share?[3] In this paper we present a model with an equilibrium in which different firms choose different share prices, smaller firms have lower share prices, brokerage commissions depend on share prices, share prices react to split announcements, the share price behavior and bid-ask spread may change following the split, the number of shareholders increases after a split, and there is cross-sectional variation in the number of analysts following different firms.

We argue that managers with favorable private information will find it advantageous to have independent third parties produce information about their firms for investors.[4] In order to avoid obvious moral hazard considerations, it is necessary that the information producers be independent of the firm.[5] This poses the problem of compensating the information producers for their efforts. We argue that the role of information producer is assumed by brokers who make earnings forecasts about individual firms and receive compensation for their efforts in the form of brokerage commissions from the investors who trade in the particular stocks. Following Merton (1987), we assume in our model that investors will only purchase stocks that they "know about", and that this knowledge is provided in the form of brokers' earnings forecasts. Thus earnings forecasts generate brokerage commissions

---

[2] ' "Stock splits are the biggest ripoff on Wall Street," contends Hans R. Reinisch, a New York investor. "The only thing that changes with a split is the brokerage commissions, and they often go up sharply. If you're an active investor, you have to take into account the transaction costs." ' (*Wall Street Journal*, October 13, 1989).

[3] For example, margin loans are not permitted on stock transactions in which the share price is less than $5.

[4] Diamond (1985) argues that firms have an incentive to make information available to shareholders in order to reduce the costs of private information acquisition.

[5] The lack of credibility of information produced by investment bankers in the employ of the corporation was discussed in a recent *Wall Street Journal* article. An associate research director at Drexel reported "The research department did our darndest to resist pressure from corporate finance. We made it clear when we had a bias, when we had an underwriting relationship. As a result, the thinking was that institutional investors using the Drexel research reports had a red flag, and unless they were completely stupid, they'd do a double check with someone with less involvement." ("Wall Street Grows Treacherous for Analysts Who Speak Out," April 5, 1990)

because investors trade only in those stocks for which the brokers forecast earnings.

In deciding whether to forecast earnings, a broker compares the cost of the forecast with the commission revenue it will generate, which depends on the size of the firm and the total number of brokers making forecasts. Given the commission rate, competition among brokers will determine the equilibrium number of brokers who make forecasts about a particular firm. We consider an equilibrium in which brokers offer a commission schedule which depends on the share price. This permits managers to influence the number of brokers who make earnings forecasts about their firms by changing the share price through a split.[6]

The major new prediction of the model, that the flow of information about firms is an increasing function of firm size and a decreasing function of the share price, is tested by examining the relation between the number of brokerage firm analysts who report earnings forecasts for a firm and its share price and size.[7] We find that the number of analysts is related to both share price and size in the predicted manner.

In the following section we summarize the previous empirical studies of splits. In Section II we present a formal model of the effect of share prices on the flow of information about a firm provided by stockbrokers. Section III discusses the data and reports the result of the empirical tests of the supply of information hypothesis. Section IV concludes.

I. Empirical Evidence on Stock Splits

There have been extensive empirical studies documenting an association between stock splits and various economic variables. We summarize here the empirical regularities that a theory of share prices must address.

Not surprisingly, stock splits follow periods of rising stock prices.[8] However, there also is extensive evidence that share prices rise further on the announcement of a split and fall on the announcement of a reverse split,[9] suggesting that the split announcement serves as a signal of management's

---

[6] A referee has suggested to us an alternative explanation for stock splits and for our empirical results. He argues that small investors who prefer low priced stocks are necessary to provide liquidity in low capitalization stocks, leading to a correlation between size and stock price. Furthermore, "a lower share price corresponds to a wider ownership and implies more potential trading commissions and therefore, more analyst following." However, this argument does not explain the observed relation between splits and subsequent earnings increases (see footnote 11).

[7] Note that our theory relates only to brokerage house analysts whose compensation depends upon stock trading commissions, and not to analysts employed by other financial institutions such as insurance companies.

[8] Fama, Fisher, Jensen, and Roll (1969) find that shares of splitting firms earned abnormal returns for 29 months prior to the split, and Lakonishok and Lev (1987) report that the shares rise by about 70% more than those of their control sample over the four years preceding the split announcement.

[9] See Grinblatt, Masulis, and Titman (1984); Eades, Hess, and Kim (1984); Lamoureux and Poon (1987); and Asquith, Healy, and Palepu (1989).

private information.[10] This notion is confirmed by the finding that stock splits are associated with unexpected increases in earnings.[11] Grinblatt et al. (1984) find that the abnormal announcement return is negatively related to the size of the firm and to a measure of information leakage over the previous week; and they interpret this evidence as consistent with an "attention hypothesis" according to which undervalued firms split their stock in order to attract attention. Arbel and Swanson (1989) find that firms that split had been followed by fewer analysts prior to the split than all firms on average, and conclude that these neglected firms split in order to attract attention from analysts. They also find that the magnitude of the price response to the firm's split announcement is negatively related to the number of analysts following the firm. Brennan and Copeland find that, as predicted by their signaling theory, the announcement return is negatively related to the target post-split share price, which they define as the pre-split price divided by the split factor.

It is commonly claimed that the purpose of stock splits is to improve liquidity and increase the number of shareholders. Despite this, several authors (e.g., Copeland (1979)) have found a decrease in trading volume following a split. However, Lakonishok and Lev (1987) show that it is the trading volume prior to the split which is abnormally high, and that it returns to normal within two months of the split. Conroy and Flood (1989) find that, despite the decline in the dollar volume of trade, there is an increase in the number of transactions, which implies that the average transaction size falls. They also find an increase in the number of individual shareholders subsequent to the split.

Stock splits also appear to be associated with increases in risk.[12] While Amihud and Mendelson (1988) attribute this finding to the discreteness of stock prices and increases in the bid-ask spread following splits, Sheikh (1989) finds an increase in the volatility implied by option prices following the split ex-date, which suggests that the phenomenon is real rather than due to measurement error. Brennan and Copeland (1988b) report a major increase in the beta coefficient on the ex-date (but not on the announcement date). Wiggins (1990) finds that the magnitude of this increase is sensitive to the return measurement interval, and explains the Brennan and Copeland finding as the result of a more rapid response of security returns to market information following the split date.

The Brennan and Copeland signaling model relies on the fact that brokerage commissions depend upon share prices. Table I summarizes the results of a study by Coler and Schaefer (1988) which compares typical commissions charged by full service brokers with those charged by discount brokers. Not

---

[10] More puzzling is the finding of additional abnormal returns on the ex-date of the split. See Grinblatt, Masulis, and Titman (1984).

[11] See Lakonishok and Lev (1987), Doran and Nachtmann (1988), and McNichols and Dravid (1990). Asquith, Healy, and Palepu (1989) find that large increases in earnings prior to the split are not reversed in the four years following the split.

[12] See Ohlson and Penman (1985), French and Dubofsky (1986), and Dravid (1987).

Table I

Typical Full Service Brokerage Commissions as Per Cent of Trade Value for Selected Transactions* (Average Discount Broker Commissions in Parentheses)

Size of Trade	Share Price				
	10	20	30	40	50
$3,000			2.600 (1.180)		
$4,000		2.625 (1.101)		2.225 (0.922)	
$5,000	2.980 (1.086)				1.940 (0.755)
$6,000			2.233 (0.846)		
$8,000				2.100 (0.700)	
$9,000			2.089 (0.716)		
$10,000		2.040 (0.734)			1.870 (0.589)
$12,000				1.850 (0.587)	
$15,000					1.720 (0.499)

*Constructed from Table 2 in Coler and Schaefer (1988).

only is the discount broker commission (in parentheses) about one-third that of the full service broker, but, for both types, the commission charged as a proportion of the trade declines as a function both of the size of the trade and of the price of the shares traded.[13] Branch (1985) argues that, although some processing fees and costs paid by brokers do depend upon the number of shares traded, these are of relatively minor importance, and the bulk of the costs to be recovered are fixed costs. He concludes that there is no justification for the current system which discourages trading in low priced stocks, and remarks that "While a company's per share price is essentially arbitrary, as a matter of practice companies with low priced stocks tend to be smaller, younger and more prone to be owned by individual investors" (op. cit., p11). He concludes that the current system discourages trading in low priced stocks. This leaves open the question why these companies choose to have low priced shares.

Since full service brokers survive the competition from discounters, they must provide additional services. According to Coler and Schaefer, the most significant consideration is that, unlike the full service broker, the discounter

[13] See Smidt (1990) for an historical perspective on New York Stock Exchange commission rates. Commission rates depended on share prices from 1919 until the end of the fixed commissions era. In 1964, the commission rate on $20 shares was 4.58 times that on $200 shares.

will not provide security recommendations or research analyses, or offer access to new stock issues. Thus it seems that the additional charge of the full service broker is to cover research costs, and that these brokers are able to prevent investors from free riding by meting out the quantity and timeliness of research they provide to customers according to their volume of trading. If the commission schedule were as arbitrary as Branch suggests, it is difficult to see how it could withstand competition. Thus, according to the evidence in Table I, a full service broker charges \$97 for a \$5000 transaction in a \$50 stock, and an extra \$52 ($= (0.298 - .0194) \times 5000$) for the same size transaction in a \$10 stock. The discounter however charges only \$16.55 extra ($= (0.01086 - 0.00755) \times \$5000$) for the transaction in the low priced stock. Therefore, assuming that this represents the incremental execution costs of both types of brokers,[14] it is apparent that the full service broker is making an additional profit of \$35.45 ($= 52 - 16.55$) on the low priced stock. It seems unlikely that this could persist in equilibrium unless there is some additional cost incurred by the full service broker for the low priced stock. In our model, this is an additional cost of research per dollar of transaction.

In summary, there is substantial evidence that stock splits serve as signals of management's private information about future earnings. They also lead to an increase in the number of shareholders, wider bid-ask spreads, and higher brokerage commissions. After the split becomes effective, the variance is higher and the response to market-wide information is more rapid.[15] However, the only attempt to explain how a split announcement can serve as a credible signal is the transaction cost model of Brennan and Copeland which is incomplete because it offers no rational justification for the dependence of brokerage commission rates on stock prices. In the following section we develop a more complete model.

II. An Equilibrium Model of the Supply of Information

In order to capture the notion that full service stockbrokers are compensated for their research costs by commissions on share transactions,[16] we consider an economy in which investors only invest in the securities of firms that they "know about",[17] and that the only way in which investors get to know about firms is through their personal brokers. Investors are loyal and

---

[14] Execution costs may be higher for small illiquid companies which typically have low share prices.

[15] Kryzanowski and Zhang (1990) find similar security price behavior for a sample of Canadian firms.

[16] "For years, big institutional investors such as pension funds and insurers have paid for Wall Street research reports by directing stock trades to the brokerage firms that produce them. The four to six cents in trading commissions that Allstate and other institutions dole out serve as payment for a variety of services, from trading expertise to research reports on the food industry." (from "Challenge to Wall Street: What's Research Worth?" *Wall Street Journal*, December 14, 1989)

[17] For a similar assumption see Merton (1987) and Arbel and Swanson (1989).

remain with brokers, receiving information from them and trading through them, as long as the charges of the broker are competitive.[18] In particular, we shall assume that brokers who charge more than the average commission charged by full service brokers lose all of their clients; moreover, clients conjecture that brokers who offer commissions less than the average of full service brokers are not providing *bona fide* forecasts. Consequently, in equilibrium all full service brokers charge identical commissions.[19] For simplicity we assume that the volume of trading done by an individual investor is determined by life-cycle considerations and is therefore insensitive to the level of brokerage commissions. The expected rate of return on a security, however, will reflect the cost of transacting in the security, so that securities in which it is expensive to trade will have low prices *ceteris paribus*.[20]

Let f denote the cost to an individual broker of making an earnings forecast for a particular firm and let t denote the present value of the total brokerage revenues to be earned from trading in the shares of the firm as a proportion of its end of period value, x. We assume that the marginal cost of transacting is zero to brokers, and consider an equilibrium in which all investors are identical, and all brokers charge the same commission and have the same number of clients. Then, since investors are loyal to their brokers and trade only in shares they know about, the total brokerage commissions will be divided equally among the brokers who make forecasts. Competition among brokers ensures that total brokerage revenue is equal to the total cost of making forecasts, so that N, the equilibrium number of brokers making forecasts for a firm with end of period value $\tilde{x}$, is given by

$$N = E[t\tilde{x}]/f \qquad (1)$$

where $E[\ ]$ denotes the expectations operator.[21] Thus the equilibrium number of brokers making a forecast about a particular company depends on both the size of the company as measured by its expected end of period value, $E[\tilde{x}]$, and the brokerage commission rate, t.[22]

---

[18] In practice brokers restrict the flow of information to investors who do not trade through them.

[19] "Also, the lack of variation in trading commissions assumes that one firm's research is as good as another." (*Wall Street Journal*, December 4, 1989)

[20] For a similar assumption see Brennan and Copeland (1988a); for empirical evidence that equilibrium rates of return do depend on the cost of transacting see Amihud and Mendelson (1987).

[21] Implicit in expression (1) is the assumption that trading volume is invariant to the commission rate. A weaker sufficient condition for what follows is that aggregate commissions be increasing in the commission rate. This condition is consistent with Copeland's (1979) finding that aggregate brokerage revenue increased following a split, despite the decrease in trading volume.

[22] A further reason that increased commissions may attract more analysts is that at many brokerage houses, trading commissions generated by analysts are used to determine the annual bonuses, which can account for more than 50% of the analysts' compensation. ("Are Analysts Putting Their Mouths Where the Money Is?" *Business Week*, December 18, 1989, p118)

Consistent with observed commission schedules discussed in the preceding section, we assume that the brokerage commission depends on the price, P, at which an individual share of the security trades, $t(P)$, where $t'(P) < 0$. Then companies with low share prices will have relatively high commission costs, and for their size, will have a relatively large number of brokers making forecasts about them. Conversely, firms that have high share prices will, for their size, have a relatively small number of brokers making forecasts about them. Moreover, by choosing the price at which their shares trade by splitting, managers are able to control the attention paid to their firms by the brokerage industry.[23]

Consider now the problem faced by the manager of a company who has private information about its future earnings and wishes to communicate it to the market. Let us suppose that there exists no credible mechanism by which the private information can be communicated costlessly to the market. One possibility is for the manager to incur communication costs, for example by employing a third party (such as an auditor) to verify the signal. However, if the third party is paid directly by the manager there is a moral hazard problem which reputational considerations will only partially alleviate.[24] The only alternative that we consider here is the manager's decision to change the stock price by means of a split. Splits affect the incentive of brokerage houses to provide earnings forecasts which serve to reveal the manager's private information, with a precision which is proportional to the number of earnings forecasts.[25]

We assume that initially all investors and the manager of the firm have homogeneous beliefs about the end of period value of the firm. The manager receives a private signal about the end of period value and decides whether to split. If a decision is made to split, the manager announces the new number of shares to be outstanding after the stock split. The stock split will change the stock price, P, which determines the rate of brokerage commission $t(P)$; and this in turn determines the number of analysts who make earnings forecasts according to relation (1). The timing of events is as follows:

τ_0: investors and the manager have homogeneous prior beliefs about the firm's final payoff, x.

τ_1: the manager receives a private signal about x and announces the new number of shares, n, through a stock split.

τ_2: N analysts gather information and announce forecasts of the end of period value.

---

[23] Note that it is the commission schedule that makes the attention hypothesis of Grinblatt, Masulis and Titman (1984) economically rational.

[24] Thakor (1982) models third-party information production by debt insurers in a similar setting of information asymmetry where moral hazard considerations preclude direct disclosure of default probabilities.

[25] The role of multiple analysts' forecasts is similar to that of multiple ratings for bond issuers. Hsueh and Kidwell (1988) find that 46% of their sample of municipal bonds had two bond ratings. They find that a second rating reduces borrowing costs.

Stock Prices and the Supply of Information   1673

τ_3: the end of period value is realized and analysts are compensated by the brokerage commission.

We assume that all individuals are risk neutral, that prior beliefs about x are represented by a normal distribution with mean x_0 and precision s_0,[26] and that the interest rate is zero. The market value of the firm at τ_0 then is

$$V_0 = x_0(1 - t). \tag{2}$$

At τ_1 the manager receives a noisy signal about the end of period value:

$$y_m = x + \tilde{\epsilon}_m, \tag{3}$$

where $\tilde{\epsilon}_m$ is normally distributed with mean zero and precision s_m. After observing the signal y_m the manager announces n, the number of shares that will be outstanding after the split. Knowing n, investors infer that the manager's signal was $\hat{y}_m(n)$. They then revise their beliefs about x in accordance with Bayes' Rule:

$$E(x \mid n) \equiv \hat{x}(n) = \frac{x_0 s_0 + \hat{y}_m(n) s_m}{s_0 + s_m}, \tag{4}$$

where $s_0 + s_m$ is the new precision. When n is announced, the market value of the firm changes to $V_1(n)$, which reflects the new information, the new commission, and the fixed administration costs of executing the split, C[27]:

$$V_1(n) = E[x(1 - t(x/n)) \mid n] - C. \tag{5}$$

In (5), x/n is the τ_3 share price. The expected aggregate brokerage commission, $T(n)$, is given by

$$T(n) = E[xt(x/n) \mid n]. \tag{6}$$

Assuming that $T(n)$ is monotonic,[28] the same information is conveyed by an announcement of T or of n, and it will be analytically convenient to assume that the manager announces T. Equation (5) then becomes

$$V_1(T) = \hat{x}(T) - T - C, \tag{7}$$

where $\hat{x}(T) = E[x \mid T]$ at τ_1.

Then, defining $F = f^{-1}$, the number of analysts who make forecasts is, from (1)

$$N(T) = FT. \tag{8}$$

The forecast of each analyst is y_i ($i = 1, \ldots, N(T)$), where

$$y_i = x + \tilde{\epsilon}_i, \tag{9}$$

[26] Precision is defined as the inverse of the variance.

[27] The administrative costs of splitting include the costs of printing and distributing new stock certificates, and the buying and selling of fractional shares.

[28] It is shown below that a sufficient condition for this is that aggregate brokerage commissions are increasing in firm size for a given number of shares.

and $\tilde{\epsilon}_i$ is drawn from an independent normal distribution with mean zero and precision s. Define $\bar{y}$ as the average value of y_i.

Then the value of the firm at τ_2, *after* all the analysts forecasts have been publicly revealed is $V_2(T, \bar{y})$ where

$$V_2(T, \bar{y}) = \frac{x_0 s_0 + \hat{y}_m(T) s_m + \bar{y} FTs}{s_0 + s_m + FTs} - E[xt(x/n) \mid T, \hat{y}_m, \bar{y}] - C. \quad (10)$$

Since the number of analysts making forecasts is increasing in T (from (8)), the effect of a higher commission T is to increase FTs, the precision of the average brokerage forecast, $\bar{y}$. Clearly then, the greater the number of analysts making earnings forecasts, the greater will be the weight that investors place on the average brokerage forecast in valuing the firm. This provides the motivation for a manager with good news to seek attention from analysts.

We assume that the objective of the manager at τ_1 is to choose the new number of shares n (or equivalently, the expected aggregate brokerage commission T), in order to maximize the expectation, conditional on his private information, of the value of the firm at τ_2 when all of the analysts' information will have been revealed. Note that

$$E[\bar{y} \mid y_m] = \frac{x_0 s_0 + y_m s_m}{s_0 + s_m} \quad (11)$$

and

$$E[\{xt(x/n) \mid T, \hat{y}_m, \bar{y}\} \mid y_m] = T. \quad (12)$$

After substituting (11) and (12) into (10), the manager's expectation at τ_1 of the τ_2 value of the firm is

$$E[V_2(T) \mid y_m] = \frac{x_0 s_0 + \hat{y}_m(T) s_m + \left\{ \dfrac{x_0 s_0 + y_m s_m}{s_0 + s_m} \right\} FTs}{s_0 + s_m + FTs} - T - C. \quad (13)$$

Note that the numerator of (13) is a weighted average of the investors' prior beliefs, what they infer about the manager's current information, and what the manager believes about the future information to be provided by analysts. The objective of the manager then is to maximize expression (13) through the choice of the new aggregate brokerage commission T.

Combining the first order condition for a maximum of (13) with respect to T with the equilibrium condition that $\hat{y}_m(T) = y_m$ yields the following differential equation for the investors' inference schedule $\hat{y}_m(T)$.

$$\hat{y}_m'(T) = \frac{s_0 + s_m + FTs}{s_m}. \quad (14)$$

The solution to (14) is

$$\hat{y}_m(T) = \frac{s_0 + s_m}{s_m} T + \frac{Fs}{2 s_m} T^2 + K, \tag{15}$$

where K is a constant of integration.

Due to the fixed costs of administering a split, not all managers will find it advantageous to announce a split after receiving private information. In order to determine the value of K, it is necessary to determine the minimum y_m which is disclosed through a split announcement. Let n_0 be the number of shares initially outstanding and let y_m^s denote the signal level at which a manager is indifferent between announcing a split and not.[29] If the manager does not announce a split, the expected aggregate brokerage commission is $\overline{T} \equiv E[xt(x/n_0) | y_m \leq y_m^s]$. Similarly, $T(n_0)$, the expected brokerage commission if the manager announces the minimum split factor of one, is defined by $T(n_0) \equiv E[xt(x/n_0) | y_m^s]$. Then the condition for the manager who receives a signal y_m^s to be indifferent to splitting is that the expected value of V_2 conditional on y_m and no split be equal to the expected value to be obtained by announcing the minimum split factor of one, less the costs of the split, or:

$$E\left[E(x | y_m \leq y_m^s, \bar{y}) | y_m^s, s(\bar{y}) = F\overline{T}s \right] - \overline{T}$$
$$= \frac{x_0 s_0 + y_m^s s_m + y_m^s FT(n_0)s}{s_0 + s_m + FT(n_0)s} - T(n_0) - C. \tag{16}$$

The left-hand side of condition (16) is the expectation of the τ_2 value of the firm of a manager who has received the signal y_m^s, when the market infers from the absence of a split that $y_m < y_m^s$, *and* receives the average analyst forecast $\bar{y}$ which has precision $F\overline{T}s$. Condition (16) and the definition of $\overline{T}$ suffice to determine y_m^s, the signal of the marginal splitting firm: note that y_m^s depends upon the prior distribution of management signals. The constant of integration in (15) is then identified by considering the inference of investors for the minimum split factor of one. Since the manager who receives the signal y_m^s will announce $T = T(n_0)$, consistent inference requires that

$$\hat{y}_m(T = T(n_0)) = \left(\frac{s_0 + s_m}{s_m} \right) T(n_0) + \frac{Fs}{2 s_m} T(n_0)^2 - K \equiv y_m^s. \tag{17}$$

The solution for K from (17) is

$$K = \frac{Fs}{2 s_m} T(n_0)^2 + \frac{Fs}{2 s_m} T(n_0) - y_m^s. \tag{18}$$

[29] For simplicity we ignore the possibility of reverse splits, which we consider in the Appendix. We assume that even an incipient stock split in which the split factor is one cannot be accomplished without incurring the fixed administrative costs.

The second order condition for a maximum of (13) is always satisfied because $\partial^2 E[V_2(T) \mid y_m]/\partial T^2 = -Fs(s_0 + s_m + FsT) < 0$.

The investors' inference of y_m is an increasing and convex function of the expected aggregate brokerage commission T (for $T > \overline{T}$). Since the inference function (15) depends upon the prior precision s_0, it differs from the more common inference schedule in signaling models where investors ignore their prior beliefs when inferring the manager's information from the observed signal. A further departure from the standard signaling model is that the manager does not care about the current τ_1 value of the firm, but is maximizing the expectation of the future value when the analysts' information is revealed.

Since investors are able to infer the manager's signal y_m at τ_1, it follows that the value of the firm at τ_1 may be written as its expected value at τ_2, conditional on $\hat{y}_m$:

$$V_1(T) = E[V_2(T) \mid \hat{y}_m(T)] - C$$

$$= \frac{x_0 s_0 + \hat{y}_m(T)s_m + \left\{ \dfrac{x_0 s_0 + \hat{y}_m(T)s_m}{s_0 + s_m} \right\} FTs}{s_0 + s_m + FTs} - T - C \quad (19)$$

$$= \frac{x_0 s_0 + \hat{y}_m(T)s_m}{s_0 + s_m} - T - C, \quad (20)$$

which is identical to expression (7).

It remains to be shown that $T(n) \equiv E[xt(x/n) \mid n]$ is increasing in n as assumed. Under this assumption we have established that the distribution of x conditional on the announcement of n (or $T(n)$) is normal with mean $x_0 s_0 + \hat{y}_m(T)s_m$ and precision $s_0 + s_m$ as shown in expression (20). Therefore the effect of an increase in n (or $T(n)$) is to shift the distribution to the right. A sufficient condition for this to increase $T(n)$ is that $xt(x/n)$ is increasing in x, or that brokerage commissions be increasing in firm size for a given number of shares.

It is easy to show that $dV_1(T)/dT > 0$, so that the post-announcement value of the firm is monotonically increasing in the signal T. Since $T'(n) > 0$, and the projected share price x_0/n is negatively related to n, it follows that the market reaction to the split announcement will be negatively related to the target share price x_0/n, as found by Brennan and Copeland (1988a).

Consistent with the evidence discussed in Section I, the model also predicts that a split will be followed by an increase in the number of shareholders as more investors learn about the firm. After the split becomes effective and brokers communicate their information to investors to stimulate trade at the higher commission rates, there will be more private information in the market. This would explain the observed increases in the bid-ask spread and the variance of returns according to the theories of Copeland and Galai (1983) and Glosten and Milgrom (1985), and Holthausen and Verrecchia

(1990) respectively. On a more speculative note, the increased attention from analysts to splitting firms could lead to the more rapid response of security returns to market-wide information as found by Wiggins (1990). Since, for a given share price the number of analysts is increasing in firm size,[30] a smaller firm must choose a lower share price in order to gain the same analyst following as a larger firm. It is likely that this accounts for the observed positive correlation between share prices and firm size. The model also predicts that stock splits will be followed by an increase in the number of earnings forecasts provided by analysts. As there is no prior evidence on this hypothesis, in the next section we turn to consider the empirical relation between share prices, stock splits, and analyst following.

An extension of the model to include reverse stock splits appears in the Appendix. We find that reverse splits convey bad news about the firm, and should occur infrequently because of the associated administrative costs. The empirical evidence on reverse splits is consistent with these predictions.

III. Data and Empirical Tests

Data on the number of analysts following individual stocks were drawn from the I/B/E/S tape for the years 1976–1987.[31] Data on stock prices, returns, and numbers of shares were drawn from the CRSP NYSE-AMEX and NASDAQ tapes. The criteria for a stock to be included in the analysis in a given year were that it was included on both the CRSP and the I/B/E/S databases on December 31 of that year, and that it was reported in the same CRSP database at the end of each of the prior five years.

Descriptive statistics for the sample appear in Table II. There is significant cross-sectional variation in the number of analysts following individual firms. The modal number of analysts for the sample firms on all exchanges for all years is one, except for the NYSE in 1987 when it is two.[32] The maximum number of analysts following a single firm is 44, and the distribution shows considerable skewness. The increase in the number of firms followed by I/B/E/S analysts over the twelve years is 60% for NYSE, 198% for AMEX, and 555% for NASDAQ. The median number of analysts is greatest for NYSE firms, which is not surprising given that these firms are larger. It also appears that NASDAQ firms have a slightly larger following

---

[30] Bhushan (1989) suggests that large firms generate more transactions, and finds that the number of analysts is positively related to the size of the firm.

[31] The authors gratefully acknowledge Lynch, Jones, and Ryan for making this tape available. I/B/E/S was developed by Lynch, Jones, and Ryan in order to systematically collect and distribute earnings forecasts from Wall Street and Regional brokerage firms. Brown, Foster, and Noreen (1985) found that, as of 1984, over 80 brokerage firms provided earnings forecasts for more than 2700 firms.

[32] Since firms are included in the sample only if they are on the I/B/E/S database, each firm must be followed by at least one analyst.

Empirical Corporate Finance I

Table II

Descriptive Statistics For the Sample for the Time Period 1976 to 1987

Number of analysts is defined as the number making one-year ahead forecasts of earnings in December as reported on the I/B/E/S database. Firm size is the total market value of equity in $ millions on December 31. Price per share is the share price on December 31.

	Number of Firms	Number of Analysts		Firm Size		Price per Share	
		Mean	Median	Mean	Median	Mean	Median
NYSE							
1976	702	7.0	4	785	314	$30.02	$26.69
1977	806	6.3	4	650	264	26.10	23.50
1978	1140	6.8	5	503	175	22.65	19.69
1979	1171	7.1	6	598	215	25.90	23.13
1980	1163	7.6	6	786	253	29.33	24.75
1981	1187	8.9	7	717	250	24.83	22.50
1982	1186	9.5	8	840	317	28.30	24.50
1983	1202	10.3	8	1011	408	29.98	26.69
1984	1202	10.5	8	1102	381	26.84	24.38
1985	1196	12.2	10	1390	436	31.48	27.25
1986	1207	12.1	10	1613	486	30.13	25.75
1987	1123	12.4	10	1731	522	25.40	21.63
AMEX							
1976	66	2.3	1	99	40	18.18	14.25
1977	82	2.1	1	86	42	17.93	17.07
1978	139	2.6	1	75	37	15.91	14.00
1979	152	2.9	1	104	50	19.35	17.76
1980	153	2.9	2	164	66	22.98	21.00
1981	173	3.0	2	112	52	17.23	15.75
1982	211	3.1	2	119	57	18.37	15.50
1983	222	3.5	2	156	79	19.06	17.07
1984	235	3.4	2	127	59	15.49	12.75
1985	218	3.9	2	165	75	17.97	13.88
1986	219	4.1	2	182	72	16.16	13.50
1987	197	4.0	2	191	63	13.51	10.25
NASDAQ							
1976	200	3.0	1	117	57	21.22	19.13
1977	265	2.8	1	90	53	20.26	17.88
1978	430	3.1	2	78	46	18.75	16.13
1979	439	3.5	2	107	58	22.27	19.31
1980	384	3.8	2	139	78	23.60	20.57
1981	476	4.2	3	130	75	20.52	18.38
1982	620	4.1	3	144	84	21.94	19.57
1983	865	4.1	3	154	80	20.14	17.63
1984	1142	4.0	2	121	60	15.90	13.00
1985	1150	4.6	3	164	77	18.70	15.50
1986	1276	4.6	3	177	75	16.53	13.50
1987	1309	4.8	3	170	60	12.91	10.25

than do AMEX firms although their size and stock price distributions do not differ significantly.

The NYSE firms are large compared to the other groups. The distributions of AMEX and NASDAQ firm sizes appear similar. The increase in average firm size over the twelve years is 121% for NYSE, 93% for AMEX, and 45% for NASDAQ, which may be due to NASDAQ firms moving onto the NYSE or AMEX as they grow.

The time-series growth in firm size is not matched by a comparable increase in share price. To show the effect of stock splits on stock prices, Figure 1 plots the time series of the logarithms of the annual CRSP equal weighted price relatives with and without adjustment for stock splits and stock dividends. It is apparent that stock prices decrease when the market goes down, but do not increase correspondingly when the market goes up. This is consistent with the prior evidence that stock splits tend to occur after a rise in stock prices.

Table III provides statistics about the firms for which there was a change in the cumulative split factor reported on the CRSP tape during the year.[33] Reverse stock splits are very rare, and stock splits occur more frequently than do stock dividends. It is clear from Table III that only a minority of firms split in any given year. These numbers appear to be consistent with the findings of Lakonishok and Lev (1987) who analyze all CRSP NYSE and AMEX firms for the years 1963-1982 and find that in most of the years, 5-10% of the firms split their stock.

In addition, as Lakonishok and Lev (1987) have found, splitting firms have higher than average share prices, with the median price for splitting firms in our sample being $42.13 for NYSE, $26.50 for AMEX, and $24.75 for NASDAQ. As our theory predicts, prices for reverse splitting firms tends to

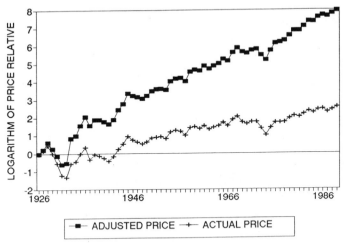

Figure 1. The effect of splits on average, 1926-1989. Logarithm of the CRSP equally weighted price relative with and without adjustment for stock splits.

---

[33] The data upon which Table III is based consists of *all* firms on the CRSP tape, not only those which are also carried by I/B/E/S.

Table III
Descriptive Statistics For Firms Listed on the CRSP Database Which Had a Change in The Split Factor in The Year

	Firms with Stock Splits					Firms with Reverse Splits					Firms with Stock Dividends				
	No. of Splits	% of Total	Max	Min	Med	No. of Splits	% of Total	Max	Min	Med	No. of Divs	% of Total	Max	Min	Med
NYSE															
1976	114	7	3[a]	1.25	2	1	0‖	5[b]	5	5	97	6	1.20[c]	1.01	1.04
1977	107	7	3	1.25	1.55	1	0	4	4	4	87	6	1.20	1.01	1.05
1978	129	8	4	1.25	1.5	1	0	4	4	4	86	6	1.20	1.01	1.05
1979	141	9	5	1.25	1.5	0					74	5	1.20	1.02	1.05
1980	183	12	4	1.25	2	0					65	4	1.25	1.02	1.05
1981	197	13	5	1.25	2	1		2	2	2	60	4	1.20	1.02	1.05
1982	84	5	2	1.25	1.5	2	0	3	3	3	58	4	1.20	1.01	1.05
1983	246	16	10	1.25	2	0	0	5	4	5	53	4	1.20	1.02	1.05
1984	121	8	5	1.25	1.5	1	0	2	2	2	56	4	1.20	1.02	1.05
1985	129	9	3	1.25	2	4	0	50	10	14	42	3	1.20	1.02	1.05
1986	237	16	5	1.25	2	6	0	50	2	10	45	3	1.15	1.02	1.05
1987	213	14	5	1.25	2						38	2	1.20	1.02	1.05
AMEX															
1976	52	5	2	1.25	1.5	2	0‖	3	2	3	96	9	1.20	1.02	1.05
1977	52	5	3	1.25	1.5	1	0	5	5	5	94	9	1.20	1.02	1.05
1978	70	7	3	1.25	1.5	1	0	5	5	5	97	10	1.20	1.01	1.05
1979	69	8	5	1.25	1.5	1	0	3	3	3	101	11	1.20	1.01	1.07
1980	108	12	7	1.25	1.5	0					110	13	1.25	1.01	1.06
1981	96	11	10	1.25	1.5	2	0	10	7.14	10	88	10	1.20	1.02	1.05
1982	58	7	2	1.25	1.5	3	0	3	2	2	66	8	1.20	1.02	1.05
1983	133	16	5	1.25	1.5	1	0	3.33	3.33	3.33	75	9	1.20	1.01	1.05
1984	43	5	3	1.25	2	0					61	8	1.20	1.02	1.05
1985	68	9	4	1.25	1.5	3	0	15	3	5	47	6	1.20	1.02	1.05
1986	67	9	10	1.25	1.5	1	0	3	3	3	42	5	1.20	1.01	1.06
1987	63	8	4	1.25	1.5	4	1	6	2.5	5	33	4	1.20	1.04	1.07

Table III—*Continued*

	Firms with Stock Splits					Firms with Reverse Splits					Firms with Stock Dividends				
	No. of Splits	% of Total	Change in Split Factor			No. of Splits	% of Total	Change in Split Factor			No. of Divs	% of Total	Change in Split Factor		
			Max	Min	Med			Max	Min	Med			Max	Min	Med
NASDAQ															
1976	152	6	5	1.25	1.5	7	≈ 0	50	1.5	5	208	8	1.20	1.01	1.05
1977	170	7	3	1.25	1.5	4	0	10	4	10	222	9	1.22	1.01	1.06
1978	260	10	7	1.25	1.5	7	0	10	2	5	227	9	1.22	1.02	1.08
1979	167	7	10	1.25	1.5	5	0	25	2.5	10	243	10	1.21	1.01	1.10
1980	273	11	10	1.25	1.5	5	0	8	2	3	210	8	1.20	1.02	1.10
1981	344	13	10	1.25	1.5	12	0	10	2	5	208	8	1.20	1.01	1.10
1982	183	6	5	1.25	1.5	20	1	50	1.5	5	193	6	1.20	1.02	1.07
1983	521	17	5	1.25	2	32	1	50	1.33	5	178	6	1.20	1.01	1.06
1984	243	7	10	1.25	1.5	31	1	40	2	10	196	5	1.20	1.01	1.07
1985	390	10	20	1.25	1.5	36	1	100	2	8	183	5	1.20	1.02	1.07
1986	527	14	40	1.25	1.5	22	1	200	2	10	164	4	1.20	1.01	1.06
1987	383	9	10	1.25	1.5	61	1	200	2	10	177	4	1.20	1.02	1.10

[a] A change of 3 means that 3 new shares are issued in exchange for 1 old share.
[b] A change of 5 means that 1 new share is issued in exchange for 5 old shares.
[c] A change of 1.2 means that a 20% stock dividend was issued.

be very low: the median is \$1.25 for NYSE, \$1.50 for AMEX, and \$0.69 for
NASDAQ.

In order to test the implication of the model that the number of analysts
making earnings forecasts about a firm is negatively related to the share
price, and positively related to the size of the firm, the following equation
was estimated by ordinary least squares for each year from 1976 to 1987 for
all firms in the sample.

$$N_{it} = a_{0t} + a_{1t}\text{Log Size}_{it} + a_{2t}(1/P_{it}) + a_{3t}\text{Var}_{it}$$
$$+ a_{4t}\text{Log } R_{it} + a_{5t}\text{Log } R_{it-1} + \cdots + a_{8t}\text{Log } R_{it-4} + e_{it}, \quad (21)$$

where

N_{it} = the number of analysts reporting a one-year ahead earnings forecast
for firm i in December of year t

Size_{it} = the market value of the equity of firm i on December 31 of year t

P_{it} = the share price of firm i on December 31 of year t

Var_{it} = the variance of returns for firm i estimated over the last 200 days
prior to December 31 of year t

R_{it} = the rate of return on the shares of firm i in year t, excluding
dividends.

The first two terms in regression equation (21) are derived from the theory
in the preceding section. We include the variance of returns because there is
prior evidence[34] that the variance is positively related to the number of
analysts and we wish to determine if the share price exerts an independent
effect on the number of analysts.[35]

The lagged log returns are included in the regression to allow for a possible
spurious relation between share price and analyst following due to a lagged
relation between number of analysts and firm size. If the number of analysts
reported on the I/B/E/S tape adjusts slowly to changes in firm size, then a
firm that earns negative returns will tend to have a larger analyst following
than that predicted on the basis of its current size (as measured by market
value of equity). It will also have a relatively low stock price, thereby
inducing a spurious relation between share price and number of analysts.
Inclusion of the logarithm of the lagged (dividend adjusted) returns is equivalent to including lagged size variables to the extent that size changes are due
to capital gains and losses rather than stock issues and retirements. In
addition, while the model predicts a simultaneous change between share

---

[34] Bhushan (1989) includes the variance of returns in his empirical study of the determinants
of analyst following. He hypothesizes that the value of private information should be positively
related to return variability because it increases the conditional expected return.

[35] Our model assigns no role to the variance as influencing the number of analysts. However,
Kim and Verrecchia (1990) show that the absolute value of price changes may be positively
related to the volume of trading. Under our assumption about competition in the brokerage
industry, an increase in the volume of trading will lead to an increase in the number of analysts.

price and analyst following, there is evidence that some of the I/B/E/S data may not be current.[36]

The regression results for equation (21) are presented by year for all firms in the sample in Table IV.[37] As Bhushan (1989) finds, the influence of the size variable is positive and highly significant, and in 10 of the 12 years, there is a significantly positive relation between analyst following and the variance

Table IV

Determinants of the Number of Analysts Forecasting Earnings for a Firm

Estimation of expression (21) for the entire sample of firms. N_{it} is the number of analysts reporting a one-year ahead earnings forecast for firm i in December of year t. $Size_{it}$ is the market value of the equity of firm i on December 31 of year t. P_{it} is the share price of firm i on December 31 of year t. Var_{it} is the variance of returns for firm i estimated over the last 200 days prior to December 31 of year t. R_{it} is the rate of return on the shares of firm i in year t, excluding dividends. n is the sample size and t-statistics appear in parentheses.

$$N_{it} = a_{0t} + a_{1t}\text{Log Size}_{it} + a_{2t}(1/P_{it}) + a_{3t}\text{Var}_{it} + a_{4t}\text{Log } R_{it}$$
$$+ a_{5t}\text{Log } R_{it-1} + \cdots + a_{8t}\text{Log } R_{it-4} + e_{it}$$

t	n	a_0	a_1	a_2	a_3	a_4	a_5	a_6	a_7	a_8	R^2
1976	967	−34.02	3.24	10.58	98.15	−3.75	0.55	−1.27	0.35	0.59	0.59
		(21.45)	(28.60)	(2.43)	(3.10)	(7.53)	(1.67)	(4.00)	(1.16)	(2.23)	
1977	1152	−29.85	2.89	6.70	152.53	−1.98	−1.60	−0.03	−0.87	0.51	0.59
		(23.75)	(30.39)	(2.27)	(4.37)	(5.11)	(4.89)	(0.14)	(3.50)	(2.14)	
1978	1707	−33.06	3.29	7.50	59.00	−0.99	−0.68	−1.34	−0.05	−0.41	0.62
		(34.39)	(44.00)	(4.56)	(4.17)	(3.82)	(2.69)	(6.04)	(0.25)	(2.33)	
1979	1699	−31.29	3.16	4.22	66.89	−2.33	−0.16	−0.22	−0.92	0.38	0.65
		(38.86)	(50.26)	(3.52)	(4.05)	(11.32)	(0.77)	(1.11)	(4.79)	(2.35)	
1980	1699	−33.85	3.35	8.17	33.11	−1.62	−1.82	0.07	−0.19	−0.49	0.65
		(38.10)	(49.30)	(5.05)	(2.09)	(7.29)	(7.93)	(0.33)	(0.91)	(2.48)	
1981	1835	−37.84	3.71	9.80	3.44	−1.55	−0.69	−0.75	0.14	0.00	0.66
		(41.02)	(52.26)	(6.67)	(0.21)	(7.30)	(3.61)	(3.68)	(0.69)	(0.01)	
1982	2016	−41.95	4.04	8.29	8.76	−0.78	−0.66	−0.06	−0.18	0.07	0.67
		(48.11)	(59.09)	(6.61)	(0.94)	(5.10)	(3.51)	(0.37)	(0.98)	(0.48)	
1983	2288	−43.82	4.19	5.26	50.99	−0.85	−0.35	−0.43	0.08	0.07	0.67
		(50.33)	(61.77)	(4.70)	(4.29)	(5.73)	(2.47)	(2.66)	(0.52)	(0.44)	
1984	2577	−40.24	3.93	4.29	33.88	−1.43	−0.34	−0.23	−0.32	0.21	0.66
		(53.91)	(65.65)	(7.20)	(4.25)	(8.63)	(2.78)	(1.83)	(2.17)	(1.73)	
1985	2560	−46.39	4.55	0.91	29.75	−3.11	−0.94	−0.47	−0.33	−0.33	0.67
		(56.88)	(69.02)	(3.50)	(5.01)	(13.45)	(5.58)	(3.51)	(2.36)	(2.19)	
1986	2700	−44.51	4.33	3.35	23.45	−2.06	−1.07	−0.74	−0.30	−0.12	0.67
		(55.07)	(67.26)	(5.71)	(4.11)	(11.48)	(5.70)	(5.29)	(2.40)	(0.97)	
1987	2628	−43.81	4.26	3.00	24.69	−1.56	−0.62	−0.43	−0.53	−0.20	0.66
		(53.27)	(65.42)	(6.14)	(5.89)	(7.57)	(4.67)	(3.17)	(4.22)	(1.73)	

[36] O'Brien (1988) and Brown, Foster, and Noreen (1985) describe characteristics of the I/B/E/S data.

[37] Results for the individual exchanges, which were included in an earlier version of this paper, are available from the authors.

of stock price. The major new prediction of our model, that the number of analysts will be negatively related to share price, is strongly supported by the finding that the coefficient of the reciprocal of share price is positive and strongly significant in each year.[38] The coefficients of the lagged return variables are negative and strongly significant for short lags, which is consistent with the discussion above of slow analyst adjustment. Since the coefficient for a lag of five years is generally insignificant and of variable sign, it appears that the adjustment is complete after five years so that share price is not a proxy for a lagged size term.

Results for the individual exchanges are similar in nature, but less significant, due to reduced sample sizes. The coefficient on the reciprocal of share price is positive for NYSE firms in 10/12 years, for AMEX firms in 11/12 years, and in 12/12 years for NASDAQ firms.

While these results are consistent with the predictions of our model, it is possible that they are due to a common factor which is associated with low shares prices and a large analyst following—for example, an industry association. In such a case, the number of analysts following a firm would not be affected by a stock split, as we hypothesize. Therefore, a more direct test of the effect of a split on analyst following is a regression of the change in the number of analysts following a firm on current and lagged values of the split factor and the capital gains as follows.

$$\Delta \text{Log } N_{it} = a_{0t} + a_{1t} \Delta \text{Log } F_{it} + a_{2t} \Delta \text{Log } F_{it-1} + \cdots$$
$$+ a_{5t} \Delta \text{Log } F_{it-4} + a_{6t} \text{Log } R_{it} + \cdots + a_{10t} \text{Log } R_{it-4} + e_{it}, \quad (22)$$

where $\Delta \text{Log } F_{it}$ is the change in the CRSP split factor in year t and, as before, R_{it} is the capital gain on the stock in year t.[39]

Under the null hypothesis, $a_{1t} = a_{2t} = \cdots = a_{5t} = 0$, whereas our model and, more generally, the Attention Hypothesis of Grinblatt, Masulis, and Titman (1984), predicts that at least some of these coefficients will be positive.

Table V reports the results of estimating equation (22) by year together with an F-test of the null hypothesis that the coefficients on the lagged changes in the split factor are all equal to zero. The null hypothesis is rejected in 7 of the 12 years at the 1% level, and in 3 additional years at the 5% level. Weighting the parameter estimates for each year by their precisions, the point estimates suggest that a doubling of the split factor (i.e., a two-for-one split) is associated with a 24% increase in the number of analysts reported by I/B/E/S in the current year, and a 54% increase by the end of

---

[38] We obtained similar but slightly less consistent results when we replaced the reciprocal of the stock price with the logarithm of the stock price.

[39] We adopted the log specification because it allows for the effect on the number of analysts of price changes associated both with returns (and therefore with changes in size) and with stock splits in a simple additive fashion.

five years. The effect is relatively weak for NYSE firms where a doubling of the split factor is associated with only a 19% increase in the number of analysts after five years. The corresponding numbers for AMEX and NAS-DAQ firms are 130% and 36%. The effect seems most consistent for NASDAQ firms for which it is concentrated in the year of the split.

The timing of the increase in the number of analysts reflects not only the predicted influence of the split, but also the efforts of Lynch, Jones, and Ryan to increase the coverage of their database. An interesting feature of the results is the large and highly significant negative coefficient on R_{it}, the log of the current year's dividend-adjusted return. While this is consistent with our hypothesis that a lower share price will be associated with a larger number of analysts, the effect seems too great for this explanation. We conjecture that analysts tend to turn their attention from firms whose stocks have appreciated either because, a major source of value having been discovered, the future prospects for further value discoveries are relatively slight, or because such firms are more likely to be overvalued and analysts tend to avoid making sell recommendations.[40] Clearly this phenomenon bears further investigation.

IV. Summary and Conclusions

We assume that investors trade only in stocks that they "know about", and trade through brokers who analyze those firms which will generate the greatest trading volume and brokerage fees. A manager with private "good news" has an incentive to attract the attention of security analysts so that they will discover the good news and inform their clients through earnings forecasts. In our model the manager does this by announcing a stock split, thereby reducing the share price and increasing the trading commission revenue which will result from research activity by brokerage houses. Investors accordingly interpret a stock split as a signal that the manager has favorable information, which explains the positive abnormal returns observed around split announcements. The model also predicts that there will be an increase in the amount of information generated by analysts after the ex-date; this may account for the increase in price volatility observed after the ex-date, the wider bid-ask spread, and the increase in the number of shareholders.

The predictions of the model are tested and confirmed on a sample of firms listed on the I/B/E/S database during 1976–1987. The number of analysts making forecasts is negatively related to share price, and the change in analyst following is positively related to the magnitude of stock splits.

---

[40] There is some indirect evidence that analysts are less willing to make sell recommendations than buy recommendations. Lloyd-Davies and Canes (1978) identify 597 buy recommendations, but only 188 sell recommendations in their study. Some explanations for this reluctance are offered by Galant (1990).

Table V

Determinants of the Change in the Number of Analysts Forecasting Earnings for a Firm

Estimation of expression (22) for the entire sample of firms. N_{it} is the number of analysts reporting a one-year ahead earnings forecast for firm i in December of year t. $\Delta \text{Log } F_{it}$ is the change in the logarithm of the CRSP split factor in year t. R_{it} is the rate of return on the shares of firm i in year t, excluding dividends. n is the sample size and t-statistics appear in parentheses.

$$\Delta \text{Log } N_{it} = a_{0t} + a_{1t}\,\Delta \text{Log } F_{it} + a_{2t}\,\Delta \text{Log } F_{it} + \cdots + a_{5t}\,\Delta \text{Log } F_{it-4}$$
$$+ a_{6t}\text{Log } R_{it} + \cdots + a_{10t}\text{Log } R_{it-4} + e_{it}$$

t	a_0	a_1	a_2	a_3	a_4	a_5	a_6	a_7	a_8	a_9	a_{10}	R^2	n
1976	-3.02	0.06	10.47	0.27	-0.23	0.16	-1.00	-3.27	-0.14	-0.02	-0.12	.08	967
	(46.06)	(0.36)	(2.34)	(1.82)	(0.48)	(1.09)	(7.62)	(3.23)	(1.46)	(0.05)	(1.40)	2.40*[a]	
1977	-1.22	0.57	0.78	-0.13	-0.00	-0.22	-1.76	-0.11	-1.03	0.08	0.61	.05	1152
	(9.77)	(1.60)	(2.19)	(0.11)	(0.00)	(0.43)	(6.38)	(0.42)	(2.26)	(0.38)	(1.47)	1.43[a]	
1978	-1.83	1.19	1.03	1.32	-1.98	0.11	-1.18	-0.51	-0.44	0.33	0.49	.04	1708
	(15.27)	(3.23)	(2.96)	(3.81)	(1.48)	(0.36)	(5.16)	(2.05)	(1.96)	(0.91)	(2.77)	7.35**[a]	
1979	-0.13	0.31	0.51	0.39	0.41	-1.07	-0.87	-0.74	-0.48	-0.20	0.39	.06	1761
	(1.91)	(1.40)	(2.25)	(1.94)	(1.83)	(1.64)	(7.28)	(5.70)	(3.44)	(1.49)	(2.05)	3.36**[a]	
1980	-0.18	0.44	0.18	0.54	0.18	-0.06	-0.40	0.04	-0.45	0.03	0.04	.03	1699
	(3.64)	(2.85)	(1.14)	(3.57)	(1.19)	(0.35)	(4.40)	(0.37)	(4.77)	(0.33)	(0.42)	4.75**[a]	
1981	-0.36	-0.07	0.76	0.68	0.83	0.41	-0.45	-0.43	-0.21	-0.54	0.03	.05	1835
	(6.31)	(0.53)	(4.13)	(3.30)	(4.49)	(2.23)	(4.32)	(4.10)	(1.88)	(4.81)	(0.27)	10.23**[a]	
1982	-0.15	0.08	0.07	-0.06	0.09	0.05	-0.73	0.06	-0.11	0.08	0.15	.12	2016
	(4.18)	(1.08)	(0.80)	(0.62)	(0.74)	(0.43)	(14.87)	(0.95)	(1.82)	(1.22)	(2.50)	0.55[a]	
1983	-0.17	0.30	-0.12	0.12	0.12	-0.03	-1.07	0.35	-0.14	0.01	0.18	.22	2288
	(4.53)	(5.23)	(1.62)	(1.41)	(1.09)	(0.27)	(21.59)	(7.70)	(2.61)	(0.27)	(3.11)	7.02**[a]	

Table V —*Continued*

t	a_0	a_1	a_2	a_3	a_4	a_5	a_6	a_7	a_8	a_9	a_{10}	R^2	n
1984	-0.42	0.29	0.12	-0.10	0.14	0.12	-0.79	-0.06	0.09	-0.08	0.05	.08	2577
	(12.80)	(4.64)	(1.96)	(1.25)	(1.61)	(1.21)	(14.41)	(1.25)	(1.98)	(1.51)	(1.12)	6.23**a	
1985	-0.01	0.19	0.10	0.09	0.06	0.11	-0.36	0.06	0.04	-0.01	0.09	.02	2562
	(0.49)	(2.71)	(1.94)	(1.81)	(0.96)	(1.63)	(6.82)	(1.48)	(1.16)	(0.20)	(2.43)	2.89*a	
1986	-0.27	0.38	0.15	0.05	-0.00	0.06	-0.71	0.14	-0.08	0.05	0.10	.11	2700
	(10.59)	(6.82)	(2.24)	(0.83)	(0.01)	(0.98)	(16.56)	(3.09)	(2.39)	(1.57)	(3.09)	9.95**a	
1987	-0.26	0.17	0.05	0.04	-0.01	0.05	-0.37	0.09	-0.02	0.03	-0.02	.03	2627
	(11.58)	(3.24)	(1.03)	(0.78)	(0.23)	(0.94)	(9.12)	(2.93)	(0.76)	(0.97)	(0.72)	2.51*a	

[a] *F*-statistic for the null hypothesis $a_1 = a_2 = \cdots = a_5 = 0$.
* Significant at the .05 level.
** Significant at the .01 level.

Appendix

Reverse Stock Splits

The model presented in Section II can be extended with minor modification to include reverse stock splits. We assume that there is a minimum brokerage commission T_{min} available to the firm, and that the next lowest commission is $T_1 = T_{min} + \delta$, where δ is strictly positive.[41] Depending upon parameter values, there may exist several different types of equilibria. Figure 2 illustrates the inference schedule for the equilibrium in which the most information is revealed, given that there is a cost of splitting or reverse-splitting. The values of $\hat{y}_m(T)$ corresponding to $T \in [(T_1, T_2), (T_3, \infty)]$ satisfy equation (15) for $K = K_1$ and K_2, respectively. The constants of integration and $y_m^0, y_m^r, y_m^s, T_2, T_3$, and $\overline{T}$ are defined as follows.

The values of y_m^0 and K_1 follow from conditions analogous to those in equations (16) and (17): that is, that the firm with the signal y_m^0 is indifferent between remaining in the pool of firms selecting T_{min}, and identifying itself by choosing T_1, and that investors make the correct inference. These conditions are:

$$E\big[E(x \mid y_m \leq y_m^0, \bar{y}) \mid y_m^0, s(\bar{y}) = FT_{min} s\big] - T_{min}$$

$$= \frac{x_0 s_0 + y_m^0 s_m + y_m^0 FT_1 s}{s_0 + s_m + FT_1 s} - T_1, \quad \text{(A-1)}$$

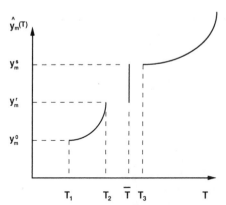

Figure 2. The inference schedule for a model of stock splits and reverse splits. T is the expected aggregate brokerage commission. $\hat{y}_m(T)$ is investors' inference of y_m based upon T. y_m^s is the signal of the marginal splitting firm. y_m^r is the signal of the marginal reverse splitting firm. $\overline{T}$ is the aggregate brokerage commission for a firm that does not split.

[41] It is necessary that δ be positive so that the pool of firms selecting T_{min} does not unravel. Since the inference schedule is convex and y_m is unbounded, a pool of firms must exist at the lower bound on T. Note that if y_m had a fixed support, the lower boundary condition for the inference schedule would be provided by the condition that the firm with the lowest possible signal would choose the minimum commission rate in equilibrium.

and

$$\hat{y}_m(T_1) = \left(\frac{s_0 + s_m}{s_m}\right)T_1 + \frac{Fs}{2\,s_m}T_1^2 - K_1 \equiv y_m^0. \qquad \text{(A-2)}$$

The value of y_m^r, the signal level of the marginal firm to choose a reverse split, and T_2 are determined by the condition that (T_2, y_2) lies on the inference schedule, and that the firm with the signal y_m^r is indifferent to announcing a reverse split and remaining in the pool of firms choosing $\bar{T}$. The conditions are:

$$E\big[\,E(\,x\mid y_m^r \le y_m \le y_m^s,\,\bar{y})\mid y_m^r,\,s(\bar{y}) = F\bar{T}s\big] - \bar{T}$$

$$= \frac{x_0 s_0 + y_m^r s_m + y_m^r F T_2 s}{s_0 + s_m + F T_2 s} - T_2 - C, \qquad \text{(A-3)}$$

where $\bar{T} \equiv E[\,xt(x/n_0)\mid y_m^r \le y_m \le y_m^s]$, and

$$\hat{y}_m(T_2) = \left(\frac{s_0 + s_m}{s_m}\right)T_2 + \frac{Fs}{2\,s_m}T_2^2 - K_1 \equiv y_m^r. \qquad \text{(A-4)}$$

Condition (A-3) depends upon y_m^s, the signal level of the marginal splitting firm. This, along with K_2, is identified by conditions analogous to (A-3) and (A-4). Finally, T_3 is defined by

$$T_3 \equiv E\big[\,xt(x/n_0)\mid y_m^s\big]. \qquad \text{(A-5)}$$

For appropriate parameter values, the nonlinear set of equations can be solved to yield the inference schedule shown. An interesting feature of the equilibrium is that no firms choose brokerage commissions $T_2 < T < \bar{T}$.[42] It is therefore necessary to show that the equilibrium is supported by reasonable beliefs about out-of-equilibrium choices of T. It is readily shown that an equilibrium in which $\hat{y}_m(T) = y_m^r$ for $T \in (T_2, \bar{T})$ satisfies the Cho-Kreps (1987) Intuitive Criterion.

Reverse splits convey negative information in this equilibrium.[43] Firms do not announce small reverse stock splits because they also are costly. Large savings in commissions are required to offset the administrative and information costs of a reverse split. Small stock splits, however, do occur in equilibrium. This implication of the model is consistent with the empirical evidence presented in Table III.

Note that as $\bar{T}$ is reduced (by reducing $E(x/n_0)$), T_2 will approach T_1 until the first continuous portion of the inference schedule is eliminated. Finally, as $\bar{T}$ declines or C increases, reverse splits will disappear completely,[44] although regular splits will continue to occur. Thus the model is consistent with the empirical finding (see Table III) that reverse splits are much less frequent than regular splits.

---

[42] Note that values of T such that $T_{\min} < T < T_1$ or $\bar{T} < T < T_3$ are technically infeasible.

[43] Lamoureux and Poon (1987) report a negative abnormal return of 3% associated with reverse stock splits. Dravid (1987) finds a decrease in the variance of returns.

[44] A sufficient condition for the absence of reverse splits is that $\bar{T} > C$.

REFERENCES

Amihud, Y. and H. Mendelson, 1987, Trading mechanisms and stock returns: An empirical investigation, *Journal of Finance* 42, 533–553.

——, and H. Mendelson, 1988, Liquidity and asset prices: Financial management implications, *Financial Management* 17, 5–15.

Arbel, A. and G. Swanson, 1989, Why do firms undertake stock splits? The role of incomplete information, Working paper, Cornell University.

Asquith, P., P. Healy, and K. Palepu, 1989, Earnings and stock splits, *The Accounting Review* 64, 387–403.

Bhushan, R., 1989, Firm characteristics and analyst following, *Journal of Accounting and Economics* 11, 255–274.

Branch, B., 1985, Low-priced stocks: Discrimination in the brokerage industry, *AAII Journal*, 7, 9–11.

Brennan, M. J. and T. E. Copeland, 1988(a), Stock splits, stock prices, and transactions costs, *Journal of Financial Economics* 22, 83–101.

——, and T. E. Copeland, (1988b), Beta changes around stock splits: A note, *Journal of Finance* 43, 1009–1013.

Brown, P., G. Foster, and E. Noreen, 1985, *Security Analyst Multi-Year Earnings Forecasts and the Capital Market*, Studies in Accounting Research #21, (American Accounting Association).

Cho, I-K. and D. Kreps, 1987, Signaling games and stable equilibria, *Quarterly Journal of Economics* 102, 179–221.

Coler, M. D. and A. Schaefer, 1988, 70% off! Discount brokers still offer big savings, *AAII Journal*, 10, 12–14.

Conroy, R. M. and M. Flood, 1989, The effect of stock splits on marketability: Transaction rates and share ownership, Working paper, University of Virginia.

Copeland, T. E., 1979, Liquidity changes following stock splits, *Journal of Finance* 34, 115–141.

——, and D. Galai, 1983, Information effects on the bid-ask spread, *Journal of Finance* 38, 1457–1469.

Diamond, D. W., 1985, Optimal release of information by firms, *Journal of Finance* 40, 1071–1094.

Doran, D. T. and R. Nachtmann, 1988, The association of stock distribution announcements and earnings performance, *Journal of Accounting, Auditing, and Finance,* 113–132.

Dravid, A. R., 1987, A note on the behavior of stock returns around ex-dates of stock distributions, *Journal of Finance* 42, 163–168.

Eades, K., P. Hess, and H. Kim, 1984, On interpreting security returns during the ex-dividend period, *Journal of Financial Economics* 13, 3–34.

Fama, E. F., L. Fisher, M. C. Jensen, and R. Roll, 1969, The adjustment of stock prices to new information, *International Economic Review* 10, 1–21.

French, D. W. and D. A. Dubofsky, 1986, Stock splits and implied price volatility, *Journal of Portfolio Management*, 12, 55–59.

Galant, D., 1990, The hazards of negative research reports, *Institutional Investor*, 24, 73–80.

Glosten, L. R. and P. R. Milgrom, 1985, Bid, ask and transaction prices in a specialist market with heterogeneously informed traders, *Journal of Financial Economics* 14, 71–100.

Grinblatt, M. S., R. W. Masulis, and S. Titman, 1984, The valuation effects of stock splits and stock dividends, *Journal of Financial Economics* 13, 461–490.

Holthausen, R. W. and R. E. Verrecchia, 1990, The effect of informedness and consensus on price and volume behaviour, *The Accounting Review* 65, 191–208.

Hsueh, L. P. and D. S. Kidwell, 1988, Bond ratings: Are two better than one? *Financial Management* 17, 46–53.

Kim, O. and R. E. Verrecchia, 1990, Trading volume and price reactions to public announcements, Working paper, UCLA.

Kryzanowski, L. and H. Zhang, 1990, Anomalous behaviour around Canadian stock splits, Working paper, Concordia University.

Lakonishok, J. and B. Lev, 1987, Stock splits and stock dividends: Why, who, and when, *Journal of Finance* 42, 913-932.

Lamoureux, C. G. and P. Poon, 1987, The market reaction to stock splits, *Journal of Finance* 42, 1347-1370.

Lloyd-Davies, P. and M. Canes, 1978, Stock prices and the publication of second-hand information, *Journal of Business* 51, 43-56.

McNichols, M. and A. Dravid, 1990, Stock dividends, stock splits, and signaling, *Journal of Finance* 45, 857-879.

Merton, R. C., 1987, A simple model of capital market equilibrium with incomplete information, *Journal of Finance* 42, 483-510.

O'Brien, P. C., 1988, Analysts' forecasts as earnings expectations, *Journal of Accounting and Economics* 10, 53-83.

Ohlson, J. A. and S. H. Penman, 1985, Volatility increases subsequent to stock splits: An empirical aberration, *Journal of Financial Economics* 14, 251-266.

Scott, D., 1983, *The Investor's Guide to Discount Brokers*, (Prager, New York).

Sheikh, A. M., 1989, Stock splits, volatility increases and implied volatilities, *Journal of Finance* 44, 1361-1372.

Smidt, S., 1990, Long run trends in equity turnover, *Journal of Portfolio Management* 17, 66-73.

Stoll, H. R. and R. E. Whaley, 1983, Transaction costs and the small firm effect, *Journal of Financial Economics* 12, 57-80.

Thakor, A. V., 1982, An exploration of competitive signalling equilibria with 'third party' information production: The case of debt insurance. *Journal of Finance* 37, 717-739.

Wiggins, J. B., 1990, Beta changes around stock splits revisited. Working paper, Cornell University.

Name Index